Doing Life

***Fledgling**, close hauled on Eggemoggin Reach*
(J. Thurston)

Doing Life

365 Daily Devotions
Finding Peace in Stressful Times

Jeffrey M. Thurston, MD, MA(BS)

JT^2 Books, Inc.
Dallas, Texas

For bulk discount (>10 copies) order at JT2Books@gmail.com

ISBN: 978-0-9892151-3-8 (Paperback)

ISBN: 978-0-9892151-4-5 (EPub)

Produced in cooperation with Sheridan Minnesota in Brainerd, MN

Printed in the United States of America.
21 22 23 24 25 26 27 7 6 5 4 3 2 1

Cover and interior book layout and design: Jill Voges

Front cover photo: *Adagio* and *Whimbrel*, Deadman's Cove (Jeff Thurston)

Back cover photo: Pumpkin Light (Otto Ratheal)

Inside front cover photo: *Caroline* on Eggemoggin Reach (Kelly Thurston)

Inside back cover photo: Windsor as a pup (Pat Thurston)

Dedication

To Mom and Dad,
Without their remarkable intelligence,
and their steadfast love, support, and guidance,
not only would the book in your hands have been impossible,
but the life that led to it would have been
far less rich and meaningful.
I love you guys!

Table of Contents

Sections Appear in this Order

Introduction

Never in my life has there been a time when more people, in every walk and station of life, felt more stressed out. At times it seems that not just our own lives are in danger of unraveling, but perhaps even the entire fabric of our society. From vitriolic political polarization, to deteriorating race relations, to non-stop natural disasters, it's been hard to find good news in any direction! Just when we thought things couldn't get worse, along comes Covid 19. Peace has never seemed so elusive.

Coincident with the viral onslaught, my own family was struck with the harsh reality of cancer in a member at the wrong end of the expected age spectrum. This was the impetus for these devotions, although the foundation was laid long ago.

I went to Medical School in the 1970's because I wanted to use my God given gifts to help as many people as possible. Looking back, it does sound impossibly altruistic, maybe even trite, but that really was my motivation at the time. The truth of the matter is, after having been raised with pets ranging from dogs and cats, to snakes, mice, birds, and turtles, I actually entered college intending to be a veterinarian! But then somewhere along my sophomore year in college, having the evangelic fervor of a newly minted Christian teen, I decided that God might better use me to treat people! (Little did I know at the time, that animals were much more likely to be both cooperative and grateful, than humans!)

By my junior year, surrounded by a culture that looked favorably on both drug use and licentiousness, I felt the tug of my new "found" faith pulling me toward the possibility of an advanced education in theology. (New "found" because despite having been raised a Presbyterian and nodding my head along with twenty other compliant teenagers, most accepting Christ because that was what everyone else was doing, I don't believe I truly accepted Christ as my *personal* Lord and Savior until my sophomore year in college, on a church retreat.) While I prayed about how I might do the most good in the world, it became a foregone conclusion that years of study in biology, biochemistry, organic chemistry, anatomy, physiology and psychology, were going to lead me to a Doctorate in Medicine rather than one in Divinity or Theology.

Nine years after that decision to apply to med school, I had my MD from Baylor, a completed residency in Obstetrics, Gynecology and Infertility, from one of the most prestigious universities in the country, UCSF, and if that were not enough, I also had a wife! After extensive interviews across the state of Texas, we chose Dallas as our home, and we returned in a UHaul, with our cat on the dash, and everything we owned in a 13 foot truck.

Seventeen years later, after two children, thousands of deliveries, thousands of surgeries, over 4,000 nights on call away from home, hundreds of thousands of patient visits, hundreds of tragic clinical scenarios, and an amicable but incredibly painful divorce, I was at the lowest point I thought one could ever be. Sitting in a parking lot behind my hospital, I seriously considered whether life was worth living. I was an elder in my church, a very successful, well respected clinician, the father of first, a remarkably gifted daughter, then a son just as amazing. I had been married to an intelligent woman who was a wonderful, loving, involved and talented mother, but nevertheless, we had both managed to be complicit in the utter mutual destruction of our marriage. Despite my standing in our church, it occurred to me, sitting in that car behind the hospital, that I really liked being well respected substantially more than I did serving the Lord! This actually came to me as an epiphany while I contemplated what a mess I had made of my life. Sure, I had helped some people along the way, but my focus on myself as I swept to success as a physician, speaker and author, had left a wide path of emotional destruction in my wake. The turbulence that resulted had certainly been suffered by my ex-wife, children and of course, my own parents.

As I sat there considering my bleak future, it occurred to me that my prayer life had become non-existent. I wasn't regularly "taking everything to the Lord in prayer" as Paul instructed us in Philippians. I wasn't taking *anything* to the Lord in prayer! All of what I taught in Sunday school about "surrendering ourselves" to the Lord was in essence, rote, never having really been applied to myself. For the first time since that church retreat as a sophomore in college, I decided then and there, to *actually surrender* myself to Jesus Christ. The first step in that submission was pretty obvious: I wept as I asked my forgotten Lord to renew in me the knowledge of the forgiveness I had been offered by Grace through faith, over 2,000 years ago, on a cross, on a hill, outside of Jerusalem!

I remembered in that instant, that "Jerusalem" meant the "teaching of peace," in Hebrew. In that same moment, I could see Jesus sitting astride the little colt on the Mount of Olives, looking out over the city, and bitterly weeping. He realized that Jerusalem, in rejecting Him, was discarding the very peace for which it had been named! Because they were blind to God's coming into their very presence, blind to the true nature of Messiah, because Jesus didn't conform to their idea of a military-political savior of Israel, but instead proclaimed that He was the Savior of all humanity whom God had always intended; because of this failure to understand, Jerusalem would be utterly destroyed! (Luke 19:41-45) It probably sounds melodramatic, but I had an epiphany, again. I realized that I had been part of that Jerusalem, part of that city that paid lip service to faith, that acted out the rituals, that was proud of their religious standing, that in essence, talked the talk, but failed to walk the walk!

I would love to tell you that life suddenly became all lollipops and roses for me after this sudden awakening, but such was not the case. Paul tells us before his execution that "I have fought the good fight, I have finished the race, I have kept the faith." (2 Tim 4:7) Life wasn't suddenly going to get easy for me. Truly DOING LIFE the way Christ requires, is to die to ourselves! We are to be crucified with Christ, and the life we are to live, is the life of Christ within us! (Gal 2:20) In his journeys, Paul faced abandonment, injustice, beatings, and in the end, isolation in a dank prison cell, begging Timothy, one of his small circle of close friends, to bring him a coat! What did he get for this? Little in this life, but the knowledge that he had lived with integrity and served His Lord unflinchingly, despite whatever hardship or affliction came his way.

My story is not over. I am re-married, have a loving family that has expanded to include my four children, their spouses, and now grandchildren. But not one little bit of that transition was without significant bumps in the road. I soon returned to my musings of 25 years earlier, and decided it was never too late to learn more about my faith in an effort to better comprehend peoples' spiritual well-being as well as their physical health. So, I went to seminary at nights, and over the course of five years, despite an 80-hour work week as a physician, earned my Masters from Dallas Theological Seminary.

I found seminary to be enlightening in more ways than I can elucidate. I learned that my young fellow students had a lot to learn about life; and that my older fellow students had learned the hard way about a lot of things, just as I had. I learned that our Christian faith is about Grace. It's about getting what we *don't* deserve and could never earn. It's about humility, and thinking of others before yourself, in the full knowledge that God loves them just as much as He loves you! I thought about writing a book like *Seminary for Dummies,* relating in a clear way the essence of what I learned in all of the Seminary disciplines, and I might still do that one day. But first, I decided to try and help others in an even wider arena than my practice. I have found the use of devotionals, well, useful! The writings of C. S. Lewis, G. K. Chesterton, Oswald Chambers, Charles Spurgeon, Bob Goff, Martha Hickman and Sarah Young, just to name a few, have aided me day to day, sometimes lifting me up, and other times challenging me in ways that I had never considered prior to that day's reading.

While there are scores of good devotionals available, I have decided to impart what I could of my own history, the history of many of my patients, the applications of scripture that either did, or might have, helped them or myself, at the time. I wanted to do so drawing primarily on the Word of God, but also from time to time, the wisdom of many great thinkers; theological, philosophical, scientific and even mathematical!

While this devotional is organized by the calendar, it also tags each devotional to a certain topic area, the index of which can be found at the front of the book. So if you are feeling stressed out by the state of the world today, or if you just have trouble with anger, jealousy, lust, coveting, loss, fear, hopelessness, exhaustion, etc. etc., hopefully you will be able to find a path toward peace in these remarkably stressful times.

And suddenly a great tempest arose on the sea, so that the boat was covered with the waves. But He was asleep.

Then His disciples came to Him and awoke Him, saying, "Lord, save us! We are perishing!"

But He said to them, "Why are you fearful, O you of little faith?" He then arose and rebuked the winds and the sea, and there was a great calm.

So, the men marveled, saying, "Who can this be, that even the winds and the sea obey Him?" (Matthew 8:24-27)

"Who indeed? Can you see why He might be the right One to turn to, when your decks are awash and you are terrified that you are about to founder? Sam Johnson once famously said, "Nothing concentrates the mind like the prospect of the noose!" Finding peace in the midst of the worst imaginable stress is all about knowing where to look for it! Hopefully, DOING LIFE will, day by day, point you in the right direction!

Topical Index

(continued...)

JANUARY

JANUARY 1

Walking Through the Valley of the Shadow of Death

"The Lord is my Shepherd, I shall not want...
Yea, though I walk through the valley of the shadow of death,
I will fear no evil; For You are with me;
Your rod and Your staff,
They comfort me." (Psalm 23 NKJV)

New Years Day! A day to recover from parties spent ringing in the New Year. A day for football, family, friends, food and a day for…cancer. What? December 31, 2019 and I was stuck on call at the hospital for the last night of the decade. With fifty-seven pregnant patients in the office and 5 in labor, I am interrupted by a call from my daughter, Kelly, the second-year cardiology fellow. (A Call, not a text. She never calls. Should have been a hint, huh?) Dad, do you have 10 minutes?/ No sweetie, swamped here./ Well, can you call me later when you do have ten minutes?/ Not gonna have ten minutes. Tell me now./ With a falter in her voice, "Okay Dad. Ian has lymphoma. All over. Everywhere. Abdomen, mediastinum, pleural cavity." Not my best moment, but I said, "What?" Cancer, dad. Ian has cancer.

My beautiful 32 year-old physician daughter's 32 year old 6'5" 240-pound former linebacker orthopedic surgeon, has WHAT? They have a two-year old, Henry, my grandson. Well, even Christians sometimes say, "Oh my God?" Hopefully I gave my daughter the loving support that she desperately needed in that moment. But New Years took on a different coloring for all of us that next day.

New Years is a time for celebration, for putting the errors, regrets and misfortunes of the past year behind us and celebrating the bright new future which holds endless possibilities wrapped up in our steadfast determination to honor our resolutions! Right? But for some of us it means cancer. Or a death on the highway. Or the loss of a job, a marriage, a parent, a sibling or a child. For some the New Year just ushers in waves of fear and sadness rather than the rising tide of new beginnings.

But "hope springs eternal," and well it should! Life will throw all kinds of curves our way, but we need to awaken each and every morning thanking God for any life at all! Every breath is a gift to be treasured. When the person you cherish more than anyone in the world asks for ten minutes, you give it to them! Never miss an opportunity to tell the ones you love that you do…every day! It's much easier to look back and see that God has turned bad to good, while it is almost impossible to see it looking forward. Faith is not always easy, but it is always fruitful! New Years Day, 2020, wasn't to be the celebration that my family expected, but it was certainly still a day to set new priorities, make new resolutions, and find new focus. Bad news doesn't have to keep us down, even if it first knocks us down. For people of faith, God is always present, always there to help and guide us. The Holy Spirit indwelt us the moment we accepted the Gift offered through Christ. We are never alone! There is always a hand right there, reaching down to help us up so that we might rise up and see the trauma through, and even, one day, understand the benefit of having gone through it! Cancer? Whatever…bring it on!

> *Prayer: I will lift up my eyes to the hills—From whence comes my help? My help comes from the Lord, Who made Heaven and Earth. He will not allow your foot to be moved; He who keeps you will not slumber. (Psalm 121:1-2 NKJV)*

JANUARY 2

When you are Utterly Lost

"Then Jesus spoke again saying, 'I am the light of the world. He who follows me shall not walk in darkness, but have the light of life.' " (John 8:12 NKJV)

It was twenty-five years ago, on a Friday afternoon in the late autumn. I was driving. It was raining hard, one of my best friends, Andy, in the passenger seat next to me. Thirty minutes before, we had hugged our little Indian Princess daughters goodbye and raced through the downpour to our car. Kelly and Jordan were in the Mojave Tribe and spending the first night of a campout without the dads present. Andy and I were headed back to North Dallas from the YMCA's Camp Grady Spruce on Lake Possum Kingdom, southwest of Fort Worth.

Now all these compass points may not seem relevant, but this was 1993. There were no iphones, no GPS, no Apple watches, no fancy satellite anything! There were maps. Remember those? The ones printed on folding paper that you bought at the Exxon station? We had one of those, as it turned out; and in the daytime, we always had the sun. The position of the sun could give you critical information re your directional orientation on the globe, and combined with the watch and map, presto change-o, you could figure out where you were! Except there isn't always the sun. Not when it's raining cats and dogs, anyway. There was a gun-metal sky, and about fifty yards visibility. That combined with a watch and a map gave us, well, a watch and a map! We knew we had headed out FM 2353 to 16, turned right on 16, and then right onto 180, back tracking the way we had come. Once we reached Weatherford, we both felt we knew the way from there. It normally took an hour to get to Weatherford in good weather, so we figured about ninety minutes.

Well, ninety minutes later we rolled into where—Albany, Texas, a place neither of us remembered ever having seen before, on this trip or any other, for that matter. Until that moment, we hadn't even known how completely lost we were! That's because like Jonah in the Bible, we had gone in exactly the wrong direction! West and East may only differ by one letter, but they sort of lead directly away from each other! In short, Andy and I had found ourselves three hours behind schedule simply because we had lost sight of the sun!

Life can certainly be like that! People get lost in depression, addiction, anger, loneliness, hopelessness, even apathy. How do they get lost? Wait for it... wait for it...exactly! They lose sight of the Son! Christ claimed to be the "light of the world." In the absence of light there is only dark, and in the dark we get lost. The writer of Hebrews exhorts us to "keep our eyes fixed on Jesus." Our Lord provides not only guidance in His words and examples recorded in the bible, but also in the light of life by His Holy Spirit within us. The light of the Son not only shows us the way to go, but also gives us the joy and peace of the knowledge that we are secure in His presence eternally!

"...And let us run with perseverance the race marked out for us, fixing our eyes on Jesus, the pioneer and perfecter of faith..." (Hebrews 12:1-2 NIV)

Prayer: Lord, You are a lamp to my feet. Remind us when we are turned around and start to panic, that You are right there next to us, and we can never be lost together! You are the light of the world, and that will suffice for me! AMEN

JANUARY 3

Feeling Guilty

"This is the covenant I will make...I will put my law in their minds, and write it on their hearts...I will forgive their wickedness and remember their sins no more!" (Jeremiah 31:33,34)

All of us have done things about which we feel guilty afterwards. Sometimes the things we do are intentional, knowing that it is easier to ask absolution than it is permission. For instance, the time that I climbed out of the second story window of our house in Tulsa, quietly opened the garage door, and proceeded to steal my father's 1968 Dodge Charger! (that's right...Bullet starring Steve McQueen) I don't even remember what I was angry about, but taking the car at age 16 and driving through the night to New Mexico was definitely intentional! It turned out to be a really bad idea too, not the least of which was evident when I ran out of gas in Tucumcari, with not a penny to my name. Luckily, no pennies, but I did have a dime, and I called the house that next day. Thank God my brother answered, and was able to sneak dad's wallet off the dresser and read me the Texaco credit card number. When I asked the lay of the land, he nonchalantly cautioned me to keep my head down, since dad had called the Highway Patrol, reported the car stolen, and neglected to mention the identity of the suspected thief! There were all kinds of reasons that I felt guilty in the coming weeks, not the least of which was the fact that I was guilty!

On the other hand, sometimes we feel guilty, despite our lack of intentional wrong-doing. You would think that after I pulled into our circle-drive in 1990, and noticed the car seat next to me in the truck (that was legal back then) instead of wondering why it was there, it might have triggered the memory of me departing the Blockbuster without my 2 year old daughter in tow. But no, my hand was on the front door handle when the shadow crossed my mind, and I drove the two miles back to the video store at about 105 mph. When I walked in, Kelly was sitting in the corner watching the *Little Mermaid* on the big screen TV with several other toddlers! I relayed the story to my wife some 6 years later, guilt plagued that entire time!

I've chosen two anecdotes that are light-hearted examples of what the ancient Hebrews called both intentional and unintentional sin. The priests would offer sacrifices for the people in multiple categories including burnt, grain, peace, sin and guilt offerings. These were to cover (atone for) *unintentional* sins. Intentional disobedience brought curses from disease, to crop failure, wild animal attacks, war and even plague. (Leviticus 1-7, 26-27) The Old Testament is the story of the Hebrew's (the Chosen People's) persistent failure to abide by the 613 Laws of Moses that he received at Mount Sinai, and the consequences.

But the prophet Jeremiah promised that God had a new plan! No longer would the people have complex rules to follow in meticulous detail depending on the priests to offer sacrifices to atone for their continual disobedience. Instead, the law would be written *on their hearts!* The Messiah would come, and conceived by the Holy Ghost, born of a Virgin, live a perfect life, and die on a cross, taking all our sins, past, present, and future to the grave with Him, as the ultimate and final sacrifice! Jesus then rose from the dead and ascended into Heaven, conquering the ultimate penalty for sin, which had been death, and clothing us in His perfect righteousness! Now there is no more reason to feel guilt ever again! The indwelling Spirit guides us, and when we ignore Him and go our own way, we are still forgiven because of His incomparable Grace and love for us! Hallelujah!

"In Him we have redemption through His blood, the forgiveness of sins..." (Ephesians 1:7)

Prayer: When the weight of our own inevitable sin weighs us down and we start to doubt our own worth even to You, remind us that Your Son took the hit for us! He paid the price of our sin, so that we are free of guilt and shame! That cross 2,000 years ago covered our sins, past, present and future. AMEN

JANUARY 4

Holding Your Tongue

"It is better to remain silent and thought a fool, than to speak and remove all doubt!" (Twain)

"A gentle answer turns away wrath, but a harsh word stirs up anger." (Proverbs 15:1)

At this writing, I am in my sixty fourth year. (Sounds ridiculous to me! Seems like high school was yesterday.) Looking back over the decades at every angry moment, every altercation, every hurt feeling, every embarrassing episode, every circumstance where I wished with all my might that I could turn back the clock; virtually every single one involved an ill-conceived or untoward remark that slipped right over my lips as though there were no central intelligence controlling the expression of my every thought! How many times in my life have I been told by colleagues, employees, family members and even people I had just met, who somewhat aghast, queried as to whether I had *any filter* at all?

I was what everyone would call "the class clown," growing up. My teachers would write in their assessments that I was clearly intelligent, but often acted in such a way as to ensure that I was the center of attention. Well, a lot of the time clowns *are* funny and entertaining right? But they are also disruptive, annoying, and counter-productive in many learning situations from kindergarten to sixth grade science class, medical school anatomy, to internship and residency, and eventually to direct patient care and teaching of students and residents! I can still hear my father saying that I needed to "engage my brain before engaging my mouth."

No matter what the nature-nurture phenomenon that led to my seeking attention in this way, if that's what I was doing, being witty often entails making a smart remark at someone else's expense. Just as I can hear my late father in my memory, I still hear my 92 year-old mother in person, often reminding me that if I am the only one laughing in the room, it might just not be funny!

So, if you are good at witticisms, you learn how to make people laugh. If you are observant, you also learn how people sometimes get their feelings hurt, and unfortunately, you can then learn how to do that intentionally. This comes up for many people when arguing with a loved one, and in particular a mate or a child. A sharp remark, particularly a sarcastic one or one that encompasses far more than the actual scope of the discussion, using words like "you always and you never" can lead to long lasting injury. No oft-quoted saying has ever been more ***incorrect*** than "sticks and stones might break my bones but words can never hurt me!"

Learning to control one's tongue, and specifically to hold one's tongue, is one of the single best pathways to peace in all your relationships from family to school to work to friends, and everyone from Solomon, to Isaiah, Paul, James, and even the likes of Ben Franklin, Mark Twain and Winston Churchill, have tried to impress this upon their readers! Think before you speak, or better yet, simply listen! It's not easy. It's just effective. Here are just a couple of hundreds of quotes that speak to this!

"Speak only if it improves upon the silence!" (M. Gandhi)

"Never miss an opportunity to keep your mouth shut." (Robert Newton Peck)

> *Prayer: Lord, we do so much damage with our tongues! Remind us that the mark of the serpent is that long flickering tongue, and bring that image to mind each time we are tempted to speak before we think! AMEN*

JANUARY 5

Little White Lies

"Let the words of my mouth and the meditations of my heart be acceptable to Your sight, O Lord..." (Psalm 19:14)

"The Lord detests lying lips, but He delights in people who are trustworthy." (Proverbs 12:2)

Every man on the planet knows that he's in trouble when he hears his wife ask the age-old question, "Does this outfit make me look fat?" It is certainly possible that a husband might respond with an answer, that by any objective criteria, was not *quite* the truth. Little untruths that we tell are referred to as "white" lies. The Oxford English Dictionary defines a "white lie" as a "harmless or trivial untruth meant to protect someone's feelings." Its origin was in the 14-16th century, when the "moral purity" that had been attached to the color white, was added to modify the 10th century term "lie" for untruth.

This is an everyday occurrence of the "ends justifying the means." You do a bad thing for a good end. There are several problems with this, not the least of which is, that for a person of basically good moral character, it can become addictive! In addition, telling little lies makes it easier to tell bigger lies, and gradually the beneficiary can switch from the recipient of the untruth to the teller.

Let's say one gradually develops an addiction. It can be to a drug, alcohol, pornography, gambling, or any number of "vices." Now when you first get into any of these pursuits, hiding them from say, your spouse, can be rationalized as protecting them from worry about what you do in your free time to release your stress. But as you sink deeper and deeper, the deceit often gets bigger and more frequent, and pretty soon you are lying all the time, not to spare the other's feelings, but to cover your own guilt and shame.

"Once we practice to deceive, what a tangled web we weave," originated in Sir Walter Scott's play, *Marmion,* and in fact, referred to a love triangle. Lies to hide an activity that we know will harm another emotionally, may seem the same as a "white lie" but they are not. Remember, that the white lie by definition comes from a morally pure place, where the *only* intent is to spare another's feelings. There is no morally questionable activity being hidden by a white lie. So, the person who is immersed in a vice to which they have become addicted, is not sparing the other party's feelings when they lie about it. They are simply lying about it to cover their own tracks, and as their lies become more frequent, they overlap, and very soon that tangled web has been woven.

There is a reason God told Moses to include "not bearing false witness" when those first ten of 613 commandments came down the mountain! Lying damages your character, the perception that others have of you. Over time, if you are not a sociopath, it will damage your own perception of self and lead to depression, anger and self-loathing, leaving you unable to pursue your normal life, let alone find the path to peace and happiness. Honesty may not *always* be the best policy when answering that question about your wife's outfit, but it is in nearly every single other aspect of your life!

"If you always tell the truth, you never have to remember anything!" (Mark Twain)

"I'm not upset that you lied to me. I'm upset that from now on I can't believe you." (Nietzsche)

> *Prayer: Lord, we ask Your Holy Spirit to lead us into all truth! If You Jesus are the truth, then it is no wonder that You command us to avoid falsehood. Have Your Spirit give us a nudge whenever a little white lie turns a shade darker, so that its motivation is no longer pure, but self-serving. AMEN*

JANUARY 6

Be Anxious for Nothing

"Do not be anxious about your life, what you will eat or drink, nor about your body or what you will wear. Is not life more than food, and the body more than clothing?....Which of you being anxious can add a single hour to his life? Therefore, do not be worry about tomorrow, for tomorrow will worry about itself. Each day has enough trouble of its own." (Matthew 6:25-28,34)

"Do not anticipate trouble, or worry about what may never happen. Keep in the sunlight." (Ben Franklin)

Let's face it. All of us get anxious. All of us find ourselves in circumstances where we wish fervently that we were anywhere but there. Sometimes it is a new situation, but often it is one that we wish we could avoid weekly, daily or even hourly. Whether it's the anticipated reaction of your boss to work you have done, the reaction of a spouse to whatever habit you have that annoys him or her, or the knowledge that something lies just around the corner for which you are unprepared or lack the resources with which to deal; they can all generate anxiety. Is it a job interview that has you nervous? Is it a public speaking engagement that terrifies you? Getting on an airplane? An elevator? Walking down a sidewalk that you know passes that big barking dog that lunges at the fence? Opening the mail, or e-mail, that you know contains the bills you are going to be unable to pay?

Maybe your anxiety relates to "bigger" things? Your company has been bought by another, and the layoffs are almost certain to leave you unemployed. Maybe you are a laborer and any sickness or injury could leave you unable to care for your family? Maybe you are an immigrant, and your pending legal status leaves you afraid of deportation? Maybe you are simply a young Afro-American man driving down the street in an affluent neighborhood, jumpy whenever you see a police car? Maybe your spouse has a serious illness and you are scared you could end up alone? Maybe you are elderly, have trouble with your memory, your eyesight, and your arthritis, and you are terrified that your children are planning on taking you out of your home and moving you to a "retirement" home?

Interestingly, anxiety is an emotion, usually extremely dysfunctional, that relates to something **that hasn't even happened yet!** That in and of itself should rob any circumstance of at least some of its power to trigger your fears. Many anxieties are actually psychopathologies like phobias, which are largely unfounded fears of events that either never happen, or happen extremely rarely (i.e. plane crashes and elevators falling.) These often require specific professional treatment. But all the other situational anxieties, like those mentioned above, can usually be handled rationally. For the Christian, rational includes first and foremost, prayer and reliance on the Savior. Trusting that God is the omnipotent creator of the universe *and at the same time* loves us beyond imagining, should alleviate most of our daily fears instantly! God has sent the Holy Spirit to indwell the believer! How incredible is that? We are *never* alone. We are *never* powerless. We are *never* without hope. God is *always* sovereign and in control. Claiming this for ourselves takes us a long way down the path to inner peace and the absence of fear while we concentrate on the now.

Someone once said, "Anxiety doesn't come from thinking about the future, but from wanting to control it."

> *Prayer: Lord, help me to remember to 'keep in the sunlight!' Worry about tomorrow is fruitless. We don't know what tomorrow brings and we certainly can't control it. Remind us of our dependence on You Lord, and help us trust that You have our backs when it comes to the future as well as the past! AMEN*

JANUARY 7

Being There

"Then they sat on the ground with him for seven days and seven nights. No one said a word to him, because they saw how great his suffering was." (Job 2:13 NIV)

It had been a particularly harrowing day. After four days out of town, I returned to find that one of my long-term infertility patients, who had finally joyously conceived, had lost her pregnancy at 22 weeks due to preterm premature rupture of the membranes, and the labor caused by the ensuing infection. My partners had done all the right things. They had behaved professionally and compassionately. They had explained everything to the best of their ability. Still, that morning, the day after her horrific loss, she burst into tears and held her arms open wide when I walked into her hospital room.

I sat on her bed and silently held her for a few moments while her sobs subsided. Her husband had his hand on my shoulder throughout, and couldn't hide his own tears. Despite a packed schedule, I spent the next thirty minutes listening to the two of them. We covered ground I knew my partners had already covered, but they wanted to hear it from me. We discussed the emotions both of them would experience, from denial to anger to bewilderment to fear and finally to a resolution. We talked about the future. We talked about whatever needed to be talked about. But mostly I listened. Despite the guilt I always feel at not being there for a patient when a crisis occurs, she called out as I turned to leave her room, "Thank you for being here. You don't know what a difference it makes!"

I *do know* what a difference it makes, to me and to the patient. I know that without the ability to touch a patient and relieve her suffering there would be no reason to do what I do for a living. The remarkable thing though, was that I *wasn't there,* I mean not really; at least not when it all went down! But here's the thing, from their perspective, I *was there* when they needed me most.

We will all encounter the anguish of loved ones and friends who face crises of health, whether by accident or circumstance, crises of loss, related to a job, their savings or even the untimely death of a loved one. Compassionate people struggle with how they can possibly help another in their darkest hour. I clearly remember the words of one of my senior seminary professors, a man in his early nineties, still teaching, still imparting knowledge about the Word of God to yet another generation of students. He said not to reach for your store of appropriate Bible verses right off the bat. Don't sit next to them, take their hand and say "let's pray together," unless of course they request that. Don't try to explain that even though their five year-old just died of leukemia, God is sovereign and it is clearly part of His plan! These are not things for emotionally devastated people to hear in the immediate wake of tragedy!

The single *best thing* you can do is ***just be there!*** When Job of the Bible, was at his very lowest, having lost his wealth, his home, his livestock and his entire family, his closest friends did what? They came and just *sat with him silently* for a week! (They only got off track once they opened their mouths!) How can you help people return to that path that leads to peace? Just be there.

When people you care about are suffering, just being there and available is the best thing that you can do to help them find peace.

> ***Prayer: Lord, when people are suffering, remind me gently that it is not my job to fix or explain their circumstances, only to love them by being present and available to them. Father, help me first to listen. AMEN***

JANUARY 8
What Are You So Afraid Of?

"What then can we say to these things, if God is for us, who can be against us?" (Romans 8:31)

All of us have things that we are afraid of, although those things will have undoubtedly changed over time. When you were small you may have been afraid of the dark, and your parents would have to leave a small "night light" on for you. As you got older, you may have been afraid something would happen to your parents and you would be left alone. You may have been afraid of going to school because of a teacher, or a mean classmate, or because you didn't think you were as smart as the other kids. In high school, you may have been afraid of what people thought about you, the way you looked, walked, talked, performed athletically or in the classroom. You may have been afraid of driving. You may have been afraid that a certain boy or girl didn't like you, or that no one would like you if you didn't drink or smoke or have sex. Eventually, you might have been afraid you wouldn't get into college, or when you got there that you would flunk out! Then you worried about whether you could get the job you wanted, or maybe even any job.

Adults are scared of other things. Will I be able to continue to support my family? What if something were to happen to my spouse, or God forbid one of the kids? What happens now that that guy I don't get along with has been promoted to my boss? As the kids grow, parents spend most of their "fearing" energy on their kids. It's scary when your kids drive, date, play sports, stay out late, experiment with drugs, alcohol and sex. It's scary when they won't talk to you.

Finally, as you face middle age with adult children and aging parents you start to have the ultimate fear. What happens when my parents die? For that matter, what if I die? Well, I'm gonna die, but what if I die *soon*? How will my spouse handle it? What will happen to me? Does it just end; I mean just like that? Is there something beyond death, some sort of consciousness, some sort of collective gathering of souls? Are all the world's religions really just mass self-deception?

God knew that our natural tendency would be to fear. We were made to have a dependent relationship with the one who created us. Recognizing that relationship is the key to conquering fear! Why would we fear *anything* if we believed that the all-powerful Creator of the Universe loved us and always had our best interest in mind? Well, what about when the bad things we fear *really do happen*? Weren't we right to have been afraid?

The Christian doesn't *fear* the bad things that can happen to them and their loved ones, because first, they know with certainty that bad things sometimes do happen 'to good people!' Second, they know in their hearts that God is sovereign, in control, and wants what is best for us. Believing that requires accepting the short game, knowing that the long game is guaranteed to come out alright! God's own Son died a horrific, undeserved, agonizing, death! He gets it! But Christ conquered death for all who accept His gift of Life! What can I truly fear?

Don't spend any time fearing what hasn't happened yet! Concentrate on what is happening today. Fearing tomorrow will knock you off the path to any peace and joy!

> ***Prayer: Father God, let me sense the shadow of your wings spread overhead, protecting me from what may come tomorrow, so that I can concentrate on today alone! You are sovereign Lord. What am I to fear? AMEN***

JANUARY 9

Exhausted

"All at once an angel touched him and said, 'Get up and eat!"

How is it, that just living our lives can be simply exhausting from time to time? It seems like working to provide for one's family, raising children, being a loving spouse, keeping oneself healthy physically, mentally, and spiritually, should just be something that comes with the territory, right? My mom used to call it *cryin' tired*. When it takes all of your effort just to get out of bed in the morning, when it's hard to put one foot in front of the other, no less fill even one of the roles listed above, that's *cryin' tired*.

When you are exhausted, it's also easy to get depressed. If you're too tired to play all your roles, then you can easily start to believe that you're just not good enough, and if that's the case, you can start to feel like you're not of much value to anyone!

All of us have occasionally experienced these feelings. Even in the absence of clinical depression, we can become so tired that the little joys of life simply escape us. When I was a resident at UCSF in the early 1980's, we would work 36 hour shifts, 12 hours off and then another 36 on, for weeks at a time. I became adept at sleeping standing up in elevators, often missing my floor several times until a kind stranger would loudly ask me my floor, often with a gentle nudge! More than once, my 1976, 5 speed stick shift Celica would roll backwards at a red light, as my foot came off the brake, briefly gathering speed before crashing into the front of the hapless driver behind me on one of San Francisco's infamous steep hills.

Decades later, I would see my eldest daughter trying valiantly to handle the overlapping total dependence of her 1 and 3 year-olds, while still trying to keep house, work, cook, clean and care for herself and her husband. I had seen this played out hundreds of times in my own postpartum patients. Physical exhaustion leads to mental exhaustion, and vice versa. During the Vietnam war, the Viet Cong would keep our prisoners awake with loud music and bright lights until their mental capacity to resist simply evaporated and they were left teetering on the edge of insanity. Such is the importance of sleep and the danger of exhaustion.

Clearly, getting enough sleep, scheduling mental breaks away from children, work, and responsibility, whether with weekly date-nights, weekends away, or simply a daily 20-30 minutes of meditation, exercise, or just quiet time, are all techniques to employ for our mental and physical well-being. But, when totally exhausted, to the point of anxiety, depression and the fear that one simply cannot go on, we need to keep the prophet Elijah in mind. Running into the desert to escape the wicked Queen Jezebel, Elijah fell beneath the shade of a broom bush and ask God to simply take his life! Remarkably, this was only days after God had proven His faithfulness with first fire and then torrential rain on Mt. Carmel. Still, the prophet was spent, to the point of mental, physical and spiritual exhaustion. What did God do? Did He boom out from the clouds a rousing half-time pep talk? Did He explain all the ways that Elijah had brought this on himself, and then detail an intricate plan to return him to full power? No. He sent an angel who provided water and a loaf of bread, and commanded him, "Get up and eat!" When he finally obeyed, he regained his strength and went on 40 days and nights until he reached Mt. Horeb, and his personal encounter with God Himself!

"The main thing is to keep the main thing the main thing." (Stephen Covey)

"You can't get second things by putting them first. You get second things by putting first things first!" (C.S. Lewis)

Prayer: Lord, when life gets frenetic and overwhelming, remind me of the angel and Elijah! All I need to do is take the next small step: get up and eat! AMEN

JANUARY 10

Mad As Hell

"A fool is quick tempered, but a wise man stays calm when insulted." (Proverbs 12:16)

Anger can be like a life-destroying volcanic eruption! It may start out slowly, just a steam vent here and there indicating the pressure building inside. Then, with what seems like no warning, that anger can spew hot ash and superheated lava, all over the people we care about. But is anger always bad? Is anger sinful?

In the iconic 1976 film, *Network*, actor Peter Finch famously screamed, "I'm mad as hell and I'm not going to take it anymore!" Paddy Chayefsky's line was meant to be humorous, but it became a nationwide cry of frustration against the industrial-military-media complex that constantly kept us in the dark with omissions and untruths. Is it wrong to vent our frustrations, when the motivation stems from oppression?

Didn't God get big time angry when the people built a golden calf while waiting for Moses to bring the Tablets down from Mt. Sinai? (Ex 32:1-28) How about Christ? Jesus was none too pleased when he threw over the tables of the moneychangers in the Jerusalem Temple, (Mt 21:12) and angry for sure, when he healed a shriveled hand on the Sabbath, in defiance of the Pharisees. (Mk 3:5) So anger in and of itself is clearly not sinful. But the anger demonstrated by God comes specifically out of *His perfect righteousness*, and always leads to a rectifying action, rather than the kind of vicious act that often comes out of humankind's anger. There are in fact, 66 passages that address anger in the Old Testament alone, and self-control seven times in the New Testament. These passages reinforce God's desire for us to overlook the wrongs done to us, forgiving the perpetrators, to avoid action or speech out of anger, and to love each other above all else!

James tells us "let every person be quick to hear, slow to speak, slow to anger; for the anger *of man* does not produce the righteousness God requires." (James 1:19) "A hot-tempered man stirs up strife, but the slow to anger calms a dispute." (Proverbs 15:18) " A man's discretion makes him slow to anger, and it is to his glory to overlook a transgression." (Proverbs 19:11) "A man without self-control is like a city broken into and left without walls!" (Proverbs 25:28)

When you find yourself rapidly getting angry, you are on the verge of making mistakes that will come back to haunt you. Instead, step away from the situation and regain control! Centuries of experience teach us that quick action in anger usually leads to the destruction or certainly to the detriment, of the one who is angry, rather than his intended target! Many great minds have addressed the danger of anger.

"No one will have time for you if you are always angry or complaining." (Stephen Hawking)

"When you are extremely angry, stop and think about how momentary is your life." (Marcus Aurelius)

"For every minute you are angry, you give up 60 seconds of peace!" (Ralph Waldo Emerson)

Prayer: Father, grant me the self-perception to realize when I am ramping up to rage, and whisper in my ear that I need to step away and breathe! Teach me to lay hurts and frustrations imposed by others at Your feet Lord, and let You rob them of their power over me. AMEN

JANUARY 11

All Alone

"The Lord God said, "It is not good for man to be alone." (Genesis 2:18)

There is perhaps no less desirable human condition than being alone for too long a time. Sure, all of us treasure some degree of silence and solitude for short periods, even on a regular basis, away from the craziness of daily life so that we can recharge with meditation, prayer, exercise, or just time with ourselves and nature alone. *"Solitude is fine, but you need someone to tell that solitude is fine!" (Balzac)* There is a reason that solitary confinement is the penalty the incarcerated fear the most. We are often our own worst enemy, and confined with only ourselves, we can quickly yearn for the company of others. Totally alone, we can spiral into rage, despair, hatred, decay, and then, eventually, into madness or even death.

The feeling of loneliness does not actually necessitate being physically alone. When you walked into that dance in high school, and you weren't part of the cool kids, you could spend a miserable couple of hours totally alone, and yet surrounded by hundreds of people. You could be in a long-term relationship, a marriage for example, see your spouse every day, even wake up next to them, and yet feel totally alone. Humans are flawed by nature. They are inherently selfish and shortsighted. Actions that they may think are to their benefit, often injure others and in the long run, end up isolating themselves. But there is a better option.

C.S. Lewis said, "Look out for yourself, and you will find in the long run, only hatred, loneliness, despair, rage, ruin, and decay. But look for Christ, and you will find Him, and with Him, everything else thrown in!" How could that be? Because if you have Christ, if you believe that Jesus is your Lord and Savior, then you are *never alone.* Not only do you never again have to face the vicissitudes of life by yourself, but in Christ you will find all the things that He promised. He tells us that He is the light, the bread of life, the living water, the gateway, and the shepherd. The greatest commands, by His own testimony, are to love God with all your heart, and to love others; impossible to do by yourself, under your own power, completely possible with the indwelling Holy Spirit!

Paul tells us that it is not even possible for us to be alone once we have claimed the free gift that is in Christ. *"For I am convinced that neither death nor life, neither angels nor demons, neither the present nor the future, nor any powers, neither height nor depth, nor anything else in all creation, will be able to separate us from the love of God that is in Christ Jesus, Our Lord!" (Romans 8:38,39)*

So, the next time you feel lonely, rejected, even sorry for yourself, remember that Christ was lonely and rejected too (Isaiah 53:3) and that He loves you no matter what your condition. (Revelation 1:5,6) He will never abandon you. He will always be by your side through whatever trials you may face, and in the end, you will be victorious, because He has won the ultimate victory over sin and death and because you love Him, you have done it with Him! (Galatians 2:20)

Prayer: Father, remind me daily of Your constant presence! When I feel sad and lonely, touch me somehow, through the wonder of nature, through an unexpected meeting, through Your Word, and return me to the joy and peace that comes from the knowledge of Your love for me! AMEN

JANUARY 12

Bad Decisions

"Trust in the Lord with all your heart, and lean not to your own understanding. In all your ways acknowledge Him, and He will make straight your paths." (Proverbs 3:5-6)

We've all made bad decisions, and some of us, very bad! Maybe you got behind the wheel after too many drinks, or felt so much pressure to pass that you cheated on that test, or just knew this person was the one for you and cheated on your spouse or partner. You may have cheated on your taxes, lied about being sick, left a store without paying for something, decided the speed limit didn't apply to you, or just set off on a hike in a canyon by yourself with no phone signal, when you knew a storm was coming! Sometimes we just feel like there is no other option, and sometimes we just don't consider the potential consequences at all.

The Bible is full of stories about people who made really bad decisions, starting with Adam, Eve, the serpent and the apple! Abraham lied and said Sarah was his sister; Lot's daughters decided sleeping with their own father was their only choice; Jonah went exactly the wrong direction; Moses doubted that God could bring water out of the rock; Saul decided to have David killed; and David decided sleeping with another man's wife, and having him killed, was a really good plan! Solomon made the decision to marry women who worshipped foreign idols, and then 19 out of 19 Kings of Israel, and 12 out of 20 Kings of Judah, did what was wrong in the Lord's sight! Even Peter denied that he knew Christ three times in a row! Why do good people make really bad decisions just like bad people do?

The simple answer is, we're human. Ever since the Fall, man has been prone to sin, good at rationalizing it, but condemned to death as the ultimate consequence. Lot's daughters were living in a cave out in the wilderness with only their aged father. If he died, they were lost and condemned to death as well. They felt like being impregnated by their father was their only choice to keep their family alive, or at least so they rationalized. Really? Why didn't they just go back to Abraham? Why don't we just study harder for the next test? Save money for our taxes? Make an effort to remember why we fell in love with our spouse in the first place?

We Christians believe that only by the Grace of God, through faith in Christ, can we avoid the punishment of sin that is death. But while not all bad decisions are sinful, there is a way to avoid them or at least diminish the frequency of them! In every one of the Biblical examples above the person making the bad decision failed to do one thing: *they never trusted or consulted God!* God's people were created by Him to be in relationship with Him and dependence on Him. Our natural tendency ever since reaching the age of two, is to *do it ourselves!* But the right way to avoid wrong decisions, is to bring them to the Lord in prayer, search the Word of God, and consult other Believers! This is why fellowship through a community of believers is critical. This is why regular study of the Word is critical. This is why prayer is critical! Growth in each of these areas will lead to decisions that bring us peace and joy!

"If anyone lacks wisdom, let him ask God, who gives generously to all without reproach, and it will be given to him." (James 1:5)

> ***Prayer: Heavenly Father, let Your Spirit awaken us every day with resolve to pause and ask your direction in prayer at each of the decisions we make daily! Help us make the time to study Your Word regularly, and to do life with others who are like-minded.***

JANUARY 13

Grief and Unexpected Loss

" The steadfast love of the Lord never ceases. His mercies never come to an end; they are new every day. Great is God's faithfulness! (Lamentations 3:22-23)

It comes in many forms, grief. It can be a silence, a contemplation of something once possessed but lost long ago. Or it can be more immediate. Then it comes in waves, rolling, relentless, inescapable. It can be so oppressive that it actually takes on physical qualities, thick, seemingly impenetrable, sometimes even suffocating. Everyone has things to mourn in their lives. We all grieve on the passing of loved ones. But the commonality lays only with expected deaths. Most people expect their grandparents to die before their parents, and their parents before their siblings or spouses, and themselves before their children.

Physicians, in the company of the EMTs, the undertakers and the clergy, must deal not only with these deaths, but also with those horrible events for which the patient and her loved one are completely unprepared. The most stressful event that a human can endure, for instance, is roundly agreed to be the death of a child. It appears to matter little whether the child is as yet unborn, five minutes old, or seventy years old. The twenty year-old mother of the term stillbirth may well understand the anguish of the ninety year-old who has outlived her sixty five year-old son!

It was in the early 80's at San Francisco General Hospital, when I first experienced the inconsolable sadness that comes from such a loss, and felt the bitter disappointment of failure as a physician. The young woman was an 18 year-old immigrant Laotian, who presented at 34 weeks of pregnancy with no prenatal care. We had to communicate to her parents, largely with hand signals, that the rapid onset of toxemia, which had led to her horrible swelling and astronomically high blood pressure, had also killed the fetus. In active labor when she arrived, she was rushed to the OR where she delivered quickly, but shortly thereafter began hemorrhaging uncontrollably, which led to a collapse of her coagulation system and fulminant pulmonary edema. Despite every medical intervention possible, she essentially drowned in her own fluids, despite being intubated.

There was no consoling the father. He shed the nurses' restraints and burst into the operating room, collapsed on the floor, screaming and then moaning, literally rolling in his own daughter's blood. What can anyone do in the face of that kind of grief?

As we alluded to previously, just being there is the answer. Whether it is someone you don't even know, a friend, or your own loved one; being silent, listening and being available are the right things to do. Explanations do little to console one in the midst of tragedy. If it is your own grief you are dealing with, then you must know as a person of faith, that "as a father cares for his children, so God cares for His own; His love is everlasting." (Psalm 103:8) Trust in Him. *Grief is a process that cannot be rushed.* It takes time to see the light again. But like the dawn after the darkness, it *will* break over the horizon one day!

"...They shall be His people, and God Himself will be among them, and He will wipe away every tear from their eyes; and there will no longer be any death; there will no longer be any mourning, or crying or pain; the first things have passed away." (Rev 21:3-4 NASB)

Prayer: Lord, let me feel Your presence in my suffering! Remind me of Your promises; assure me of the dawn! AMEN

JANUARY 14

The Blame Game

"A person's own folly leads to their ruin, yet their heart rages against the Lord!" (Prvb 19:3)

I was thirteen years old and my brother was fifteen. We were living in a rent house for one year in Chappaqua, New York. While my parents had grown up in that town, dad was in the oil industry and my brother and I had lived in Pennsylvania and Texas as well, and the following year would find the family moving to Tulsa, Oklahoma, a true unknown for us. But in any event, my brother and I were playing ping pong in the basement playroom after school one day. There was a foot of snow on the ground and another storm just around the corner, with the bitter wind whipping up something fierce. Indoor entertainment was looking considerably more attractive than any outdoor options, even to two teenagers.

Things got a little wild and violent as they do with teens, even though it was only ping pong. In a tight game, with emotions running high, when the ball rolled out of reach behind a marble table top which was stored leaning up against the wall, we scrambled on our hands and knees to retrieve it and in the process, the heavy table was pushed away from the wall and then slowly lost its balance and crashed to the cement floor, fracturing in multiple places. Both of us knew immediately that the other one was responsible! (This episode was remarkably similar to the one which took place in Tulsa a year later, wherein we were doing flips on my parents' king size bed when my heel crashed through the wall. It was my brother's idea to move the painting down and to the left to cover the hole. That worked for about thirty seconds later that night, when my father walked into their bedroom.)

In both cases, we were quick to point the finger at the other. Unfortunately, shifting blame is a common maneuver for all of us. When fighting with a spouse you try to shift the blame to them. When a problem occurs at work, it was the previous shift's responsibility. When your assignment isn't completed on time, there were extenuating circumstances, and the *real fault* lay not in your procrastination but the difficulty of the assignment, or your malfunctioning computer. These are all mere variations of "the dog ate my homework!" People are not very good at accepting blame. They don't want to suffer the consequences for whatever went wrong, including feeling bad about themselves; so, they blame someone or something else.

Humans have had many eons to perfect what began in the garden. After God caught Adam eating of the forbidden fruit, he immediately claimed it was the woman God had given him who was responsible (implicating God as well as the giver of this faulty gift!) When He turned to Eve, she pointed at the Serpent who had deceived her! (Genesis 3:12-13) Everybody has an excuse and rationalization for sin, and shifting blame is one of the common modalities for attempting this. This shifting, by necessity involves judging the other guilty. And it doesn't have to be another person! When things go wrong, who do we get mad at? God! We go right to the top and blame God! How could He let this happen? Even though we made the bad investment, ignored the speed limit, blew past our credit limit, or ignored our children!

We Christians are commanded specifically not to judge others, lest we be judged by the same faulty standard! (Matthew 7:1-5) Take responsibility, and where necessary, ask the Lord's forgiveness as well as the forgiveness of any you may have injured. It only hurts briefly, whereas shirking responsibility damages your character forever!

Prayer: Lord, help me to accept responsibility for my own actions, and resist the temptation to shift blame. Remind me to forgive myself, recognizing that You forgave me even before my error. AMEN

JANUARY 15
Stuff and Success

"Do not lay up for yourselves treasures on earth, where moth and rust destroy and where thieves break in and steal; but lay up for yourselves treasures in heaven... for where your treasure is there will your heart be also." (Matthew 6:19 NKJV)

I don't know if you've noticed, but Americans accumulate a lot of "stuff!" In fact, all Westerners seem to accumulate a lot of stuff. Perhaps this is an outgrowth of our capitalist economic system, or affluence in general, or the rapid progression of technology where new toys, games, gadgets, phones, cars, etc. etc. are available daily, that have never been available before. It probably doesn't help that we live in an instant gratification world either. Most millennials can hardly remember a time before AMAZON could deliver anything to your door, usually on the same day. Even worse, anything you buy online can usually be bought with a credit card, or Paypal, or Applepay, so that unfortunately, a lot of people accumulate stuff they really didn't have to pay for...at least not yet!

Recently, I was at one of my daughter's houses just after Christmas. Looking around the living room and family room, it was hard to find a square foot not filled with some toy belonging to either my five year-old granddaughter or her eight year old brother. (I remember when their mom, aunts and uncle were really little, say under four. We would give them toys that they would be enamored with for, oh, maybe three days tops! Then after a week of non-use, we would silently confiscate that toy to be re-wrapped the next year and re-gifted! I'm not sure they ever really caught on!)

I have colleagues at the hospital who drive extremely expensive cars and live in extremely expensive houses, and take extremely expensive trips, which I guarantee most of them haven't paid for, but instead have financed at ridiculous interest rates. Why on earth do we in the West accumulate so much junk? Could it be that we have somehow mixed up owning stuff to indicate our wealth, with being successful? On a mission trip with our church to India in 2014, we visited the slums of Mumbai. There, in the midst of poverty almost impossible for Americans to conceive, we prayed and sang and gave thanks in house churches made of tin, with boxes for furniture, hotplates the only kitchen, and mattresses on the floor the only "stuff" they had. Some of the sweetest, happiest, loveliest people we have ever met were in those hovels. Surely their wealth demonstrated a different idea of success. My father carried a faded, wrinkled, newspaper article, folded in his wallet for sixty years, and I've now carried a copy in mine for at least forty, entitled *The Sanibel Success Story*.

> *"Success is a word for which there could be a thousand definitions. A great many people equate success with money. The fact is that there are millions of affluent failures and an equal number of successes who have nothing in the bank. One definition of success is to win the respect of intelligent persons, the affection of children, the approval of honest critics and to endure the betrayal of false friends. To appreciate beauty, to find the best in others, and to have accomplished at least one rescued soul. To have played and lived with enthusiasm and seeing with exultation, to know that even one life has*

breathed easier because you have lived. This is to have succeeded."

"Success is going from failure to failure without losing enthusiasm." (Winston Churchill)

"Success is not the key to happiness. Happiness is the key to success. If you love what you are doing, you will be successful!" (Herb Cain)

Prayer: Father God, keep us mindful of your commands to love You and to love each other! As sure as the ocean meets the shore, both our self-perception and the perception of others with regards to our success, will be in direct proportion to our ability to help others breathe a little easier! AMEN

JANUARY 16

Faith

"Now faith is confidence in what we hope for and assurance about what we do not see" (Hebrews 11:1 NIV)

What is faith, really? I mean we have faith that the sun will rise in the east every morning and set in the west, and faith that our next breath will come. Is that faith? Or is faith our attitude toward intangibles like faith in the love of a spouse, or our children, or our parents? Is the believe that we Christians have in God as the Creator and His Son as our Savior, also intangibles, what we think of as faith? The Oxford English dictionary says faith comes from the Latin word *fides*, and means first confidence, or belief, especially reliance on something without evidence or proof. In theology, it says faith means the spiritual apprehension of divine truth or intangible realities. Hmmm, not sure that helps most of us.

If we Christians believe that we are "saved by Grace through faith" (Eph 2:5,8-9) and not by being "good," then understanding what "faith" means seems pretty central to our religion. The author of Hebrews defines it in our opening quote above. There are realities for which we have no objective evidence, though they are no less real for that. (Before Copernicus did the math, the earth still revolved around the sun and not the reverse. It has always been real, whether you believed it or not!) Faith allows us to know that these realities exist, while we have no certainty apart from faith. The word "assurance" in the NIV, is often translated as "conviction," (ESV& Voice) or "evidence," (NKJV,MEV, and others) or even "proof." (CEB) These terms can be taken either in their legal or scientific sense. Legally, "proof" means an objective set of facts that demonstrate a reality. In the scientific sense, the author means that faith is not only the basis of what we hope for, but it is also the way by which we test things we cannot actually see. The things that extend beyond earthly physics, cannot be tested with the five senses, but must instead be tested by faith.

The author of Hebrews was discussing faith as an introduction to a long list of Biblical figures who were made righteous not by their actions, but by the faith which their actions demonstrated. Christ, however, defines the ultimate faith by confirming the belief of the Centurion in Matthew 8:5-13. The Centurion (a Roman soldier and not a Jew), went out on the highway to meet Jesus, having heard that He was coming, in order to plead with Him to heal his servant, who was paralyzed. When Jesus said that He would come and heal him, the Centurion had a remarkable response! He told Jesus that he himself was a man under authority and had men over whom he had authority in turn. These men did what he commanded without question. Thus, there was no need for Jesus to physically come to the Centurion's village, only to say the word, and his servant would be healed. What Matthew assumes the reader understands is that the Centurion is acknowledging his absolutely solid conviction, that Jesus is the Son of God, who has ultimate authority, and that Jesus Himself, has authority over everything else; angels, demons, life, disease and even death! This to me, is the best demonstration of what faith means, and in fact, Matthew says that Jesus *marveled,* and said He had never seen such great faith anywhere!

Faith means *knowing in your heart* that something is true, even if it is a reality beyond the capability of our senses.

> *Prayer: Dear Heavenly Father, direct Your Spirit within us to strengthen our faith to match that of the Centurion! Your Son's eternal power is quite simply a reality, the ultimate truth, and faith in that is the undoing of Satan and death, and our only path to be reunited with You in the peace and joy that You promise! AMEN*

JANUARY 17

Jesus Loves Me

"Jesus loves the little children, All the children of the world. Red, brown, yellow, black and white, They are precious in His sight. Jesus loves the little children of the world!" (Krieger and Root)

Well, okay, you think, sure He does! Who doesn't love little children? They're innocent and usually adorable and harmless, right? So how hard is it to love the little children? What about you though? How does *that* work? I mean you clearly see most of the seven deadly sins as familiar, right? You've lied to your parents, your friends, your spouse, at least from time to time. You've cheated on a few tests, fudged a little on your taxes, looked intently at that girl in your office, *from behind.* You've felt more than a pang of jealousy at your brother's big house, and wondered why *you* don't get to drive a Ferrari, like the one in your neighbor's driveway? You take your family to church, and you put money in the basket, right? (Turns out about 1-2% though, not that tithing thing that everyone says they do.) You spend a lot, and I mean a lot, of time on your phone following all of the sports data you can find. You check your stocks about twenty times per day. You used to take your wife on date nights once per week, but lately the grind at the office keeps you late and there's no way you're going to fall behind and miss out on that promotion that you know you deserve. So, "*Yes, Jesus loves me... the Bible tells me so.*" But that seems like a big 'maybe' to you. I mean what's there to love, right? A mediocre human at best. Not so sure you deserve the love of the Creator of the universe.

Here's a newsflash, *YOU DON'T DESERVE IT!* That's what Grace is about. God demonstrated His love for us in the most graphic way possible: He allowed the crucifixion of His Son as the sacrifice that took away your sins and granted you forgiveness. Then he rose from the dead, conquering the death, the punishment for your sin, forever! This is the Gospel, the Good News! We are saved by Grace through Faith. That means those who believe, get not what they deserve, which is eternal punishment for their sins, but freedom from guilt and shame and eternal life together with Christ! He imparts His righteousness to us, so that we may stand before the Creator God, blameless!

Even so, you might ask, how can He love a wretch like me? The answer comes more easily to all of us who have children. When my daughter was born, my world changed in an instant! There is nothing I wouldn't do for her, nothing. Yes, I love my parents and my wife and my friends, but not the same as I love my children. We do truly love our kids unconditionally! I think about her often, I pray for her, I treasure time with her, even if it's Facetime! And I crave the love she returns to me like I do that first breath of air when you've swum a little too far underwater! What if God loves us like that? What if He craves our love for Him like that? What if that's what the song writers wanted you to understand? Jesus loves the little children of the world because they are His children! When we accept Christ's offer of redemption, He says that we have been adopted into His family! Do you know anyone with adopted children? If you do, have you any inkling that they love their adopted children less than others love their biological children? God loves us just as we love our own children, wildly, sacrificially, exuberantly, uncontrollably! He wants you to love Him back, that's all; and when you do, you'll find that your neighbor's Ferrrari doesn't look so great anymore and a date with your wife every week is worth a lot more than a promotion.

Prayer: Father, remind me today why we call you "Father!" Not just because You are the Creator, but because when you gave us Your Son, You adopted us into Your own family, and Your love is thankfully, unconditional!! AMEN

JANUARY 18

It's the Little Things

"It has long been an axiom of mine that the little things are infinitely the most important." (Sir Arthur Conan Doyle)

It was snowing at our house in Dallas; big, lazy, slow flakes, the kind that would have accumulated were we not, well, in Dallas! A storm front had passed through the night before, with heavy rain, thunder and lightening. The kind of storm with the embedded tornadoes that had so recently ravished North Dallas and destroyed many of our friends' homes. My ninety-one year old widowed mother lives in Baton Rouge during the winter and Maine in the summer.

I frequently text with her, and she informed me this morning that the front had reached Baton Rouge and there were terrible high winds and pouring rain; too much even to take, *Tilley,* her little Tibetan Spaniel out to do her business. I told her about the snow here and we exchanged exclamations of relief that my son-in-law's lymphoma turned out to be, on final pathology, just the "run of the mill" diffuse large B cell lymphoma, rather than the absolutely most dismal sub-types.

Shortly after we signed off, my twenty-nine year-old son, who also lives in Dallas, checked in via text and asked if Nana was alright in Baton Rouge, since he'd been watching the national weather and realized the storm had just passed through southern Louisiana. I told him we had just "spoken" (a 21st century euphemism for texting, which remarkably, even my mother prefers) and that she was fine, but I suggested that he text her himself and inquire. I shared that if he did text her, she'd be so thrilled that she would be telling me and everyone else about it for the next week! My son texted back a "HaHa" emoji and commented, "It's the little things, isn't it?"

If you want to stay on the path to peace and joy, it's the little things indeed. If I write my wife a little post it note with "417" on it (secret code..well, not so secret now… for 'I love you'…417 is our sailboat's sail number). I will often find that post-it note mysteriously moved from her steering wheel, or the refrigerator, or her computer screen, or where-ever I had stuck it, to the back of her closet door, where she might appreciate it for months.

As I write this, the mail lady just left us a package and continued around the cul-de-sac in the snow. I opened the door and hollered for her to wait a second, I had something more to give her. I whipped up a hot chocolate in the Keurig and brought it out to her. She of course had expected more mail. Her huge smile and laugh were reward enough for an entire day. It's the little things. Say "hi" or even "thank you" to the invisible people in your office, or the airport, or the hospital, or wherever you work. Who are the invisible people? If you have to ask, you missed them. They're cleaning the public bathroom, they're mopping the floor, they're picking up the trash, they're standing in the street outside your multi-level parking, directing traffic, they're handing you your breakfast sandwich at the drive-through, they're drying your car at the carwash, they're bagging your groceries, they're fixing the pot holes on your street, they're answering your technical questions, albeit in a foreign accent, on the phone, they're checking your rental car in as you hurry to your flight. Try giving a $20 bill to the person cleaning the bathroom in the airport terminal along with a compliment on how nice it looks. It'll change their week…and yours.

"I tell you the truth, whatever you did for one of the least of these brothers of mine, you did for me." (Matthew 25:40 NIV)

Prayer: Father, use Your Spirit to remind me every day, that You love all Your children! It is so easy for us to pass that love to those around us, if we just look for them, and remember to do it! AMEN

JANUARY 19
Forgiveness

"To Err is human, to forgive, Divine!" (Alexander Pope)

Everyone has had their feelings hurt. It may be a sarcastic comment made right to your face, or it might be something you overheard, that someone else said about you. Oddly enough, it's usually someone close to you like a good friend or a family member, or even more commonly, your spouse that makes the damaging remark. If you are slighted by the guy who cuts you off in traffic and then makes an obscene gesture at the next light, as though it were your fault, you might get momentarily angry; you might even say somethings under your breath, or louder, that you know you shouldn't, but you won't be *hurt* by the incident. No, it's those that mean something to us emotionally that usually cause the pain. The expression "you always hurt the ones you love," became an expression for a reason!

Forgiveness *seems* like a very hard thing for us to do. After all, we didn't do anything wrong, right? They were the ones who broadened the attack during an argument to include various aspects of your character, rather than sticking to the facts. As we've mentioned in previous devotionals, words can be incredibly damaging, and if you are the recipient of someone's vitriol in a particularly painful emotional circumstance, those words can be indelibly seared into your memory. What if it isn't words alone? What if you have a partner who stole from you and destroyed your corporation? What if your teenager gets into drugs or alcohol and after your last screaming fight, tells you they *hate you*, they're moving out and never want to see you again? What if it's your spouse, and you catch them lying to you about an addiction, or even worse, lying to you about their infidelity? There are really *big hurts* out there!

Well, luckily God knows exactly how hard it is to forgive! He gave His Son's life to forgive us! Think about sacrificing your own child in a particularly gruesome way in order to forgive someone else, who doesn't even deserve forgiveness! Yet, Christ tells us that if we can find a way to forgive others, our Heavenly Father will forgive us, and if we can't, neither will we be forgiven! (Mt 6:14,15) Is this paradoxical? Weren't our sins forgiven unconditionally when we accepted Christ? So how can our forgiveness of others be a condition of our own forgiveness? Because we are saved by Grace through *faith!* If we have faith in Jesus, and love Him, then we will keep His commandments. He is awfully clear when He tells us we must forgive! This includes forgiving oneself, the very hardest thing to do.

Let me tell you a secret about forgiveness: You think it is something you give to the other person, but it's really a gift to yourself! You may be releasing the other party from guilt, but you are releasing yourself from the tyranny of anger and resentment! You will feel immediately better. We are commanded to love, not like. Love expresses itself in forgiveness. If you just feel you can't do it, then ask God to help you do it, and He will. That's why it's part of the Lord's Prayer! (Matthew 6:12)

"You can't forgive without loving. And I don't mean sentimentality. I don't mean

mush. I mean having enough courage to stand up and say 'I forgive you. I am finished with it." (Maya Angelou)

"Sweet mercy is nobility's true badge." (William Shakespeare)

> ***Prayer: Father God, We can never adequately express the gratitude we feel in the sacrifice of Your Son for the forgiveness of our sins. The best that we can do is to forgive those who have injured us. Let Your Holy Spirit guide us to do so every day. AMEN***

JANUARY 20

Breathe

"Looking for peace? Close your eyes, take a few deep breaths...that inner connection and peace are always there, available to you at any moment." (Nanette Matthews)

I remember getting my first Indiglo Watch back in the early 70's. It was possibly the coolest thing ever! Not only did it glow at night, but it was *digital!* That's right: the numbers changed like magic. There were no little hands to march around the face in a circle, and no guessing *about* what time it indicated. It told you *exactly* what time it was to the digital second! That's all it did. It just told time and you could see it at night, oh, and you never had to wind it! WOW!!

Last evening during the national championship football game my wrist tingled for a moment as my Apple watch vibrated silently. When I turned my wrist to see the face, a beautiful blue flower twirled and pulsed as it got larger and larger. Instructions on the face told me it was time to breathe; informed me when I had last breathed; gave me a total of time I had "breathed" today and announced my pulse in red. My watch shows me the stock market, the weather, the news, the sports, my calendar, reminders, my bank statement, how many calories I've eaten, how many steps I've walked, how long I slept last night, displays pictures, plays music, opens my car doors and can turn my car on, controls the lights and temperature in my house among other things. OH! And it tells time.

I was struck by the irony here. The most technologically advanced piece of equipment, probably ever, at least in regard to its size, was reminding me to breathe, to close my eyes, to separate myself from the chaos brought on by, well, technology! It seems odd but true, that we *have to remind* ourselves to breathe! Not of course the automatic mechanical act of moving oxygen into our blood, but the conscious act of intermittently clearing our minds, focusing on the gradually increasing volume of measured, meditative breathing. The peace one feels, even momentarily with deep breathing and clearing one's mind, is well demonstrated and very real. Just try it!

Once you've cleared your mind and begin to calm yourself, try something else. Jesus promised to give us His peace, not as the world does, but so that our hearts would not be troubled, and we need not fear. That pervasive peace comes from the forgiveness of our sins, and the knowledge that we have been reunited with God, no longer enemies as we were before Grace found us! The Apostle Paul told us what we should think about in these few moments that we give ourselves. (See Phil 4:8 below) I've found a shortcut though. I breathe deeply several times, concentrating on emptying my mind and focusing on my breath. Then I simply count my Blessings instead of sheep! Reminding yourself at least once or twice a day, of the ways in which God has Blessed you, whether it be health, children, your spouse, your job, your pet, your house, your yard, or just the cardinal on the branch outside your window, is guaranteed to bring you peace.

"Finally brethren, whatever things are true, whatever things are noble, whatever things are just, whatever things are pure, whatever things are lovely, whatever things are of good report, if there is any virtue, and if there is anything praiseworthy—meditate on these things." (Phil 4:8 NKJV)

Prayer: Heavenly Father, let Your Spirit remind us, with or without a Smart watch, that we need to pause, clear our minds of daily chaos and worry, and reflect on every good gift that comes from above! We thank you for Your Grace and the path back to peace through Jesus! AMEN

JANUARY 21

Names

"You are a name, not a number. Never forget that." (Jane Yolen)

My wife left me a note the other day. It was on a post-it, sitting on the kitchen isle when I came home from a night on call at the hospital. She was out for the morning, and I was barely upright, ready to fall in bed when it caught my eye. "*Just a head's up, Tony will be here about 9 AM. He probably won't need to come inside, but he knows where the key in the rock is! Try not to 'shoot to kill' if you wake up to someone upstairs!*" Now, I am sure that note made perfect sense to my wife, because my wife is a name person. I, on the other hand, had not a clue who Tony might be! She, on the other hand, knows the first name of every person that she's ever met or worked with. To me, I have to admit, these are usually the "tree guy," or the "AC guy" or the "pool guy." I do my best to interact when needed, to be sure and say thanks, to ask if they need anything, whenever I encounter someone working around our house. But I have to be honest, I am just not good with names!

But there is no question, being "good with names" is a wonderful social skill. My wife, (Pat…there, see I can remember names) has some of the best interpersonal interactions with scores of people who I can smile at, but simply have no idea of their names. Knowing someone's name, it turns out, is important! A person's name, when recalled, allows us to bring to mind that whole incredibly complex creation that is a man or woman! When used with them face to face, it imparts the sensation that you think they are more than a number, or worker, or client, or patient, but instead someone with hopes and dreams and problems and issues, just like you have!

How important are names? Scripture gives us over 950 names for God! *Abba (daddy,) Adonai (my Lord,) Advocate (intercessor,) Almighty (ruler of all,) Alpha and Omega (beginning and end,) Ancient of Days (old one,) Anointed (chosen Messiah,) Author of faith (creator of faith,) Bread of Life (Jesus,) Bridegroom (Jesus married to church,) Cornerstone (foundation,) Comforter (Holy Spirit,)* and the list goes on and on! Scripture uses these different names because they represent different aspects of the Holy Trinity: God the Father, God the Son and the Holy Spirit. Knowing someone, necessarily includes knowing their name. God knew us, and our name, before He formed us in the womb! (Jeremiah 1:5) That means He knew us before anyone, even before our parents! When you want someone to really listen, you go to the one who knows you the best, right? Maybe that's why prayer is such a good idea!

So, names are important for all kinds of reasons. Strive to know people's names whenever possible. Realizing that when someone knows your name, it makes you feel a little more validated, and it does the same when you know there's! While you're at it, study the names of your Creator when you get a chance. It'll help you get to know Him a little better as well! Knowing other people, not to mention God, on a first name basis, is one of the paths to joy that you can discover!

"Integrity: A name is the blueprint of the thing we call character. You ask, 'what's in a name?' I answer, 'Just about everything you do." (Morris Mandel)

> ***Prayer: Abba, guide us in our study of the Word to learn the many facets of Your character. Aid us in making a conscious effort to learn the names of those people with whom we regularly interact, realizing that to do so shows a certain level of respect for them as individuals. AMEN***

JANUARY 22

Self-Driving

"In their hearts, humans plan their course, but the Lord establishes their steps. (Proverbs 16:9 NIV)

They say in just a few years, we will all have "self-driving" cars. Am I the only one who thinks that this prospect isn't all that great? *I like driving!* I remember anxiously anticipating my sixteenth birthday, just so I could get behind the wheel, and let's face it, be able to get away from home, see my friends, and have *something* be under my own authority, even if it was only a 1969 Pontiac Tempest. And self-driving is an oxymoron anyway; it won't be "my-*self*" driving, it will be, well, a robot. As Elon Musk says, it's way better to call it "being on autopilot" than "self-driving." But no matter what we call it, we are in fact, ceding control of the vehicle, and actually, our very *lives*, to a computerized machine!

Maybe the joy of the open road isn't really the issue here. Maybe the issue is in that word "control?" Man craves independence, freedom, and the right to make his own decisions about every aspect of his life. Our Declaration of Independence says it in its title, before we even read the first paragraph! Men and women, in general, do not want to have others make decisions for them, or tell them what to do at work, or at home, or in their relationships. Owning an automobile has been a manifestation of the American Dream, since the early 20th century; and not just as a symbol of wealth, but as the means, for a modicum of independence. Self-driving cars may promise efficiency, increased public safety, more free time, or any number of advantages for society, but they diminish our sense of control over our own destiny.

But what if that sense of "control" is just that, a sense, not *actual* control? If all the cars were theoretically driverless, AND all of the robots in control made errors say, a billion times less often than humans, wouldn't we in reality be "controlling" our destinies to a much greater extent than when we were the only decision maker behind the wheel? Besides, when we're driving, it's often the *other guy's lack of control* that puts us in grave danger, right?

Coming to the realization that we are, in fact, *not* in ultimate control of our destiny is called "providence" to the Believer. God is sovereign over *all* of His creation. An age-old theological dilemrna lands right in the middle of this. If God is all-powerful and all-knowing, where does free will come into play? Is "pre-destination" correct? Has God chosen who He will save regardless of any human choices we make? Not surprisingly, that falls just outside the scope of a five-minute devotional. But what we can say is this: If an all-powerful God who loves us, and wants the best for us, and who can see the long road ahead far beyond our own horizon, wants to take the wheel, maybe we should just let Him? There is both joy and peace to be found in realizing that we can turn any issue over to God in prayer, and, *know*, that in His own timing, He will work things out for the best.

"The Lord works out everything to its proper end—" (Proverbs 16:4 NIV)

"I make known the end from the beginning, from ancient times, what is still to come. I say, 'My purpose will stand…' " (Isaiah 46:10-13)

Prayer: Father God, we want You to direct our paths! Help us examine our own will, and when we make decisions, submit our will to Yours! Remind us Lord, that if You be for us, nothing can stand against us! AMEN

JANUARY 23

Empathy

"Nobody cares how much you know, until they know how much you care." (Theodore Roosevelt)

Mine is a sailing family and always has been. For four generations, we have been sailing off the coast of Maine on Penobscot Bay. Our little ones have all been pictured at the helm of one boat or another, clinging to the wheel, before they could even walk with a steady gait. When I was in my late forties, having practiced obstetrics by then for fifteen years, my father, my older brother, and I, had all decided to sail to an offshore island, about thirty miles from our cove, anchor there, and spend the night. When we set out, it was a beautiful, crisp, sunny, early July morning with a steady southwest breeze of 12-15 knots. We made excellent time, had the perfect sail, arrived at our destination, anchored, cooked dinner and had a fun evening exchanging stories over the meal and then coffee. We bunked down early as the night chill set in. The plan was to cook an early breakfast on the mooring, and head back about mid-morning.

We awoke to pea soup fog, and not a breath of wind. After a quick breakfast of oatmeal and coffee, we weighed anchor under motor, and moved out of the sheltered anchorage to the body of the Bay, where we immediately encountered four-foot rollers. The boat pitched relentlessly, as our course took us directly into the waves. And then something happened that had never happened to me. I got seasick. I struggled to the bow so as not to vomit in the cockpit, where I proceeded to hang an arm and a leg over the gunnel, dry heaving off and on for the next six hours. I remember thinking that even in July, you can only live in the water for fifteen minutes or so, in Maine, and that if I just pushed over the edge this would all be over in no time! *Then*, I had the real epiphany: what if my pregnant patients felt like *THIS?* OMG!

I returned to Dallas a week later and the first patient I saw was one of those unfortunates, still with morning sickness at 32 weeks. I related the story above, and told her that I *finally understood* what she was going through. She looked up from the exam table and said, "Really? How long did you say you were sick again?" I answered, "For over six hours!" She responded with a weak smile, "Oh, I misheard you, I thought you said six months!" Maybe I didn't quite understand what walking a mile in her shoes was all about, after all!

Empathy is the ability to mentally identify with another person and so fully comprehend their outlook. Martin Luther King said "*Pity is feeling sorry for someone. Empathy is feeling sorry with someone.*" The bible is full of references to empathy. Paul tells us to "*rejoice with those who rejoice, weep with those who weep.*" (Rom 12:15 ESV) Peter tells us to "*have unity of mind, sympathy, brotherly love, a tender heart and a humble mind.*" (1 Peter 3:8 ESV) Christ says the entire Law and Prophets is summed up in this, "*Do to others what you would have them do to you.*" (Matt 7:12 NIV)

But remember this above all, Christ is the ultimate empathizer! As we are told in Philippians 2, Christ, being part of the Trinity, could have simply imposed His will on mankind. Instead, He humbled Himself and took the form of the lowliest of men, took the nature of a servant, was tempted but never succumbed, and was obedient even unto death. Jesus experienced our feelings, dilemmas, temptations, joys, sorrows, pains and loss. In short: *He gets it!* Our God is an awesome God indeed, but also one who knows what you are going through, and will stay right there beside you! That's empathy.

Prayer: Lord, let your Holy Spirit reveal opportunities to empathize with others. We know that walking in another's shoes is the only way to fully understand their perspective, and thus love them the way that they need to be loved. AMEN

JANUARY 24
Darkness

"This is dark. This is like, serious dark..." (Sylvester Stallone, Rhinestone 1984)

You have to be way out in the country on a moonless, overcast, night to understand what Sylvester Stallone was referring to in this little remembered 1984 romantic comedy. (And, you have to *hear "serious dark"* drawled slowly, and in Stallone's voice*!*), 'Serious dark' is when there is not one single photon waving its way in your direction; not one single lumen in the square meter on which you are standing. And when you experience it, it is at the very least, *uncomfortable*, and at the very worst, *terrifying*.

Why should the total absence of light have such a negative effect on us? First, because we live and move and function with the aid of our vision. Without it, we naturally fear that we could easily misstep, and seriously injure ourselves. But, don't blind people get along without it? They can, but no one says it's easy, and it takes time. That's why it's considered a 'handicap.' Blind people learn to compensate for the lack of sight in many ways over time, and many blind people can at least sense light and dark. Second, not only do we fear our own missteps in the total darkness, but on some primal level, we fear being attacked. Predators hunt at night. They did a 100,000 years ago, and they do today. We feel defenseless in the dark. Third, we all fear being lost. If we are completely lost, then we face the fear of death in another way, for we as humans need food, water, and the companionship of others, and with no directional sense, we fear we may never make it back to that safety and security.

God knows our history with darkness. In the beginning God created the heavens and the earth, right? What did He do next? *"Then God said, 'Let there be light' and there was light. And God saw the light, that it was good; and God divided the light from the darkness." (Genesis 1:3-4 NKJV)* Ever since the dawn of man, light has been good, and its absence, the darkness, has been the opposite. When God chose to become incarnate, to live among us as a man, He described Himself as *the light of the world*. He promised that those who follow Him need not ever walk in darkness, but have the light of life! (John 8:12) He even told His followers that they too, were the light of the world! (Matt 5:14) Jesus was standing beneath sixteen lit bowls of oil, elevated on lamp stands when He claimed this. It was at the Temple, during the Feast of Tabernacles. The spectacular display of lights was to remind the people that God had led them out of slavery through the desert, providing the pillar of fire as a guide. The world into which Jesus arrived was in darkness, signifying evil, sinfulness and ignorance. Light symbolizes God, and His holiness, throughout the scriptures. (Acts 9:3; 1 John 1:5) Jesus was telling the people that He was not just another light, He was ***the** light, the one true light*. (John 1:9) When He says that following Him, believing in Him, obeying Him, you need never walk in darkness any longer, He means you need not live in sin, and evil and shame. If you come to Christ, accept the gift of Grace in the salvation offered, you can start to live this life *abundantly. (John 10:10)*

A lot of theology is hard. This is not. Man sins perpetually, separating himself from God, moving into and hiding in the shadows, even when that is not his original intent. Evil lurks in the shadows. But so does loneliness, anxiety, depression and desperation. But we have a chance to scatter the darkness, and never fear it again! Look for the Light in the Word, tell a friend how you feel, ***don't be afraid to ask for help!***

"The light shines in the darkness, and the darkness has not overcome it." (John 1:5)

"Whoever says he is in the light and hates his brother, is still in darkness." (1 John 2:9)

Prayer: Lord, let Your Word truly be a lamp for my feet and a light on my path. When we are afraid that we are slipping into "serious dark," let Your Holy Spirit, that is Light, awaken within us. Remind us to search our hearts for what the Lord has written there, and in that Light, love each other better. AMEN

JANUARY 25

Dogs and Grandchildren

"My fashion philosophy is, if you're not covered in dog hair, your life is empty!" (Elayne Boosler)

My first degree was a BS in Biology from Rice University. The workings of life from the molecular level on up have always fascinated me, and to be honest, continues to be the staunchest argument against atheism that I know. Did you now that Francis Crick, who with James Watson discovered DNA, has proposed that life must have arrived on particles from outer space, since it is too complex at even its most basic level, to have arisen spontaneously! (So, Francis, where did *those* building blocks come from?) Genetic similarities have of course led to the now 150 year old debate on evolution, intelligent design, etc. etc. But no matter where you fall on that argument, some similarities remain remarkable! Did you know that we share 98.6% of our DNA with chimps, 98% with gorillas, roughly 97% with orangutans, gibbons, bonobos, monkeys, and Lemurs? We share 97.5% of our DNA with *mice!* How about this one, we share 90% of our DNA with cats, and only 84% with dogs! (Okay, that's just *not right!*)

Despite these amazing genetic discoveries, I have yet to read about the etiology of the remarkable similarity between dogs and grandchildren! Once you've become a parent, you will testify that you love your children unconditionally. All those things that Bruno Mars sings he would do for his girlfriend, like step in front of a train, take a grenade, etc. etc., we would actually do for our kids in a heartbeat. We may not love them exactly the same, but we do love them unconditionally. Do they love us *unconditionally?* I'll let you parents ponder that one for yourselves. But there are two other creatures whose similarity in this regard is phenomenal, and I find it hard to believe they only share 84% of their DNA! That's right, you got it, dogs and grandchildren.

When you've had the worst day of your life; you just got fired, or at least you let your boss have a piece of your mind and you know you'll get fired tomorrow; you left the house that morning after a spat with your spouse; you had a flat on the way to work, or a wreck on the way home; you got terrible news about a friend or loved one's health; you lost a big client, or worse, you lost a patient; who runs to the door when they hear you open it, smile on their often drooling face, tail wagging uncontrollably, prancing on their front paws like the hard wood floor is burning hot? (It's Windsor the Labradoodle for me!) Check your ARLO or RING cameras if you have them, and look at your own face when Rover greets you!

Well, it's the exact same expression you would see on your face when you walk through the door at your kids' house and one of your grandchildren has heard the door open. They race across the house to get to you, big smile, throw themselves on you with a hug, and all of a sudden, the world is a safe and happy place again!

What you are experiencing from your grandchild and your dog is called *unconditional love!* When you're grumpy, they think *they* did something wrong, and try to make up for it lavishly! Maybe you don't have a dog. Or maybe you don't have a grandchild, or even a child. Here's a cool fact: you are still loved unconditionally! *"For God so loved the world, that He gave His only begotten Son, that whoever believes in Him should not perish but have everlasting life!" (John 3:16 NKJV)* Try and wrap your head around that each and every morning before you do anything else.

"Child of my child, heart of my heart. Your smile bridges the years between us…I am young again through your eyes!" (Author Unknown)

"Dogs have given us their absolute all. We are the center of their universe. We are the only focus of their love and faith and trust. It is without a doubt, the best deal man has ever made." (Roger Caras)

Prayer: Heavenly Father, thank you for loving us! Help us to greet others in our lives the way our dogs and grandchildren greet us: joyously, exuberantly, consistently. AMEN

JANUARY 26

Laughter

"Among those I admire, I can find no common denominator, but among those whom I love, I can: all of them make me laugh" (W.H. Auden)

Who says that laughter is the best medicine? Well, actually King Solomon the wise, probably said it first, *"A cheerful heart is good medicine." (Proverbs 17:22)* But down through the centuries there have been many a pundit who agreed. *"Laugh whenever you can. It is cheap medicine." (Lord Byron)* I can tell you I felt better immediately and for the rest of the day, when at Thanksgiving this last year I went to use the rest room in my sister in law's home, and the toilet water glowed in rotating colors when I lifted the seat! (AMAZON $8.99 for real.) Like-wise, at Christmas, I went to do an exam on a long-term patient (remember I am a gynecologist) who was already in the stirrups when I entered the room. When I lifted the sheet, there were two small red felt clad, black booted Santa feet projecting from…yea, from there! (also for real!)

Okay, I'm gonna go a little medical on you for a minute. Multiple studies have shown that more frequent laughter reduces blood sugar, reduces pain from surgery, injury and chronic conditions, lowers blood pressure, and improves complex problem-solving ability and boosts creativity. Extensive evidence suggests that couples who laugh have stronger, longer marriages. Apparently, laughter creates a positive emotional environment and strengthens a sense of connection between two people. (Psychology Today, June 2016)

Dr. Michael Miller of University of Maryland showed recently that laughter acts on the endothelial lining of the blood vessels, causing them to relax, expand, and improve blood flow. In fact, laughter was as effective as aerobic exercise! The endothelium not only regulates blood flow to the brain and heart, but it secretes chemicals that affect clotting, wound healing, and response to infection and injury. It is unclear if the effect is due to the rapid movement of the diaphragm with laughter, or perhaps the release of endorphins from the "happy" brain. It could be that nitrous oxide, which plays a role in vessel dilation, is decreased by mental stress and increased by laughter and relaxation.

Everybody has a slightly different sense of humor. My dad's favorite joke was illustrative. "Do you know why one side of the V is longer when geese fly over in formation?" Answer: "More geese on that side." Or maybe a one liner from the late Mitch Hedberg: "What about refried beans? Maybe fried beans are just as good, and we're just wasting time!"

God created laughter. Any serious student of the bible will tell you that there is laughter throughout. Much of the Old Testament is in "acrostic" where the first and sometimes last letters of lines of prose spell out a word. Often, this formed a play on words or a hidden joke. God laughed at the defiant nations. He brought laughter to Sarah with the birth of Isaac in her old age. He created us to laugh. *"There is a time to laugh…"* (Eccl 3:4) God's sense of humor? He made the platypus and the armadillo right? Jesus was fully man and fully God. He had to laugh. He told funny stories called parables. A plank in your eye? Fitting through the eye of a needle? Tell me He didn't chuckle turning water into wine at the wedding.

Laughter is just flat out a good thing all around, as long as it isn't at the expense of another.

"The secret of life lies in laughter and humility" G. K. Chesterton

"If we couldn't laugh, we would all go insane." Robert Frost

"The earth laughs with flowers" Ralph Waldo Emerson

Prayer: Lord, let Your Holy Spirit help us to lighten up. Help us remember not to sweat the small stuff, and that it's all small stuff, as Richard Carlson said. Spur us to lighten someone else's load with a laugh. AMEN

JANUARY 27
Aging

"We don't stop playing because we grow old. We grow old because we stop playing." (George B. Shaw)

I am sixty-four years old. I've had three back surgeries, and four eye surgeries. I have intermittent muscle spasms that knock me to the ground for several days. I can't really run anymore, I can't golf anymore, and let's face it, skiing has become just too dangerous. When my late father turned 80, I asked him what it was like to be 80. He thought about it for a long time, maybe 15-20 seconds, looked up at the sky and finally said, "I guess about like 70." I said, "Come on dad! You can do better than that! What was it like turning 70?" He thought again for a bit, and said, "I guess about like 60." Well, I was 52 at the time, and I found this extremely hard to believe. Was he trying to tell me nothing changes, cause my back and knees told me otherwise. "Ok dad, so what was 60 like?" This time he answered instantly, "Its nothing like 50, cause everything goes to hell after 50!" But he was laughing when he said it, and I took this as a hopeful sign that maybe at 60 you plateau for a couple decades!

My mom is 91 at this writing. She drives, texts, walks the dog, teaches painting three times a week, goes to lunch club, book club, and she's taking French this year...you never know right? Mom spends 4 months of the year with her Tibetan Spaniel, in our little cabin on the ocean in Maine (with no electricity...propane stove, refrigerator and lights) down a 1.5 mile dirt road with only a next door neighbor who happens to be my completely deaf 90 year-old uncle who still drives, texts and sails his 105 year old sailboat on the ocean.

Marie Dressler said, *"It's not how old you are, but how you are old!"* As we get older, and hopefully wiser, we come to realize that not only are the best things in life free, but they are better appreciated when you've outgrown a lot of your *stuff!* Eventually you're gonna die, and you won't be taking any of your stuff with you. Even Christ made this clear in the parable of the man who was focused on storing more and more stuff in his barns! (Luke 12:16-21) No, like we said earlier in the year, success is measured by how many people you have helped to breathe easier in this life, not by the accumulation of material wealth. (Matthew 6:19-21) If you wake up every morning, thanking God for the new day of opportunities, and then go out there looking for ways to have fun and help others doing it, you really can be young at heart, and physical limitations will hold no power over you.

Jesus tells us we have TWO things to do. TWO! How hard is that? Love God and love each other! You actually get better at both with age, and paradoxically, you feel younger and energized! In any event, God will sustain us, if we let Him. *"Even to your old age and gray hairs I am He, I am He who will sustain you. I have made you and I will carry you..."* (Isaiah 46:4) The way you let Him carry you, is by loving others in any way you can, every day.

"Those who love deeply never grow old; they may die of old age, but they die young!" (Ben Franklin)

"None are so old as those who have outlived enthusiasm." (Henry David Thoreau)

"Just remember, once you're over the hill, you start to pick up speed!" (Charles Schultz)

Prayer: Lord I trust You as I age. Help me greet each new day intent on helping someone else, and listening for Your guidance, I know You will sustain me! AMEN

JANUARY 28

What About Me?

"He who is humble is confident and wise. He who brags is insecure and lacking." (Lisa Edmondson)

We live in an odd time in America. All around us we see the erosion of personal responsibility, but at the same time, a pervasive focus on "the self!" Everyone sees a problem with the education system, the family, the environment, big business, the banks and financial institutions, the police, the government on all levels, and the media. Solutions fall into the "N.I.M.B.Y." category, where all sorts of steps are proposed, but when others try to implement them, it's okay as long as its "not in my back yard," where the solution might actually require *sacrifice from you, personally!* (That's crazy talk, right? I mean it's not *your* fault.) Sixty years ago, Leonard Bernstein saw it coming and expressed it in *West Side Story.* The gang kids weren't delinquents, that would mean it was their fault! No, they had a "social disease" exemplified in the deplorable circumstances surrounding their home-life. No one wants to take responsibility for their own bad behavior.

Recently I backed my large Toyota Tundra into a small sports car in the mall parking lot on a noon run from the office. I couldn't even see it, until I felt the crunch! I had not a dent on my truck, but the trailer hitch pretty much filleted the rear end of the parked car. I jumped out, took pictures, left a note with my insurance info and my cell phone. On the way home, I called my insurance agent (relax… it was 'hands free.') She listened to the story and then said, "Why on earth did you leave a note?" I was, well, stupefied! "Why what?" I said. She explained how it wouldn't have cost the company anything if I had just left and never given it a thought! When the very nice young lady whose car it was, called that night, she had the same question. "Why might I ask, did you leave a note?" This is for real, people. Am I just old?

While society deteriorates to this low level, our children's role models in college and professional athletics, are doing gorilla dances in the end zones, pointing to themselves, pounding on their chests, fake posing for pictures, because all that they have achieved is clearly due to their own efforts! (Not their parents, their coaches, not even the linemen whose blocking made their spectacular runs possible.) Politicians stand up and take credit for any improvement in society, while making excuses for the riots that took place on their watch, or the kick back payments from government contractors that somehow ended up in their accounts without their knowledge.

This focus on self and lack of true personal responsibility, isn't a new thing, just more prevalent, or more visible, due to social media. Jesus had to deal with this. At the Last Supper of all places, once the disciples know that one of them would betray Christ, they skip right past it, and start arguing about which one of them is the greatest! Once again, Jesus has to explain what is meant by a servant heart, and that the last shall be first and the first, last, in the Kingdom of Heaven. (Luke 22:23-27) Peter even claims that he would follow Jesus to death with no hesitation, (read: how cool a disciple am I?) when the Lord informs him that he will deny him three times in the next 12 hours! (Luke 22:34)

You want peace and joy? Then stop focusing on yourself! Paul makes it very clear in the letter to the Philippians. Humility. Placing the needs of others before yourself. Considering others in fact, better than yourself! Do nothing through selfish ambition or vain conceit! Have the mind of Christ, who humbled Himself while God, choosing to live as a simple man, serving others. (Phil 2:1-11)

"A man is called selfish not for pursuing his own good, but for neglecting his neighbor's." (R.Whately)

"The World says, "You have needs. Satisfy them. Indeed, expand them and demand more. The result for the rich is isolation and suicide. The result for the poor, envy and murder." (F. Dostoevsky)

Prayer: Heavenly Father, let Your Servant Son be our model every day. When we strive for the betterment of our circumstances, remind us not to do so at the expense of others. AMEN

JANUARY 29

Eating

"To share a table with someone is to share everything." (Paul Krueger)

One of our favorite TV shows, (if you can still call it that, when watching it on Netflix or Hulu) is Blue Bloods, starring Tom Selleck, Bridget Moynahan, and Donnie Wahlberg. If you've never seen it, the story, now in its tenth season, centers around four generations of an NYPD family. Sure, it's a cop show, so good guys, bad guys, some of that is predictable. But what's different with this show, is that it's all about this Irish Catholic family, the Reagans, who, despite their inter-family squabbles, always reach out to each other before anyone else. They put their family first. They always have each other's backs. One of the ways they do that, is keeping a family ritual: Sunday evening dinner at the family home. This is a commitment that they have all agreed to, whether tacitly or proactively, and they show up, come hell or high water! Every meal begins with the saying of Grace. Around the dinner table there is then an unspoken truce from the outset. Whatever disagreement, whatever hurt feelings, whatever difficult issue an individual might be dealing with currently; they can unload it on the fam, get input from the people they love, and do so without feeling criticized or put down!

While my grandparents were born in Belfast, and they thought of themselves as Irish, they were Irish orange, (Protestant) not Irish green, (Catholic.) But whether you genuflect when you say grace or not, the fact that a family has decided to laugh, cry, argue and celebrate together, around the dinner table, each week, is an anathema in today's culture. Everything moves fast today, from cars to the internet, to the way we eat. America was an agrarian society until the late 19th century. Meals were a big deal, especially at the end of the day. People worked *hard, all day,* to literally put food on the table, harvesting or hunting or slaughtering; not to make money to go to the grocery. I remember eating together as a family every night while growing up, unless my dad was away on business, and then my brother and my mom and I still ate together. But with my own children, starting in about junior high, there was almost always *something* that kept that from happening. It might have been, and often was, sports commitments, music commitments, too much homework to be done, or meetings of some kind or another. That precious time together just seemed to vaporize as the kids got older.

Now a new study from the University of Antwerp, Belgium, shows that eating together as a family yields more children who grow up into altruistic adults, than families who don't eat together. Eating together as a family makes you *better* people! (Charlotte De Backer, *Appetite, 2014)*

Another American phenomenon is the growing tendency to eat out at restaurants. Growing up, my parents were frequently having dinner parties at our house, where mom prepared the meals, or they were attending a dinner party at someone else's house. People just seem to entertain differently in this rapidly moving, social networking, online society. I mean who brings out their good china anymore?

Many cultures place much more emphasis on eating together than contemporary America. In China, one of the most common greetings translates best not as "Hello," but instead, "Have you eaten yet?" Spain, France, Italy and all of the Mediterranean cultures from Lebanon to Morocco have either the noon or evening meal as a centerpiece of their family life. This was clear in Biblical times as well. Many major events recorded in the life of Christ were at gatherings for meals, from dinner with tax collectors and sinners (Luke 19:1-8), to the feeding of the 5,000 (John 6:10-14), to the Last Supper itself! (Luke 22:14-18) You can learn a lot by eating with someone!

Consider making a special effort to gather your whole immediate family at the table, if not every night, then at least once per week. Even if you have teenagers who are disgruntled and say little. Years later they will remember these times as a time when they knew they were loved.

"Sharing food is the very best way to create memories." (Noopur Sorti)

" If you really want to make a friend, go to their house and eat…the people who give you their food give you their heart." (Cesar Chavez)

Prayer: Lord, remind us to gather at the table with friends and loved ones whenever we can. We will find that we share much more than food, and that is a way to love, as You command! AMEN

JANUARY 30
Flexibility

"No battle plan survives first contact with the enemy." (Helmuth von Moltke, the Elder)

General von Moltke led the Prussian army prior to WW I. Battle tested, he understood that while well thought out plans are important, circumstances tend to change immediately once hostilities actually begin. That meant that the original plans might well have had to be altered. In other words, commanders needed to be flexible. Sun Tzu understood this, 2400 years earlier, when he wrote his *Art of War*. He said, *"Don't flail against the world, use it. Flexibility is the operative principle in the art of war."* Many a battle of the American Civil War, both World Wars, Korea and Vietnam, might have had completely different outcomes, had one side not been able to adapt their plans to changing circumstances.

You might well find yourself in shifting circumstances right this minute. Perhaps you or your spouse has just experienced a tectonic shift in your work environment, perhaps with new management; or maybe one of you has even lost their job altogether; or maybe someone you love has just been diagnosed with a life-threatening disease and you're facing a long, possibly difficult road ahead; perhaps a parent has died, or a child, or you're facing infertility, or your marriage is coming apart, or one of your kids is in real trouble. Whatever the situation in which you find yourself, it will be dynamic and shifting, because life is just that. If you want to continue to live life abundantly, helping those around you by lifting them up to the best of your ability, then you need to be flexible. The Generals know what this means. So does Albert Einstein. He defined insanity as *"doing the same thing over and over and over again and expecting different results."* Flexibility then, means trying something radically different, perhaps something you've never thought of trying? Does it mean giving up the Thursday night poker game and substituting a date night with your wife? Does it mean a radical change in expectations, and maybe an altered career path in order to care for a loved one? Does it mean finally considering adoption a viable option? Does it mean supporting your adult child's decision, even if you think it's the wrong one? Does it mean celebrating the loss of your job because now you are free to finally go in a completely different direction?

There are scores of Biblical examples, but the flexibility spoken of is possible only because of their heart-felt faith in God. That flexibility allows for *contentment* in every circumstance, no matter how dire it may first appear. (Philippians 4:11-13) Paul, the New Testament crusader for Christ, adapted to his circumstances by doing things that were radical departures from his training and upbringing, in order to achieve the goal he sought, the spread of the Gospel! He said, to the Jews he became like a Jew, to the Gentiles he became like one not under Mosaic law, to the weak he became weak, in fact, he became all things to all people, in order to offer salvation to as many as possible. (1 Cor 9:19-23)

My personal conclusion about flexibility is that far from being an in-born character trait, *it is an acquired ability that results from persistence in reaching for a goal.* If what you are doing day in and day out isn't working, ***don't be afraid to try something radically different!*** Remember, developing flexibility in your body protects your muscles and joints against injury. Developing flexibility in your approach to obstacles, protects your self-perception, your sense of purpose, and improves your outcomes!

"Flexibility: in all aspects of life, the person with the most varied responses 'wins.' " (Kelly Perdew)

"Flexibility makes buildings to be stronger, imagine what it can do for your soul." (Carlos Barrios)

"Flexibility is always being open to the fact that you might be on the wrong track." (Brian Tracy)

> ***Prayer: Father, let your Holy Spirit lead us to new approaches for attaining our goals, and let those goals always include lifting others up more than ourselves. Grant us contentment Lord, no matter our shifting circumstances, knowing that you are our Rock, our Fortress, and our Deliverer in Whom we may always take refuge. AMEN***

JANUARY 31

Time

"Time is an illusion created by the mind to aid in our sense of temporal presence in the vast ocean of space. Without the neurons to create a virtual perception of the past and the future based on all our experiences, there is no actual existence of the past or the future, only the present." (A.Naskar)

I don't know if you've ever noticed this, but men aren't very good at time. They are often quite good at space, at knowing where things are in relation to other things. But when it comes to time...well...ask my wife. I came out of our bathroom recently into sort of a sitting area, that is part of the master bedroom. On the wall to the right, over the keyboard that sits there, were some dried flowers. Now, in general, I'm just not really a fan of dead stuff hanging on the wall; flowers or moose heads, doesn't really matter, just not a fan. But, I had to admit, these flowers sort of matched the wall color, went with the loveseat, even looked okay with the oriental on the floor. Overall, they looked pretty good, or at least good enough that I noticed and commented on it.

My wife said, "Really?" I, sensing a trap, said, "Yea, really. What, have they been there for three months or something?" There was a noticeable pause and I believe, a quiet snort of incredulity. "Seven years. They've been hanging there for seven years!" Oops. So, I'm not sure this demonstrates my poor grasp of time, or my failure to notice things that my brain classifies as incidental and not critical to survival. (Like noticing your wife's haircut...*that's* critical to survival.) In any event, our perception of the passage of time can vary tremendously.

When you are waiting for the end of the day in seventh grade, the clock moves at a glacial pace. When you are trying to finish your MCAT exam to get into medical school, the hands move so fast they're a blur. The week you spend with your new bride in the Virgin Islands flies by, while the one dinner you spend with her parents seems to take at least as long! My parents always told me that looking back, your youth would fly by. In my youth, it sure didn't seem that way. Now at sixty-four, I think they may have understated the facts!

But there is a consolation for those of us that are Christians. We know that this earth is not really our home! We have been adopted into the family of the eternal Creator Himself, and while there is much opportunity to help others in this life, this lifetime is only a blink of the eye compared to the eternity we are inheriting! Still, Ecclesiastes tells us there is a time for every purpose under heaven, for birth, death, to plant, to reap, to kill, to heal, to break down, to build up, to weep, to laugh, to mourn, to dance, to throw stones and to gather them, to embrace and not to, to gain, to lose, to keep, to throw away, to tear, to sew, to be silent, to speak, to love, to hate, for war and for peace! (Ecclesiastes 3:1-8) As we enter into each of these seasons, we need to remember that, as my mom always said, "This too shall pass," and we'll move into the next season! It may be bumpy. It may be emotionally traumatic. But transition will come. We simply need to remember whose we are, and knowing God as Abba, Daddy, face every new phase secure that our family is right there with us! This gives us the strength to grasp every opportunity to help others, no matter our own circumstances.

"The world and its desires pass away, but whoever does the will of God lives forever." (1 John 2:17)

"Time passes slowly if you are unaware of it, and quickly if you are." (Marc Bolan)

"The trouble is, you think you have time." (Buddha)

"Never give up on a dream because of the time it will take. Time will pass anyway." (E. Nightengale)

Prayer: Father, we know that you have adopted us into your family for eternity! Let us use this security to step out in each phase of our lives, and use our time effectively to help others! AMEN

FEBRUARY

FEBRUARY 1
Simplify

"The simplest solution is most likely to be the right one." William of Ockham (1287-1347)

When I was attending Dallas Theological Seminary a few years ago, while in my late 50's, I had a 93 year-old professor of New Testament Theology (we'll call him Dr P.). In one series of eight lectures he was covering the book of Revelation. There were four or five of us in the class of about forty, who were in our "autumn" years, but all the rest were definitively 'wet behind the ears' millennials who had a lot to say, but often not much life experience to back up their dogmatic perspectives. It gave us seniors on the back row a quiet chuckle from time to time. However, when it came to the study of Revelation, we found ourselves in the same leaky boat as the youngsters!

The Apostle John penned Revelation as a letter to seven churches, while exiled to the Isle of Patmos, off the coast of present-day Turkey, probably around 95 AD. There are as many interpretations of John's prophetic vision, as there are people intelligent and inquisitive enough to read it. The opinions run the gamut from an allegorical and symbolic dream, dealing with near future events for the nation of Israel in the 1st century AD, to incredibly arcane and complex predictions of the future end times, with multiple signs of the apocalyptic end to the world as we know it, currently extant and identifiable. Through a sequence of interwoven and overlapping visions, warnings and judgments flow from on high involving, bowls, trumpets, scrolls, fantastic beasts, multi-colored horses, and the final battle between good and evil. Down through the centuries people have seen their own, or others' leaders, depicted by the beasts, and have even assigned incredible detail to each symbol, like dragonflies representing Apache helicopters!

Well, Dr P told us that as a young seminarian in the 1940's at Denver Seminary, he and his fellow students would often play basketball at lunchtime. There was a high school gym just down the street, and they would get an hour or so in between morning and afternoon lectures. Day after day, he noticed an older gentleman of color, sitting on the top bench of the empty bleachers, a large, worn text open across his lap. He had his thermos on his left and his lunch box on his right, and usually held a sandwich in his right hand while he studied. One day, Dr P threw a towel over his neck and climbed the bleachers just to say hello. He greeted the older gentleman, who looked up and returned the greeting. He said he was the janitor, and usually took his lunch break while the boys played. Dr P thanked him for looking after the place, and asked him what he was reading. "I's readen da Rebullacion." Dr P said, "Wow, Revelation is a hard book to understand, don't ya think?" The old gentleman nodded his head and ventured that he guessed that was true for some, sho 'nough. "Well, do you think you know what it means?" asked an intrigued Dr P. "Well, I don tink. I knows what it mean!" Dr P was taken-aback at the octogenarian's confidence in his interpretation. "Well, what ***does*** it mean?" The old gentleman slapped his palm down on the worn leather Bible open across his knees. A giant grin blossomed over his old wrinkled cheeks and he looked right up at Dr P. "It means ***JESUS GONNA WIN!!!***" The two of them laughed together, and I'm sure if it had been a thing back then, they would have high-fived!

"If you can't explain it to a six year-old, you don't understand it yourself!" (Albert Einstein)

"There is no greatness where there is not simplicity, goodness and truth." (Leo Tolstoy)

> ***Prayer: Lord, we praise You! We thank You for making it so incredibly simple! Love God. Love each other. Through Your Grace this is made possible. Through Your Grace we are confident of Your ultimate victory over evil, and thus our ultimate victory as well. Hallelujah! AMEN***

FEBRUARY 2

The Hundred Acre Wood

"I praise You, for I am fearfully and wonderfully made...Your eyes saw my unformed substance; in Your book were written every one of them, the days that were formed for me, when as yet there was none of them!" (Psalm 139:14-16)

Hopefully, children today continue to be exposed to Winnie the Pooh, House at Pooh Corner, When We Were Very Young and Now We Are Six, the original classic short story collections by A.A. Milne, first released in England in the 1920's. They chronicle the adventures of Christopher Robin's stuffed bear, Pooh, as he roams the Hundred Acre Wood, interacting with his animal friends. While regrettably there is no Ground Hog to speak of on today's auspicious date, Pooh's world included other actual stuffed animals belonging to the author's son, Christopher. These included Eeyore, Tigger, Piglet, Kanga and baby Roo. Owl and Rabbit, on the other hand, came solely from Milne's imagination. "Winnie" was the name of a much-loved bear in the London zoo, donated by a soldier who had brought him back to London from his time in Winnipeg, Canada. "Pooh" as Milne explained himself, came from the fact that Pooh's little arms were so stiff that whenever a fly came along, Pooh Bear would have to blow the bother away, and thus the name, "Pooh."

While Pooh is, by his own admission, a bear of very little brain, he does come up with some remarkable insights on life. In fact, these even stimulated a little book published as *The Tao of Pooh* some forty years ago, by Benjamin Hoff. For the most part, Pooh knows how to stay happy and calm under all circumstances. Hoff insists that all the Winnie the Pooh stories are really Taoism, or a philosophy of life that emphasizes naturalness, simplicity, spontaneity and the Chinese Three Treasures: compassion, frugality and humility. He proves it in the Foreword:

> *Piglet: Pooh, when you wake up in the morning, what's the first thing you say to yourself?*

Pooh: What's for breakfast? What do you say, Piglet?
Piglet: I say, I wonder what's going to happen today that's exciting!
Pooh nodded thoughtfully.
Pooh: Same thing, he said.

There is much to be learned from all of Pooh's adventures and from all of his friends, but it's Eeyore and Tigger that most affect me. My wife will tell you that after 40 years of taking night call, when my turn is approaching in a day or two, I become noticeably Eeyore-like. Eeyore has the remarkable ability to see absolutely everything as the cup ½ empty, and to never be content with his circumstance. He has a dim view of all the other animals, a fondness for his detachable tail, which is frequently lost, and a droopy outlook mirrored in his long floppy ears. Tigger on the other hand is all energy and optimism. He always sees the cup ½ full! As he is fond of telling everyone:

The wonderful thing about Tiggers, Is Tiggers are wonderful things
Their tops are made out of rubber, Their bottoms are made out of springs
They're bouncy, trouncy, flouncy, pouncy, lots of Fun, fun, fun, fun, fun
But the most wonderful thing about Tiggers, is
I'm the only one!

None of us can be totally Tigger all the time, and wouldn't want to be, because in his enthusiasm for life, he does often display a dangerous lack of judgement. But his inner joy and peace come from one realization: He's the only one! Once we realize that we are unique and wonderful as well, created by the God of the Universe with a purpose in mind, it's hard to stay stuck in Eeyore mode very long!

Prayer: Thank you Father that You value me so highly as to create me unique among your creations! Use me Lord, to love others, exactly as only I can, and give the Glory to You alone! AMEN

FEBRUARY 3

Thank God!

"When morning gilds the skies, my heart awaking cries, 'Let Jesus Christ be praised!" (Tune-Joseph Barnby)

The other day I received a text from my daughter, the one whose husband was recently diagnosed with lymphoma. In it, she related having taken little 2 ½ year old Henry to his grandmother's house early Monday morning. She cares for him some days and Kelly typically drops him off on her way to the hospital. This particular morning there were clouds on the eastern horizon, and the rising sun was painting them pink and gold before it actually crested the horizon. Little Henry spotted the pink clouds and spontaneously broke into a rousing chorus of stanza 3 of John Denver's *Thank God I'm a Country Boy!* For those of you millennials, and whatever it is that comes after you guys, who don't know this entire song by heart, the third stanza goes like this:

"Well, I got me a fine wife, I got me old fiddle, When the sun's comin' up, I got cakes on the griddle. And life ain't nuthin' but a funny funny riddle......thank God I'm a country boy!"

'Spotify' it, if you don't know the tune, but trust me, it's an exuberant outpouring of joy and peace, in celebration of the simple! John Denver wrote many songs that celebrated the simple pleasures to be found in experiencing nature, (*Rocky Mountain High*) or even right in front of us (*Grandma's Feather Bed*). Maybe it's the incredible capacity for small children to appreciate the simple joys in life that so attracted Jesus to them. They are so busy being immersed in absolute *wonder* at the world around them, that they are impervious to evil thoughts. When once, His disciples tried to keep the little ones away from Him, He made it clear in no uncertain terms, that not only did He want the kids to come be with Him, but that their chance of entering Heaven was far superior to that of the self-righteous rule followers, such as the Scribes and Pharisees. (Mark 10:14-16)

We grown-ups may not lose the capacity to wonder, but perhaps we fail to take advantage of most of the opportunities. Get up early tomorrow, especially if it's not your routine to do so. Find a place in your house, or maybe somewhere in your neighborhood, where you can sit quietly and watch the sunrise for the 5 minutes before the actual scheduled time on your Apple watch, to 5 minutes after the posted time. Now, try and do that and either imagine being, or sadly, continue being, an atheist. Hard to do ain't it? Sure, you can dissect it to the physics involved, but you can't deny the glory of it, can you? Why does it make you feel the same way it made John Denver feel, and little Henry? Hmmmmmm.

The opening quote is from an anonymous German hymn published in The Catholic Songbook, Wurzburg, 1824. I've sung it all my life, even raised as a Presbyterian. There are 14 stanzas, but only 6 were translated into English for the first 150 years. The song is based on Psalm 5:3; Psalm 34:1 and 1 Corinthians 10:31. The second line is, *"Alike at work and prayer, To Jesus I repair; May Jesus Christ be praised!"* The author's intent is clear: if we look with eyes wide open, we see God's handiwork in all aspects of our lives! From the first moment of dawn to the darkness of midnight, we must recognize that not only our lives and livelihood, but our eternal lives through His Grace, and everything that makes up our lives, is a gift from above that is worthy of praise to God!

Prayer: Father God, let Henry teach us to start every day with wonder! Let us start every day grateful for the life we've been given and the life we are promised, and let the splendor of Your creation remind us that we are truly Blessed to witness it, even if for one more day! AMEN

FEBRUARY 4

Weakness

"My grace is sufficient for you, for my strength is made perfect in weakness." (2 Cor 12:9 NKJV)

In the mid 90's my family had a lake house in east Texas. You may not know it, but northeast Texas is beautifully green with rolling hills, especially as one nears the foothills of the Ozarks. Our house was on Lake Cypress Springs, and besides towing behind the ski boat, sailing on our board boat, *Zuma,* was a favorite of the kids. Kelly, who went on to be one of my two accomplished, sailor children, used to head out with me on particularly windy summer days. We would have that little boat heeled over to the max, water streaming in over the low side, while she and I hiked way out over the high side. I would have the tiller extension in one hand, the main sheet in the other, and Kelly would lean back holding onto the jib sheet and side stay. She knew full well that at any moment, all I had to do was pull that sheet in a little more, or hike a little less, and we were going over! She was an awesome swimmer by age five and we always had life preservers on, but as we zipped along on the ragged edge of stability, Kelly shrieking into the wind, I used to yell the same question at her each time.

"Sweetie, are you a man or a mouse?" I would jerk the main sheet, tipping us even more instantly, asking her by my motions whether she wanted to get dunked! "I'm a mouse daddy, I'm a mouse!!" she would cry out giggling uncontrollably. "Really?" I would ask. "You're just a little bitty mousey that wants to stay dry?" "Yes, daddy, yes!! I'm a mouse! I'm a mouse!" Usually, as I flipped over the boat to her screams of delight, I would yell back something like, "I can't hear you……"

The origin of the dichotomous phrase "man or a mouse" goes back to at least the 16th century. Google searching it, you will find a bewildering array of possible origins and essential meanings. It was sometimes meant to distinguish between human and animal, but most often carried the connotation of brave versus cowardly or strong versus weak. In our American heritage, founded on the strength of a victorious fight for independence over the world's largest and strongest army, we clearly value both strength and independence. It is almost an anathema to think of weakness as in any way good, or a quality to be sought after. Biblically, even David was ridiculed for his weakness when first he went up against Goliath.

Yet, we as humans are intrinsically weak. That's why "*there is strength in numbers.*" (Ask any lion on the Serengeti if he'd rather take on one man or a village!) But we are not just a physically weak species, man is weak when it comes to resisting temptation as well. There is a certain moral code, that many, such as C.S. Lewis for instance, believe is imprinted upon us by our Creator, and not just a result of socialization. Yet we, if it serves our immediate desires, whether greed or lust driven, seem to have little compunction about breaking that code repeatedly. The Mosaic law proved, over centuries, that man is too weak to achieve righteousness before God by following a set of rules. That's why we need a Savior! Putting our faith in God, as little David the shepherd did, makes perfect God's strength! God promises to use His strength when we are weak, if only we have faith. The Apostle Paul was reminded of his own weakness by a "thorn in his side," a physical malady, given to him by the Lord. It was there to remind him that it is God's power that persuades and convicts, not he in his own strength! We are strongest, when we submit our weakness to the Lord.

"I am the vine; you are the branches. If you remain in me and I in you, you will bear much fruit; apart from me you can nothing!" (1 John 15:5 NIV)

"God is faithful; he will not let you be tempted beyond what you can bear...he will provide a way out so you can endure it!" (1 Cor 10:113)

Prayer: Lord, when we fully recognize our dependence on You, and admit that we can do nothing in our own strength; that is surely when You use us most effectively, and Your power is demonstrated! AMEN

FEBRUARY 5

Be Still

"Be still, and know that I am God; I will be exalted among the nations, I will be exalted in the earth." (Psalm 46:10)

There is a difference between being silent and being still. We've mentioned the inestimable value of holding your tongue before. That's where "silence is golden" comes from. The entire 18th century phrase used by Thomas Carlyle, "speech is silver, silence is golden," probably has its origin in ancient Egypt. Gold being more precious and valuable than silver, refraining from responding to another verbally, is almost always better than blurting something out. As Abraham Lincoln said, "*Better to remain silent and thought a fool than to speak and remove all doubt.*"

But "stillness" is a receptive posture. One can be silent and not listening, but to be "still" carries with it the connotation of silence in the service of awareness. We have a 15lb cat named Sterling. He's not supposed to be 15 pounds, but his parents tend to be a little careless with the treats. His favorite game involves stalking a 10 foot-long felt ribbon attached to a 3 foot plastic stick. I wield the stick, and for the most part, the cat of little brain is unaware and focuses only on felt mouse tied to the end of that ribbon. I will lay it out on the hardwood floor for example, and Sterling will stealthily creep around the end table to approach the unsuspecting mouse, in order to catch it "unawares." Initially he puts his head down, haunches in the air, and wiggles his rear, twitching his tail. He looks left, looks right, and then resumes the crouch but now, all is concentration, and he is absolutely dead still. He is absolutely motionless while he waits and listens and watches for any movement whatsoever from his prey. When he is absolutely sure it is unsuspecting, he pounces!!

When you gaze at the stars at midnight, or you stand on a porch and watch the breeze move the aspens across the valley, or you sit on the beach watching the sunrise, hearing only the waves and the gulls; this is a time to be still. You are not simply quiet. You are also *aware*, your senses are heightened, taking in your surroundings more fully because your appreciation of them is unsullied by your own movement and speech.

This is what the Lord your God wants you to do with Him. He wants your undivided attention. Think of yourself on Holy Ground when you pray and when God addresses you. Do you think perhaps God had Moses' undivided attention when he gazed at the burning bush? Why do you think the Lord leads us beside still waters? It is there He can restore your soul just as He restores the sheep with drink.

"Hear this O Job, STOP, and consider the wondrous works of God." (Job 37:14)

"Stand still, that I may plead with you before the Lord concerning all the righteous deeds of the Lord."(1 Sam 12:7)

"Don't let the enemy keep you bound with fear. The devil is a liar. Stay in faith and trust the process. Be still. God has a plan!" (Germany Kent)

"When we are still, all settles into place. We take time to see the beauty, time to see the heart. And we naturally gravitate to others that resonate that inner calm. When we are still." (Tom Althouse)

> ***Prayer: Lord, we know you have good reason when you tell us to be still! We have a tendency to think we are most productive when we are constantly in motion; but You know that's not the case! Thank you Lord that You grant us the wisdom to realize clarity comes when distraction goes. AMEN***

FEBRUARY 6

Be Perfect

"Be perfect therefore, as your heavenly Father is perfect." (Matthew 5:48 NIV)

Recently, I had the pleasure of watching the 2020 U.S. National Figure Skating Championships from Greensboro, North Carolina, on TV. It was the women's final free skate that had me, once again, transfixed. Now, this was the figure skating championships mind you, not ice-dancing, but if any of you are even near my age, you can't watch any skating without remembering Jane Torvill and Christopher Dean's 1984 Gold Medal skate, to Ravel's *Bolero*. It was, quite simply, perfection. (YouTube it!) But the other day it was Mariah Bell, two-time U.S. bronze medalist, in third place after the short program, who skated to *Hallelujah*, and well, took my breath away, along with the rest of the world! Pull out your Oxford English Dictionary and look up the words determination, grit, perseverance, grace, beauty, ecstasy, and maybe tears of joy, and they will all have an accompanying photo of Mariah, face in her hands, sobbing and grinning at the same time, after a long awaited perfect program. I have watched it multiple times now, and I tear up every time. In the end, she took the silver, fourteen-year old phenom Alysa Liu defending her title successfully with simply impossible quads. But it was Mariah that brought the crowd to their feet a full 20 seconds before she had finished the final Biellmann spin, skate in hand, high over her head, as she whirled at a blurring, dizzying, pace.

The 23 year-old Bell began skating at age 4. Every day of her life for 19 years she has practiced for hours, undoubtedly sacrificing all sorts of things that other teenagers took for granted. Seven times in her young life she has finished second or third in important international competitions. Perfection is the goal of all Olympic quality athletes. It's what in the old scoring system a 10/10 meant! From her stunning triple lutz, triple toe combinations, to her breathtaking fluidity, to her undeniable joy in her pursuit of her dream, Mariah Bell simply was ***perfection***, and everyone watching knew it.

So why does it bring tears and a grin to my face just as it did to hers? Perhaps because only an infinitesimal percentage of people on the planet will ever achieve in sport, anything even close to what this young woman has, and we get to share it with her! We have all worked hard at something in life, so that we can at least incompletely identify with the feelings that accompany such an accomplishment.

But we also know that if perfection is the goal for the rest of us, well, Salvador Dali hit the nail on the head when he said, *"Have no fear of perfection; you will never reach it!"* Leo Tostoy remarked that *"If you look for perfection, you will never be content."* Steve Mariboli points out in his book, *Life, the Truth and Being Free*, that like the snowflake, we are all uniquely, imperfect, but perfect for our particular journey, and no one else's. He contends that we are all universally headed in the same direction, and by that I believe he means death, in the end.

But are we? Why does Christ, the only man who ever lived a sinless life, command us *"Be perfect, as our heavenly Father is perfect?"* The reference Christ makes is to Leviticus 19:2 where God tells Moses to speak to all Israel, and tell them to *"Be Holy, because I am Holy."* God wants our moral code to evolve from His nature. Well, the history of man from the Garden demonstrates that man is incapable of meeting this standard, whether in adherence to Mosaic Law, or to the Sermon on the Mount! Jesus tells us to *be perfect*, not expecting us to succeed in our own strength, but by putting our faith in Him! In Grace He sent us the Spirit that is indwelling! We don't *strive* for perfection, we *love* to perfection, and the Spirit, when we allow Him, leads us to do the righteous thing! And through His Grace, we who believe, are actually headed in a different direction, in the end. Hallelujah indeed!

Prayer: Father, focus our being on You, Your Son and in Your Word! The Perfection You desire of us can be attained in no other way. AMEN

FEBRUARY 7

Tiny House

"Two things I ask of you Lord...Give me neither poverty nor riches, but give me only my daily bread. Otherwise, I may have too much and disown you, saying, "Who is the Lord?" Or I may have too little and steal, and so dishonor the name of my God." (Proverbs 30:7-9 NIV)

We spent today driving through the Hill Country, near Fredericksburg, Texas. For those of you unfamiliar with Texas who picture huge flat expanses of near desert, bathed in oppressive heat, and devoid of recognizable life, you either need to actually visit our great state, or at least read a book. South central Texas has rolling hills, deciduous forests mixed in with towering cliffs which overlook mesquite, rock and cactus strewn valleys, intertwined with hundreds of wineries and thousands of acres of farmland crisscrossed by creeks and rivers and dotted with lakes. It's actually hard to even imagine until you've seen it. A well-known highlight of the area is the awe-inspiring **Museum of WW II in the Pacific**, dedicated to local boy made good, Admiral Chester W. Nimitz. But we also enjoyed a tour of a nearby collection of "Tiny Houses" made famous by HGTV exposure.

The "Tiny House Movement," found its origins with Lester Walker's book, *Tiny Houses* (1987) and then really took off with Sarah Susanka's tome, *The Not So Big House*. (1997) Jay Shafer popularized putting the tiny house on wheels, and has founded several companies, the most recent of which is Four Lights Tiny House Company, Inc. All three, credit inspiration from Henry David Thoreau's classic work, *On Walden Pond*. (1854) Tiny houses originated in Fredericksburg as weekend lodgings, called "Sunday Houses," for farmers who would travel many miles to town, to shop, visit and attend church, and then would return to their farms Sunday evenings. Tiny Houses are usually defined as less than 400 sq ft., while the "Small House" is 400-1000 sq ft. Costs range from $20-55,000 in general, with homes constructed of standard building materials intended to last, unlike "mobile homes." The average American home has mushroomed from 1700 sq. ft. in 1978, to 2700 in 2014. With the economic downturn of 2008, combined with the rapid expansion of a sustainable, reusable, public mindset, living with less stuff in much smaller spaces, has increasing attraction. The Tiny House movement dovetails with those who advocate the health-saving advantages of minimalism in general.

My wife and I have long been attracted to this scaled down idea of living, although admittedly as a concept for a second home, on a lake or in the mountains somewhere, i.e. the bourgeois version. But we are attracted and intrigued, nevertheless. I joke about where my grandmother's grand piano will go, but other than that, I am all in! Joking aside, we are trying, at least now that our kids are grown, to divest ourselves of so much of our, well, junk. We really do believe what Christ tells us in Luke 12:15, "*Be on your guard against all kinds of greed: life does not consist in an abundance of possessions.*"

We admired the compact genius of one tiny house, noting the central AC, climbing the ladder-stairs to a bedroom loft with a three foot ceiling; inspecting a fully functioning kitchen that takes no more space than a front hall closet; marveling at the living room-kitchenette of no more than 50 sq. ft., finding a *study* by the bathroom/utility room of about 35 sq. ft., and admiring the attached covered front porch. We agreed that we could *absolutely live here*, with a big part of it however, being the view from that little front porch!

After two minutes in the car, our minds went to the same place, and at the same instant we both said, "Remember Mumbai..." Our 2013 trip through the slums showed us loving, truly happy families, living in aluminum huts, often with no electricity, all with no running water or plumbing, crowded together along filthy muddy paths. These people would view a "tiny house" as a veritable palace, but they lived abundantly with almost nothing. Who knew? It's not their stuff that made them happy. Christ was right, again.

Prayer: Dear Lord, focus us outward. Make us aware daily that living abundantly has nothing to do with owning an abundance of stuff. Remind us that our identity is in You, not in things. AMEN

FEBRUARY 8

Soldiering On

"The first virtue of a soldier is endurance of fatigue. Courage is only the second." (Bonaparte)

We visited the WW II Museum of the Pacific in Fredericksburg, Texas, yesterday. It's located there, because Admiral Chester Nimitz, supreme commander of allied forces in the Pacific, was born there. A generous donation from WW II veteran and 41st President of the United States, the late George H.W. Bush, renovated it and greatly expanded it recently. If you've never been there, you need to go. It is easily as impressive any of the Presidential libraries, and if you leave there, unmoved by the sacrifices of "the Greatest Generation," well then, there's something seriously wrong with you.

Over and over again our young soldiers faced certain death, whether dive bombing Japanese aircraft carriers, storming the beaches of Iwo Jima, Guadalcanal, or Okinawa, facing the machine guns in pillboxes and caves on the Island of Peleliu, or suffering interminably in Japanese prison camps. How was it even possible? Someone once said that *"a soldier perseveres not out of hatred for those before him, but out of love for those behind him."* The four-hour tour through incredibly well conceived exhibits leaves one with a bittersweet taste, harkening back to a time when we all pulled together as Americans instead of tearing each other apart as we seem to be doing today. Our brave soldiers fought specifically to defend the right of all to express their opinions in our society, without fear of retribution, verbally or physically! Now we have colleges, universities, and a press, whose embrace of diversity extends only to skin color and not to diversity of perspective or opinion. Could our young men today fight for the society we've become, as our grandfathers did in WW II? Would they?

The term 'soldiering on,' references the fighting man's determination to keep going, no matter the hardship encountered. He has to have a reason to do so, and presumably it is love of family and country that drives him or her. I have examples of soldiering on in my own family. My father lived for years as Parkinson's advanced, yet he gave up his loves, like sailing and walking, grudgingly, but still showed his love to all of us in any way he could. My mother, having been married for 64 years to my late father, has emerged from grief more determined than ever, driving, texting, painting, and becoming involved with friends from her neighborhood and her church. Her constant encouragement of the rest of us is humbling indeed. My uncle, losing his partner of decades to pancreatic cancer, has continued into his 90's still an avid reader, writer, traveler, teacher and sailor. Even after a battle with Meniere's Disease followed by deafness in one ear and surgical removal of his cancerous other ear, he learned to communicate with cochlear implants in a fraction of the time predicted. Now my son-in-law battles lymphoma, while carrying on as a husband, father, and orthopedic surgeon. Thinking of the obstacles overcome in my own family makes me fatigued, no less thinking of the perseverance of our military from WW II, or of those overseas today.

The bible is replete with verses encouraging us to "soldier on." The rationale is the same as for those boys in WW II; love, not hatred. We love God by loving others, through thick and thin as it turns out, just as He commands us. Loving is its own reward, but eternity waits for those of faith.

"Blessed is the man who remains steadfast under trial, for when he has stood the test, he will receive the crown of life, which God has promised to those who love Him." (James 1:12 ESV)

"We glory in our sufferings, knowing that suffering produces perseverance, perseverance, character; and character, hope. And hope does not put us to shame, because God's love has been poured out onto our hearts through the Holy Spirit." (Romans 5:3-5 NIV)

Prayer: Thank you Lord that the reward for endurance is love, and for love, eternity. AMEN

FEBRUARY 9

Technology

"Before you become too entranced with gadgets and mesmerizing video, let me remind you that information is not knowledge, knowledge is not wisdom, and wisdom is not foresight. Each grows out of the other and we need them all." (Arthur C. Clarke)

I remember in 1969 when we landed on the moon and the entire world was overwhelmed that such technology, determination and bravery existed. My grandmother, then 68 herself, joined in our family discussion of technology. She asked us if we could guess what the most fantastic technological advance had been during her lifetime. Was it the telephone? The record player? Was it the radio? Talking movies? The television? How about the automobile? The airplane? Was it jet travel? Space travel? She shook her head no to all of these. She gave us a hint. She said it was in the kitchen of their house in New York. My mom, dad, brother and I all guessed one thing after another. The oven? Was it the refrigerator-freezer? The electric lighting? The toaster? I know... the electric blender? How about the dishwasher? Gran shook her head, 'no' to everything we came up with. "Give up?" she asked. Exasperated, even my mother threw in the towel, and she'd grown up in that kitchen. "The water," Gran said with a grin. "It was the running water coming right out of the faucet!" I remember we were speechless that she had ever worked in a kitchen without running water!

Our kids are in their 30's now and we made a brief list of technology that they were unfamiliar with, these things having disappeared since their childhood. Millennials have never seen an 8-track tape, a super 8 movie camera, or a shoulder held video camera for that matter. They never saw a computer punch card or a 5 ¼" floppy disc. They've never seen a cassette, or a black and white TV, or the TV station sign off screen at 1 AM. They never waited a whole year for the Wizard of Oz to come on! They've never seen roller skates with four wheels that strapped onto your shoes and adjusted with a key. They never needed a handle to roll up a car window, or rode in a car without seat belts and head rests and airbags. They've never used a slide rule, an adding machine, an SR-11 calculator, or a portable typewriter, or even an IBM selectric! They've never seen or heard a cash register with keys and a spring drawer.

They've never used a dial telephone. They've never even seen a cell phone with an extendable antennae, or a telephone answering machine. They've never used the Yellow Pages, or a phone booth with a pay phone that took a dime, or a folding map. They've never known a world without microwaves. They've never seen a Brownie camera, no less used one. They've never owned or seen a palm size transistor radio. Millennials have never heard of S&H Green stamps. They have no idea that TAB existed before Diet Coke. They never had to climb a rope to the top of the gymnasium, nor did they ever have "duck and cover" drills for nuclear war. Millennials have never had a Pet Rock. They've never seen glass milk bottles delivered to their doorsteps and the empties collected from the "milk box or chute." None of them has ordered from a Sears Catalog. No millennial had a preference for BetaMax or VHS, because they never saw the former and DVDs replaced the latter in their early childhood. Many cannot read an analog clock, or write in cursive, or know where to buy a stamp if they ever even wrote a letter, cursive or not.

Today, your smart phone could have run the entire Apollo moon program with gigabytes to spare. Soon, our AI technology may well outstrip our understanding of how to control it. But we are "stuck with technology, because we want stuff to work,"(Douglas Adams)

God created man smart and He wants us to use our intelligence. All we have to do is remember the foremost thing for which we are to use it! We are to *love God with all our heart, soul and* **mind**. *(Mt22:37-38)*

> *Prayer: Father God, thank You that You gave us a mind made in Your image! Guide us to direct our mental energies first to loving others in order to demonstrate our love for You. Let us use our intellect developing the technologies needed to guard the home you have given us in earth, to lift up those in need, and to explore the inner and outer reaches of the universe You have created. AMEN*

FEBRUARY 10

Pay Attention

"Caves have two great things to teach you: Light is sacred; silence is to integrate with eternity." (Mehmet Murat Ildan)

I'm not sure I even know the difference between a cave and a cavern. I have the feeling the former might just be smaller, but I'm not sure. I do know that the rooms of the *Natural Bridge Caverns* just north of San Antonio, are, in a word, big. We visited in winter, so the constant 70F and 99% humidity as we worked our way 200 feet underground, felt more than warm. We were soaked by the time we began our ascent an hour after descending the wet, at times slippery and extremely narrow path. If you've never been to any caverns, like these, or *Carlsbad, Mammoth, Jewel, Wind, Fisher Ridge*, etc. etc. (36 states in the USA have more than three caverns open to the public,) you need to find a way to go.

There is something magical about these fantastic worlds hidden beneath the surface. They can explain about how shallow seas covered central Texas 120 million years ago, and thick deposits of calcium carbonate from dead sea creatures accumulated on the sea floor. Scientists tell us after millions of years of compacting, limestone and dolomite were formed. A mere 20 million years ago, the earth cracked at the Balcones Fault, forming the Edwards Plateau, which extends hundreds of miles to the west across the hill country. Running water then formed river valleys through erosion. Rainwater that seeps through the ground along the joints and faults becomes CO2 enriched, forming a weak carbonic acid, which drains into the underground water flow, and erodes cavernous spaces in the more soluble rock. Carbonic acid rich water which drips into these caverns over centuries, form the fantastic stalagmites and stalactites that every school child struggles to keep straight in their mind! (Stalactites hold "tight" to the roof!) They form majestic structures, named things like the Watchtower, and the King's Throne.

Seeing the tiny opening that four St. Mary's college students crawled through in 1968, and then returned with flashlights to crawl over the rough wet caverns, millions of bats overhead, gives one the hebbie-jeebies, to say the least! But today, 50 years later, with all of the passages well lit, and railings along cement walkways, you can concentrate on the phenomenal beauty that this natural occurrence has created! But why is it phenomenal? Why is it so moving, so beautiful? I think the answer lies in the realization that the caverns, like the sunrise, like a mountain range, like the seashore, like a flower, like a snowflake, like an eagle, like the night sky, despite our technological advancement, lie completely outside the spectrum of our creative abilities. In point of fact, if we really pay attention, all of these *natural* wonders, are just that, wonders! They are awe inspiring.

For those of us who see more than a random cohesion of atoms developing in complexity over impossibly long times, i.e. those of us who believe in a creative intelligence, the Bible explains that feeling of wonder we get. Our God is indeed an awesome God! All we have to do is pay attention to His creative works that surround us every moment. You can literally see God everywhere you look! So go ahead; pay attention!

"Who among the gods is like You Lord? Who is like you-majestic in holiness, awesome in glory, working wonders?" (Exodus 15:11 NIV)

"The Heavens declare the Glory of God; the skies proclaim the work of His hands." (Psalm 19:1)

"Look deep into nature, and you will understand everything better." (Albert Einstein)

"Those who contemplate the beauty of the earth find reserves of strength that last a lifetime."(Rachel Carson)

> *Prayer: Lord, let us not pass quickly by the wonders of Your creation! Remind us to take a moment to truly contemplate the aspects of nature all around us, and when we do, fill us with awe at the complexity, expanse and beauty that Your hand has wrought! Thank you for the little joys that Your creation gifts us every day, from an eagle soaring in a blue sky to the early morning sunrise. AMEN*

FEBRUARY 11

Rude

"Rudeness is the weak man's imitation of strength." (Eric Hoffer)

You know when you are accelerating on a freeway on-ramp, your turn signal is on, and there is a guy in your rear-view mirror who actually accelerates into your blind spot as you try to merge? Your only choice is to slow down, annoy the people behind you, and try to re-accelerate into another spot, after the rude guy is gone. Frequently, he or she will make an obscene gesture as they fly by just to add insult to injury. Why would *anyone do* that? Why would someone hit your car in a parking lot and *not* leave a note? Why do some people let the glass door to the office slam closed in your face when you are right behind them? Why would someone sit 12 inches from the back of your head in the waiting area for your gate at the airport, and carry on a spirited hands-free phone conversation at a decibel level appropriate for a stock car race? The term "common" courtesy may be turning into an oxymoron.

It costs you virtually nothing to be nice to people, and the old adage "*you catch more flies with honey than vinegar,*" is as true today as it was when Italian Giovanni Torriano coined it in 1666 (Often mis-attributed to Ben Franklin in his 1744 edition of *Poor Richard's Almanac.*) Try this next time you call one of those high-tech support lines for one of the FAANG companies. (Facebook, Apple, Amazon, Netflix, Google.) Odds are the person you speak with might well have an accent, and if you are calling in the daytime here, they are helping you at 3 AM where they live. Instead of being annoyed when they start out asking you to turn your device on and off, just laugh and tell them 'yes, I did this time, but you'd be amazed how often I forget to try that!' Somewhere in the conversation, thank them for working in the middle of the night and maybe ask them where they are. Next time you get pulled over by a police officer. Don't argue. Don't offer an excuse. Thank the man or woman in blue for reminding you it *really isn't* safe, even to roll through a stop sign at 3 mph! Engage them a little, rather than being defensive. After he explains the situation and you thank him, ask him how his shift is going tonight or if there's a good place to eat nearby, or tell him you wish your 8 year old was with you because he absolutely loves police cars! It might be even harder with that TSA agent who confiscates your tiny keychain Swiss Army Knife for the 60th time, but try. Laugh instead of getting angry, and thank them for keeping our plane travel safe. Part of being polite, is showing an interest in people, which oddly enough, makes them feel like you think they *actually are people*!

Here's a tougher assignment. Next time someone is incredibly rude to you; offers a universally understood hand gesture, yells an obscenity at you, cuts in line or cuts you off in traffic; don't respond in kind! Apologize even if it isn't your fault, or if you can't do that, say nothing. If it's on the road, just slow down and get out of their way. You have absolutely no idea what horrible thing might have just happened in their lives to cause them to act the way they are at that particular moment. So, when a woman has her six kids under 7 years old, 200 feet below ground in the caverns, talking, pushing, and crying incessantly so you can't even here the tour guide, don't get annoyed! Put yourself in her shoes. Imagine you had to corral those six by yourself! Express your sympathy to her, or even ask if there is anything you can do, like carry something? You'll be amazed how good you both feel if you do.

"A gentle answer turns away wrath, but a harsh word stirs up anger." (Proverbs 15:1 NIV)

"A gentleman is someone who does not what he wants, but what he should." (Haruki Murakami)

"Politeness is a sign of dignity, not of subservience." (Teddy Roosevelt)

Prayer: Father God, keep us mindful of the fact that all people are your creatures, your children. When we are rude, or react in kind to those who are rude to us, we are actually showing disrespect to You, and a complete lack of empathy for whatever they might be suffering. Lord, keep us kind. AMEN

FEBRUARY 12

Dancing

"Dance, then, wherever you may be, I am the Lord of the dance said He, And I'll lead you all, wherever you may be, And I'll lead you all in the dance, said He." (lyrics-Sydney Carter)

Why, do you suppose, that first dance between husband and wife is such a highlight of every wedding? (Not to mention the father-daughter dance which I've been incredibly Blessed to do three times!) Why, do you suppose, that first electric touch with that girl or boy you liked in middle school, happened at a school dance? Why, do you suppose, one of my fondest memories of my now cardiologist daughter, is from when she was less than 6 months old and I would hold her in my arms and dance her around the living room to George

Strait and Randy Travis? And how about that Valentine's dance with her, when she was six? Why, do you suppose, a favorite memory from my own childhood is "*do-si-do and allemande left*," square dancing at Buck's Harbor Yacht Club in Brooksville, Maine? Why, do you suppose, it is that when people just need a break from the daily grind, they often hit on this idea, "Hey, let's go dancing!"

I'll tell you why: ***Because it feels good, that's why! It feels like we are free!*** Music and movement form an extremely powerful combination. Other than possibly scent, there is no more potent motivator of memories than music. And it's not only memories associated with the tune that affects us, but the lyrics as well. Ever noticed how someone can ask you the lyrics to a familiar song and you can come up with virtually nothing, but if you hear the first few bars and words, you may be off to the races on a song you listened to fifty years ago! And movement brings in your kinesthetic sense, which is tied into muscle memory. We are designed to move fluidly, although it becomes more difficult with age. But add music, and all of a sudden, a lot of that stiffness seems to disappear!

Well, life is a dance, different events and emotions weaving in and out, ceaselessly. And it's a dance, even if you don't recognize it as such. The sad thing is, if you fail to recognize it, you will most certainly fail to enjoy it. Every low is followed by a high, or it wouldn't be a low. People that recognize that, and flow with it, cope a lot better in this world.

There's a reason the songwriter refers to Christ as, *the Lord of the Dance*. He is our Creator, and by definition, the dance we move to, is His. Living a life of faith has been mistaken by many through the ages as rule-following. Nothing could be further from the message of scripture. The entire Bible is a demonstration of how "living a moral life" has nothing to do with what God desires for us. Our Pastor used to call that "marching." It didn't work for even the most "religious" like the Pharisees and Sadducees. In the lead up to the parable of the Good Samaritan, Christ is asked what a person must do to inherit eternal life? Jesus answers, "Love the Lord your God with all your heart, soul, strength and mind, and love your neighbor as yourself." (Luke 10:25-27 NIV) Loving is not marching to a set of orders. What is love, if not a dance? God created marriage so that we could live and reproduce together. He used marriage as the metaphor for Christ's relationship with His own church. What's the highlight of that wedding celebration again? *That first dance*. Looking for peace? Dance.

"Christ has truly made us free! Stay free and let no man put a yoke on you again... You are cut off from Christ who would have righteousness by the law: you are turned away from Grace!" (Galatians 5:1,4 BBE)

Prayer: Father God, You are all about love. Correct in us everyday Lord, the misperception that we can work hard, serve better, study the Bible more and somehow march to our Salvation! Your love is Grace, a free gift undeserved, and it sets us free from our guilt and shame and sin! Remind us that the freedom should make us feel like dancing the night away!! AMEN

FEBRUARY 13

Waves

"Waves are inspiring not because they rise and fall, but because each time they fall, they never fail to rise again." (Josh Billings)

Why are we transfixed by the surf at the shore? Why is the sound of waves breaking on the beach the most popular sound soother for people trying to go to sleep? What is it about rhythmicity that so attracts the human brain?

When I was a child spending the summers on Penobscot Bay in Maine, I used to lie on the foredeck of my grandfather's 26 foot Dark Harbor 17. She was built around 1930 and now belongs to my ninety-year old uncle, who still sails her every summer. *Fledgling is all* teak and mahogany with wooden sail rings, wooden mast, boom and gaff, and halyards and sheets that are all manual with no winches or jam cleats. She is a sailor's sailboat with very little freeboard, and a long, overhanging bow and stern, with only 17 feet touching at the waterline. Lying on the deck with my head turned to the side, I could hear the water rushing under her hull, and the waves slapping against her bow. I remember it as more of a whispering gurgle, the sound of muffled conversation in the distance, since on most compass points my father and grandfather were downwind in the cockpit, and barely audible. The sun baking on my back, the ice-old water rushing underneath, even as a supercharged ten-year old, I would still drift off to sleep. Only a change in tack, with the jib sheets brushing over my body, would awaken me. This memory is from 55-60 years ago, and yet as clear as if it were yesterday.

Waves are the result of unseen forces, and to most of us non-physicists, their unending pattern of rise and fall, terminating in the repetitive curl of breakers on the beach, all across the world, has in it, well, the feel of the miraculous! Sound also travels in waves, and as those waves hit our tympanic membranes, the vibration is carried from our middle to inner ear and then on to the brain. Sound soothers may also emit pink, red, brown, white and black "noise" depending on the frequencies of the sound waves that are combined. While these can be helpful, for my family of sailors, it's definitely the rhythmic sound of the surf that puts us out!

Energy travels in waves: sound, light, and all other electromagnetic impulses as far as we know. As a biologist, I can tell you, just like the physicist and the chemist can, that nature has a phenomenal tendency to express itself in repetitive patterns. There are nine recognized natural patterns including symmetries, trees, spirals, meanders, waves, foams, tessellations, cracks and stripes. Many can be modeled mathematically. Those of us who believe in an intelligence guiding the creation and course of the universe, see it expressed all around us, all the time! We see God in all these natural patterns, just as we do in the ocean waves.

I think the sound soother works, because it transports us mentally to a place where God is, and that place is where we were created! That place, we call, home. That place is safe and comforting. Even if not all of us remember our earthly home as a good place, I believe there is a place in all of us, that recognizes where we came from and Who made us. The loving home that some of us are blessed enough to have as a memory, is only a weak foreshadowing of what it will be like when we *really* go home. We all need sleep. If you have trouble getting there, try out the waves on the beach! It might just help you on that path to peace.

"I lay down and slept, yet I woke up in safety, for the Lord was watching over me." (Psalm 3:5 NIV)

"When you lie down, you will not be afraid...your sleep will be sweet." (Proverbs 3:24 NIV)

"Come to me, all you who are weary and burdened, and I will give you rest." (Matthew 11:28)

Prayer: Lord, let me find rest in You. Let the remarkable natural patterns found all around us reassure us of your omnipotence and plan, and in that reassurance, cause us to relax. You got this God! AMEN

FEBRUARY 14

A Little Sweetness

"The best and most beautiful things in the world cannot be seen or even touched. They must be felt with the heart." (Helen Keller)

Some people dislike Valentine's Day. They say it's a holiday designed by Hallmark and Ghiradelli to ramp up their profits. Well, is there a "Bah, Humbug," equivalent for February 14? Most people love Valentine's Day, and that's because most people have someone to love and be loved by, or at least somebody in mind! And a lot of us humans aren't very good at expressing, or even remembering to make the effort to express, our feelings for the people closest to us. Consequently, they welcome a little help at least once per year.

Valentine's Day started in the late 5th century AD when Pope Gelasius replaced the pagan celebration of spring and match-making rituals of "Lupercalia" with the new holiday. There are multiple accounts of which Saint, named *Valentine*, is honored in the holiday's designation, but the most likely is a bishop from Terni, who in the late 3rd century was said to have secretly married couples, exempting the husbands from military conscription for at least a year, and thus avoiding any ongoing wars. The exchange of cards on February 14, containing messages professing affection, became common as early as the mid 1500's! Since emotions were thought for centuries to arise in the heart and not the brain, candies and images on cards taking the shape of the heart became popular, as did depictions of Cupid (Roman God of Love) shooting his arrows into the heart designated by an admirer, in order to capture it for them.

Virtually all creatures like at least a bit of something sweet from time to time. (Well, okay, they say cats can't taste sweet...maybe, but it sure seems like our cat can!) In fact, we are so attracted to it, that this designation of one of the four primary taste areas on the tongue, has become associated with acts of kindness or even features of one's personality. And this concept of sweetness, of being kind to one another, has extended even to our children who celebrate Valentine's day right down to Kindergarten!

I like the idea of being kind to each other, and so does God! Recall that loving your neighbor is the second half of the greatest commandment. (Matthew 22:37) Sure, you can express it with flowers, chocolates, dinner out and a card; but you could just as easily write your affections on a post-it note. In fact, you could promise to do a specific nice think for the recipient daily, or weekly, or monthly or whatever you come up with! Everyone can appreciate kindness. Mark Twain said, "*Kindness is the language the deaf can hear and the blind can see.*"

Every kindness you extend to others will be appreciated, but it will have an even more powerful effect on your own peace and happiness.

"*Beginning today, treat everyone you meet as though they will pass away by midnight. Extend to them all the care, kindness and understanding you can muster, with no thought of reward. Your life will never be the same.*" (Og Mandino)

"*Doubt thou the stars are on fire. Doubt that the sun doth move. Doubt truth to be a liar. But never doubt my love.*" (William Shakespeare)

"*Anyone who says, 'It's as easy as taking candy from a baby,' has obviously never tried to take candy from a baby.*" (Unknown)

"*'Stressed' spelled backwards is 'desserts.' Coincidence? I think not.*" (Chandler, on Friends)

Prayer: Lord, You are all about love. Scripture tells us You are love. Guide us to lighten our hearts for this man-made holiday and spread a little sweetness as intended. AMEN

FEBRUARY 15

What Does God Want?

"He has shown you, oh mortal, what is good. And what does the Lord require of you? To act justly and to love mercy and to walk humbly with your God." (Micah 6:8)

Frequently, I wake up thinking, "what can I do for God today?" I forget momentarily, that this is exactly the wrong question! Man-kind has struggled to determine what would please God down through the ages. And it only took one generation for Cain to murder Able over their respective efforts to please God! God gave Moses a detailed set of ordinances far beyond the 10 Commandments, and He made it clear that righteousness meant obeying *every rule, all the time.* (Deuteronomy 6:2) The destruction of first the Northern Kingdom of Israel, followed a couple of centuries later by the destruction of the Southern Kingdom of Judah, made it clear that the Chosen People failed miserably and repeatedly at what they believed God wanted of them. In fact, they missed the point entirely.

Many non-Christian societies have tried to please their Gods in a variety of ways, from human sacrifice among the Aztecs, Mayans, and even many of the original Canaanite societies. Animal sacrifice served for centuries for the Hebrews, while ritual prostitution was adopted by Rome from its conquered cultures. American Indian tribes strove to please God with ritual dances, festivals, and at times sacrifices. The real question is, has all that much changed today?

Those of us in Western culture may no longer practice human or animal sacrifice, but we certainly have rituals to please God. For centuries different churches have worshipped in only rigid prescribed forms, prayed in certain mandated patterns, or made promises to live in silence, chastity, service etc. in order, often honestly, to try and position themselves as worthy before God. Many Christians today, believe that the degree to which they dedicate themselves to the study of the Word, to consistent quiet time, to the service of their church, or their charity to the poor, all combine to earn them favor in God's eyes. This leads not only to those who become prideful for their great contribution, but also to those who feel unworthy in comparison.

Paul spends all of his epistles, making up the majority of the New Testament, explaining that this is simply *not the case*. God's love is unending, and offered in Grace to all, and the only requirement is faith! (Ephesians 2:8) The Hebrews of the Old Testament, even when obedient, were obedient in ritual only. Their hearts were "uncircumcised," meaning they had no faith behind their ceremony. (Jeremiah 9:26) If we as Christians, have faith in our Savior, then there is nothing we can do to make God love us more or to make Him love us less. (Romans 5:8; 8:35)

So, what does Micah mean? God wants His people to obey Him because they ***want to***, not because they are constrained by ritual. God showed them three things that were "good." ***Act justly***, means simply to be fair to others in their dealings; ***Love mercy***, means to carry through on commitments to meeting other's needs, and to ***Walk humbly***, means the absence of prideful arrogance in your relationship with God! Micah relates this, centuries before the birth of Christ, and yet the message is unchanged! Micah 6:8 merely spells out *how* we are to love God completely, and how to love our neighbors as ourselves. (Matthew 22:34)

So, when I wake up in the morning, a better questions is, "what love can God demonstrate through me today, that I might glorify Him?"

Prayer: Father, remind us every day that "it's about the relationship, dummy!" Let us pray, study and serve because in loving You, we want to do these things, not because we want to try and earn the approval that Your Grace has already given us through faith! AMEN

FEBRUARY 16
Reach Out

"Reach out and touch, somebody's hand; make this word a better place, if you can!" (Diana Ross by Ashford Nikolas)

It was 1968. The war in Vietnam was raging and so were the youth of America, as demonstrations became volatile across the country's college campuses. Dr. Martin Luther King was murdered in April, and Bobby Kennedy shot down in September. The entire nation was at a boiling point, and many of the young felt hopeless. We were embroiled in a much-reviled war, and the civil rights movement had taken a violent turn in response to Dr. King's assassination. The epicenter of unrest was the Bay Area, and at the center of that, was UC Berkley.

It was in this atmosphere that Dr. Jerome Motto returned to the Bay Area and joined the psychiatric faculty at UCSF. After serving as a Captain in the Battle of the Bulge in WW II, Jerry finished his undergraduate studies at Berkley, received his MD from UCSF, and then did a residency at Johns Hopkins in Baltimore. Once his training was complete, he made the trek home to San Francisco. Dr. Motto received a grant from NIH to study attempted suicide admissions to SF hospitals that tumultuous fall of 1968. Dr. Motto set up a controlled study to follow up these patients after release. The study design was simple. One half of the patients would receive a brief, typewritten note at one-month intervals initially dropping to quarterly after six months. It would be signed by the patient's direct caregiver from the hospital, and the message was the same each time. It simply stated that the team was wondering how they were doing and wanted them to know that they were always available should the patient need to contact them. The other half received no communication. The outcome startled the entire psychiatric community.

The result of this "Caring Letter" approach as it became known, was a better than 50% reduction in suicide over the ensuing several years, compared to the non-communication group. At the time, there was not a single proven method of reducing suicide attempts in the medical literature.

People of faith have turned to God to fill that communication void for centuries, and they have not been disappointed. David wrote seventy-three Psalms in which he poured out his heart to God. (For example Psalms 3 through 8.) Surely a man, having murdered another man in order to get away with adultery, betrayed his own daughter in law, who was raped by his own son, and then been set upon by another son in a coup attempt, had much about which to be depressed. And yet God, through the prophet Samuel, referred to David as "A man after God's own heart." (1 Sam 13:14) Psalms are just one more example of evidence that God sends us those "Caring Letters" whenever we open one of His notes! Some people call that collection of notes from our Father, "The Bible." Imagine what it would mean to someone in need, if you just dropped them a spontaneous text or e-mail, that let them know you were thinking about them? Try it. It's one more step on the path to peace.

"Never underestimate the lingering effects of a dash of spontaneous comfort!" (Gina Greenlea)

"If I take the wings of the dawn, if I dwell in the remotest part of the sea, even there Your hand will reach me, and Your right hand will lay hold of me." (Psalm 139:9-10 NASB)

Prayer: Father God, we are Blessed to be adopted into Your family and treated as one of Your own! Thank you for reaching us every day in Your Word, reminding us that we need to reach out to others in kind. AMEN

FEBRUARY 17

Becalmed

"Never sail out farther than you know you can row back!" (Danish Proverb)

Sometime when I was in my forties and the kids were small, we slipped our mooring in Deadman's Cove, sailing *Fledgling* out into the Reach on a gorgeous, sunny, breezy day. We headed toward the Deer Isle bridge on a broad reach, with a brisk southwest breeze on our starboard quarter. *Fledgling* is the all wooden, gaff rigged, century old, sleek racing boat, that has passed down from my grandfather to my uncle. She is a beautiful sailor indeed, low to the water, excellent at pointing (sailing close to or almost toward the wind for you lubbers,) but powered by the wind alone. Our sailboat back in north Texas was a bit larger, but more importantly, happened to have an in-board diesel engine. Not a small distinction to forget.

There are a few things true sailors must consider before heading out, particularly on an ocean shore like mid-coast Maine. The tides move 12-13 vertical feet every six hours, and on Eggemoggin Reach, a narrow body of water at the head of Penobscot Bay, the current changes direction with the tide and moves at a very good clip indeed. There are untold numbers of rocks, invisible at high tide, and thus a potentially lethal danger to a fast-moving hull. In addition to the tides, currents, and hidden dangers, the skipper of course, has to know the forecast for the day; including projected temperature, wind direction and strength. Now the wind on the Bay comes up reliably about 1 PM, and every sailor knows it. But when it will die down is, to put it mildly, much less predictable. My grandfather warned me about this. My father warned me about this. My uncle warned me about this.

Throughout the 18th and 19th century, ocean going ship Captains had to be sensitive to seasonal weather changes, and especially to changes in the trade winds, that were very much latitude related. In fact, the "horse latitudes" is a term that refers to latitudes 30-35 degrees, both north and south of the equator, where constant high pressure leads to calm or often non-existent winds. Ships that became trapped in these latitudes were "becalmed," with no wind to move them out of the oppressive heat and humidity for weeks or months at a time. The predicament was so severe, that sailors were often forced to eat their virtually indispensable horses, and hence the term.

On this particular Maine Blue Day, I sort of forgot that *Fledgling* was powered by the movement of the air alone. Any sailor ought to know that if you sail largely down wind, and the wind dies, you've got a problem on your hands that is directly proportionate to how far you sailed away from your mooring. We sat in the heat and the brilliant sun without a breath of wind, baking in our own sweat, for over four hours.

The larger metaphor for the faithful of course, is that we are constantly making plans, big and little, without a thought to consulting the One Who created us and already has a plan for us! Try pausing for one moment next time; think about what your father may have advised you, then clear your mind and ask your Heavenly Father for the guidance of the One who is already within you! You may well be surprised that you find yourself in your own little "horse latitudes" less often!

"The one who is wise is cautious…but a fool is reckless and careless." (Proverbs 14:16 NIV)

"Consider generations long past. Ask your father and he will tell you; your elders… will explain."(Deut. 32:7)

"A person's steps are directed by the Lord. How can anyone understand their own way?" (Proverbs 20:24)

Prayer: Father, we know that all things are possible with God. But we also know You want us to use our minds and hopefully have the sense both to listen to our elders, and to think ahead when we step out into the world. Let our judgment be guided by Your Word, through prayer and by the Holy Spirit. AMEN

FEBRUARY 18

Tai Chi

"Whatever things are true, whatever things are noble, whatever things are just, whatever things are pure, whatever things are lovely, whatever things are of good report; if there is any virtue and if there is anything praiseworthy---- meditate on these things" (Philippians 4:8 NKJV)

Unfortunately, I have a bad back. It started with my first ruptured disc after a rebound my junior year in high school, when an opposing player came down across my neck and hyper-flexed my back. That was forty-seven years ago and it's been downhill since! Through the years I've had countless epidural steroids and multiple surgeries, all of which helped…*some*. But what I needed was something to strengthen my core without causing yet another injury. Enter author Dr. Paul Lam and *Tai Chi for Beginners and the 24 Forms*. Add to that the beautifully instructive videos by Kriss Brooks, *24 Forms Tai Chi-The Basics*, and my life began to change.

Tai chi exists in many forms, but the ancient Chinese martial art seeks integration of mind, body and spirit, through standard sets of exercises performed on a regular basis. The essential principles of mind/body integration include fluidity of movement, control of breathing and mental concentration. The central focus is to enable the *qi*, or life force, to flow smoothly and powerfully throughout the body. The idea is that this integration of mind and body leads to total harmony of inner and outer self. I practice *qigong* exercises every morning followed by the twenty-four standard moves of *Yang Tai Chi*, the most popular form found in the West.

While once, many in Western society fiercely resisted any integration of the ancient beliefs and practices of Eastern cultures, the 21st century has seen a rapid crumbling of the wall between these cultures. I stumbled upon *Tai Chi* shortly after completing seminary in my late fifties, still practicing medicine full-time. *Tai Chi* is based on an ancient Chinese holistic view of medicine, combined with the physical principles of an inward focused martial art. The goal is for people to exist in complete balance with nature, in both a spiritual and physical sense. *Tai Chi* improves cardiovascular fitness, muscular strength, and joint flexibility. Literally hundreds of studies have shown its effectiveness in helping conditions including arthritis, heart disease, and diabetes. It definitively improves balance and markedly prevents the risk of falling. It has been shown to reduce every physiologic indicator of stress.

For me, it was remarkably easy and effective to integrate *Tai Chi* with meditation on both scripture and those things on which God would have us concentrate. I'm sure that many theologians and philosophers would have kittens if they knew I find the concept of *qi* as 'life force' not all that distant from what the indwelling Spirit is for the Christian, although Believers know our life force to be the Holy Spirit Himself. When I first focus on slowing my breathing, and then making my movements fluid and consistent, I find that I can then easily begin to meditate on either a bible verse I have selected, or the issue I wish to discuss with my Father. For me, a prayerful conversation comes naturally during *Tai Chi*, when I have no distractions whatsoever. Personally, I prefer to perform Yang to the accompaniment of calming music written for Tai Chi, which one may find on Spotify. *Tai Chi* may or may not be your cup of tea, but God knows, you need some way to slow down and meditate prayerfully, and you need it everyday!

"I will meditate on Your precepts, and contemplate Your ways." (Psalms 119:15 NKJV)

"My eyes are awake through the night watches, that I may meditate on Your Word. (Psalms 119:148)

"It is good for me that I have been afflicted, that I may learn Your statutes." (Psalms 119:71 NKJV)

"The more you read and meditate on the Bible, the more you will be astonished with it!" (Charles Spurgeon)

Prayer: Lord, help us find a way to quiet our hearts in the midst of our hectic lives, and spend a few moments every day in receptive meditation. We know that this will strengthen our awareness of the life force within us all, which is You! AMEN

FEBRUARY 19
Fetch

"The fruit of the Spirit is love, joy, peace, long suffering, kindness, goodness, faithfulness, gentleness and self-control." (Galatians 5:22 NKJV)

We had a black lab while the kids were growing up. Now we have Windsor, the standard Labradoodle. My brother and one of my daughters have yellow labs now. If you weren't a Christian, and you had no familiarity whatsoever with the Bible, then when you read of the nine qualities above, you certainly wouldn't think they described the average man, but you might think they described your own dog!

So, what is it about dogs that makes them better companions than other humans? Perhaps it's their absolute, unshakable, lifelong dedication to one goal alone…pleasing you! Let's look at the fruits above one at a time with Rover in mind. If you've never owned a dog, then you truly have limited experience with being on the receiving end of unconditional love. Dogs can ***DO love***, believe me. When you come home each night, you would have to be blind not to see the **joy** just bursting out of every fiber of their being when they run to the door! When you sit quietly anywhere, gently petting the dog curled up next to you as you both look out over the water, or watch the sunset, or just fall asleep by the fire; that my friend, is **peace**. How many times has your dog put up with your bad moods, or forgetting to feed him, or even getting swatted for an imagined indiscretion or disobedience? Our labs could have taken our arms off at the shoulder if they chose to, but instead they take our abuse, even in their innocence. That is **long suffering**. Our lab played with our cat, shared food with him, even protected him when threatened. He would lick an injury on the cat or on you, if you let him. That's awfully close to **kindness** in my book. When you train a lab to do something, even something that's part of his nature, like fetching anything you care to throw, he does it reliably, each time he's asked, even when he's exhausted. He'll protect your family without being told. He's showing you what **goodness** looks like. Our lab would walk across hot coals or across the whole country, just to serve our family in any way he could. But it was our family he loved and protected; and ours specifically. That's called **faithfulness**. When you snuck him a table scrap, he would **gently** take it from your fingers, careful not to grab your hand along with it. Finally, even though he had to be taught, once he knew what you wanted of him, he never had an accident inside, when you told him to come, he would, but he would also stay, until you released him. That's **self-control**.

Now, imagine if you woke up every morning just as excited about seeing God and doing His bidding in order to please Him, as your dog is about seeing you and doing your bidding, in order to please you? No one really knows what makes a dog so, well, dog-like! But we do know that people do **NOT** exhibit these qualities consistently, with anywhere near the reliability of this creature with whom we share only 84% of our DNA.

But Paul tells us, as he tells the Galatians, that there is a way to make it happen. If we accept Christ as our Savior and receive the gift of the indwelling Spirit, then God will exhibit His own qualities ***through us!*** All we have to do is let Him. In order to do that, we have to know Him, and in order to do that, we need to read the owner's manual He gave us. Your puppy wasn't so good at many of these qualities until he understood exactly what you wanted and how you wanted him to serve you. We're not so good at it either, until we study what God has to say, discuss it with friends, and then talk to Him about it ourselves!

Prayer: Lord, thank you SO MUCH for dogs! In Your wisdom you gave us the perfect best friend; one who, without even trying, shows us every day how You would have us love others in order to love you! Thank you for Your Word, Lord. There is no question being a human is easier with an owner's manual! AMEN

FEBRUARY 20

That's Not Fair

"I am not being unfair to you friend. Didn't you agree to work for a denarius? Take your pay and go. I want to give the one I hired last the same as I gave you. Don't I have the right to do what I want with my own money? Or are you envious because I am generous?" (Matthew 20:13-15)

Why is it that when you hear someone cry out, in their too loud voice, "*That's not fair!*" that you immediately think of a child? And yet, do we not know of adults who are constantly comparing themselves to others, and complaining that they are somehow being treated unfairly? Have we not done it ourselves? Perhaps we think of a child, because young children have not learned consideration for others yet. They are primarily focused on themselves and their own immediate needs. If someone comes and takes the toy they have monopolized for thirty minutes on the playground at recess, they are likely to scream about how unfair that is! They might complain to the teacher with a story like, "Johnny just came and stole my truck! (the fact that it isn't his truck and it wasn't "stealing" are lost on the four-year old!) When I was perhaps six and my brother, nine, and he would beat me at chess, I would angrily flip over the board and claim through my tears that "*he was cheating!*" Clearly unfair, right? (never mind that he was just better at it, and no cheating was necessary to beat me!) To me, it just wasn't fair that he won all the time.

Someone close to me recently quit their job, not because he was unhappy with his company's assignments, but because another employee was doing essentially the same job, but getting paid considerably more. In other circumstances, and medicine comes to mind, because that is my field, there are health care professionals that perform the same task as others, but because of their differing level of education, get paid more or less, than the one who really fulfills the same role. Of course, here are legitimate societal grievances. Women often get paid less for the same job as a man. People of color may either get paid less, or have less opportunities than whites in the same community. But even in these circumstances where unfairness truly does exist, comparisons certainly don't breed happiness. And it's not always about money. Children feel that their sibling gets more toys or more attention or more ipad time! Teens complain that their punishment or restriction is "unfair" because their sibling *never* had to do this, or give up that. Why should they be grounded, when *all their friends* are doing the same thing! (Whatever it might be!)

All of these scenarios have a common thread: *comparison*. In Jesus' parable of the vineyard workers, all had *agreed* ahead of time to work for one denarius. It was only in comparing themselves to those who had been in the field less time, that those who had worked the longest hours, felt they were being treated unfairly. Jesus not only makes the point that it is the vineyard owner's money to do with as he pleases, but that all had *agreed* to work for one denarius. Those who think that is unfair afterwards, are not as good as their word. A deal is a deal. "Envious [*ophthalmos in* Greek] of my generosity," literally, means 'jealous side-eye or evil eye' as in, 'begrudge' or 'resent.'

Jesus told this parable to illustrate several points. First, God is sovereign, and rewards are under his purview alone. Second, your perceived self-importance by worldly standards, may have nothing to do with your salvation and eternal reward. *"The last will be first and the first will be last."* Third, it is wrong to resent someone's generosity simply because you are not the recipient! The Pharisees could not possibly imagine a Gentile entering the Kingdom of Heaven! How could they possibly *deserve* it? (No one *deserves* it; but that's about Grace!)

Christians find their identity, and their worth, in Christ alone. We have been adopted into God's family, and we have put on the righteousness of the Son! There *are no comparisons!*

Prayer: Dear Heavenly Father, help us all to see that our value to You is in our union with Your Son, not in the amount or type of work that we do, not in the color of our skin, and not in our bank account. Comparing ourselves to others is the quickest way to unhappiness, and the quickest way to lose sight of the good gifts you have bestowed on us all! AMEN

FEBRUARY 21

Practicality

"You have heard that it was said to people long ago, 'You shall not commit murder, and anyone who commits murder will be subject to judgment.' But I tell you anyone who is angry with a brother or sister will be subject to judgment!" (Matthew 5:21-22 NIV)

G.K. Chesterton lived in the late 19th and early 20th centuries in England. He was famous in his own time, as a theologian, literary and art critic, and comedian. Known as the "prince of paradox," he was well known for often making his point by turning popular sayings, proverbs and allegories upside down and inside out.

Here is a tiny taste of his wit:

"Obviously the reason angels can fly is they take themselves lightly."

"The poets have been mysteriously silent on the subject of cheese."

And a taste of his beliefs:

"Tolerance is the virtue of the man without convictions."

"The Christian ideal has not been tried and found wanting. It has been found difficult; and left untried."

And a taste of his observations on life:

"The world will never starve for wonders; but only for want of wonder."

I maintain that thanks are the highest form of thought; that gratitude is happiness doubled by wonder."

"One sees great thing from the valley; only small things from the peaks."

Today, the few that are familiar with Chesterton are either well-read, or they watch *The Father Brown Mysteries* on Netflix, of which he was the author! If you have read or seen the tails and travails of Father Brown, then you have a better idea of Chesterton's remarkable mind. His most famous work, comparable to CS Lewis' *Mere Christianity*, is called *Orthodoxy*, and every Christian should read it once in their life times.

In his fifties, as a well- respected newspaper columnist and theologian, he was once asked by a reporter, "If you were to be stranded on a desert island, all alone in the middle of the ocean, and you could have only one book salvaged from the wreckage, what would it be?" All of course, expected his answer to be 'The bible' and the only speculation was to what translation he would prefer. Chesterton reportedly tilted his head, gave the matter a moment's consideration, and then responded, "'I should think Lewis Brown's *Guide to Practical Ship Building,'* would suit nicely!"

One of the last five hundred years' most erudite theologians offered a valuable lesson by his response. Chesterton, like Christ, advocates practical approaches to life, not religiosity leading to empty ritual. Yes, Jesus in the Sermon on the Mount, certainly used hyperbole. God doesn't actually expect you to pluck out your eye if you look at a member of the opposite sex lustfully! He's not threatening you with hell for yelling at your brother. He understands that simply *proscribing sin* isn't practical because it doesn't work on humans! But, He does want you to understand that it's not the *breaking of the rule* that is to be avoided, but the orientation of your heart that *allows* you to break the rule in the first place! Jesus isn't saying that you are going to hell for adultery or for arguing with your brother; He's saying that *if you follow Him*, you will move toward extinguishing your desire to do anything hurtful; because that's not part of loving each other and that's not part of treating others the way you would like to be treated! And following Him includes being already forgiven when you fail!

Prayer: Thank you Jesus for coming to live among us so that You have felt our temptations, you know our joys and our sorrows, and for offering us a practical solution! Faith in You gains us the Holy Spirit who will guide us into all truth, and consequently to the peace and joy we seek! AMEN

FEBRUARY 22
Mirror, Mirror

"Mirror, mirror, on the wall, who's the fairest one of all?" (Evil Queen, Snow White)

I would venture to say that most people around the world are familiar with Jacob & Wilhelm Grimm's 1812 fairy tale, *Snow White and the Seven Dwarfs*. Without relating the entire story, suffice it to say that the Queen, who was the wicked stepmother of Snow White, needed reassurance every day that she was the most beautiful woman in the Realm. Only when she received an answer that she wasn't looking for, did she go on her murderous rampage.

One of the many reasons this particular story has caught the imagination of the world for more than two centuries, is of course, that we see ourselves in it. We often literally look in a mirror, hoping to see how attractive we appear. Unfortunately, the modern aluminum glass mirror, in its perfect reflection, tells the truth more often than we would like! Used often for personal grooming, we hope to find near perfection, but often find near disaster!

Interestingly, there is another mirror available to us, and while it shows the same glaring imperfections we would rather not see, it does offer a quick fix that involves neither botox nor filler. I'm talking, of course, about the Bible! Never has there been a more representative, truthful, yet horrifying reflection of ourselves than the scriptures! Take the Hebrews at Mount Sinai, only weeks after having been rescued from four hundred years of slavery in Egypt. Moses and Aaron served as the conduit for the delivery of TEN horrific plagues on Egypt, necessary to finally convince Pharaoh to release the people and their livestock. The Hebrews witnessed this! Then, they WALKED through the Red Sea, held open for them by God Himself, and followed a pillar of fire and column of cloud into the desert after the entire pursuing Egyptian army had drowned. Then, at the foot of Mount Sinai, impatient for Moses to come down from his meeting with God, and fearing they would starve or be destroyed by enemies in the desert, they convinced Aaron to let them create, and then worship, a Golden Calf! (Exodus 32:1) ***Are you kidding me?*** How stiff necked can a people be? Immediately following miracle after miracle performed right before their eyes, they turn away from God and decide to go their own way, and follow a God *they made themselves?* As you are probably aware, that didn't work out too well for the ring leaders, shortly thereafter.

Is it so hard to see yourself in that story? Have you ever been very aware of God's blessings, indeed thankful in prayer, until the next week you find yourself in a very tight spot, don't think God is handling it well or responding quickly enough, or more likely, you never even ask Him about it in the first place, and decide to take matters into your own hands? Sort of *forgetting* to speak to God happens over and over in the scriptures. Moses, Aaron, Saul, David, almost all of the Kings that followed, the list is endless; all *forgot* to ask God every now and then, and what always followed was the outcome of their own disastrous decisions!

How about Peter, the Rock on which Christ built the church? He doesn't just forget Jesus, he actively denies Him three times right after His arrest! (And before we're too tough on Peter, where are the other ten remaining disciples; that's right, *not remaining*…they split!) (Matthew 26:56,75) Peter was so zealous, that he swore he would die alongside of Jesus, remember? Then, when the cock crowed, he looked in the mirror. What he saw was the flawed human that we all are.

But there's good news, and a very quick fix, if you choose it! Romans 10:13 tells us that our imperfect selves, reflected in that mirror, can be made *perfect* in God's eyes, and in only an instant! All we need to do is call on the name of the Lord, and all our blemishes vanish in *His righteousness*. Poof! Instant Snow White!

Prayer: Heavenly Father, we love You! We know that You first loved us, because in our perpetual imperfection, You offered us Your Son, that through His sacrifice for our sin, and our forgiveness, we might find our back to You, clothed in the perfect righteousness of Christ. AMEN

FEBRUARY 23

The Depths

"Out of the depths I cry to You Lord; Lord hear my voice. Let Your ears be attentive to my cry for mercy!" (Psalm 130:1-2 NIV)

Have you ever noticed that we have a tendency to call on God more urgently and more frequently when we have hit rock bottom? When the money is good, the job is secure and going well, the family is healthy, heck, you're healthy, and your leisure time is even plentiful; well, man usually feels that he is doing just fine thank you very much, without God. Prayer seems sort of silly, and let's face it, who even remembers to pray when everything is going swimmingly?

But those of us who occasionally put God on a back burner until we *really* need Him, find to our surprise, that He is still there waiting! Our God is a faithful God, and He offers *hesed,* the Hebrew word used 248 times in the Bible, meaning 'unfailing love.' Charles Spurgeon, the famous English, Particular Baptist, preacher in the last half of the 19th century, looked at our trials and tribulations as proportional to our mercies or consolations. It is always darkest before the dawn, and Spurgeon felt you could see the light much brighter if you were emerging from the inky blackness. Being driven to the depths tends to make a man humble, and on your knees is a good posture to receive the Lord's Grace. Our trials make more room for consolation. Great troubles are critical for the development of great hearts. Spurgeon puts it this way. *"God comes into your heart and finds it full...He begins to break your comforts and to make it empty; then there is more room for grace."*

When things start rapidly coming apart; you or a loved one receive a bad diagnosis; a family member dies, you lose your job; you lose a friend, or your marriage is in real trouble; God comes to us even before we beg for Him to do just that. The realization dawns on us that doing things our way, in our own power, has led us right to the bottom of the well. This realization then leads to a rejection of the idols with which we have surrounded ourselves. The money, the power, the fancy car, the alcohol, the porn; none of these objects of our intermittent worship, leads anywhere but down. And when we hit bottom, it tends to wake us up to what's actually important in life.

Joseph's brothers threw him in a well and then sold him into slavery. Even after working enslaved in Egypt, things got worse when Potiphar's wife accused him of sexual assault and he was thrown into prison. (Genesis 39:11) Can't get much worse off than that, right? But God provided Joseph with an opportunity by empowering him to interpret dreams, and although Joseph gave the credit to God, still it was he who was rescued from slavery and put in power over all of Egypt!

The prophet Jonah didn't forget about God, he just flat ignored Him, and went in the opposite direction from Nineveh, where God had directed him! Read the story again for the details, (Jonah 1-4) but suffice it to say that when the sailors threw him overboard in the midst of the storm, and he sank like a rock, things were not looking well for his immediate future as a prophet, or any future for that matter! But far from punishing him for rank disobedience, God provided a great fish to swallow him and take him to shore! Whether literal, or metaphorical, the message is clear: God is there for you even if you don't ask 'till you're desperate! That's what His *hesed* is about!

"As for you, you meant it for evil against me, but God meant it for good in order to bring about this present result, to preserve many people alive." (Joseph-Genesis 50:20-21 NASB)

"I sought the Lord, and He answered me, and delivered me from all my fears." (Psalm 34:4 ESV)

"Because he holds fast to me in love, I will deliver him; I will protect him because he knows my name. When he calls to me, I will answer him; I will be with him in trouble; I will rescue him." (Psalm 91:14 ESV)

Prayer: Dear Heavenly Father, We want to praise you Lord, for all the good gifts we receive, that we know are from You, even though we forget! When we only seek you in the rough times, thank you for loving us anyway! AMEN

FEBRUARY 24

Really Hard Stuff

"If you're doing something safe, something you already know can be done, you're wasting your time." (Astronaut Scott Kelly)

A few weeks ago, we had the privilege of hearing Captain Scott Kelly, the NASA astronaut, tell us about how a mediocre, unmotivated high school student became the American to spend the longest time in space, as of 2016 at 520 days total. He spent 340 days in a row aboard the International Space Station (ISS). [Since then, astronaut-biochemist, Peggy Whitson, has broken that record.] Scott's identical twin brother, Mark, was also an astronaut, and spent 50 days in space. As such, they were the perfect choice to study the effects of weightlessness and radiation exposure over periods as long as those necessary to reach Mars and return.

Scott, like his brother, was both a Navy F-14 fighter pilot and subsequently a test pilot, before joining the astronaut corp. They grew up in West Orange, New Jersey, where their father was a police officer. Scott claims he was a poor student, and if they'd had the diagnosis of ADHD in the early 70's, he would have been the poster child. Scott reluctantly applied to, and then attended U of Maryland, Baltimore County, where still a poor student, he read Tom Wolfe's, *The Right Stuff* about the original NASA astronauts, and found his inspiration. Transferring to SUNY Maritime on a NROTC scholarship, he eventually went on to an engineering degree, a Naval commission, flight school, piloting the F-14 Tomcat off an aircraft carrier, test piloting, then as a NASA astronaut, flying two shuttle missions and two ISS missions. Before his final lift off in Russia, for his year-long flight, a Russian Orthodox priest blessed them and threw Holy water over them. Kelly said he figured a blessing couldn't hurt before rocketing into space on a Russian Soyuz!

While Scott was inspired by reading *The Right Stuff,* he says what gave him strength whenever he thought he just couldn't take it anymore, was the fact that his mother became the first female police officer in Orange, New Jersey, largely by conquering a backyard obstacle course that his dad had helped her construct. It took a year for her to meet the physical requirements for academy admission, but she was out there every day, rain or shine, until she could climb over that last wall. She never gave up. During his weightless year in space, Kelly monitored body functions every day, and experienced distention and thickening of carotid arteries, huge swings in biochemical indicators of stress and his immune system, changes in 7% of his DNA including inversions, translocations and telomeric lengthening, and he had accelerated bone turn over. Two liters of fluid shifted from the lower to upper half of his body, altering neuro-optic function and even emotional perception. The most abrupt changes happened during his re-entry in the tiny Soyuz capsule which he described as "going over Niagara Falls in a barrel that's on fire!" But, from his first day in community college, to his last day in space, he never gave up.

In his book, *Endurance: A Year in Space, (2017)* Captain Kelly drills home some advice from lessons that were hard earned. 1) If you are going to do anything, pick the really hard stuff 2) Be willing to make mistakes 3) Control whatever you can and ignore the rest 4) Make your goals really, really high 5) Test the status quo and lastly 6) Never, never, never, give up!

God created man to endure. We are one of the weakest mammals on the planet, and yet we were ordained to use our ingenuity to subdue the earth. In the Bible, Paul was given the task of bringing the Gospel to the Gentiles, despite the fact that prior to meeting Christ on the road to Damascus, he was Saul, a Pharisee, and chief persecutor of this new Jewish sect called The Way! What Christ called Paul to do seemed, well, *really hard stuff*! Yet, with the guidance of the Holy Spirit, willingness to fail, impossibly high goals, and the commitment of never, never giving up, he travelled by foot, at least three times across the entire known world, starting churches with whom he stayed in touch by letter. Shortly before his execution in Rome, he penned these words, *"I have fought the good fight, I have finished the race, I have kept the faith." (2 Timothy 4:7 NKJV)*

Prayer: Father God, thank you that we are each "fearfully and wonderfully made!" Let your Spirit keep urging us to meet our potential,

and use the gifts you have given us to achieve tasks that at first, seem impossible, but in actuality, are just really, really, hard! AMEN

FEBRUARY 25

The Star-Spangled Banner

"Blest with victory and peace, may the heaven-rescued land, Praise the Power that hath made and preserved us a nation. Then conquer we must, for our cause is just, And this be our motto, 'In God is our trust.' And the star-spangled banner forever shall wave, O'er the land of the free and the home of the brave!" (Francis Scott Key)

Not many of us recognize the end of the fourth verse of our national anthem, but there it is! Today, there seems to be much debate about the religious persuasion of the Founding Fathers. There are those who insist that our nation, founded in revolution, was not, in fact, founded as a "Christian" nation, nor were those who formulated our constitution necessarily Christian, but many were universalists of some sort. We fought a bloody terrible war, we continued to permit enslavement of our fellow man after our independence was secure, and we structured a government that favored the preferences and input of the wealthy over the poor.

Maybe. I think it only shows that we are a nation made up of fallible, inherently self-concerned people, just like those that have populated the world since the beginning of recorded history. But, at the same time, we are a phenomenally diverse group of people, from all different ethnic, cultural, and yes, religious, backgrounds, who came together to throw off the tyranny of a few, and overturn the system of oppression that had been the world's predominant form of government for many centuries. In doing so, we acknowledged in the Declaration of Independence, that we formed a nation 'under God.' As such, the founders, as we do today, value the monotheistic *precepts* of freedom, love for God and each other, equality, independence and community! (Speaking of community, did you know that Article III of the US Constitution clearly delineates a "league of friendship" between the states, and that they will provide for the common defense, secure each other's liberties, binding themselves to assist each other against all forces? Should we remind everyone before the OU-Texas game each year?)

These musings came to mind when I noticed one of those huge American Flags that often fly over places like car dealerships, hanging limply in the cold rain this morning. For some reason, whenever I see the Stars and Bars snapping in the wind, at right angles to the pole, on a sunny day with the blue sky in the background; well, I just feel *better!* In contrast, this morning, the flaccid flag just kind of, I don't know, bums me out a little. Is that just the weather? I guess the weather is part of it. But I think the bigger part, is that when I see that flag, flying proudly in a brisk breeze, it speaks of energy and determination and history and sacrifice and freedom and a people bound together by common beliefs and values.

While I was mulling that over later, it occurred to me that every one of those things are common to our Christian faith. Christ sacrificed Himself specifically for our freedom; Freedom from sin and guilt and shame and fear. He left us the Holy Spirit to energize us in our determination to spread the Gospel and to love our neighbors as we want to be loved. We were adopted into His family, as equals, and thus are a people bound together by common beliefs. Lastly, there are now almost 2000 years of Christian Church history, during which we have both failed miserably and been horribly misguided, as well as triumphed and brought hope to millions.

So, America might not be a *Christian* nation, we still struggle with racism, class distinction, crime and immorality, but at least we struggle. It's still a darn good country to live in, if you want to be able to express your opinion and worship as you choose. Here's to the flag!

Prayer: Dear Heavenly Father, we know that You love all Your children all over the world; and yet we thank you every day that Your Providence has allowed us to live under a flag that declares to the world, "we are a free people, able to speak and worship as we please." AMEN

FEBRUARY 26

That's Just WRONG

"Quarreling means trying to show that the other party is wrong. There would be no sense in trying to do that, unless you both had some agreement as to what Right and Wrong actually are." (C.S. Lewis)

Earlier today I was at the Home Depot. This particular store, has parking spots where some Machiavellian humorist evidently drew the lines on the ground. Knowing that eventually, I would need to pull my SUV out into this river of humanity, vehicles and speed bumps, I pulled past the open space, with my blinker on, and began to back into its rather narrow confines. Luckily, my truck has all those warning bells and whistles that sound when something crosses the rear-view camera, or I wouldn't even have seen the corvette that zipped into the spot while I was executing my carefully planned maneuver!

Now, let's all say it together. **That's just *WRONG***. Everybody, (including the guilty party involved) can agree that this is simply not done. But why not? He was quicker. He had something he needed at the Home Depot too. Why shouldn't he just slide into that space while I was aligning my ship like the shuttle docking with the International Space Station? Or let's take, perhaps, a clearer example. Why is everyone so outraged that a certain movie producer coerced scores of actresses into having sex with him in order to help their careers advance? He saw an opportunity for self-gratification and took it. What's wrong with that? Or let's bring even more clarity to the question. When 276 young girls were kidnapped by the radical Islamist group, Boko Haram, from their school in Chibook, Nigeria, in order to use them as cooks and sex slaves, the world was outraged!

So why the outrage? Who determines that it's "wrong?" Here is the simple truth. No one would think that either the man who stole my parking space, or the man who kidnapped and raped young girls, had done anything "wrong" unless there were some universal idea of what is permissible among humans who live in society with each other. In other words, there appears to be a standard of what is "wrong" and what is "right." Yes, there are of course cultural variations, and huge ones that have changed down through history to some extent or another. But certain things have *always* been considered wrong; among them stealing stuff and raping children. At one time, we called these distinctions between right and wrong, the "Laws of Human Nature." It was called a law of human nature, because people thought that everyone knew these rules of how we *ought to behave,* innately, and did not need to be taught. It does *not* mean however, that this is *how* we do behave, because we all break these laws of decent behavior every day.

The late Briton, C.S. Lewis, perhaps the most renowned former atheist, apologist, professor, and author, of the last two centuries, remarked that although man is inevitably subject to the *Laws of Nature,* like gravity, or heredity, or chemistry; he is not so bound by the *Laws of Human Nature*. These laws he may choose to disobey. His seminal work, *Mere Christianity,* is really a collection of radio addresses given in England during the blitz, when the Nazis were bombing London indiscriminately, killing thousands. "*What is the sense of saying the Nazis were wrong, unless Right is a real thing which the Nazis, at bottom, knew as well as we did, and ought to have practiced? If they had no notion of what we mean by right, then we might fight them, but we could no more have blamed them for that than the color of their hair!*"

The atheists will object. They will say our ideas of right and wrong are an evolutionary outcome based on self-preservation. (Difficult to explain the soldier who throws himself on the hand-grenade to save his fellow soldiers, though.) There are other objections and we will dive deeper on another day. But C.S. Lewis drew one conclusion: This universally understood standard of right and wrong was created, and that standard is above the actual facts of human behavior. It appears to be a real Law, that we did not create ourselves, and yet know we ought to obey. It is in fact, a strong argument for God.

Prayer: Dear Heavenly Father, direct Your Holy Spirit to guide us in such a way that our actions reflect Your character! We know right from wrong, because of Your love for us! If we loved each other as we want to be loved, we would never have to experience that feeling of having wronged another. AMEN

FEBRUARY 27

Top of the World

"Though you have not seen Him, you love him; and even though you do not see Him now, you believe in him and are filled with an inexpressible and glorious joy! (1 Peter 1:8-9 NIV)

Okay, every now and then I just can't help doing this. Yesterday, I had a period of melancholy; which I guess really means sort of 'worry.' We all know what Christ had to say about worry; it gains you nothing so why don't you just not do it? (Matthew 6:25) But I have friends and relatives facing critical health situations, my mother is in her nineties, much of my family is far away, there are stresses at work and stresses in my body, and I guess I just got down for a little while.

But then I was listening to the radio and on came a song I had just learned on the violin. It's a dear old friend from the 70's, so maybe a lot of you don't know it. It took four minutes to totally change me around, put a smile on my face and restore my usual (hopefully) attitude toward life. Here is *On Top of the World*, from 1973, sung by Karen Carpenter and written by her brother, Richard.

Such a feelin's comin' over me
There is wonder in 'most every thing I see
Not a cloud in the sky, got the sun in my eyes
And I won't be surprised if it's a dream

Everything I want the world to be
Is now comin' true especially for me
And the reason is clear, it's because you are here
You're the nearest thing to heaven that I've seen

(Chorus) I'm on the top of the world lookin' down on creation
And the only explanation I can find
Is the love that I've found ever since you've been around
Your love's put me at the top of the world

Somethin' in the wind has learned my name
And it's tellin' me that things are not the same
In the leaves on the trees and the touch of the breeze
There's a pleasin' sense of happiness for me

There is only one wish on my mind
When this day is through I hope that I will find
That tomorrow will be just the same for you and me
All I need will be mine if you are here

(ChorusX2)

There's not much question this is a love song! It's also simply impossible to listen to it without a smile coming to your face and a sway to your shoulders. (PLEASE SPOTIFY now if you don't know it!) But I was struck by the fact that Christ's love for us, and the overwhelming joy we feel when we learn to love Him back, fits every verse of this song! Capitalize each 'You' and this could have been written by John Wesley or even Matthew Spafford! Next time you get down, play this, and remember who loves ya baby!

Prayer: Dear Heavenly Father, We praise You for the genius of approaching Your people with love first. Love lifts us all, and music moves us like no other experience! Thank you for the gift given to people who write the lyrics and the music that instantly help us refocus our eyes on Your Son! AMEN

FEBRUARY 28

Pascal's Wager

"If there is a God, He is infinitely incomprehensible, since, having neither parts nor limits, He has no affinity to us. We are then incapable of knowing either what He is or if He is..." (Blaise Pascal 1662)

There is a common thread whenever I have a discussion with an atheist about God. By definition, the atheist has a belief system, just as surely as I do, as a Christian. He *believes* that there is no supernatural intelligent Creator just as firmly as I believe that there is. One would think that an impasse!

Not long ago, I was having this sort of discussion with an atheist colleague of mine. Unlike the agnostic, who is unsure if there is or isn't a God, the atheist is quite sure, despite his or her inability to prove a negative. Surprisingly, he was not familiar with Blaise Pascal, the 17th century mathematician, physicist, philosopher, and Catholic theologian. One of the inventors of the mechanical calculator, he was also known for pioneering work in geometry (at age 16) and for later work with Pierre de Fermat on probability theory, which influenced modern thought on economics and social theory. After a religious experience in 1654, Pascal began to write on theology and philosophy, and one of his most famous works, published posthumously, was called *Pensees.*

It may seem less remarkable now than it was in the 17th century, but Pascal's writing incorporated perhaps the first formal use of probability and decision-making theory, pragmatism, existentialism and voluntarism. (Feel free to Wiki them all should you be so inclined!) But the gist of what became known as Pascal's Wager is this: *Humans bet with their lives on whether or not God exists!* A similar idea had been posited by Pope Innocent III as early as the 12th century, and much more recently by C.S. Lewis in his radio addresses, later compiled as *Mere Christianity.* His logic was as follows:

1. God is or is not
2. In short, heads or tails as in a coin flip
3. Wagering is mandated in life
4. Weighing gain or loss for either option: If you gain, you gain all; if you lose, you lose nothing!
5. If there are equal chances of gain or loss, and the possibility of infinite gain, wager that He is!
6. Those who do not or feel they cannot believe, should endeavor to convince themselves.

Pascal contends that while humankind can discern an enormous amount of truth through reason and the scientific method, of which he was one of the most articulate and ardent proponents, on the question of God, we are simply forced to gamble! **Believing in God, you have everything to gain and nothing to lose! An atheist, who does not believe, has nothing to gain and everything to lose!**

Many today would use the expression, "a leap of faith," in reference to such a gamble. Maybe. For me, not a very big leap. Over forty years, I have seen thousands of six week pregnancies, looking like peanuts on ultrasound, turn into fully formed little people at ten weeks, delivered thousands of babies, and seen my own children grow and mature. My undergraduate degree is in evolutionary biology, and yet the complexity and intricate patterns of the natural universe, from the sub-atomic to the cosmologic, constantly *reinforce* my belief in the Creator. So go ahead, make a bet!

Prayer: Dear Heavenly Father, thank you for the wonders of the universe with which we are surrounded every day! Let the Holy Spirit use those everyday 'miracles' to lead the lost back to You through Your Son, and recognize there is infinite gain to be had! AMEN

FEBRUARY 29

Garbage

"Consider the lilies of the field, how they grow: they neither toil nor spin; and yet I say to you that even Solomon in all his glory was not arrayed like one of these!" (Matthew 6:28-29 NKJV)

The Egg was slippery with dew, and it rocked back and forth in the pre-dawn shadows, wobbled really, like a toddler's rubber ducky in the tub. Pop was already seated on the middle bench, his right hand, protruding from his ever-present grey, woolen jacket, grasping the dock to stabilize the tiny boat. He reached up with his left to take my hand, waving impatiently even as I grabbed a hold of it. "Come on Jeffy, just step in, for God's sake!" He barked at me in his low gruff voice, mumbling in that way that an old man does with his ever-present mahogany pipe clasped loosely between his teeth. Come to think of it, there was a lot of "ever-present" stuff about Pop that I think I even recognized at age eight.

The Egg was our dinghy's name, appropriate for the tiny tender which served to take us out across Deadman's Cove to *Fledgling's* mooring. This particular morning in July, 1964, we weren't headed out for a sail. Instead, as I used the oversized sponge to bail the last of the night's rainwater from the bottom of the Egg, squeezing it over the gunnel as directed, Pop placed the wooden oars in the brass locks, and began pulling for our Sea Skiff. Another classic wooden boat, the Skiff was a 14 foot mahogany outboard, which was used to ply Eggemoggin Reach whenever we needed to go to town or out to the islands. Our little town was and still is, South Brooksville, Maine, the very same made famous only a few short years before, by our neighbor, Robert McClosky, author of both *Blueberries for Sal*, and the even better known, *Make Way for Ducklings*.

As Pop shipped the oars and swung expertly parallel to the starboard aft quarter of the Skiff, I clambered up into the bigger boat without prompting this time, always anxious to avoid Pop's growl, even though not always able to discern when it was good natured and when it was critical. He used one hand to grasp the gunnel of the Skiff, and the other to swing the three paper grocery bags of garbage up into my waiting hands. I piled them where directed, behind the front bench, on the wooden floor slats, just out of reach of the inch or so of rainwater in the bilge of the runabout. As usual, the Skiff needed a bit of bailing as well, and as Pop pulled the Egg forward in order to tie her painter to the

Skiff's mooring line, I began scooping the frigid water from the low point in the stern, up and over the side with the square wooden scoop my grandfather had made just for this purpose. (Plastic milk jugs, that we would later use for this purpose, did not yet exist in 1964.) Pop climbed aboard, stepping adroitly over the middle bench to the opposite side from where I was bailing, balancing the boat in the process.

The sky was gradually lightening in the east, a grey hue creeping over the hill between the cove and Walker Pond, but instead of the other boats and the shoreline becoming increasingly clear, the dim light served mostly to reveal the thick layer of fog that stretched over the cove and out into the Reach. The water was smooth and black as glass. Back in the 60's, the temperature hovered around 50-52 degrees Fahrenheit every morning, fog or no fog. It wasn't uncommon to have a fire going every morning all through the summer. That particular morning it was just after 7 AM, and the chill in the air was only worsened by the fog that fell over us like a wet blanket draped over our shoulders. The early morning stillness was only broken by the approaching sound of the big diesel engine on Mr. Parker's lobster boat, as it rounded the point and crossed the opening of the cove, heading southeast along the shore. His wake entered the cove, rolled inexorably towards us, gently rocked the Skiff back and forth, then hit the dock with a slapping sound, and finally ran up onto the rocky beach with a shushing hiss.

Pop motioned for me to climb onto the foredeck, while he took a seat in the stern next to the engine. Then, kneeling somewhat precariously on the slippery, curved and varnished wood, I prepared to cast off on his command. I looked over my shoulder from my hands and knees, and watched as he released the tilt on the 6 hp Mercury, then gently lowered the drive shaft into the vertical position, leaving the prop in the water. He then set the choke, pumped the squeeze ball on the feed line from the big red gas can sitting on the floorboards, set the throttle to start, and pulled smoothly back on the starter rope. (I was determined to memorize the sequence for that glorious future day when I might be allowed to start the engine.) The Mercury made a half-hearted grumble, as though annoyed at being awakened from its overnight slumber. My grandfather pulled on the rope again and this time got a little more reassuring sputter, only to die after a few seconds. On the third pull, as I had come to learn was usually about right, the engine coughed into life, immediately emitting a high-pitched whine which Pop instantly quieted by twisting the throttle on the handle away from himself. After running for a good minute, he motioned with his hand to cast off the mooring line, just as he moved the toggle switch forward into drive. As the Skiff moved forward, I did as ordered, but realized too late that while the loop of the heavy mooring line was indeed overboard, the narrow line extending from that loop to the float, had caught on the foredeck cleat. Pop turned to look forward just as the Skiff jerked suddenly to the side, having over-run the mooring and then been suddenly arrested by the trapped buoy line.

"Jeffy, good God Almighty, what in the tarnation are you doing?" he half shouted over the little outboard's rumble. When the Skiff jerked to a stop and swung sideways, it had set me sliding backwards off the deck and down onto the front bench seat with an unceremonious thump.

"Sorry Pop!" I scrambled back onto the foredeck and was only able to free the float line when Pop reversed the little outboard and created some slack. My Grandfather shook his head and said just loud enough for me to hear, "That boy doesn't have the brains God gave geese!" I sank back down onto the seat and hung my head as I pulled my puffy orange life preserver over my red sweater. Tears welled up in the corners of my eyes and I desperately tried to wipe them away before the old man saw. It wasn't so much his anger that upset me, as much as knowing that once again, my chance to run the motor had just gone out the window for the umpteenth time!

The Skiff slowly negotiated the obstacle course created by the boats moored in our cove, sequentially emerging from the slowly dissipating fog. Pop pointed the prow SSW, directly across the Reach, toward Pumpkin Light. Off to starboard, the Eggemoggin bell chimed irregularly with the motion of sea, and the foghorn situated beneath it, blew its mournful tone for a full ten seconds every minute. Visibility began to rapidly improve however, just minutes out into the Reach, a little unusual for this early. The breeze picked up a bit. Eggemoggin Reach is a roughly eight by one mile stretch of seawater that runs NW to SE, between Deer Isle and the mainland. It forms the head of East Penobscot Bay, the head of the West Bay being the Penobscot River that runs up to Bangor and beyond. This narrow stretch of sea, right at our front door, is called *The Reach* because the word "reach" has a special meaning to the sailor. In the lexicon of sailing, "reach" means moving at, or nearly at, right angles to the wind. Since the prevailing wind is from the SW in Penobscot Bay, a line drawn down the center of the Reach is almost exactly perpendicular to the wind. Hence, sailing the Reach, in either direction, one is always likely to be "reaching."

The ritual which found me accompanying my grandfather to the center of a body of salt water, in a small boat loaded with garbage, which involved dumping said garbage into the Reach, would today, land us in the Hancock County jail only long enough to be transferred to the state prison, only long enough to then be transferred to the Federal prison in Augusta! But in 1964, it was what everybody did, and I mean everybody. We first diligently burned our waste paper in the fireplace, but our diligence on the water consisted only of making sure we filled the tin cans and glass bottles with water, one at a time, so that they would sink the hundred or so feet to the bottom of the Reach. In all honesty, I remember no plastic whatsoever. I'm not really sure it even existed at that time.

But none of this had anything to do with why I waited all week, why, I in point of fact, begged all week, to be the one who accompanied Pop on this seemingly mundane Wednesday chore. No, the reason I remember it clearly half a century later, and the reason I could hardly sleep the night before, would shortly become evident.

Fifteen minutes or so into our excursion, Pop cut the engine and we drifted to a halt, somewhere near the center of the Reach. This was a relatively safe spot. The lobster pots were all buoyed in closer to either Little Deer Isle, or the mainland, and it was too early in the morning for the schooners from Camden, Rockport and Dublin to be heading for Acadia. The big motor cruisers loaded with wealthy Bostonians and New Yorkers wouldn't come barreling down the Reach until the sun was well up and the warming, such as it was, was well established. Once we glided to a halt, it was absolutely silent except for the gentle lapping of the small waves against our wooden hull, and the distant chime of the bell at the harbor entrance. The foghorn was so common an accompaniment of morning in coastal Maine, that one really hardly heard it at all.

"Jeffy, start picking the cans and the glasses out of that one there, and sink them." I climbed over the back of the front bench and sat on the middle one, the garbage bags on the floorboards between Pop's feet. For the most part, the gooey garbage, truly worthy of the term, had already been separated from, what would one day in the distant future, be dubbed re-cycling. Two bags held cans and glass jars, and two held coffee grounds, egg- shells, vegetable peelings, corn husks, lobster shells, fat and bones from meat, and grease from the coffee cans used to pour it off the frying pan. He picked the other bag without goo, and we both leaned over opposite sides of the Skiff to sink the items one at a time.

It was about now that you could hear the first distant calls of the gulls. "Pop, how do they know? The fog hasn't even cleared! Can they really smell it for miles?" My grandfather hefted one of the two remaining full bags and handed me the other. "Don't know. Hear it maybe? You go ahead," he said, pipe still held in his teeth, though the bowl of the Meerschaum hadn't been lit once all morning long, as far as I could tell. I turned over my bag and the clumps of wet smelly garbage plopped into the water. The eggshells, lobster shells and coffee grounds floated immediately, but it looked like the other food particles would quickly sink.

They never had a chance.

In an instant, literally scores of screaming gulls dove at our boat from out of nowhere! What had been a few, seemingly distant, calls only seconds before, were now a roaring cacophony of squawking screams and furiously flapping wings. The birds dived right at us, only to spread their wings wide and hockey stop right above our heads, looking like giant hummingbirds as they hovered and swerved. Most ignored us and headed right for the floating treasures, alternating beak grabs from low altitude and quick landings in the midst of the goods, torn between fighting off their rivals and gulping down whatever they were closest to!

I sat, mouth hanging open, shielding my eyes from the brilliant sun, which seemed to leap over the hill behind the cove, where only moments before it had seemed hesitant to challenge the cloak of fog that hid the tree line. Through the melee of feathers, beaks, and yellow feet, I could now see patches of brilliant blue sky directly overhead.

As quickly as they had appeared out of the fog, the seagulls dispersed and were gone in every direction. The boisterous outburst of sound that had accompanied their frenzied arrival dissipated with equal rapidity.

"How 'bout that?" growled my grandfather. "Ain't that somethin' to see every single time?" I simply nodded my head as I looked around in every direction to see if I could figure out where they had gone. There was absolutely no sign of them. None. They had literally vanished in an instant, just as they had appeared.

It was, indeed, "something. "

I remember the wonder of those brief moments as clearly as if they had happened yesterday, and yet they occurred fifty -six years ago! What was it about that sudden, overwhelming, burst of life that overtook us on those garbage runs, that so mesmerized me at the time and seared the images and the sounds and the smells into my mind? Was it just my youth and inexperience that played the major role? That may account for a part of it. But I don't think the major part.

Pop stood up from the seat by the engine, and motioned for me to trade with him. Was this really happening? The second miracle in less than ten minutes! He crab-walked to the middle seat, port side, and I swung over to the little seat to the right of the outboard.

"Okay Jeffy. Let's see if you were paying attention. What do you do now?"

I looked at him wide-eyed for a moment and then turned to look at the engine. I turned the throttle to start, squeezed the gas bulb, and reached for the choke.

"Don't need to choke it. She's already hot." I nodded my head and pulled the handle so the engine angled toward me and I could reach the pull rope. Pop must have known there was no way I could generate the force to pull that rope fast enough to turn the engine over. He gently put his hand over mine.

"We'll pull together. On three; one, two, three..." We pulled the rope out quickly and the outboard gave its sputter and whine. I quickly throttled back and then flipped the gear into forward.

"Let's head for the barn, son," my grandfather said, nodding his head aftward. I turned the Skiff back toward the mainland, her prow high in the air with Pop and I in the back. I must have had a pretty big smile on my face.

"What you grinnin' at boy?" growled Pop around his pipe. He actually grinned a little himself and took out his tobacco pouch. He dipped the bowl in, tamped the brown clump in with his thumb, and then placed the stem back in his mouth as he bent down out of the wind to light up. He came up squinting at the sun and puffed big blue, sweet smelling clouds over his head that disappeared quickly in the breeze.

All of us have memories of our childhood, some wonderful, some not so good, some confused and unclear, some crystal. Why does the memory of garbage day still make me tingle, and when I really, really, concentrate on it, literally make me tear up? Why is the memory so phenomenally clear? Why was that odd event such a happy recollection despite the gruffness of my grandfather, the cold, the wet, the mistakes I made that I thought disappointed?

We are all the accumulation of our experiences, overlaid on a body and soul that are "fearfully and wonderfully made," as David tells us in Psalms. (Psalm 139:14) If our consciousness is thus formed by life events, then it follows that all of them have something to teach us. I prefer to believe this process is guided by the supernatural, and of course, there are others who choose not to believe that. But to me it makes more sense that our Creator wishes to communicate with us through the people and events that we encounter every day of our lives.

Dumping garbage seems to many, I am sure, mundane in the extreme. Furthermore, dumping it in the ocean seems to many today, I am sure, not just mundane, but criminal! Yet God had something to teach me, something to show me, that has shaped me and stuck with me all my life.

There is beauty in the ordinary.(Matthew 6:28-29)

Lewis Thomas wrote several wonderful works on just this topic, beginning with *Lives of a Cell*. It is possible, I suppose, to have lived through that morning in the cold, wet, early morning fog of the Maine Coast, exposed to a grumpy old man, smelly garbage, and screaming gulls, and come away simply glad to be ashore again and finished with an onerous chore. Instead, I came away stupefied by the miraculous mobility and exuberance of life demonstrated by those frantic gulls, and warmed by the way a surly old man showed me that he loved me. *There is beauty in the ordinary, and it surrounds us everyday. All we have to do is be aware.*

Being aware. My response to that morning in Maine remains indelibly imprinted in my recollection, not simply because of the sequence of events, but because of the sounds, the smells, the sights, and the emotions that surrounded those events. Observation involves a sense of *wonder* that the phenomenal complexity and functional beauty of the world around us must have been ordered somehow! The bible tells us that man, from the very beginning, has had the evidence of a supernatural Creator all around him everyday, if only he would choose to notice and be thankful! (Romans 1:20)

But it wasn't just the fog and the sun and the water and the gulls and the smells and the sound of the buoy bells, foghorns and frantic birds that I observed; it was the tenderness of a gruff old man that many thought surly. It was an easy leap for many to think Pop T unloving. But he *let me drive* the skiff, and he helped me pull the rope, and he showed me that even grandfather didn't really know how the gulls knew we were there! Those were the observations above and beyond nature.

While the observations of nature made me acutely aware of a Creator, as they always have my entire life, the observations of my grandfather opened the door to interpretation in my schoolboy mind. My grandfather loved me! Even though he seemed gruff and unapproachable at times, (many times actually,) the correct analysis was that he loved me. Maybe this seems like it should have been a forgone conclusion for a grandson, but it wasn't. My awareness of the subtlety of our interaction that day, and my subsequent conscious consideration of the experience in retrospect, led me to a conclusion that, once applied in my young life, altered our relationship for the better, until the day that he died, many years after a stroke that left him paralyzed and unable to speak. Our parents, and our parent's parents, have much to teach us, that will enrich our lives in a myriad of ways, and they deserve our veneration. (Exodus 20:12) Maybe that is the real reason I remember that day so clearly decades later. The love of a grumpy old man might have been totally missed had I not really lived that day. Living means actively participating and observing. Like I've said before, "Pay attention!"

Prayer: Dear Heavenly Father, We love You! We praise You for Your marvelous creation and all that it has to teach us! Make us more aware of the love You show is every day, if only we pay attention! AMEN

MARCH

MARCH 1

Pick Me

"But Moses said, 'Who am I that I should go to Pharaoh, and that I should bring the children of Israel out of Egypt...suppose they will not believe me or listen to my voice; suppose they say, 'the Lord has not appeared to you...Oh Lord, I am not eloquent, neither before nor since You have spoken to Your servant; but I am slow of speech and slow of tongue.'" (Excerpts Exodus 3:11-4:10)

Do you remember in third grade when you wanted one of the team captains to pick you right away for Dodge ball? You were disappointed if you didn't go in the first round, and down-right embarrassed if you were the last to be picked for either team! For many of us though, this gradually changes through high school, maybe college if you went, and then certainly extending into our work lives. Some people are always the first to volunteer. They are happy in the spotlight, confident in their ability to lead the way! But truthfully, that's not most of us. Most of us enter a lecture hall today and sit somewhere near the back, and this is especially true, if you know they might be "calling on" people for answers or maybe to 'volunteer.'

So, what's happening here? Have we lost confidence since third grade? Is it just the desire to be included and perceived as valuable that made us jump up and down to be picked back then, and now, not so much? As we become adults, perhaps we start to understand the weight of responsibility. If we are picked, sure, we are 'included' in a way, but now we are depended on to perform a task, and we know that others may be unhappy or disappointed in us if we fail. Fear of failure keeps a lot of people from reaching their potential, as you will recall astronaut, Captain Scott Kelly, emphasized in an earlier devotional.

Many of the Bible 'heroes' did everything they possibly could to avoid stepping up and doing what God asked them to do! Moses made every excuse he could think of, even while standing in front of the burning bush with God *promising him* that He would be right there with him! Jonah didn't just refuse to obey, *he ran the other direction* as fast as his little legs and a ship would carry him. Then even after God rescued him from drowning, and he finally preached to the wayward city of Ninevah, Jonah didn't like the outcome and so was furious with...you guessed it...God! Sarai, Abram's wife, was told she would bear a son in her old age, from whom would come untold numbers of descendants. Her reaction. She laughed, i.e. "I don't think so!" When the Lord called on the prophet Jeremiah, telling him that He had known him, even before He formed him in his mother's womb, what does Jeremiah answer? Something along the lines of, "Ah, Lord, You've got the wrong guy. I am too young, and I am not what you would call a good speaker!" (Jeremiah 1:6) Immediately after Peter correctly identifies Jesus as **the Christ**, and Jesus tells Peter and the disciples that He must suffer and die, and then rise after three days, Peter takes him aside and *chews him out! Really?* At the Last Supper when Jesus is demonstrating servanthood by washing the disciples' feet, Peter refuses. *Really?* He jumps to the front of the line at the Last Supper and says, "*I will lay down my life for Your sake!*" Then, after Jesus' arrest, just when we think Peter has finally figured it out, he goes and famously denies, *three times,* that he even knows Him! *Really?* (John 13:38)

Why do we love Peter like we do? Why did Jesus? Why did Jesus make him the "Rock on which I will build my church?" *Because Peter is us, and we are him.* We need to remember, that with God all things are possible! We need not fear failure, but instead be willing to, from time to time! We can safely return to that excited anticipation we felt in third grade when we so *wanted to be picked!* When God picks us, we need not worry that we will let Him down, as long as faith and obedience guide us. So, go ahead and pick me Lord! Pick me!! I'm ready.

"Be strong and courageous. Do not be afraid; do not be discouraged, for the Lord your God will be with you wherever you go!" (Joshua 1:9 NIV)

"The Lord is my light and my salvation; whom shall I fear? The Lord is the strength of my life; of whom shall I be afraid?" (Psalm 27:1 NKJV)

Prayer: Lord, when opportunity knocks, and we prayerfully consider the leading of Your Holy Spirit, let us go forth boldly, knowing that the Creator of the Universe has our back! We might fail sometimes along the way, but God is in it for the long haul. AMEN

MARCH 2

Light

"You are the light of the world. A town built on a hill cannot be hidden. Neither do people light a lamp and put it under a bowl. Instead they put it on a stand and it gives light to everyone in the house." (Matthew 5:14-15)

Thirty years ago, I was getting ready for the impending cardiac arrest, requiring CPR and then cardioversion, of a 28 year-old woman. No, she hadn't just been freed with the jaws of life, extricated from a crushed vehicle on the highway, and then rushed in by air ambulance. She wasn't a pre-eclamptic with HELLP syndrome. She wasn't a viral pneumonia with whited out lungs. She wasn't any of these things. No, she was a healthy young woman in labor, at term gestation, whose blood pressure was too low and now the baby was having heart rate decelerations because it wasn't getting enough oxygenated blood from the placenta.

Back then, emergency medicines weren't locked up in an automated, passcode locked, Pixus, which would only dispense the drug if the proper order was entered in the electronic medical record. The drugs were in a fishing tackle box that was in the room, next to the patient's bed. The labor room was dark, as they often are. I gave the order for ephedrine to up her BP, and one of the two RNs in the room opened the tackle box, removed the dark, brown, glass vial and handed it to me. I snapped off the top, drew up the appropriate amount into the syringe, and quickly injected it into the patient's IV. I expected some increase in the patient's pulse and tremulousness, but not what we got. The patient began shaking violently and clutching her chest, her pulse and blood pressure both shot through the roof, and she began complaining both of chest pain and shortness of breath. Her EKG suggested coronary ischemia. In short, she seemed to be having a heart attack. I was flabbergasted at her response to a single dose of ephedrine, as we put her on oxygen, called anesthesia, and prepared for the worst. Just as I was sure she would arrest, standing in the well-lit hallway, waving the anesthesiologist into our room, I pulled the glass vial out of my scrub pocket and looked at it closely.

It wasn't ephedrine, it was epinephrine...good old straight adrenaline! The two cardioactive drugs used to be manufactured in *identical* little brown, single dose, glass vials. Only holding them to a bright light, and reading the label with care, avoided potentially catastrophic errors. Thankfully, her symptoms resolved in under four minutes, her baby's heart rate recovered, and she went on to a normal delivery of a healthy baby. I can tell you however, that my coronary arteries were squeezed, at least as much as the patient's that night!

You see errors get made in the dark. And errors get made if things are either poorly labelled or labelled incorrectly. Unfortunately, man has made most of his decisions in the dark since the Garden of Eden! And man is well-known for applying labels that miss-characterize his fellow man. Prejudice and racism are alive and well today all over a dark world in which so many, fail to see clearly that God loves us all equally! Christ is, in fact, the light of the world. He even calls Himself this. Those who put their trust in Him, then become lights themselves, and they can then pass His message of love and peace on to others. There is no reason to fumble in the dark, and maybe make a fatal mistake, when you can rejoice in the light every single day! The path to peace, is in fact impossible to see without His forgiveness in Grace, shedding light on each step that we take.

Prayer: Father, lift our eyes so that we might fix our vision on the Source of the light that has saved us from the pain, misery, and guilt of our own repeated mistakes, always made in the dark, and through the Holy Spirit, let us be a light to all those around us. AMEN

MARCH 3

Apparent Wind

"The pessimist complains about the wind; the optimist expects it to change,; the realist adjusts the sails." (William Arthur Ward)

There is a phenomenon with which all sailors are familiar, called '*the apparent wind.*' The word apparent means "plainly visible, evident, obvious or palpable." Now, the first reaction of a non-sailor might be, if you see and feel evidence of the wind, isn't the apparent wind the same thing as the true wind?

Well, it is, if you are motionless. But sailboats, being sailboats, are usually moving if there is any wind, and only motionless when there isn't! That means that when you are in a moving sailboat, some of those confusing mathematical concepts that come out of Einstein's theory of relativity come into play.

For example, let's say you are 'heading into the wind,' which of course, you can't really do in a sailboat. If you head directly into the wind, the air pressure on either side of your sails is the same and well, you don't move. So 'heading into the wind' for a sailor, usually means about 30 degrees off the wind, to one side or the other. If your objective is 'upwind,' then you have to zig-zag back and forth, called *beating*. The boat will *heel* or lean more and more, as the wind increases. Real sailors like the thrill…for a while! If the wind and or current, is very strong, there is significant side-slip, and you make very little progress over time. In order to make the boat go forward efficiently at 30 degrees off the wind, you have to pull the sails in close to the axis of the hull. We call that *close- hauled*, because the *sheets*, which are the lines that control the sails' lateral movement, are hauled in tight. With this sail set, the wind is more or less, constantly, in your face.

Now without getting too hung up on vectors, realize that the motion of the boat cutting into the air, creates its own "wind." On land, if you go from standing still, to jogging, you can feel this artificially created 'wind' on your face, right? Same thing in a sailboat. Roughly speaking, if the actual wind is 10 knots, and your boat is moving into, or nearly into it, at 6 knots, then the *apparent* wind you feel on your face is 16 knots, right? Now, let's say you are sailing away from the wind, or *downwind*. Your sails are out at right angles to the axis of the hull, i.e. the opposite of close-hauled. The wind is coming from *behind you* at 10 knots, but you are moving *away* from the wind at 6 knots. *Now the math is different and so is the sensation!* The apparent wind is only 4 knots; not 16 knots! That's a four-fold difference in movement sensation, *even though the boat is still going 6 knots and the actual wind speed is still 10 knots!* Although you feel like you are going slower, you are actually moving through the water at the same speed. If your objective is downwind, you can run straight at it with no zig-zagging, so even though your boat speed is the same, you get there much quicker!

I'll bet you can see the lesson in here without me even telling you! How one experiences a given circumstance depends largely on one's perspective! If you encounter a major set back at work, or in your health, or in your marriage, or in raising your kids, or in any number of life events, then you might well view that set back as a deal breaker, as insurmountable, as the straw that breaks the camel's back. That can lead to anger, discouragement, depression, and a downward spiral, from which it is extremely difficult to recover. It's like you are close-hauled, heeling all the time, cold spray and wind in your face, muscles taught on the sheet and helm, zig-zagging over and over, yet making very little progress.

But what if you see the set-back in the light of faith in God's Providential plan for your life? Not in a Poly Anna way. You may still be suffering. But looking at it from Your Savior's perspective, if He's the one that "puts the wind in your sails" and the one who "floats your boat," (couldn't resist) then you can rest easy! He's got you. He knows your true destination, even if you don't! Adjust your sails as Mr. Ward says. You may need to just go with the flow for a while. Let your sails out and head downwind for a bit. Relax your muscles, rest your mind, and get your balance back. When things are coming apart, you may need to take a new direction, a new strategy, or maybe only take a break. When something isn't working, you try something different, right? You may have to try it the boss' way for a while. You may have to swallow your pride and apologize to your co-worker, spouse, child, whomever, even if you think you were in the right. You may need to forgive someone whom you've just never been able to bring yourself to forgive. Even with the same wind direction and speed, i.e. the same circumstances, if you keep your eyes fixed on the cross, ***it will feel different***. It will feel a lot closer to being on that path toward peace and happiness.

And who knows, maybe the wind direction will change shortly, and you'll find yourself sailing straight downwind to your objective after all!

"A person's steps are directed by the Lord. How can anyone understand their own way?" (Proverbs 20:24 NIV)

Prayer: Father we know that faith doesn't lead to an easy life, it only leads to an abundant life, with all its ups and downs. Help us to remember that man makes plans, but our steps are directed by the Lord. Sometimes we need to look at our situation in a different way, adjust our sails, and rest secure in the knowledge that you both know our destination and how we are to get there. AMEN

MARCH 4

Life is Real

"Life is real, life is earnest, and the grave is not its goal! Dust thou art to dust returnest, was not spoken of the soul!" (Henry Wadsworth Longfellow)

My family is one for passing down the expressions of our ancestors, and often, their favorite quotations or lines of verse. *A Psalm of Life* was penned by the famous American poet, H.W. Longfellow, in the mid 19th century. Those familiar with the Bible, know that the scriptural Psalms express praise, anguish, joy, anger, frustration, doubt, fear, and faith, among virtually every other possible human emotional state. Each has a different message for us about our relationship to a loving, faithful, reliable God. Longfellow in his own Psalm, takes a look at life as a whole, and addresses that universal question, "Why are we here?" Forgive me for reproducing it here in full, but it was my mother's favorite, and today it hangs prominently in our home, where we see it each and every day.

Tell me not in mournful numbers, Life is but an empty dream!
For the soul is dead that slumbers, And things are not what they seem.

Life is real! Life is earnest! And the grave is not its goal;
Dust thou art to dust returnest, Was not spoken of the soul.

Not enjoyment, and not sorrow, Is our destined end or way;
But to act, that each tomorrow, Find us farther than today!

Art is long, and time is fleeting, And our hearts though stout and brave;
Still, like muffled drums are beating Funeral marches to the grave.

In the world's broad field of battle, In the bivouac of life,
Be not like dumb driven cattle! Be a hero in the strife!

Trust no future, howe'er pleasant! Let the dead Past bury its dead!
Act, act in the living present! Heart within, and God o'erhead!

Lives of great men all remind us WE can make our lives sublime,
And departing, leave behind us Footprints on the sands of time;

Footprints that perhaps another, Sailing o'er life's solemn main,
A forlorn and shipwrecked brother, Seeing shall take heart again.

Let us then be up and doing, With a heart for any fate;
Still achieving, still pursuing, Learn to labor and to wait.

Longfellow understood what many Christians do not. Doing good works to please God demonstrates a complete misunderstanding of Biblical teaching and certainly doesn't represent Christ's message. Christianity consists not merely of accepting God's forgiveness, offered by Grace through faith in the cross, but living out that second chance every day! Yes, we are born anew in that instant, and yes, we receive the assurance of salvation in that instant. But welcoming the gift of the indwelling Holy Spirit, means much, much, more. It means that in being born anew, we will be anxious to extend the gift of the Gospel to others, and to do so in the context of actively loving them! Yes, we do good works, but we do them because we *desire to do them! ACT!* That is what Longfellow reminds us! It is your actions, not your words that may cause that shipwrecked brother to "take heart again!"

Prayer: Thank you that you have adopted us into your family! We benefit from Your gift of freedom because of the cross, every day of our lives. Let the urging of Your Holy Spirit remind us daily to "pass it forward" in the active way that we love our brothers! Let them truly know us by our fruit, Lord! AMEN

MARCH 5

Pea Soup

"Let the morning bring me word of Your unfailing love, for I have put my trust in you. Show me the way I should go, for to you I entrust my life." (Psalm 143:8)

Several years ago, my daughter and I sailed out to Buckle Island from our cove on Eggemoggin Reach. You may recall the 'Reach' is the long, narrow, body of ocean at the northern most aspect of Penobscot Bay, in mid-coast Maine. It's 13.9 nautical miles from our mooring to the inlet where we usually anchor, on Buckle Island. As is so often the case, our sail out on a Thursday morning was gorgeous; a Maine Blue Day (MBD) as our family refers to it. Wind SSW at 12 knots, temperature 71F, and not a cloud in the sky. After exiting the Reach, we crossed the minefield of lobster pots on choppy Jericho Bay, anchored about noon at Buckle, rowed the dinghy into the beach, and spent a few hours exploring the 25-acre island. In the evening, we had steak sandwiches, fried potatoes and hot coffee, onboard *Malachite*, our 31-foot Island Packet. As we swayed gently at anchor, in the shadow of Acadia National Park's Cadillac Mountain, we quietly took in the spectacular sunset and thanked God we were alive!

The next morning, we were blanketed with fog. Not the kind of fog you see inland, where intermittently there are hints of light and shadow, and occasionally a landmark. No, this was 'pea soup' fog as they say; thick, impenetrable, wet and oppressive. There seemed to be not a breath of air. As we wiped down the dew-soaked cockpit with towels in order to eat breakfast, only the huff of the nearby seals and the intermittent cry of the gulls could be heard. We had a compass and the chart of course. That year was before GPS on your Smartphone, and we had only an old radar that was, to be kind, not terribly reliable and quite difficult to interpret. The best course was to wait for the fog to lift. We waited. It didn't.

We fired up the inboard diesel and eased forward to slacken the anchor chain. Kelly hauled it aboard. The initial compass heading was easy enough from our known position, and once clear of a few scary rocks close in, we headed back across Jericho Bay. Even at dead slow though, you couldn't see the lobster buoys that could foul the prop, until the very last second. Of course, the real danger began as we headed northwest into the Reach. Rocky shores on either side, bell buoys, lobster pots, hidden reefs, changing current and tide, not to mention the possibility of other boats travelling in both directions. Sure, there were foghorns on the buoys which marked the entrance to each harbor we slipped past, but even sound direction is difficult in the thickest of fogs, and somehow their mournful blare actually added an edge to our nerves. The only way to allay one's fear in pea soup, is to stop and listen. So, intermittently, we shut off the big diesel and coasted. As the hull rapidly slowed and the bow wake dissipated, we strained into the dense blanket of grayness, alert to the sound of an engine, a wake, a sail flap, or another voice.

When you're lost, and in a fog, the only safe thing to do is stop, and listen! Hmmmm, see any application to your life anywhere here? When people are lost, confused, blinded by whatever it is in their lives that has them frightened and indecisive, they often simply pick a direction and strike out, hoping that they don't collide with a hard object. Unfortunately, people get hurt that way. Christians know that what they ought to do is stop, and listen. Take a breath and then be still. The answer will come, if you pay attention. The body of Christ is made up of the people around you. The answer to prayer when you are lost, may well be very nearby. Just listen!

"Be still and know that I am God…The Lord Almighty is with us; the God of Jacob is our fortress." (Psalm 46:9-11 NIV)

"God is our refuge and strength, an ever-present help in trouble. Therefore, we will not fear, though the earth give way and the mountains fall into the heart of the sea." (Psalm 46:1-2 NIV)

"Whoever listens to me will live in safety and be at ease, without fear of harm." (Proverbs 1:33)

Prayer: Dear Heavenly Father, quiet our beating hearts in our fear and confusion. Let us take a deep breath and listen for You, when in doubt. Guide us through Your Holy Spirit to a faith that soothes, and takes us in the direction You would have us go. AMEN

MARCH 6

Elevators

"Trust in the Lord with all your heart, and lean not to your own understanding." (Proverbs 3:5 NKJV)

I was ten years old. My parents were taking my older brother and me on yet another driving/camping trip, which we did a lot in the 60's. This time we were making our way across the Colorado Rockies. Having been raised in the northeast until I was nine, the mountains were as breathtaking the first time as they would be the twentieth. But then dad thought it would be a great idea to drive up the, let's face it, *one lane road,* that wound around Pike's Peak to the very top. I'm not a hundred percent sure, but I believe my life-long fear of heights probably started here. Of course, I was in the back seat, and right behind mom while dad drove. There were no seat belts back then and I could easily get on my knees and look straight down over the edge of the crumbling road to the valley floor thousands of feet below. It was pretty clear I was terrified, and my brother was no help, since it seemed he was always on the *inside* facing the mountain and not oblivion, like I was! Luckily my mother could turn and see I was near panic. In a calm voice, that I'm not completely sure came spontaneously, she told me to *trust my father,* that he was the best driver in the world. I survived, and I guess that must have helped.

Have you ever thought about the things we trust every day automatically without giving it a thought? Why do we trust? Because we *know* things have been reliable in the past. When you brake for a red light, you *trust* that the 4,000 lb hunk of steel you are driving will come to a halt. When you step in an elevator on the 67th floor of your office building, you *trust* that you won't plummet to your death in the next few seconds. When you walk down the gangway and get onto a 100,000 lb. jet plane, you *trust* that the nose of that aircraft will lift into the air at about 104 mph. When you fill your glass from the tap in your office building, you *trust* that the water won't poison you. And let's bring it on home: when you go into labor, you *trust* that the training and experience of the nurses and doctors will bring you and your baby safely through the ordeal.

So why do we find it so hard to trust the Creator of the universe? The same God who assures us that, *"Before I formed you in the womb I knew you, before you were born I set you apart..."* (Jeremiah 1:5) Paul tells us in Romans 1:20, that, *"since the creation of the world God's invisible qualities-His eternal power and divine nature-have been clearly seen, being understood from what has been made, so that people are without excuse."* And so, they have been understood. Those Colorado Rockies took my breath away in the same way that the coast of Maine did the first time I saw it. The wonder of the night sky, the flowers, the trees, the birds, the animals, is indeed spectacular, but even they pale in comparison to holding a newborn made in the very image of God, when she first cries out!

In the 60's there was an ad on TV for the drain cleaner, *Draino.* Their slogan was, *"You can trust your pipes to Draino!"* If we can so easily trust the everyday man-made things of this world because of their reliability, can we not trust the Creator who made us, gave us each other, gave us a planet, and loved us enough to give us His only Son, just so we could have a way to come back to Him when we wandered off? If my mom were here, I bet she'd tell me that ***God's the best driver in the world!***

> ***Prayer: Lord Jesus, You have shown us over and over again how marvelous is Your creation, through the wonders of nature, and the wonder of human life! You have been faithful to us and the definition of reliability. Come Holy Spirit and lead us to trust the One who created us, and then saved us! AMEN***

MARCH 7

Pop's Checkbook

"God made him who had no sin to be sin for us, so that in him we might become the righteousness of God!" (2 Corinthians 5:21 NIV)

When my grandfather was the age I am now, I was seven years old and living in a two story, 1100 square foot, Cape Cod cottage, on an old apple orchard, in Chappaqua, New York. Gran and Pop lived a few miles away in an area called Deep Wood. I remember their house as being gigantic, up on a forested hill, surrounded by birch, maple and oak trees. There was a long gravel driveway, a good sized lawn all around, a huge (or huge to a seven year old) screened in porch with flagstone flooring, and an inside that I vaguely remember as gray-green carpet with lots of wood railings, furniture, stairs, and the smell of Pop's cigars throughout.

Pop was a meticulous, retired executive from ESSO, the precursor to what you know as EXXON today. He used to sit at his desk before a large window and go slowly over his ledgers with his mechanical ESSO pencil and his gold bifocals in place. The only time he ever used a pen, was to write a letter, or to write out checks when he paid bills. Now, the check was a complete mystery to me at age seven, even after Pop tried to explain it to me more than once. Evidently, Pop could just write the date, the name of the person he was paying, a dollar amount, sign it, and *voila*, it became *money!* I just didn't get it. I understood money, both paper and coin. Pop collected coins from all over the world, so I really had the money concept down. But how could he just write a dollar amount on a piece of paper, sign it, and hand it to someone for payment? What's more, why on earth would they accept it?

Pop tried to explain the concept of the bank's involvement, but my idea of a bank came from Mary Poppins as a place to store your toppins, and certainly not a magic place that made your hand- written note turn into money! Eventually, as I grew older, I came to understand how it worked. The check was more like a *promise* to the recipient, that if he/she brought *it to a bank*, they would then give them the cash it represented, or put it directly into their account. The actual money came from the payor's bank, which would then send it somehow, to the recipient's bank.

There is a faith analogy here! When you attend any scripturally based, Christian church in the world, you will hear the Gospel preached. You can also read the Gospel message in your Bible. In essence, when you first hear the Gospel, it's as though someone hands you an envelope with the word *FORGIVEN* written on the front. It's a reminder that Jesus paid the price for our sin, which had been death, ever since the Garden of Eden. Man's rebellion against his creator earned him the death penalty, and over the centuries it became clear that no amount of effort at following the rules was able to make him righteous enough, in God's eyes, to avoid that penalty. God, in His infinite love for us, became incarnate, coming to earth in the form of Jesus, who was fully man, and at the same time, fully God. He lived a perfect life among us, and then became the once and for all sacrifice for our sin, forgiving all who would believe in Him. With all our sins forgiven, it's as though they never even occurred! In God's eyes, we become as *righteous* as Jesus, the perfect Son, the instant we accept Him as Lord and Savior! God has offered this by *Grace,* meaning He gives us this way back to Him, even though we don't deserve it at all.

Receiving the envelope is becoming aware of this Gospel story. *Opening* the envelope is acknowledging that we are sinners and need a Savior. The check we find inside has our name on it, dated today, and the dollar amount is *INFINITY! Eternal life!* On the notation line at the bottom left is written: For *Righteousness*. Jesus' death on the cross and subsequent resurrection, imparts His perfect righteousness on believers and proves His power over death. Cashing that check by asking Jesus to save us, returns a receipt as well. It's a He, called the Holy Spirit. All of us who have cashed that check have the indwelling Spirit to guide us in this life.

I know for a fact, that my grandfather understood this. He didn't talk about it as much as people do today, but Pop knew where he was going when he died, and he made sure I knew too. As I said, he was meticulous that way. He knew exactly how to write a check...as well as cash one.

Prayer: Dear Heavenly Father, how you love us! We are indeed saved by Grace through faith in Your Son, and we are eternally grateful that You thought to send us that check! AMEN

MARCH 8
Circumcision

"In Christ you were also circumcised with a circumcision not performed by human hands. Your whole self, ruled by the flesh, was put off when you were circumcised by Christ..." (Colossians 2:11 NIV)

Turns out people get a little squeamish when they hear the word 'circumcision.' I, on the other hand, have performed several thousand circumcisions on newborns and don't even flinch when the topic arises! Most commonly, couples ask me my opinion on whether their son should be circumcised. I go through the facts with them; that there is no clear cut medical indication; that it's been done for thousands of years among Jews and Muslims as an outward sign of their devotion to God; it is extremely uncommon in Europe and Asia, and variable in Africa today; there are no public funds available for circumcision in the USA since the late 80's, so there are many more children of every race who are not circumcised than there used to be, and about 25% of our male population are uncircumcised.

However, I do feel that 'like father like son' is something to consider. When my son was four, his weenie was about the most important thing in the world and comparison to dad was inevitable! Most importantly, I emphasize that the decision is *permanent*. You could wait to do a circumcision until the child is older (not a particularly good idea,) but once you have it done, there is no turning back!

In the Bible, God commands Abraham to have the males among the Chosen people circumcised on the eighth day of life. This is to signify the everlasting covenant made between God and Abraham and his descendants. In it, God promises that Abraham will be fruitful, the father of many nations, and that the Chosen People will receive the Land of Canaan as an everlasting possession, and in return, YAHWEH will be their God. (Genesis 17:6-11) God intended circumcision to be an *outward sign* of their inner devotion. His Chosen People, were to be set apart, Holy, and the circumcision of, let's face it, a very significant part of a man's body, would be both a constant reminder, and a sign of their faith to outsiders.

Unfortunately, the entire Old Testament is the story of the Chosen People messing up, and the Lord forgiving them, in a cycle repeated over and over, until finally God has had enough, and He allows both Israel and Judah to be destroyed, and the remnant forced into exile. The people forgot what circumcision even meant. In fact, they forgot what all of the rituals related in Leviticus meant! They started to believe *the action* of their sacrificial ceremonies, like circumcision, were *earning* God's favor rather than the sign of their inner orientation of heart! They started to believe that *they were special* because of these things, not because of their loving relationship to God.

As *The Way*, by which Christianity was initially known, began to spread, a dispute between Paul, Barnabas, and some of the Pharisees now following Christ, arose. Many of these early Jewish-Christians felt that the Gentiles should have to be circumcised in order to join their sect. Eventually, this was so contentious an issue, that it had to be adjudicated by the Jerusalem Council. They concluded rightly, that circumcision was an outward sign only; that it was the *heart of the individual* that determined their adoption into God's family via Christ! Circumcision was not required of Gentiles. (Acts 15:7-9)

Circumcision on the eighth day wasn't magic. It marked the person permanently, but it was the parents who were instructed to teach the child and bring them to faith. True children of Abraham were those whose inner being, whose heart, had been circumcised, no matter their ethnicity. (Deut 30:6) That same permanence is intended for the circumcision of the heart today, which happens *immediately after* a person truly comes to faith! So next time you fail, next time you begin to doubt your faith, next time you start to think you aren't good enough, remember that the moment you accepted Christ, you became a new person, *permanently!* Despite the opinion of a minority, you can't lose your faith! God's love for you *does not change, and even your faith is a loving gift from God!*

Each one of the thousands of circumcisions I have done is permanent. Christians aren't perfect. They sin every day. But for those of us whose faith is real, well, we've been circumcised in the heart, irrevocably. So, as we allow more and more control by the Holy Spirit, those mess ups we make daily, will, *God willing*, diminish!

Prayer: Dear Heavenly Father, Thank you that Your Grace is everlasting! Once born anew, with a circumcised heart, our desire to glorify You with our actions will continue to grow, permanently! AMEN

MARCH 9

Hypocrisy

"So, when you give to the needy, do not announce it with trumpets, as the hypocrites do in the synagogues and on the streets, to be honored by others." (Matthew 6:2 NIV)

When you look around a big city like I live in, there are signs of philanthropy everywhere; evidence of wealthy individuals who have donated money for the creation of this park, or that arts center; this hospital wing, or that museum. Even in churches, I will see organs, or buildings, or chapels that bear the name of individuals or families, or better, the name of someone they wish to honor. For the most part, I know that these individuals provided the funds, for the simple reason that the entity bears their name. On the websites for many charitable organizations, through which you may donate with the click of a button, you will be given the option of "anonymous" or "show my name." I often just don't know what to think about this.

In reading The Sermon on the Mount, it becomes pretty clear, pretty quickly, that God takes a dim view of hypocrisy. Jesus comments on public charity in our opening quote, and goes on to condemn those who pray in public, whether it be in church or on the street corner, if done in order to bring attention to themselves. Fasting was a more common form of devotional self-sacrificing in the 1st century, than perhaps it is now, but Jesus also denounces those who fast, but make sure that everyone *knows* they are fasting. So, what are we to conclude? Does Christ frown upon *all* philanthropy, or public prayer? Is it *always* bad to deny ourselves things, perhaps as we do during Lent, in many Christian traditions? Is that what Jesus is saying? Of course not.

If you really want a better sense of how Christ defines hypocrisy, check out Matthew 23:13-39, where Jesus addresses the Pharisees and teachers of the Law, gathered at a dinner, as a "brood of vipers." These are by far the most respected, revered men, in Jewish society of the first century! Jesus likens them to Serpents, the very emblem of Satan, himself? These paragons of virtue he accuses of following the letter of the law in little things, but ignoring matters like justice, mercy and faithfulness! Metaphorically, he says they clean the outside of a cup, but the inside is full of greed and self -indulgences! If they clean up "on the inside," then they will automatically be clean on the outside! Seven times Jesus says, "*Woe to you, teachers of the law and Pharisees, you hypocrites!*" You can read the words and just hear the anger in His voice!

Proverbs 16: 18-19, tells us that "*Pride goes before destruction, and a haughty spirit before a fall. Better to be of humble spirit with the lowly, than to divide spoil with the proud.*" Now, does giving to a worthy charity or civic project and allowing your name to be published as a donor mean you lack the requisite humility? Does it mean it is you Jesus is denouncing in the Sermon on the Mount? The answer has to do, as it always does with God, with the ***orientation of your heart!*** Scripture tells us repeatedly that God sees into your heart, no matter what your outward actions. If you donate to a cause and want others to know about it *as an encouragement for them to donate as well*, then clearly your motives are pure! If you are honoring a loved one, and that is made clear in the publication or on the plaque, well then clearly your motives are again unreproachable. If on the other hand, you make receiving *credit publicly*, a condition of your charity? Well, you tell me what Christ would think about that? Your giving in that instance, is *really motivated* by trying to get something for yourself!

Philippians 2 defines humility for us. God chose incarnation as a baby born to a poor carpenter, who would grow up to live as an itinerant teacher, before eventually submitting to a horrific sacrificial crucifixion on our behalf, while totally innocent Himself! The very message of the Gospel is self-denial, literally becoming a new person through whom Christ can work, and to do so as a humble servant just as our Savior showed us! Pride tends to go hand in hand with hypocrisy. When crediting ourselves, we easily forget that every good gift comes from above, and our pride makes the requisite posture of humility impossible.

So, just TAI, (think about it, as an old seminary professor used to say!) Next time you do a good thing, charity, leading worship in prayer, fasting or the equivalent, make sure your intention is to glorify God and not yourself. Then you can avoid falling in with a brood of vipers! (Harrison Ford hated that in *Raiders of the Lost Ark!)*

Prayer: Father, when we start to feel proud of ourselves and our good works, lead Your Holy Spirit to remind us it is You who deserves the credit! The chief end of man is indeed, to glorify God. Let us strive to remember that daily! AMEN

MARCH 10

Faking It

"Jesus said to him, "'If you can? All things are possible for one who believes." Immediately the father of the child cried out and said, "I believe; help my unbelief!" (Mark 9:23-24 ESV)

I don't know about you, but every now and then I just totally feel like I'm faking it! And I mean life; like I'm faking different parts on different days. I have been a physician for forty years come this June. I have operated on thousands of people, delivered thousands of babies, and seen hundreds of thousands of patient visits in the office. Yet, even now, I can be involved in some aspect of my practice and think to myself, "Can I really do this? Am I really *the* doctor doing this surgery, right now?"

From time to time, faith can feel the same way. In my heart, I know I have accepted Christ, but I don't always feel the indwelling Holy Spirit. In my heart, I know that I have been saved, but from time to time, I question the very veracity of Christianity intellectually! Despite years in my church, years professing my faith, even years in seminary, I find myself occasionally dissecting my stated beliefs from the logical and scientific perspectives that made up large parts of my education.

It can even make you more uncertain, when you have doubts, to look at the miracles of Christ in the Gospels! Not once does Christ ever perform a miracle where he attributes the occurrence to His own power. Every time he either attributes the miracle to the faith of the ones involved, (Luke 5:12; 7:7-8; Matthew 8:2-3; 8:8; 9:20-22; Mark 9: 16-21; 9:27-29) performs the miracle to instill faith in an individual for the first time,(John 4:46; 5:1; Mark 1:23) or performs a miracle to teach a lesson to the Pharisees. (Matthew 9:2-8)

A Centurion wished Jesus to heal his servant, but had such faith, even as a Roman soldier, that he was confident the Messiah could do so with just a word, not even coming to his house! (Mt 8:5-13) A woman in Gennesaret, who had been bleeding for twelve years, thus completely cut off from her family and community as ceremonially unclean, had such faith that she knew just the touch of Jesus' cloak would heal her! (Mt 9:20) And so it did! Two blind men in Tyre, who couldn't even see the Lord, were absolutely sure that He could restore their sight, and so He did! (Mt 9:28-29) Time after time, it is people's faith that makes them well. Sometimes, I just can't help but wonder how I got into this club, I mean me, the one who questions his faith on a somewhat regular basis? Lucky for me, scripture addresses my doubts.

Mark 9:16-29 tells the story of a man whose son has been demon possessed since childhood. It took complete control of him, rendering him unable to speak, and often throwing his body into the fire or the water to try and kill him. The father says to Jesus, "If you can do anything, take pity on us and help us!" Jesus responds, ***"If I can? Everything is possible for one who believes."*** Immediately the boy's father responds, ***"I do believe! Help my unbelief!"*** Jesus commands the persistent demon to leave the boy's body, and he does.

Here is a critical element for those of us that feel like we are faking it sometimes! When our belief wavers; when our faith isn't as strong as it once was, or as strong as we think it should be, the One person who can help, is also the object of our faith! Jesus promised to send a Helper after he ascended to heaven, and He did! The Holy Spirit is immediately at our disposal to help 'our unbelief.' We have only to ask! Yes, the unwavering faith of some is rewarded with miracles. But it's nice to be reminded that the majority of us, who do in fact waver, need never think our faith unequal to the task of acquiring Jesus' help! He will not only hear our prayer, but strengthen our belief in the meantime!

Prayer: Father, thank You that we have the Holy Spirit at hand to strengthen our faith! AMEN

MARCH 11

Prejudice

"Prejudice means you don't see the other human being anymore, but only your own concept of that human being. To reduce the aliveness of another human being to a concept, is already a form of violence." (Eckhart Tolle)

When I hear the word "prejudice," I think first of racism. Prejudice comes from the Latin, *prae (pre) + judicium (judgment), to pre-judge*. Essentially, that means forming a conclusion about *anything*, without first ascertaining the facts. That, quite frankly, is insane, when you really think about it. What if we formed conclusions on how to go to the moon without first finding out how far away it was, the details of its orbit and our rotation, the thickness of the atmosphere, the strength of gravity on earth and the moon, and any of a myriad of other facts, before we strapped three men into couches on top of ten million pounds of explosives? Would you buy a car for its appearance with no thought of the engine, the ergonomics, the reliability, the warranty, or even the price? Would you pick a mate for life from a picture? I mean there are people that do, but that doesn't make it wise. Similarly, racism is the act of coming to conclusions about an individual, or an entire group of people, based on no facts other than their skin color or their place of origin!

We are a country still struggling out from under not only 450 years of slavery, but another 150 years of oppression through prejudicial laws, prejudicial enforcement, prejudicial structure of everything from housing to schooling to opportunities, after the United States came into existence. And this is not just a black-white issue. Talk to a few native Americans, or Vietnamese, or Cambodians, or Indians, or Latinos, or LGBTQs, or the obese, or the unattractive, or any group that doesn't look like they were the King and Queen of their Iowa high school homecoming. *But, at least we are struggling in the best sense of the word.* My children's generation is much, much closer to 'color' blindness than was my parent's generation.

But appearance isn't the only area in which prejudice arises. How about politics? What ever happened to the politics of President Ronald Reagan and

Speaker Tip O'Neal? Mutual compromise was their approach to problem solving. Our political climate has become so polarized and nasty in America, that most of the talk I hear is about personalities, and not about issues which need effective solutions. In fact, political discourse today sounds more like an acrimonious divorce trial than a reasonable arbitration. Are my Christian acquaintances any better than the general populace when it comes to this rhetoric? Am I? Maybe. Some. But it often doesn't sound like it. We're quick to make statements about the opposing side's character, and less likely to critique their approaches.

Christ was pretty clear on this issue. He could care less who the pious Jewish hierarchy thought were dirty sinners. He saw them with the same loving eyes as His Father, and He wanted to spend time with them. The scribes and Pharisees asked the disciples, "*How is it that He eats with tax collectors and sinners?*" When Jesus overheard, he said, "*Those who are well have no need of a physician, but those who are sick. I did not come to call the righteous, but sinners." (Mark 2:15-17)* I guess I ought to be able to understand that metaphor as a doctor. Paul makes it clear that Christ didn't just hang out with sinners, but that He saw no difference in people based on their skin color, ethnicity or religious background. "*There is neither Jew nor Greek, there is neither slave nor free, there is neither male nor female; for you are all one in Jesus Christ." (Galatians 3:28)*

"*Judge not, that you be not judged. For with what judgment you judge, you will be judged; and the measure you use, it will be measured back to you."(Matthew 7:1-2)*

Prayer: Dear Heavenly Father, Help us to see our biases, especially those we are sure we don't have! Let us see people through Your lens, as their Creator. Next time we denigrate someone's character, instead of listening to what they have to say, remind us of Your words in Matthew 7:1! AMEN

MARCH 12
Birthdays

"Today you are you! That is truer than true! There is no one alive who is you-er than you! (Dr. Seuss)

Today is my birthday. It's also my only son's birthday. The number associated with my age is substantially larger than the number associated with his. Sigh...On the bright side however, there still are numbers associated with mine! As Steven Wright once said, "*I intend to live forever. So far so good!*"

Birthdays have been celebrated since ancient times, from Egypt to Persia, Assyria, China and throughout the Roman Empire. But in the Judeo-Christian tradition, the celebration certainly got off to a slow start. While over the centuries the majority of Rabbi's felt a person's birth should be celebrated, in the first several centuries of Christianity, the celebration of one's birth was viewed disparagingly as pagan, and inappropriately focused on the flesh. Common Medieval Christians began invariably including a name for their child that belonged to one of the Saints. They then celebrated on that "Saint's Day," which was the day of that Saint's earthly death, but heavenly "birth!" (Some parents would pick the Saint's Day that fell on the biological birthday of the child, thus combining the celebrations...very sneaky!) Medieval nobility however, always celebrated the day of their actual birth. Modern Christians, and particularly Orthodox from Eastern Europe, accept both the pagan celebration of physical birth and celebration of their Saint's Day. Islamic tradition has opposed any celebration of birthdays as pagan, but some sects, and many Westernized Muslims, have accepted the birthday traditions of the countries in which they reside. Hindus, Buddhists, and Sikhs have somewhat more complicated traditions. For instance in India and Nepal, on a child's first birthday, their head is shaved to cleanse the child of evil from past lives!

One's birth *date* is used for all sorts of 'rights of passage.' In the USA, examples include the Latin/Portugese tradition of *quinceanera* at a girl's fifteenth birthday, *bar and bat mitzvahs* on a Jewish child's thirteenth birthday, driver's license at sixteen, legal age of majority at eighteen, allowing one to vote, serve in the military, have sex, marry without parental consent etc. And there are a myriad of different 'rights of passage' in different cultures across the globe.

The birthday celebration, including a party, birthday cake, candles, and the giving of gifts, is certainly my family's tradition. As I age, I have also found the best part of having my son's birthday on the same day, is that it takes the focus off of the old man! Even if there is a pagan origin for our tradition, it feels like a celebration of *life*, and a recognition that every day of it is a *gift!* Some early Christian philosophers were still struggling with philosophical perspectives that viewed the physical world as *bad*, and the spiritual world as *good*. But after the beginning of the 5th century and the influential writings of St. Augustine, Christians were able to focus more clearly on the Gospels and the Epistles of Paul, which clearly celebrated our earthly life as not only a gift, but one to be used for the benefit of others.

So, I welcome my sixties! I thank God that I am healthy, able to continue helping others, and surrounded by a loving family. The tennis player Anna Kournikova said, "*Why are people afraid of getting older? You feel wiser, more mature, like you know yourself better. You would trade that for softer skin?*" One of my favorite birthday stories involves the late comedian George Burns. On his 100th birthday, a reporter noted that most people surveyed had no desire to live to 100. George thoughtfully removed his ever-present cigar and responded, "*Exactly how many 99 year-olds did you speak to?*" Taylor Swift released a song earlier this year whose chorus is *"I promise that you'll never find another like ME... I'm the only one of me, baby that's the fun of me; You're the only one of you, baby that's the fun of you!"* George understands that we all cling to this earthly life as long as possible, and Taylor understands why! King David said it in Psalm 139:14, *"I will praise you, for I am fearfully and wonderfully made; Marvelous are Your works, And that, my soul knows very well."*

Go ahead! Have a party on your own birthday! And try to celebrate whenever you can with others, on their special day! You're *alive!* The world is a great, big, beautiful, wonderful, fascinating place full of every type of person, animal, plant and vista. Celebrate what you've experienced and achieved thus far, but no matter your age, party down about the possibilities on the horizon! You have to get older to know all the advantages! Wisdom, the perspective that comes with time, is freeing, and it makes you feel, well, young!

"It takes a very long time to become young." (Pablo Picasso)

Prayer: Dear Heavenly Father, How can we ever thank you for this life, this world, the people you put in our path? The day of our birth was a priceless gift to us, to our parents and families, and to the people whose lives we were yet to brighten. Thank you Lord. AMEN

MARCH 13

Zamboni Drivers

"Then Caleb quieted the people before Moses, and said, 'Let us go up at once and take possession, for we are able to overcome it." (Numbers 13:30 NKJV)

I saw a story on the national news the other day, about a 42 year-old Zamboni driver from Toronto, named, David Ayres. He is not a professional hockey player by any stretch. When he did play, it was for a local league team and they went 0-8 in his last season. But that didn't stop David from signing up as an NHL 'emergency goalie.' NHL teams normally travel with two goalies. In the extremely unlikely event that they are both injured, there is an emergency goalie on call. Last week, the Carolina Hurricanes asked Mr. Ayers to step off his Zamboni and fill in against his home-town team, the Toronto Maple Leafs. Not only did he play with heart, but after allowing two goals, he stopped the next eight shots and the Canes went on to victory. He is the oldest man to have ever played in an NHL game.

If you look carefully enough, you will find there are now, and have been throughout history, Zamboni drivers who were ready to step up! Let's start with Mr. Ayers namesake, one teenager destined to become Israel's great King David, and the ancestor of the Messiah. David was a shepherd boy with three older brothers who had gone to fight with King Saul against the Philistines. It happened that David was also accomplished on the harp, and had been called upon in the past to play for King Saul, so he was known in the royal camp. David's father, Jesse, instructed him to leave the sheep, and carry bread and cheese to his brothers and their commanders. David did so, and found the entire Hebrew army terrified of Goliath, the giant Philistine who had challenged Israel to one on one combat to decide the dispute. Despite his brothers sneering denigration, little David said this, *"Who is this uncircumcised Philistine, that he should defy the armies of the living God?....Let no man's heart fail because of him; your servant David will go and fight the Philistine!" (1 Samuel 17: 26,32)* The rest, as they say, is history!

Or what of Caleb, who is quoted in today's opening? Moses sent twelve men, the heads of the children of Israel, from the Wilderness of Paran, up into

Canaan to reconnoiter. On their return forty days later, they reported a fantastic land of fruit and flowing with milk and honey as the Lord had promised, but a people of giants living there who would be impossible to overcome! Then the Zamboni driver stepped up. Only Caleb and Joshua understood that with God's help, anything was possible. But the Children of Israel shouted them down, and would pay a terrible price for their lack of faith, wandering in the desert one year for every day that Caleb was spying in Canaan. Forty years later, Rahab, the prostitute, saved the lives of two Hebrew spies by lowering them in a basket out of her window in Jericho. She could have driven a Zamboni ! (Joshua 2:15)

There are less obvious Zamboni drivers as well. Ruth the Moabitess, and her sister-in-law Orpah, set out to return to Judah with their mother-on-law, Naomi, after their husbands had died. Naomi urged them to return to Moab and find new husbands, for she was an old woman and could have no more sons for them to marry. Orpah took her advice. But Ruth stepped up, and would never allow her mother-in-law to go on all alone! The story ends with yet another Zamboni emergency goalie named, Boas. You'll have to read the Book of Ruth for the whole story, but Boas steps up in chivalry and in duty, to marry the Moabitess despite the fact that she was a foreigner. Once again, they are in the ancestral line of the Messiah.

They asked David Ayres what he *felt* as he stepped onto the ice in his only NHL game. He said, "Excited, but then nervous. I didn't want to embarrass myself, or more importantly let the other guys down." Well, He didn't.

Prayer: Dear Lord, help us to see the opportunities to 'step up.' They are everywhere around us everyday, and we ask Your Spirit's direction. Help us to realize that loving our neighbors as ourselves means overcoming the risk of embarrassment and failure, and going on to not let others down. AMEN

MARCH 14
Just Keep Swimming

"Be joyful in hope, patient in affliction, faithful in prayer." (Romans 12:12 NIV)

We have a fish tank at our house. Well, okay, a 125 gallon corner-tank aquarium. It is filled with the most colorful, interesting, varied fresh-water fish. While I spent ten years tending a salt-water tank, which required the most effort and expense in keeping the plants and corals alive, not the fish, I finally discovered the world of *cichlids,* endemic to Lakes Malawi and Tanganyika in Africa, to the Amazonian delta in South America, as well as some high water lakes in Mexico and the slow moving waters of southeast Asian rainforests. Every morning I feed them, and every evening I play violin in front of them, for which they dutifully line up at the front of the glass. (Probably some sort of weird vibration thing, not the quality of play.) They are fascinating to watch. One of the things that always catches my attention however, is their seemingly calm perseverance.

Back and forth, in and out, up and down, they journey through the plants and rocks, the plecas even burrowing into the gravel or attaching to the glass so their entire mouths and undersides are plainly visible. I guess the word that comes to mind is *tireless*. Definitely not boredom, because they are always up to some new antics with each other; but *tireless*.

Many of you with children and grandchildren will remember the fabulous 2003 film, *Finding Nemo*. Dori, the Regal Tang, voiced by Ellen Degeneres, was beautiful and kind, but lacked a significant short-term memory. Famously, she taught Marlin, the distraught Clown fish dad, that when things get you down, the thing to do is *just keep swimming!* Her buoyant attitude no matter what the circumstance, along with Marlin's determination, allow them to rescue Nemo against impossible odds.

You don't have to look too far today to find new circumstances, that many view, as terrifying, the solutions desperately sought, against seemingly impossible odds. Viral pandemics and market crashes come to mind! But so do a few other stories played out in the past. An America, devastated by economic collapse, clawed its way back to prosperity in the 1930s. From the battle grounds of the Revolutionary War to the shores of Europe, Africa, and the islands of the South Pacific, the overpowered forces of freedom faced immense forces of oppression, and yet triumphed. How did they do it? They put one foot in front of the other, that's how.

The early Christian fathers followed on the heels of the Apostles themselves, spreading the Gospel throughout the known world. For nearly two centuries, almost all faced gruesome deaths at the hands of the world's most powerful empire, bent on the destruction of the fledgling Christian faith, and yet they still promoted it. Martyred by being thrown to wild animals, crucified, beheaded, torn apart on the rack, and burned at the stake, were first the disciples, then the likes of Ignatius of Antioch (60-115 AD), Justin Martyr (100-165), Origen (186-250), and many others. If the resurrection had been a hoax perpetrated by the disciples, would they and their own students have gone on to die for expounding the truth of it? Of course not. Did the execution of these heroes of the faith testify to their failure? Far from it. Their persistence, generation after generation, led not only to eternity for each of them, but to the world-wide spread of a religion that came into being through a baby born to impoverished parents, in a backwater town, in a backwater district of a backwater corner of the Roman Empire! What did these martyrs do when persecuted throughout their lives? They just kept swimming.

We can face things like viral pandemics and economic chaos because our hope is in Christ, and our home is in eternity! We can deal on a daily basis, by just continuing to swim, to do what we know how to do, to be productive and helpful members of society, and then to go home and share the love of our families.

"We are afflicted in every way, but not crushed; perplexed, but not driven to despair; persecuted, but not forsaken; struck down but not destroyed!" (2 Corinthians 4:8 NIV)

Prayer: Dear Heavenly Father, we praise You that You never abandon

us! Guide us as we deal with crises in our lives and in the lives of those who make up our society, to just keep swimming, and trusting You to direct our paths! AMEN

MARCH 15

The Violin

"God sees us through the eyes of a Father. He sees our defects, errors and blemishes. But He also sees our intrinsic value." (Randy Alcorn)

My father passed away just over six years ago now; hard to believe. The last time I saw him alive, one month before his death and debilitated by the ALS that was slowly stealing his vitality, he made me a gift of his beautiful violin. My father had played violin literally, for seventy years. Almost all of that time was at home, practicing. He was a chemical engineer by training, and worked in marketing for Ethyl Corporation, his entire working life. In the twenty-eight years since his retirement, he had only played publicly, every summer Sunday, in the little Methodist church in South Brooksville, Maine. He did play at my wedding, and occasionally I believe, at a few retirement homes. I think he would tell you that he was never very good, but I can tell you that he was better than most!

He played only his mass production high school violin made in 1928, until in 1986, he decided to spend some money and purchase a "good" instrument. The violin he bought in Philadelphia, is a 1956 Louis Ganora, from the famous violin region of Monfalcone, Italy, near the Slovenian border on the Gulf of Trieste. My teacher for the last four years, both a lawyer and musician, is just totally in love with the sound of my dad's violin. So is his partner and brother, an airline pilot and luthier who makes violins and cellos. While valuable as most personal instruments go, it has nothing of the dollar value of those played in major symphonies. He says mine has a much better sound than many of those instruments worth hundreds of thousands of dollars, but their value comes from their provenance, i.e. knowing who made them, how long ago, and who has owned them ever since. Some of those instruments had been damaged, lost their luster as their varnish faded, warped over time with exposure to heat and moisture. But, if adequately restored, that damage wouldn't even be detectable, nor alter the provenance, and thus the value.

As I work every night for at least an hour, to bring out the beautiful sound that springs from the instrument whenever my teacher takes the bow, (or when my father took it, in my memory,) it has occurred to me that *our value* is determined in a similar fashion! For those of us that believe the Bible, we know that we were "*fearfully and wonderfully made*" (Psalm 139:14) by a God who saw fit to make us in His/Her image! (Genesis 1:27) Despite being made in that image, our reflection of the Creator became flawed, *warped* as it were, by our perpetual defiance. God gave us a way to reclaim that original image, as it was in the Garden of Eden before Adam and Eve sinned. That way, of course, is *The Way,* faith in His Son, Jesus Christ. Jesus is the way, the truth and the life, and those who accept Him, are given His righteousness before God. (Ephesians 4:24) They are in effect *restored* to life!

Our identity is in Christ and Christ alone. It is He, via the Holy Spirit, that has indwelt us ever since we accepted His gracious offer of forgiveness! Christ is from everlasting to everlasting, the alpha and the Omega, the Great 'I AM' that Moses heard from the burning bush. We not only know Who made us, but we know our provenance as well! We have always been the clay and He the potter, but since the incarnation, perfect life, sacrificial death, and resurrection of His Son, we have been adopted into His family as sons and daughters. Our value is inestimable! *The Creator made us, and we've belonged to Him for eternity,* since He knew us before we were formed in the womb. We were damaged, flawed, before we accepted Christ, but now we are completely restored through His Grace!

The next time someone puts you down, or you put yourself down, because you don't think you're good enough at your school, your job, in your relationships, or just in the mirror, remember **who** is being criticized! You are now, literally, a perfect child of God and a member of His intimate immediate family! You are so much more than a Stradivarius or a Guarneri or an Amati!

Dear Heavenly Father, Thank you that while we were yet sinners, You offered us Salvation through Your Son and granted us perfect righteousness in Your eyes! Help us not to forget our value and especially to not forget what determined it! We can live abundantly because we know that You love and value us above everything else, no matter what the world may say! AMEN

MARCH 16

Deep Breath

"Unteachable from infancy to tomb-There is the first and main characteristic of mankind." (Winston Churchill, May 21, 1928)

In my experience, there are three ways to react to a perceived crisis: (1) You can hide your head in the sand and hope it goes away (2) You can panic and in doing so engender panic in those around you (3) You can ascertain the facts. Personally, I think the lattermost is a good idea. When for instance, you are told by every possible form of media that you are in the midst of a viral pandemic, you can choose any of these responses. If you flew to rural Alaska last week and decided to camp along a riverbank for the next three months, you can safely put yourself in group (1). If you now have a garage that is packed to the ceiling with toilet paper, bottled water and hand sanitizer, such that your cars are now both exiled to the driveway, you can safely count yourself in group (2). If however, you ignored social media, only referred to reliable sources such as the CDC and the WHO, and took the time to learn a little history, then you can take a deep breath, plan on going to work tomorrow, and safely put yourself in group (3).

We attended our north Dallas mega-church online yesterday, because we complied with the local government request that groups of over 500 not congregate. It was different, but still an effective hour of learning and worshipping. When I arrived home, I received an e-mail link to a historical review of pandemics, put together by Nicholas LePan and published online at visualcapitalist.com on March 14, 2020. There is an excellent article on how diseases spread and how scientists have improved their understanding of the mathematics involved in both recording and predicting transmission rates and geographic expansion. The history of pandemics is perhaps germane to taking that deep breath we spoke of above, especially in a time when people would think it better not to breathe in at all! Certainly, the plague or black death as it was called in the mid-14th century, takes the prize for the most horrific infectious disease process known to man, with estimates of 200 million deaths. The same guilty party, the rat born bacteria, *yersinia pestis,* was also responsible for the 30-50 million deaths of the Justinian Plague in the mid 6th century. Of the sixteen "pandemics" that have killed over 100,000 people, there are only nine known to have killed over a million worldwide and by far the next biggest contenders after the plagues, were the New World smallpox outbreak beginning in the early 16th century, that took at least 55 million, and the Spanish flu outbreak of 1919, that claimed 50 million. HIV/AIDS has probably killed over 35 million. True, seasonal influenza kills 500-600,000 people every year world-wide,(CDC 2019,) but the viral outbreaks that seem to cause panic, other than the eradicated smallpox, include SWINE FLU, SARS, EBOLA, MERS and now COVID-19 and, at the time of this writing, these have killed roughly 215,000 *combined.* (At publication in Fall, 2021 over 650,000 had died of or with, COVID-19 in the USA.)

Certainly, the things that an advanced society can do to protect the elderly, those with underlying heart and pulmonary disease, and the immune-suppressed, should be instituted. Perhaps even taking draconian measures like many of the world's nations have now done, including the USA, to blunt the curve of the inevitable spread of coronavirus 19 in order to maximize efficient use of facilities and equipment like respirators, could even make sense. However, terrorizing people via the traditional media as well as social media, with dire predictions of apocalyptic outcomes and government failure is both irresponsible and dangerous. The end of the world-ers will buy all the toilet paper, bottled water and ammunition, for sure. But panic spreads in societies much faster than viruses, and panic can cause people to make really poor decisions that truly damage our economy, our governments, and the very structure of our society.

Winston Churchill didn't actually say, *"Keep Calm and Carry On,"* although his face appeared famously, on a poster in the 70's, produced long after WW II, but there is no question he would have approved of the sentiment! Keeping calm can be difficult for everyone in a crisis, but at least Christians have the bible to turn to, also known as B.I.B.L.E. or Basic Instructions Before Leaving Earth! In it, you will find an example of how to deal with life-threatening pressure, without panicking. There's this guy see, named Jesus Christ, who even knew while growing up, that He was destined to die a horrific death on a cross, before He reached His 35th birthday! Read the Gospels. Read Paul's Epistles. Is there ever a moment when you saw Him panic? Well, why NOT? It sure seems like He had more reason to than most.

He never panicked because He had complete and utter trust in His Father.

"For I have come down from Heaven, not to do my own will, but the will of Him who sent me." (John 6:38 NIV)

"I and the Father are one." (John 10:30 NIV)

"My Father, if it is possible, let this cup pass from Me; yet not as I will, but as You will." (Matthew 26:39 NIV)

We need never panic, because we have the indwelling Holy Spirit and we have the Word as a guide.

"In the beginning was the Word, and the Word was with God, and the Word was God." (John 1:1 NIV)

"The Helper, the Holy Spirit, whom the Father will send in My name, He will teach you all things and bring to your remembrance all that I have said to you." (John 14:26 ESV)

"Even the Spirit of truth, whom the world cannot receive, because it neither sees Him nor knows Him. You know Him for He dwells with you and will be in you." (John 14:17 (ESV)

"Whoever dwells in the shadow of the Most High, will rest in the shadow of the Almighty. I will say of the Lord, 'He is my refuge and my fortress, my God, in whom I trust.'" (Psalm 91:1-2 NIV)

"Trust in the Lord with all your heart and lean not to your own understanding; in all your ways submit to Him, and He will make your paths straight." (Proverbs 3:5-6 NIV)

"When I am afraid, I put my trust in You." (Psalm 56:3 NIV)

We can act sensibly in an effort to secure the health of our families and those with whom we come in contact. But we can also use our heads, be cognizant of the past, calm in the present, and hopeful for the future. And we can trust in the God who gave us His Son, and promised that, quite frankly, it will all work out in the end.

Dear Heavenly Father, We love You! We thank you that you gave us the intelligence to deal with the challenges we face unexpectedly in this life, and the certain knowledge that You are Sovereign, and our faith is the rock on which we stand. AMEN

MARCH 17

Freedom

"It is for freedom that Christ has made us free! Stand firm then and do not let yourselves be burdened by the yolk of slavery!" (Galatians 5:1 NIV)

As a young believer I can remember being frustrated by this kind of reflexive phrase that the Apostle Paul seemed to use so often! What on earth does that first sentence mean? And to be honest, the following sentence didn't help me a lot either. At that time in my life I had no "study bible" with commentary in the footnotes, and truthfully, few even existed in the 1970's. Today, you would simply look at the footnote in any study bible and understand that Paul was referring to the enslavement by *the law.* And as a mature Christian, this might be obvious without the help of a notation. But at the time, the only help I had, came from an old, very worn, leather bound version of a book that belonged to my grandfather. It was called, *Morning by Morning.*

Charles Hadden Spurgeon (1834-1892) was the pastor of London's Metropolitan Tabernacle for over thirty years. It is estimated that during his lifetime he preached to over 10 million people, remarkable in the age before radio even existed. He was known as the "Prince of Preachers," for his passion, his theatrics, and his unswerving ability to preach complete, entertaining, moving and effective sermons entirely without notes. He also expressed more than once that he would rather immerse himself in a few verses of scripture each day, than "wash his hands in several chapters." (Patricia Klein, Forward to Hendrickson's Edition of *Morning by Morning*) Today, you can choose from many different Daily Devotionals like those of Oswald Chambers, Eugene Peterson, C.S. Lewis, Max Lucado, Sarah Young and Bob Goff. But in 1860, there were virtually no guides for daily study and devotion until Spurgeon's, *Morning by Morning,"* was published. The original title was *Daily Readings for the Family or Closet,* paying homage of course, to Matthew 6:6. In it, I found a little about *freedom.*

If you believe in an intrinsic, God-given, Moral Code, as we have discussed elsewhere, then you will feel guilty from time to time. Whether or not your guilt is a fact, or an offense you have altered in your own mind, you will feel a weight that interferes with your daily functioning on every level. If you have committed an offence of which others become aware, especially if you had hidden it, then shame is added to your sense of guilt. Or, if you, in your understanding of the moral code, believe that following all the rules is essential to your "good-standing" in God's eyes as well as other people's, then you are in fact, enslaved by that set of rules. The Chosen People of the Old Testament knew those elaborate and extensive rules as "the law." So, *what can we do* when we fail, and we carry this burden of guilt and shame? Try *harder to be good?* Make bricks without straw, as Pharaoh forced the Hebrew slaves to do?

No, Spurgeon clarifies the answer for us. We don't have to *do anything!* Christ already did it for us on the cross! We are free from condemnation. (Romans 8:1) Christ, through His sacrificial crucifixion and resurrection, has freed us from enslavement to the law! We are saved, made righteous in God's eyes, by Grace through Faith, not by anything we do, ever. So, what do we do when we fail? There is nothing *to do* but enjoy the freedom we have, to approach the

Throne of Grace unobstructed! We can bring anything directly to God through our unity with the Risen Christ! All our feelings of guilt, or our wants, needs, desires, and difficulties in life, we can bring to God in prayer. It matters not one bit how much, or in what way, we have sinned; our faith frees us from condemnation and from the weight of guilt! Lastly, we are free to enjoy all the Blessings promised in scripture, not the least of which is God's faithful love. "(*hesed* in Hebrew) "*For the mountains shall depart and the hills be removed, But my kindness shall not depart from you, nor shall my covenant peace be removed, Says the Lord who has mercy on you.*" *(Isaiah 54:10 NKJV)*

"*Therefore, if the Son of Man makes you free, you shall be free indeed! (John 8:36 NKJV)*

> ***Prayer: Dear Heavenly Father, We love you! We praise you for understanding that we enslave ourselves by marching to the rules, failing daily to keep step, instead of dancing as we should, to Your Grace! Let the freedom You have granted us in Christ, be the music that helps us keep time to each movement of the dance! AMEN***

MARCH 18

What Comes Out

"Nothing outside a person can defile them by going into them. Rather, it is what comes out of a person that defiles them," (Mark 7:15 NIV)

Have you ever thought highly of someone, and then in an unguarded moment you see them say or do something that shocks you, maybe even permanently alters your opinion of that person's character? All of us sin. Anyone who believes in God, Christian, Muslim, Jew, all agree that we sin. And we all recognize in different ways, that God can be forgiving. But sometimes we have a lot more trouble with that forgiveness part when we suspect that the person in question's righteous exterior actually has nothing to do with their immoral interior. In other words, there's a difference between what we perceive as a Christian whom we see sinning, and someone claiming to be of faith, whose actions indicate that they really have little, or perhaps, no faith at all!

While the two things might at times be hard to distinguish, some things so clearly smack of hypocrisy that it is very hard to overlook. I recently overhead someone I know and respect, laughing about how they had cheated the IRS, and done so on many occasions, as a routine! Another time I was told that a highly respected, very conservative cleric, was seen on more than one occasion stepping furtively out of a Quick Stop, having, once again, slipped a pornographic magazine into his robes. A Christian man I had known for twenty years, who had been married for all of that time and more, reported to me once, somewhat sheepishly, that he had had over 220 sexual partners! I asked him how that was even possible? He responded with a shrug, "I travel for work." How many times have we heard of mega-church pastors who were caught in adulterous relationships with church members or were found to frequent prostitutes? Why were the congregations so shocked? We all sin, right?

Over and over, scripture condemns hypocrisy. A great portion of Jesus' teaching is devoted to illustrating that the entire Old Testament is the story of God's Chosen People mistaking the keeping of the letter of the Mosaic law, for righteousness in God's eyes. The Pharisees and Scribes taught that to be "ceremonially unclean" required correction through various rituals, before they could come in contact with others, eat meals, take part in worship, or even in many daily activities. Many of these rules were actually Traditions of the Elders, and not per se, written in Mosaic Law which came from God. When Jesus' disciples were seen eating without first washing their hands, rendering them ceremonially unclean, the Pharisees were aghast! They asked Jesus how it was possible that he permitted this? He called them 'hypocrites' to their faces and said Isaiah was right about them when he wrote, "*These people honor me with their lips, but their hearts are far from me. They worship me in vain, for their teachings are merely human rules. You have let go the commands of God and are holding to your human traditions.*"*(Mark 7:6-8 NIV)*

Christ goes on to teach the crowd that nothing outside a person that goes into them can defile them, but only what comes out of a person. This is an absolutely stunning statement for the 1st century Jew to hear, whose every move all day long is guided by rituals, like what is allowed to eat and even how to eat it! He tells them that it is "*from within, out of a person's heart, that evil thoughts come, sexual immorality, theft, murder, adultery, greed, malice, deceit, lewdness, envy, slander, arrogance and folly. All these evils come from inside, and they are what defiles a person.*" (Mark 7:19-23 NIV; See Fruits of the Spirit: Galatians 5:22) In other words, even when a person scrupulously observes ritual laws publicly, it is what he thinks, and the orientation of his heart, that makes him unclean. We know that God sees into the heart. "*The heart is more deceitful than all else, and is desperately sick; who can understand it? I, the Lord, search the mind and test the heart...*" *(Jeremiah 17:9 NASB)*

Once again, it is our heart that matters to God! Christ was talking about more than food when he says that things on the outside cannot make you 'unclean.' The books you read, the movies you watch, the company you keep, are all things on the outside. Can they influence you? Can you be tempted to sin because of them? Absolutely. But those *things* outside of you don't *make you defiled* in God's eyes. But for those people who have no faith, though they pretend to, well, the evil thoughts that come out of their heart, as well as those things they do because of them, are not hidden from God. A Saint who sins, is different in God's eyes than one who pretends to believe, but is faithless in his heart.

Prayer: Father God, Thank you that You hear our heartfelt confession of sin, desire for repentance, and acknowledge when we accept the gift of Your Grace in Jesus! We are reborn, and we ask the Holy Spirit to guide our thoughts such that the desires of hearts and the meditations of our mouths will ceaselessly match! AMEN

MARCH 19

The Devil Went Down to Georgia

"My prayer is not that You take them out of the world, but that You protect them from the Evil One." (Jesus...John 17:15) "Count it all joy, my brothers, when you meet trials of various kinds, for you know that the testing of your faith produces steadfastness. And let steadfastness have its full effect, that you may be perfect and complete, lacking in nothing." (James 1:2 NIV)

I was raised as a Presbyterian, but now have attended both an evangelical non-denominational church and an evangelical seminary, over the last eighteen years. Prior to the last two decades, I had never even heard the term "the Evil One," the common denominational designation being Satan or the Devil. But far more important than the name by which the Fallen Angel is called, there seems to be some confusion about his role in our daily lives.

It is impossible to switch on any form of media and not have the first word you see be *coronavirus,* in recent days. There are those who tell me this pandemic is the work of the Evil One. There are others who tell me it's punishment from God for mankind's own evil and disobedience. Recently, I spoke with a woman whose job was in jeopardy due to circumstances beyond her control. The stressors in her life were causing conflict with her spouse, and she was afraid it might even lead to divorce. On top of that, she has a son who was just sent to drug rehab for the fourth time, and a daughter who was killed three years ago in a car wreck. She and her husband are both Christians, and she made the comment to me that the Evil One seemed to be assaulting her on all sides. Is Satan the cause of her problems? Did the Evil One cause this pandemic? I didn't say it exactly, but my thought was, *maybe, but probably not!*

There seems to be what I believe to be, a common misconception in the Christian community, and it actually may extend to the other monotheistic communities as well. Many people feel that when things go horribly wrong in life, it is not due to the confluence of circumstances, and certainly not due to choices they have made personally, but instead due to supernatural interference by the Evil One. Oddly enough, some Believers, who find themselves in almost identical circumstances, are just as likely to 'blame' God, feeling that their tough times are either punishment, or the discipline that the author of Hebrews promises. (Hebrews 12:4-11) There is no question, **Satan is the one that tempts us to sin in our reaction to hard times**, but I think we give him too much credit when we place the creation of all life's difficulties at his feet. Conversely, there is no question that God may discipline as a loving father, but there are certainly theological complexities in how that might play out, and He will never tempt us to sin, but instead help us to resist temptation. (1 Cor 10:13 & James 1:13)

I am much more inclined to take the 'big picture' approach, looking first at the ***character*** of God. We know that God is loving, faithful, long-suffering, and slow to anger. We know He has chosen to forgive us of all our sins, past, present and future, if only we place our faith in His Son, thereby putting on His righteousness. Are we too quick to confuse God's provision with punishment, or even the work of Satan? A pastor of ours recently pointed out that getting thrown overboard and swallowed by a great fish, as happened to Jonah, might certainly appear to Jonah as a bad thing! But it was that very circumstance, in God's providence, that both saved his life and eventually set him in the right direction. The prophet Jeremiah found himself at the bottom of a well in his old age, thrown there by the King's officers, but this cruel act allowed for his providential rescue and subsequent prophecy to the King! (Jeremiah 38) The apostle Peter was imprisoned by Herod and awaiting death, but if not for his arrest, he couldn't have been providentially freed by the angel, a miracle that brought faith to many. (Acts 12:1-19) A similar miracle freed Paul and Silas from prison in Philippi after being beaten with rods. That providential arrest and miraculous release, enabled Paul to lead the jailers, their families and eventually hundreds of others to faith in Christ! (Acts 16:16-34)

Really, really, bad stuff can happen to us during our life here on earth. As you've heard before, we live in a 'fallen world' full of imperfect, sinful people who are often rotten to each other, and even rotten to the planet itself. ***The Devil's style is to draw you away from God.*** Scripture tells us he is a lion crouching at your door, waiting for an opportunity to take you down. (1 Peter 5:8) He is a liar and the father of lies. (John 8:44) **The Devil went down to Georgia remember?** Did he want to fight Johnny to the death in that contest of skills? No, he bet Johnny a golden fiddle against his *soul!* The pandemic is a gleeful time for the Evil One indeed, because he will cause people to act solely in a manner that they think is ***in their own best interest***. He will ***sow panic.*** He will encourage you to ***hoard*** so others have nothing. He will intensify your ***fear of death*** and loss. **BUT THE DEVIL IS A LIAR!** Believers know that God, despite seemingly hopeless, horrific circumstances, can work bad for good! (Gen 50:20) There have been unimaginably awful wars, enslavements, tortures, natural disasters and every manner of calamity since the beginning of recorded history. But a 'big picture' analysis reveals that overall, societal good can come out of such traumatic events. God wants you to trust Him. Satan wants you to not.

Christ tells us how to react to a pandemic. ***Do not be afraid of those who kill the body but cannot kill the soul. Rather be afraid of the One who can destroy both body and soul in hell." (Matthew 10:28 NIV)*** You are commanded to love your neighbor! This is the time to pull together, as one nation, as one world, and do whatever we can to help each other, not simply look out for ourselves! Those Believers who actually perish in the strife, know that this life is but a moment in the eternity we are promised! The prophet, Micah, says, "*But as for me, I will look to the Lord; I will wait for the God of my salvation; my God will hear me. Rejoice not over me, O my enemy; when I fall, I shall rise; when I sit in darkness, the Lord will be a light to me." (Micah 7:7-8)* King David says, "*The steps of a man are established by the Lord, when he delights in his way; though he fall, he shall not be cast headlong, for the Lord upholds his hand." (Psalm 37:23-24)*

Dear Heavenly Father, Thank you that You have provided the Holy Spirit, and if we just allow Him free rein, He will resist temptation through us, and the devil will indeed flee! Help us to see that no matter what our current predicament, You are faithful, and You will bring us through to better times and an abundant life, whether in this life or the next! The Devil went down to Georgia, but he went away a loser. AMEN

MARCH 20
Abundant Life

"Focus on a good life, not a good living!" (Mary & David Compton)

There is no question, this advice rings a little more true in some societies than in others; perhaps a gross generality might be that it applies more in the West than in the East, although even that is now changing rapidly. In America we learn, without even being taught specifically, that this is the "land of opportunity," and so it is! But there is a subliminal message in all of our media, whether it be television, social media, radio, magazines and newspapers, even billboards, that your happiness will be enhanced if you will just buy _____________! (Feel free to fill in the product.) The obvious, pre-requisite, is that you have the wherewithal to purchase said item. The average American is taught from an early age that excelling in secondary school will lead to university, and that excelling in university will lead to a job, and then excelling at that job will lead to an even 'better' job, meaning one where you can make even more money! The problem comes when people start to actually believe the advertising intrinsic to a capitalist system. They start to think their satisfaction in life, their fundamental happiness and peace, will be enhanced the more stuff they acquire!

Not only does it turn out that this simply isn't true, there is some pretty good evidence that it is antithetical, meaning sometimes the opposite might be true. If we use suicide rates as a marker, there is overwhelming data that poverty, joblessness, divorce, depression, and other mental illnesses increase the suicide rate. But interestingly, once the income rises above the poverty level to the point where all basic needs are met in terms of food, housing and employment, further increases in wealth have no effect on suicide rates. In other words, greater wealth doesn't bring greater happiness. Also interesting, the suicide rate in the abject poor is low and constant, if *everyone is poor.* Similarly, of two individuals with exactly the same income, one living in a wealthy neighborhood and the other in a less wealthy neighborhood, the one with the richer neighbors is more likely to commit suicide. (J Sanburn, Time, 11/2012)

What does all this mean? It means that not only does money not necessarily make you happier, but that *comparing your income to others* is what leads to discouragement, depression and suicide. Keeping up with the Joneses turns out to be a really bad idea! When we went through the slums of Mumbai several years ago, there was a vibrant, lively sense of life there, despite their lack of what we in the west would consider basic necessities. The family unit was strong. Faith was strong. But expendable cash was non-existent and everyone worked just outside the slums for subsistence wages. The WHO found that the suicide rate in very high-income countries was almost the same as that in the poorest of countries. Also, the suicide rate was highest in Western Europe and North America, and lowest in the Eastern Mediterranean and Africa. (WHO April, 2018)

Christ said there would be poor always, and that we were free to help them whenever we want. (Mark 14:7 NIV) But he also said, "*I have come that they may have life, and that they may have it more abundantly. I am the good shepherd. The good shepherd gives his life for the sheep.*" (John 10:10 NKJV) So, what is the life more abundant? The context of Christ's teaching had nothing to do with money. He was comparing the hypocritical Jewish hierarchy with thieves and robbers, who cared nothing for the good of the people, but only for their own power and wealth. He then says the thief comes in the night, to kill and destroy, further comparing false teachers to the wild animals that attacked flocks in the night. But they need not fear, for He would guard them, and even give up His life for theirs! Jesus cancelled our sinner's debt on the cross, forgiving us in one final act of perfect sacrifice. We who accept the gift of Grace, are then clothed in His righteousness, and thus are welcome in the very presence of God the Father!

It is this Gift of the Gospel that grants us a more 'abundant' life. The Greek word in scripture is *perissos*. It means overflowing; plentiful; more than sufficient, and beyond measure. What Christ purchased for us is a life with no guilt and no shame! If we just believe what He promises, it is also a life without fear, without isolation, filled with brothers and sisters; a life in community. The Greatest Commandment was simple: Love God, love each other. While we have God given abilities to use, God is more interested in our availability than our ability. Living the abundant life means being available to serve others, which the indwelling Holy Spirit will lead us to do at every opportunity. This is a formula for Biblical 'joy.' An abundant life doesn't mean *happy* all the time, but it does mean a life that is *fulfilling*.

So, there is an easy way to get rich quick: ***count your blessings!***

"No one can serve two masters. Either you will hate the one and love the other, or you will be devoted to one and despise the other. You cannot serve both God and money." (Luke 16:13 NIV)

"Do not store up for yourself treasures on earth, where moths and vermin destroy, and where thieves break in and steal. But store up for yourselves treasures in heaven…for where your treasure is, there your heart will be also." (Matthew 6:19-21 NIV)

> ***Prayer: Dear Heavenly Father, we love you! We confess that we take our eyes off the prize when are distracted by the power of money. Remind us daily of the widow who's two pennies in the offering which were worth more to You than all the gold and silver piled high! It's the servant's heart that You value, and You have enabled all of us to have just that, if we remember just how abundant our life becomes when we focus it on Your Son. AMEN***

MARCH 21

Get Out of the Boat

" 'Take courage, it is I. Don't be afraid!' 'Lord, if it's You, tell me to come to You on the water.' 'Come,' he said. Then Peter got down out of the boat, and walked on the water and came toward Jesus." (Matthew 14:27–29)

All through college and medical school, when I was on my way to take an exam, I would cough. Some people internalize their nervous fear and then display physical manifestations like tremor, or nausea, or diarrhea, or in the form of a headache, or muscle spasm. I cough. Now, whether I had legitimate reason to fear or not, was irrelevant. Like my older brother and in fact, most of my colleagues, we excelled academically. But my history of fear with tests goes much farther and deeper, than education at the higher levels. My mother could tell you I was a nervous wreck before every test I ever took from kindergarten to the end of high school, even though I invariably did well.

There of course, are seemingly much more legitimate reasons to fear in life. A friend at church has his contract at work expiring next month and he knows it won't be renewed. He's worked at the same bank for twenty years and is now facing unemployment and the attendant uncertainties. I've mentioned my daughter and son-in-law who deal with fear and uncertainty as they battle his recent lymphoma diagnosis, now compounded by the very real fear of Covid-19 for someone immune suppressed. There are individuals every day who face impending bankruptcy, potential homelessness, literal starvation, legal entanglements, bad diagnoses followed by bad prognoses, and injury whose severity threatens to radically later daily life.

As I write this, there is fear, like rarely before, on a global scale. The coronavirus outbreak is now fully a pandemic. In the last weeks, stores have emptied of bottled water, toilet paper, and hand sanitizer in what certainly appear to be apocalyptic fears, on at least a part of the populace. The stock market is in its third week of free fall as manufacturing and travel are drastically curtailed in the wake of nationwide quarantines, and those restrictions are now spreading to other continents. People are watching their investments, sometimes representing their life savings, dwindle drastically overnight. Hourly workers fear they are permanently out of jobs with all restaurants, gyms, malls, music events, and sporting events halted indefinitely, and they have rent and food to pay for. Mothers are dealing with homeschooling 50 million kids in our country alone.

We've discussed this before. Remember that *fear*, by definition, is an emotion largely based on something that *hasn't actually happened yet*. The world's efforts to contain this virus are unprecedented, and yes, drastic measures are being taken, but mortality rates in the average person are still extremely low. As soon as I sat down and began taking my exams, my cough would always stop. My friend at church is still the same person he was before he found out about his contract not being renewed, and he will find a job, but it's the fear of the unknown that he's really experiencing. (If you've had a wreck going too fast around a certain curve, and you are anxious when you next encounter it, such that you slow down, that's not really fear, it's wisdom!) You can fear a bad prognosis, but it's only a prognosis, not the fact. You can fear financial destitution, or you can fear the complete collapse of society due to a pandemic, but none of that has actually happened and you don't know what tomorrow will bring.

In a way, all fear is fear of the unknown, because only God knows the future. *But right there is the key!* If you come to have a relationship with God through your knowledge of Christ and your experience of Him via the indwelling Holy Spirit, then you know God is unfailing in His love for you and that He has plans for you! So, when only God knows the future, that is actually *the most reassuring realization*! When Peter stepped out of the boat, he did it because *he believed the Lord!* He took the initiative to step out in faith and try something that everyone would have said was impossible! (Ask, say, Sister Theresa, if you could, about what is possible and what is impossible!) ***He conquered his fear with his faith!*** When he took his eyes off of Jesus and looked at the wind and the waves, he panicked, panic breeds a downward spiral of fear and he began to sink. But even when his faith wavered, and even though Jesus rebuked him for his little faith afterwards, notice that *Jesus rescued him anyway*! Jesus never abandons us. He is there to rescue us even when our faith wavers. "I believe, help my unbelief, right?"

By the way, as you may have figured out, Peter is *my person* in scripture. Everybody's too hard on him in my opinion. So, he sank when he got scared! Did you see *anyone else stepping out of the boat?* A little shout out for Peter in my opinion! So, step out of the boat today! Help your neighbor who is self-isolating by not being one of the hoarders! Practice self-distancing. Dive into work and school from home to whatever extent you can. Health care workers do what we were trained to do: save lives at the risk of our own, but be smart and diligent and do it right. Everyone do what you can to help your neighbor, and today, like never before, the whole world is your neighbor!

The message is simple really. There is no reason to fear the unknown for the person who is united with his Savior! The remarkable thing however, is the only way this knowledge will assuage your fear in the future, is *if you really believe it!!*

"There is no fear in love; but perfect love casts out fear…" (1 John 4:18 NKJV)

> *Prayer: Father God, strengthen in us every day our faith in Your Son and the perfect love that He is for us! When we acknowledge that 'God only knows,' may that be a reassurance and not an expression of frustration. Let it calm us with the certainty that we are firmly in the midst of Your Providential will for us, and let fear be cast out! AMEN*

MARCH 22

A Miracle

"Then Peter came and said to Him, 'Lord, how often shall my brother sin against me and I forgive him? Up to seven times?' Jesus said to him, 'I do not say to you up to seven times, but up to seventy times seven!'" (Matthew 18:21-22)

It's hard to move someone under general anesthesia, and its particularly hard to roll them over. We had just delivered her 30-week premie twins by Cesarean, and now we had to remove her right kidney. The tumor was simply too big, not to remove the entire kidney. The hope of course, was that the pathology would prove benign. Unfortunately, that was not to be the case. Not only did the pathology come back the next day as malignant, but as a rare malignancy for which there was no cure.

After the initial shock, grief rolled in like a tidal wave for all of us. I sat on the edge of her hospital bed and held my sobbing patient for a long time, until her disbelieving husband took my place at her side. Initially, there was nothing I could do, but be there and listen. She was discharged a in a few days, but was back multiple times per day to see her twins in the NICU. She told me weeks later, that she had begun a series of videos for the girls, one for each on their birthdays, for the next eighteen years. She had been told it would be extremely unusual for her to survive even two years, with her type of cancer. She was a psychologist and her husband an attorney. They did what any couple would do. They went to M.D. Anderson in Houston, for a second opinion. They were given the same dismal prognosis there and told there was really no treatment that held any hope of extending her life. The doctor in Houston did mention in passing, that they hadn't had a chance to review her actual pathology slides however, since they hadn't received the shipment from Dallas by the day of their consult.

This was long before cell phones, and when my patient arrived back in Dallas after the five-hour drive, there was an urgent message on their answering machine. They were to call the doctor's office at M.D. Anderson, as soon as they got home. They tried, but the office was closed for the day. They had him paged at home, as they'd been instructed in the message. When they finally reached him, they could tell he was jumping out of his skin! Her slides had arrived right after they had left, and they had reviewed them just to be sure. Not only was it not the type malignancy they'd been told, but it showed a completely benign, quite common, renal tumor! She was not going to die. She was going to live! It turns out the pathologist in Dallas had mistakenly read the slides he was preparing for a lecture, rather than hers! He then dictated the pathology report in error! Her actual slides were then forwarded to M. D. Anderson for review.

Even thirty years ago, one would think this would have led, invariably, to a lawsuit against every possible defendant the plaintiff's attorney could find. But it didn't. In fact, the opposite happened, if there can be an opposite to a lawsuit. The couple had a party called, *Celebrating Life*, and they not only invited their friends, but all the medical personnel involved, including the guilt-ridden pathologist! By that simple act of forgiveness, they undoubtedly changed his life forever. I like to think it changed all our lives forever. In short, it was a miracle!

Forgiving another isn't just the *right* thing to do, it's really the *only thing* to do, if you've accepted the gift of Christ's sacrificial forgiveness for yourself! Perhaps the most memorable line from the wonderful novel, *The Light Between the Oceans*, was this: "*You only have to forgive once. To resent you have to do it all day, every day! You have to keep remembering all the bad things. I would have to make a very, very, long list and make sure I hated the people on it the right amount...It is much less exhausting to forgive. We always have a choice. All of us.*" *(M.L. Stedman)* As anyone who has ever carried bitterness in their heart for any length of time, knows, offering forgiveness when we've been wronged, is the *only way* to reclaim one's own life! It is absolutely the only path to freedom and peace.

Prayer: Dear Heavenly Father, guide to us to reflect Your love for us in the way we love each other. You saw to forgive us in Your Grace; let us forgive each other graciously and free ourselves from bitterness. AMEN

MARCH 23

Awesome God

"Our God is an awesome God. He reigns from heaven above, with wisdom, power and love. Our God is an awesome God!" (Rich Mullins 1955-1997)

Not many people know Rich Mullins' story, even though millions of people sing his song in worship every Sunday. Amy Grant, in her tribute after his sudden death in an automobile accident at age 41, called him "the uneasy conscience of Christian music." I think you need to know a little about his life. Richard Wayne Mullins was one of five children born to a tree farmer and a Quaker mother near Lynn, Indiana. The family attended the Arba Friends Meeting, a Quaker church, in his early years. Then in third grade, his family moved, and began attending Whitewater Christian Church, where "Wayne," as his family called him, was baptized. It was his great grandmother that taught him about four-part harmony, and how to play hymns, building on the piano lessons he received from a Quaker teacher in elementary school. But his real love was the *Beatles*, and John Lennon became a major influence for his music. In high school, he was the pianist and songwriter for the *New Creations*, a touring Christian choir which eventually led to the creation of a church and secondary school.

From 1974-1978 he attended Cincinnati Bible College, where he supported himself with the band *Zion*, which he formed, and for which he wrote the music. At the same time, he served as a youth pastor at a Methodist Church. He continued touring with *Zion* until his 'big break' when Amy Grant recorded his song, *Sing Your Praise to the Lord*, in 1981. He moved to just north of Nashville, got engaged to be married, and planned to start his solo career. His fiancé broke off their engagement a year later, but he continued to write music and perform in the Nashville area. His first two albums in 1986-87 sold poorly, but a single off the third album, entitled *Awesome God,* flew to the top of the charts. Its simplistic lyrics were totally out of character for Mullins, who was known for complex instrumentation and metaphorical lyrics that heavily stressed his Quaker roots of peace and social justice.

In 1988, Mullins moved to Wichita, Kansas, where he attended Friends University, planning to eventually be a music teacher on a Navajo Reservation. While obtaining his degree in music education, he served as a choir director at West Evangelical Free Church. In the early 90's, Mullins also formed the *Ragamuffin Band*, with his best friend and co-writer, Beaker. (David Strasser) He later co-wrote a musical, *Canticle of the Plains,* based on the life of St. Francis of Assisi, for whom he had a lifelong admiration. St. Francis' influence played a major role in his decision after graduation from Friends in 1995, to move to Tse Bonito, New Mexico, to teach children music on a Navajo reservation. When asked why he left his former life and moved to a reservation he said, "*I think I just got tired of White, Evangelical, middle class perspective on God, and I thought I would have better luck finding Christ among the Navajos.*" (Wikipedia) While on the reservation, in the final years before the accident, Rich became more and more fascinated with Catholicism. He found the common ground with Protestantism was much greater than he had been led to believe but still had issues he could not resolve. The advice he got from an elderly Protestant Minister whom he respected, was not to get bogged down in that. Christianity is about following where Christ leads. Period.

Immediately before his death, he summed up his personal philosophy this way. " *Jesus said, 'whatever you do to the least of these, you've done to me.' And this is what I've come to think. That if I want to identify fully with Jesus Christ, who I claim to be my Savior and Lord, the best way that I can do that is to identify with the poor. This I know goes against the teachings of the popular Evangelical preachers, (name it and claim it) but they're just wrong. They're not bad, they're just wrong...Christianity is about learning to love like Jesus loved and Jesus loved the poor and broken-hearted."* (YouTube video)

Here is a man who was influenced by the Quakers, Evangelicals, Methodists, the Beatles, and St. Francis' version of Roman Catholicism, who gave away all the profits from his tours and sale of music, to charity. He was able to see past the denominational differences of Christianity to the heart of his faith. I would be willing to wager that most of the Christians who stand and sing *Awesome God* with gusto, have no idea of the ecumenical mind behind its composer! The next time you catch yourself forgetting Matthew 7:1, and perhaps being a little too critical of another Christian denomination, or just another Christian for that matter, remember Rich Mullins' perspective. No, we don't have to give away everything we own, and no, we don't have to dedicate our lives solely to the poor. But it would be a good idea to remember that our love of Christ calls us to submission, and that means making sure every day, that we get ourselves out of the way, so the Holy Spirit can love through us! Our God is a big God. He loves all kinds of people *just as much as He loves you!* Remember that.

"Father, may they be all one as You are in Me and I am in You; may they be in Us, for by this unity the world will believe that You sent me." (John 17:21 Voice)

Prayer: Dear Heavenly Father, We love You! Make us more and more aware every day, when judgmentalism creeps in! Help us keep the Main thing the Main thing. We need to focus on Your Son, and the Good News we have to share with others!

MARCH 24

Fight Like a Man

"Get down on your knees, and fight like a man!" (Mary & David Compton)

"Do nothing from rivalry or conceit, but in humility count others more significant than yourselves." (Philippians 2:3 ESV)

In modern Western society, the idea of what it means to "be a man" has rarely been aligned with what Christ would consider manliness. What the Latino might describe as *machismo*, is certainly not restricted to south of the U.S. Mexican border. The social paradigm in which the male partner in a marital, or marital-like relationship, is dominant in every sense of the word, persists widely.

Down through the eons one might posit this circumstance evolved because men were physically larger and stronger, and have been involved in violent activities like hunting and fighting, or physically demanding field work, since humans became partially agrarian. Physical dominance translated naturally to decision-making dominance when the female was unable to fight back effectively, and unable to survive on her own.

While Christ promoted equal treatment of men and women and minorities, the Christian church that evolved since Rome made Christianity the official Roman religion in 323 AD, certainly failed to do the same. The church hierarchy was developed to largely exclude women from church leadership. Even 1200 years later, after the Protestant Reformation made scripture available to the masses in their own languages, passages like those in Paul's Epistle to the Ephesians 5:22, were grossly mis-interpreted and mis-applied. "*Wives submit to your own husbands as to the Lord,*" for example, was, and still is, used to justify every type of male dominance from sexual abuse, to domestic slavery, secondary to financial control. Nothing could be further from Paul's meaning or the Lord's intent. Like everything scriptural, *a text out of context is a pretext for a proof text.* The two verses immediately previous prove the point. "*...giving thanks for all things to God the Father in the name of our Lord Jesus Christ,* ***submitting to one another in the fear of God!"*** How much clearer could it be? But in case you missed it, Paul makes it even clearer to the man in Ephesians 5:25: *"Husbands,* ***love your wives*** *just as Christ also loved the church and* ***gave Himself for her."***

Not only are men supposed to submit to their wives, just as they submit, but they are to love their wives ***sacrificially.*** Gary Smalley wrote a classic book forty years ago called *If Only He Knew* that develops this point into a practical guide to loving (and fighting) with your spouse, as God intended. Trust me, most men don't understand what it means to love sacrificially. It means putting the interests of your spouse ahead of your own. It means daily practicing the same humility that Christ demonstrated in Philippians 2. It means falling to your knees to wash the feet of the one you love, just as Christ did at the Last Supper. It means striving to listen first and understand before even speaking and certainly before acting.

Real men don't just eat quiche, they seek to understand rather than to get even. The scriptures are filled with verses urging this demeanor. "*Be completely humble and gentle; be patient bearing one another in love." (Ephesians 4:2 NIV) "Above all love each other deeply, because love covers a multitude of sins." (1 Peter 4:8 NIV) "My command is this: Love each other as I have loved you." (John 15:12)* Of course, the attitude which Christ urges us to take, applies not only to relations with the opposite sex, but to relations with literally everyone! There will be times, perhaps daily, where you interact with someone who you feel demeans you, insults you, talks about you behind your back, or just in general treats you like they are spoiling for a fight! Euphemistically, getting on your knees to fight, may actually look like taking a deep breath and channeling my mother's advice whenever things get heated, simply say, "*You might just be right. I'll think about that.*" Even when you are furious and sure you are in the right, remember Proverbs 29:11 *"A fool vents all his feelings, but a wise man holds them back," or "A gentle answer turns away wrath, but a harsh word stirs up anger." (Proverbs 15:1)*

While you may feel yourself momentarily robbed of the 'joy of victory,' you will find that the true victor is the one who allows the Holy Spirit to have His way with them! They will be the ones free from anger and bitterness and reliably on that path to peace and joy!

Prayer: Father God, we confess that our natural reaction is often to fight back when attacked, verbally or physically. Turning the other cheek is not intuitive. But that's why we crucified our old self with Christ and now the life we live is in Him! Strengthen us that so we might be weak, knowing that Your strength is made perfect in our weakness! AMEN

MARCH 25

Make 'Em Laugh

"Make 'em laugh, make 'em laugh, Don't you know everyone wants to laugh? My dad said, 'Be an actor my son, But be a comical one!' They'll be standing in lines for those ole honky tonk shines. Oh, you could study Shakespeare and be quite elite, And you could charm the critics and still have nothing to eat, Just slip on a banana peel, the world's at your feet! Make 'em laugh, make 'em laugh, make 'em laugh!" (Donald O'Connor in Singin' in the Rain)

My son-in-law was diagnosed with lymphoma earlier this year. Ian and Kelly have a 2 ½ year old, Henry, my grandson. They are both doctors, so they both know too much, which probably makes everything a little harder. Everyone who hears their story of course immediately says they will pray for them. But one physician with whom I work mostly at nights, since she is a hospitalist, offered both prayers and something else. She wanted to send me a joke every day to pass on to Ian and Kelly. You know, something along the lines of, "*Why do you never see hippos hiding in the tops of trees?*" *Answer:* "*Because they're really, really, good at it!*" Ba dum dum! For the most part, she remembers everyday. She texts me the joke with a long empty space after the set up, so I can't see the answer until I scroll down. You know, like, "*Where does Noah store all his bees?*" (Imagine a large blank space here!) *Answer:* "*In an ArkHive!*"

Now, I am sure that most of the people who said they would pray for our kids actually remembered to do so. In fact, whenever I say I will pray for someone, I usually try and do it right then, or I might well forget. Whether or not someone really did pray for Ian and Kelly is essentially invisible to me. But not Lisa's jokes! Those, I see almost every day, and then Ian and Kelly see them too! I know they make me smile, and there's a pretty good chance they make the kids smile too. There are certain situations in life that are just so dire, so emotion filled, so tense, that only laughter has even a chance of improving things. A 2020 study showed that laughter relaxes your whole body, relieving physical stress, it boosts your immune system, triggers endorphin release that relieve pain and increase sense of well-being, improves cardiovascular fitness, burns calories, and it helps change perspective and release bitterness and resentment. A Norwegian study showed that those with a good sense of humor outlived those who didn't laugh, and this was particularly statistically significant in those battling cancer.

God has a sense of humor, and he wants us to use it! How do I know that? Because scripture is awfully clear about us being made in the Creator's image! And believe me, that refers to character, not looks, 'cause I am pretty sure God and I bear only a passing resemblance! ☺ Do you really think when Adam and Eve are hiding naked in the garden and God comes looking for them, calling out, *"Adam, where arrrrreeeeee you???"* that He doesn't already *know* where they are? It's the Creator's version of *"Come out, come out, wherever you are!"* Take Ecclesiastes 10:19, *"A feast is made for laughter, wine makes life merry, but money is the answer for everything!"* No question that was tongue in cheek! Tell me there's not a little humor in the boys jeering at Elisha and calling him "baldy," then his curse leading to their being attacked by a bear! (2 Kings 2:23) Ever been in church and the minister droned on a little too long? In Acts 20:9-12, Paul literally bored a young man, name Eutychus, to death with his sermon! Eutychus fell asleep, and falling from a third story window, possibly died on impact! In any event, the service came to a screeching halt, and Paul ran downstairs and hugged the boy, miraculously reviving him! There's a little chuckle in there somewhere! When frustrated by protesters in Galatia while preaching about no longer needing physical circumcision, Paul exclaims essentially, if they are such big fans of this, why don't they just go ahead and cut their own *cojones* off! (Tell me *that* didn't get a laugh from the crowd! (Galatians 5:12) And you don't smile when you read about Balaam's donkey talking back to him? The donkey that can see the angel in the road, when Balaam can not? (Numbers 22)

You can look throughout scripture and find humor. But Proverbs and the Psalms make it crystal clear that God is an advocate of the smile and the chuckle!

"A cheerful heart is good medicine; but a crushed spirit dries up the bones. (Proverbs 17:22 NIV)

"Clap your hands all you nations; shout to God with cries of joy!" (Psalm 47:1 NIV)

"The One enthroned in Heaven laughs!" (Psalm 2:4 NIV)

"I will turn their mourning to joy, I will comfort them and give them gladness for sorrow."(Jer 31:13 NIV)

"So, I heartily recommended that you pursue joy, for the best a person can do under the sun is to enjoy life! Eat, drink and be happy! If this is your attitude, joy will carry you through the toil every day that God gives you!" (Eccl 8:15 Voice)

"Our tongues were filled with laughter; our tongues were spilling over into song… the Eternal has done remarkable things!" (Psalms 126:2 Voice)

It is impossible to read of the joy throughout the New Testament and not picture smiles on the faces of Christ and His disciples!

"All you who weep now are Blessed, for you shall laugh!" (Luke 6:21 Voice)

"Although you have not seen Jesus, you love Him. And even though you do not

see Him now, you believe in Him and rejoice with an indescribable and glorious joy!" (1 Peter 1:8 NIV)

Some churches have even instituted laughter Sunday across the country. We close today with a song often used, sung to the tune of *Be Thou My vision.* (Feel free to use it as prayer instead!)

Give to Us Laughter (Walter Farquharson)

Give to us laughter, o source of our life,
Laughter can banish so much of our strife!
Laughter and love give us wholeness and health.
Laughter and love are the coin of true wealth!

Give us to laughter as sign of deep joy;
Let us in laughing fine Christian employ,
Joining with stars and with bright Northern Lights,
Laughing and praising and sharing delights!

Even in sorrow and hours of grief,
Laughter with tears brings us healing relief!
God, give us laughter, and God give us peace,
Joy of Your promise among us increase!

> ***Prayer: Dear Heavenly Father, at this writing, the doctor who sends me the jokes to forward to my son-in-law has since contracted Covid-19 herself. We pray for her, her family, all our medical personnel and first responders, and our entire world, Lord, as it struggles with this pandemic. Strengthen our brothers and sisters Lord, so that they may step into this bad situation and wrest good out of it, by showing that sacrificial love to each other that our union with You allows us to do!! AMEN***

MARCH 26

Bravery

"I learned that courage has nothing to do with the absence of fear, but only with the triumph over it. The brave man is not one who does not feel afraid, but he who conquers that fear." (Nelson Mandela)

Thirty years ago, my family and I were graciously invited to the owner's box at Cowboy Stadium for a game. At the time, I was on call for our group, and it just wasn't possible for anyone to cover for me. As a consequence, I respectfully declined. I later discovered that Nelson Mandela, newly elected President of South Africa, had also been a guest in the box that afternoon! My kids could have sat in Nelson Mandela's lap!

Nelson Mandela was arrested in 1963 and sentenced to life in prison, allegedly for being involved in sabotage against the apartheid South African government, but in retrospect clearly a political prisoner. He served twenty-seven consecutive years in jail, mostly in the horrific Robben Island Prison, before finally being released by President F.W. de Klerk in 1990, due to incredible international pressure to end the racist policy of apartheid. Mandela was first arrested in 1956, charged with High Treason. The white security police dragged him from his home in handcuffs, in front of his terrified children. Even though released that time, by 1963 "political prisoners" could be held indefinitely without trial, and he was sentenced to life. Even when a trial was held, South African law did not guarantee the defendant a right to an attorney, so many were convicted with no understanding of the procedures whatsoever.

Most of Mandela's prison time was spent in a tiny cell in the island prison. Every day, for almost thirty years, he faced the possibility of beating and execution. Any guard could claim a prisoner violated a regulation and the prisoner was then punished with isolation, loss of meals, or loss of exercise privileges. He was punished arbitrarily, himself, and forced to watch others suffer as well. Multiple times through the years he would spend long periods in solitary confinement. But then, when finally released in 1990, a man who had spent three decades in the worst prison in Africa, came out and worked tirelessly, ignoring threats to his life, for a society of racial equality. He advocated forgiveness, in keeping with his Christian faith, for the white society who promulgated the unjust and often murderous subjugation of the majority black African population for well over fifty years. He became not only President, but a national hero, revered by the black population and respected by the white, even if often grudgingly. He was awarded the Nobel Peace Prize, the Presidential Medal of Freedom, among hundreds of other honors. You can read details of his remarkable life in his autobiography, *The Long Walk to Freedom*.

What is bravery really? It's doing what you know to be right, despite awareness of the potential negative consequences. There are hundreds of moving, true stories, from every war in which the U.S. has participated. Stories of men who ran up a hill, dove their planes, stood their ground, waded onto beaches, knowing that death was likely, but doing it anyway, because of what they believed was right. And of course, there are everyday heroes who run toward fires, who halt violent crime, who raise a child alone, or who just wake up every day and do their job in the middle of a viral pandemic! The Bible is full of stories of bravery. There are obvious ones: Abraham and Isaac on the mountain altar; David and Goliath; Daniel and the Lions' Den; Joseph and Pharaoh's dream; but there are more subtle ones as well. After Jesus was crucified in a very public, humiliating fashion, a member of the Jewish high council, Joseph of Arimathea, a secret follower of Christ, came and asked Pilate for his body. He then buried this 'rebel' who was reviled by the other members of the Sanhedrin, in his own tomb! In short, he risked the loss of everything he had in the world, including his reputation, in order to do the right thing.

Faith plays a big part in bravery for many. Nelson Mandela, over decades in prison, realized that forgiveness was the only way forward. Heroes of the bible did what they did, secure in the righteous, loving, nature of God, who would watch out for them providentially, guiding them through this life, or sometimes, into the next! Those with the indwelling Holy Spirit don't have to think about the right thing and the consequences, they just do the right thing because it seems the only reasonable choice.

When you know the right thing to do, do it. Whatever you risk in making that choice, will be more than compensated by the most powerful force in the universe. That's what it means to store up treasures in heaven. They are untouchable.

"Be strong and of good courage, do not fear nor be afraid of them; for the Lord your God, He is the One who goes with you. He will not leave you nor forsake you!" (Deuteronomy 31:6 NKJV)

"So do not fear, for I am with you; do not be dismayed, for I am your God. I will strengthen you and help you; I will uphold you with my righteous right hand!" (Isaiah 41:10)

"Do not fear those who kill the body but cannot kill the soul." (Matthew 10:28)

Prayer: Dear Heavenly Father, grant us the strength to conquer our immediate fears when we make the choice to do the right thing. Give us calm resolve, secure in the knowledge that You have our back. In fact, we know You go above us to watch over us, below us to support us, behind us to encourage us, next to us in friendship, and before us to lead the way! AMEN

MARCH 27

What, No Dance Lessons?

"Sometimes, I think there are only two instructions we need to follow to develop and deepen our spiritual life: Slow down and let go!" (Oriah Mountain Dreamer)

Yesterday, still in the midst of the Coronavirus pandemic, all of the Dallas Fort Worth area had been placed on lockdown, euphemistically called, "shelter in place." My wife was out taking a walk, on an uncharacteristically warm and sunny day for March. She went the old loop we used to use with our late German Shepherd "Buddy," after he grew lame. Not very far. It is maybe a quarter of a mile at most, down a short street to a cul-de-sac on a small lake, then back and through an alley to another street near our house. I had skipped this walk, because I was resting after both my commercial pilot son and myself, had enjoyed an incredibly rare simultaneous day off. We'd gone sailing on Lake Texoma with a perfect 17 kt. breeze, under blue skies, with the temperature hovering around 90F. We both figured the likelihood of my spreading the virus asymptomatically, as a physician still seeing many patients, was limited by several thousand acres of lake and a brisk wind! Anyway, I was giving the couch a work-out while she went on her walk.

When my wife returned, she remarked on how many people she had passed on her walk. They were out jogging, pushing strollers, biking, or chatting (six feet apart) on the sidewalks. Usually at 6:30 PM on a Thursday, we might pass two or three people. She counted 31. She overheard three women discussing the incredible joy of their day, simply because they had all been *forced* out of their busy routines. They couldn't believe how stress free a day could be without taking the kids to school, being there at lunch or volunteering for this or that, then taking one to dance lessons, picking another up after basketball or soccer or baseball, shopping in-between, and then, preparing dinner, on top of all that! One woman who worked full time out of the home, remarked it had been similar for her. Her routine normally, was showering, putting on make-up and dressing for work, gulping down an instant something for breakfast while making the kid's breakfast and lunches, then dropping them off at school, and trying to get to work on time, hustle from one meeting to another, lunch out with a client, back to the office for another meeting and trying to finish a report before fighting her way home in the traffic, and then usually having to make dinner for everyone anyway, since her husband couldn't boil an egg! Instead of all that, she leisurely took a shower, the kids slept late, she had coffee with her husband, they both had conference calls a little later while the kids did online assignments themselves, they ate lunch together at the table on the deck in the back yard, took a nap while the kids had screen time, checked in with a few more things remotely at the office, then all had dinner together! It was, well, unbelievable!!!

Winston Churchill once said, "*We shape our buildings, and then our buildings shape us.*" Through our ingenuity, we have created this technocracy where everything, and I mean everything, is *instant*. When everything works so fast that we cut the microwave short because we can't possibly wait for the full ninety seconds, there is a huge amount of stress built into every day that has never existed in the history of man before the last twenty years or so. Tom Golway, chief technologist at HP, says we have shaped our technology to be more responsive and productive, and now our technology is shaping our behavior so that we are "*always on-demand.*" I am old enough to remember not just a day before smart phones, or a day before digital pagers, but a day where if you weren't sitting by your phone at home, well, whoever was looking for you just had to *wait* until you became available again! Imagine!

The viral pandemic will undoubtedly change our society in many ways, not unlike 9/11 did. But there may also be a sort of Renaissance re-awakening that ripples through our franticly mobile, overachieving, workaholic, 'always connected" country. What if people rediscover the value of quiet? What if they re-discover the occasional beauty of solitude? What if they re-discover *their families?* What if they re-discover *their Savior?*

Our Lord understood the value of solitude. He understood the necessity to *get away* from the busyness and the crowd. He understood the importance of prayer. As One with the Creator, He understood the value of *rest* (Hebrew *Sabot* from which we get Sabbath), because He invented it! Ward Cushman notes, in *To Every Nation,* that Jesus rested, often in solitude, to prepare for a major task (Luke 4:1, 14), to pray (Luke 5:16), to recharge after a hard day (Mark 6:30) , to work through His own grief Matthew 14:1-13), in times of distress (Luke 22:39-44), and before important decisions (Luke 6:12).

Disconnecting from the crazy busy, interactive, instant communication world, that the device we all hold in our hands, even while driving, has created, can be a tremendously freeing event! Not a single one of the 31 people my wife passed was on their iphone! Not one. When was the last time you saw that on a walk, or anywhere for that matter? They were happy and relaxed. When we relax, we can often communicate better than when we are in a rush to "be productive." We can use this newly discovered state of being, called *relaxed,* to connect with those we love, and for us Christian types, that means connecting with God through prayer. Remember, when you go in that closet and pray, you are not alone! That's the whole point. The Person that's in there with you loves you more than you can begin to imagine! Maybe you should take a moment and really have a conversation, you know, where you talk and then listen? Prayer in a rush, has the same effect on God, as speaking to your spouse does when you do so without even looking at him/her because you are in too big a hurry to get something done, or head out the door, or get on the phone or…whatever!

Let the pandemic give you something good. Let the complete alteration of routine truly turn your world upside down! When you turn stuff upside down, all sorts of things fall out! Maybe turning your world upside down will drop out the frantic, drop out the overworked, drop out the instant connectedness to everything! Maybe as the dissemination of *actual facts* helps us get a grip on our anxiety about this pandemic, we can get a grip on our everyday performance, connectedness anxieties, and then see the value that comes from stepping back, taking a breath, and slowing down!

"Come to me all you who are heavy burdened, and I will give you rest." (Matthew 11:28 NIV)

"Then God Blessed the seventh day and made it Holy, because on it He rested… (Genesis 2:2-3 NIV)

"Jesus said to them, 'Come with me by yourselves to a quiet place and get some rest." (Mark 6:31 NIV)

Prayer: Father God, we love You and confess that this technological world we have created has benefit for mankind, but it also tears us away from the things that are truly important. When we slow down and step away, even if we are forced to do so by a virus that completely disrupts society as we know it, there are unexpected joys that bring us closer to the ones we love and closer to You, Lord. Thank you for hidden blessings!! AMEN

MARCH 28

Practice, Practice

"A couple was walking down Broadway toward Columbus circle in New York City. Disoriented by the tourist map they struggled to unfold in the wind, they stopped and asked a street musician if he knew how to get to Carnegie Hall? The man

stopped playing and looked up from his old worn guitar, 'Everybody knows that... practice, practice, practice!'" (Anonymous)

This is my fourth year of taking violin lessons. I took it up at age fifty-nine. I ask my teacher recently, when would I go from someone who *plays the violin* to being a *violinist*? He laughed. Hmmmmmmm. My musical education started with trumpet, the cornet technically, in the sixth grade. I remember clearly putting shelf paper on the outside of my worn case to make it look better on my bicycle rack while I rode the two miles to school. I went on to play the horn all the way through college. Probably because I could read music, I became involved in choir by high school, and have sung bass in some group or other ever since. Along the way, I picked up a little piano, a little guitar, but never really became at all proficient in either.

No, the violin was to be my first real musical effort since the trumpet, and I was anxious to learn an instrument that I could play quietly, perhaps calming myself, without driving other people out of the house, as a trumpet is wont to do! My initial concentration was on simply learning the proper left -hand position, the location of the notes on the fingerboard, and the proper bowing technique. As my rudimentary skills accrued, I became more and more aware of the subtleties of every aspect of play. I recalled a conversation from twenty years ago with one of the Julliard post-doctoral students, who attend Kneisel Hall every year, in Blue Hill, Maine. We were sailing on my father's Island Packet, and I ask this 22 year-old Asian violinist, how often did she play a wrong note? Through my uncle, fluent in Chinese and Japanese, who was acting as translator, she made it clear that she didn't understand the question. Uncle Don put it to her in slightly different words, and she laughed out loud! Turns out that she hadn't played a "wrong" note to her recollection, since she was perhaps, five years-old? She thought by 'wrong,' I had meant poor *interpretation*. She said the violinist learns technical proficiency through practice, that is true, but what she learns eventually is that one has to let the intent of the composer *come through* your playing. It's about letting the instrument sing, but doing so not just with the correct notes, but with the *feelings* that the composer wished to express. In one sense, the violinist needs to get out of the way, and let the emotions that the writer intended shine through, but in another, she admittedly learns to overlay her own feelings onto the interpretation when she plays. So, practice becomes not about technique, but about being a conduit for the genius of the composer.

It occurred to me, that in our Christian faith, a similar situation arises. Many people think that by being 'good,' that is to say by both resisting temptation and proactively serving others, that they are becoming better or more accomplished Christians. As their good works accumulate, they start to think that they are earning faith brownie points! They create a pressure on themselves to never miss a quiet time, or journaling, or church service, or committee meeting, or choir practice, or food pantry serving line, or whatever it is. They castigate themselves when they 'sin' with an expletive, or an uncharitable thought, or give in to lust or alcohol or gambling or any other addiction. They think that *practicing* the technical aspect of Christianity, i.e. being good, is *sanctification*.

Sanctification is used in several different ways theologically, but generally refers to *holiness*, either as a process or a state of being. Different Christian denominations use the term with slight variations. It can refer to the Sanctifying Holy Spirit indwelling at the moment of conversion, but more commonly refers to the process whereby we become more and more Christ-like. If one views this process as simply doing more good works and resisting temptation, it becomes that practice of technique, that might lead to the right notes, but misses the *essence* of what God intended. God gave us Jesus for a reason; not only as teacher and example, but the ultimate living sacrifice, who would take away our sin, and grant us forgiveness in a life eternal. But God also gave us the Holy Spirit, and the idea is to let the Spirit work *through us*! We are the vessel. We are the aqueduct. We are the violinist that can hit the right notes, but also the one who allows the love of the Spirit to flow outwards in our daily lives! The music we produce with good deeds will be just notes on a page, unless we let the love of the composer shine through, and then the melody may soar with the heart of the Composer! If sanctification is viewed as an ever-increasing series of good works, then Christianity becomes a "do religion." That's not Christianity. Christianity is about *Grace*, about getting what we never deserved in the past and don't deserve now. It's about our love relationship with the composer of all our music! The good we do in the world needs to be because we are so in love with Jesus that we *can't help but do good!*

"The Spirit of Truth will guide you into all the truth. He will not speak on His own; he will speak only what He hears…the Spirit will receive from Me what he will make known to you." (John 16:13, 15)

"No branch can bear fruit by itself; it must remain in the vine. Neither can you bear fruit unless you remain in me." (John 15:4)

Prayer: Father God, we love You because You first loved us and brought us into Your family as adopted sons and daughters. Help us to allow the Holy Spirit, Who embodies Your love for all mankind, to flow through us to others. Let others see the music of a loving Creator shine out of us, giving the Glory to the composer and not the musician! AMEN

MARCH 29

Pray

"If you worry, why pray? If you pray, why worry? Worry is a waste of the imagination. When life knocks you to your knees, just pray there! The closest distance between a problem and its solution is the distance between your knees and the floor!" (Mary & David Compton)

Prayer used to confuse me. I mean, I know we are supposed to be able to ask God anything, and He will listen. (Philippians 4:6) But I also learned early on, that God sees into our hearts and judges us not on our actions, but what He finds on the inside. (Luke 16:15; Proverbs 21:2; Jeremiah 17:10; 1 Samuel 16:7) On top of that, God already knows what I want or need before I even ask Him! (Matthew 6:8) So, what's the point?

It took well into adulthood for me to figure out that if God told us to pray, over and over again, throughout the bible, that he probably had a good reason. Combine that with the startling realization that God's love is perfectly faithful, and it started to dawn on me that maybe praying is ***good for us,*** like exercise, or fiber, or avoiding processed sugar! The New Testament is pretty relentless in driving home the point that the whole Gospel thing is really about the *relationship.* Even the best-known verse in the entire Bible, the verse that people know who haven't cracked another chapter *ever,* know that *"God so loved the world that He gave His one and only Son, that whoever believes in Him shall not perish but have eternal life." (John 3:16)* Why did God do *that?* Because He so *loved* the world!

Well, what do you do when you love someone? Stare at them from across the room? Gaze at a picture of them all day? Ask other people if they think that certain someone likes you? No. If you love someone ***you tell them!*** True, you tell them because you want them to know. But even if they already know, you tell them *because it* feels good to tell them, and it feels good for them to tell you! In short, when you are in love with someone, you want to be with them as much as possible, you want to talk to them and tell them all your feelings, and you want to know what they think and hear what they have to say! I guess you can figure out how you do that if the one you love happens to be the Creator, your Savior, and the Spirit that dwells within you, all at the same time, right? You guessed it. Prayer.

I don't think Christ would have been as specific as He was in Matthew 6:5-15, if He didn't think the process was important for our health. He wanted to make sure we didn't pray in public if our *motivation* became self-aggrandizement after being praised for our wise words; He wanted us to pray in private so that He, who knows what we do in secret, might reward us. He said not to use a bunch of big words and long drawn out prayers to impress people, because He already knows what we need before we ask. Instead, pray simply, like the Lord's Pray He gave us demonstrates!

I was taught to always pray A.C.T.S. which stands for adoration, confession, thanksgiving, and supplication! True, all of these things are good to contemplate, and doing so from time to time will provide spiritual nourishment, but it's okay to just have a conversation with God, just as Jesus did multiple times in the Gospels. *Daily prayers lessen daily cares!*

Next time you pray, think about what it means to love your own children, if you have them. Think about how much you want them to know that you love them! Your children may tell you that they know you love them, or they may tell you that they love you. **But when they unburden their hearts to you, because they trust you and want your guidance, that's when you really feel their love!** God may already know what's on your mind, but telling your Creator and Savior what's on your heart...well, that just has to make Him smile. And after you have, remember to stop, look and listen. You will get an answer.

"May these words of my mouth and this meditation of my heart be pleasing in

Your sight, Lord, my Rock and my Redeemer! (Psalm 19:14 NIV)

"May the Lord answer you when you are in distress, may the name of the God of Jacob protect you. May He send you help from the sanctuary, and grant you support..." (Psalm 20:1 NIV)

Prayer: Dear Heavenly Father, Thank You that You love us, that You have a plan for us, that You want to hear from us, and that You have told us it's okay to approach a very Big God with any issue we have, and know that it is pleasing to You to listen and respond! AMEN

MARCH 30

Family

"Someone told Jesus, 'Your mother and your brothers are just outside, and they want to speak to you.' Jesus asked, 'Who is my mother? Who are my brothers?' Then He pointed to his disciples and said, 'Look, these are my mother and brothers. Anyone who does the will of my Father in heaven is my brother and sister and mother!'" (Matthew 12:47-50 NLT)

In the presence of our families, we are often somewhat different people than we are in the outside world. As a child, your parents, and as an adult, perhaps your spouse, have seen and heard you not looking and sounding your very best! In fact, they may well have experienced a 'you' that no one else really has, and that you certainly don't care to have anyone on the 'outside' experience! Our families are the place where we can 'let our guard down,' knowing that if attacked, we might get mauled a little, but no one wants to take us down all the way! Do we fight with family members? You bet. And often, and not to our credit, we fight 'dirty' with family members when we would never do that with those from the outside world. Why? Because we know how to push all the right buttons! We know where the soft underbelly of our sibling, or parent is!

But we also usually love our families with a deep, abiding love, that transcends all the squabbles and jabs. We know deep inside, that when it really starts to come apart, like for instance, in a pandemic, we will *always* be able to count on our brother, or sister, or mom or dad, to *have our backs!* Jesus felt the same way. Yes, some members of your family might drive you to distraction from time to time. Others will be so far out there to be barely recognizable by the standards of sanity the rest of your family tacitly establishes. In fact, some of your family members, though from the same gene pool, may bear no more resemblance to you, than a teapot to a squirrel. Still, they're your *family,* and we're just wired by our Creator to make that very significant.

So why does Jesus seem to deny His own family, waiting outside the door, on His visit back to Nazareth? It reminds one of when He stayed back in Jerusalem at age twelve to talk with the learned scribes in the Temple, with seemingly no concern for the terror he caused His parents when they discovered Him missing! By no means! His actions were not a denial of his biological family, but instead an affirmation of who He is, and why God chose to become incarnate! Jesus is totally at one with the Father. As He tells us Himself, He can only do what He sees the Father doing. (John 5:19). Still, the last verse of our opening passage above, may add to the confusion for some. Does it mean He considers only those who obey Him, to be members of His family? Is that what He means elsewhere, when He says, "*If you love me, you will keep my commands.*" (*John 14:15 NIV*)

Whenever these types of questions come up, never forget the *character of God,* well established through all the Wisdom Books of the Scriptures! God is love, and perfect love at that. The statements that make it sound like obedience is a condition of Jesus's love, must be understood in the tense and syntax of the original Greek or Aramaic. Far from obedience being requisite for receiving the love of God, wanting to do the Father's will is an *outgrowth* of the love we have for our Lord! *If you love Me, you will do as I command!* A better rendering in common English might be, *Since you love me, I know you will do as I command!* Similarly, *anyone who does the will of my Father is my brother and sister and mother,* might better be translated, *Anyone who does the will of my Father shows him/herself to be my brother, sister and mother!*

Family is there for you in the final analysis. That's why the epistles tell us repeatedly, that our acceptance of the gift of Grace, through which we obtain forgiveness, and belief in Christ as the risen Lord, allow us to be adopted into the family of God, as sons and daughters! (Romans 8:15) Adoption in the ancient Middle East, imparted all the rights and privileges of biological sonship on the recipient! Think of how a human father loves his children, even though he makes mistakes along the way. Imagine now, the love of a Perfect Father, who never makes mistakes! That's the kind of love you receive when Jesus considers you a member of His nuclear family, and that nuclear family is multi-ethnic, yellow, brown, red, black and white! When you realize the privilege of being in that inner circle, it will *definitely* make you yearn to do the will of the Father. And what is that will? Love your neighbor. Your neighbor may not look like you, or sound like you, but they may well be your adopted nuclear family! Argue sure, but be there for your neighbor, just like you would for the people that share your name.

Prayer: Father, Your love overwhelms us! It's not in an attempt to earn Your favor that we try to do what's right! It's because of Your favor, in extending Your grace to us, that we want to do what's right! Let the Holy Spirit make us constantly aware of the needs of our brothers and sisters in Christ, and make us ready and willing to step up! AMEN

MARCH 31

Change

"The only constant in life is change!" (Heraclitus of Ephesus, 500 BCE)

It is somewhat remarkable that a man known as the "dark philosopher" for his frequently expressed utter contempt for other pre-Socratic philosophers, should be quoted commonly 2500 years later. Heraclitus put forward the assertion that 'life is flux.' He claimed for instance, that "*The way up and the way down are one and the same. Living and dead, waking and sleeping, young and old are the same.*" Needless to say, such statements drove the average reader to distraction. But Heraclitus had stumbled upon a central tenant of life. These things are the same in that they are all subject to change at any time! Life is characterized by the pull of opposing forces, that many equate with struggle, but that Heraclitus contended were simply the normal flux of events, shifting like the flow of a river.

Let's take say, oh I don't know, a *pandemic* as an example! Most people would be willing to take 2020 back to Walmart and exchange it for almost any other year! At least the entire world now has something they can get behind, and they seem to be a little more motivated than they have been with climate change. Different people and different cultures are reacting somewhat differently, but they are all reacting.

God's people are familiar with change, and they have been from the very beginning. Getting tossed out of the Garden, whether euphemistic or literal, certainly represented a big change. The flood that destroyed the known world and led to Noah's Ark, certainly represented a big change. And for the Chosen People, freedom from Egypt after 400 years of enslavement represented a big change. Once out in the desert of Sinai with their children, elderly, livestock and tents, the Hebrew people were never still. Often daily, they broke their camp of hundreds of thousands, and followed the pillar of cloud wherever it led. When dark, the pillar of fire would mark their intended encampment. Can you imagine doing that for forty years? Carrying all your stuff on foot, through valleys, over mountains, across wide open scorching desert, never knowing where you would end up, and what you would find at the next campsite? Once they had defied God, even to His limit, by refusing to enter the Promised Land of Canaan, they spent the next entire generation wandering in the wilderness.

But even after that, they had one constant other than change, despite the perspective of Herculitis: God. God's love is faithful and unchanging. (Malachi 3:6; Hebrews 13:8; Revelation 1:8) The Hebrew word is *checed,* sometimes trans-alliterated as *hesed,* and means steadfast love, loving-kindness, or unfailing love. It is used 240 times in the Old Testament, and when God is the subject of the verb, it is always associated with the covenant. Thus, the word refers to God's love for His people, specifically. God's people may have moved constantly in the wilderness, but they always dwelled in just one place, and that was God. Moses began his famous prayer on behalf of the people, reaffirming this fact. "*Lord, you have been our dwelling place in all generations!" (Psalm 90 NKJV)*

Christians today have the same assurance, and in fact God has doubled down on that! He chose to become a man and live among us, live a perfect sinless life, and then sacrifice Himself for our sins, to show us just how constant that love is! Our lives can change in an instant. We can go from healthy to cancer overnight; healthy to critically injured in an accident; rich to poor in a week, as the stock market plunges; in love to separation and heartbreak; and exactly the opposite can happen as we are cured of an illness, healed of our wounds, fall madly in love or have wealth restored overnight! But we have no change with regard to God. There is nothing we can do to change God's love for us. No way to increase or decrease it, because it is unchanging and frankly, beyond our comprehension! We may roam the earth, and the winds of change may merely ruffle our hair, or they can blow the house down with all our worldly possessions. But we are safe and sound, and at home with God! He lives in us and we in Him!

"Or do you not realize about yourselves that Jesus Christ is in you?" (2 Corinthians 13:5 NIV)

"I am crucified with Christ; and it is no longer I who live, but it is Christ who lives in me." (Galatians 2:20 NIV)

"That Christ may make His home in your hearts through faith." (Ephesians 3:17 NIV)

"Who dwells in the shadow of the Most High, will rest in the shadow of the Almighty." (Psalm 91:1 NIV)

"Under His wings you will find refuge; His faithfulness will be your shield and rampart." (Psalm 91:4 NIV)

Prayer: Dear Heavenly Father, We thank you for the security of Your unchanging love for us! Let Your Holy Spirit keep us aware that a rapidly changing world will never alter our relationship to You, Our Creator and Savior. AMEN

APRIL

APRIL 1

Masks

"We refuse to wear masks and play games. We don't maneuver and manipulate behind the scenes. And we don't twist God's word to suit ourselves. Rather, we keep everything we do and say out in the open, the whole truth on display, so that those who want to can see and judge for themselves in the presence of God." (2 Corinthians 4:2 The Message)

If you have travelled to any major destination city in the world in the last fifteen years, San Francisco, New York, London, Paris, Rome, you name it, you will have seen Asian tourists wearing masks everywhere they go. It actually became an identifying mark for an Asian of any nation, even from a distance. Their cultures had incorporated the precautions necessary during the SARS viral outbreak of 2002. SARS spread by airborne droplet, skin to skin, and surface transmission, just like Covid-19. But rigid adherence to interrupting human to human transmission was able to keep worldwide deaths to only 800. It became axiomatic in Asian nations that masking was a good idea. But, in the rest of the world, it became the punchline to many jokes. Those crazy Asians! Huh. Not so funny now, is it?

So much of the way humans socialize is dependent on close contact, and on the reading of non-verbal cues from facial expression. Many have heard the oft quoted statistic that 93% of our communication is non-verbal. This is derived (and misinterpreted) from Albert Mehrabian's studies at UCLA in the late 1960's. The verbal component of his experiments was actually only one word repeated with different facial expressions and tone of voice. So, the 7% rule, as it's called, is probably not valid for thought-containing full sentences with which we communicate all the time. But, animal studies do verify that much information can and is communicated non-verbally, especially by primates. Communication between humans who don't speak the same language is nearly completely non-verbal.

Clearly our syntax pays homage to the importance of non-verbal communication with phrases like, turn your back on, keep at arms-length, get it off your chest, keep a stiff upper lip, shoulder the burden, face up to it, put your best foot forward, hand over fist, or a rule of thumb! Let's face it (there we go again!) covering our faces with a mask just feels *wrong!* It makes us feel hot, claustrophobic, itchy, and it keeps us from kissing each other! It hides our smiles, frowns, laughter and grimaces. It even muffles our verbal communication, our speech.

Wearing masks plays an important role in the cultural history of many peoples, from worship, to ceremonial dance, even to subtle seduction as in the masquerade ball. But hiding your face in a mask whenever in public seems to scream out against everything normal within us! God made you in His/Her image for a reason, both spiritually and physically. No wonder we hate wearing them for this viral pandemic! As Paul points out in 2 Corinthians above, God hates deception, and as we've discussed before, Satan is the father of deception. We all wear masks euphemistically, especially when we want to hide our feelings from others, or we hide what we feel to be our true identity. Probably most of our tendency to do so stems from our own insecurities, and even confusion about our real identities. Where do our own insecurities come from? Well, at least partially from not believing that we truly are "fearfully and wonderfully made," (Psalm 139:14) by a God who loves us unfailingly. (Psalm 36:5-7)

When you accept the Gift of Salvation by Grace through faith, you are adopted into the immediate family of Your Savior. That means you have a new identity, and one that is clothed in the righteousness of Christ! You are of inestimable value to God! Once you truly accept your true identity, claim that confidence, you will feel less of a need to wear a mask with others! Eventually, trying to be who you are not to please someone else will feel as itchy and uncomfortable as the masks we wear during this pandemic.

Don't get me wrong: we all need to mask when appropriate during this pandemic, to keep ourselves and others safe. No one *likes* wearing a bicycle or motorcycle helmet; no one *likes* wearing a seat belt; no one *likes* bringing their seat to the full and upright locked position and storing their tray tables; no one even really *likes* sitting at red lights, but we do it!

So, wear your paper mask for protection. But learn not to wear that other invisible mask! Most good people will love you for who you are, and those who don't, well, that's their issue not yours. Just remember what Telly Savalas, as Detective Theo Kojak from the TV series in the 1970's, always used to say, "Who loves ya, baby?" I'll tell you. God does!

> *Prayer: Dear Heavenly Father, we love You! Why do have so much trouble remembering that You loved us first!! We are Blessed that we are created in Your image, and we should realize we have no good reason to hide who we are from others! Even sharing our weaknesses and our own failings with others is redemptive, and better for us than hiding what we perceive as our faults. Help us Lord as we negotiate the shifting sands of this pandemic, wearing our paper masks on the outside, but letting the love we have for our neighbor showing clearly on the outside! AMEN*

APRIL 2

Ingenuity

"Never tell people how to do things. Tell them what to do and they will surprise you with their ingenuity." (General George S. Patton)

My five-year old granddaughter, no wait, SIX-year old granddaughter, Allie, had her birthday yesterday. Remember your birthdays when you were a kid? Remember your own kids' birthdays when they were little? Well, a viral pandemic reaches its ugly tentacles into every single tiny crack of our lives. It reminds me of the pyracantha that I once had to strip from our brick walls growing up in Tulsa. It latched onto every little crevice, and when you went to pull it out, it made every effort to impale you with its razor-sharp thorns. Well, needless to say there was no birthday get together party for little Alllie. The virus saw to that. But there's an extensive school/neighborhood Facebook presence in Prosper, Texas, and a bunch of moms decided this particular viral incursion would simply not go unanswered. So, my daughter knew when to take Allie out in front of the house at the designated time and watch the parade of cars drive by with happy Birthday signs, balloons and blaring the Birthday Song out the windows.

My 31 year old niece, who works for Facebook and lives in the stricken Bay Area, had a ZOOM party for at least twenty, as I scrolled the live feeds on my Macbook. We've all seen videos that bring tears to our eyes, of weddings in the back yard with only parents and preacher, and then a parade of 100 cars of well-wishers passing slowly by the house as the newlyweds come out the front door to head for their car. Our church, life group and office have all been meeting for weeks using ZOOM and our laptops. My brother and I both attended Rice University in Houston as undergraduates. Today, I received an e-mail from my brother, with a link to an article about a 22 year old RICE University engineering student who whipped together a ventilator for less than $20, using existing ambu-bags, and will be mass produced as early as next week!

There is an old Platonic expression my grandparents used to use constantly, "*Necessity is the mother of invention!*" Even in 380 BC when it first appeared in Plato's *Republic,* the ingenuity of man, when faced with adversity, was known as one of our species' defining characteristics. Why is that the case? Because whether you believe in the literal Creation story or an evolution guided by our Creator, somebody made us humans *really smart!* The bible is full of stories of man's ingenuity. (Ruth 3:1-18; 1 Kings 3:16-18; Joshua 8 etc.) God wants us to love Him how? With all our heart, soul and *mind.* We've said it before, but as the Westminster Catechism clarifies for us, the chief end of man is to Glorify God! Scripture tells us over and over again exactly how to do that. We do it by loving God and by loving our neighbor!!! (Matthew 22:36-39) It is remarkably, *just that simple!*

When circumstances get you down, especially when you think everything's literally going to "hell in a handbasket," (another favorite expression of my grandparents,) remember what magnificent creatures God has made man to be! Man is one of the weakest, slowest, mammals with the least powerful senses. Yet, in the midst of a pandemic, who's going to help you get through to the end? Is it true that it's ***all going to be okay?*** You can bet it is! Because there are literally hundreds of millions of people, all of whom are worried and scared just like you are, but they are all *imago dei,* made in the image of God! God said, "*Let us make man in our own image, according to Our likeness; let them have dominion over the fish of the sea, over the birds of the air, and over the cattle, over all the earth and over every creeping thing that creeps on the earth." (Genesis 1:26)* Trust me, I have a biology degree. That includes Coronavirus-19, the creepy little bug! Mankind is well equal to the task and more equipped than ever technologically, even if transiently short on toilet paper and ventilators. When 22 year-olds can design a functioning ventilator on the work bench in their college laboratory in a matter of days, and people can figure out ways to get together for celebrations and worship without, well, getting together, than just give it a few weeks. Do what you can to help. Then you're going to see the Glory of God like never before when we not only defeat a virus, but make the world a more loving place where hugs are finally recognized for their value.

Prayer: Dear Heavenly Father, We love You!! How Blessed are we that You saw fit to make us in Your image, unlike all the creatures of the world! Thank you that You have given us a mind creative enough to both love You and solve any problem thrown our way. There are no problems, only solutions waiting to be found! AMEN

APRIL 3

I Need That

"For everything in the world, the lust of the flesh, the lust of the eyes, and the pride of life, comes not from the Father, but from the world." (1 John 2:16 NIV)

We all get confused sometimes about what we need versus what we want. We live in Dallas, Texas. The DFW metroplex is 9,286 square miles. We have an above ground light rail system with only 93 miles of track on four lines. People from New York often ask me why we drive everywhere? Why do you think you *need* a car? Well, Manhattan is 22.8 square miles, with 850 miles of track to it and the surrounding boroughs. The comparison usually helps them understand. In short, we *need* a car.

Now, do we *need* a brand new $70,000 GMC Yukon and an $80,000 Lexus RX 350, or do we just, well, *want* them? I think you know the answer. If we really do think we *need them*, then there's a problem. Feeling like we really *needed* them would mean we worshipped their power, or their prestige, or their sex appeal, or their dominance on the road. One of the few benefits of a pandemic, like we are experiencing in 2020 with the Coronavirus, is that we start to recognize that some of the things we felt we really needed, we don't actually need at all. Funny how the fear of becoming sick or falling into the poverty level, teaches us what we actually need to live!

We had a pastor who was a good basketball player in college. He told us once he was cleaning out his closet under a marital edict when he came across his old college basketball sweatshirts. He *really had trouble* parting with them, even though he hadn't worn them in years. Why? They represented a day gone by when he could run and shoot and bring the roaring crowd to their feet! They represented a time when he was a hero. They felt like they represented *who he really was..is...I mean was!* He felt like he just, well, *needed* those sweatshirts! Understandable, right? But as he pointed out, building your identity on anything but God is a big mistake, and it even has a name: *idolatry.*

Isaiah 44:16-17 describes the carving of an idol out of the wood not burned in a cooking fire. He eats the meat, warms himself at the fire, and then proceeds to carve a 'God' that he subsequently worships! We want to cling to idols because we let ourselves believe they can help us! In the Old Testament '*deliver me or save me*' usually means from a predicament, not from damnation. When the people fell on hard times, they clung to idols out of desperation, because they had forgotten their own Creator.

Today Christians still turn to idols, and even those who truly accepted the Gift, and were rewarded with the indwelling Spirit! Just having the Spirit within doesn't mean we don't still sin and go our own way, from time to time. There are plenty of idols to choose from nowadays: drugs, food, porn, shopping, religious works, exercise, occupation and the money it generates, approval and all kinds of media idols. We turn to idols in order to cope with everyday life that we can't seem to handle. It's our old false friend Satan, who deftly augments our fear of failure. He loves to feel your insecurity. His goal, as always, is to *draw you away* from the One True God. He does that by enticing you with worldly things that he makes you think you need in order to feel good, and in particular, feel good about yourself! You feel like a failure at work? Maybe get yourself hooked on gambling so intermittently you can feel like a winner! Failure with the opposite sex? Porn can provide the most awesome partner that you can satisfy every time, in your mind. Grew up poor and never want to feel that way again? Then you would feel good if only you could make more and more money, even at the expense of losing your family. Are you a little guy? Always bugged you to get picked last in 4th grade? Then buy yourself a Ford F-350 duale!

Get the picture? Our idols comfort us and make us feel better, for a little bit. And when it starts to fade, Satan just suggests that you *do it some more, or buy some more!* But it never works. It never brings long lasting peace and happiness. In fact, it brings just the opposite. Idols are inanimate! They are powerless! But you can't see it. And as you become more and more insatiable and more and more unsatisfied, you are an easy mark for Satan indeed.

The bible warns us of the futility of idols over and over and over, again. What's more, the first of the Ten Commandments that Moses brought down from Sinai, and the first of the Greatest Commandments according to Jesus, carry the same meaning. *"You shall love the Lord your God with all your soul, and with all your heart and with all your mind." (Matthew 22:36 NASB) "You shall have no other Gods before me…You shall not make for yourself an idol." (Deuteronomy 5:7-8 NASB)*

The prophets warn us of the foolishness of idol worship. *"All whom form idols are nothing; the things in which they delight are worthless…Who forms a god and casts an idol that will prove worthless?"* Actually, the next 14 verses go on to make clear how utterly foolish idol worship really is. *(Isaiah 44:9-23 NET)* Samuel tells us, *"You should not turn aside after empty things that can't profit* and *can't deliver since they are empty!" (1 Samuel 12:21 NET)*

So, you may want something you really don't need. It might be an indulgence. You can treat yourself now and then. But be careful not to confuse your wants with your needs! When you start convincing yourself that you really need anything to make you feel better, or whole, or complete, and it isn't Christ, you'll find yourself in a very unhappy place before long.

Prayer: Lord, let Your love and Providence be more than enough for

us! Give us ears to hear and eyes to see that the things we fall into fervently desiring, are things that pull our eyes off of You, and there lies only darkness. AMEN

APRIL 4

God Might Just Use You

"But seek first the Kingdom of God and his righteousness, and all these things will be added to you." (Matthew 6:33 ESV)

Any of you that fiddle around (violin joke :) with an instrument, have probably strung together some random notes and thought, "Hmm, that might make a pretty good tune." It turns out that many song writers do just that. Some just feel a melody come out of them, put it down on paper and then write words to fit, or someone else writes the lyrics. Others start with lyrics, essentially a poem, and then write the music to fit like a screenplay composer might do while watching a movie with no music embedded yet. But most successful songwriters have at least one thing in common, they didn't train to be songwriters, and they certainly never thought they would meet with any success.

Andra'e Crouch is a good example. Raised in East L.A. in a working-class family, he managed his family's dry-leaning business as a young man. His father was an ordained minister in the Church of God in Christ, pastored a small church, and ran street, prison and hospital ministries. At age 11, his father called him up in front of a church where he was guest preaching and asked his son to play piano for the choir. Andra'e was self-taught by ear, but found he could play along in the right key. A piano was donated to his father's church, and with no hymnals available, he began composing melodies that were easy for the congregation to sing. One of his earliest was ***Bless the Lord O My Soul*** based on Psalm 103.

He of course, went on to international fame as a singer, songwriter, producer, arranger, choir director and pastor. His second group, *The Disciples*, formed in 1965, toured 68 countries, recorded seven albums, and appeared in Carnegie Hall and on the Tonight Show, before disbanding in 1979. He went on as a solo artist, and to produce for or with, the Winans, Diana Ross, Quincy Jones, Elton John and Rick Astley; to have his songs covered by Elvis Presley, Chaka Khan, Sheila E, Stevie Wonder, Bob Dylan, Barbara Mandrell, and Little Richard. Michael Jackson used the Andra'e Crouch singers for albums like *Bad, Dangerous, and Invincible*. Crouch performed his song, ***Soon and Very Soon,*** at Jackson's public memorial service in the Staples Center in 2009.

Crouch's personal life was not without some failings, but there has only been one person ever who had none of those. He suffered tragedy as well, losing his father, mother and older brother in one year, after which he and his twin sister took over the pastorship of his father's church in Pacoima, California.

God used a minority teenage boy from East LA, who banged out a few bars on a donated piano, to become what Michael W. Smith called at his funeral, "my greatest inspiration, and a man whose depth of influence on Christian music is incalculable." David taught himself to play the lyre and King Saul used him. That put him in a position to use his only other self-taught skill, the sling-shot, to go on and save a nation and change the world. Matthew was a tax collector, reviled by everyone, and God used him to write one of the four Gospels. An old woman put the only two pennies she had in the offering, and led Jesus to exclaim that she had contributed more than all those who had donated, combined. Her gift was given not out of abundance, but out of poverty. (Mark 12:41)

The next time you hear yourself thinking, "Oh, what can I do? I don't know much, or I don't know many important people. How can I make a difference? I have no influence!" Stop and remember that God has his eye even on the sparrow, and you are of much more worth to Him than that. (Matthew 10:29-31)

Bless the Lord

"Bless the Lord, O my soul, and all that is within me, Bless His holy name." (Andra'e Crouch)

Soon and Very Soon

"Soon and very soon, We are going to see the King, Hallelujah, Hallelujah!
No more crying there, We are going to see the King, Hallelujah, Hallelujah!
No more dying there, We are going to see the King, Hallelujah, Hallelujah!
Should there be any rivers we must cross, Should there be any mountains we must climb,
God will supply all the strength that we need, Give us Grace till we reach the other side…" (Andra'e Crouch)

Prayer: Dear Lord, we love You and we need to remember You loved us first, so that we should never believe we are too little to bring Glory to You! In everything we do, in everything we say, let it be to Your Glory Lord, and with whatever it is, You may do great things! AMEN

APRIL 5

My Will or His?

"For you have need of endurance, so that when you have done the will of God you may receive what is promised." (Hebrews 10:36 ESV)

There is a perception among many Christians, that when we feel confident that our actions are consistent with the will of God: if we have listened and prayed; if we feel in our hearts that the Holy Spirit is, in fact, leading us in a certain direction; then the end result will be a great success! Often, in what appear to be the vicissitudes of life, however, this turns out not to be the case at all! That can lead to disillusionment and doubt. What is it about our relationship with Christ that makes us think we are striking a deal when we pray for guidance, that somehow the earthly outcome we desire must be exactly what He has in mind as well? What if the direction we are led by the Spirit reveals a totally different outcome than the one we were hoping for? We may see the steps we take as a process whereby we reach the goal we have in mind. But what if the goal God has in mind ***is the process?***

It is awfully easy for us to forget that we are dependent on God, not equal partners with the Trinity. *"For my thoughts are not your thoughts, neither are your ways my ways,' declares the Lord. 'As the heavens are higher than the earth, so are my ways higher than your ways and my thoughts than your thoughts."(Isaiah 55:8 NIV)* Yes, when we accept Christ, He lives in us and we in Him. We are righteous before God because we *put on His righteousness*, not because somehow, we have *achieved it* ourselves through our own strength. But even when we have properly perceived the direction the Lord would have us take, it doesn't mean the short-term result will always be what we expected or wanted! Remember, there is no *reward* for obedience to His will. You are not earning favor by doing the right things, for that is seeking salvation under the Law of Moses, not the Law of Grace!

There is an old joke that is one of my favorites, that derives from the Westminster Catechism. What is the chief end of man? Answer: To glorify God. And how do we glorify God? By doing His will! **So, all men seek to serve God, but it turns out, most of us wish to serve primarily, in an advisory capacity!** What is the proper perspective on God's will for me? The answer is simple. The execution is not. The answer is that ***God's will for me is total dependence on Him!*** That's what Paul means whenever He speaks of 'dying to ourselves, and living to Christ!'

Do you remember when Christ rebuked Peter with the seemingly incredibly harsh, *"Get behind me Satan!"* Jesus had just explained, yet again, to the disciples, that God's will for Him was to be tortured and killed at the hands of the Chief Priests, but then He would rise again on the third day! Peter was appalled that this could be the will of God! (Mark 8:31-33) Shortly thereafter, at the last supper, Christ tells Peter that he will deny Him three times before the rooster crows. Once again Peter contradicts his Lord, and tells Him even if he has to die with Him, he would never disown Him! (Matthew 26:34) Here is Peter, the Rock on which Christ will build His church, but even He thinks He knows the will of God better than God does!

So, there are two potential sources of error here. First, we misperceive the will of God. Second, we perceive it correctly, but are then shocked when the outcome is not what *we had planned.* In either case, there is a reason that Jesus sets the example in the garden when He prays for what He would prefer, but ends with, *"Not my will Father, but Yours!"* Whether we have inadvertently negotiated an outcome we desired in exchange for following the will of God, or we have mistaken our own will for His, our orientation of heart must always be the same: *total dependence on the Lord!*

Charles Spurgeon liked to put it this way. If we can stay calm, faithful, and clear-headed in the midst of life's rough patches, then the goal of God's purpose is being accomplished in us! We glorify God in the process, not in the outcome. What the world sees and envies, is the manner in which the Christian handles the adversities in life, not the whether he succeeds in a worldly sense. What people think of as preparation, God may well see as the goal itself. Obedience to God should have nothing to with an earthly goal for us. Obedience to God is exactly what Christ told us it is: the way we show our love for Him! (John 14:15)

Christ is your Lord and Savior *right now. Right this very minute. Jesus is concerned with the now!* Loving God, loving our neighbor, is the moment by moment obedience that we need to pay attention to. We should have no concern for the immediate outcome of our obedience in worldly terms. Its' not about whether we get the job, get the girl or guy, receive the healing, or our loved one receives whatever they may need. It's about the relationship. It's about loving in obedience every moment of every day. Let tomorrow worry about tomorrow, I believe it was your Lord who told you that!

Prayer: Father we do love You. But we fall into the trap all too often of thinking that when things work out the way we want, it was Your will, and when they don't, it wasn't! Remind us Lord to depend on You and stop worrying about tomorrow's outcome! Success in a worldly sense may not be Your purpose for us. Your purpose may be totally in how others see us handle the lack of it! AMEN

APRIL 6

Meet in the Middle

"In essentials unity; in doubtful matters liberty; but in all things charity." (Variably attributed to St. Augustine, John Wesley, or others)

Recently, my daughter related to me the gist of a discussion she had had with our then five-year old granddaughter. It seems that on a beautiful evening last fall, Allie wanted to go outside after dinner and play for another hour, even though the sun was setting. My daughter told her that no, she had to take a bath, get her pajamas on, and then they could read books. Her five-year old looked at her very seriously, folded her arms in front of her on the dinner table, and said, *"Mommy, couldn't we just meet in the middle on this?"* Of course, the real difficulty for my daughter and her husband was to keep from laughing so hard, that they injured themselves!

It is interesting to me, that in a society where *"tolerance"* is roundly agreed to be the societal goal most treasured in the twenty-first century, that *"compromise"* seems to have fallen by the wayside. Last fall, long before the pandemic refocused our priorities, there were students who not only boycotted speakers who held different political perspectives, but actually had episodes of violent protest. Really? Now even our college campuses seem to value "tolerance" and "diversity" as long as that applies only to ethnicity and skin color, and not to opinion! We have a congress so polarized that they are viewed largely with disgust by a population whose own reasonable moderates seem to have been screamed into silence by the radicals of both left and right! What's happening to us? What happened to 'political discourse,' that leads to solutions via, you guessed it, *compromise?*

Perhaps, the problem is that the issues over which the most vitriol is spewed, like gun control, abortion rights, and illegal immigration, all are viewed as moral *essentials* with regard to our opening quotation today. I have many acquaintances who fear the "slippery slope" in approaching any of these controversies. They feel like giving any ground at all will result in an even worse societal norm. What is worse, is that people have begun to denigrate the *characters* of those with whom they disagree, rather than trying to counter their arguments on the issue. We saw this widely in the 2020 Presidential campaign. For example, if two people differ on any of these hot button issues, for one to then question the patriotism, or even the fundamental sense of morals of the other, is a common occurrence today.

Abraham Lincoln said, *"Discourage litigation. Persuade your neighbors to compromise whenever you can."* He was undoubtedly echoing a directive from our Lord in Matthew 5:25. *"Settle matters quickly with your adversary who is taking you to court. Do it while you are still together on the way..."*

Take a quick look at the following relevant scriptures as well.

"A gentle answer turns away wrath, but a harsh word stirs up anger." (Proverbs 15:1 NIV)

"Don't give in to worry or anger; it only leads to trouble." (Psalm 37:8 GNT)

"In your anger do not sin. Do not let the sun go down while you are still angry, and do not give the devil a foothold." (Ephesians 4:26-27 NIV)

"The tongue is a blazing fire seeking to ignite an entire world of vices." (James 3:6 Voice)

Give the devil a foothold. That's a key phrase. What does Satan want to do again? He wants to deceive and destroy. He is a murderer and a liar and the Father of Lies. So, when we defame the character of someone, just because they hold a different view, it's very likely to hurt them and make them angry. We give the devil a foothold. Then they may have a tendency to fight fire with fire. Pretty soon instead of figuring out how to put out a house fire, you're both siphoning all the gas out of your cars to throw on the fire! That results in two things happening: the building burns down and neither of you are going anywhere!

St. Augustine wanted certain things to be inviolate. Christians must be united in their belief in Christ's divinity, his atoning sacrificial crucifixion and His resurrection, for example. These are non-negotiable. That's what he meant by '*in essentials unity.*' Now, does the wine actually turn into the blood of Christ during communion? Does a *rapture* really occur before the second coming of Christ, and does that happen before or after a period of tribulation? These are a few of hundreds of things that Christians may seriously disagree on. They are free to believe whatever they like, if it doesn't affect the Gospel itself. That's what he means by '*in doubtful matters liberty.*' But, what the author of this quote, whether Augustine or John Wesley, really pleads for is, the final phrase: '*but in all things charity.*' That means that when you disagree on how to handle illegal immigration, you can agree to disagree, after discussion, without calling names, without insulting the other's intelligence or patriotism or even common sense! Because if you can't do that, eventually you will be doing more than giving the devil a foothold, you'll be holding the door for him and directing him down the red carpet you've laid out for him, that leads right to the middle of your heart.

When you think your disagreement is about essentials, and there is just no room for disunity, perhaps remember ***Aslan.*** Aslan is the great lion, the Christ character, in C.S. Lewis' seminal work, *The Lion, the Witch and the Wardrobe*, book 1 of the *Chronicles of Narnia*. When Lucy asks if the lion is safe, Mr. Beaver responds, "*Safe? Who said anything about safe? 'Course He isn't safe! But He's good. He's the King, I tell you.*" What that means for us Christians is this, He can defend Himself! We should argue our positions rationally, but when the one with whom we disagree remains unmovable, then move on. Shake the dust from your sandals, the bible says. God can handle His detractors by Himself. He's a big God. A very big God, in fact.

It turns out that my five-year old granddaughter had listened to the song *The Middle, (Zedd, Marin Morris, Grey)* about fifty times that day, so her exclamation was slightly less than miraculous. However, even a five-year old was able to intuit the meaning, and then apply it correctly to a situation where two sides had a different opinion. Maybe we could all *Spotify* it next time we get hot under the collar, and instead of giving him that foothold, slam the door in the Devil's face for once.

Prayer: Dear Heavenly Father, You are the Creator of the Universe, the Almighty! Feel free to remind us from time to time that You can defend Yourself! Let us depend on the Holy Spirit to lead others to truth, and realize that it isn't really our job. You've asked us to love, not to convince. AMEN

APRIL 7

You Sleep, Do you Rest?

"Out of nowhere a vicious storm blew over the sea. Waves were lapping over the boat, threatening to overtake it! Yet Jesus was asleep." (Matthew 8:24 Voice)

After 35 years of private practice I've seen a lot of people who have trouble sleeping. Either they have trouble falling asleep, or they awaken at about 3 in the morning. Both groups have one thing in common, however. Most of these insomnia sufferers lie there in bed and just can't clear their mental desktops. The can't fall asleep group are either, going over all the things they have to do, all the things they haven't gotten to yet, but meant to; or they are fretting about being simply overwhelmed and what the consequences might be. The early morning group are slightly different. They often have lists as well, but their thoughts are whirring about in spirals, flitting from one potential disaster to another. My mother always called these the 'wolf hours,' when everything seems so bad, so hopeless, that everything feels like the wolf is right at the door, ready to devour you! Turns out my mother wasn't the actual origin, but instead Swedish and Finnish folk lore. Wolves were central to Scandinavian mythology and were thought to have a special relationship to witches, hence the alternate term "the witching hour," although this more commonly refers to midnight.

Obviously, while worrying and awake, we are not *resting*. Rest carries the implication of both physical and mental/spiritual replenishment. While the common English meaning of the word *rest* certainly overlaps with that of *sleep,* scripturally, the word for sleep, (*katheudo in Greek,*) was more often a euphemism for death. *Rest* on the other hand, always carried a good connotation. The derivation of course, is the Sabbath, the seventh day, when God *rested (Sabot in Hebrew)* from the labor of creating the universe. So, *rest* carries with it the meaning of cessation from labor. But *rest* also connotes the cessation or absence of fear. Fear is really just a word for worrying about the future, about things that might happen, but haven't yet. *"Yes my soul, finds rest in God; my hope comes from Him. Truly he is my rock and my salvation; he is my fortress, I will not be shaken." (Psalm 62:5-6 NIV)* Another example: *"In peace I will lie down and sleep, for You alone Lord, make me dwell in safety." (Psalm 4:8 NIV)*

While the Hebrew Old Testament is full of references to resting in God's protection, the New Testament allows us to hear directly from God incarnate Himself. Jesus entreats, *"Come to me all you who are weary and burdened, and I will give you rest. Take my yoke upon you and learn from me, for I am gentle and humble in heart, and you will find rest for your souls. For my yoke is easy and my burden is light." (Matthew 11:28-30 NIV)* Jesus of course was emphasizing that accepting God's gracious gift of salvation through faith, is a much easier burden than trying to follow all 613 Mosaic Laws! Can you imagine if your salvation was dependent on how closely you followed hundreds of obscure rules? Talk about exhausting! Not only that, but there would be a constant element of fear and worry as well.

In our opening verse, the disciples are completely flabbergasted that Jesus can be sleeping peacefully in the bottom of the boat, when they feel they are all about to be drowned! They *still don't get it!* Perhaps those of us panicked over current events don't get it either. Christ has power over the wind and the waves just as He does over pandemics. Can you imagine Christ hoarding toilet paper and hand sanitizer? You know the disciples would be, because they thought they were going to drown while the Creator of the Universe was sleeping in the boat right next to them! I am not suggesting that Christians need to be Pollyanna about the current state of events. Follow the guidelines that the government has laid out for minimizing the effect of this viral pandemic. Keep yourself and others as safe as reasonably possible. But in order to have peace, you need to actually *believe* what you say you believe, about Christ! God is Sovereign. He has really *got* this, and the end result will be just as He wills it. All things *really do* work together for good, for those who love God! (Romans 8:28)

Belief is not just a word. Faith is not just a word. Trust is not just a word. They are matters of the will, just as love is. True, faith is a gift from God, but it is we who must actuate it and allow the presence of Christ to manifest Himself fully in us. That means when you are lying in bed and your thoughts are racing at midnight and you still haven't slept, that perhaps you are allowing your fears and your worries to overwhelm you, forgetting that if you allow Christ to live in you, no storm can overturn your boat. In the early hours of the morning, when the wolf is at the door, and everything seems worse than it really is, perhaps you are forgetting that you don't need to fear the wolf, when Aslan, the great lion of Narnia, is sleeping on the floor next to your bed!

Prayer: Dear Heavenly Father, let us find our rest in the shadow of Your wings! Let Your Holy Spirit fill us Lord, so that there is no room for fear of something that can affect only the physical body! Grant us the sleep that we need to awaken refreshed each day. Remind us that we are one with the Eternal, and that this is for real! Satan is the liar that makes us panic, live in fear, and lose precious sleep. Show us again that all we need do is resist the devil, and he will flee! AMEN

APRIL 8

Who Reads the Bible?

"All Scripture is God-breathed and is useful for teaching, rebuking, correcting and training in righteousness, so the servant of God may be thoroughly equipped for every good work." (1 Timothy 3:16 NIV)

As a physician, I often have the privilege of seeing patients for many years in a row. More and more often the new patients I see are ones whom I helped to bring into the world themselves, and now I am getting to deliver yet another generation. These older patients, many of whom I have known for thirty years, will exchange updates with me about their jobs, spouses, kids, schools, homes, and the general state of their lives. In the course of these discussions, I will often mention a good book I have read recently or inquire what they have read recently. More and more often, the response I'll get is, "Oh, to be honest, I don't really read! We're more of a movie type family. I do read the news apps on my phone though, and I admit, I do keep up with Instagram." This used to just floor me, since I have been addicted to reading since preschool, but now it has become almost the norm.

What I've discovered, is that only a tiny minority of people read any version whatsoever of the Bible on a regular basis, and only a minority of people *read any books at all!* Of those who have read the bible, only a few read daily and almost none report having read the entire Old and New Testaments, even once! Now admittedly, I went to seminary and thus have perhaps a somewhat skewed perspective. I had read through the bible several times, before even attending seminary at age fifty-three. Since then, I have discovered the podcast and App for ***Daily Audio Bible, by Brian Hardin.*** If you feel you cannot possibly devote even the twenty minutes necessary to read and study a few verses a day, reading at least the text and foot notes of a good study bible, then you could try listening to this podcast during your commute! Brian reads an OT passage, a NT passage, one from Psalms and a Proverb, and then gives a short ten-minute discussion on the interpretation and application of one of them. He progresses through the entire bible in one year. My wife and I have done this now for eleven years in a row, and we are actually starting to know where to look for things in the bible! ☺ (You can also download the **NIV Passages Bible** from Kindle, which paces the broadcast day by day with an abbreviated discussion.)

When we are tempted by Satan, where do we turn? Trust me, he is stronger than we are alone. Remember the description of the Devil: he is a murderer, a liar and a deceiver. The latter is the most dangerous. Eve wasn't stupid. The serpent just made a convincing argument that what he was saying made more sense than what God had told them! How do you know when you are being deceived? Why do so many people lose their life savings to scam artists? Our pastor's father used to work in an English bank before WWII. His job was to ferret out counter-fitters of British paper currency. How many counterfeit bills did he study in his training? NONE. Why? Because the only way to know a fake, to know when you are being deceived, is to study the *real thing, the truth*, over and over and over until you know it like the back of your hand. The bible is our source for the truth.

How do you know when you are being tempted, being drawn inexorably away from God? The Bible is the one sure way to discern this. When Satan tempted Jesus three times in the desert, where did Our Lord turn for the authority to rebuke the devil? To the Scriptures (Luke 4). When Jesus was locked in debate with the learned men of the Jewish hierarchy, the scribes and pharisees, where did He turn? To the Scriptures. (Mark 11:27-12:17) Every time, Christ was able to turn the tables on the Pharisees or on the devil, by using the words of the Hebrew Scriptures against them. If we learn the Bible, and we believe it to be inspired by God, then our opening verse is both valid and essential to our lives! The Scriptures won't help you one iota in life unless you know what's in them or at least how to look up what's in them! More than that, the Bible can remind you who you actually are, not to mention *whose* you are!

"We know that anyone born of God does not continue to sin; the One who was born of God keeps them safe, and the evil one cannot harm them! We know that we are children of God...and we are in Him who is true by being in His Son Jesus Christ. He is the true God and eternal life." (1 John 5:18-20 NIV)

Read the Bible. Pick an easy version if you want. The Message, the Voice, or the Common English Bible. But if you could, at least buy one Study Bible, either online or as a softback. Try any of these: New International Version (NIV,) the New English Translation (NET,) the New Living Translation (NLT), the English Standard Version (ESV,) the New King James Version (NKJV,) or the New American Standard Bible (NASB.) There is a reason B.I.B.L.E. stands for Basic Instructions Before Leaving Earth!

Prayer: Dear Heavenly Father, We love you Lord. Thank you that You have inspired men to write a record of Your thoughts for us, and that they have been preserved through the centuries. Inspire us now Lord to take the time to learn what You have to tell us! Let all of us realize that our Maker might just have some important things to say to us! AMEN

APRIL 9

Winches

"Mechanical advantage is a measure of how much force is multiplied, while efficiency is a measure of how much the work you do actually goes to the thing you are trying to move. In other words, efficiency is the difference or ratio, between energy input and energy output."

Fledgling is my uncle's century old sailboat, which I have mentioned before. She spends every summer moored in the little cove adjacent to our houses, on Eggemoggin Reach, in Penobscot Bay, Maine. She is indeed a beautiful thing; all teak and mahogany, wooden hull, sky blue deck, wooden sail rings, gaff rigged like all the sailing ships of the 19th and early 20th century. (I was going to try and describe *gaff rigged,* but believe me, it's better you Google Image it!) She has little freeboard, meaning her gunnels are close to the water, and her over-all length far exceeds her water line, so she appears incredibly sleek as her bow slices through the sea.

Raise Me Up is our sailboat on Lake Texoma. She is fiberglass, top to bottom, with aluminum mast, boom and hydraulic vang. She's Marconi Rigged, like almost all modern sloops. (Google Image again, land lubbers!) She's comfortable, beamy, (wide) and stable in a high wind, but not nearly as sleek in the water as a fast-moving boat like *Fledgling.*

But *Raise Me Up* has something *Fledgling* does not have, *winches.* A winch is a metal drum, around which you wrap a *sheet* or *halyard* (lines on a boat for controlling sail or hoisting sail, respectively,) to gain mechanical advantage. You crank the winch with a removable handle that fits in the top. Some winches are even bi-directional, meaning you can both pull and push the crank, and the winch still winds the line in. Why does one *need* a winch? Because, depending on your angle of attack to the wind, there are tremendous forces on your sails. Obviously, there is enough vector force transmitted to the hull to move a boat that weighs many tons through the water. *Fledgling* requires a crew member with sufficient upper body strength to actually bring the jib sheet all the way in when close hauled and heading up into the wind. You may think that easy until you either try it, or better yet, *get older*, and then try it! On *Raise Me Up,* which is admittedly a larger, heavier boat, tightening the jib sheet all the way in, even in a 12- knot breeze, is essentially impossible without a winch. Believe me, I've tried. It's hard enough on *Fledgling. RMU* even has a 2-speed *power winch* for the mainsheet and halyards! (That way your *wench [aka 1st mate,]* can literally trim the mainsail with her one finger on the power *winch* button*!*)

The Apostle Paul tells us that Christ's power is made perfect in our weakness. (2 Corinthians 12:9) It occurred to me that faith is a multiplier, sort of like a winch! In reality, I can do nothing without Christ! *"I am the vine; you are the branches. Whoever abides in me and I in him, he it is that bears much fruit, for apart from me you can do nothing."(John 15:5 ESV)* Believers realize that their re-birth means they have died to their old selves and now the life they lead is in Christ. The chief end of man is to glorify God in everything we say and do; and glorifying Him means loving Him and loving others, the way He showed us and commanded us! I promise you, I could do absolutely *nothing* to control *RMU's* sails and thus move forward, in any significant wind, without her winches! (My son could testify to this after recently attempting *manually* to shift a jib sheet to the opposite side to run "wing and wing." Without the winch, the line raced through his hand when the wind caught, and burned his fingers, blistering instantly!)

I try to start each day with this thought, even before I get out of bed to do that Tai Chi we talked about: "*Lord, let me be the instrument of Your will; use me to lighten someone else's load today.*" Of course, some days I simply forget, and this isn't my first, or even my last, thought! But on the days when I remember, it somehow keeps me more conscious that the most powerful force in the universe knows who I am and is using me that day. That's an awesome feeling, if you've never experienced it! Ask my first mate how much fun it is to just lay her finger on that button, and through that winch, in her own weakness, harness the phenomenal power of the wind to move a 7-ton sailboat through the water! We can harness the power of the Holy Spirit, just like we do that winch!

Prayer: Dear Heavenly Father,
What a thrill to realize that You know us personally through Your Son! What's more than that, His power is made perfect through our weakness! Just as I am totally dependent on that winch to effectively move forward, I am totally dependent on my Savior to move forward in every aspect of my life! Thank You that Your Son is made available to us through the Holy Spirit every day. Help us to be diligent about wrapping the lines of our life around the winch of Christ!! AMEN

APRIL 10
Ashes

"Then I turned my face to the Lord God, seeking Him by prayer and pleas for mercy with fasting and sackcloth and ashes." (Daniel 9:3 ESV)

Six weeks ago I was sitting in a business meeting with my partners and representatives of our hospital, discussing the potential for our group playing a role in the hospital system's attempt to penetrate new markets. Several minutes into the meeting, I noticed what I thought was a bruise on one of my partner's foreheads. I looked at her from several different angles, and I became more and more convinced that she must have injured herself, and her make-up simply failed to conceal the bruise. I contemplated this for several moments before noticing a similar bruise on the forehead of one of the hospital administrators. That's when it dawned on me that it was Ash Wednesday, and my colleagues had attended a service where ashes had been rubbed onto their foreheads in the sign of the cross!

When I realized that this was the beginning of Lent, the day after Fat Tuesday down in New Orleans, where Mardi Gras is King, I first thought of what I would give up, and then I felt a tinge of regret that I no longer marked my own head with ashes. In fact, since attending a non-denominational church, beginning seventeen years ago, none of my close friends even celebrate Ash Wednesday, because our church makes no mention of the season of Lent. Bible churches often eschew any traditional celebrations that may have originated with the Roman Catholic church, feeling that ever since the Reformation in the mid-17th century, if a tradition isn't mentioned in the scriptures specifically, then it shouldn't be included in the body's formal worship, nor reflected in its calendar. Having once been an Elder in the Presbyterian church, but having also attended an evangelical non-denominational seminary, I can see both perspectives. But personally, I like the tradition. This was just pre-pandemic. Little did I know then, what we would soon all be forced to give up, let alone what we might have chosen to give up for Lent.

Easter of course, celebrates the resurrection of Jesus Christ on the third day after His crucifixion, and despite what commercial America would have you believe, has very little to do with chocolate bunnies and colored eggs (although I certainly looked forward to both as a child, as did my children!) The date on which Easter is celebrated can vary yearly, from as early as March 22 to as late as April 25th, and consequently, the date on which Ash Wednesday marks the start of Lent varies as well.

Ashes are associated throughout the Old and the New Testaments with mourning, fasting, grief, humiliation, and repentance, often being placed on the head when tearing clothes and then putting on sackcloth. Christians who have those ashes in the sign of the cross on their foreheads, are symbolizing both their mourning over their own sins and the death required of Christ to pay for them. Additionally, the cross marks them as belonging to Christ.

Lent derives from the Anglo-Saxon word for "lengthen" and refers to the increasing daylight hours associated with Spring. Christians as early as the second century AD, felt that the importance of Easter deserved more than one day of celebration, and in fact required a period of penitence and fasting beforehand. By the middle of the millennium, forty days became the accepted length for "Lent," reminiscent of Jesus' forty days of fasting in the desert when tempted by Satan. (Matthew 4:1-2) Fasting on Sundays was never accepted in the early church, so the forty-day period excluded them, making the actual length of Lent, forty-six days prior to Easter Sunday. The early Christian church used this time, not only for repentance and reflection, but also for teaching the children who were preparing to become Christians with public baptism traditionally held on Easter morning. Paradoxically, this baptism of believers tied to Lent, faded away as churches moved to infant Baptism. The very non-denominational churches that today do not celebrate the Lenten season, are among the ones practicing baptism of adult believers, rather than infant baptism.

As a physician, the sight of the ashes on the forehead always triggers contemplation of the physical aspects of Christ's sacrifice. He was beaten, flogged and then crucified. It was a horrific way to die, and it was described in detail by Edwards, Gabel and Hosmer in 1986. (JAMA 3/21/1986) Everyone should read that article or at least the summation of it, in Lee Strobel's *The Case for Christ*. Christians need to understand just *how much* they are loved, and non-Christians need to read it, as at least one more piece of evidence for man's inhumanity to man.

In my mind, a devotional is really just something to contemplate in the hope that doing so might bring you a little more peace or joy as it helps you get through yet another day. Well, if that's the case, you might think reflecting on crucifixion as at least an unorthodox approach to experiencing either of those states of mind. But joy for the Christian, is about contentment, no matter the circumstance. Peace (*eirene* in Greek) for the Christian, is not only about safety, and security, but about all that Christ did through the cross and resurrection. Good Friday and Easter together mean that man is finally reconciled to God, once and for all. The cross is in fact, is the only thing that can truly bring peace and joy to all mankind, for all eternity!

Dear Heavenly Father, As we approach the celebration of Easter, let our mindfulness of the magnitude of Your love for us permeate our thoughts each day! In this uncertain time, when a viral pandemic will force us to 'give up' celebrating Easter together for the first time in a century, reassure us with Your presence that the life we enjoy will last for an eternity. More than 'giving something up' as a Lenten reminder of Christ's sacrifice, let the understanding of just what He went through for us, bring us the contentment and security we have in the knowledge of our Salvation. AMEN

APRIL 11

Hopeless

"Father, if you are willing, take this cup from me; yet not my will but yours be done. An angel from heaven appeared to him and strengthened him. And being in anguish, he prayed more earnestly, and his sweat was like drops of blood falling to the ground. When he rose from prayer and went back to the disciples, he found them asleep, exhausted from sorrow." (Luke 22:42-45 NIV)

Last week one of my patients showed me a virtual map on her iphone that updated moment to moment. Unfortunately, it wasn't a weather map, or even one of those maps that shows you real time earthquake activity. It was of course, a map of new Covid-19 cases, represented as expanding red dots. Another showed the death toll with little expanding black circles. "How can anyone be happy in a situation like this? It seems like no matter what we do it keeps spreading and even when it slows, it bounces right back!" We had a discussion then about joy vs happiness, and the nature of hope. You're probably thinking, well that is just amazing at a gynecology visit! Don't be too amazed. It helped that I had four patients scheduled all day, since our office wasn't seeing routine anything in spring of 2020. Gave us a while to talk. I told her laughingly, we could take an hour to discuss her rash, if she would like!

Happiness, is an emotion that is more transient and related to circumstance, just like *sorrow*. *Joy*, at least for the Christian, might better be translated "contentment," no matter what the circumstances. Now, don't get me wrong. I think there is a place for cheerfulness and especially humor, even in the face of a pandemic. (See Devotionals Laughter, January 26, *Just keep Swimming, March 14 and Make 'Em Laugh, March 25.)* But the Apostle James uses joy, with the meaning that really counts for us. *"Consider it pure joy, my brothers and sisters, whenever you face trials of many kinds, because you know that the testing of your faith produces perseverance. Let perseverance finish its work so that you may be mature and complete, not lacking anything." (James 1:2-4 NIV)* Now was James just a lunatic? No one is *happy* that they are going through all kinds of tough times, but we can by *joyful,* and James tells us why! We benefit from going through difficult circumstances while trusting in God completely! We can rest assured that in His providence and sovereignty, *IT WILL ALL BE OKAY,* as the signs say going up in many of our cities. Our joy comes from exactly that, *resting assured* in the final outcome. That is what can leave the Christian content, or joyful, no matter the apparent desperation of the circumstance.

Hopelessness means that there is no way out! Whatever horror; whether war, pestilence or natural disaster, fearing you cannot be saved in that situation, renders you "hopeless." Jesus' followers were both unimaginably sad, scared and *feeling hopeless* on that Saturday after the crucifixion. They had the Lord's words, but they didn't understand. We've talked about fear before. Fear is really the emotion attached to something that hasn't happened yet. On that Saturday, they feared they had lost Him forever. They feared that all the good He had done in just three years, would now amount to nothing. They feared that they had been wrong, that Jesus was a good man, a good teacher, but not the Messiah after-all.

The difference for Christians, is that *we already know the end of the story!* We have the Resurrection in the rear-view mirror, and ***that changes everything***! Christ told us not to fear the one who can kill our bodies, but only the one who can capture our souls. If we've accepted Christ already, as our Lord and Savior, the devil has no real power over us. If we can't be torn away from Christ, then we are already victorious over death!! In other words, it just isn't possible for the Christian to be hopeless.

It is possible for us to be very sad. The disciples were very sad, and afraid. They undoubtedly prayed in their anguish. The Resurrection hadn't happened yet for them. It is also normal for us to pray for an alternative to our current circumstance, just as Christ did in the Garden. He was fully human as well as fully God. He didn't want to die right then any more than we do!

When Christ feared death and begged for an alternative, how did God respond? He sent an angel to strengthen even our Savior! How does He do that for us? He did it with the gift of the Helper, whom Christ promised would come to indwell us after His resurrection. We have only to look inward when we are afraid, or starting to feel hopeless, and the Holy Spirit will direct us to the truth, which is, that we actually have nothing to fear! Then we will remember that we are ***"in it to win it,"*** and in Christ, we've already won!!

> ***Prayer: Father God, You gave us this life, and it is precious to all of us, so it's natural that we would cling to life desperately! When we fear for our lives, there is a tendency to let hopelessness and utter despair creep in. And yet, You have already given us the gift of eternal life in Christ! There is a reason that martyrs for centuries have of-***

ten marched to their deaths singing, or at least silent. The hope that gives us that contentment, that joy, even during every type of trial, cuts through the momentary panic and fear and lifts us to remember the one certainty, as that old janitor in Denver taught us earlier in the year, in the final analysis, JESUS GONNA WIN! AMEN

APRIL 12

He is Risen!

"Why do you look for the living among the dead? He is not here. He has risen! Remember how he told you, while He was still with you in Galilee: 'The Son of Man must be delivered over to sinners, be crucified and on the third day be raised again.' Then they remembered His words! (Luke 24:6-8 NIV)

A few years ago, our Pastor had given his usual Easter sermon, and it was as inspiring and uplifting as ever. At the close he asked rhetorically, believing he was quoting scripture, "Why do you look for the dead among the living?" This was in preparation for his closing, shouted declaration, a yearly ritual, "HE IS RISEN, to which every Believer knows the response, "HE IS RISEN INDEED!" But that year, he stopped himself right before that final joyous proclamation. Wait a minute! Did I just say, "Why do you look for the dead among the living?" The congregation murmured and some chuckled and some called out, "Yea, you sort of did!" The Pastor stood stock still flabbergasted. "I think I've said that wrong my entire life! And when you think about it, it's sort of a significant error! Let's try that one more time. "Why do you look for the *living* among the dead? HE IS RISEN!" And a thunderous roar came from the 3,000 congregants, "HE IS RISEN INDEED!"

Easter is by far the most significant, most joyous, celebration of the liturgical calendar year. I realize it won't be celebrated on this date every year in the future, and people reading the DOING LIFE-April 12th devotional on this date may not be celebrating Easter that day. But perhaps this will remind that future reader of the Easter when the world was hurting like never before. Yes, there have been multiple plagues that killed more people, the most recent of which was the Spanish Flu in 1919. But now, with a world infinitely more interconnected via the internet and overseas air travel, no matter the mortality rate, the draconian methods to contain the outbreak, are taking a massive toll on the world's economies, and have drastically altered every single facet of society.

For the Christian, the celebration of Christ's resurrection after dying on the cross in our place, is in fact, a celebration of hope; and hope seems one of the many things in short supply, at the moment. The apostle Paul defines faith for us in Hebrews 11:1, *"Now faith is confidence in what we hope for and assurance about what we do not see." (NIV)* Our hope, our *only hope* actually, is in our Savior, Jesus Christ! That hope is salvation, our reunion with the Father. When Christ died for us on that cross, in a sacrifice we in no way deserved, He took our sins on Himself, and in so doing, clothed us in His perfect Righteousness.

That means we can appear directly before the Creator of the Universe unblemished by sin, and no longer under the penalty of death meted out when we first disobeyed. We can't see Heaven, but we are assured of where we are headed. We are free of shame and free of guilt! His resurrection proved Him not just a prophet, but the Son of the Living God, with authority over life and death. He emerged from that tomb victorious!!

Mary and the others were indeed, unknowingly, looking for the living among the dead, and not vice-versa! As Christians, the Resurrection is the central tenant of our faith. Without it, Jesus was a good man, a teacher, and someone who died an undeserved horrific death for absolutely no reason. In fact, as C.S. Lewis, author of *Mere Christianity* purported, Jesus, who claimed to be divine, was either a liar, a lunatic or God. Well, the Resurrection would suggest he was neither of the former! Gary Habermas PhD in philosophy and well known author, claims the evidence for the Resurrection of Jesus is incontrovertible when the known facts are taken as a whole. There are five facts from scripture which are undisputed, but also verified by local Roman authorities at the time, and later historians such as Josephus, Tacitus, Lucian, Mara Bar-Serapion, Clement of Rome, Polycarp, Ignatius, Dionysius of Corinth, Tertullian, and Origen among others. They are these: 1) Jesus was crucified publicly 2) the disciples believed he arose from the dead and subsequently appeared to them, and then all were willing to suffer and die for that belief 3) the Christian persecutor Saul was suddenly converted, becoming the Apostle Paul 4) the skeptic James inexplicably became the leader of the Jerusalem church 5) the tomb was definitively empty that Sunday morning.

Arguments that the Resurrection was fraudulent are easily undermined. The disciples didn't lie or steal the body, for men will die for a lie they believe to be true, but never die for a lie they know to be a lie. There is no rationale for someone else stealing the body, and even if they had, it would not explain the conversions of Saul, James, and hundreds of others who claimed and later wrote about Christ's appearance to over five hundred of them. Were Mary and the others at the wrong tomb? That doesn't explain their encounter with the angels, later testimonies of His appearances, nor the conversion of Paul who never even saw the empty tomb. Was Jesus only apparently dead? Not if you read the Journal of the American Medical Association March 21, 1986, and understand what crucifixion really means. Did the Roman or Jewish authorities remove the body? If so, all they had to do in order to destroy the fledgling faith called the Way, was to produce the body! One more point, given the station of women in the ancient middle east, it would seem an exceedingly odd choice for the writers of the Gospels to have chosen the testimony of women with regard to so essential a fact as the empty tomb!

Ah, but I digress as they say. A physician friend of mine told me why the usual sermon was like a Longhorn Steer: just two points, far apart, and a whole lot of bull in between! Here's what I want you to think about today. We are living through an indescribably scary time with this viral pandemic. But we are also seeing people pull together, while forced to be apart. We are seeing people rediscover neighbors and families despite being unable to embrace them for the first time in their lives! We are seeing people who just recently were polarized politically almost to the point of physical blows, come to the realization that we are literally all in this together, just six feet apart!

God can make good out of bad. (Genesis 50:20) We've seen it in every war our country has fought. We saw it with 9/11. We're seeing it with Covid-19. Why is there reason for hope? Even non- believers know how John 3:16 starts: *For God so loved the world..."* And Christians know that it doesn't matter what gets thrown at us, nothing can separate us from that love! When you believe that the most powerful force in the Universe, in fact the force that created the Universe, loves you, personally, and so much so that He sacrificed His Son for you, well, I can't find a better argument for hope than that.

"Who will separate us from the love of Christ? Shall trouble, or hardship, or persecution, or famine, or nakedness, or danger, or sword?....No, in all these things we are more than conquerors through Him who loved us. For I am convinced that neither death nor life, neither angels nor demons, neither the present nor the future, nor any powers, neither height nor depth, nor anything else in all creation, will be able to separate us from the love of God that is in Christ Jesus, our Lord!" (Romans 8:35-39 NIV)

Prayer: Lord, we love you! We thank you for this beautiful world. Help us learn the lessons of Covid-19. Let it remind us that you require only two things of us ever: Love You and demonstrate that by loving others. When the world is suffering, there is a great opportunity for comforters. Let Your Holy Spirit open our eyes and ears to ways in which we can be exactly that! Every human fears suffering alone. Thank you that Easter reminds us we need never be alone again! Christ is in us, and His Spirit goes below us to lift us up, behind us to encourage us, above us to watch over us, beside us in friendship, and before us to lead the way! AMEN

APRIL 13

Human Touch

"Let the little children come to me; do not hinder them, for to such belongs the Kingdom of God...And he took them in His arms and blessed them, laying His hands on them." (Mark 10:14-16 ESV)

I have now been a physician for forty-one years. Babies I have delivered range from newborns to 38 years old, as of this writing. But, the ones I get the most follow-up on, are the teenagers. Their mothers are usually reaching the end of their reproductive years, but they still require birth control, and at least yearly visits, so we have an opportunity to catch up on each other's families. One of the things I hear most frequently nowadays, is that kids reaching age sixteen, are not really interested in Driver's Ed! Moms tell me they have seniors in high school, who just haven't gotten around to getting their licenses. Now, *maybe* I could understand this if we lived in New York City where you can live your entire life without an automobile, but this is *Texas!* We don't go to the 'corner store' without driving, for the simple reason that the corner store may be several miles away!

When I was growing up in Texas and Oklahoma, we could not WAIT to get our Driver's Licenses! We wanted to spend time with our own peers, not with *old people* like our parents, who listened to terrible music, kept talking about this war or that war that we'd never even heard of, and kept making rules about everything from homework, to what we wore to school, to how much time we could spend on the phone! We wanted privacy with friends. We wanted to go on dates! We *could not wait* to get out of the house!

So, what's going on? Are teenagers that different nowadays? Do they suddenly want to spend more time with their parents? I don't think so. I don't think they feel the pressing *need* to get out of the house to see their friends. Why? Because in order to see their friends, they only need to FaceTime, or ZOOM, or SKYPE, while lying around their bedrooms, with their parents on the other side of a door!

But something ironic has happened, in the midst of a pandemic that has much of the world literally confined to their small living spaces. Suddenly, we are all *forced to communicate* over the internet! For those of my generation, leaning into this technology is truly a miracle, even though it may have been available for years. After all, our kids know all about it, right? As we revel in the ability to see our friends and relatives, and in my case, patients, over our computer screens, those same teens have become miserable in their confinement! And now, after the shine of this technology has worn off for the rest of us, we too long to once again be able to gather in groups, and maybe even get closer than six feet to the people we care about!

Why? Because *human touch* is essential to our health! God has designed us as communal, social beings, who enjoy touching and being touched! The Scriptures are replete with examples like the one above from Mark above. Social psychologists will tell you that primate experiments ever since the late 50's have shown the critical importance of touch for infants. Newborns raised without being touched and held, develop multiple physical and social deficits. Our need to physically touch each other is inbred and overwhelming. Touching is of course, a fundamental component of courtship and mating, but also an essential part of greeting everyone, from new acquaintances to closest friends.

So, if you have a longing in the midst of the pandemic for normalcy, that itself, is normal, and centered on the desire to be able to physically contact our fellow humans. Of course, we are worried about the economy, both for the nation, as well as for our own gainful employment and ability to provide for our families. But, there is a *yearning* that can be satisfied only with a hug! A handshake will have much more significance in the future. We will place new value on the ability to have a birthday party, a wedding, a funeral, or to worship in the presence of others.

The critical importance of touch is making itself felt like never before. This, pandemic, perhaps more so than many other crises in the last couple centuries, will have the beneficial effect of causing us to value what we formerly thought of as *the little things*. Christ knew they weren't little. He commanded us to "*Greet each other with a Holy kiss!*" *(Romans 16:16 ESV)* In one of His most often quoted parables, Christ tells us of the prodigal son's return after wasting away all of his inheritance: *"While he was still a long way off, his father saw him and felt compassion, and ran and embraced him and kissed him!"* (Luke 15:20 ESV)

All of us hunger for another's touch as this scourge plays out. We can persevere, remembering always, that God knows our hearts! He made us the way we are. There is comfort in knowing that a loving Father knows what we need, and that He has sent us the Holy Spirit to lead us to truth in difficult times. Soon, we will once again be able to greet each other with a handshake, but I have a feeling a lot of those will rapidly convert to hugs! We may even find that our teenagers actually *want* to get their Driver's Licenses now!

Prayer: Precious Lord, We love You for loving us so well! We trust in You as we traverse these dark hours when human contact has become a liability, that soon the Son will shine again, and we will welcome our brothers and sisters in a way none of us has ever done before! AMEN

APRIL 14

New Normal

"And He said to them, 'Follow me and I will make you fishers of men.' Immediately, they left their nets and followed Him." (Matthew 4:19-20 ESV)

I don't know about you, but I don't really care for that term, "the new normal." As everyone's life is disrupted by the seemingly never-ending coronavirus pandemic, people have taken to calling the adjustments we have made, "the new normal." The word, *normal,* comes from the Latin, *normalis,* which means "made according to a square or perpendicular." Definitions include conforming to a standard, regular, usual, typical, ordinary, conventional or in a medical context, healthy! I'm gonna go with absolutely *none* of these for the current viral pandemic! Believing that this is what life will look like from now on is not only unsupported historically, it's just too depressing to even consider!

No, instead, I would say that we have been taken out of our *routine*; and we were yanked out of it suddenly indeed! It is a credit to our society, and to Americans specifically, that a country as geographically vast, and as varied as is our populace of 330,000,000, could so drastically change their routine that they now largely stay isolated at home with their families, still work from there or go to a workplace if in an essential industry, have converted literally overnight to home-school 50,000,000 children, at all times practice physical/social distancing, have learned to wash their hands...*a lot*, and in general have a new awareness of *"watching out for the other guy"* as the drive-safe commercials of the 1970's implored drivers to do.

All of us have some sort of daily routine, from showering, to exercise, to work, to meals, to interacting with our children, to evening leisure activities, to bedtime. Some of us have routines that are very occupation driven. I have spent some portion of every summer on mid-coast Maine. As the sun rises, several days/week, often in thick fog, you will hear the deep rumble of the engines and then limited conversation of the lobsterman who are checking their pots right in front of our house. I'm not absolutely sure when these folks get up and then eat breakfast before heading to the dock, but I'm guessing it's in the 4AM range at the latest. There's undoubtedly a routine for checking each pot in a certain order and making sure you are pulling only your own colored buoys, for re-baiting and lowering the pots, putting the boat to bed, off-loading and storing the catch (live in the case of lobster,) getting the catch to market, then prepping for the following day.

Peter and Andrew had a routine, before Jesus called to them to leave their nets and follow him. They were fisherman who rose early every morning, undoubtedly while it was still dark, to ply their trade, day after day. For three years, they set that routine aside and applied a new one, as they followed their teacher around Israel, absorbing His ways, listening to His teaching, and applying His parable lessons. Interestingly, although Jesus promised to teach them to be fishers of men, after His crucifixion and burial, they went right back to fishing on the Sea of Galilee! Despite His promise to rise again, which He told them in plain language (Luke 9:22,) Jesus finds them throwing their nets over the side of the boat (the wrong side, as it were ☺ John 21:6) only days later, right back in their old routine! But once they had seen the Risen Lord, only *then* did they truly experience a new normal. Peter went on to preach the Gospel throughout the known world, and became the Rock on which the Church was founded. But Andrew also brought the Gospel to what would become most of Eastern Europe, as well as Spain and Scotland in the west!

When coronavirus plays out; when we have acquired enough immunity on our own or through a new vaccine; when rapid accurate testing is available across the country; we too will return to our old routine. We will go to work every morning, shop in stores, meet at the water cooler and talk about sports, (remember sports?) drop our kids off at school, exercise without fear of coming too close to another person, meet friends for lunch or dinner in a restaurant, and start to travel again. The world eradicated small pox, and did essentially so with polio; and did it with much less refined computing capacity and a far smaller knowledge base. God willing, we will stop this pandemic, and be better prepared for the next bug, but we will return to normal!

No, the "new normal" for Believers occurs when they experience the freedom and peace and joy that accompanies their re-birth in Christ! Normal never looks the same for those whose guilt, whose shame, whose feelings of unworthiness, are washed away like mud off of hands dipped in a clear rushing stream! We are re-born into a life with the Holy Spirit as an integral part; a life where we view things through a new lens. We can suddenly see that *all men* were created by God, that all could be brothers and sisters, and that all are just as undeserving, but in need of salvation as we once were! Then our new "normal" includes sharing, by our attitudes and way of life, as well as our words, the Good News! We share that best by lending a hand to those in need whenever we can, and by encouraging others that they can own the hope that we have, by accepting the gift offered by a loving God, through His Son.

Nope, we may reap some benefit from a pandemic; learning the benefits of solitude; learning how it feels to help others sacrificially; learning the value of more time with the family; learning the value of slowing to take a breath; but social isolation, economic deterioration and a mask every day is *not* the new normal! The *old normal is coming back…just new and improved!!*

"Do not be afraid, for behold, I bring you good tidings of great joy which will be for all people! For there is born to you this day in the city of David a Savior, who is Christ the Lord." (Luke 2:10 NKJV)

"If you keep my commandments, you will abide in my love, just as I have kept my Father's commandments and abide in His love. These things I have spoken to you that my joy may be in you, and that your joy may be full! (John 15:10-12 NIV)
"Your life will be richer if you take joy in the people whom you love and who love you back!" (The Good News)

"I tell you there will be more joy in heaven over one sinner who repents than over 99 persons who need no repentance." (Luke 15:7 NIV) "We believe in a forgiving God; take joy in that knowledge! (The Good News)

> *Prayer: Dear Heavenly Father, we thank you that you abide with us as we work our way through this present hardship that alters our routine and seems never-ending! But we rejoice in the knowledge that you are at the helm and sovereign, and our lives will return to something like they were, only kinder, and more understanding of others. Let Your Holy Spirit guide us so that we might share with others what a new normal really looks like, once we accept the gift of Salvation in Christ! AMEN*

APRIL 15
Safe in the Harbor

"But do you not know, O foolish man, that faith without works is dead? Was not Abraham our father justified by works when he offered Isaac his son on the altar? Do you see that faith was working together with his works, and by works faith was made perfect?" (James 2:20-22 NKJV)

Perhaps you are tired of hearing by now, that my family is a sailing family! C'est la vie! It's going to keep happening from time to time in these devotions. My father owned four sailboats over his lifetime, but he sailed six, if you count my grandfather's boats. I've had five of my own, but eleven that I've sailed, if you count my father's and grandfather's! That sounds bourgeoise I know, but a lot of them were either very small, or very old, and sometimes both, so it's not nearly as Great Gatsby as it sounds!

But it does mean I've been moored in several different harbors during my lifetime. A harbor is by definition, a place that protects boats from the wind and the waves. For many years I have had a photo of a schooner in my office. She's negotiating her way past an iceberg on a sparkling blue sea. The caption reads,

"A ship in the harbor is safe...but that's not what ships were made for!" (John A. Shedd, 1928)

Sailors understand that while the wind and the waves can be their deadly enemy at times, the former is the only thing that gives life to a boat, and the latter simply must be dealt with in order to get anywhere. Most of the world's commerce was carried by sailing ships for thousands of years before the mid 19th century. In fact, for the world's economy to function at all, a certain subset of humanity, known as sailors, had to learn to effectively harness the power of the wind. Yes, there is danger on the high seas, but there is no reason at all to build sailing ships if they always have their sails furled, sitting at anchor in a harbor. It is the ability of the sailboat to move, and to carry crew and cargo, that make her worthwhile. If she never *moves*; if she *never does* anything; well then, she's a waist of good metal and timber!

Yet again our Christian faith finds itself in the midst of a sailing metaphor! Let's suppose we have accepted Christ, and thus launched our life of faith. We read the bible. We listen to sermons and podcasts. We come to understand the Gospel message and the essence of our salvation found in the final work of Christ on the cross and His subsequent Resurrection. Then what? If our faith is analogous to this beautiful, gaff rigged, teak and mahogany sloop, like my uncle's *Fledgling*, would we choose to never hoist the sails and leave her on her mooring in the cove for a hundred years? Of course not. That would be absurd! So, why have there been arguments among believers about the epistle of James ever since the Reformation? We have to ***do something*** with our faith! Galatians 2:16 affirms that justification before God comes through, faith, not through *works of the* law! But Paul is telling us that trying to follow a set of rules perfectly, in the absence of faith in Christ, will never save you! That doesn't mean you do nothing with your faith! The very same book of Galatians also says to *walk by the Spirit!* (Galatians 5:16 ESV) It doesn't say, sit on the couch in the Spirit! Why does Jesus say, *"Assuredly, I say to you, inasmuch as you did it to one of the least of these My brethren, you did it to Me!" (Matthew 25:40 NKJV)*? And why would our Savior say, *"If you love me, keep my commandments." (John 14:15 NKJV)*? The answer is obvious to a sailor! If you never hoist the sails, tighten the sheets, and cast off, you're not going anywhere!

Christ doesn't want us to understand what He did for us intellectually, and then sit on the couch eating potato chips and watching re-runs of Gilligan's Island! He wants us to take our ship of faith out there and show other people what it's all about! He wants you to help people understand that simply by accepting the Gift of Grace He offers, they too can have a beautiful sailboat of faith! They can use that faith to travel the city in which they live, or travel the world, and bring comfort, sustenance and hope to a world desperately in need of a Savior!

"So, walk by faith, not by sight." (2 Corinthians 5:7 ESV)

"If a brother or sister is poorly clothed and lacking in daily food, and one of you says to them, 'Go in peace, be warmed and filled,' without giving them the things needed for the body, what good is that?" (James 2:14 ESV)

Prayer: Father God, we know that faith is a gift from above like every good thing! Remind us that You gave it to us for a reason, and that reason is to use it in loving our neighbor! May we demonstrate our faith through our works; may our light shine on a hilltop; may our salt not lose its taste; as we show the world the abundant life and hope we have in Christ! AMEN

APRIL 16

Showers

"And I will make them and the places all around my hill a blessing, and I will send down the showers in their season; they shall be showers of blessing." (Ezekial 34:26 ESV)

So, have you had a shower today? Do you usually shower in the morning or the evening? Showering, in fact, is such a normal part of North American culture, that one can assume if you are anything but homeless, you have likely showered in the last twenty-four hours. Even the homeless have public facilities available to them to shower, should they choose to do so. And honestly , is there *anything* better than a hot shower, either in the morning to get the stiffness out, or after a workout, to wash away the sweat and get back to feeling fresh and clean? The feel of the spray on your exposed skin, coursing through your hair, tingling on your face; it's all, just so, awesome!

I have been involved with an organization called *Water Is Basic* for several years now. The nonprofit concentrates on well digging and delivery of purification systems, including portable personal ones, for distribution in South Sudan. Not only is that part of Sub-Saharan Africa continuously war torn, but literally hundreds of thousands of people have no, or extremely arduous, access to freshwater. As in other under-developed areas of the world, women may walk many miles carrying water jugs back to their villages, from whatever source is nearest. Even then, the water source is often contaminated with human and animal feces, and a potential source of diarrhea, cholera, dysentery, typhoid and even polio. Globally, 1.8 billion people have access only to water that is contaminated with raw sewage. It is estimated that 500,000 people die annually from dehydration secondary to diarrhea. Believe me, that hot shower you take at least once a day, has *never* been experienced by millions and millions of people!

There is a reason that the word "shower" has pleasant connotations for man. *Shower* implies light rain only, but enough to nourish the new growth of spring. *Rain,* on the other hand may be associated with devastation and flooding in many monsoon areas of the world. Christians often speak of being "showered with blessings," and we all know what it means to be "showered" with love and affection. But we also speak of being "flooded with troubles," and "when it rains it pours!" Scripturally, showers are a good thing. We as Christians believe that "all good things are gifts from above," (James 1:17 NASB) and showers of course, come from above, and bring life-giving fresh water for drinking, for crop irrigation and for bathing.

A big part of our faith involves gratitude. We are indeed grateful for the Grace that allowed us to be saved while still sinners, through the atoning sacrifice of Jesus Christ, Our Lord and Savior. But we should also follow Bing Crosby's lead when we can't sleep, and maybe count our blessings instead of sheep! Every day when you get into that shower and adjust the flow and temperature to just your liking, keep in mind those people that are walking miles roundtrip in the heat, to hand-carry heavy containers of feces infested water for drinking, cooking and bathing. And while you're thinking about it, and hopefully praying about it, remember that faith without works is dead. ***Do something to help!*** If you want to do what I do, then get online and donate at *Waterisbasic.org*. It's hard to lead someone to the "living water" that is Christ, when they are watching their children die for lack of fresh water! The first step toward salvation, is making sure people don't die before they've even heard the Good News! There are plenty of other organizations working to make water available around the world, just Google it!

"If you knew the gift of God and who it is that asks you for a drink, you would have asked him and he would have given you living water." (John 4:10 NIV)

"Thousands have lived without love, not one without water." (W.H. Auden)

"When the well is dry, we will know the worth of water." (Benjamin Franklin)

Prayer: Dear Heavenly Father, We love You! Forgive us when we so easily forget to express the gratitude we feel everyday! Showers of pure clean water should indeed remind us that every good and perfect gift is from above. But You want us to be the Lord's hands and feet, and that means that we need to be the source of the showers that fall on the less fortunate, and we can literally be that source when we work to preserve water and to make it available to those in need. AMEN

APRIL 17

A Dark Tunnel

"The Lord is my light and my salvation-whom shall I fear? The Lord is the stronghold of my life-of whom shall I be afraid? When the wicked advance against me to devour me, it is my enemies and my foes who will stumble and fall. Though an army besiege me, my heart will not fear; though war break out against me, even then I will be confident." (Psalm 27:1-3 NIV)

Many people are familiar with the story of Dietrich Bonhoeffer, the German evangelical pastor who was a vociferous anti-Nazi dissident. He is the author of the now classic work, *The Cost of Discipleship*. A vocal opponent of antisemitism, he boldly opposed Hitler's genocidal persecution of the Jews. Eventually, he was executed, only months before the war's end, in the Nazi concentration camp of Flossenburg. Accused of being involved in the failed plot to assassinate Hitler, he was hung by the Nazis, even knowing that their cause was lost. Bonhoeffer has since become a household name among Christians worldwide. But far fewer people have ever heard of Titus Brandsma.

Brandsma was a Dutch Carmelite friar and then a Catholic priest, and by 1923, a professor of philosophy at what is now Radboud University in Nijmegan, Netherlands. He was a leader of the resistance to the policies of Hitler, during and after the invasion of Holland in 1940. While some churches believed cooperation, for the safety for its members, was the right move, Titus was vociferously opposed to collaboration in any way, and as a journalist, as well as theologian and philosopher, his views were on public display. He was an outspoken critic of persecuting the Jews, and referred to Nazism as the "new paganism." After 1941, the Nazis refused to allow any Jews to attend private schools in Holland. Brandsma was President of the Association of Catholic Secondary Schools, and openly opposed the Nazi edict. When the new government insisted that his Catholic papers print Nazi propaganda, he refused outright. He was arrested and sent to Dachau Concentration Camp, renowned as one of the most inhumane in or out of Germany. Despite filth, starvation and torture, survivors report that Brandsma was often witnessed continuing in both prayer and meditation, and appeared, remarkably, to harbor no bitterness toward his captors. *Butler's Lives of the Saints* quotes him as telling fellow prisoners, "*We are in a dark tunnel that we must pass through. Somewhere at the end shines the eternal light.*" He fell sick in Dachau, and at age 61, was sent to the infamous hospital within the camp, known for its experiments on inmates. He was murdered with an injection of acid.

We are going through a dark time as a nation and a world, where this time the enemy is not a twisted mind like Hitler, bent on extermination of anyone unlike himself, but instead, an insensate single cell creature that would spread inexorably, at great cost to humanity, in the "single-minded" pursuit of its own survival. Of course, dark times existed on the personal level for many, even before the pandemic. There are those who are coping with other diseases whose prognosis is far more dismal, those who are coping with divorce and betrayal, those who are dealing with financial ruin, joblessness, and homelessness. All however, have a common thread; fear of the future, and the hopelessness that can well up as the result.

People of faith have an advantage in these circumstances. If you believe that you are simply a phenomenally complex evolution from more fundamental organisms, and they from inanimate elements themselves, then you are hopeless indeed, for you are entirely at the mercy of unseen and random forces that may or may not spare you and your loved ones. Furthermore, your fear is based on the deterioration of your experience in this life, or the loss of it altogether. The Christian may fear from time to time, but the indwelling Holy Spirit will bring about repeated course corrections. We have a Savior who suffered and died, undeservedly, for our benefit. Who then conquered death and lives within us, and we in Him! Belief that you are in fact, not only within the family of the Savior, but that He is within the very fiber of your being, makes the fear of earthly consequences at most, transient! There is indeed an eternal light at the end of the dark tunnel! When you're in the tunnel, you need to look up and keep your eyes fixed on the One who claimed to be the Light of the World, and then you'll be granted enough light to take the next step, and the next, and the next.

There is an expression: "*To know the strength of the anchor, you need to feel the storm!*"

We'll close today with a song by Bob Kauflin, *Anchor Beyond the Veil,* as our prayer. Recall that "the veil" in Old Testament times was the curtain that separated the sanctuary from the inner Tabernacle, the dwelling place of God.

Prayer:
My hope is not in this life, nor this passing world's reward, But my hope is in a life that will never fade; my hope is in you Jesus, Risen King, Ascended Lord, Even death itself could not Hold you in the grave!

And Jesus You've gone before us, And Your faithfulness never fails in the darkness. You reassure us, You're an anchor beyond the veil! And when the storm is raging, And I'm battered by The waves, You're my refuge and my strength. I shall not be moved;

And when the night surrounds me, And I cannot see my way, You will guide me in Your righteousness, And Your truth. And though we cannot see You, We await that glorious hour, When this earthly veil is finally stripped away; And when we hear that trumpet, And You come With awesome power, We shall gaze upon the radiance of Your face. AMEN

APRIL 18

Insecurity

"I will put my law in their minds and write it on their hearts. I will be their God and they will be my people...For I will forgive their wickedness and will remember their sins no more." (Jeremiah 31:33-34 NIV)

I played basketball in high school. Those of you actually *from my high school,* might recall that I wasn't very good. Actually, you wouldn't recall that at all, because I was usually on the bench anyway, and if I did play it was usually only for a few moments. But when I did play, I was usually pretty nervous. After all, this wasn't practice. There were referees and a clock and they were most definitely keeping score! So, even if I was only on the court for a short time, I was fully aware that I could mess up and that in a close game, I might even be the reason we lost!

Fast forward to forty-five years later. I am 64 years old and about to take my first "virtual reality" violin lesson, courtesy of the never-ending pandemic with SARS-coV-2. I am not giving a recital. There is no audience. Even my wife will make herself scarce, as she does when I am practicing. She will go to the other end of our house with the doors closed, probably in an effort to safe-guard her hearing faculties. But despite this, I will become anxious right before the lesson begins, as I always do, even when face to face in my instructor's studio. Why? There is no clock, no score keeper, no referee really. My instructor is the nicest, most patient, softest spoken man ever. The game does not hang in the balance.

The reason I become anxious is that I put all of these non-existent factors into play inadvertently, and mentally, since they don't actually apply. I am a Type A, achievement oriented individual, not unusual in a physician. Every note that I know I will get wrong, every bowing that wanders up to the bridge, every poorly executed vibrato are all failures, right? Even if no one else is keeping track, I am aware of the cumulative weight of my self-apparent ineptitude!

Before the "shelter in place" order for the Dallas area, before the corona-virus was even being called a "pandemic," we attended one of my eight-year grandson's basketball games. It was played with a smaller round ball, and there was a hoop and net involved, but otherwise it bore little resemblance to what I remembered from high school. Those second graders went out there and, well, *had fun!* While there was a clock, referees and even a score board, they were blissfully unaware that any of these elements carried much importance. There were no tears, no swearing, no serious injury, no bruised egos. Even when one team defeated the other by say, 28-2, for example, the losing players were not visibly upset. In fact, I'm not sure most of them were aware who had won and who had lost.

There might just be a reason Jesus wanted the little kids to come to Him after all. (Matthew 18:3; 19:14) It seems that they "play the game" just for the enjoyment of it! They are in fact "free" of the insecurities and embarrassment and shame that will inevitably come from errors when they "grow up." Christ said unless we could be like the little children, we certainly wouldn't be seeing the inside of the Kingdom of Heaven! God has showed us the way into His presence! He has forgotten our sins as though they never existed; as far as the east is from the west! (Psalm 103:11-12) He is not an angry coach, but is instead, slow to anger and will not treat us as our constant mess-ups deserve! (Psalm 103:8-9) My violin teacher doesn't get angry with me, I do! I'm the one who's insecure. If the children aren't too hard on themselves, maybe we shouldn't be either! Once we have accepted Christ and understand that He took our sins on Himself, that He suffered the death penalty that we deserved, and that He then conquered death, well, then as Paul says in Galatians, "we are free indeed!"

We need to live life a little more like the second graders. God isn't keeping a record of our sins and short-comings, nor should we. We should wake up every morning, thank God for His Grace that granted us salvation, and prepare ourselves to make sure that every word and deed of the coming day glorifies our God! Hallelujah! I really do like bouncing that ball, making a pass, and shooting at that hoop, a lot more than I do keeping score!

"If you Lord, kept a record of sins, Lord, who could stand? But with you there is forgiveness, so that we can, with reverence, serve you!" (Psalm 130:3-4 NIV)

Prayer: Dear Heavenly Father, we love You because You first loved us! We thank you that just as we avoid putting pressure on and shaming our second-graders when they make errors, we should avoid shaming ourselves and becoming more and more insecure as adults. Knowing that You have forgiven us, and don't even remember us ever sinning, allows us to come before You feeling clean and refreshed! Let Your

Holy spirit energize us with this knowledge, so that we might alleviate the guilt and shame of others who mistakenly feel they aren't "good enough" for anyone, and especially for You! AMEN

APRIL 19

Pleasing God

"Without faith it is impossible to please God, because anyone who comes to him must believe that He exists and that He rewards those who earnestly seek Him." (Hebrews 11:6 NIV)

This comes as quite a blow to many. It means that no matter your largesse with charities, your consistent tithing, your kindness to co-workers, your sacrificial love for your spouse, your volunteer work, your excellent parenting, your daily bible reading, your Sunday School teaching, your careful avoidance of foul or spurious language, prurience, and violence, and your meticulous adherence to the best of your ability to the Ten Commandments, you have nevertheless, failed to please God in any significant way!

How can that be? I mean, if you try really, really, hard to be a good person, doesn't that count for anything? Of course, being a 'good' person is desirable for lots of reasons, not the least of which is that people will tend to like us back, and on top of that, Jesus commanded us to treat each other as we would like to have them treat us. So, it does 'count' for something, but being good to others doesn't *earn* your righteousness. Following the rules will never do it, and you can't follow all the rules all the time anyway, as Old Testament Israel discovered!

The author of Hebrews is trying to make a point, after which he is going to extol the faith of a score of Biblical heroes from the past. He does so by pointing out that it wasn't their good deeds that brought them salvation, but their faith, which in fact, was demonstrated through those very same deeds. It's not that all those good deeds mentioned in the first paragraph *can't be pleasing to God*, it's just that they *aren't pleasing* unless they come from a *faithful posture of the heart!*

Eric Liddell is a name known not quite as well as *Chariots of Fire*, the movie about his refusal to run the 100 meter dash, for which he was favored, one Sunday in the 1924 Paris Olympic games. Even the musical score which became hugely popular in the early 1980's, is better known than the actual man in whose honor it was written. Even so, had Eric Liddell agreed to run the 100, and even if he had won the Gold Medal, no one other than another Scot would probably recognize his name at all today. He did win the gold medal for the 400 meters, however, if not for the movie about him, even fewer would know that trivia today. Much of the material below is distilled from the book, *Seven Men,* by Eric Metaxes.

Eric was a man of strong faith, even at age 22, having been born in China to Scottish Christian missionaries. At age 5, the family returned to Scotland on furlough, and although his parents would return to China, Eric, his older brother, and baby sister were not to return. Their mother remained with them in Scotland for one year to get them settled, and then rejoined her husband in China. The boys were enrolled in Eltham, a school for Christian missionaries just outside London, where they would remain through secondary school, their parents abroad the entire time. Eric was a quiet, thoughtful boy, but exuberant on the playing field. He was an outstanding rugby, football and cricket player and placed first or second in the 100 meters, long jump and high jump, reliably. At age 16, he won the school championship for 100 meters, the quarter mile and the high jump, and placed second in every other track event! Graduating with the Blackheath Cup for the best all-round sportsman, Eric went on to excel in track and field at University of Edinburgh, despite a heavy course load centering on chemistry and physics.

Eric most certainly had phenomenal God-given talent. His unorthodox running style, wind-milling his arms and throwing his head back as he approached the finish line became his athletic trademarks. He was also known as a complete gentleman, always shaking hands with each competitor before a race and congratulating them afterwards. Known as Scotland's pre-eminent sprinter, he was also known to be a Christian, though a shy one! During his junior year, the Glasgow Students' Evangelistic Union ask him to speak to a group of 80 coal miners. He agreed reluctantly, since he abhorred public speaking. The next day, Eric Liddell's little sister Jenny happened to send him this verse: *"Fear thou not, for I am with thee; be not dismayed; for I am thy God; I will strengthen thee; yea, I will help thee; yea, I will uphold thee with the right hand of my righteousness." (Isaiah 41:10 KJV)* He told those coal miners in his quiet Scottish brogue, that all of his strength and ability came from the assurance he had of God's unfailing love. Word spread quickly that the fastest man in Scotland was speaking publicly about his faith. Soon he had engagements after class all around Edinburgh.

Near the end of his life, Liddell recalled wondering how running fast as a talent could possibly enable him to glorify God? He thought that perhaps it was that in his popularity, he had a bully pulpit. But in that last year of college, he joined the Oxford Group, young Christians who advocated a quiet time daily, and living by the Four Absolutes: absolute honesty, purity, selflessness, and love. He says he lived by these principles the rest of his life. Running, and usually winning, ended up, despite its competitive nature, being exactly the formula for Eric to glorify God! His fame made him a much in demand speaker for Christ! When he won the remarkable 440 in 1923 where he was knocked down right out of the blocks and came back from 20 yards behind, he gave the glory to God, exclaiming that in the first half he ran as fast as he could and in the second half he ran faster with God's help!

A year later, when Eric refused to run the 100 meters on a Sunday, he told the British Olympic Committee that the Sabbath was to be kept holy and that meant 'set apart to God.' Sunday was a day for rest and worship and he absolutely refused to run. The British Olympic Committee was furious. They tried everything to convince him and then they appealed to the IOC to move the 100 meter heats, but they were denied. They thought he would give in, but he felt he knew God's feelings on the subject. Even if he faced a lifetime of ignominy, he was not changing his mind. God would sort out the consequences, but he would be obedient. Unlike in the movie, Liddell knew 8 months ahead that the

100 meter was to be on Sunday, so he started training for the 400 meter instead.

On the day of the Olympic 400 meter final, Liddell was assigned the worst position, the outermost lane. In addition, he'd had little rest since winning the Bronze in the 200 meter the day before. Even worse, the American named Fitch, had set a new world record in the 400 semifinal earlier that same day. But as he entered the Olympic stadium, a British team trainer handed him a note. *"It says in the Old Book "Him that honors me, I will honor." (1 Samuel 2:30)* Liddell not only went on to win, despite setting a pace everyone thought way to fast at the outset, a typical sprinter error; but he went on to win by an unheard of 5 meters, setting a new World Record of 47.6 seconds. Shortly after graduating from University of Edinburgh, later that year, he stunned the world again by announcing that he was finished with running, and would study theology in order to teach in China as a Christian missionary. The Olympics taught Eric that God would use both his refusal to run on Sunday and his later victory in the 400 meters, to bring people to him, whom he could then lead to the Lord. He gave up certain gold in the 100 meter, and the personal glory that would undoubtedly have brought, for the opportunity to glorify God, by keeping the Sabbath.

Liddell was reunited with his family in China, taught multiple subjects and led Bible studies, fell in love with another young Scot named Florence, proposed, but agreed to let her first get her nursing degree in Canada, which meant three years before they could wed. Eric returned to Scotland after a stop-over to see Florence in Canada, in 1931. He entered seminary and became an ordained minister in 1932, visiting Florence once more in Canada, on his way back to China. They finally married in 1934 when she returned to China as well. They had two daughters there, but not long after the Japanese invasion of China, they left for Toronto on furlough. In the summer of 1939, the Nazis invaded Poland and the European war began. Eric returned to Scotland alone, fearing for his family due to German U-boats. But the girls followed, and they had four months together before returning to China despite the Japanese occupation. Separated by his assignment as a pastor to a rural village there, Liddell did what he could among villages where the Japanese had killed all the men, raped all the women, and set all the buildings afire. They decided the girls should return to Canada, and Liddell accompanied his family to Japan where they boarded a ship for Canada, his wife pregnant with their third child. He never saw them again.

Returning to Tientsin at the same time as the Japanese bombed Pearl Harbor, Liddell and all the other foreign missionaries were instantly confined, and then shipped to an internment camp 300 miles away. He wrote a daily devotional called, *Discipleship*, which is still in print. Conditions were beyond deplorable, but Eric taught in the camp school, organized sporting events, and planned worship services throughout the freezing winter of 1943. He was able to send a 25 word "Red Cross Letter" to his family once a month. He was known as Uncle Eric to the internees, and spent his time settling disputes, and befriending everyone, once giving his famous Olympic running shoes to a man who survived and told the story. He began suffering terrible headaches in the winter of 1945, then suffered a minor stroke in February. After a month's rest, he felt he had recovered. As he was finishing a letter to his family, a teenage kitchen worker he had befriended, dropped in to visit. They discussed surrendering one's will to God in all things including our attitudes, she recalled. In the midst of the word 'surrender' he slumped into a coma and died later that night at age 43. An autopsy revealed an inoperable brain tumor.

When daughter Patricia was middle-aged, she recalled wondering why God would have separated her dad from his family during the last years of his young life. She realized from his letters that he had instead become a father to all the children in the internment camp who had lost their own parents. The girl who was with him when he died commented, "He made Christ's life so relevant- and made it feel like we who followed Christ must do what He asked, no matter your situation." His friend in the camp, A.P. Cullen, said this at his memorial, "He was literally God-controlled, in His thoughts, judgments, actions, and words, to an extent I have never seen surpassed and rarely equaled."

It wasn't Eric Liddell's actions that *earned* him God's love. It was faith in God's unfailing love that drove his every action! What is the necessary component to pleasing God, to Glorifying God? Faith.

Dear Heavenly Father, it is Your love for us that leads us to glorify Your name in all that we say and do! Lead us not into the temptation of believing that our actions alone glorify you, for the world is full of non-believers who do good things for others. Remind us Lord that it is the demonstration of faith to others through our actions and inactions that give Glory to You! AMEN

APRIL 20

Wrong Way

"But Jonah ran away from the Lord and headed for Tarshish. He went down to Joppa, where he found a ship bound for that port." (Jonah 1:3 NIV)

Have you ever had the experience of earnestly seeking the Lord's guidance, believing you have an answer, and then deciding that maybe your own course of action was really the way to go? Sounds kind of silly when you say it like that, but I believe it happens a lot more than we would like. You are faced with a choice, staying with your company and keeping your family close by, or moving to the coast and getting a big raise with a new firm; you finally think it's time to ask this girl to marry you, she's wonderful, but there are just a couple things about her that really bug you; you can stay in the military and all the job security it offers, knowing your path to advancement, or you can leave after your time is up and head back to school, with a promising but uncertain future; or maybe you know there is really something wrong with your boss, the way they are acting, the bad decisions they've made recently, and you can either confront them, or go over their heads.

The choices we are faced with every day, in every walk of life, are ones that we want to make the right decision on! Some of us go to God in prayer as well as sometimes discuss the choices with people we love and trust. Some of us make the call on our own. But as we've addressed before, knowing the will of

God isn't always as easy as it was for Jonah. Jonah knew perfectly well that the Lord wanted him to go and preach to the Ninevites and seek their repentance. Only problem was, Jonah despised the Ninevites and didn't think they deserved an opportunity to be forgiven. So, he decided to *specifically* go exactly in the wrong direction, as far and as fast as he could. Why he thought God wouldn't notice is beyond me. In any event, through a series of events orchestrated by his God, Jonah was brought grudgingly back onto the correct path.

While there is certainly a difference between purposefully opposing God's will for us and simply mistaking what we believe to be His will, both *can happen* to the Believer. **Remember, that we can't determine in retrospect, if a choice was compatible with the will of God, simply by the outcome.** The move to the coast might be disastrous. You might leave a good job and local family only to find that the start-up you signed on to fails, shortly after you've moved your entire life! Or the opposite might happen, and it be a fabulous success! You might decide not to ask her to marry you, and then watch horrified as she moves on and finds someone who is more sure about her than you. You might also decide not to marry her and find you are more relieved than you could possibly have imagined.

You simply cannot tell if your moves are consistent with the will of God or not, ***unless through them you are always seeking to Glorify God!*** It sounds like a broken record I know, but God sees into your heart! He judges by your motives not your actions. For instance, you might make a wrong decision, suffer an apparently bad outcome, but stay steadfastly in a posture of gratitude anyway. In that case, "*If God be for you, who can stand against you?*" Just because you had what you perceive to be a bad outcome, doesn't preclude that being part of God's will for you in the long run. That might well be the will of God for you, and through it over time, you will learn what God had in store for you, and it will reaffirm that God works all things together for good, for those who love Him! (Romans 8:28) On the other hand, if you purposefully make a decision while the orientation of your heart is *rebellion* against God, then you might find yourself like Jonah, in the midst of a storm-tossed sea on a sinking ship! Yes, making a decision prayerfully, making a decision with reference to the Word, making a decision with guidance from loved ones and other Believers are *all good ways* to seek the will of the Father! But nothing is sure except this: **His love is unfailing! It is in fact, a sure thing!** No matter what the outcome you encounter on the basis of your decisions in life, demonstrating through it all, the peace, the calm, the joy, the assurance of your salvation and your security in knowing that God is Sovereign, is the way to Glorify God! Others will notice. Understanding the chief end of man, and acting accordingly, will get you out of a lot of hot water!

"'For I know the plans I have for you,' declares the Lord, 'plans to prosper you and not to harm you, plans to give you hope and a future.'" (Jeremiah 29:11 NIV)

"Give thanks in all circumstances; for this is God's will for you in Jesus Christ." (I Thessalonians 5:18 NIV)

"Trust in the Lord with all your heart and lean not to your own understanding; in all your ways acknowledge Him, and He shall direct your paths." (Proverbs 3:5-6 NKJV)

Dear Heavenly Father, May Your Spirit within us lead us to all truth, but Lord, no matter how well we do with that, let us acknowledge Your Sovereignty and Your love for us in everything we do and every choice we make, no matter the outcome. We know that You work all thing together for good, for those who believe! AMEN

APRIL 21
Day and Night

"And God said, 'Let there be light,' and there was light. God saw that the light was good, and he separated the light from the darkness. God called the light, 'day,' and the darkness he called 'night.' And there was evening, and there was morning-the first day." (Genesis 1:3-5 NIV)

Throughout man's history, light has been associated with 'good' and dark with 'bad.' Yet, it is clear that God created them both, although He made them such that one would be separated from the other. Daytime allows us to see by the light of the sun. That means we can avoid missteps, avoid all those things like predators that might hurt or kill us. The 'dawn,' when the light takes over from the dark, has been, throughout the record of human thought, whether in writing, song, or personal experience, the time when one's heart lifts and hope floods in. Jesus Christ said, *"I am the Light of the World. He who follows me shall not walk in darkness, but have the light of life."* (John 8:12 NIV) One of my favorite hymns opens with these words, *"When morning gilds the skies, my heart awaking cries, let Jesus Christ be praised!"* (Anonymous)

Darkness, on the other hand, has always been associated with 'bad.' In the dark we can easily fall and hurt ourselves, and we become easy prey for predators, whether animal or man. Darkness has been associated with evil, from Biblical times to today. In Isaiah, *"Woe to those who deeply hide their plans from the Lord, and those whose deeds are done in darkness." (Isaiah 29:15)* The Apostle John tells us that, *"This is the judgment, that the Light has come into the world, and men loved the darkness rather than the Light, for their deeds were evil." (John 3:19 NIV)* Specifically, scripture tells us that the hypocrites are lost in the dark. *"If we say we have fellowship with Him and yet walk in darkness, we lie and do not practice the truth." (I John 6:6 NKJV)* So, no question, darkness gets a bad rap!

Then why did God create the light and the dark? Is it like beauty and ugliness? If there were not one, the other could not exist? Or is there more to it than that? When things are going well, when we are bathed in the warm light of success, health and happiness, we might praise the Lord for His Blessings, or we might not! There is a tendency to forget that *"all good gifts come from above," (James 1:17NIV)* when in fact, we are being showered with those very gifts at the moment. Likewise, the night. In the dark, it is true, there is fear, there is danger, a time where evil can abound more freely than in the light of day. We have a tendency to beg God for His assistance and protection in the midnight of our challenges, but we don't often praise Him! The darkness of night also gives us the brilliance of the stars and the indescribable beauty of the moon as it crosses the heavens!

There will be day and night perpetually, until our Lord returns and *"There will be no more night. They will not need the light of the sun, for the Lord God will give them light." (Revelation 22:5 NIV)* While we wait and watch for that glorious Day, we can praise the Lord even in the darkness of adversity. Who has not seen both a gorgeous sunrise and a gorgeous sunset? Both the coming of the light and the coming of the dark, are times to praise Him, because *all times* are times to praise Him! If we, as Believers, will learn to be content in all circumstances, as Paul tells us in Philippians, then we can praise the Lord even in the darkness of a pandemic. Charles Spurgeon says we must believe that the night is as useful as the day. He says, *"The dews of Grace fall heavily in the night of sorrow. The stars of promise shine forth gloriously amid the darkness of grief." (Morning by Morning)*

Here in the United States, as we enter the third month of this worldwide scourge due to the Coronavirus, each and every day you see more and more people coming to the realization that there are plenty of reasons to praise Him, even in the dark! We are learning by keeping our distance, how desperately we long to be close and touch, and what a Blessing that is! We are learning to be innovative technologically, in our gatherings from a distance. Many are learning the advantages of working from home, with family at hand. Others are learning that family at hand constantly can be challenging indeed, but all are learning ways to adapt. We are learning to treasure the natural beauty of the outdoors and how critical it is going to forward, to protect our planet. We are learning that the world can act together in concert for the benefit of others, despite our political boundaries. We are learning to value once again our own heroes, who risk their lives to benefit others.

The list of Blessings that can come out of this present darkness is as long as the list of Blessings that we have often ignored, when the light of ease and success and health is shining upon us! The obvious conclusion then, is that we should be thanking God for all our Blessings, whether we are doing it on a bike ride in the sun, or lying on the grass in the darkness, gazing up at a spring moon.

Maybe God made the day and the night for a reason, after-all!

"I will extol thee at all times; His praise will ***always*** *be on my lips. My soul will boast in the Lord; let the afflicted hear and rejoice!" (Psalm 34:1-2 NIV)*

Prayer: Dear Heavenly Father, we love You Lord and we thank you for the light of Day and even the dark of Night! Direct Your Spirit to lead us to contentment even in the darkness of a pandemic as we count the Blessings that were formerly hidden! AMEN

APRIL 22

Shut Ins

"And they went into the Ark to Noah, two by two of all flesh in which is the breath of life. So those that entered, male and female of all flesh, went in as God had commanded him; and the Lord shut him in. Now the flood was on the earth 40 days." (Genesis 15-17 NKJV)

When I was in high school some forty years ago, my father used to volunteer for Meals on Wheels in Tulsa, Oklahoma. On one occasion, I got to accompany him as we delivered meals to "shut-ins." (I don't remember exactly, but I bet as a 16 year-old in the '70's, 'got to' is probably an inaccurate phrase. 'Strongly encouraged to,' was probably closer to the truth.) In general, these were older people who could no longer make the trip to the grocery, even accompanied by someone else. But sometimes they were chronically disabled, mentally or physically, wheelchair or bed-bound, or sometimes just too poor to afford to feed themselves. In any event, their situation was not considered enviable. Just the term "shut in" implied darkness, and perhaps even confinement against one's will. Meals on Wheels provided a much-needed service, no doubt. I remember two things from that afternoon: the smell of old people's homes, and the broad smiles, many of them essentially toothless, when they realized who we were upon opening the door or peering out the window to a rickety porch.

In April of 2020, we have become a world of 'shut-ins.' The pandemic certainly feels dark, and we are definitely confined against our will, across the entire planet. The members of the younger generation, especially in the west, who have never truly known privation, who have never experienced a world war, or polio, or smallpox, voice their discontent from time to time at being 'cooped up' inside. I've heard complaints of how "unfair" it is! Many of these young people are "shut in" to their comfortable home with central AC and heat, running water, refrigeration, WiFi access and big screen TVs. It's not exactly a prison sentence, as those who have ever seen the inside of a real prison could tell you. Yes, it's an uncomfortable adjustment. But it's transient, and it really isn't the end of the world.

Noah was confined to the Ark with only his family and the animals. The rains fell for 40 days, flooding the earth and killing every living thing. But he and his family's movements were limited to the odiferous confines of a constantly rolling, pitching, dank and dark habitation for between 364 and 377 days, depending on how you calculate the length of a year. But remember, there was a reason they were confined. God "shut them in," in order to preserve them! They were confined for their own safety, God being well aware of what would happen in a world-wide flood were they not on the Ark. In their isolation and detention however, they were not alone, for God was with them! When they exited the Ark, Noah immediately built an altar, and sacrificed to God. God made a covenant with Noah that He would never again destroy the earth by flood. He blessed Noah and his sons, and reiterated their descendant's dominion over every living thing.

God is indeed Sovereign. When we find ourselves in a circumstance like the one brought about by this pandemic, remember that God uses evil for good. He has a long history of this throughout the Bible. As we hopefully approach the end of this particular episode in man's history, there can be no question that isolation and confinement have not only saved the majority of the world's population, they have awakened them to blessings they may have forgotten or ignored! We may have viewed "social distancing" and restriction to our own homes as terribly onerous at first. But gradually we have been reawakened to the joys of family, of taking a breath and slowing down, of enjoying what nature has to offer us right in our own backyards, of the camaraderie that comes from making a united effort as a community, a nation, and a world.

God is making good from evil, and in the process, He is re-focusing mankind on the fragility of its society and infra-structure. It would be a blind man indeed, who failed to see both our strength in moving together as humankind, and our phenomenal weakness on a universal scale. Both should point us toward a loving God. The wars, the political hatred and vitriol, the petty arguments among nation states, have virtually ground to a halt, even if only for a moment. People of different nations, cultures, ethnicity, races, religions are reaching out across the oceans to share their expertise, their experiences and their supplies. Perhaps the world has matured enough to recognize the Blessing they have been given in the guise of a pandemic. Maybe more leaders will concentrate on keeping the main thing the main thing! After all, that's all Jesus asked us to do, love Him and love each other.

Dear Heavenly Father, How clearly You love us! How clearly we need to see our dependence on You for every aspect of our lives, which in and of themselves, are gifts of inestimable value. Help us to understand what You would have us do when faced with a glimpse of the apocalypse: love each other and in so doing demonstrate our love for our Creator. Thank You Lord, even for a pandemic, where we grieve the loss of so many, but we rejoice in the knowledge that You are our Rock and our Fortress, a very present help in trouble! Holy Spirit lead us to all truth. Lead us to the realization that what we see just a glimpse of, for a moment, in the middle of this catastrophic event, people loving and enjoying each other and the planet, is what You intended for us all along! AMEN

APRIL 23

Inheritance

"Blessed be the God and Father of our Lord Jesus Christ, who according to His great mercy has caused us to be born again to a living hope through the resurrection of Jesus Christ from the dead, to obtain an inheritance which is imperishable and undefiled and will not fade away, reserved in heaven for you." (1 Peter 1:3-4 NASB)

My paternal grandmother, Polly, started coming to Maine with her family in the very earliest part of the 20th century, even before WW I. Her father, my great grandfather, Herbert Moore, was a pediatrician in Boston, and had property on the Benjamin River, in Sedgewick, Maine. The river flowed into the north side of Eggemoggin Reach. Polly would spend summers as a child at the farm, sailing on the Reach between the mainland and Deer Isle, and just as her descendants would, fell in love with coastal Maine. She married my grandfather in 1922, and eventually introduced him to the area, which he of course, fell in love with as well. Shortly after WW II, they purchased a small cottage and the plot of land next door, some five to six miles up the Reach from the old Moore farm. When my father retired in 1986, my parents then built another small house on that plot, adjacent to the old cottage.

I have spent some part of 59/64 summers sailing those same waters and eating "lobster on the rocks" which we boil in seawater, right in front of the house. My children and my brother's children did the same, and now our grandchildren have started coming. Visitors love the beauty and serenity of rural Maine as well, but it's just not *in their blood,* as it is in our family's. Coastal Maine feels like home to those who grew up there in the summers, and home is where the heart is! It's rustic beauty and the timeless nature of the waves crashing on the rocky shores, never seems to change. The brutal winters in Maine, combined with insects in the spring, and the difficulty of access, have kept development to a minimum, compared to our nation's southern shores. Its unspoiled nature combined with spectacular summers, are what render it truly priceless to those who really know it.

My father passed away in 2014 and my mother is 91 at this writing. My father's little brother, who owns half the property, is 90. When the Lord takes them home, the property will be inherited by my brother and myself, although to hear our children's plans for the place, you would think skipping a generation was an integral part of those plans! But the point is, of all that might be involved in an inheritance, the thing that is nearest and dearest to our hearts, is the thing that has remained virtually unchanged for a thousand years. Soon this sanctuary will pass to the sixth generation in our family. Incredible. That's the thing about an inheritance. It's family. It's secure. It's loved. It's something that you can count on in a world of uncertainty.

We are promised just such an inheritance, but on a far grander and more significant scale! Jesus is God incarnate, who walked on this earth, experienced what it meant to be fully human, but without sin, and then died on a cross in our place. Jesus' sacrificial death atoned for our sins, and we were redeemed, no longer separated from our Creator! We have put on His righteousness so that we can come directly into the presence of God. Scripture tells us that once we have accepted this Gift, offered in God's grace to sinners who did nothing to deserve it, we live in Christ and He in us! United with the Only Son of God, we are adopted into the Royal Family indeed! That means that the eternal life that is His, becomes ours! In the ancient middle east, adopted children shared equally in the inheritance of their siblings. We inherit His perfect righteousness and eternity! That glorious promise is as true today as it was 2,000 years ago. Its beauty is indescribable and unspoiled. That inheritance can occupy a place in your heart even more treasured than coastal Maine is for us *summer people!*

The inheritance of eternity is indeed a spectacular outcome of faith, but it's the *assurance* of its reality that comforts the Believer day to day. Just as I know that beautiful spot in Maine is promised to me and my descendants, we Christians know the glorious reality of living forever in the presence of the Creator, is promised to us. You may not have a piece of property to inherit, or anything at all of a worldly nature to inherit, but when you accept Christ as your Lord and Savior, you instantly become the rightful heir of something of much greater value! Hallelujah!!

"In my Father's house are many mansions, if it were not so, I would have told you. I go to prepare a place for you. And if I go and prepare a place for you, I will come again and receive you to Myself; that where I am, there you may be also." (John 14:2-3 NKJV)

"For you did not receive the spirit of bondage again to fear, but you received the Spirit of adoption by whom we cry out, 'Abba, Father!'" (Romans 8:15 NKJV)

"I pray that the eyes of your heart may be enlightened in order that you may know the hope to which he has called you, the riches of his glorious inheritance in His holy people." (Ephesians 1:18 NIV)

> *Prayer: Dear Abba, we love that You are our Father just as Christ is Your Son! Holy Spirit remind us daily, when we are down-hearted, that we have a glorious inheritance awaiting us that is beyond our imagining, but as sure as Your love is for us! AMEN*

APRIL 24

Cheap Grace

"But because of His great love for us, God, who is rich in mercy, made us alive with Christ even when we were dead in transgressions—it is by Grace you have been saved...For it is by Grace you have been saved, through faith—and this is not from yourselves, it is the gift of God—not by works, so that no one can boast." (Ephesians 2:4-5; 8-9 NIV)

Once, during my years at Dallas Theological Seminary, I was sitting on an airplane returning from a medical conference in San Francisco. This was back in the day when it felt slightly less like a cattle car, and there was actually an open seat between me, on the aisle, and a gentleman slightly older than myself seated by the window. At some point during the flight, we introduced ourselves and began to chat, as one does on a long flight. It turns out that he was a software salesman returning from his own conference in San Francisco. He noticed the book I had been reading, *Orthodoxy*, the famous Christian manifesto by G.K. Chesterton, and inquired if I was a Catholic, as he was. He had never read the book, but assumed by its title that it was referring to Catholicism. While G.K. Chesterton was an Anglican theologian, philosopher, humorist and journalist in early 20th century England, who did eventually convert to Catholicism, the book is by no means about the split in the Christian church, but instead about the central tenants of the early church that have been obscured across all denominational lines.

When my seat mate learned that I was both a physician and attending an 'evangelical' seminary, he confessed that he just didn't understand how Protestants could have the whole thing so backwards! How could we believe that just because we were under Grace, that we were no longer obligated to pay any attention to the law at all? If our sins were forgiven once and for all, weren't Protestants free to just keep on sinning? Why didn't they understand that they had to take communion regularly to be forgiven continually? I did mention that Paul had addressed this directly in Romans:

"What shall we say then? Shall we go on sinning so that grace may increase? By no means! We are those who have died to sin; how can we live in it any longer?" And a few verses later, *"For we know that our old self was crucified with Him so that the body ruled by sin might be done away with, that we should no longer be slaves to sin---because anyone who has died has been set free from sin."(Romans 6:1-2, 6-7 NIV)*

The Christian, who by definition has been saved by Grace through faith, far from ignoring the law, now lives *in the One who perfected the law!* Yes, we are now clothed in the righteousness of Christ and thus presentable to God, but because we have *died to our old selves, we no longer want to sin!* In other words, we are no longer slaves to sin. Christ said, *'It is finished'* from the cross, because His perfect sacrifice was all that was needed to reconcile man to God, to forgive our sins, past, present, and future. But, said my new friend, where is it then mandated that you change your sinful ways? I think at this juncture, I pointed out that a heart of repentance was part of accepting Christ to begin with, but that really didn't sell him. Not surprisingly, we didn't solve 400 years of differences between Catholics and Protestants on a portion of a 4-hour flight, but we did part as friends!

Dietrich Bonhoeffer, the famous German Christian theologian and anti-Nazi, who lost his life by hanging in Flossenburg Concentration Camp only weeks before the Allies liberated it, coined the term ***Cheap Grace,*** that was perhaps at the heart of that airborne discussion, years ago. Non-believers, Muslims, Jews and Catholics alike, frequently view Protestant Christians as those who claim to have accepted Christ as their Savior, further claim that they are without condemnation as in Romans 1, and *then continue to act as though they are thus free to sin*! It is not hard to see where the confusion lies, if in fact, a large number of those claiming Christianity are in effect, hypocrites, not unlike the Pharisees and Scribes that so drew the wrath of our Lord! These are those who cheapen the concept of Grace, in Bonhoeffer's view. *Cheap Grace is "preaching forgiveness without repentance, baptism without church discipline, communion without confession, absolution without personal confession, grace without discipleship, grace without the cross and in effect, grace without Jesus."* In short, cheap grace is **"characterized by belief without obedience, hearing without doing, and intellectual assent without commitment."**

Cheap Grace, rather than a gift from God, is the grace we give ourselves. Claiming grace alone for salvation has become a justification for disobeying the commands of Jesus. Grace for the great streams of scornful and unbelieving demonstrated the Christians' care for humanity, but any mention of 'the narrow way' was lost.

True Grace, while a gift from God, is nevertheless costly! It is costly because we are called **to follow Jesus.** It is costly because it costs our very lives! It is costly because it condemns sin. But it is Grace because we are called to follow the personification of perfect love, the only source of a true complete life of peace and joy. It is Grace because while it condemns sin, it justifies the sinner, and that reconciles us to God!

A misunderstanding of Grace is often accompanied by a misunderstanding of the cry of the Reformation, *"Not by works, but Grace through faith alone!"* When James claimed that *faith without works is dead,"* he didn't mean that works were necessary to earn your salvation, he meant that if you have the faith that renders God's grace, you will demonstrate it by the way that you live! ***There is the narrow way! (Luke 13:24)***

Okay. Seems like I've gone and gotten all theological on you! Well, it's a big topic for one devotional! But it comes down to what we've said all along. Christ sent us a Helper in the Holy Spirit. Why would we need a Helper at all, if Grace meant we were free and clear to behave in any way we felt, sinful or not? Dying to sin in accepting Christ means we have died to our old selves and no longer ***have to sin.*** It doesn't mean we won't sin. And it doesn't mean it's just okay to go on sinning! Christ said that people will know us as His followers by our love! (John 13:35) He said, if we love Him, we will follow His commandments. (John 14:15) That doesn't mean we earn our salvation by following the rules as the Chosen People of the Old Testament attempted and failed, it means that ***our love lived out will exclude a life of sin!***

Prayer: Every morning, let my first thought be, Lord, direct Your Spirit to show me how I might love You, by loving others at every opportunity. That means that I long to be obedient! I want to act in a way and do the things that let me be that salt and light that You want me to be! Don't let me fool myself about a Grace that cost the death of Your Son to offer me, and cost the death of my old life to claim! Romans 1 assures us that there is no condemnation for those in Christ Jesus, not for those who just claim to know You but live in a way that demonstrates they have cheapened Your Grace by turning it into an excuse for their own sin. AMEN

APRIL 25

Providence

"We know that all things work together for good to them that love God." (Romans 8:28 NKJV)

Not long ago I visited with a long-term patient. We'll call her Marie. She was simply in for an annual, but she was awfully bubbly for some reason!

The joy of just living seemed to be all over her face, and it was a welcome and somewhat unexpected thing to see. Only six years ago, Marie was in the depths of despair, being treated for depression, and on the verge of suicide. Her son and husband had been killed in a horrific car wreck on Christmas Eve in an ice storm. Their daughter had died of leukemia at age 8 several years before that. I had delivered both of those children. Almost incredibly, she had lost a brother and both her parents in the year that followed the car wreck. She is a Christian, but the consolation and counsel of those at her church seemed unable to pull her from the incredible depths to which she had sunk.

This time, I could barely tell her 'hello' before she was showing me pictures of a man with two school age kids, maybe 12 and 9, boy and a girl. The man was, well, just an average guy, glasses, medium height, maybe a little overweight, but with a big smile and his arm around his kids. "Who're these folks, then?" I asked her. "This is my fiancé Rick and his kids Caleb and Michelle! Aren't they just darling?" She had a finger on her iphone, and started swiping right with picture after picture of the same three, but now often with her in the shot as well. They were all taken outside, trees and rolling green hills in the background."When's the big day?" I asked. She beamed up at me from the exam table. "Twenty-three days, but who's counting?"

Turns out, Rick wasn't her old high school flame. He didn't meet her in a support group or at church or even in a bar. One rainy night eight months ago, she had a flat tire on a farm road east of Dallas. She was coming home from a weekend stay with a friend from work, who like others in her life, was struggling to return her to the light. A man in a pick-up truck, with two kids in the front seat, stopped, got out in the rain, and offered to change her tire in the downpour. When she asked him why he stopped, he simply answered, "Who wouldn't stop? You looked like you needed help." You know the rest of the story without hearing it. His wife had died of breast cancer four years ago. The rest is history, or maybe Providence?

Providence is defined by the Oxford English dictionary as *"Foresight, anticipation and preparation for the future; prudent management. Also, the foreknowing and protective care and government of a spiritual power; special providence being direct Divine intervention."* I like to think it is a concept directly tied to Sovereignty. The Christian believes that God Almighty has his hand always on the tiller. The winds of fortune may blow a gale from time to time, but if the Sovereign guides our ship, we need not perpetually despair. With God firmly in control, we can rest assured that despite our current circumstances, even if they involve a tragedy, that God will work all things together for good. The rub of course, is that He will do that in His own timing. (Psalm 27:14) We know that God is wise; in fact, the source of all truth. We know that God is loving, and in fact, equated with love, by His son. (1 John 3:1; 4:7,16) We know that God brings good out of evil as He did with Joseph in Egypt.(Genesis 50:20)

That means that no matter what happens; if like Job, you should lose literally everything, your job, your wealth, your family, your home, and your health; it is better that you lose all, if God wills it, because an omnipotent, wise and loving God will have His reasons! ***We must trust to His judgment, even if we don't understand***. It is always good to bear in mind what the Lord says in Isaiah 55:8, *"For My thoughts are not your thoughts, Nor are your ways My ways, For* *the heavens are higher than the earth, So are My ways higher than your ways, and My thoughts than your thoughts."* It is of course extremely hard to see that in the midst of disaster. But like Horatio Spafford, the author of *It is Well with My Soul*, one can recover even from the loss of one's children at sea, still trusting in the Lord.

Marie may not have received the happy ending that she has. If she had not, the Lord had a reason for that as well, and a plan to utilize that circumstance. But as it is now, I was just happy for Marie, and thankful to our God!

"Say not my soul, From whence can God relieve my care? Remember that Omnipotence has servants everywhere. His method is sublime, His heart profoundly kind, God never is before His time, and never is behind ." (Charles Spurgeon)

Prayer: Dear Heavenly Father, We know that You sent the Spirit to us for just this reason, to help us in our hour of need! Lord when things look the very darkest and our hearts are downcast, direct Your Spirit to whisper in our ear that Abba's love will never fail, that we are never alone, and that in God's providence, and in His timing, good will come from evil. AMEN

APRIL 26

Cardinal Virtues

"Shall I come before Him with burnt offerings, with calves a year old? Will the Lord be pleased with thousands of rams, with ten thousand rivers of oil? Shall I offer my first born for my transgression, the fruit of my body for the sin of my soul? He has showed you O man, what is good. And what does the Lord require of you? To act justly and to love mercy and to walk humbly with you God." (Micah 6: 6-8 NIV)

This is my life-verse; my favorite verse in all of scripture. We spend a lot of time, sometimes a lifetime, wondering why we are here and what God intends for us to do. C.S. Lewis in his seminal work, *Mere Christianity,* which you will recall is actually a compilation of radio addresses to the British public during WW II, addresses what God intends for us, exploring the concepts of right and wrong, what it is that Christians believe, and the behavior that stems from those beliefs. This behavior is an outcome of our Christian morality, which is made up of three components: the way we are internally, the way we relate to each other, and the way we relate to God.

Lewis leads off this discussion with the story of a small boy, who when asked what he thought God was like, answered that He's *"the sort of person who is always snooping around to see if anyone is enjoying himself and then trying to stop it!"* He contends that many people view morality as a set of rules designed to do just that, keep us from having fun! In reality, moral rules are there to prevent a breakdown in the human machine. Moral precepts are actually *freeing* for the Christian, for only when one lives by them, is one free to live abundantly, as God intended.

As you've picked up on this year, I come from a sailing family. Thus, any sailing analogy hits home with me! Lewis suggested that we think of humanity as a fleet of sailing ships in formation! (*No wonder* he's my favorite Christian philosopher!) The success of our mission on earth, depends not only on the seaworthiness of each individual vessel, but on the certainty that they will not each go off course and thus, collide with each other. Repeated collisions would lead to hull damage, and that, to the lack of seaworthiness! Ships would sink. So, the success of mankind depends not only on the seaworthiness of each of us, but our tiller and rudder and helmsman! Lastly, the entire fleet's ultimate destination is critical to the overall success of the mission. That mission is the purpose of humanity!

So, morality involves fair play and harmony, a sound internal structure to each of us, and the general purpose of humanity as a whole. But, men and women *generally* think only about the first one of these, that is, fairness between individuals, teams, or nations. But fairness, even if dictated by written laws, will be meaningless if the individual ships are riddled with self-conceit, cowardice, greed and meanness! *"You cannot make men good by law; and without good men, you cannot have a good society."* These first two aspects of morality are then clear. But what of the third, the ultimate purpose of mankind? C.S. Lewis contends that different religions assert different ideas as factually true. Christians believe that our bodies are not our own, and that our lives are eternal! You can be an atheist and believe in fairness, feeling that as long as your actions don't hurt anyone else, then you are in the right. But that man thinks what he does with his own ship, is only his business. The Christian, on the other hand, is to view himself as a living sacrifice and his body as a temple! (Romans 12:1) He is created in the image of God, by God, and in point of fact, belongs to Him!

Moral behavior classically was described by the Greeks as falling into four categories: prudence (common sense), temperance (moderation), justice (fairness), and fortitude (courage). These are the *cardinal (Latin for pivotal or hinge) virtues.* Paul's teaching added faith, hope and love. (1 Cor 13; Gal 5:22; Phil 4:8; Col 3:12) But *acting* in a virtuous manner and *being* virtuous must not be confused as the same thing in any way. *Right behavior, done for wrong reasons, won't help build character and clearly isn't what God desires.* (Matthew 6:1-18) God doesn't want us to simply follow a particular set of rules. He wants us to be a particular type of person! Consider the tax collector and the Pharisee, both coming to pray in the synagogue. Jesus shows us that between the self-righteous rule follower and the humble repentant sinner, it is the latter who is justified before God. (Luke 18:10-14) It may sound like a broken record, but *God sees into your heart. Yes, God wants us to use our minds, for we are to love Him with all our heart, souls and minds. He gave us an intellect for a reason. But he wants us to have the heart of a child.* (Mark 10:14-16)

What does the Lord require of us? Act justly. That means be fair. Don't cheat, don't lie, don't steal, don't take advantage. Love mercy. That means be kind. Don't gossip, don't use sarcasm as a weapon, don't demean. Walk humbly with your God. Don't boast, don't act out of self-interest, don't put yourself before others, submit your will to that of the Father. Micah says it all as far as I'm concerned. Micah 6:8. You can live by it. Memorize it. I wanted it as my license plate, but some other darn Christian got it first!! ☺

Prayer: Dear Father, We know that You look into our hearts, Lord! Thank you for sending us the Holy Spirit to indwell us, so that the cardinal virtues reflected in Micah's words may become more and more a part of our characters. This is the sanctification we crave, Lord! Let us be more and more Christ-like every day, so that our behaviors flow naturally out of the character that you would have us all perfect. AMEN

APRIL 27

Good Ship and True

"We also glory in tribulations, knowing that tribulation produces perseverance; and perseverance, character; and character, hope." (Rom 5:3-4 NKJV)

On the Reach, sailing was and is, simply *what one does*. Whether manning the helm and demonstrating the matchless grace of a well-trimmed sloop, heeled over, stiff breeze, blue sky, white caps scattered over the surface, slowly working your way upwind toward Pumpkin Light, or skippering a boat that is hove-to (stationary) in a pea soup fog, listening intently for hints that might reveal the treachery of a nearby rocky shore or an approaching craft, the sailor has a special connection with the natural environment. Coastal Maine simply gets into the sailor's blood.

Why is that? Can't anyone observe the interplay of sail, wind and waves standing on the shore and achieve that same connection or at least a similar one? While it is true that the non-sailor can observe in just such a way, and thus experience in a two-dimensional sense, what it means to sail, only the sailor understands the reality of his interaction with the forces of nature. The sailor knows where his/her skill and judgment end and the unalterable and irresistible forces of nature begin. The sailor understands that the tides and the currents and the winds themselves, are beyond his control. He can only hone his expertise at the art of adaptation to circumstance. She can learn the intricacies of her ship, and she can come to know the waters in which she sails, with respect to predictable hazards of tide and rock. But in so doing, over years of experience, she develops not the adversarial relationship with nature that one might expect, but instead, an almost symbiotic understanding. The sailor, out in the elements, in command of a "good ship and true," no matter her size, feels more at one with nature, and thus with his Creator, than at perhaps any other time in his life! The constant shifting of circumstances produces that perseverance, and that perseverance the character required in the competent Captain.

It's difficult to explain to anyone who doesn't sail, even if they have occasionally been on a boat, sailed by someone else. As your fund of knowledge increases, commensurate with your years of experience, the sailor comes to *feel* not only what his vessel *wants* to do, but he *senses* what mother nature has in store as well. He learns to read the clouds, the wind, the waves, the currents, the tides, and makes a myriad of moment to moment observations, judgments and adjustments, on the basis of sensory input often so subtle, that he himself is not even aware of its influence. Many a time I have tried to teach novices a simple task like how to use the wheel or tiller to steer a straight course. What I discover anew each time, is that the ability to make minute changes in helm, to compensate for wind, waves, drift, yaw, and momentum, are not per say, *teachable*. I in fact, make these changes unconsciously and automatically because I *feel* what is required.

But the sailor also has the humility to recognize his limitations. Once he was dependent on observations of the stars and the sun and the moon to determine location and course, and often inaccuracies or poor computation led to considerable and sometimes fatal navigational error. Only a few years ago, we carried charts aboard, sealed in plastic against the salt air. There were many tense moments growing up, as we approached a known area of hazard, when that particular chart was franticly searched for, because *someone* had not put it back where it belonged!! Knowing the exact location of that chart was critical, as was the guidance it could provide.

Today, instruments are of more practical aid to the sailor than ever in history. His GPS has virtually supplanted his paper chart, ruler and protractor. His chart plotter, digital speedometer, depth meter, anemometer, wind vane, radar, cell phone, and radio, all aid him immeasurably in successfully navigating any chosen voyage.

But despite his experience, expertise, and instrumentation, the sailor is constantly aware that his journey, his goal, his safety, and in essence his very life, are dependent on forces much greater than himself. He can adapt to a certain degree, but in the final analysis, the sailor knows he is dependent on the elements. This may seem intuitive, but it is not a daily facet of life for most people. Most, at least in developed nations, are blissfully unaware of the natural forces around them. They drive their cars or take mass transit to work, leave their climate-controlled vehicle and walk into their climate-controlled workspace for the rest of the day. Their success, and certainly their survival, do not seem to them, to be obviously linked to those unseen forces.

The analogy to the Christian life is clear. We can adapt to events in our own strength, just as the secular world does, or we can recognize that our Creator has made us not only with a purpose in mind, but with a built-in dependence and need to acknowledge Him! In doing so, in openly acknowledging and professing our belief, dependence and repentance, we receive the indwelling Holy Spirit, and are granted His guidance while negotiating the vicissitudes of life. We of course, then "sail" through the challenges of life buoyed by the peace that accompanies the knowledge of salvation. James tells us to *"Count it all joy, when you fall into various trials, knowing that the testing of your faith produces patience." (James 1:2-3)* **We have the serenity of the knowledge that whatever weather threatens to alter our course, the sail set we choose, the adjustments we make, will eventually take us to a destination where our new perspective permits us to understand the good that has actually come out of hardship.**

Living by faith, in no way precludes learning practical approaches to negotiating the optimum path, through the myriad of challenges that will come our way in life. In fact, were we not to avail ourselves of the knowledge of those who have gone before us, then we practice a "blind faith," and no part of scripture has ever advocated that. *"Test all things; hold fast to what is good." (1 Thess 5:21)* We will make decisions based on our past experience. We will stand at the helm. But we should remember to adjust our course only after consulting the One who can calm the seas with a simple command. Thanks to the Helper that indwells us, we don't have to look far to find that guidance.

"I may not have gone where I intended to go, but I think I have ended up where I needed to be." (Douglas Adams)

"Faith is our foundation and our guiding compass, navigating us through life." (Kim Ha Campbell)

Prayer: Dear Heavenly Father, We love You! We thank You that You have provided us with a mind that can grasp the subtleties of our circumstance and make considered decisions; but Holy Spirit keep us constantly aware that the Father is Sovereign, and we need to prayerfully contemplate each course change in our lives before we can feel confident that we are submitting our will to His! AMEN

APRIL 28

Hole in the Roof

"And when they could not come near Him because of the crowd, they uncovered the roof where He was. So, when they had broken through, they let down the bed on which the paralytic was lying. When Jesus saw their faith, He said to the paralytic, 'Son, your sins are forgiven you.' (Mark 2:4-5 NKJV)

Not long ago a friend, call him Jack, related a story about his efforts to reach out to a Muslim couple with the Good News. My friend works for a large high-tech chip manufacturer in Dallas, which does a lot of defense contracting. One of the places available for lunch on campus is a Mediterranean Style Deli, and one gentleman and his wife have been running it for the last 31 years. Jack knew them well enough to say 'hello' when he ordered from Sadia, and wave to her husband Ahmed, who was usually behind the sandwich counter or visible through the pass-through in the kitchen. They seemed like a happy, hard-working couple, who smiled a lot and joked about sports and the weather with many of the employees, as they picked up their meals. The food was outstanding, and the little Deli had a good reputation.

Jack had some passing involvement with missionary work in north Africa, and was truly interested in finding out more about Iranian culture and religion. One day, when he had finished eating and the lunch crowd had mostly cleared out, he approached Sadia and asked if she and her husband could teach Jack and his wife something about their culture in Iran. She smiled, and waved her husband over. Their English was excellent, even if accented. She passed on the request to her husband and he looked delighted! *"No one is ever asking about our culture! Please, we would love to have you and your wife over to dinner at our home and we will talk, not of Iran, but of Persia, which is the land of our ancestors."* Jack was a little taken aback, not expecting to be invited to their house, but after a moment's hesitation, responded that he would check with his wife, but he thought it would be marvelous! *"How about this Sunday afternoon? It is our only time off...say 5 PM?"* Jack told them as far as he knew that would work!

That Sunday, Jack put on nice jeans and a sport coat, and Sarah, his wife, wore a below the knee dress, with a colorful scarf. They were both a little nervous, having never been in the home of a Muslim family. Ahmed and Sadia lived on a quiet residential street about five miles from the plant. When they ushered them into the cool, darkened interior, there were several other people present. Ahmed introduced his sister and sister in law and his mother in law. All of whom nodded their welcome, but spoke considerably less English than their hosts. They sat and had tea and pita with humus, as well as yogurt and spinach dip, Tzatziki, and delicious Falafel wraps with Tahini sauce. Jack and his wife learned of Ahmed's narrow escape from Tehran, traveling to the Turkish border and seeking asylum in the Canadian Embassy, during the revolution. The Shah had been deposed and was in exile, and the Ayatollah and his Revolutionary Council had taken over. It was months before his fiancé, at the time, Sadia, could escape as well, and make her way to Canada. Through family connections, they sought asylum in Texas, and they never left. Sadia and Ahmed told of their heartbreak over infertility, of their families still in Iran, who, being westernized, were constantly under suspicion from the radical Islamist government. They learned that Persia's age-old religion was Zoroastrianism, and not Islam, and that most citizens were forced into an Islam that they viewed as imposed by foreigners from Saudia Arabia. Most of the citizens are not even practicing Muslims.

It turns out that Sadia has a sister who married an American and converted to Christianity. They were open to discussing it and promised to get together with Jack and Sarah for a visit to their church.

All of us who have put our trust in Christ, have experienced the joy and the freedom from guilt, shame, and the power of sin. We have the promise of eternity with a loving Father to turn to whenever times get dark. That peace is something we really want to share, but for whatever reason, we are usually extremely hesitant to bring up Jesus, to someone whom we know could benefit. Instead of thinking about bringing Jesus to the unbeliever, try the opposite, as the men in the passage from Mark did with their friend the paralytic. Bring the unbeliever to Jesus, no matter what's in the way, crowd, roof, or our own hesitation! Don't let embarrassment, or shyness, or fear of what others might think of you, act as obstacles to possibly bringing someone the joy of receiving Christ! Jack used a passing acquaintance with someone to ask more *about them!!* Opportunities to share anything, including your faith, tend to present themselves frequently, if you learn to *listen first*. That's how you make the hole in the roof! Listen first. That's how you *break through*. Find out where people are coming from in their own experience. Only then is it possible to use your story as a way to lower them through the roof and put them right in front of the Savior!

"My dear brothers and sisters, take note of this: Everyone should be quick to listen, slow to speak and slow to become angry." (James 1:19 NIV)

"When people talk, listen completely. Most people hear and never listen." (Ernest Hemingway)

"Most people don't listen with the intent to understand; they listen with the intent to reply." (Stephen R. Covey)

> ***Prayer: Lord, help us to overcome our insecurities about sharing the Good News! Remind us of the men who didn't let a crowd or a building keep them from getting their friend to Jesus. And direct us to listen first, to those with whom we would share, recognizing that people are validated and receptive when you acknowledge their stories. AMEN***

APRIL 29

It's None of My Business

"Those who consider themselves religious and yet do not keep a tight rein on their tongues deceives themselves, and their religion is worthless." (James 1:26 NIV)

All of us know someone who frequently begins a sentence with the phrase, *"It's none of my business but..."* These people make it easy to spot when they are on the verge of saying something about someone else, often of a not so subtle judgmental bent. Would that all of us, when gossiping, were kind enough to fly this yellow warning flag at the start of our transgression! Most of us were taught by a parent or a grandparent that if we can't say something nice about someone, we shouldn't say anything at all. Imagine what our political discourse would look like if everyone listened to their grandmother's advice!

But "gossip" doesn't have to be judgmental. It doesn't even have to be ill intended. Oxford English Dictionary defines it as tattling, unrestrained idle talk or unfounded rumor. Certain localities are even known for the presence of gossip, whether a hair salon or the gym. The problem of course is that when you speculate about what are often the private affairs of others, you can do real and sometimes irreparable damage. You can damage the reputation of the object of your discourse, based completely on erroneous information. When your words inevitably get back to the person about whom you were speaking, you can severely hurt their feelings and damage whatever relationship you might have had or ever hoped to have with them. Even well-meaning speculation can be dangerous. Recently a large church in Dallas lost its senior pastor of more than 25 years. The circumstances under which he left were never made entirely clear, and few have had any communication with him or his family since then. There was discussion among what I believe to be good, moral, devout people, who nevertheless would throw out all kinds of speculation, very little of which was based on any fact whatsoever. Some of those suggestions would definitely have been hurtful should they become known to the object of the discussion, or to people who had a close personal relationship with our pastor.

Let's take it a step further. During the pandemic of Coronavirus 19 in the Spring of 2020, you could hardly speak to anyone without them repeating something that they had heard about who has it, how they got it, why they got it, what the mortality rate was, how many were going to die, or what so and so was doing wrong. Gossip is *unfounded rumor* about events as well as individuals, and it can often be mixed into conversations where some things are factual, and others are completely made up or misunderstood. The consequences can be essentially fear-mongering; the kind of thing that stirs up crowd panic, emotionally just like the kind of thing that can lead to stampedes and people being trampled to death! In essence, gossiping can be just like yelling *fire* in a crowded theatre!

There is a reason that gossip is listed by Paul in his letter to the Corinthians among discord, jealousy, fits of rage, selfish ambition, slander, arrogance and disorder. (2 Corinthians 12:20) In his letter to the Ephesians, he admonishes them to *"let no unwholesome talk come out of your mouths, but only what is helpful for building others up according to their needs, that it may benefit those who listen." (Ephesians 4:29 NIV)* Believe me, we are all guilty of this particular sin, no matter who you are. It is important to remember that when you are talking about *anybody,* even a family member to another family member, and *that person is not present* and part of the conversation, it may well be gossip. So, the easiest thing to do is pause before you speak. *(A LOT of people reading this, who know me, will laugh at ME giving this advice!)* In that pause, ask yourself 1) is the person about whom I am speaking present? 2) if that person were present, would my words be uplifting for them? If the answer to these questions is 'no,' it would better if you remained silent. Similarly, if someone starts a sentence with, "It's none of my business but..." then make an excuse to not listen, and turn away. Whatever they have to say is not something that's going to be uplifting for anyone.

"Do not let any unwholesome talk come out of your mouths, but only what is helpful for building others up according to their needs, that it may benefit those who listen." (Ephesians 4:29 NIV)

"Take ships as an example. Although they are so large and driven by strong winds, they are steered by a very small rudder...likewise the tongue is a small part of the body...Consider what a great fire can be set on fire by a small spark. The tongue also is a fire, a world of evil among the parts of the body. It corrupts the whole person, sets the whole course of his life on fire, and is itself set on fire by hell!" (James 3:4-6 NIV)

"A perverse person stirs up conflict, and a gossip separates friends." (Proverbs 16:28 NIV)

"Rumors are dainty morsels that sink deep into one's heart. (Proverbs 18:8 NLT)

Prayer: Dear Heavenly Father, Remind us to adhere to the advice of our elders, who have already travelled the routes in life which we find so circuitous! When our grandmother tells us not to say anything, if we can't say something nice, lead us to recognize true wisdom when we hear it! Even those who have little to say are regarded more highly than those who prattle on about things of which they know little, or about another's business that they undoubtedly would have preferred to remain private. AMEN

APRIL 30

Time

"Time is free but it's priceless. You can't own it, but you can use it. You can't keep it, but you can spend it. Once you've lost it you can never get it back." (Harvey Mackay)

One of the things I keep hearing during the Covid-19 quarantine of 2020, is "I've been reading a lot more books than I used to!" No matter where you are sheltering in place, house, apartment, out in the country; and no matter where you are sheltering geographically, New York, Detroit, San Francisco, Dallas, or some other region, *most* of you will find yourself with more unassigned time than before. Even if you are now working from home, or you've become not only mom, but mom-homeschool teacher, you'll have all the time you used to spend commuting or ferrying children, whether that was on the train or in the car or on the bus, that now needs to be filled. People are playing board games, doing family puzzles laid out on the dining table, playing charades or trivia games with distant family and friends via ZOOM or some other sharing platform. Birthday, funeral, wedding, anniversary, and soon graduation celebrations are all happening over the internet. Through it all, people are spending more time, often than ever before, with their immediate family members, and often with family who live far away. Kids are home from school, teens and young adults are home from college. Many people are home with their families because they have lost their jobs, or they have been temporarily furloughed. And yet…

Home. *Home is where the heart is!* How many poems, how many songs, how many books, how many musicals, how many plays, how many movies have been made whose central theme was either the desire or the struggle to find the road home? Even Dorothy reached only one conclusion after her fantastic adventure in the land of Oz: *"There's no place like home."* For many "home" just means the current roof over their head, but for others that roof is the one in which their parents live or lived, and in which they were raised. It has special meaning, because of the people with whom you shared that part of your life, and the memories that were generated there.

Despite all the negative effects on our personal and national economies, the tragic loss of life, the induction of fear and uncertainty, the disruption of everything from schools to universities to all manner of sports, the small businesses that may never recover; all of us have recognized at least some of the good. The humor of the American public has staggered me with its diversity and adaptability! Who knew toilet paper could be *that funny?* The degree of compliance with truly draconian restrictions put in place by our governments has been nothing short of remarkable. And we have been given this *gift of time at home* that would otherwise have never happened! My parents, and probably all parents at all times, have warned the younger generation that life is short. And now, looking back from 64, let me reiterate, *life is short!* Author John Green wrote, *"One day you're 17 and planning for someday. And then quietly, without you ever really noticing, someday is today. And then someday is yesterday."*

The point perhaps, is *carpe diem!* "Seize the day!" Those were the words of Horace, the Latin lyric poet, in his collection, *Odes,* published in 23 BCE. From ancient Greek Epicurianism to the 17th century English Metaphysical poets, to modern writers, the concept is of enjoying life in its current circumstance. Solomon tells us as much in Ecclesiastes 3:1-10, where he outlines examples demonstrating that *"there is an appointed time for everything. And there is a time for every event under heaven..."* The Bible encourages us to concentrate on the good we can do and the love we can show to others, *right now,* without worrying about tomorrow. (Matthew 6:31-34) While we may struggle through some tough times financially in the midst of the pandemic, it's clear that the Lord wants us focused on Him, dependent on Him, trusting Him, and not becoming preoccupied with money. (Hebrews 13:5)

So, read that book, watch that movie you haven't had time to watch, binge that series everyone is talking about, and do it with one of those poor sots trapped in the house with you! Walk that dog more than he's ever been walked in his life. Do that puzzle that's been in the closet for 10 years and might stay another ten, unless you do it now. Go totally crazy and write a *hand-written letter* to your grandparents, parents, or even children. For the latter group, it might be something they've never even seen before! Show a little love to those neighbors you may never have met, while you're out walking. A wave and a smile and a conversation can all traverse 6 feet distance with ease! If you have money that you can donate, do it now, while charities and non-profits of all sorts are tapped out and desperate.

Here's a thought about what you can do with a little extra time to kill; pull your Bible down off that upper shelf and dust it! Maybe you've never actually read anything in your bible since Sunday School as a child. Maybe you've never opened one at all. Maybe there isn't one in your home. Luckily, in the time of this pandemic, we have the internet! Go to the App store and download YouVersion, or Olive Tree, or Open Bible, or Blue Letter Bible, or a myriad of others, and Read Matthew 5, the Sermon on the Mount. If that peaks your interest, read John, and then Romans. You'll be off to the races!

You will probably never be given a gift of time like this again in your life! Think how *much time* you men in particular, used to spend talking about sports! This is one time in your life where you actually have the opportunity to *really listen* to your children, or your spouse! Carpe diem!!

"Time is a sort of river of passing events, and strong is its current; no sooner is a thing brought to sight than it is swept by and another takes its place, and then this too will be swept away." (Marcus Aurelius)

"Life is not the passing of time. Life is the collection of experiences and their intensity." (Jim Rohn)

"You may delay, but time will not." (Ben Franklin)

Prayer: Father God, we thank you that there is a time for everything under the sun! Now in this time of fear for many, uncertainty for all, let us seize the day and take advantage of what we may never have again...time at home. We ask Your Holy Spirit to guide us in our use of such a precious commodity of time. Lead us to opportunities to show our love for family and friends as we all pull together, even though apart. Anyone who has ever loved knows that distance cannot separate two hearts! AMEN

MAY

MAY 1
Total Dependence

"I am the vine, you are the branches. He who abides in Me and I in him, bears much fruit; for without Me you can do nothing." (John 15:5 NIV)

There was a Friday a few weeks ago that was one of the better days of my adult life. I saw patients only in the morning, and the afternoon was 70F, sunny and breezy, and I texted my son and asked if he had time to take me up? Andy's a CFI or certified flight instructor and a commercial pilot. Flight operations were deemed "essential industries" during the 2020 pandemic, and as such, people employed in that industry were still allowed to go to work. I too, as a physician, worked in an essential industry, but that Friday, I had the afternoon off. Andy had offered long ago, to take me up in a Cessna, but I am basically a flight chicken and had declined to this point. But what the hey, it was a perfect day to give it a shot!

I met my son at the small regional airport where the flight school was located. While I filled out paperwork, he walked down the line of aircraft and began pre-flight checks on the brand new Cessna 172 Skyhawk S we would be taking up. I had flown on a 10 seat DHC 3 Twin Otter in Belize last year, but prior to that, the last time I had been in a light aircraft was 36 years ago! When I arrived at the plane, Andy showed me how to get in, adjust the seat, work the door and window, and then took me outside to do his walk around with him. He checked mechanical function of the rudder, elevators, ailerons, and flaps; checked that all wing lights and strobes were functioning, sampled the fuel from below the wing tanks at 13 separate ports, looking for water or contaminants, checked the air speed sensor, tire inflation, and in addition, washed the windshield! He patiently explained the functionality of each wing surface and the ways the various flap adjustments would affect lift. I listened equally as patiently, remembering that engineering physics at Rice University had *almost* kept me from Med School!

Once we were settled in, Andy on the right, since he was now more used to flying from there as an instructor than in the pilot's seat, he began the instrument pre-flight check. He made sure I knew where the fire extinguisher was, where the button on the yoke was to allow me to communicate with ATC if for some reason he was unable to, and then he went through the very sophisticated avionics displays, and functioning of throttle, choke, yoke, and pedals; none of which did I have even the slightest desire to touch! Then we got out, attached the tow bar and pulled her out onto the accessory pavement which would lead to the taxiway. Two planes had to pass while we waited to line ours up. We got in, buckled up, adjusted our headphones and microphones, started the engines, and then Andy methodically went through another check list reviewing engine function. Next, he checked the appropriate frequencies, set the altimeter to 640 feet above sea level, and we began to taxi. My son explained subtleties of taxiing including rules and courtesies that all experienced pilots were familiar with. Due to the skeleton staffs mandated by the pandemic, the tower controller for ground and air was the same person! We pulled into an area to wait for our take-off clearance, as three before us set out on runway 15, almost directly into the 20-knot breeze. It was 1700 hours.

The take-off roll is remarkably quick in a Cessna 172 with V-1 at only 55 mph, so we were in the air within an instant! It didn't take too long for us to be buffeted by convection updrafts as the thousands of acres of cement that is DFW reflected the afternoon heat. Andy explained each movement of the aircraft, laid down some ground rules, like his index finger in the air meant silence while he talked to approach control or tower, and then further explained how engine rpms, control surfaces, and angle of attack, all affected the movement and heading of the Cessna. He had the calmest most reassuring tone to his voice when he spoke to me, and a professional efficiency and courtesy when he spoke to ATC. Each of his movements were perfectly conserved and purposeful. He asked me if I wanted to stall, and I respectfully declined, but he did demonstrate a glide and then steep turns that generated enough G's that my phone felt heavy in my hand! He received permission to circle our house and I texted my wife who came out to our cul-de-sac to wave and acknowledge our wing waggle. On the return run directly into the sun, we struggled to see an approaching aircraft directly ahead and only 500 feet below us, according to our GPS. He passed rapidly under our right wing, appearing as if magic out of the glaring sun and it momentarily reminded me of how difficult a dogfight must be going 8-10 times faster than we were!! Andy explained the various types of approach and as expected we took base left and came straight into runway 15 with a 24-knot headwind. Despite that, he brought the Cessna down right on the center line with barely a bump.

It occurred to me afterwards that the tables had turned. I have a 100-ton Masters License from the US Coast Guard, and whenever any of my children were on our boats, I was definitively in charge. They were, in almost all respects, totally dependent on me and on my decisions. Twenty-five hundred feet in the air, with Andy at the controls, I was now totally dependent on my son! The absolutely coolest observation afterwards, was that I loved it! I felt completely comfortable, unafraid, not even nervous really, as I thought I would be. My son had the knowledge and both the flight and interpersonal skills, to put me completely at ease! But it wasn't just that. It was more than that. Part of my enjoyment, part of my calmness, stemmed from the fact that I loved and trusted my son. I knew in my heart that he would look out for me, protect me. In short, I knew he always had my best interest in mind and he would use his considerable talents to make sure I got the most out of this experience!

Once we recognize as people of faith, that we are totally dependent on the Son, we can take a big breath and turn it all over to Him. I had no power at all to control my own destiny or destination while in that aircraft. My son guided me, taught me, lifted me, and kept me safe, not only because he could, but because he loved me. Could there be a better metaphor for our Christian life? If we can just remember that the most powerful Being in the world, the One who created it, us, all the laws of physics, and went on to save us from our sins because He loves us, is the same One we depend on day to day, well, it makes it easier to take a breath and relax!

"I will wait patiently for God to save me; I depend on Him alone. He alone protects and saves me; He is my defender, and I shall never be defeated." (Psalm 62:1-2 GNT)

Prayer: Dear Heavenly Father, We love You! We depend on Your Son to teach us, Your Spirit to Guide us, and You to love us unfailingly, every day! What a joy to depend on One whom we know loves us and always has our best interest in mind! We can endure all hardships, knowing that You loved us enough to sacrifice Your own Son to bring us back to You. AMEN

MAY 2

Let 'Em See You Sweat

"Admitting a mistake is not a weakness; on the contrary, it shows an openness of heart. Only a strong well-balanced individual with clarity of mind can do so effortlessly." (Vishwas Chavan)

Doctors are in no way infallible. In fact, our mistakes may be more evident than in most professions, because of the nature of our work. If in a frenzied moment we make a flawed judgment, the good doctor recognizes his error, makes appropriate changes, and moves on. But you can't learn from mistakes if you won't acknowledge them. The patient must view the doctor as even-keeled, but the med school admonition of "never let 'em see you sweat," is bad advice for the doctor and the patient. A patient can't trust a doctor who perceives himself as infallible, because inevitably the doctor will prove that he is not—perhaps at the patient's expense.

I was awakened one night at about 3:30 AM when on call at San Francisco General Hospital as a junior resident in OB/GYN. This was unusual only in that I was actually asleep, and miraculously had been for over 45 minutes! The three interns covering L&D and the ER were either in total control, or alternatively, had nothing to do. Anyway, the page was from a senior internal medicine resident, screening intern presentations in the ER. He listened to the case of a Laotian woman writhing in pain, hands clutching her abdomen, who evidently had a large pelvic tumor. Unfortunately, it was not uncommon for non-English speaking indigent patients to arrive in the ER with advanced malignancies in a crisis stage. The medicine chief had diligently examined the patient himself and confirmed that there was a rock hard mass at the apex of the vagina, which seemed to extend in an irregular mass all the way to the sternum. The cervix had a small amount of blood exuding, but otherwise looked normal.

When I arrived in the tiny curtained space in the packed emergency ward, I discovered what can only be described as bedlam. The patient who appeared about 16 years old, was sweating heavily, flushed, and agitated. There was a woman by the head of the bed in tears, with her arms and upper body thrown across the thrashing patient's chest. The tiny space contained not only these two, but the intern, a nurse, two security officers restraining the girl's father, who was babbling unintelligibly and gesticulating wildly as he yanked first one then the other arm away from the security personnel trying to restrain him. He seemed to be hurling most of his Laotian invective at our hapless internal medicine resident. The doctor had evidently, at least been able to communicate the internationally recognized word, 'cancer' to the distraught father. In this quiet group of competent professionals, they needed me?

Anybody appraising this situation objectively, could agree on one thing immediately; there were just too many people screaming in this tiny space. I asked security to remove the older gentlemen, and the two other physicians to step out and give me a moment alone with the nurse, the patient and her mother. I knew no Laotian, but I did know many of our Laotian patients also spoke French. When the noise level was down to only the patient's groans and the mother's sobs, I asked the only thing I knew how to say in French, "*Quand etait tes dernieres regles*?" The teenager looked up and responded, *"Je ne sais pas,"* which was the only other phrase I knew in French. The patient allowed a brief bimanual exam to confirm the impending birth, and with some international sign language, I communicated the 'good' news to her mother, who immediately began to sob once again.

The other two physicians were of course, mortified almost to the point of self-vaporization. It became clear that only the patient suspected her diagnosis, while her parents had been practicing the Eastern version of Western denial. They maintained it was not possible, since their daughter had not yet enjoyed sexual congress. I was tempted to tell the translator that she may not have enjoyed it, but she'd definitely had it. I remembered my professional code of conduct at the last instant and refrained.

This is not as outrageous as it seems. Doctors are no more omniscient than they are infallible, and many a patient has intentionally or inadvertently misled those caring for her. In this case, denial was so manifest that this Laotian family either really didn't know what was happening, or considered it so unlikely as to deny the logical findings of their own senses. Thanks to their demeanor on arrival, the intern was sucked in completely. Who can blame him? All doctors have seen patients with large undiagnosed cancers. The family's level of agitation told the intern that something extremely grave was going on, and it made it easy for him to overlook her youth, the fact that her pain was coming in waves, or even that the pelvic mass felt just the way a baby's head would feel! The resident, reviewing hundreds of cases, had simply bought what the intern had told him.

Before the girl was transferred to L&D, the translator managed to straighten out the confusion. The father screamed something in Laotian, threw his hands in the air, and we thought he was going to hit the intern, who tried to back up quickly. Instead the father gave him a bear hug, and began crying tears of joy and thanking the flabbergasted intern over and over. The translator related his words carefully. *"We are not so terrible parents as we thought! Even you did not know our daughter was pregnant!! We are so happy that there is no cancer!! I bet you will never make this mistake again!"*

Being a good doctor, like a good pilot, requires the cool clockwork rationality of the flight computer—and more. While the pilot must recognize his own fears, but never show them to the crew or passengers, the doctor learns that his own emotions and fears are the same as his patients' and that occasionally revealing them can be beneficial to the doctor patient relationship. Achieving the desired outcome while still remaining human requires both compassion and self-discipline. Every now and then, let 'em see you sweat. They won't trust you completely if you don't.

Christians have the Great Physician to rely on. But if He were just an omnipotent force that no one had ever seen, a force that your parents told you to believe in, to have faith in, would you? When you are the object of someone else's cruelty, or disease, or injury, or just bad circumstances, would you trust a God you had never seen? God chose to be incarnate. Jesus was born in humble surroundings to a teenage unwed mother. He grew up to live a sinless perfect life, but he got angry in front of the disciples. He got sad and wept in front of the disciples. He was tempted and undoubtedly shared it with the disciples. Our Savior died for our sins on that cross, a death we deserved. But He also understood us. He was fully man. God knew we needed a Savior to whom we could relate. God and heaven couldn't just be pie in the sky for a whole world to come to faith. God wanted us back! He thought of the perfect way. He became one of us. And when He did, He let us see Him sweat!

"Jesus wept." (John 11:35 NASB)

"And He looked around at them with anger, grieved at their hardness of heart." (Mark 3:5 NASB)

"And making a whip of cords, He drove them all out of the Temple...and overturned their tables." (John 2:13-18 NASB)

Prayer: Dear Heavenly Father, thank you that You decided to send Your Son to live among us, so that we could see and hear with our own eyes and ears that You understand us! You know our temptations, our frustrations, our anger, our sadness, and our sinfulness, and still You loved us enough to give us a way back home!! We love you back!! AMEN

MAY 3
A Wink

"Jesus said to them, 'Assuredly I say to you, if you have faith as a mustard seed, you will say to this mountain, 'Move from there to there,' and it will move; and nothing will be impossible for you." (Matthew 17:20 NKJV)

We have a 16-pound cat named, *Sterling*, and he is not fat; he's just big. They tell us he's a tuxedo because of his black and white markings. While there are varying opinions about what is more humane, *Sterling* is an indoor-outdoor cat with a cat door to the back yard and another door in a back gate that allows him to go, well, cat around. We live on a creek, so he spends a good portion of each day doing whatever it is cats do during a good portion of the day prowling around the heavily wooded banks of a creek.

A few days ago, I was off after being on call. I have trouble sleeping in the morning, even if I've been up all night at the hospital, but that day was sunny and warm and I fell asleep on a chaise lounge in the backyard. I was awakened by my wife calling the cat's name, and then asking me if I'd seen him? I looked up, shaded my eyes, and said, I hadn't seen him lately. One minute later, after my wife had gone into the house, I heard a soft thud behind me as *Sterling* jumped onto the deck from the top of the fence, distaining the door in the gate placed there for his use. He then strolled past me, heading towards the back porch, and in the glare of the bright late morning sun, it looked suspiciously like he had a tail at both ends! I got up and he scurried beneath a rocking chair on the porch, where he proceeded to deposit the young squirrel, who evidently, hadn't been quite fast enough.

I called to my wife, who came out the back door, rapidly assessed the situation, and retreated to the interior just as rapidly. She did at least, bring me a plastic bag which she handed carefully through a cracked door, presumably afraid that the squirrel might re-animate. I took care of rodent removal, using a broom to separate *Sterling* from his kill, prior to bagging. Later, my wife expressed her relief that this particular episode of *Wild Kingdom* had occurred while I was home. In fact, what she said was, *"There's no question God winked at me on this deal!"*

I started thinking about that. How often have you heard someone say, *"That was just totally a God-thing!"* Is it? Maybe. Maybe not. But Believers tend to look at things differently than nonbelievers. Atheists believe in coincidence. Period. The atheist will tell you that Christians are just kidding themselves when they assign a favorable coincidence to the hand of God. Christians can believe in coincidence too, but there is a difference. Christians know that the Sovereign God is just that, Sovereign. He is in control. (There's an old saying, *"If God is your co-pilot, you need to switch seats!")* If you had left for work two minutes earlier, you would have been in that pile up on the freeway, and possibly not even around to speculate! Was that Providence? Coincidence? Was that a *"God-wink?"*

I honestly think the answer is, maybe. If the answer is "definitely," then you are expressing a theology known as *Determinism*. Jonathon Edwards was a famous 18th century preacher in America who espoused this perspective. (Most famous Sermon: *Sinners in the Hands of an Angry God)* The problem with this perspective of course, is one of free will, or more accurately, the lack thereof! If God has fore-ordained every detail of our lives, if He decided whether or not you had an English muffin this morning, then why did He give us the command to love Him with all our heart, soul, strength and *mind*? If everything was fore-ordained, then all choice, all events, would simply be beyond our control. Most Christians don't believe that today.

But that is different from believing that God never intervenes supernaturally. If God never intervened, then intercessional prayer might seem pointless, unless the extent of that prayer was never anything other than *thy will be done*. But even Jesus prayed for an alternative to His crucifixion, if God would allow it.

My conclusion is that there are probably *"God winks"* all around us every day. To what extent the omnipotent, omniscient Creator of the Universe chooses to intervene is quite frankly, up to Him! God being Sovereign means He may intervene whenever He feels it is right to do so. We believe He has a plan for us, and that *all things work together for good for those who love Him. (Romans 8:28)* That means quite simply, that things work out in the long run exactly the way He wants them to, but perhaps not exactly the way we want them to nor with the exact timing we would prefer! When my wife and I were dating 35 years ago, I once complained of a headache that had persisted for a couple of days. She immediately asked me if I had prayed about it? At the time, perhaps due to my conventional Protestant upbringing, I thought there were certain things God wanted us to handle on our own! Now, more than three decades later, I have come to realize that what God wants of us is to trust Him! He wants us to depend on Him at all times. (Psalm 62:8) Paul makes it pretty clear that we are to bring *anything* to God in prayer. (Phil 4:6) That means that while it may not always be the case, something as seemingly inconsequential as a persistent headache resolving might be a kind of "God wink!"

Most of us need look no further back than a few days, to identify multiple events that might have the fingerprints of the Creator on them! You may have received an unexpected payment the day before a bill was due that you knew you wouldn't have been able to pay; you may have missed a plane that made you late for a job interview, forcing you to meet with someone else who thought you were just stupendous and recommended you; you may have decided you wanted Chinese food the other night and read about the food poisoning from unwashed lettuce at the Mexican restaurant you originally planned to attend. Each of you can make your own list in all likelihood.

But, watch-out! It's important to remember, as we've noted before, that you can't determine God's will by the short-term outcome. The "God-thing" that happens in your life could be the *opposite* of each of the examples above. That doesn't mean that God is against you, or wants harm to come to you. ***It means He knows what He's about and you don't! His thoughts are not your thoughts.*** (Isaiah 55:8-9) You have to **trust** that even if what has happened seems bad, that in the long run, for those who love and trust Him, it will turn out for the good!

We may not know exactly when God has intervened in the course of our daily lives, but we do know that He loves us with a love that is beyond human comprehension. We know that He has a plan for us that is good, not bad. (Jeremiah 29:11) And that means that **we give God the Glory at every turn!** So, the next time you wonder if something that occurred was coincidence or "a God thing," err on the side of the "God wink" in my opinion. Maybe He intervened at that moment, maybe He didn't, but He is Ruler overall, and He wants what's good for you. Trust me, ***trust Him!***

"Have faith in Him in all circumstances, dear people. Open up your heart to Him; the true God shelters us in His arms." (Psalm 62:8 VOICE)

Prayer: Dear Heavenly Father, We love you and because you first loved us, we trust you. Help us Lord, to fully realize that we can trust You in the small things as well as the big things. We cannot understand how Your Providence works because Your thoughts are not our thoughts.

But we don't need to understand how, only that it does; and know that we can trust in that Providence no matter our moment to moment circumstance. AMEN

MAY 4

The Shema

"Jesus answered him, 'The first of all the commandments is, 'Hear O Israel, the Lord our God, the Lord is One. And you shall love the Lord your God with all your heart, with all your soul, with all your mind, and with all your strength. This is the first commandment. And the second like it is this: You shall love your neighbor as yourself. There is no other commandment greater than these.'" (Mark 12:28-31 NKJV)

Over and over again in the Bible, we are commanded to love God. In fact, a version of the above response to a lawyer who sought to test Jesus, occurs nine times in scripture; three times in the synoptic Gospels, and six times in the Old Testament. Interestingly, the Old Testament verses, which occur in Deuteronomy and Joshua, mention only loving God with all your heart, soul and might. (Deut 6:4-9;10:12;11:13; 30:6; Joshua 22:5) Jesus, in quoting the first of three parts of the *Shema*, the core Hebrew prayer in the Siddur, or Hebrew prayer book, alters it slightly. Interestingly, He adds the word *mind*, to heart, soul and strength. More about this in a moment. In Jewish culture, there is special emphasis given to the first six words of the Shema, ***"Shema, Yisrael, Adonai eloheinu, Adonai, echad,"*** found in Deuteronomy 6:4, which is followed by a six word response, and then a recitation of the remaining Deuteronomy 6:5-9, in which we are commanded to love the Lord with all our heart, soul and might. While the first part of the ***Shema***, is called the *Shema* as well, the second and third parts have their own titles.

The second part of the *Shemah* is called the ***Vehayah*** (Deuteronomy 11:13-21) and relates the blessings and consequences of obedience and disobedience to Adonai, respectively. The third part is called the ***Vaiyomer*** (Numbers 15:37-41) and concerns the use of the *tallit*, or prayer shawl with the four tassels called *tzitzit*, on the corners. It is designed to remind the faithful Hebrew to follow all of the commandments.

So, why all this focus on one line of scripture? Jesus was asked by a scribe (lawyer,) impressed by all he had overheard, a sincere question. The rabbis taught that there are 613 individual statutes with 365 prohibitive and 248 positive directions! Jewish historians tell us that those who studied the law, were constantly seeking to know which were the more important and which could be emphasized in hopes of simplifying the code. Jesus first quotes those opening six words of the *Shema*, which affirms two things: the unity of God and His covenant relationship with the Hebrew people. They are to love God completely, with every fiber of their being, because He alone is God and He has chosen a special relationship with the Jewish people. But Jesus goes further, and reminds the listeners of Leviticus 19:18, commanding them to love their neighbor as themselves, clearly intending to communicate that this is the natural outgrowth of loving God completely.

The Jews of Jesus' time had a very narrow view of who their neighbor might be, not unlike many people of all different ethnic groups do today. To the Jews, their "neighbor," deserving application of the Golden Rule, clearly meant, well, other Jews! In Luke 10:25-27, Jesus responds to a similar question, but one He knows is not asked out of sincerity this time, but out of guile, intended to trick Him. The question from this lawyer, was what must he do to inherit eternal life? Jesus answered with the second phrase of the *Shema*, and tied it into the Leviticus reference known as the Golden Rule. When the scribe, seeking to justify or defend himself, then asked who exactly was his neighbor, Jesus responded with the famous story of the Good Samaritan.

Recall that there was no more reviled group than the Samaritans, which the Jews of Judah viewed as mongrels who inter-bred with pagans. The Samaritans were half-breeds both physically and spiritually. But in the parable, the priest walks by on the other side of the road, as does the Levite, both avoiding the naked, bleeding, injured man in the street. They are the most respected and revered in Jewish society. Both had sacred duties to perform and perhaps felt they couldn't risk becoming ceremonially unclean by touching the man. (We tend to demonize the Pharisees and the Scribes for their role in the Lord's eventual crucifixion, but remember, they simply had no ears to hear or eyes to see who the Messiah really was, and what the coming of the Kingdom really meant!) The fact that the Samaritan was the one who showed mercy, and was clearly the one Jesus defined as a neighbor, would have been extremely hard to swallow for the listeners. As one of our pastors put it a couple years ago, imagine an American Indian helping an injured cowboy who was shot full of arrows, putting him on his own horse, and then riding into the doc's office in Dodge City!

Our Lord has compassion on those in need, on the wounded, the hungry, the poor, and the sinners. These were the ones who needed the help of a neighbor! The religious leaders in Judah had no compassion for anyone who was not like them, members of their tribe, and even then, not to those who lived a life of sin. Instead of leading sinners to redemption and salvation, they condemned them by a law that only one person ever could follow completely; Jesus, the One who fulfilled the law.

Why is the *Shema* so important then, for the Jew and the Christian alike? Because it reminds us every time we think of it, or every time that we recite it, that our God is the only God, and that He loves us, and we are to love Him with everything in us! But Jesus chose not to let the Shema stand alone. He expanded on it by adding the word *mind*, and by tying it to Leviticus 19:18! The Jews have Leviticus as a part of the Torah. This should not have been news to them. Jesus makes it clear what we have stated over and over, the way to love God, is to love the people he made in his own image! He wants us to use our *minds* and not just our emotions and our tribal instincts! Who are those people made in His own image? Who are your neighbors? Remember what my 90 year-old seminary professor used to say, TAI (think about it!) Your neighbors are those in need, anyone in need, no matter the color of their skin, their gender, their ethnicity, and especially not their religion!

"You shall not take vengeance, nor bear any grudge against the children of your people, but you shall love your neighbor as yourself: I am the Lord." (Leviticus 19:18 NKJV)

Prayer: Dear Heavenly Father, How easy it is for us to hang with only people like ourselves. How easy it is to criticize and look down on people who are not like ourselves. Direct Your Holy Spirit within us to remind us everyday that ALL PEOPLE are made in Your image!! Your Son, Jesus, commands us to love our neighbors as ourselves, and we need to remember that our neighbor isn't just the person who lives next door in a house that looks just like ours, and has skin that looks just like ours, and speaks just like we do, but our neighbor is ANYONE IN NEED. AMEN

MAY 5

Mine

"Do not store up for yourselves treasures on earth, where moth and rust destroy, and where thieves break in and steal. But store up for yourselves treasures in heaven...for where your treasure is there your heart will be also." (Matthew 6:19-21 NASB)

"There are two ways to have enough. One is to accumulate more and more. The other is to desire less." (G.K. Chesterton)

My wife and I are approaching our mid-sixties. I still practice OB/GYN full-time, but in the common vernacular, 'it ain't easy!' As we creep toward my retirement, a fixed income, and an ever- increasing number of grandchildren, we are considering moving to smaller digs. We are Blessed to live in a large two-story English Tudor, overlooking a creek and a pond, on a cul-de-sac, in North Dallas. It has a large pool, a deck, a hot tub, and it was the perfect house in which to raise our four kids. But our youngest is now thirty, and we have begun seriously contemplating downsizing. This brings up questions of, well, what to do with all our...possessions!

I mean, there are a few things I *really, really, like*. For instance, I am a bibliophile. My study has bookshelves that are chock full of treasures, in my estimation. For instance, I own the full set of 50 Harvard Classics, 1902 edition, that were my great grandfather's; all 22 volumes of Calvin's Bible Commentary; all 13 volumes of the Expositor's Bible Commentary; the full PNTC Bible Commentary; the five volume Complete Sermons by Charles Spurgeon; nine bound translations of the Bible; the Easton Press *100 Greatest Books Ever Written*, hardbound, embossed, and illustrated, with gold leaf pages! During seminary, from 2010 to 2014, I acquired almost all of the theological works in digital form as well. That means that currently, I almost never, physically open, a single one of these books! (Reading was just easier on my Kindle, my iphone, or my ipad, particularly before I had my cataract surgeries.)

So, this is a no-brainer for my wife, the practical, organized half of our marriage...If we downsize, the books will need to go!! If you can't hear my scream from there, I must have put this devotion on 'mute!' ***My books?*** These books are ***mine!*** You'd give away my books? Just because we won't have the room? Are you, I don't know, CRAZY? The same argument applied to our 1906 Mason & Hamlin Grand Piano that belonged to my grandmother. Yes, the sounding board had to be repaired, and yes, the action had to be rebuilt, and yes, it doesn't stay in tune very well despite that, and yes, it takes up a lot of space, and yes, a Yamaha Upright would sound way better and would cost 1/3 of what we could get for the grand piano in trade...but it's ***my*** PIANO!! Don't even get me started on the 120 gallon corner fish tank.

How about my reaction to the wrecks involving all those cars I've purchased for family members down through the years? Why would those mishaps upset me at all, as long as the family member wasn't injured? Why do any of us even bother to spend hard earned money on cosmetic repairs to our vehicles, when the damage doesn't affect their ability to get us from point A to point B?

Why are we so attached to these ***things***? I mean they are really just, stuff! Sure, there is some emotional attachment to Granny T's old piano, but let's face it, even she left it on a screened-in porch for twenty years! Couldn't my commentaries be better used by a current seminary student? Couldn't the piano work for someone with the necessary space after we moved to a townhouse or even a high-rise condo or apartment? But, wait a minute...that stuff is *mine, right?*

When our kids were little, we noticed that the new doll, game, toy, or gadget they received for Christmas engaged them for a day, maybe several days, and then it ended up in a pile on the floor of the playroom. Remember how your one year old had way more fun crawling in the cardboard boxes than playing with whatever toy came in them? Well, why was it again, that Jesus wanted the little children to come to Him? Why did He tell the disciples unless they became like one of them, they could never enter the Kingdom of Heaven? (Matthew 19:14-15) I'll tell you why. Because little children are humble, faithful, transparent, without guile, and seem to treasure their experiences and their relationships more than their stuff! It's only as they grow and learn our bad habits that they start to think they ***need*** new and cool stuff. It's only as they grow, that they start to believe certain things ***belong*** to them and no one else has a right to them. We adults tend to forget that ***all of our possessions,* and in fact *every good thing,*** is a gift (loaner actually, when it comes to the physical objects ☺) from above! (James 1:17) We tend to forget that we are actually stewards, even of our land, not owners, of everything that we think of as our own! (Col 3:23; 1 Peter 4:10; Matthew 25:20-21)

Being a steward does not mean our possessions are of no value to us; and there is nothing intrinsically wrong from getting enjoyment from what we possess. The problem comes when those possessions become not useful, not just enjoyable, but ***objects of our affection.*** The problem comes when we **forget to give God the Glory** for whatever we possess, and start to congratulate ourselves for the excellent work we've done in obtaining them!

How might we give Glory to God? We give Him thanks and we praise Him and we share that with others, but primarily we need to use our *stuff* to do what we're commanded to do: Love God and love others. It sure seems to come down to that every time doesn't it? So, when we have possessions that have served their purpose for us, and they could be useful or bring joy to another, we need to find a way to make that happen.

"No one can serve two masters; for either you will hate the one and love the other, or you will be devoted to the one and despise the other. You cannot serve both God and money." (Matthew 6:24 NIV)

"Take care and be on your guard against all covetousness, for one's life does not consist in the abundance of possessions." (Luke 12:15 ESV)

"For the love of money is the root of all kinds of evil." (1 Timothy 6:10 ESV)

"But f anyone has the world's goods and sees his brother in need, yet closes his heart against him, how does God's love abide in him?" (1 John 3:17 ESV)

> *Prayer: Dear Heavenly Father, We all know in our hearts that 'the best things in life are free,' and yet we lust after new models of everything from cars to phones to computers. Direct Your Holy Spirit to point us to the sunset, to the moon and the stars, to the ocean surf, to a walk through a garden on a sunny day, to remind us that all good things come from above and we are only caretakers. Lead us from temptation Lord, keep us from allowing possessions to take on an importance that turns them into little idols in our path. Help us to use the gifts with which You have trusted us, to love others and advance Your Kingdom here on earth, giving You the Glory and the Praise! AMEN*

MAY 6

Stonecatchers

"Now Moses, in the Law, commanded us that such [adulterers] should be stoned. But what do You say?....He raised Himself up and said to them, 'He who is without sin among you, let him throw a stone at her first.'" (John 8:5,7 NKJV)

I recently finished a book entitled, ***Just Mercy,*** by Bryan Stevenson, which I believe every school in America should have as required reading. For the most part, it recounts several cases that represent phenomenal miscarriages of justice, wrought by a legal system that is clearly broken. More startling still, is the documentation provided that such travesties have left the poor, the ethnic minority, the young, and the disabled, as their often, completely helpless, targets. The author relates the story of the ***The Equal Justice Initiative,*** a non-profit which he founded in Alabama, nearly forty years ago, and its tireless efforts to halt the executions of individuals who were clearly wrongfully convicted. More often than not, this happened as a result of bigotry and malice, rather than simple failure to ascertain the truth. The actual facts that demonstrated the truth, were often known, but simply withheld or distorted in order to obtain a conviction. Over time, they also took on hundreds of cases in an effort to stop first, the death penalty, and second, the sentence of life in prison without parole, for juveniles. One would have to read the book to comprehend the depth of the hatred, fear and prejudice which have grown first out of slavery, then the collapse of Reconstruction, then a Jim Crow society tailored for oppression, and finally out of disproportionate and extreme levels of mass incarceration. To call the stories 'heartbreaking" is like calling the ocean "big."

At one point, when Bryan is especially disheartened and contemplating quitting, he saw an old woman sitting on a bench outside the courtroom, whom he had seen on multiple previous occasions. They made eye contact and she motioned him over to sit with her. He assumed she was there for a relative. No, she told him, she just comes there because "she's supposed to." What did she mean he asked her, as she looped her arm in his? She told him how her grandson had been murdered by two other kids, years ago. She had come every day for two weeks to that trial and in the end, the judge sent those two children to prison forever, with no chance of parole. At first, she thought that would make her feel better. But eventually she found her tears were for those boys as much as her grandson. She started coming to the courthouse just to comfort families of the victims. Then she realized that many of the people crying in the halls were families of the accused. *"I started letting anybody lean on me who needed it. All this grief and violence...people shooting each other and hurting each other like they don't care. I don't know, it's a lot of pain. I decided that I was supposed to be here to catch some of the stones people cast at each other."*

The author came to realize that self-righteousness, fear, and anger have led to even the Christians hurling stones at people who have fallen down, despite knowing they are called to forgive and show compassion. No, like the old woman at the courthouse, we all have to become *stonecatchers*! We are all broken. We all sin. ***And yet, all of us are much more than just our worst act.*** If you tell a lie, you're not a liar, you're someone who lied. If you steal, you are more than just a robber. If you kill someone, you are more than just a murderer. How else can we Believers be Saints who sometimes sin? Instead of being defined by our unity with Christ, we would simply be sinners and nothing more, defined only by our crimes.

Mercy is often confused with Grace. Mercy is when punishment is withheld, that *we do deserve*. On the other hand, Grace is when we are given a gift, that *we don't deserve*. When Christ died for us on the cross, it was a mercy because the punishment we deserved was withheld, but it was Grace as well, because God offered His Son to obtain our forgiveness while we were still undeserving. Stevenson calls *"just mercy"* that which we offer to the undeserving, creating reconciliation and love. *It is when mercy is least expected that it is most potent.* It is what we need to break the cycle of victimization, retribution and suffering. He says that all of us are caught in a web of hurt and brokenness in our lives, but that can also be a web of healing and mercy.

Stonecatchers. I love that term! Jesus turned away the self-righteous by challenging those without sin to cast the first stone at the adulteress. I think we are more likely to come upon situations where the first stones have already been cast. When we see someone different than ourselves; a different skin color, a different nationality, a disabled person, mentally or physically or both, a homeless person; we need to be stonecatchers, not throwers. Don't think the worst of people. Don't assume the street corner beggar is just looking for money to buy drugs or alcohol. He might be. But he might not be. When someone mistreats you; they act rudely or insensitively, or they make fun of you publicly, you have no idea what has led to their behavior. More often than not it is something painful that has happened to them. Try not to throw a stone back. When you see another being picked on, or gossiped about, or prejudiced against, catch the stone and come to their defense.

If you keep John 8:7 in mind, along with the command not to judge others in Matthew 7:1, you'll go a long way toward becoming more Christ-like and finding that peace and joy we keep talking about!

"He has shown you O man what is good; And what does the Lord require of you, But to do justly, to love mercy, and walk humbly with your God?" (Micah 6:8 NIV)

Prayer: Dear Heavenly Father, we know that You love us! Why do we have so much trouble loving others not like ourselves? What are we so afraid of? Direct Your Holy Spirit to not only keep us from throwing the first stone, but to catch the stones that others throw before they hurt their intended target! AMEN

MAY 7

Suffering

"Either God wants to abolish evil and cannot; or He can, but does not want to. If He wants to but cannot, He is impotent. If He can, and does not want to, He is wicked. But if God both can and wants to abolish evil, then why is there evil in the world? (Epicurus 300BC)

Can you remember the last time you found a baby bird, hopping limply around on the ground after having been blown out of its nest? Or perhaps you found a baby squirrel in roughly similar circumstances. Some of us have had the unfortunate run in with somewhat more imposing creatures, like encountering an injured dog, coyote or fox on the side of the highway. As you approached to see how you might render aid, I'll wager they all exhibited the same response…terror. They either tried to get away, or they tried to bite you or both. Why would they do that when all you were doing was trying to help? The obvious answer is that in their agony and pain and fear, they have no idea that you are *trying to help*.

When Professor of Philosophy at Boston College, Peter John Kreeft, PhD., was confronted with the question of how could there be such suffering in a world where there is supposedly an omnipotent loving God, he drew on a metaphor using similar imagery to that of our injured wild animal. Dr Kreeft, the author of the acclaimed book, *Making Sense Out of Suffering,* was interviewed by Lee Strobel who was writing *The Case for Faith,* and researching responses to the eight great objections to Christianity, the most common of which is, why is there suffering. Dr. Kreeft was presented with horrific examples of suffering, everything from WW I nerve gas, to the Holocaust, the slaughter of Nanjing, the killing fields of Cambodia, the Rwandan genocide, Serb-Croat horrors, to the torture and disappearance of an entire generation in South America. How could a loving God even exist? Dr. Kreeft first noted that claiming God *could not possibly exist,* was the height of intellectual arrogance. It assumes that God, in His infinite wisdom and complete knowledge of the future, sees things the same way we see things, in our very finite and limited understanding, with no knowledge of the future. That is of course, absurd.

Dr. Kreeft posits that we imagine a bear caught in a trap. A hunter, who wishes to free this particular animal, approaches with a rifle, tranquilizer darts, and rope. The bear will become even more angry and agitated and fearful. The hunter then shoots the bear with a dart in order to render him defenseless while he frees him. In so doing, he actually has to push the leg further into the trap in order to get the jaws open and release the injured appendage. If the bear were not adequately sedated, it would undoubtedly kill the hunter, misunderstanding his attempts to free him as attacks. Why did the bear react this way? Because he's not nearly as smart as a human. Dr. Kreeft suggests there is logically a much greater gulf between the infinite intelligence of an omnipotent God and man, than there is between the man and the bear! We know no more about the motivations of God than that bear does about us. But, just as the bear could choose to trust the man, we can choose to trust God, despite the suffering we don't understand.

We won't put the question of suffering in the world to rest, in one devotional. Suffering in our world, often seems to come from the free will we have been given. God created us good, but with the potential to do badly, which we appear to do every day. Strobel says that if we ask God, "Why do you allow people to suffer in pestilence and starvation?" He could very well respond with, "I was just going to ask you the same question!"

The answer to the question is not philosophical. The answer is a person: Jesus Christ. Jesus suffered and died a horrific death when He was innocent, taking our sins onto Himself, abandoned on a cross on a hillside. But then He conquered death, and turned what man meant for evil into what God meant for good!

The next time you contemplate suffering, like the ancient Greek philosopher in our opening quote, whether on a worldly scale or because a loved one is suffering very near to home, remember that ***we are the bear***. Combine that with your faith that the Word is true, that God will work everything for good for those who love Him, (Romans 8:28) and you have stumbled upon the recipe for hope, peace, and the contentment that we call, joy.

"For by Him all things were created, in heaven and on earth, visible and invisible, whether thrones or dominions or rulers or authorities—all things were created through Him and for Him." (Colossians 1:6 NIV)

"Where were you when I laid the foundations of the earth? Tell me if you have understanding?" (Job 38:4 NKJV)

Prayer: Dear Heavenly Father, forgive us our arrogance when we question Your very existence simply because our understanding is so limited! Remind us through Your holy Spirit that Your thoughts are not our thoughts and Your ways are not our ways! We beg You on behalf of those who are suffering Lord, bring them relief, if not in this life than the next! Bring them the assurance that You are indeed Sovereign, and that good will win out over evil, no matter the time frame, just as You have promised us in your Word. AMEN

MAY 8
Doubt

"Are faith and intellect really incompatible? Is it possible to be a thinker and a Bible-believing Christian at the same time? Some don't believe so." (Lee Strobel)

This is essentially the question that has been asked of me since graduating from medical school forty years ago! These questions only intensified after I finished seminary in 2014. There are those who just feel that the findings of modern science on every front, from geology, to biology, to archaeology, even to astrophysics, have made Biblical precepts untenable. They feel that belief in an all-powerful, loving, God, is simply what Karl Marx said it was, an opiate for the masses. Others, while not abandoning the *possibility* of an omnipotent force beyond our conception, still have serious doubts about the Judeo-Christian basis for our faith, not the least of which is an adherence to the Bible as the ultimate source of truth.

No less than the author of the *Narnia Chronicles*, C.S. Lewis, had these kinds of serious doubts. He was an agnostic until mid-life, when, largely through the influence of his good friend J.R.R. Tolkien, he became a Christian while a professor at Oxford University. The Reverend Billy Graham, perhaps the most influential Christian evangelist of the twentieth century struggled with these doubts, finally leading to a split between himself and his best friend, Charles Templeton. The latter had been a journalist who became a Christian following a night at a sleazy strip joint with co-workers. His self-loathing led him to an awakening in prayer, that actually resulted in him quitting journalism and turning to ministry. He later toured with Billy Graham, but doubts began to plague him, and he became convinced that his conversion was driven simply by youthful emotion. When he began to chip away at his friend's faith that the bible had been inspired by God, Graham began to doubt literally everything about his faith. He searched the scriptures, he prayed, he contemplated all the things that modernity tells us are in conflict with the Bible.

In spiritual crisis, one night before the Los Angeles Crusade that would launch his world-wide ministry, Strobel tells us in *A Case for Faith*, from which our opening quote is taken, that Graham was walking at midnight through the San Bernadino Mountains when he finally just dropped to his knees, bible in hand. He confessed to the Lord that He couldn't answer many of the philosophical, scientific and psychological questions that were seeding his doubts. He prayed, *"Father, I am going to accept this as Thy word—by faith! I'm going to allow faith to take me beyond my intellectual questions and doubts, and I will believe from now on that this is Your inspired word!"* Graham testified many times later in life, that he felt a spiritual battle had been fought and won that night. He believed not all his questions had been answered, but that a bridge had been crossed.

You don't have to be in the sciences like I am, to have doubts. What could be more implausible than the Creator of the Universe deciding to come to earth as a poor infant in a backwater corner of the known world, to live, teach and be executed, and then be raised from the dead? While there are those who have devoted their lives, research and writings to proving that is, in fact, exactly what happened, for most of us, *believing takes faith by definition!* If God had chosen to reveal Himself in an absolutely incontrovertible fashion for all the world, all the cultures, all the ethnic groups, in order to save us from ourselves, well, that wouldn't require any faith would it? If it required no faith, and it required no free will, then His self-revelation would be a Star Trek episode, not a work of the Spirit, and we would be automatons, not humans.

There are many in the modern sciences who have bridged the gap between the objective findings of their disciplines and faith. Frank Morison's Classic from 1930, *Who Moved the Stone?* and Gary Habermas' *The Case for the Resurrection* (2004) both make convincing historical arguments for Christ's resurrection. Dr. Francis Collins, current head of the NIH, penned the *Language of God* after becoming the first to sequence the human genome. Dr. Kenneth Samples has written *Without a Doubt,* tackling many of the philosophical objections to the Christian faith. Canadian astrophysicist, Hugh Ross, has written many books detailing the scientific veracity of the Bible, not the least of which was *The Creator and the Cosmos.* His organization, ***Reasons to Believe,*** has strived to demonstrate that each new discovery across many scientific fields builds the case for faith rather than undermining it. Particle physicist, Michael Strauss, PhD, from the University of Oklahoma, has written and lectured extensively on what he feels to be the utter implausibility of atheism. Jeff Zweerink, a PhD in high energy astrophysics, has written *Is there Life Out There?* Fazale Rana PhD, in biochemistry, has written books exploring evolution and faith such as *Origins of Life, The Cell's Design,* and *Creating Life in the Lab.* There are of course, hundreds of others.

But if you are just now exploring Christianity, or if you accepted Christ decades ago, you will, without a doubt, have doubts! That is the nature of faith. *"Lord, I believe, help my unbelief!"* This is the cry of the anguished father who brought his child to Jesus. (Mark 9:17-23) This needs to be our cry as well! It is normal to have doubts. It is okay to have doubts. But don't let them overwhelm you. Don't let them sink your boat like the storm-tossed sea of which James speaks. (James 1:6)

Instead, perhaps bring the image of Billy Graham to mind, on his knees, in the dark, in tears, with just his bible in his hand; and then rising up, renewed, refreshed, and resolute, prepared to do just what he did, walk humbly, love mercy, act justly, and give God the Glory for the next sixty years.

"As an astronomer, my investigations into both the cosmos and the bible, have

shown me a more wondrous personal God behind nature than I could ever have imagined." (Hugh Ross, PhD)*

> ***Prayer:** Dear Heavenly Father, we love You and we trust You! When we have doubts about what we cannot see, remind us of all that we believe so firmly without sight or understanding, from gravity to subatomic physics to love! In the year of my grandmother's birth no one believed we could fly. In the year of my mother's birth, no one believed a picture could be transmitted through the air. In the year of my birth, no one believed we could ever reach the moon. Let history teach us to believe in the things we can't conceive of! As we learn more, we understand that we know very little. Let the Holy Spirit strengthen our faith rather than diminish it as we take our stuttering steps toward knowledge. AMEN*

MAY 9

Warning

"If you ever forget the Lord your God and follow other gods and worship and bow down to them, I testify against you today that you will surely be destroyed" (Deuteronomy 8:19, NIV)

Many of you reading this may not be old enough to remember the twenty years that Andy Rooney spent doing weekly spots on 60 Minutes, but they were a bright spot in the week for those of us that do. Andy was a humorist with a dry sardonic wit. He used observations of everyday occurrences as the basis for his humor. I remember once he told a story of having realized just as the train pulled out, that he had dropped a glove on the train platform. It was a freezing cold winter day in NYC. His seatmate was astonished to see him slide down the window and toss a leather glove out, to land on the platform. "Why on earth did you just do that?" Andy responded, "Well, I just realized I had dropped the other glove by mistake before boarding. Whoever finds it, now has a chance of finding its mate and making his day! They were expensive gloves!"

There is a fabulous book of his entitled, *A Year of Minutes*. One of the entries is about warning labels. He points out that all these companies spend millions on advertising and labelling to try and get you to buy and use their product, and then the government insists on a label to tell you all the ways it could kill you! I mean, do you *really need* a label that tells you not to drink varnish? Do many people really iron their clothes while wearing them? Is there really a mother who would fail to remove her baby from the stroller before collapsing it? One label said, "DO NOT USE THIS PRODUCT IF YOU HAVE HYPERTENSION, DIABETES, THYROID DISEASE, GLAUCOMA, OR ASTHMA. DO NOT USE THIS PRODUCT IF YOU ARE ON A MONOAMINE OXIDASE INHIBITOR." *Really?* Andy Rooney had no idea if he was taking a monoamine oxidase inhibitor, but he knew it would be bad to use this stuff if he were! He suggested a label on all products that says simply, "BE CAREFUL IF YOU USE THIS, CAUSE

THERE'S A GOOD CHANCE IT WILL KILL YOU."

The Bible is replete with warnings. Let's not overlook the very first warning in scripture informing Adam and Eve what would happen if they ate of the fruit of the tree of knowledge of good and evil! (Genesis 2:16-17) Many chapters of Deuteronomy, as the above verse demonstrates, are particularly onerous. There are many proverbs that warn what will happen if you take a certain path or say certain things. *"A man who hardens his neck after much reproof, Will suddenly be broken beyond remedy." (Proverbs 29:1 NIV)* There are 26 more warning passages in this chapter alone! Some people just exploring Christianity, or at least the Bible for the first time, could get the impression that our God is an angry one seeking to punish us at every turn!

The mature Christian understands however, that the Bible is a progressive revelation of God's character, and that the 613 laws He provided to Moses would naturally generate lots of warnings re the consequences of ignoring them. God created us in His image, loves us, and wants the best for us, despite the fact that humanity has rebelled against Him from the start. (Romans 1) The law showed us clearly that perfect adherence to it, was humanly impossible. Once we finally realize that, we also recognize the need for a Savior! The penalty for continually sinning has always been death, ever since the Garden of Eden. Avoiding that fate requires reconciliation with God, and the Mosaic Law clearly demonstrated that we weren't going to achieve the righteousness to do that by trying and failing to follow all the rules! In His Grace, God offered us a way back to Him, through the atoning sacrifice of Christ on the cross. He took our punishment for us, and then conquered death in His resurrection. We are now clothed in His righteousness and through Him, achieve eternity!

Does that mean the warnings of scripture are not for us? Of course not. The punishment for failure to adhere to them, still applies for those who are not yet saved by Grace through faith in Christ. They will die. But for those of us who are Christians, we have been granted eternal life. However, remember that Jesus told us He came to fulfill the law, not to abolish it. (Matthew 5:17) Paul admonishes us that Grace given to us, while completely undeserving, certainly does not mean we can go on sinning, i.e. ignoring the Law! (Romans 6:1)

So, when you're looking for guidance, take a look at Proverbs. Rather than thinking of these verses as warnings, think of most of them as just plain old good advice for living abundantly! And I would think about using the *Message* or the *Bible in Basic English* translations. Proverbs is not poetry like Psalms. Its good hard truth, and understanding the verses is more important than enjoying them for their fluidity! Take Proverbs 19:7 as an example: *"The person who tells lies gets caught; the person who spreads rumors is ruined."* The Ten Commandments tell you not to lie too, and the punishment used to be stoning. Here's how to think of it. In light of our salvation, better to understand that your sins are now forgiven, once and for all, but now you have the heart of Christ and the Holy Spirit indwelling to help you catch yourself when you, for example, start to spread gossip or set out to tell a little bit of an untruth!

The Bible's warning labels are usually more sensical than *"Do not eat the buttons on your shirt, or you may need a doctor."* God wants you to know that to live the life He wants you to live, there are certain parameters you should stay within! Think of many of the warnings you read in scripture as God telling you,

"If you really love Me and want to love others as I've asked, then I would seriously consider NOT doing..."

"What then? Shall we sin because we are not under the Law but under Grace? May it never be!" (Romans 6:15 NIV)

"Let angry people endure the backlash of their own anger; if you try to make it better, you'll only make it worse." (Proverbs 19:19 Message)

We humans keep brainstorming options and plans, but God's purposes prevail." (Proverbs 19:21 Message)

> ***Prayer: Dear Heavenly Father, thank you for caring enough to give us rules to live by; and thank you for loving us enough to realize we can never comply fully in our own power. You have forgiven us even before we sin, but also given us the Holy Spirit so that if we have ears to hear and eyes to see, we will choose the better option each time. AMEN***

MAY 10

Vibrato

"There is nothing more rare, nor more beautiful, than a woman being unapologetically herself; comfortable in her imperfection. That is the true essence of beauty." (Steve Mariboli)

There are many complexities involved in making beautiful music come from a stringed instrument.

First, there is the instrument itself. There are the types of wood used: for instance the backs of maple and the tops of spruce; the actual shape of the instrument; the type and heaviness of varnish; the types and caliber of strings; the cut of the bridge; the shape of the sound holes; the quality of the fittings from pegs to neck to nut to bridge. Next, there is the type of wood and shape and flexibility of the bow, and the type of hair used. Finally, the type of shoulder rest and the actual size of the musician relative to the size of the instrument utilized.

Second, there is the technique and proficiency of the player. The quality and type of their instruction over time, is of course, related to their quality of play, but also their innate gifts in terms of hearing and coordination..

Third, there is the interpretation of the music itself. A written score can only go so far in dictating the sound which comes from the player's instrument. Subtle alterations of rhythm, bowing, and finger placement can make for remarkably different auditory experiences derived from the very same piece of music!

Let's take *vibrato* as an example. Vibrato is the technique of rolling a finger off and on a specific note on the string, creating oscillations in the pitch. Perfect intonation, or the ability to place your finger on the fingerboard and hit *exactly* the desired pitch, particularly in the upper positions on violin or even viola, is literally impossible. While each note might be reliably clear, it will not be *absolutely* reliable in pitch; although a very good violinist and can be very, very, close, nearly all the time. Oscillating the pitch with vibrato, adds *color* to the melody, allows different moods to be communicated by the same written notes, and will include the *exact* correct pitch in the sound produced. For instance, a wide, slow vibrato creates a rich, darker, chocolatey tone, where a narrow fast vibrato creates a tone that seems almost to shimmer in the light! These different tonalities may be what the artist feels were intended by the composer, or they may simply be the personal preference of the performer to communicate his or her own feelings!

While vibrato doesn't *have to be used* to communicate the notes which the composer wished to have played, it is used to some extent, by the best violinists, on almost every note played. Why? The simple answer is: *it just sounds better!* While not the specific goal per se, vibrato does oscillate the pitch, thus technically obfuscating the intended pitch. In other words, vibrato, which all agree can add beauty and emotion and color to music, is really built off of imperfection!

Christians are the same way! We are most certainly imperfect, and it is our imperfections that lead us to dependency on the only One who is perfect! Not only that, but Christians are meant to be together! How much more glorious is the worship of the Lord when exercised with others? While a solo singer can be inspiring, how often does the magic happen when there are multiple voices singing together, just as the vibrato recruits multiple surrounding pitches! There are life applications as well. Often in marriage, the strengths of one seem to perfectly balance the weakness of the other. While the imperfections of each help define their individuality, together they form a new being whose synergism is more perfect even than it is additive! Just like marriage, developing a beautiful vibrato comes not without effort. I can tell you that there is some pain involved. But the end result is a more beautiful, stronger, more joyful noise, even though the *exact pitch* is only a part of what the ear hears! Christians, working and worshipping *together, is exactly* what the Lord intended. His love for us, ours for Him, and our love for each other, all combine to make a sound that is more perfect in the combination of our imperfections! *Vive la difference!*

"'My Grace is sufficient for you, for My strength is made perfect in weakness.' Therefore, most gladly I will rather boast in my infirmities, that the power of Christ may rest upon me." (2 Corinthians 12:9 NKJV)

"To banish imperfection is to destroy expression, to check exertion, to paralyze vitality." (John Ruskin)

"Do not forsake meeting together, as some are in the habit of doing, but let us encourage one another." (Hebrews 10:25 NIV)

"I praise you, for I am fearfully and wonderfully made!" (Psalm 139:14 NIV)

Prayer: Dear Heavenly Father, we thank you that You love us in our imperfection! Your Grace is indeed sufficient for us. Remind us daily as well, that we are better together, just as we are better united with You! Each of us in our varied imperfections, united in purpose, make a more joyful noise than we ever could apart! AMEN

MAY 11
Dintism

"What you have learned and received and heard and seen in me---practice these things, and the God of peace will be with you." (Philippians 4:9 NIV)

Recently, my brother, the retired heart surgeon now accomplished potter, classical guitarist, bridge player, sailor, and novice cellist, among other things, sent me a copy of a speech delivered by the late classical cellist, Lynn Harrell. Twenty-five years ago, he gave the Commencement Address at the Cleveland Institute of Music. He was the principle cellist of the well-respected, Cleveland Symphony Orchestra, from age 20-27, but went on to teach at many institutions including the Royal Academy of Music for many years, and became one of the most sought after and best loved classical musicians in the world. He passed away several days ago at age 76, on April 27, 2020.

He was of special interest to me, since he grew up in Dallas and attended Denton High School. His father, an operatic baritone died of cancer when Lynn was only 15. Three years later, his mother, a classical violinist, died in a car wreck on her way to Fort Worth to perform a recital. By then Lynn had already studied at Juliard in the summers and had had his debut at Carnegie Hall. At age fifty and internationally renowned, he was invited to give the commencement address mentioned. The person that posted it on Facebook titled the post "*Keep Going.*" While it wasn't clear if that had been Mr. Harrell's title for the address, it is nevertheless appropriate.

When he joined the Cleveland Symphony at age 18, he remembers thinking that he had "made it," just sitting in the back row as a third cellist, proud of his technical proficiency, and his youth when many of his friends were still in music school. But he quickly began feeling empty inside, contemplating forty years of being invisible, playing along with the herd! Was this really it? Not too long after joining the symphony, the director, George Szell, kept him after practice and literally read him the riot act in an absolute tirade! He told Lynn he was unprepared, unschooled, and apparently bored, and there is no such thing as boring music, only boring people! Right then and there he woke up and began studying the score closely, practicing the *music* and not just technique. He studied the architecture of the whole piece, the lines weaving through all the other instruments. But mostly Szell taught him to take pride in his playing once again, not the narcissistic type, but by immersing himself in the psyche and personality of the composer, and truly understanding the music. There is never a moment in a lifetime of music when you can say, "this is the moment, now I have arrived." There are frustrating pauses, whirlwind advances and many times when you just feel totally lost. But Lynn Harrell learned a secret one day.

The secret lies in the concept behind the English term "DINTISM." It means you learn "*by sheer dint of doing.*" You just have to keep going. It isn't a competition. It's only about yourself. It's about one practice after another, after another, after another, and coming to eventually understand that you never understand it all! Mr. Harrell was asked once if he got bored playing the same Dvorak Concerto over and over? Bored? Are you kidding, he responded. At twenty he had thought he knew everything there was to know about that concerto. At fifty, he had long since realized that he learned something new every single time he either played, or heard someone else play, the piece. He once heard Pablo Casals, perhaps the most famous cellist who has ever lived, play the piece when he was in his 90's. His technique couldn't even be called 'good' anymore, and it was difficult for the master to even hold the bow, but Harrell said it was the most moving, dynamic, powerful rendition he had ever heard! It was alive with soul and Casals' own belief in music!

Christians often have the same perspective as the young musician who thinks he has learned what he needs to know about a piece of music. So, you understand the Gospel message, and now it's well, a little boring to hear it or read it over and over again. *Really?* I am sixty-four years old and have either read through or heard the bible read through completely, roughly twenty times. Yet, you could put your finger on any set of verses in scripture, even the familiar famous ones, and if I spent twenty minutes prayerfully studying them, looking at commentaries, reviewing the context, I would then see things *I had never seen before*. This is what Paul is talking about in our opening quotation! Paul wants you to keep learning, keep receiving, keep listening and then *put what you are learning into practice, over and over and over again!* That is where the Peace of God lies! Immerse yourself in the Word if you are going to read it at all. As Lynn Harrell learned, you can read the notes on the page and play them along with everyone else, or you can study their patterns, their feeling, the emotion of the composer, and then you can really bring the music to life!

We need to study the Word, read it, hear it, discuss it with others, seek out the *Composer's* intention, and then pass it on by living it ourselves!!

"For the things we have to learn before doing them, we learn by doing them." (Aristotle)

"You don't need to justify your love, you don't need to explain your love, you just need to practice your love. Practice creates the Master." (Don Miquel Ruiz)

"Practice doesn't make perfect, Practice reduces the imperfection." (Toba Beta)

Prayer: Dear Heavenly Father, we love You and the incredible world You have created! Forgive us when in our arrogance we think we understand it all, when in reality what we have yet to learn is endless! This applies in music, in science, in personal interaction, in any endeavor of life; and we know it applies to our relationship with Christ! Spur us to take some portion of each day and learn more about You Lord and what you would have us understand! AMEN

MAY 12

For Granted

"When it comes to life the critical thing is whether you take things for granted, or take them with gratitude." (G.K. Chesterton)

Let's see now. How far back do I have to think before realizing I have taken something for granted? Oh wait, it might have happened fifteen seconds ago when I started typing this on my MacBook Pro, in my environmentally controlled office, sitting in my comfortable, leather, swivel chair, with my steaming Starbuck's at my left hand! Oh, and I have a job where they pay me to help people; and I have a that job in the middle of a pandemic that has left 21 million unemployed, and...

You get the picture! I could go on for the next several hours thinking of things that I take for granted every day. Now, admittedly, there isn't anyone I can easily contact on my new iphone to thank personally for my MacBook Pro, or my chair, or even really, my office. When I got up this morning, (out of my Sleep Number controlled softness bed) and took a hot shower, I followed that up with my Qi Dong exercises and my 24 move standard Yang Tai Chi. But then I opened my top drawer, took out my underwear and a rolled up pair of socks, and then my neatly folded scrubs from the drawer below, and dressed in my closet before quietly exiting the bedroom to go feed the cat, feed the fish, and get my first cup of coffee (from the automated pot that came on at the prescribed time, while I was in the shower!)

Why I am telling you all this? Because not only am I Blessed beyond credulity in terms of my career, my home, and my life circumstance in general, but *somehow my laundry got folded neatly and magically appeared exactly where it always does, especially for my convenience!* Was it a miracle? Well, in a way, it was a miracle, because it was my wife's doing! When I look around our home, almost everything I see is something whose position, condition, or very existence is something I have taken for granted, but in fact, should be thanking my wife for daily! Of course, my health, our beautiful weather, the people with whom I work, my children and grandchildren, my mom alive and well at 91, my brother, and my friends are all things that I need to be thankful for every day.

Even though I said I don't know who to call on my iphone to thank for my computer, my chair, my office, or even the weather, or my health, there is of course someone I can thank! The Bible tells us that every good and perfect gift comes from above! (James 1:17) Well, in our modern world of science, we know that God is not "above" per se, but that's what the metaphor means! We need to thank all the people around us whose actions enrich our own lives; and we need to thank our God for them! When we take things for granted, those things tend to slip by unnoticed. When I thank my wife for always taking care of me, and having my scrubs in the drawer, or food in the fridge, or food on the table for that matter, *then her service takes on the significance it deserves!* The same is true with our heavenly Father. When we walk out the door on a sunny, breezy, day and enjoy our walk to the car on the way to lunch, the beautiful day seems just part of the everyday routine. But if we take a moment, just a fleeting moment, to think a silent prayer, thanking the Lord for the spectacular natural world He has given us, then we appreciate Him in a way that would have been lost had we just let the moment pass.

Say "thank you" more than you have in the past. Don't take the people in your life for granted. Say "thank you" to God more than you have in the past. Don't take the God that gave you life, for granted either!

"In taking life for granted, we completely fail to notice it." (Stephen Batchelor)

"Give thanks to the Lord, for He is good; his love endures forever" (1 Chronicles 16:34 NIV)

"Rejoice always, pray continually, give thanks in all circumstances; for this is God's will for you in Christ Jesus." (1 Thessalonians 5:16-18 NIV)

Prayer: Dear Heavenly Father, have your Holy Spirit stop us in our tracks the next time we think on how lovely a day, situation, or person we have encountered, but fail to give You thanks! AMEN

MAY 13

Starting the Subaru

Starting the Subaru at Five Below *(Stuart Kestenbaum)*

After six Maine winters and 100,000 miles, when I take it to be inspected,
I search for gas stations where they just say beep the horn and don't ask me to
Put it on the lift, exposing its soft rusted underbelly.
Inside the record
of commuting: apple cores, a bag from McDonald's, crushed
Dunkin' Donuts cups,
A flashlight that doesn't work
And one
That does, gas receipts
Blurred beyond Recognition.
Finger tips
Numb, nose
Hair frozen, I pump the accelerator
And turn the key. The battery
Cranks,
The engine gives 2 or 3 low groans and
Starts. My God it starts. And
Unlike
My family in the house, the
Job I'm
Headed towards, the poems in my briefcase,
The dreams I had last night,
There is
No questions about what Makes sense.
White exhaust billowing
From the tail pipe,
Heater blowing, this car is
Going to
Move me, it's going to take
Me places.

Ever had a day where you just can't have one more thing go wrong? One thing after another, and often one thing exactly at the same time as another, just doesn't work. It, or maybe they, just didn't do their job and as a consequence, your life just got a little harder! You feel like the camel just waiting for that last spine crushing straw, that will finally break your back.

I'm having a day like that today, but I'm using lunch to write down these thoughts. Some days are just so frustrating. It seems like everything you touch falls apart, whether that be a railing on your backyard deck, a tool, a project or even a relationship! You just want to stop and say, "GOD! Could you pleeeaaasssse throw me a bone here? Could you give me a break for one minute?

Evidently the poet Stuart Kestenbaum was having just this kind of a day. He just couldn't make sense of his family, his job, the poems he'd written, or even the dreams he'd had! But through all that emotional and intellectual turmoil, he could rely on one thing: that old Subaru. It started just like it always did, and it got him from point A to point B.

Just about everybody in Maine owns a Subaru; just like we noted when visiting Montana. Even my nephew who lives in Blue Hill owns a Subaru. So maybe they will forgive me when I draw this analogy. *Jesus is just like your old Subaru!!* Okay, at least someone reading this will think it blasphemy. But what I mean is this: when you're down in the dumps, when you're disheartened, discouraged, frustrated, exhausted and maybe even scared, your Savior is *right there with you!!* Incredibly, He's been through *much worse than you are experiencing* and He came out the other side! More than that, He's promised to be there for you to the point that He has taken up residence right in your heart in the form of the Holy Spirit! When you really need Him, when you turn the ignition key with prayer, which is really just calling out His name in your head, He starts right up! In fact, He starts up every single time, no matter how cold it is where you are.

There's a wonderful little book called, *My Heart, Christ's Home,* by Robert Boyd Munger. Munger takes you on an imaginary tour of his home, greeting Jesus in the living room, asking to help you clean out the junk in your closets, discussing your various appetites in the kitchen. Well, it's a memorable metaphor, but Munger never takes Christ to the garage, at least as far as I recall. If he had, He might have found an old Subaru there, and Christ would have smiled as He encountered it. He would have said that He'd once heard of a crazy guy who said that He, the Savior, the Creator of the Universe, was like this beat up old Subaru! When He asked the owner if the old car was reliable, the owner would have answered, "She's not much for looks, but yea, she starts every time!" I like to think Jesus would have laughed then, and exclaimed, "Well then, I guess that crazy guy was right!"

"The servant grew up before God—a scrawny seedling, a scrubby plant in a parched field. There was nothing attractive about Him, nothing to cause us to take a second look. He was looked down on and passed over, a man who suffered and knew pain firsthand. One look at Him and people turned away... He took the punishment, and that made us whole. Through His bruises we are healed." (Isaiah 53:2-6 Message)

Prayer: Dear Heavenly Father, we are truly Blessed that you love us

as You do, completely, passionately, and above all, reliably! When all seems lost Lord, we can remember that all seemed lost for Your Son as well, and for His disciples, but through Grace, You turned night into day; You started that engine again and it's been starting every day since!! AMEN

MAY 14

Audible Books

"You're never too old, too wacky, too wild, to pick up a book and read to a child!" (Dr. Seuss)

My absolute earliest memory as a child is sitting on the basement stairs watching the moving men place the washer and drier in our little Cape Cod cottage in Chappaqua, New York. I was four. I know. Not a gripping tale, but factual none-the-less. But there is a flood of much warmer memories that came shortly after that, with one or the other of my mom or dad, sitting on the edge of my bed, reading to me at night. Mostly I remember stories from the original A.A. Milne, Winnie the Pooh books, such as *When We Were Very Young, Winnie the Pooh, The House at Pooh Corner,* and *Now We Are Six.* Published in the mid-20's, my grandparents had read them to my parents when they were very young as well! Other favorites were Watty Piper's *The Little Engine that Could,* and Rudyard Kipling's *The Jungle Books,* also stories my parents remember from the early 30's. My children were introduced to these same stories in the early 90's and now, my grandchildren are learning them in the new century.

Most of you will be able to think back to your own childhood and remember what it was like to be read to. There is a comfort, a warmth, a security, almost as cheesy as it sounds, a fuzzy glow that surrounds those memories. If you have your own children who are now at least adolescents, you should have no trouble at least remembering when you read to them! (Admittedly, my kids might have those memories interrupted with visions of dad frequently falling asleep in mid-sentence, long before they achieved dreamland themselves!) That feeling you remember; that sense of wonder at the story and comfort from the nearness of a loving parent, is what makes you want to repeat the sensation generation after generation. There is something special about being read to. I am addicted to reading and have been from an early age. I was raised by other bookophiles, and they instilled in my brother and I an intense love of reading the written word. But when you are read to, it is a different experience. That part of your intellect that must work to interpret the written word, is now put to rest and another part of your brain performs a similar, but different, task on the audible word.

All of this is to say that hearing a story read to you, is just very different experience from reading it yourself. The reader puts their own interpretation and inflections into it, much as a musician does when playing from a score. And if that reader is someone who loves you unconditionally like your parent, then the experience takes on multiple levels of significance.

I bet you see where this is going too! There are multiple ways for you to hear the greatest story ever told, audibly! And I promise you, if you have never tried it, the experience is totally different from reading it yourself. The Bible is the revealed Word of God to the Believer. That means that it represents an inspired message from the One who created you; the One who loves you unconditionally and eternally. Listening to the Bible read in a voice that you enjoy and appreciate is a beautiful experience that can augment both your desire to go through the Bible and to augment your understanding. Recognizing that the voice you hear reading, is really reciting the contents of a love letter from God to you, can make you feel the same as you felt curled up in your pajamas, resting in the crook of your father's arm, as he revealed a whole fantastic world to you, right before you went to sleep!

You can download the Audible app to your iOS device of course, and hear virtually any translation of the Bible read to you, just as you can the vast majority of Kindle books available from Amazon. (HINT: Try *The Dutch House* read by Tom Hanks!) Alternatively, you can listen to Daily Audio Bible (DAB) another app which you can download to your iphone or ipad or computer, and have the reader take you through the Bible in a year! There are many, many other platforms to choose from if you simply search online.

Reading aloud to your child, or to any child, is one of the very most valuable, loving and enjoyable gifts you can give! Let your Father in Heaven have a shot at the same thing. You'll be glad you did!

"If you cannot read all your books…fondle them…peer into them, let them fall open where they will, read out loud from the first sentence that arrests the eye, set them back on the shelves with your own hands, arrange them on your own plan so that if you do not know what is in them, you at least know where they are. Let them be your friends; let them at any rate, be your acquaintances." (Winston Churchill)

"Vocabulary and coherent sentences can't be downloaded onto paper unless they've first been uploaded to the head—by reading or being read to." (Jim Trelease)

"Fairytales do not tell children that dragons exist. Children already know dragons exist. Fairytales tell then that dragons can be defeated." (G.K. Chesterton)

Prayer: Dear Heavenly Father, thank you that You saw fit to tell us Your story, and to do it in a love letter just for us! Let us remember the Bible's intent, before we make the mistake of neglecting to hear what You have to say! Just like our angst in a movie when the love letter that would make all the difference gets lost or worse, is purposefully unread, we ask Your Spirit to nudge us so that we will make the effort to curl up in the crook of Your arm and let You read to us! AMEN

MAY 15

Drowning

"Why are you so downcast, O my soul? Why so disturbed within me? Put your hope in God, for I will yet praise Him, my Savior and my God." (Psalm 42:5,11; 43:5 NIV)

When you sail a boat on the open water, especially a big boat, it's important that you frequently review your "man overboard" drill. Whether we're on the 35 foot *Raise Me Up*, on Lake Texoma, or the 25 foot *Adagio*, on the coast of Maine, we go over the steps almost every time we go out. You begin with a life preserver of course, and if not always worn, it must at least be readily accessible, and everyone aboard needs to know where theirs is stored. In a tiny boat the risk is capsizing and the only safety precaution is your life preserver. In a larger boat, the risk is falling or being knocked overboard, and the safety precautions include a set series of actions.

First, one person yells out "man overboard" so that all eyes turn aft to keep the victim in sight, at the same instant, throwing a floatation ring or cushion overboard. On the open ocean, this should include a life ring with attached whistle, 8 foot pole, strobe light and orange flag. Now, the next steps are critical. If equipped with an inboard engine, you turn it on. Release the sheets, rather than dropping sails, and come about, reversing course as quickly as possible. If the person at the helm is an accomplished sailor, and there is no engine, they come about immediately under sail, in order to retrace their course as nearly as possible. Whether one tacks, or jibes, in order to keep eyes on the swimmer depends on wind, waves, and heading at the time. Recovery is easier if you come from windward, unless high seas may drive you over the swimmer. It's a judgment call. The sailboat must then stop, using one of several methods, but most often 'heave-to.' Actual recovery technique depends on consciousness, strength, injury, and fatigue of the victim, as well as available lines, winches or ladders.

In short, its more complicated than you might think! My wife and I have gone over this, multiple times. She gets almost every step correct, and in the correct order, and virtually every time. She only forgets one thing...she ***never*** remembers the first step is to throw me a life ring! (Yes, I know there's a marriage joke in there somewhere!) But the fear of literal drowning, or of a loved one drowning, is a very real, very intense, gut reaction. Fear generated not by a valid physical danger, but by an altered emotional/psychological state, is just as intense and gut-wrenching as fear of physical danger. This fear of course, can generate exactly the same physical response, fight or flight, and exactly the same autonomic response with sweating, tremulousness, heart racing, shortness of breath, nausea and even chest pain. This anxiety or panic attack can be an accompaniment of a longer standing depression, or seemingly come out of the blue with an as yet unidentified trigger and underlying cause. A person close to me described her panic attacks as 'feeling as though her life force was being drawn out of her right through her feet." In short, you can feel like you are drowning!

Professional counseling is, and should be, the mainstay of approaching depression and anxiety. But Christians do have an advantage that others may not. Our faith in Christ can lead us to *a renewing of the mind,* as the Apostle Paul tells us in Romans 12. When we have offered our whole selves to God, in response to His Grace through Christ, the experience of His mercies in our lives can lead us to think differently about everything! Paul urges us not to be conformed to what the world does and thinks is important, not to act as others do, but instead to be *transformed by the renewing of our minds.* Our minds control our thoughts, feelings, attitudes and actions. Our lives then, in all aspects, through the influence of the Word, the Spirit and fellowship with other believers, can and do become more Christ-like!

For the Christian, there will be an intimate interplay between professional counseling and spiritual guidance as they climb out of the depths of depression. The timelines will differ for everyone. While simple platitudes or bible verses tossed out to the one drowning in depression and or anxiety, will be inadequate and often even rejected, meditating on certain scriptural passages can be a true solace for the Christian who feels that desperation one would feel with the water closing in over your head. The Psalms contain 150 songs and prayers collected over hundreds of years, many of which can remind the one hurting of God's inconceivable love for them, and of their inestimable value in their Creator's eyes. Being sensitive to the timing, the appropriate Psalm might be the life ring to which the desperate, hurting, believer can cling.

When In Fear: *"The Lord is my light and my salvation; whom shall I fear? The Lord is the stronghold of my life; of whom shall I be afraid? Wait for the Lord; be strong, and let your heart take courage; wait for the Lord!" (Psalm 27:1,14 ESV)*

When Discouraged: *"Why are you cast down, O my soul, and why are you in turmoil within me? Hope in God; for I shall again praise Him, my salvation and my God." (Psalm 42:5,11; 43:5 ESV)*

When Grieving: *"I am weary with moaning; every night I flood my bed with tears; I drench my couch with weeping...[my eye] grows weak because of all my foes...the Lord has heard the sound of my weeping. The Lord has heard my plea; the Lord accepts my prayer." (Psalm 6:6-9 ESV)*

When Overwhelmed: *"God is our refuge and strength, a very present help in trouble. Therefore we will not fear though the earth gives way, though the mountains be moved into the heart of the sea...Be still, and know that I am God!" (Psalm 46:1-3, 10 ESV)*

When Terrified: *"When I am afraid, I put my trust in you. In God, whose Word I praise, in God I trust; I shall not be afraid. What can mere flesh do to me?" (Psalm 56: 2-4 ESV)*

(Verses suggested by Micah Maddox from BibleStudyTools.com)

Prayer: Dear Heavenly Father, we love you, but in our fear and insecurity and anxiety we sometimes forget how much you love us! Help us to keep focused on Your Son, so that we are not conformed to this world, with all it contains that would draw us away from You! Once we have accepted the Gift of our salvation, let Your Spirit strengthen us,

in the face of any trial that brings us down or makes us anxious, in the knowledge that absolutely nothing in this world can separate us from Your love and eternal protection! AMEN

MAY 16

Don't Spit Into the Wind

"You don't tug on Superman's cape, You don't spit into the wind, You don't pull the mask off that old lone ranger, And you don't mess around with Jim." (Jim Croce)

You don't have to be very old before you learn by personal experience that the adage, "You don't spit into the wind," made famous by Jim Croce's ballad, *You Don't Mess Around with Jim,* (1972) can be taken both in a literal and a figurative sense. The expression means of course, that one shouldn't engage in activities that are either futile, or extremely likely to be a detriment to one's health. While the land-locked person may not realize it, the idiom certainly didn't originate with Jim Croce. Instead, it is a euphemism for the slightly more vulgar original, which was a common British nautical expression. That's right, it came from sailing! The folk rock song substitutes the word "spit" for the original four letter slang word related to a bodily function, and any sailor can tell you, that when you are out with just the boys, and the girls are nowhere to be found, no *true* sailor goes below decks to use the head! Early on however, the male sailor learns to assess the tack first, be aware of wind direction, and select the side of the boat most amenable to staying dry!

The same principle of flow dynamics behind not expectorating directly into the breeze, presents a problem for the sailor. There are 360 degrees to the compass, but in general, about 60 of them are eliminated as a directional heading by the forces of nature! Roughly 30 degrees to either side of the wind direction (direction always being the compass point from which the wind *originates*) cannot physically be the heading for a sailboat, no matter the rigging, no matter the skipper, no matter the size of the craft, no matter when in history! You simply cannot sail directly into the wind, and not exactly for the reason that most people think. We will however, delay our discussion of the physics of sail for a moment, and take you back to my childhood experiences in Maine.

The Reach, is so called, because the prevailing southwest breeze blows *across* this body of water, so that sailing up or down the Reach, usually means you have the wind coming over the beam, or side of the boat. This is 'reaching.' But if you start out at our Deadman's Cove, and you want to head out across the Reach for West Penobscot Bay, and furthermore, let's say specifically, you plan to head for Pumpkin Light, then, well, you usually have a problem. You see, Pumpkin lies just west of south, from our cottage. That means the prevailing wind often comes directly from the lighthouse!

We were in *Fledgling* on a brisk, sunny, summer afternoon, heading for Pond Island and a planned picnic. Pond lies on a heading of 240 degrees, right through the slot between Pumpkin and Little Deer Isle. Pop and I and Uncle

Don were in our classic, gaff rigged, wooden sailboat, while my dad was in the sea skiff with mom, Granny T and my brother, Scott. It was about 1964. I was eight, which means I was protected from the cold ocean spray by the bulbous orange life vest draped around by neck and tied across my chest, as dictated by the life-saving technology of the era. My grandfather was sitting on a flotation cushion on the floor of the wooden cockpit, back against the gunwale of the high side, pipe smoke streaming aft behind him. I was on the high side as well, but too short to support myself in a steep heel with my feet against, well, anything, so I was hiked up onto the narrow strip of decking surrounding the cockpit, holding onto the cleated jib sheet for stability. My uncle was relaxed on the low side, the cold water streaming past, right behind his shoulders, breeze ruffling his hair and sun on his face.

We were on a port tack, (wind coming over the left side of the boat.) Our sails were hauled all the way in, both the boom, which is the cross bar sticking aft from the mast to which the foot of the mainsail is anchored, and the jib up front, controlled by the ropes (called *sheets*) on the clew (aft corner of the triangular sail) which led back through pulleys along either side of the boat, to one cleat for each.

"Pop, I thought you said we had to go right next to Pumpkin?" I asked over the sound of the water streaming off the bow, as *Fledgling* cut cleanly through the waves.

"Yup." This was his usual gruff mono-syllabic answer, and was delivered in a tone which seemed to communicate his awareness that a stupid question would undoubtedly follow this simple observation.

"Well," I said innocently, "why aren't we pointing at it?"

Pop looked away from the telltales and right into my eyes. There was a twinkle in his, despite his roughness. He held the tiller with his right hand, keeping it toward him, with some significant effort, against the unseen forces of wind and water acting on the rudder below. With his left hand, he carefully removed the pipe as if to speak, and then coughed with that hack that so many smokers seem to have.

"Watch," he said as he replaced his old Meerschaum. "Ready about," he said to my Uncle. He pushed the tiller away slowly and Fledgling turned to port, toward the wind, and to a heading which pointed directly at the slot between Pumpkin and Deer. At first the boat heeled even more, and I scrambled to hold onto my now precarious perch, but that only lasted a second. Immediately, the boat leveled out and a tremendously loud snapping, popping, noise filled the air. As my uncle released the sheet on the starboard side, the boat pointed into the wind, which now blew past us on *both* sides of the sail. No longer at a flat angle against the port side of the sailcloth, the jib and main began flapping furiously in the wind. Despite the cacophony of the sails, and the seeming disarray of jib and main sheets flopping back and forth rapidly on the deck, you could feel the boat's way give off. In other words, she quickly slowed. Pop worked the tiller to try and keep her into the wind for longer than one would normally on a tack, or turn into and through the wind. But *Fledgling* bucked on the waves like a mare confined to a paddock she distained, and despite Pop's efforts, she completed the tack.

Now the wind came over our starboard or right side, just forward of the beam. He finally pulled in the mainsheet, bringing the boom almost parallel to the boat again, and this, with some considerable effort. Uncle Don put an end to the flapping of the jib by hauling in the sheet on my side, and then leaning on his knees across the cockpit, cleated it home. Suddenly, I was on the low side! My grandfather had deftly moved to the high side as he reigned in the mainsheet, and my uncle had stayed where he was. I didn't like the low side, so close to the rushing water, and I may have even begun to cry a little. Uncle Don put out his hand and pulled me up next to him.

"Here kiddo, plenty of room on the high side for all of us!"

That was my grandfather. It was typical that he had demonstrated the answer to my question, never uttering a response beyond, "yup and watch." It dawned on my eight-year old brain, that you can't sail directly into the wind, no matter how much you may care to. Pretty clearly, spitting into the wind would be just as ineffective!

Christians experience the same thing going through life as Fledgling did going through the water. Certain headings are simply not possible in our own power, no matter how sincerely we desire them! (John 15:5) It is faith that allows us to steer a reliable course through the peak and trough of life's waves without foundering. (James 1:6) It is faith that keeps us beating to windward, knowing that our destination is attainable, even if not directly in front of us. Spitting into the wind is exactly what tends to happen when we make our plans without God. (Proverbs 16:3,9; James 4:13-17) Our relationship to Christ is the only true constant, and ***depending on Him,*** as the sailor depends on physics, is the only choice that always works in life! Just as the vector forces on the weighted keel beneath the hull, keeps you from capsizing, keeps you from slipping laterally, and always moves you forward, so too the Holy Spirit in our lives! (John 14:16,26 1 Corinthians 3:16) Just as I depended on Pop T to steer the best course toward our island destination, we depend on Christ, the one who loves us, and has a plan and a direction for us. Just as Pop T had my best interests at heart, so too The Lord works everything together for good for those who love Him. (Romans 8:28)

"I am the vine; you are the branches. Whoever abides in me and I in him, he it is that bears much fruit, apart from Me you can do nothing." (John 15:5 ESV)

"People do their best making plans for their lives, but the Eternal guides each step." (Proverbs 16:9 Voice)

Prayer: Dear Heavenly Father, we do love You, but then we turn and immediately depend on ourselves rather than You! Holy Spirit, whisper in our ears each time we plan a course without consulting the Lord, Who has made Himself, through Grace, immediately available to us 24/7 for counsel! AMEN

MAY 17

Good News

"Just once I'd like to see the headlines say, 'Not much to print today, can't find nothin' bad to say,' because Nobody robbed a liquor store on the lower side of town, Nobody OD'ed, nobody burned a single building down, Nobody fired a shot in anger, nobody had to die in vain, We sure could use a little good news today." (Anne Murray)

I have this habit of reading out loud. It's a good thing for putting grandchildren to bed, but not quite as good, when scrolling through the news apps on my phone while my wife is trying to do something else. It's not so much that she doesn't want me to share in general; it's more that nothing I can find to read out loud seems to even remotely qualify as good news. Last night I read a story about an employee of a Dollar General who was tasked with enforcing the state's rule on donning a mask before entering an essential business, during this never-ending pandemic. Evidently, he told a young woman her daughter couldn't enter without a mask. The woman swore and spat on him and then screeched out of the parking lot in a pick-up truck. Some short time later she returned with her husband and teenage son, who began screaming at the employee. In the midst of this, the teenager took out a gun and shot the store employee in the back of the head. The deceased was the father of eight.

The horrific things that man will do to man have been chronicled since Biblical times, right back to the tortures inflicted by the Chaldeans on anyone they conquered. Daily, we are surrounded with examples of man's inhumanity to man, and in this age of modern instant communication, you hear about every one of them on the news or through social media. This only intensifies and even exaggerates the reality. One of my patients is an FBI Special Agent who works with child abduction. When I was little, fifty-five years ago in Houston, I rode my bike two miles to elementary school every day. No one in an urban area would even consider that today. But she assured me that the child abduction rate in Texas in 1965 was exactly the same as today. The difference is that every five miles on the freeway there's an electronic billboard that will give you the Amber Alert, even if it's 2,000 miles away in New Hampshire. The end effect is that you feel like kids are getting abducted all the time.

We stopped watching the televised National News eight months ago. It didn't help much, because you can't pick up your phone or turn on your computer without being inundated with bad news. In short, it's bad for the psyche. There are attempts to counter it, like the Good News Network, that strive to bring you only uplifting stories from around the globe, but to be honest, these outlets are drowned out by a cacophony of negative reports from every direction.

Scripture addresses this issue. While recognizing the sinful state of humanity emphasizes our need for a Savior, dwelling on it constantly depresses the mood and increases our cynicism to the point of almost wanting to give up. In his letter to the Colossians, Paul tells them, *"Set your minds on things above, not on earthly things...Therefore, as God's chosen people, holy and dearly loved, clothe yourselves with compassion, kindness, humility, gentleness and patience. Bear with each other and forgive one another..."* (Col 3:2,12 NIV)

In today's media driven world, this requires a conscious effort! The books we choose to read, the movies we watch, the TV shows we binge watch, all have an effect on our daily outlook. This doesn't mean watching a crime drama is in itself a bad thing. But perhaps immersing yourself in things of that ilk may not the best idea. Some of our favorite TV shows are of the genre like *Anne with an E*, or *Call the Midwife*, which deal with real life situations and emotions, but focus on the good that God can bring out of evil.

This devotional isn't intended to provide you with recommendations for your daily news sources or Netflix viewing. It is only intended to remind you that we who are born again, are not of this world, even though we are in it. We have the ultimate Good News which is the Gospel of our Lord! Commanded to love God and love each other, we are to go forth and make disciples of all the world; but the way to do that, is always by loving first. Being conscious of the fruits of the Spirit in our own lives, will enable us to do just that! Contemplating the things that Paul suggests, makes it much easier for us to avoid the cynical view of the world that can be promoted by a constant stream of 'bad news.'

Yes, the world is hurting. Yes, there are a lot of questions about how to fix it. But the answer is always the same. It's not an approach, it's a person, and that person is Jesus Christ. And that's the best reason in the world for optimism!

" What I need first of all is not exhortation, but the gospel, not directions for saving myself but knowledge of how God has saved me. Have you any good news?" (J. Gresham Machen)

"Worry looks around. Faith looks up."

"Nothing to be thankful for? Check your pulse."

"finally, whatever things are true, whatever things are noble, whatever things are just, whatever things are pure, whatever things are lovely, whatever things are of good report, if there is any virtue and there is anything praiseworthy—meditate on these things." (Philippians 4:8 NKJV)

Prayer: Dear Heavenly Father, we love You and we know we are called to love the world and spread the message that they are all loved by You! Help us to focus on Your Son, and in so doing, avoid being conformed to this world, avoid being overwhelmed by the bad news that floods in upon us every day; and instead strive to be conformed to the mind of Christ. Then we will be the Good News, and it will be expressed in us through the Fruits of the Spirit! AMEN

MAY 18

Before Dawn

"It is always darkest just before the day dawns." (Thomas Fuller, 1650)

All of us have experienced the dark. Darkness by definition is the absence of light, and it is light that gives us life. Life that comes from the warmth and nourishment of the sun. It is the light that allows us to see and make our way in the world. Metaphorically, it is Christ whom we Christians proclaim as the light of the world; who saves us from the powers of darkness and who guides us through this life and the next. No wonder darkness is associated with both evil and fear! There's a reason Darth Vader wore black! But darkness is also associated with depression. Many of us have found ourselves overwhelmed by circumstances, unable to cope any longer with the vicissitudes of life. As it seems that our options contract, we may slip gradually into a state of hopelessness, and that we know as, depression.

The darkness we experience can be in many forms. All Believers have periods of doubt, times when they think that maybe they weren't really saved after all! They look at their own actions, and seeing the sin that we all find in ourselves, become convinced that their repentance was false and their rebirth a fiction! Some have the darkness descend when they lose a loved one, or receive a bad prognosis themselves, or have lost a job, or see a family relationship deteriorating. Maybe the darkness you feel is that oppressing the entire world, with secularism on the rise, the faithful dwindling, especially in the West.

Yet, in all these scenarios, scripture rings true. We are not promised an easy life when we accept the Gift of the Gospel. *"Many are the afflictions of the righteous: but the Lord delivers him out of them all." (Psalm 34:19 NKJV)* And our Lord assures you Himself, *"In this world you will have tribulation; but be of good cheer, I have overcome the world!" (John 16:33 NKJV)* While you may feel it your darkest hour yet in this life, yet on this world; still, you may be confident that the dawn arrives *reliably,* and that the sun will rise again!

Thomas Fuller, the English historian and theologian coined our opening quotation. But King David put the concept to paper first, in Psalm 30:5, *"Weeping may endure for a night, But Joy comes in the morning."* Our perspective during the dark of night, whatever the cause, should be the same. We wait with **patient endurance** for the dawn, for as long as God deems it necessary. We wait **hopefully,** like the sailors of old, with our gaze turned toward the east, just as we are patient and hopeful for our Lord's return! We wait **in stillness**, unchanging in our beliefs, unchanging in our position, knowing that as adopted members of Christ's immediate family, He will ultimately rescue us from whatever our infirmity or insecurity, either in this life or the next. The dawn will come. Wait for it.

"Therefore, I will look to the Lord; I will wait for the God of my Salvation. My God will hear me." (Micah 7:7 NKJV)

"For the Lord is a God of justice; Blessed are all those who wait for Him." (Isaiah 30:18 NKJV)

"Be strong and of good courage; do not be afraid, nor be dismayed, for the Lord your God is with you wherever you go." (Joshua 1:9 NKJV)

"The Lord is good to those who wait for Him. It is good that one should hope and wait quietly for the salvation of the Lord." (Lamentations 3:5 NKJV)

Prayer: Dear Heavenly Father, we can talk a good game, but let's face it, it's hard to stay strong and patient when life throws us into the gutter, in the dark. But the light wouldn't be the light if there were no dark, and the Son wouldn't need to be the light of salvation if there were no darkness or evil. Direct Your Spirit to strengthen us in our waiting through whatever circumstance has plunged us into darkness. That strength may come from the assurance that dawn is just around the corner, and with it, the bright light of our freedom in Christ! AMEN

MAY 19

Fighting Words

"I am the Way, the Truth and the Life. No one comes to the Father except through Me." (John 14:6 NKJV)

"I am absolutely against religion that says one faith is superior to another. I don't see how that is anything different than spiritual racism!" (Rabbi Schmuley Boteach)

I remember writing a paper in high school about individual rights. I don't recall the title, but the theme was basically that in any civil society, my right to swing my fist stops right when it meets your face! In other words, I was free to act in any way that expressed my desires, as long as it didn't personally harm anyone else. (See DOING LIFE April 26) Logically, the right to free speech in the United States, would be expected to follow the same pattern, but legal challenges in the last several decades have sought to define exactly what constitutes "harm." There are certain words spoken in public, such as racial epitaphs, that are considered "fightin' words," and some states consider these harmful enough to restrict the use of such terms, if in fact they have tremendous potential to incite a violent response.

The claims of Christ to be the only route to salvation and reconciliation with God, fall exactly into that category, for some people, and as such, the Christian claim to exclusivity is one of the common objections to Christianity. That claim is in fact, viewed as offensive to those of other faiths: *fightin' words!* There are "moral" and very "good" people who devote their entire lives to helping others, who in fact profess no faith at all! How can it be that a belief in Jesus Christ as the Son of God, can be the only route to heaven? This claim is at the very least, politically incorrect in our current relativistic, pluralistic, society, that values tolerance over every other virtue.

For the Christian, devoting a few moments to contemplating this extremely common objection is well worthwhile. The following points are worth consideration. First, many religions claim exclusivity. Muslims believe Islam is absolutely the only valid faith, and that the Koran, in Arabic, is the only legitimate written revelation of God. Hinduism professes that the law of karma, reincarnation and the authority of the *Vedas*, are inviolate. But, Buddhism for example, was born out of Gautama Buddha's rejection of those very same *Vedas!* Sikhism, on the other had, rejects both Buddhism and Hinduism as false. Judaism claims worship of the one true God, and rejects all other worship as false. Atheists reject any religious belief as false. Every one of these perspectives is just as exclusivist as Christianity.

Second, truth, by very definition, is exclusionary. If one thing is true, then anything that contradicts it must be false. Truth excludes its opposite, as philosophers tell us.

The late Ravi Zacharias, D.D. LL.D., internationally renowned author, lecturer and theologian, admits that Christians have a checkered history down through the centuries, of presenting the truth with arrogance, not under-girded by love, and their condescension has often led to rejection and violent opposition. There is an Indian proverb he relates often. "*Once you cut off a person's nose, there's no point in giving him a rose to smell.*" Mahatma Gandhi was fond of saying, "*I like your Jesus Christ very much. It's just your Christians I don't care for.*" But despite Christians' frequent cultural insensitivity, Dr Zaharias points out in Strobel's The Case for Faith, that he knows of no Christianized country where one's life is in danger for professing another faith, as it is for Christians in some Muslim and Hindu countries today.

Many men have claimed to be God, from Caesar to multiple cult leaders, so why believe Christ?

Recognizing that Jesus never made a claim shown to be untrue, and showed no signs whatsoever of mental illness, C.S. Lewis famously stated that Christ was either a liar, a lunatic or Lord, and there was just no evidence for the first two! Theologians tell us all religions may be examined for coherence, in terms of origins, morality, meaning and destiny. Christianity asserts man was created by God, fashioned in His image, with a moral code derived from God's character. The Christian derives meaning from loving God with all his heart, soul, strength and mind. Their destiny is eternity with their Creator, made possible by the historically verifiable and widely witnessed resurrection of Christ, who conquered death and allows Believers to do the same. No other religion has coherent, non-contradictory, positions in all four of these areas. But does this invalidate the world's other religions? Aren't they basically the same? Don't they all teach about a loving Father God and the brotherhood of man?

The answer to that is an unequivocal and resounding, "No!" Buddhism believes in no God. Hinduism believes we *are God.* Brotherhood is restrictive in both Islam and Judaism. The world's religions do not teach anywhere near the same things, and while they each have aspects of truth in them, they are mutually exclusive and missing the big picture. It's really not like the blind men exploring the parts of the elephant and having their own truths. *The seeing man knows there is only one truth: it's an elephant!* Philosophers who believe all religions have a part of the truth ignore the possibility that God revealed Himself to mankind, and He did, in the incarnation of Jesus Christ! Jesus *is the truth.*

How can Christians believe a man like Gandhi may not go to heaven, but a redeemed mass murderer can? Because we humans see justice from our own standpoint. From God's standpoint, we are *all deserving of death*, ever since we rebelled and rejected Him! ***If we all miss the mark by sinning, then God's Grace becomes the most important aspect of life, not strictly our behavior.***

God has offered a way back to Him, and it's not by being as good as possible, because we can never be as good as required! The way back came through His Son, and our faith in Him, leads to our own repentance, forgiveness and redemption. ***Then we are seen by God as having Christ's perfect righteousness!*** All the world's religions except one, offer a set of instructions on how to climb the mountain to God, Nirvana, or some ethereal concept of perfection and peace. ***Only Christianity teaches that God came down the mountain to us, became fully man, and offered us salvation as a gift that we in no way deserved!*** How God deals with Gandhi is up to God, but what He has offered us through Christ is made clear in the Word.

What about the person raised in a culture where they never hear the Gospel, never meet a Christian, have never heard of Christ? Romans 1 tells us that God's attributes and eternal power have been on display since creation, exhibited in all of nature every single day! If Pascal is right, and there is a "God-sized hole" in all of us, a person of any culture and from any place can fall on their knees and beg to know God. In both the Muslim and Hindu worlds thousands have come to Christ through dreams and visions, even having never met a Christian. There is always a way in which God can respond to those who earnestly seek Him, and make them aware of His Grace.

In your quiet time today, examine your own thoughts and deeds. My guess is you will find aspects of your life that you don't feel are stellar examples of morality. We are all sinners, and those of us who have recognized it, and accepted God's grace through Christ on the cross, have conquered death already. That is peace. It's this love God has shown to us, that allows us to love our fellow man.

Prayer: Dear Heavenly Father, we ask, How can we ever thank you for the Gracious Gift of Christ, and the redemption we have been granted through faith? Help us to remember that the answer is loving You with our entire selves, and passing that love onto those around us! Guide us Spirit, so that when we tell others of Christs love, we find a way to do that without seeming arrogant or rude or condescending, but instead broken hearted for those that are missing that peace of which we are assured! AMEN

MAY 20

Freedom

"If you abide by My word, you are My disciples indeed. And you shall know the truth, and the truth shall make you free." (John 8:31-32 NKJV)

Freedom seems like a concept with which most Americans should be familiar. I mean, we are the Home of the Brave and the Land of the Free! As citizens of the United States, we enjoy freedom of speech, freedom of religion, freedom of the press, freedom of association, freedom from taxation without representation, and freedom of travel, among others. So, we ought to "get it," right? Why then, do you suppose so many Christians have trouble understanding our opening quotation from Christ Himself? Jesus says not only that the truth shall make us free, but he also says that He *IS* the truth! (John 14:6) How does He make us free, and free from what?

Steve Brown, in his fabulous book, *A Scandalous Freedom,* opens with a story from the 2000 Presidential election. A reporter noted to Joe Lieberman, the Democratic VP candidate, that many of his views seemed not too different from the Republican Presidential candidate, George W. Bush. Joe laughed and said that was like saying there's no real difference between the taxidermist and the veterinarian, because in both cases, they give you your dog back when they've finished! Steve's point in relating the story, is that the freedom experienced by most Christians today, is as different from what Christ meant by freedom, as the difference between a stuffed dog and a real dog!

Many who grew up in Christian homes, attended Sunday School, maybe even attended a Christian school, were encouraged by their parents and well-intentioned teachers to become more obedient, more pious, more...holy. They wanted us to witness to the world about the way life should be lived. Steve Brown notes that you might have been told that *freedom* really just meant you were free to be *good*, and that *Grace* is good, but you shouldn't take advantage of it! You were held to a *higher standard*, and pretty soon freedom didn't feel very free; it felt more like restraint and struggle to toe the line. Somehow people had you believing that you could live up to heightened expectations because with Christ's strength, you could do all things! (Philippians 4: 13) All you had to do was be a Christian, and you would become a 'Super-Saint!"

When you finally figure out that you are human and a sinner, it can come as quite a blow; disillusioning in fact. Had we just taken Christ's word at face value, we might be enjoying that true freedom instead of trying to walk our stuffed dog! Freedom means "exemption or liberation from control of some other person or some arbitrary power." **Christianity is not about obeying the rules, doing religious things, and being nice to people! Christianity is about, well, Christ! Go figure!** Somehow, many Believers have gotten it in their head that *freedom* doesn't mean that you are free to do whatever you want. Well, actually, it does! That's *exactly* what it means, otherwise you aren't truly free and you are trying to follow a set of rules just like...oh wait...that's right...just like they tried and failed for 2,000 years in the Old Testament!

Paul teaches that people have a choice. *"'I have the right to do anything,' you say, but not everything is beneficial...not everything is constructive. No one should seek their own good but the good of others." (1 Corinthians 10:23 NIV)* They really *are free* to do as they choose, but some choices are better than others! We tend to teach new Christians *'not to'* a lot. We tell them not to curse, not to do this or that or they might weaken their witness! Really? When Paul was faced with this issue with regard to eating meat sacrificed to idols, he told them to do whatever they wanted, but they might *consider* action that would not be offensive to others. ***Hypocrisy is what spoils witness. Pretense is what spoils witness. False piety is what spoils witness.*** Steve Brown writes that "living your life with such joy and freedom that it disturbs uptight Christians" is exactly what will draw the seeker to Christ!

Freedom, for the one who has accepted the Gift that none of us de-

served, means that God loves us no matter what we do or don't do! His love for us is unconditional, like your love for your own child. (Romans 8:1) BUT, the more we experience His Grace, the more we understand His love for us, the more we will WANT to please Him! That means that while we are free from the bondage of sin, free from the law, free from guilt and shame, we will gradually discover that we just DON'T want to sin! That is the beauty of the indwelling Holy Spirit, the Helper Christ promised to send each of us!

Christians unfortunately, have somewhat of a reputation for being cold, critical, judgmental and sometimes downright mean. Christians who act that way either don't understand their faith, or aren't really people of faith to begin with! This is the opposite of what our Lord wanted when He said His followers would be known by their fruit! It is the opposite of what Paul teaches us about the Fruit of the Spirit! Perhaps we don't live free, because many of us don't believe in a God who loves us enough to give us our freedom! The Christian who acts judgmentally, criticizing others, whether believers or not, clearly missed the message behind Matthew 7:1, and furthermore, lacks even a rudimentary understanding of the freedom we have been granted by Grace!

As you think about what it feels like to be truly free, maybe think about *not trying* so hard to be better! We try to be more loving, more compassionate, more understanding, over time, but consider asking your spouse how that's working for you? Sanctification in our own strength leads to disappointment and frustration. If you improve in one area you get prideful, if you fail in another, you get self-absorbed. John Wesley, the founder of Methodism, realized after years of attempted self-improvement in terms of piety, that he had made no improvement whatsoever! The end result was that he became much easier to live with! When you finally give up, you stop being so focused on yourself! ***Nip your obsession with self-improvement in the bud, and start getting obsessed with Jesus!***

We had a pastor once who focused an entire sermon series on the beauty of Believers who were free to dance through life, rather than march to a strict set of rules. The Gospel frees us from obsessive concentration on commitment, attempts to be good, spiritual disciplines, correctness, and moral judgment of ourselves and others! The Christian moralist has been duped into believing our righteousness comes from good behavior! Our righteousness is the perfect righteousness that Christ passed to us on the cross! It is that imputed righteousness that is irreversible and makes us free! We can come before the Creator of the Universe, perfectly Holy, not because we never sin, but because on this side of the cross, God has removed our sin from us, as far as the east is from the west! (Psalms 103:12) That my friend, is called *FREEDOM,* and that leads to both joy and peace!

"Either we give up trying so hard to be good, or we become very unhappy indeed!" (C.S. Lewis)

"What then? Shall we sin because we are no longer under the law but Grace? Certainly not!" (Romans 6:15 NKJV)

"Therefore, if the Son makes you free, you are free indeed!" (John 8:36 NKJV)

Prayer: Dear Heavenly Father, when will we ever really learn what Your Son meant when He said on the cross, "It is finished!" Christ has taken our sin on Himself and left us pure as the driven snow, and only faith achieves this, not effort! Holy Spirit help us to avoid both judging others and ourselves, for not "behaving" in the way that we think we should. Instead, help us concentrate on our understanding of, and relationship with, Your Son! How much more freeing, how much more joyous, is dance than lock step! AMEN

MAY 21

Aslan

"Wrong will be right when Aslan comes in sight, at the sound of His roar, sorrows will be no more, When He bares His teeth, winter meets its death, And when He shakes His mane, we shall have spring again." (C.S. Lewis in The Chronicles of Narnia)

Susan, Lucy, Edmund and Peter are trying to save Mr. Tumnus from the White Queen, in *The Lion, the Witch and the Wardrobe*. Mr. and Mrs. Beaver have come to their aid, but they tell the children if there's any hope at all, their salvation must come from the ruler of the forest, Aslan.

"Is he a man?" asked Lucy. *"Aslan, a man!"* said Beaver sternly. *"Why certainly not. I tell you He is the King of the Wood and the Son of the Emperor Beyond the Sea. Don't you know who is the King of the Beasts? Aslan is a lion, the lion, the Great Lion!"*

"Ooh," said Susan, *"I'd thought he was a man. Is he quite safe? I should feel quite nervous about meeting a lion!"*

"That you will Dearie, and make no mistake," said Mrs. Beaver...

"Then he isn't safe?" said Lucy.

"Safe?...Who said anything about safe? Course He isn't safe, but He's good. He's the King I tell you."

C.S. Lewis' incredible *Chronicles of Narnia,* is a seven volume allegory for man's relationship to God, and the salvation that has been offered to him by Grace through faith in Christ. Aslan, the great lion, is of course Christ. The Beaver's quote above, is one of the most theologically astute and significant, in all of literature. Why on earth would anyone think of the Son of God as simply safe? Sometimes, it is convenient for Believers to forget that the God of the Old Testament is the same as the New. Christ is "I AM." He is part of the Trinity, the Alpha and the Omega, and was there before the formation of the world! Would one not tremble before the Creator of the Universe?

Yes, He is the loving, compassionate, forgiving, humble, servant Christ of the incarnation, but He is also the God who destroyed the Egyptians with plagues, and the inhabitants of Canaan before the armies of Israel. More than that, He was there when Adam and Eve rebelled; He was there when Moses was on the mountain and Aaron allowed the people to worship a Golden Calf;

He was there every time the Chosen People forgot Him and turned to other God's down through the centuries. He is the same God who punished those who rebelled with often horrific deaths, over and over. It was He that used the surrounding nations to eventually utterly destroy both Israel and Judah when time and time again they failed to repent. They certainly *feared* the Lord in the sense that they were afraid of Him. They would go through the prescribed rituals to try to keep Him appeased. But this was no different than what the Moabites, Amorites, Ammonites, Philistines and others, all did with their made-up Gods! They had no sense of a loving God who made rules to keep them safe. They only knew the terrible might of the Gods who could destroy them in a moment! The Israelites could certainly see that their Great Lion wasn't safe, they just forgot that He was also good!

Those of us who were raised in the Protestant Church are familiar with the Apostle's Creed. *"On the third day He arose from the dead and siteth on the right hand of God the Father Almighty, from whence He shall come to judge the quick and the dead!"* Even as a child I remember distinctly being conscious of Jesus not as just Savior, but as Judge as well! What I didn't understand until later, was that while fear for Christ is appropriate, in the sense of awe, we need not be frightened of Him as the judge! He is our perfect High Priest, our perfect intercessor, and our faith has clothed us in His righteousness, so that we can come before the Judge unblemished and Holy, and unafraid! Hallelujah!

Not only will we be judged favorably because we are in Christ, and there is no condemnation for us, (Romans 8:1) but The Lord is *"a very present help in trouble!"* Don't ever mistake our Savior for a pussy cat instead of a lion! People love to quote James 4:7, *"Resist the devil and he will flee from you."* Do you really think that when you stand in front of Satan and tell him where to go, that he will run from *you?* Do you really think that's true? You think the Devil is afraid of you? Trust me. He won't flee. He'll swallow you whole! How can that be? Because the verse that everyone quotes is usually recited incompletely. Verse 4:7 opens with these words, *"Therefore submit to God..."* Believe me, the devil won't run when he looks into *your* eyes, but he will certainly turn and hightail it when he notices who's right behind you. The devil understands the fear of the Lord when he sees that you are standing securely between the mighty forelegs of Aslan!!

"'Aslan,' said Lucy. 'you're bigger.' 'that is because you are older little one,' answered the lion. 'Not because you are?' 'I am not. But every year you grow, you will find me bigger.'" (C.S. Lewis in Vol 4, Prince Caspian)

"You would not have called to me unless I had been calling to you." (C.S. Lewis, Aslan in Vol 6, The Silver Chair)

"If one is nervous, there's nothing like having your face towards the danger and having something warm and solid at your back." (C.S. Lewis in Vol 3, The Horse and His Boy)

Prayer: Dear Heavenly Father, help us not to make the mistake of the Israelites in simply fearing Your power, but forgetting Your goodness! Your love for us is what allows us to face hardship and evil in the

world, knowing that you are as warm and solid at our back as Aslan's mighty chest! AMEN

MAY 22
Miracles

"Skeptics tell us that miracles are contradicted by the realm of science and therefore cannot be true... But miracles lie outside the realm of science as opposed to contradicting it, just like ethics." (William Lane Craig, paraphrased)

The miracles recorded in the Bible seem to be a major stumbling block for some people on their quest for faith. Interestingly, only those who don't believe in a Creator have any problem with miracles! Believers in an omnipotent Creator have no issue with them at all, whether or not their field of interest is in the sciences! The famous British philosopher David Hume, who died one month after the American Declaration of Independence, felt that miracles absolutely contradicted natural law. But like many philosophers who say they insist on following the evidence wherever it might lead them, Hume refused to follow any evidence which led to supernatural intervention. In other words, if the logical conclusion is supernatural intervention, then the evidence must be simply rejected! William Lane Craig, analytical philosopher and theologian from the Talbot School of Theology at Biola University, provides a classic example, in his 1994 classic *Reasonable Faith*. Gravity is universally accepted as a law of nature. If an apple falls from a tree and is intercepted by your hand, then the fact that it didn't fall to the ground is not breaking a law of nature, it has simply been altered by a willful, purposeful, intervention on your part. What if the willful intervention is on the part of the entity *who created the natural laws?* God's willful intervention may often be seen by man as miraculous!

Why don't miracles occur when we diligently ask God to provide them? Craig himself has a progressive neurologic disease that kept him from the sports he excelled at in his youth. He prayed repeatedly for miraculous healing, but it never occurred. He feels in retrospect, that the absence of that healing, is exactly what drove Craig to excel academically, throughout his career. Had he been healed as he requested, he is absolutely sure that he would not have become the world-renowned theologian and apologist that he is! Once again, our ways are not His ways, and His thoughts are above our thoughts! (Isaiah 55:8)

When one contemplates miracles, one has to accept that an inability to explain the occurrence scientifically, doesn't necessarily undermine its veracity. In fact, it may be seen to reinforce it. Reason and belief are not contradictory. C.S. Lewis, J.R.R. Tolkein, G.K. Chesterton, Lee Strobel, Timothy Keller, Ken Samples, Gary Habermas, Hugh Ross, and William Lane Craig are just a few who have researched the available evidence and drawn the conclusion that the Creator not only exists but is alive and active today. There are many findings of modern science that strongly point to the validity of an omnipotent Creator. Certainly, the universal acceptance of the Big Bang theory of the origin of the universe points directly to a Creator, as does the phenomenal fine tuning of the cosmos to even allow life on the third planet from an insignificant star. There are over fifty mathematical constants that cannot vary by a thousandth of a percentage point, or humanity, and the earth on which we live, simply could not exist. No variation can exist for example, in the Weak Nuclear Force, the force of gravity, the shape of our orbit around the sun, the mathematics of magnetism, or the universe's rate of expansion. That's a lot of coincidence.

The existence of moral law has always been another argument for the deity. Atheists believe that morality evolved as a product of soicio-biology; but if this is the case, then raping and murdering children is simply a choice, like eating cauliflower; ok for some, not for others. Sounds absurd doesn't it? And that's because some things are simply objectively wrong, and that suggests that God exists and His moral character traits, including a sense of what is right and wrong, have been instilled in man from the beginning.

There has never been a miracle more thoroughly documented than the resurrection of Christ, and the empty tomb. Not only is there independent attestation from the owner of the tomb, Joseph of Arimethea, a member of the powerful Sanhedrin, but the government felt it necessary to lie about the body being stolen despite the guards in place, to explain the empty tomb. Jesus appeared to over 500 people, many of whom wrote about the experience. The disciples were convinced enough to all die for their beliefs, as martyrs. The miracle of Jesus' resurrection is also believed by over 3 billion people, 2,000 years after the event!

Personal experience has also validated the veracity of miracles for untold numbers of people down through the ages. Philosophers like Craig, call this a "properly basic belief" like the certainty that the external world beyond yourself exists: impossible to prove, but nevertheless rational!

So, as you have your quiet time today, and hopefully you have a conversation with God in which you actually take time to listen as well as make your requests known, listen for God's prompting in terms of His active involvement in the world! If you say that you believe in an omnipotent loving God, it should be no leap whatsoever to believe that the actions He might choose to take and take in His own timing, actually occur, and will appear as miraculous to us!

"If you don't believe in miracles, perhaps you've forgotten you are one." (Anonymous)

"There are only two ways to live your life. One is as though nothing is a miracle and the other is though everything is as miracle." (Albert Einstein)

"You have to see miracles for there to be miracles." (Jandy Nelson)

"Miracles are not contrary to nature, only contrary to what we know about nature." (St. Augustine)

"It is possible that a miracle was not what happened to you, but what didn't." (Jodi Picoult)

Prayer: Father God, let Your Spirit remind us that we need ears to hear and eyes to see that You are present in our world! The world is trying to convince us that if we believe in miracles, we are somehow weak minded or naïve. Give us the strength to withstand the distain of those who don't know You, and yet ironically think they know more than those of us with faith! Thank you, Lord, that You surround us with miracles every day, and in Your Grace, permit us to see You in every one of them! AMEN

MAY 23

Convictions

"And when he saw that, [Jezebel's threat], he arose and ran for his life, and went to Beersheba, which belongs to Judah, and left his servant there. But he himself went a day's journey into the wilderness, and came and sat down under a broom tree." (1 Kings 19:2-4 NKJV)

We've all heard the expression, "to have the courage of your convictions." When your New Year's resolution is not to eat French Fries anymore, then when you're out with your grandchildren at a burger joint and they all order fries; well, that's when one needs the courage of their convictions! But there's a two thousand year history of people who had the courage of their convictions when it really counted; like when your life is on the line.

There is a famous listing of the Catholic Saints down through the centuries, with brief biographies, entitled *Lives of Saints,* by Alban Butler, first published in 1894. Many of these men and women went to their deaths because they had the "courage of their convictions" and refused to deny their faith in Christ. One thinks of Dietrich Bonhoeffer, the German evangelist who was executed by the Nazis at the very end of WWII for opposing the extermination of the Jews, among other things. There are online lists available right now of people who die for their Christian faith all around the world today. The answer as to how many actually do is: it depends! It depends on who is counted as a Christian, how you categorize the circumstances of their deaths, and it depends on how you count them. *The Center for the Study of Global Christianity* has documented an average of 26,000 people killed per year worldwide, specifically for their Christian faith. As many as 70,000 more, largely in Africa, have been killed in Tribal conflicts with other religious groups, but not specifically for their faith. *Open Doors,* a member of the Religious Liberty Partnership, has firmly documented 3,066 cases for 2017, while the Institute for Religious Freedom documented 6,000 killed in the same period. Whether it is 3,000 or 26,000, it's clearly too many!

On February 15, 2016, twenty-one Coptic Christians were beheaded on video by Islamic State militants, and broadcast around the world. A new book, *The 21: A Journey into the Land of the Coptic,* by Martin Mosebach, relates the surprising pride and happiness of the families of the martyrs who have a very simple, but very real, understanding of theology. Nevertheless, the belief that "martyrdom" has been consigned to the history books, is still a widespread mis-perception.

The term "martyr" is derived from that Latin word for "witness." Remarkably, during the first several centuries of the church, the Roman persecution of

Christians was so widespread, that the word for one who testifies about the Gospel, became the same word as one who died for their faith: *martyr.* This persecution was typified by the very real slaughter of thousands, for primarily entertainment purposes, in the Colosseum. Many were killed with no option, no matter what they said. But, the people who were given the opportunity to save their lives by recanting their faith, and chose to stand firm, are the people of whom we say, they had the "courage of their convictions."

Take Biblical Elijah. He's a bit of an enigma. Here is a prophet of the Lord, and yet, did he have the courage of his convictions? After a magnificent demonstration of God's power on Mount Carmel, Elijah ran for his life when Jezebel threatened to have him killed! The very Gods she worshipped he had just shown to be powerless! Nevertheless, sitting under the broom tree in the Negev desert, Elijah was so disheartened that he prayed for his own death! (I Kings 19:4) Incredibly, or maybe just *humanly,* Elijah had forgotten the multiple times Yahweh had rescued him in the past, and now was distraught over his current circumstances. He lay down and slept, convinced that he had failed God in the end.

But God doesn't read him the riot act! Instead He sends an angel with bread and water, who simply tells him to get up and eat. It's just a little miracle, right? But that's not uncommon for our God. A big God can carry out big His plans with just little miracles! The next time you promise yourself to avoid a repetitive sin; the next time you dedicate yourself to a spiritual discipline; the next time you swear that you absolutely will *never, ever, do that thing again:* be assured, you will fail from time to time.

Remember the Transfiguration on the mountaintop? Moses, Jesus and who? That's right, the third one is Elijah. Elijah, who forgot who God was and ran! Elijah. So cut yourself some slack. It's a dance, not a goose step. *Never forget that God sees into your heart. He sees beyond your actions.* He saw into Elijah's heart, overlooking his actions, gently corrected him, and sent him on to complete his mission! Once you've accepted the Gift of the Gospel and you are in Christ, believe me, you can expect the same treatment! You won't always have the courage of your convictions; but if you really *want to,* with faith in the One who indwells you, you will stand your ground more often than not.

"Have convictions. Be friendly. Stick to your beliefs as they stick to theirs. Work as hard as they do. (Eleanor Roosevelt)

"The man of character is the persistent man, the man who is faithful to his own words, his own convictions, his own affections." (Maria Montessori)

Prayer: Dear Heavenly Father, we know that You see into our hearts! Forgive us when we forget that You have provided us with the means to have the courage of our convictions by sending the Holy Spirit as our helper! In our own strength, we will often fail to stand firm! Like the thousands of martyrs that have come before us, we pray that we would despise the world enough to choose our faith, even if threatened with death for the choice, and we pray for all those around the world who may be facing that choice tomorrow. AMEN

MAY 24

On Call

"From whence comes my help? My help comes from the Lord, Who made heaven and earth. He will not allow your foot to be moved; He who keeps you...shall neither slumber nor sleep." (Psalm 121:1-4 NKJV)

This year, 2020, marks the fortieth year that I have taken night call. It started with various rotations and schedules during my third year of medical school and continued to a much more intense schedule my first two years of residency, and then settled down to every third or fourth night until the last decade when it averaged 1-2 nights per week. For the first year of residency at UCSF, we were on call (at the hospital) for 36 hours straight, then off for twelve, then on another 36 with one Sunday off per month; i.e. every other night. My second year, we were on for 36 hours, off for twelve, on for twelve, off for twelve, then on for 36 again; i.e. every third night. Heading home at night, I used to fall asleep at almost every red light in my 1976 5-speed Toyota Celica. That usually meant rolling either backwards or forwards, down the steep San Francisco hills, until being halted by the car either behind or in front. Luckily, the Celica was small, and the traffic was always heavy and close together, so there was *almost* never any damage.

At age sixty-four, when I look back over my entire adult life, virtually every aspect of it was dictated by call. In the 80's I was never without a voice pager on my hip while in the hospital; in the 90's it was a small radio pager on my belt, in or out of the hospital; through most of the 2000's it has been a cell phone of one kind or another. Every dinner date, every event, every trip, every holiday, every family gathering had to be planned around my call schedule. For the first three decades after medical school, this was complicated by the fact that everyone I knew was also a doctor, including my brother, and thus all of the possible items to be scheduled, had to be interwoven with someone else's schedule as well! On top of this, there was the added stress of knowing that your beeper or cell phone had the potential, inevitably realized, of going off at the *very most* inopportune times possible: just let your imagination run wild! For the last two decades, my daughter and her husband became physicians with call schedules as well, further complicating any family gathering!

It occurred to me only recently, while sitting at this keyboard at 0348 AM in the hospital, (that's right, on call again,) that the One we rely on, when in need, is *always on call!* It may seem silly, but that realization just dawned on me! By Grace through faith in Christ, we have been granted *direct access* to our heavenly Father! That means that He is not accessible only in church, or only in a Bible study, or only at family meals, or only during your quiet time. God is available to us *at all times*! That's what it means when it says He neither slumbers nor sleeps. How often has your lowest moment come in the pre-dawn hours of the morning? Good thing you can rest assured that the Big Guy's awake and listening, huh? On top of that, the Creator of the Universe handles sleeplessness way better than we do. You won't see Him rolling backwards down a hill in his '76 Celica. What's more, you won't find Him irascible and unreasonable either. Lucky for us, *"the Lord is merciful and gracious, slow to anger, and abounding in mercy," (Psalm 103:8 NKJV)* even though He never gets any sleep!

"God is our refuge and strength, a very present help in trouble. Therefore, we will not fear..." (Psalm 46:1 NKJV)

"He never sleeps, our Shepherd never slumbers. He knows no night, His watch care never ends. He sees beyond the danger of this moment. We need not fear what lies beyond the bend." (Stephen Adams; recorded by FotoSisters)

> *Prayer: Dear Heavenly Father, thank You that we can rely on Your help at all times. There is no time and no situation where, should we cry out to you, in anguish, in need, or in joy, that You are not available to us! Even when we cannot articulate our needs or organize our thoughts, You have given us the Holy Spirit to intercede on our behalf. Thank you for being on call Lord, 24/7 !! AMEN*

MAY 25

Known

"He knows your name, and speaks it to His Father, His thoughts are with you, each moment of the day. He is no stranger, to your hurt, your heartache. You're in His care, the Shepherd knows your name." (Stephen Adams, recorded by FotoSisters)

I don't know how many of you have a childhood home that you remember fondly. I pray more do than don't. For at least some of us there is a place that is so tied up with our first memories, with the love of our parents, with the play of our sisters and brothers, with our first sights and sounds and scents, that coming in contact with those memories brings tears to our eyes. Those tears aren't necessarily sad. They aren't really for loss or time that has slipped by. To me they are just tears of indescribable emotions that simply well up unbidden with those often-fleeting thoughts. I think those emotions are, perhaps, associated with the simple beauty of knowing and being known; and being known feels just like *home*.

One of the three daughters with whom we are Blessed, is a licensed professional counsellor. A few years ago, when she and her husband were searching for the perfect name for her practice, they considered and rejected a panoply of possibilities. But after much prayer and consideration, they came up with *Known Counselling*. I'm sure there were many reasons behind their choice, but one of them undoubtedly had to be the realization that *being truly known*, to yourself of course, but to another as well, somehow develops in the seeker those feelings of security, of comfort, of warmth, of intimacy, that we associate collectively with being *home*.

So, when I walked into my study this morning, the first thing my eyes fell upon, was the CD, *What Lies Beyond, by The FotoSisters, 2017*. I love Katelyn, Adelyn, and Gaylyn, for many reasons, not the least of which is that they play the violin, viola and cello, respectively. The opening quote this morning was taken from their song, *The Shepherd Knows Your Name,* (words by Stephen Adams; music by Phillip Keveren.) I popped it into the now rarely used CD accessory for my iMac, and it opened with this, *not the first track*. No idea why. Well, *I do have an idea* why, but sadly not everyone believes *that* is possible! In any event, it struck me that much of the comfort and security we get from our Lord, is the knowledge that no one knows us better, *and* that He is constantly watching over, protecting, and leading us. He is the Shepherd. He is the One that leaves the ninety-nine to come search for us when we are lost. He is the only Son of the Father, who gave Himself up for each of us personally! He is the God who knows us, completely, and wants desperately for us to know Him. Whether the tune, the words, or the accompanying revelation did it, I was crying quite freely by the time the song ended!

When you feel lost and alone; when you feel like no one understands you; when you feel like you're a complete failure; when you feel like you don't even know who you are; then remember that the most important Someone in the world *knows exactly who you are!* You can rest assured. You can be secure. You can feel the same comfort and warmth and intimacy that those special, poignant, memories of home cause to wash over you, because *Jesus Christ has got you*, He knows what is right around the bend, and *He is your forever home.*

"My sheep hear My voice, and I know them, and they follow Me. And I give them eternal life, and they shall never perish; neither shall anyone snatch them out of My hand! My Father who has given them to Me, is greater than all; and no one is able to snatch them out of My Father's hand. I and My Father are One." (John 10:27-30 NKJV)

Prayer: Dear Heavenly Father, we love You!! Thank You so much for deciding to come to us as our Shepherd! The Shepherd keeps us under His watchful eye, and we know that He knows each one of us and keeps us safe. The Shepherd is the One who can lead us home; and we keeping our eyes on Him, will always be our safest course. AMEN

MAY 26

Call Mom

"Got a call from a friend about a friend, It's news no one ever wants to hear. It hit me like a punch, it took my breath. He was just getting into his best years. Yeah something like that'll shake you up, Wake you up...I thought of home, grabbed my phone from my pocket, And I called mama. (Tim McGraw)

I was drivin' pretty fast this afternoon, trying to get from my office to the hospital for a very emergent Cesarean section on a patient of mine who had rapid onset severe pre-eclampsia. The radio happened to be on in my truck, and a familiar voice was singing about how he had got to thinking about what was really important in life, and he needed to call mama right away, and tell her that he loved her.

Maybe they were playing this new song by Tim McGraw because it was off the first new album he'd made in several years. Or maybe they were playing it just because Mother's Day was celebrated, pandemic style, only a few days ago. But no matter what the reason, I could identify with Tim. My mom is going strong at 91. My wife's mother died at 42, when she was only 19. Many a time I have thought of how Blessed I am to have the love and counsel of my mother for so many years more than most! There's just something special about moms, and it's a little hard to articulate. Maybe it's because when we were completely helpless as an infant, she did everything for us, and held us when we cried, and rocked us to sleep with a song sung softly. Maybe it's because when we got a little older and started in school she packed our lunch, cleaned our clothes, made us eat breakfast, picked us up after school or after practice, read us books at night, and comforted us when we fell, or failed, or somebody was mean to us. Maybe it's because when we got even older, and meaner, and talked back, and asserted our teenage version of independence, she loved us anyway. Maybe it's because one day, even though we were her whole world, she let us go.

How I thought all these things while changing into scrubs and putting on all the extra Covid-19 personal protection equipment, I have no idea. But it was afterward, while I was sitting at the computer putting in orders that John 19 crossed my mind. I'd never really thought this specific thing before, but the last thing, the very last thing that, Jesus Christ did on this earth, was to make sure his mama was taken care of! Hanging from the spikes through his wrists, struggling to draw in breath through what must have been indescribable agony, He called out to His best friend who was standing near His mother, *"'Woman, behold your son!'" Then He said to the disciple, [John] 'Behold your mother!' And form that hour the disciple took her to his own home." (John 19:26-27 NKJV)* The following verse starts with, *"After this, Jesus, knowing that all things were now accomplished..."* Yes, John meant that Christ realized His sacrifice was complete and that He was in fact, taking on the sins of the world, so that we might be redeemed; he also meant Jesus had done all He needed to do, in order to go. But, the last thing to be taken care of, to be absolutely sure about, was mom.

Perhaps, like my wife, you may have to substitute your mother-in-law, or your aunt, at Mothers' Day. But for those of us lucky enough to still have our moms, make sure you remember that your mom has cared for you every single day of your life from your first breath! That means that every day is Mothers' Day. So, whether you are hit with sudden bad news, like Tim McGraw was, or you have something really wonderful happen in your life, call your mama. She wants to know either way, and she wants to give you her advice, even if you stopped taking it long ago. You don't have to take her advice. But you do need to listen, because that's the way you make sure she knows that you love her now, you always have, and like your Savior, you'll love her to your dying breath.

"Mother is the name for God on the lips and in the hearts of little children." (W.M. Thackeray)

"Life doesn't come with a manual, it comes with a mother." (Anonymous)

Prayer: Dear Heavenly Father, we love You and we love that You saw fit to give us mothers! We love our dads, and we need our dads, but You

made it different from moms. Moms are special. Their heartbeat was the first we ever heard. Their touch, the first we ever felt. Their voice, the first we ever heard. Holy Spirit, remind us to call our mamas. They deserve it, and we need it. AMEN

MAY 27

Others

"Apologize to her."
"For what?"
"It doesn't matter. It shows strength not weakness."
"I can't just go and apologize for nothing."
"Well, it wouldn't be for nothing would it? It would be apologizing for arguing with someone you like, who's nice."

My wife and I have recently been watching the Netflix British TV Show *AfterLife*, starring Ricky Gervais. We were put off by the language initially, but soon came to appreciate the local Wales expressions as they were intended. The story line is about Tony who has recently lost his wife, Lisa, to breast cancer. He is in his 40's and works as a feature reporter for their local free paper. Tony never had higher career aspirations, because he figured there couldn't ever be anything as good as living with Lisa, in their little town, with their German Shepherd. Every day he watches a bit of her last instructional videos for him, knowing he is helpless without her. But still her death leaves him desperate, lost and bitter. He was angry at everyone and everything. His new superpower was annoying everyone else because there was nothing anyone could do to him to make him hurt more.

One day while Tony and the Shepherd are visiting Lisa's grave, he meets Ann, sitting on a bench across from the headstone next to Lisa's. It turns out she comes there every day to visit with her Stan, to whom she was married 48 years. Tony and Ann strike up an unlikely friendship, and through her gentle, loving, listening, she leads him gradually on the road back to life! The quote above comes after Tony admits he yelled at the nurse who cares for his father with Alzheimer's, and Ann picks up on the fact that he's sweet on her.

Every few days they meet in the graveyard, and Ann teaches him to laugh again, and he makes her laugh in return. One time she role plays with him on a mock date. What would he say to her?

"I'd just be honest. Tell her my situation, tell her what I'm gong through, be honest up front and…"

"So, just all about you then?"

"I can't win can I? I don't want to date again. I don't want to live without Lisa."

"But it's not just all about you, is it? That's what I'm saying. What if a nice date made HER feel good? That might feel nice, right? We're not just here for us. We're here for others…all we've got is each other. We've got to help each other through until we die."

Neither Ann nor Tony are Christians, as far as I can tell. Neither recognize that this very principle of putting others before you, is straight out of scripture and thus straight from God's mouth to our ears! But in this story, part of the beauty, is that they discover the concept of putting others first, for themselves! One day perhaps, someone could lead them to the source.

Ann is teaching Tony humility; the lack of self-centeredness; the death of pride, the importance of others. This is the very epitome of the servant mindset. This is the mind of Christ we are to adopt, described in Philippians 2:3-8. Once Tony finally gets it, every aspect of his world changes. His mean streak turns into compassion, his sarcasm into concern. It is the key to success in life. Not an episode ends without my eyes being moist.

"Let nothing be done through selfish ambition or conceit, but in lowliness of mind let each esteem others better than himself. Let each of you look not only for his own interests, but also for the interests of others. Let this be the mindset in you that is also in Christ Jesus."

Prayer: Dear Heavenly Father, we love you! Help us remember that you love not only us, but all of your creation! Awake in us a servant heart Lord where we strive first for the betterment of others! Truly the joy we receive from this will far outweigh anything we could do for ourselves! AMEN

MAY 28

Discipline

"For the moment all discipline seems painful rather than pleasant, but later it yields the peaceful fruit of righteousness to those who have been trained by it." (Hebrews 12:11 ESV)

When we head out onto the open water in a sailboat, there is a certain protocol applied that is remarkably similar to the one in place when my son prepares to take off in one of his company's aircraft. Sailors and pilots both have checklists to go through, even if only mental, that they perform in order to ensure their own safety and the safety of their passengers. These checklists have to do with availability and functionality of emergency equipment, structural integrity of the hull or fuselage, structural integrity and functionality of control surfaces and their connections, whether ailerons, flaps and rudder, or main and jib sheets, halyards, winches, helm and rudder. These checklists review integrity and functionality of the engines, oil, and fuel levels as well. In short, the safe pilot or sailor, exercises a certain *self-imposed discipline* prior to every trip. Absent employment requirements, no one is forcing me to go through such a checklist before I cast off. I'm not following a rule. I'm dong it because I *want to* be at peace when I am out on the ocean.

People head out every morning and live their lives, facing all manner of eventualities. Their joy, peace, and in fact, safety, depend on how they have chosen to educate themselves, prepare, and respond to different situations, which are often interpersonal. Christians approach each day a little differently than others. We awaken each day and make ourselves available to the Lord so that hopefully everything we do and say might bring Glory to Him. In order to do that, most of us exercise some spiritual discipline.

Now, we are indeed saved by grace through faith. We are not *under the law* anymore, meaning our righteousness is not achievable by following a given set of rules. Instead our salvation, our ability to stand before God Holy and set apart, is because we have been granted the perfect righteousness of Christ by accepting His sacrifice for us. Part of the confusion for some, is then believing that obedience *need not* be any part of our lives, and nothing could be further from the truth! Christ Himself said He came to fulfill the law not to abolish it. (Matthew 5: 17) Our deeds, while not earning our salvation, do still matter! James was certainly correct when he exclaimed that faith without works is dead! (James 2:20.) If, we are people of faith, then our works are an expression of our desire to be obedient to God's will, best expressed through becoming more and more Christ like! That is the process of *sanctification*.

Well, that doesn't just happen magically. Sanctification is not absorbed through your pillow at night. There is personal volition involved. That means some degree of self-discipline. I am not suggesting you journal, or have a quiet time, or study the bible, or volunteer, or pray *because you think you have to in order to be obedient.* What I am saying, is that if you structure your day so that you give yourself the opportunity to do the things that you enjoy, which also serve to aid in your sanctification, you will find yourself happier and more at peace! If you have a daily quiet time and find one day that you just don't have the time, or don't feel motivated, there is no reason to feel guilty at all; instead hopefully, you just simply miss the joy that it normally brings to you! But still, some self-discipline is required to set the time aside for it in the first place! Get up every morning and consciously make room for God in your life!

"Have nothing to do with irreverent silly myths. Rather train yourself for godliness…" (1 Timothy 4:7 ESV)

"Train up a child in the way he should go; even when he is old he will not depart from it." (Proverbs 22:6 ESV)

"Sow for yourselves righteousness; reap steadfast love; break up your fallow ground, for it is time to seek the Lord, that He may come and rain righteousness upon you." (Hosea 10:12 ESV)

Prayer: Father God, we confess that sometimes we are tempted to just sit on our salvation and be grateful that You love us enough to have sent Your Son!! But use Your Holy Spirit to lead us toward a self-discipline that enables a deeper relationship with You in prayer, study of the Word, and a quiet time to listen for Your Voice! AMEN

MAY 29
Irish Horses

"Therefore we also, since we are surrounded by so great a cloud of witnesses, let us lay aside every weight, and the sin which so easily ensnares us, and let us run with endurance the race that is set before us, looking unto Jesus, the author and finisher of our faith..." (Hebrews 12:1-2, NKJV)

My wife and I travelled to Ireland a few years back. At the time, the economy was booming and all of Europe referred to Ireland as "The Celtic Tiger." We stayed our first night in the beautiful, modern, Zuni Hotel, in Kilkenny. When we arrived, on a dappled sunny evening, the afternoon rainstorm having just ended, we noticed that the streets were full of thousands of people celebrating. I asked our host once we were settled in our room, what on earth all the celebration was about? "Well, we won the All Ireland Hurling Championship, didn't we? It's a big deal around here!" I inquired as to where the team was at the moment, and he said, "Still in Dublin, they'll be arriving on the train tomorrow, and then the celebration will really begin!" Begin? "It seems like everyone's had a wee bit to drink already, by the looks of the streets," I said. "Has Kilkenny ever won the national championship before?" He laughed as he handed us a map and some pamphlets. "Well, you might say a few. This is the 34th time!"

We walked up the stairs to our second-floor room to change, take a nap, and decide on where to eat our first night in Ireland. On the landing, I noticed an oil painting of a horse race, splashing colors, mud flying, perfectly reflecting the feeling of speed and abandon with which the powerful animals thundered around the track. After our rest, we descended, ready to walk down the hill to town in the cool evening air, and in the lobby, I noticed another painting, similar to the first, of a race-track presumably somewhere in nearby. After stew in a pub nearby, we walked along Bateman Quay beside the River Nore, and headed toward the famous Kilkenny Castle, now lit up for the evening, standing out against the darkening sky. Along the way, I mentioned to my wife that I hadn't realized horse racing was such a popular sport in Ireland, noting that yet again there were paintings of a race-track hanging in the pub. I had always pictured Irish horses as these huge, stalwart stallions, that were either pulling a plow or carrying a Knight into battle, not running around a track with blinders on. Still something else *bothered me about those pictures*, but I just couldn't put my finger on it.

The next morning, we had a fabulous Irish breakfast of fried tomatoes, black pudding, baked beans, fried eggs, bacon rashers, buttered toast and bangers! (You can have my black, pudding to be honest!) As I looked out the window on people walking down Patrick Street toward the river, I saw yet another horse race painting hanging in the breakfast room, and it finally hit me! ***The horses were all running the wrong way around the track!*** Not only do they drive on the other side of the road in the UK, but at least in Ireland, the horses run *CLOCKWISE* around the track! As we checked out, I asked the front desk man about it, and he chuckled. "Don't see too many Irish horses on American racetracks do ya? They'd all cross the finish line first alright, but they'd cross it headin' the wrong direction right out of the gate, now wouldn't dey!"

As we drove along the River Nore, and then followed the River Barrow down to rural *Hook Head Light,* I thought a lot about this oddity. The author of Hebrews likens our lifetime on earth as a great race of endurance, where we are to shake off the sinful nature that weighs us down and holds us back, and as saints who went before us look on, head for the finish line with our eyes fixed on Jesus! Paul tells Timothy as he nears his execution in a Roman prison, "I have fought the good fight, I have finished the race, I have kept the faith!" (2 Timothy 4:7 NKJV)

All of us have a tendency to "go with the flow" or maybe "run with the crowd." We settle into certain patterns of behavior that become routine, and we are comfortable because we know what to expect and perhaps what is expected of us. **But we might be racing around the track in the wrong direction!** In college one might drink too much, party too hard, get involved with drugs, or sex with multiple changing partners. A young business professional might get caught up in the race to advance, coupled with the race to make more money. They might start cutting corners, "borrowing" someone else's data or work or conclusions, or possibly making money on illegal trades or real estate or other shady investment. A professor might plagiarize someone else's writing, perhaps long dead, just to publish more and obtain tenure earlier. An athlete might use performance enhancing drugs 'cause "everyone else does."

The freedom and forgiveness that comes from accepting Christ, is a freedom from guilt and shame and fear. It is also freedom from the tyranny of sin, meaning while we might still sin, we certainly don't have to, and we no longer want to. The compassionate humility that Christ would have us model, once Grace has bestowed His righteousness on us, is like suddenly being moved to the right racetrack! Before faith, we might have been like an Irish racehorse on an American track, free to run, but never to succeed, because we were running in the wrong direction, our eyes fixed on the wrong goal. Scripture tells us repeatedly from Job to Proverbs to Psalms to the Sermon on the Mount: life isn't about a race for money, possessions, power or influence. Life is about the chief end of man: Glorifying God! He has told us how to do that through our Savior, love God and love each other by putting each other first! The prophet Micah makes it simple in our closing quote.

"And what is it that the Lord requires of you, but to do justly, to love mercy, and to walk humbly with your God?" (Micah 6:8 NKJV)

Prayer: Father God, we love you! Forgive us when we run the race in the wrong direction, forgetting that we cannot love both God and money at the same time! Direct Your Holy Spirit within us to reign us in, pull our heads around and get us running in the right direction, our eyes fixed always on Jesus! AMEN

MAY 30

Everyday Miracles

"I think that I see something deeper, more infinite, more eternal than the ocean in the expression of the eyes of a little baby when it wakes in the morning and coos or laughs because it sees the sun shining on its crib." (Van Gogh)

I have delivered somewhere around 8,000 babies and been in attendance at the birth of at least 3500 more. That ought to mean I have seen just about everything you can see related to the birth of a child, right? Wrong. Every single one is a new experience for the parents, the nurses, the baby and for me. I've contemplated many times, making a book of photographs that are nothing but the parents' facial expressions when they see their child for the very first time. Tears, grins, laughter, shouts, faces looking heavenward, faces looking downward, covered with hands, (now even masked faces in the pandemic) and audible sobs. You name it. I've had a father who literally dropped to the floor, rolling back and forth, and thanking God over and over! Many I time I have noted that while there may be no atheists in foxholes, you'll be hard pressed to find any in delivery rooms either.

Consider that a baby starts as two microscopic cells somehow finding each other in a dark expanse, analogous to two ping pong balls hitting each other when released randomly into a space the size of the SuperDome! That should be miracle enough! But then to have that tiny bundle of dividing cells turn into the phenomenally complex and responsive creature you hold in your hands at delivery; well, having both a Bachelor of Science in biology and a Doctorate in Medicine, provide me with far less understanding than my Masters in Biblical Studies!

I really just want you to take a moment and enjoy some of my favorite baby quotes below, and while you are doing that, consider what a Master stroke it was for God to choose the incarnation of His Son as a baby! There could have been no better way for us to see both the character of God, and the perfect model of humanity, than through a Savior born to a woman but conceived by the Spirit, who was both fully man and fully God. Talk about a miracle! Would you not love to have had an Arlo camera in the corner of that manger! As an obstetrician, I can totally understand why Ricky Bobby likes to pray only to the *Baby* Jesus in the movie, *Talladega Nights*, even if, as his wife points out, He grew up and had a beard!!

"There are no words to describe the euphoria you feel when your baby recognizes you for the first time and smiles." (Jared Padalecki)

"Making the decision to have a child is momentous. It is to decide forever to have your heart go walking around outside your body." (Elizabeth Stone)

"Children see neither the past nor the future. They enjoy the present, which very few of us do." (Jean De La Bruyere)

"It is a moment of pure ecstasy and satisfaction when you see a smile flicker on a baby's lips, just as they gently pass into deep slumber." (Unknown)

"All those cliches, those things you hear about having a baby and motherhood—

all of them are true. And all of them are the most beautiful things you will ever experience." (Penelope Cruz)

"Even when freshly washed and relieved of all obvious confections, children tend to be sticky!" (Fran Lebowitz)

"If evolution is really true, how come mothers only have two hands?" (Milton Berle)

"The most precious jewels you'll ever have around your neck, are the arms of your children." (Unknown)

"When your first baby drops her pacifier, you immediately sterilize it. When your next baby drops her pacifier, you tell the dog, "Fetch!" (Bruce Lansky)

Prayer: Dear Heavenly Father, thank you for the everyday miracle that is a baby. It's true. A baby changes everything! Remind us every day that One special baby changed everything for all of us, those of us with children and those without. Thank you that believing in Your Son adopts all of us into Your family for eternity, and You become to us, not only God, but Dad. AMEN

MAY 31

Spirit of Power

"For God has not given us a spirit of fear, but of power and of love and of a sound mind." (2Timothy 1:7 NKJV)

I can only think of three times in my life when I was really afraid. The first was when I was about ten years old and our Lido 14 capsized in the Houston Ship Channel. There was a race going on and a group of what I perceived as "huge" boats slicing through the water headed right for us. That was the last thing I remember seeing before struggling to the surface, battered by waves, and trapped beneath the mainsail.

The next time I remember being truly afraid, was after the death of a newborn thirty years ago. The Texas Medical Association board review found that I was not responsible, but there was a subsequent lawsuit and tremendous angst over a long period. My grief for the couple was coupled with my paralyzing fear of losing everything, my house, possessions, savings, my children's futures, my family's security, all because our civil justice system left defendants open to damages that were not solely based on treatment issues, but on "emotional trauma," and thus could be absurdly high.

The third time I was truly afraid, was only a few years ago, when I was terrified that I had lost the love, and perhaps had never had the respect of someone I loved unconditionally.

Paul tells Timothy that while we are not given a spirit of fear, we are given the spirit of *power, of love and a sound mind.* Fear of course, can be a legitimate and useful emotion. That's what fight or flight is all about on a primal level, and fear can work to keep us safe. But Paul isn't talking about our emotions, he's talking about the character of the Holy Spirit. The indwelling Spirit enables us to approach life with power, love and a sound mind. A spirit of power of course, enables us to influence our own circumstances, resist temptation, and make choices with confidence. A spirit of love is the primary means by which can exercise that power, and influence other people. "Sound mind" in Greek, is *sophronismos,* and literally means "moderation, or self-control." Recall that love and self control are two of the Fruits of the Spirit spoken of in Galatians.

A spirit of self-control under the sail of the capsized Lido 14, would have meant staying calm, treading water, and waiting for my dad. In litigation, self-control might have meant exercising another fruit of the spirit, patience, and not "going off half-cocked," when feeling unjustly accused. Regarding the fear of losing a relationship in my last example above, the spirit of power, love and sound mind have allowed me to seek first to understand before speaking. It would have allowed me to think, before reflexively defending myself. It would have allowed me to lovingly focus on the needs and feelings of the other person, not on myself.

Christians once again, have an advantage over others when it comes to fear. We have a Savior who promises, *"Fear not! For I am with you always."* (Isaiah 41:10; 43:5; Jeremiah 46:28) Christ is present specifically in the form of the Spirit, whom we can call on as our Helper, who indwells us ever since our re-birth. All of us are afraid from time to time. Dwelling on that fear and letting it control us is called worry, and Christ told us in no uncertain terms, not to do that. (Matthew 6:25) When you find yourself afraid, pause and call upon the power, love and level headedness that God has promised you! Recall the verses that reassure you, no matter what the threat in this world, the God of the Universe has your back every second. How could you be more secure than you in Christ and He in you?

"For He himself has said, 'I will never leave you nor forsake you.' So we may boldly say: 'The Lord is my helper; I will not fear. What can man do to me?'" (Hebrews 13:5-6 NKJV)

"Be strong and of good courage, do not fear nor be afraid of them; for the Lord Your God, He is the One who goes with you!" (Deuteronomy 31:6 NKJV)

'God is our refuge and strength, A very present help in trouble. Therefore, we will not fear, even though the earth be removed and the mountains be carried into the midst of the sea…" (Psalm 46:1-2 NKJV)

"Do not be afraid of those who kill the body, and after that have no more that they can do…Fear him who, after he has killed, has power to cast into hell…

Prayer: Father God, we love you. Forgive us in our fear of daily occurrences. How easy it is for us to forget the promises You have made! We have eternity before us, and this life only to demonstrate Your love to those who don't yet know it. When we fear Lord, remind us to call on the Spirit You have put into us, that we might draw on that power, that love, and that calm demeanor. AMEN

JUNE

JUNE 1

Uncertainty

"Now faith is confidence in what we hope for and assurance about what we do not see." (Hebrews 11:1 NIV)

My wife is a light sleeper. I am not. Most obstetricians learn early on to sleep comfortably standing in an elevator. My wife on the other hand will awaken when she senses those butterfly wings flap 12,000 miles away in North Africa! Recently, we discussed sleeping in different bedrooms, maybe once to twice per week, because even though I always sleep soundly, evidently, I flop around like a bass on a dock and occasionally make breathing noises reminiscent of a moose! With the kids grown and gone, we have alternative places to sleep. I figured that since I sleep at the hospital once or twice per week, another night was no big deal, so last night I stayed up watching Netflix and let my wife fall asleep. I checked on her, turned out the light, and went down the hall to one of our daughter's old rooms and climbed into that bed.

About 5AM, shortly before we would normally awaken anyway, she came quietly into the room and sat on the bed with a sigh. I asked what was wrong. She said that she didn't know where I was! She had awakened about midnight, and laid awake waiting for me to come to bed. Then she fell asleep for a while, awakened about 2AM, and was alarmed when I wasn't there. She'd gotten up, checked the TV room, checked the rooms upstairs, and finally realized I must be in Allison's old room. By then there was no hope for sleep, and she lay there awake for 2 1/2 hours, not wanting to wake me!

In short, my compassionate decision to sleep elsewhere was a complete bust! Why? *Uncertainty*. Pat was uncertain whether I was coming to bed, had fallen asleep on the couch, was sleeping in a kid's room, or not too unlikely, had been called back to the hospital and wasn't actually in the house at all!

We are faced with uncertainty every day, and it is always uncomfortable. Will you get the job after the interview? Does the X-ray show that the problem has resolved? Are we part of, or excluded from, the next round of furloughs? Will this pandemic EVER end, or will it just get worse? Will the fabric of society be rent apart over race-relations? Is my loved one going to survive this bout of cancer? What happens if I die? Am I aware of my circumstances? How will my family do without me? Uncertainty. Not knowing. It is something everyone deals with and nobody likes.

But Christians have an assurance that others do not. Unbelievers have no guarantee of an after-life. Unbelievers have no guarantee of salvation. They have no guarantee that they will see loved ones again in that afterlife, no matter how they perform in this life! That assurance brings a peace and a freedom to Christians that others may not feel.

What Christians need to do is ***remember it!*** As we face the ups and downs of our relationships, our jobs, and our health, we need to keep in mind that all of what we are experiencing is first transient, and second, not an admissions test. Our salvation is a gift to the undeserving! Once we have realized this, repented, accepted Christ, and become open to the working of the Spirit, there is no "failing grade" that will keep you out of heaven! That is the nature of our assurance. The ultimate uncertainty, "is this all there is, what happens after this," is one with which we never have to deal! Thank God!

"I have written this to you who believe in the name of the Son of God, so that you may know that you have eternal life." (1 John: 5:13 NLT)

"I tell you the truth. Anyone who believes has eternal life." (John 6:47 NLT)

> ***Prayer: Dear Heavenly Father, what an incredible Gift you have given us in the assurance of our Salvation and an eternity with You waiting for us! Let us awaken every day with the Holy Spirit whispering in our ears, "How will you show the Father's love to another today? Who will hear the word 'Jesus' on your lips today, and ask about Him in your life?" We are blessed indeed to have certainty replace insecurity in our lives! Hallelujah! AMEN***

JUNE 2
WWJD

"Ask in all cases, 'What would Jesus do?' That unties the knot of all moral difficulty in the most practical way, and does it so simply that no great wit or wisdom will be needed. " (Charles Spurgeon, 1891)

Anyone born before about 1980 will recall the *What Would Jesus Do Movement* of the early 1990's. Specifically you might remember that literally millions of young people wore wrist bands engraved with the acronym W.W.J.D. If you want to know what to do in any circumstance, imagine Jesus in your position, and then ask yourself what your Savior would do? The next step is easy. Do it.

People laboring under the illusion that this approach was an invention of the late 20th century, might be humbled to know that Charles Spurgeon, the renowned Baptist orator and author of late 19th century London, quoted the phrase in a sermon he gave in 1891. It came from the book *Imitatio Christi*, by Thomas Kempis, written in 1418! The movement seemed to have lost steam in the early 2000's, perhaps because of the evangelical emphasis on faith over works; a shame in my opinion. WWJD is more needed conceptually in today's world than perhaps ever before.

Rev. Martin Luther King, Jr. expressed his dream for America in 1963, first lamenting that 100 years after the end of slavery, after the presumed end of their long night of captivity, the black man is still *"crippled by the manacles of segregation and the chains of discrimination, living on a lonely island of poverty in the midst of a vast sea of prosperity.*" Reconstruction, a century of Jim Crow laws, prejudicial exclusion from voting and representative government, institutionalized discrimination in housing, education, job opportunities, and disproportionate mass incarceration, have left us with the legacy of a society unequal in almost every way, despite a Constitutional promise that we as a Republic would never tolerate such a society.

In Acts 15, the Jerusalem Council took steps to put an end to Christian prejudice at the get go. When Jewish Christians insisted that Gentiles would have to be circumcised like them in order to "join" The Way, the leaders of the fledgling church, like James and Peter and Paul, made it abundantly clear that this was *not what Jesus would do*, and thus was unacceptable. We as a people of faith, in-dwelt by the Holy Spirit, are called to love God and love each other. There is no definition of who "each other" means and who "our neighbor" is, other than that offered by Christ when making crystal clear in the parable of the Good Samaritan, that the one who is least like you is your neighbor and deserving of your love and respect. (Luke 10:25-29)

At this writing, yet another unarmed black man has been killed in a horrific manner, by a person in the position of authority held by our police, in a seemingly endless stream of similar injustices. While protests erupt across America, streamed on every media platform, America's premier reality entertainment show, America's Got Talent, was showcasing a black man who was unjustly convicted, imprisoned in Louisiana for 37 years, 20 of which were in solitary confinement, until released last year on DNA evidence. The evidence of his innocence was overwhelming at the time of his trial, but in the deep south, a white jury dealing with the rape of a white woman, wasn't interested in exculpatory facts. We are shocked and horrified at his story, and yet our society has kept true freedom out of the hands of an entire race of our citizens for eight generations! As long as a black man walking in a white neighborhood leads to suspicion as the initial reaction, we should be just as shocked and horrified as we are at each finding of the Innocence Project!

What would Jesus do? Jesus was not a political activist. Those who thought he would lead a revolt against the Roman occupation were sorely disappointed. Would He march in a protest, maybe, maybe not, but He surely wouldn't condone the violence and looting of a mob either. No, Jesus would sit anyone down who would listen and teach them what it means to love. He would probably do it with a story. But the moral of that story would be that every one of us that loves what America stands for, and loves what Our Savior died for, would find something to do to help.

The parable would begin with a man who was so sure of his own righteousness, that he was blind to the prejudice within himself, that had become automatic, completely unrecognized and unacknowledged. Next, it would have that man becoming more aware in conversation, listening better to others, and doing so while gradually recognizing the unsuspected prejudices in his own perspectives. After listening, he would seek to teach his children and grandchildren all of America's history, the good, the bad and the ugly. The man would start to recognize the inequalities all around him, and draw his friends into community efforts to ensure equal job and educational opportunities, training those with all backgrounds for jobs of the future. Becoming more active in his community and government, the man could use the ballot box to pick government officials who would seek to eliminate police who demonstrate their race hatred and/or poor judgment, officials who would concentrate efforts on transforming poor neighborhoods by providing green spaces, sidewalks, public safety measures, and decent housing. This is the tiniest of starts, in what would undoubtedly be a long parable indeed.

Christians have put on a new self, "which is being renewed in knowledge in the image of its Creator. Here there is no Gentile or Jew, circumcised or uncircumcised, barbarian, Scythian, slave or free, but Christ is all, and is in all." (Colossians 3:10-11) Our Savior is truly color-blind, and as we conform ourselves to Him, we must be as well. Our Pastor always used to say, "When you see a 'therefore' be sure and note what it's there for." Verse 12 states, "Therefore, as God's chosen people, holy and dearly loved, clothe yourself with compassion, kindness, humility, gentleness and patience. Bear with each other and forgive one another..."

What would Jesus do? Pretty sure He would do that.

"Now is the time to make real the promise of democracy. Now is the time to rise from the dark and desolate valley of segregation to the sunlit path of racial justice. Now is the time to lift our nation from the quicksand of racial injustice to the solid rock of brotherhood...We must forever conduct our struggle on the high plane of dignity and discipline. We must never allow our creative protests to degenerate into physical violence...I have a dream that my four little children will one day live in a nation where they will not be judged by the color of their skin but by the content of their character...I have a dream... (Rev. Martin Luther King, Jr. 1963)

Prayer: Dear Heavenly Father, thank You for loving us despite our constant failure to emulate Your Son! Knowing that we are saved by grave through faith in Your Son, in no way means that our actions need not reflect His teachings! James was right indeed, faith without works is not genuine. Let Your Holy Spirit move mightily within each of us to speak out against injustice when we see it, engage others in conversation, enlarge our circle of friends to include those who don't look or sound like us, and to wake every morning with heightened awareness for opportunities to demonstrate Your unfailing love. AMEN

JUNE 3

Discouraged

"They who wait for the Lord shall renew their strength; they shall mount up with wings like Eagles; they shall run and not be weary; they shall walk and not faint." (Isaiah 40:31 NIV)

I was a freshman at Rice University in Houston in 1974. I had graduated from Holland Hall in Tulsa, Oklahoma, second in my class, and a National Merit

Scholar. My SATs were nearly perfect. In short, I thought I was, in today's parlance, "just all that."

A perfectly good number really, seventeen. Could be the chapter number in a book, the number of years that I considered thirty five to be 'old,' the age at which sex was an all consuming interest, the number of billions the federal government borrowed in a week, the number of games the dallas Cowboys won in the '92-'93 season, the age of my Siamese cat, or any number of things.

It was not, however, a particularly good number to have scrawled in red across the top of my first chemistry test in college. While the public perception of physicians may have changed in the last forty years or so, in some ways it remains unchanged. Most graduates of medical school are not dummies. They may have the bedside manner of Bobby Knight or Donald Trump, but they're not supposed to be stupid. Even the average high school student knows that if you ever want to have "M.D." after your name, you better not ever see seventeen written at the top of anything you do!

Rice's incoming class of 1974 was over 90% class valedictorians and about the same for National Merit Scholars. In fact, it was a little embarrassing to have been salutatorian, even from an extremely academically challenging private school. Still, I thought I was pretty "hot stuff." It took exactly nine days for Rice University to disavow me of that illusion. For you *Top Gun* fans, it turns out I was *Maverick* on the first hop at Miramar, and Commander Mike Metcalf had just ceremoniously cleaned my plow! Lo and behold, it turned out there were kids from all over the country with considerably more cerebral firepower than moi!

Seventeen? I of course assumed that must be the number I had gotten wrong...nope. Then I assumed it would be graded on a curve...nope. In the immortal words of astronaut Gus Grissom, accused of letting his Mercury capsule sink in the Pacific after panicking and blowing the hatch too soon, I had "screwed the pooch." This was literally the first time in my life (other than handwriting in third grade) that I had not received an "A." It may seem silly to you non-anal retentive, non-compulsive types reading this, but this was *huge* to a pre-med student! Discouraged is probably not an adequate adjective.

All of us have times in our lives when we are down-hearted. Often, it is the result of what we perceive as our own failures, or at least our own inadequacies. Had I been a person of faith as a freshman in college, a seventeen might have made much less of an impact than it did. Why? Because I would have known with certainty, that I was "fearfully and wonderfully made." (Psalm 139:14) Because I would have known with certainty that, "God had plans to prosper me and not harm me, plans to give me hope and a future." (Jeremiah 29:11) Because I would have known with certainty that, "In all things, God works for the good of those who love Him, who have been called according to His purpose." (Romans 8:28) Believe it. Even when life deals you a seventeen.

"Why my soul are you downcast? Why so disturbed within me? Put your hope in God, for I will yet praise Him, my Savior and my God." (Psalm 43:5 NIV)

Prayer: Dear Heavenly Father, we love You and praise You for Your steadfastness! We can always rely on You to work things out according

to Your will and our betterment. When we are disappointed in ourselves, let Your Holy Spirit remind us that there is nothing we can do or fail to do, that would make You love us any more or any less! AMEN

JUNE 4

Waiting

"Do not be quickly provoked in your spirit, for anger resides in the lap of fools." (Ecclesiastes 7:9 NIV)

A couple weeks ago I was operating in our outpatient surgery center. Elective surgery was once again permitted with severe restrictions, during this stage of the relentless pandemic. Not only were we all required to wear personal protective gear including N95's and shields, but once a patient is intubated or extubated, no one can open the operating room door for 21 minutes. (Don't get me started on the controversial arguments behind that particular draconian rule!)

In any event, shortly into the procedure I discovered that the scrub nurse had pulled the wrong trocar for the case, such that the laparoscope and camera would not fit down the sleeve. Normally this was a 10 second fix by switching out the trocar for the next size up. With Covid-19 however, we had to wait another 15 minutes before anyone could open the door to go get the correct trocar. Are you *kidding me?*

My mother used to quote a phrase that came immediately to mind. "***Patience is a virtue. Possess it if you can. Seldom found in woman...never found in man!***" Waiting is not something I am particularly adept at. Delayed gratification is just not my thing. This could be the reason for AMAZON being my one major stock holding. But the fact is, waiting isn't comfortable for anyone.

Of course, there are much bigger waits than delivery of a trocar. Waiting for a baby to arrive comes to mind. (Poor elephants!) Waiting to see if the cancer's all gone; waiting for the biopsy results; waiting for your teenage child to return when it's already long past curfew; waiting for Christmas when you're eight; waiting till your father comes home; (Yikes!) waiting in a surgery waiting room; waiting to see if your name is on the list of layoffs; waiting for someone missing to be found. Those my age and older remember waiting for the spacecraft to come back into contact after traversing the dark side of the moon; or waiting to see if the parachutes opened during re-entry. The list is, quite naturally, infinite. Waiting can be excruciating.

When a close friend is waiting in that surgery waiting room, it is often best to just be there, as Job's friends in the bible were; more a comfort in their silent presence, than they would be in giving "helpful" advice or platitudes. Waiting can go hand in hand with patience, or hand in hand with anger and frustration. I can tell you from personal experience that option "A" works better. The *Message* translation of our opening quote illustrates this well. *"Don't be quick to fly off the handle. Anger boomerangs! You can spot a fool by the lumps on his head."* Other scriptures can tell you too.

Hopefully, at one point, you will have gone to Galatians 5:22 and memorized the nine Fruits of the Spirit. Number three: patience. Now, recall that these are not talents to be developed and honed, they are outgrowths of the indwelling Holy Spirit, when we give Him free reign in our lives. That means that as we become more Christ-like, in other words, as we are *sanctified*, these fruits will manifest themselves more fully in our actions and daily demeanor. We become more Christ-like by getting to know Him intimately. We get to know Him intimately through prayer, study of scripture, observation of His magnificent Creation all around us, worship, fellowship with other believers, and obedience.

Waiting can be tough. Waiting on the Lord can be tough. Often we would certainly prefer that God acted on our timetable rather than His! As I've said before, "All men desire to serve God, just most would prefer to do so in an advisory capacity!" But Christ has gifted us with patience when He gifted us with the Holy Spirit! We can "work on being patient" with various tricks from counting to ten all the way to furious exercise, but that won't be as effective as keeping your eyes focused on Jesus to the very best of your ability.

"So Jacob served seven years to get Rachel, but they seemed like only a few days to him because of his love for her." (Genesis 29:20 NIV)

"Love is patient, love is kind. It does not envy, it does not boast, it is not proud." (1 Corinthians 13:4 NIV)

"A hot tempered person stirs up conflict, but the one who is patient calms a quarrel." (Proverbs 15:18 NIV)

"Wait on the Lord; Be of good courage, And He shall strengthen your heart; Wait I say, on the Lord." (Psalm 27:14 NKJV)

Prayer: Dear Heavenly Father, we know that your ways are not our ways and your thoughts are not ours, but it is still hard to wait sometimes. Holy Spirit remind us that the Lord waits patiently on us every day, to come to Him when He calls, and to grow into obedience. Grant us the peace of mind to wait on outcomes in faith, not worrying before things have even occurred. Are not the flowers of the field clothed and the sparrows fed? AMEN

JUNE 5

Frenetic

"Ignorant zeal is worthless; haste makes waste." (Proverbs 19:2 ESV)

My drive to work each day is only 6.6 miles, of which 2.5 is on a freeway. Almost every day, I am surrounded by the same cars, since I routinely leave the house at the same time, and presumably a lot of them do too. Almost every day the same red Honda Civic ends up behind me at a red light, about 1 mile north of the freeway on-ramp. He tailgates immediately after we start off on the green, until I pull over a lane, and then he surges forward to tailgate the next guy. He never changes lanes to pass, just pushes the person in front until they move and then he rushes forward again. He takes the same freeway exit I do, but he is usually half a mile ahead when he does. But by the time I turn into the hospital, he is almost always pulling up to the red light just beyond the driveway into which I've just turned. Occasionally I get a glimpse at his ever-present scowl.

Aside from the fact that he will undoubtedly be involved in a rear-end collision one day, he just seems, well, unhappy. With apologies to *Aesop*, it seems that ***slow and steady wins the race*** (or at least ties!) It's not so much that we arrive at the same point at the same time that matters, but that he is usually unhappy at the start of his day, and I am not!

I remember as an intern at UCSF in the early 1980's, there would be nights when I was simply frantic that I was so far behind! I just couldn't believe another emergency was walking through the door when I hadn't begun to sort the ones I was already dealing with. One of my senior residents took note of my distress one of those nights at about 2 AM when my world was falling apart. She motioned me into an empty room for a moment of quiet. "What's going on?" she asked me. "I'm swamped, that's what's going on. I mean this is impossible!" I was near tears. Not too manly in the eighties. She realized immediately what the problem was. "Forget the paperwork. Just take care of the patient. You can catch up when things quiet down." She was so right. It changed my world, and I've never forgotten it. Today you might phrase it this way, ***"Keep the first things, first!"***

Get up every morning and thank God that you are alive and have been given another opportunity to demonstrate His love through your care for others. Ask Him to direct His Spirit within you to lead you to opportunities, to do your job well, and to take just one step at a time. The author of Hebrews encourages us to run the race with endurance, keeping our eyes fixed on Jesus! He says nothing about leaving the other competitors in the dust. I'm not suggesting you need to plod along, or even imitate the turtle, or the sloth, I'm just suggesting that you put Christ first in the morning, involve Him all through the day, and just concentrate on doing your best with what's in front of you and not fretting about what you have to do next!

"Adopt the pace of nature. Her secret is patience!" (Ralph Waldo Emerson)

"Let us lay aside every weight, and the sin which so easily ensnares us, and let us run with endurance the race set before us, looking unto Jesus, the author and finisher of our faith…" (Hebrews 12:1 NKJV)

"The plans of the diligent lead surely to abundance, but everyone who is hasty comes only to poverty." (Proverbs 21:5 NKJV)

Prayer: Dear Heavenly Father, we love that You are there with us first thing every morning! As we work our way through each day, taking opportunities as they come to ease other's burdens, let Your Holy Spir-

it make His presence known, calming us, slowing our frenetic pace with self-awareness when necessary. Help us keep first things first Lord. AMEN

JUNE 6
Rufous

"For His invisible attributes, namely, his eternal power and divine nature, have been clearly perceived, ever since the creation of the world, in the things that have been made." (Romans 1:20 ESV)

My wife and I often sit on the window seats in our breakfast room, sipping coffee, and looking out at whatever we can see. Most often this is at first light, or right as the sun is setting, the former before breakfast and the latter after dinner. The other evening, *Sterling,* our large Tuxedo cat, was sitting on the sill at the open window, only a screen protecting the object of his intense but quickly shifting gaze. We humans are usually watching the bikers and dog walkers on the trail across the street. *Sterling* is more closely interested.

This particular evening, when we looked closely to see what had his tail twitching back and forth, it was a hummingbird drinking from our salvia. Now, we don't see many hummingbirds in Dallas, Texas. We see them frequently in the summer months in coastal Maine, but rarely here. So, me being me, I had to look this little fella up on iBird plus. Turns out he was a male Rufous Hummingbird whose summer range is northwest Canada, and whose winter range has only a tiny sliver on the map that comes through Dallas, extending from West Virginia meandering all the way down to the Rio Grande. It is May as I right this. He better get with the program if he's gonna be in northwest Canada by June 21st!

Have you ever thought about some of the wonders of nature like this one? How on earth does this little guy cross 3,000 miles, 14,000 foot mountains, and arrive on the Pacific Coast of lower Alaska? Ever seen a flock of hummingbirds flying over? I haven't. How high do they fly? Do they travel at 100 feet above the ground or 5,000 feet above ground? The iBird app says they nest further north than any hummingbird in the world, and travel as far as Mexico in winter. While they are rarely seen in groups very large, there are words for such gatherings: "bouquet, glittering, hover, shimmer, and a tune," have all been used for this. We found information on their feeding, nesting, and breeding habits. We found maps of their range, migratory patterns, and descriptions of their preferred habitat. We found not one word about how in the heck they get from Mexico back to Canada with their tiny little wings and tiny little bodies! They must use an awful lot of energy! No wonder they have to make frequent nectar stops!

Look around you every day. You will see miracles at every turn. Things that might just pass you by are actually fascinating, if you take the time to look into them! It just never ceases to amaze me that there are people who watch a hummingbird, even for a moment, and doubt the existence of God! Try reading

Lewis Thomas' classic book, *Lives of a Cell,* to boost you along, if you have any trouble being fascinated by the world around you!

"I think nature's imagination is so much greater than man's, she's never gonna let us relax!" (Richard P. Feynman)

"Those who contemplate the beauty of the earth find reserves of strength that will endure as long as life lasts." (Rachel Carson)

"Sovereign Lord, You have made the heavens and the earth by Your great power and outstretched arm. Nothing is too hard for You." (Jeremiah 32:17 NIV)

"The heavens declare the glory of God; and the firmament shows his handiwork." (Psalm 19:1 NKJV)

> ***Prayer: Father God, how wonderful and mysterious are Your creations! Who has followed the hummingbird when she migrates? Who can count the stars in the skies, or the quarks, neutrinos, or electrons in the palm of our hands? Help us keep our awe in front of us every single day that we are privileged and two live in a nd care for this magnificent world You have made for us! AMEN***

JUNE 7
Bluetooth

"For Christ has not entered the Holy Places made with man's hands, which are copies of the true, but into heaven itself, now to appear in the presence of God for us!" (Hebrews 9:24 NIV)

I recently had a first world problem. I needed a power cord to connect my iPhone 10s to the stereo on my sailboat. (Told you it was first world!) You see the recent iPhones, once again, have switched to a different kind of connector, and the old one neither powered nor could connect my phone to the stereo. Similarly, I was missing the 9 or 11 or 14 pin connector, or whatever it was, needed to give a Power Point lecture with a projector intended to be connected to my Apple Powerbook. I subsequently dug through the second right hand drawer of my desk at home, searching for both of these elusive, yet essential, intermediaries. What I found was a rat's nest of twisted cords of different colors, lengths, diameters, and power sources!

Now, even though the reader probably thinks I was alive when the earth was cooling, most of my electronics, from Bose Minis to Google Home, to Alexa, to my truck, are all equipped with Bluetooth, which allows them to communicate with my iOS devices. How did we ever even exist before Bluetooth? Even my house's incredibly poor internet and wifi connectivity, (are ALL houses at the very *edge of the fiber optic cable's* service area?) does nothing to stop the power of the magical Bluetooth.

As a child, my wife used to picture talking to God like a tin can held to your mouth attached to another tin can held to God's ear, with a really really long string in between! Luckily, we we don't have to depend on a string. We don't even have to rummage through a drawer in a desperate attempt to find the right way to connect! We actually have our very own dynamic Bluetooth to connect us to God, that is actually a 'who' rather than a 'what!' Jesus Christ is our intercessor, our advocate before God the Father! Where once God's people had to depend on the High Priest to enter the Holy of Holies in the Tabernacle to offer sacrifices on our behalf, we have the Perfect Sacrifice Himself both indwelling us and standing before God at the same time! Christ promised to send us a helper, and He did, in the form of the Holy Spirit! The Holy Spirit intercedes for us when we don't even know what to pray! Even though we can speak directly to God the Father, Christ knew we would need help. The Spirit intercedes on our behalf with Christ, who is our advocate in the very presence of the Creator of the Universe! How's that for solid, reliable Bluetooth connection?

"In the same way, the Spirit helps us in our weakness. We do not know what we ought to pray for, but the Spirit Himself intercedes for us through wordless groans. And He who searches our hearts knows the mind of the Spirit, because the Spirit intercedes for God's people in accordance with the will of God." (Romans 8:26-27 NIV)

Prayer: Lord Jesus, thank You for standing before the Father on our behalf! We know that You look into our hearts rather than at our actions, and thus the Spirit knows what we want to say to You even when we can't find the words. We can come before You in our minds, and sometimes simply listen for You, since the Spirit has already interceded on our behalf! What a Blessing! AMEN

JUNE 8

Opportunity

"When life gives you lemons, add melted butter and dip some lobster in it!" (Stuart Scesney)

Last night I was on call at the hospital. I arrived home at 6:30 AM. After a brief recovery, we put the e-bikes on the rack, and took them to a park trail about fifteen miles away, planning a picnic after our ride. It is Saturday, of Memorial Day Pandemic Weekend, and I am writing this missive, post shower and nap.

Before our excursion, while I was prepping and loading the bikes, helmets, water bottles, etc., my wife was making lunch. Instead of the usual sandwiches, she made individual salads in Tupperware to pack into the bike bag intended for the rear of my bike. I walked into the kitchen just as she finished. The salads looked fabulous, with lettuce, spinach, arugula, red onion, glazed pecans, grape tomatoes, Gorgonzola cheese, and a home made vinigrette. I asked if we needed napkins, and she grabbed a couple and handed them to me. I asked if there were plastic forks in the containers, and she said we had real ones! We put cold packs in the bottom of the bike bag, threw in the salads (knowing the ride would toss them) and zipped her up!

The park trail was one we had never ridden, and much of it was beautiful. The partly cloudy morning turned quickly sunny and warm, and there were lots of people meeting in lawn chairs, not too terribly compliant with social distancing, as restrictions are easing rapidly in North Texas. As noon approached, and we grew hungry, we found a park bench in the shade, next to a Rec Center. It had a beautiful view of different types of trees blowing in the brisk breeze along the edge of a flowing creek. There were song birds flitting all around, squirrels dashing about, and people walking dogs, as we unloaded our water and salads and got comfortable. That's when I asked where the forks were.

"What do you mean, 'where are the forks?' I told you to pack real ones when you asked!'" I responded with a slightly exasperated, incredulous tone, "I asked you if you needed plastic forks and you said you had real ones!" My wife shook her head and said, "That may have been what you heard, but it is most definitely not what I said!" This is one of those critical moments in a marriage. We both looked at the very tossed vinigrette covered salads in our laps, and burst out laughing. Pat said, "Well we can just eat with our hands like they do in the Middle East!" I said, "Those two Triscuits you included look like perfect "sporks" to me!" We watched the birds and the breeze in the trees and ate our salads more carefully and thoughtfully than ever-before. I think we commented on how delicious every component was as we worked to get each into our mouths, and not on our shirts. We both agreed, that it was possibly the best lunch we had ever had, and the first salad we had ever, in our cumulative 128 years of life, eaten *without a fork!*

Someone once said, "When life gives you lemons, make lemonade!" See each unplanned obstacle as an opportunity! The Bible is full of life lessons that follow this pattern. Job took the sour bitterness of loss, and with his faith, turned it into the sweet renewal of his life and family. Joseph was thrown into a pit and sold into slavery by his brothers. He took that circumstance and turned it into the second most powerful position in all of Egypt, and a platform to show his brothers love and forgiveness. Moses was found floating in a river, adopted, but then wanted for murder, and yet became the savior of the Chosen People, leading them out of slavery to the Promised Land. David was a shepherd boy, disparaged by his older brothers, but a boy who knew how to sling a stone, and he used that skill to kill Goliath and defeat the Philistines. There are literally scores of scriptural examples. Peter denied Christ three times at a critical moment, and yet used that human weakness as a part of his testimony to become the Rock of the Church which Christ had intended for him.

But, you say, in each of these examples, God intervened supernaturally to help the individual who turned his situation around! I say to that, ***exactly!*** God has given you a Spirit of Power, not of Fear! (2 Timothy 1:7) He wants you to use it and He wants you to do so by ***trusting and depending on Him!***

Now, did my faith in God *really* help with the fork situation? You bet it did! God gave me a help-mate to depend upon, and *I had faith in her!* Taking advantage of a bad situation, whether it is big or small, and turning it to good, requires certain qualities. It requires calm, not anger; patience not frustration, gentleness and kindness, not bitterness and blame; self-control, not fury; love not hatred; and finding the joy in any situation, not the sadness. Oh wait! Those sound an awful lot like the Fruits of the Spirit! (Galatians 5:22) Oh, and my wife has them in spades!

You should try eating a salad with a Triscuit!

Prayer: Father God, thank You for the Spirit! If we would just give Him reign in our lives, we could always eat the salad with a Triscuit instead of the loss of a fork ruining our day!! AMEN

JUNE 9

Anchored

"'I will surely Bless you and I will surely multiply you.' ...this hope we have as an anchor of the soul, a hope both sure and steadfast, and one which enters within the veil, where Jesus has entered as a forerunner for us, having become our High Priest forever..." (Hebrews 6:13-19 NASB)

June

One who has sailed for any reasonable length of time, has had the experience of heading into a desired cove to spend the night, anchoring, dropping sail, and securing the boat for the night. The inexperienced sailor learns quickly however, that like everything else on a sailboat, there is a fine art to anchoring effectively. The novice believes that either the weight of the anchor, or the shape of the part that rests on the sea floor, holds the boat in place, resisting the force of both wind and waves. Not quite. The experienced sailor, on the other hand, knows this is not the case, but occasionally forgets it! Cruising in my father's 32 foot sloop off the coast of Maine, my son and I were reminded that in a high wind, your boat is going to move from where you want it to stay, unless you pay particular attention to assessing the situation carefully when anchoring. (Be calm! No animals or boats were seriously injured in the process of re-acquiring this bit of seafaring knowledge. Enough said.)

There are whole categories of anchors like the *drogue*, made of cloth and used as a sea anchor to drag behind a boat, slowing and directing its passive movement; the *mooring* anchor, usually made of cement and used in a permanent location to hold a boat in place; the *working* anchor, usually made of steel and intended to be dropped in the water on a chain and/or rope, to counter the effect of wind and current for a short period of time. These anchors are of all different types, weights and shapes, often depending on the type of seabed most commonly encountered.

Working anchors can be heavy storm anchors, lightweight lunch hooks, or medium weight for typical overnight use. All of these can be either *burying or non-burying,* the former designed to dig into soft muddy bottoms and the latter to sit on a hard bottom. There are over twenty types of anchor in widespread use. Most yachts or larger sailboats, however, use either the popular *Danforth* with sharp flukes that articulate around the head pin, or for heavier boats and stronger currents, the older *CQR or Plough* anchor. Both are attached to a chain lead and can be stored on a bow roller. That's two. There are eighteen more. Not as simple as you might think.

But here's the most important part. None of them work at all if you simply drop them into the water directly under your boat! They all require a length of rope and chain, called the anchor *rode,* and the amount of rode required depends on the wind, waves, current, weight of the boat, type of the anchor and quality of the seabed! Furthermore, the rode is a combination of chain and rope that allows it to sag (called *catenary*) and lie almost horizontally near the anchor, but also strong enough and stretchy enough to absorb the shock of the boat jerking in the waves without pulling the anchor out of the bottom. The *scope* is the ratio of the length of anchor line let out in relation to the depth of the water from the deck to the sea floor. In rough water or overnight, the scope should be at least 5:1, so that in 20 feet of water, at least 100 feet of anchor line would be required.

The author of Hebrews assures us that God's promise of Blessing is an anchor to our soul that will hold fast! Knowing that we are neither condemned by God (Romans 8:1) nor abandoned, (Deuteronomy 31:8) is surely a hope that will keep our boat from splintering on the rocks of a lee shore, and us from drowning in the sea of circumstance we know as life! But we know that anchor, that hope, is worth nothing if placed incorrectly! The author of Hebrews goes on to say that our hope, our anchor, has been *carried forward,* beyond the veil (inner Holy of Holies within the Temple, where God resides) by Jesus, our High Priest! *Christ Himself, then set our rode according to the correct scope*! He, like sailors of old, rowed forward in a dinghy, carrying the anchor of our hope with Him, in order to place it exactly!

The anchor of our soul is our hope in the Promise of God's Blessing, but that anchor is worthless without Christ! It is Christ who has become our intercessor, who allows us to come into the presence of God, only because we are clothed in His perfect righteousness! It is He who sets our anchor. If we drop our own anchor too close, right beneath the boat, the line is too taught, and the first wave will set us adrift! If our anchor, our hope, isn't carried forward, with Jesus, then we are like one striving to be Holy, striving to keep every rule, attempting in our own power and wisdom to earn the righteousness God requires. Israel and Judea went this route, and ended up utterly destroyed and in exile.

We are saved by Grace alone, through faith alone, in Christ alone, but in growing more Christ-like, we have to permit the Holy Spirit within us to move and stretch and sway. Christ has made us free through His redemptive act and resurrection. Free not just from the hold of sin, free not just from guilt and shame, but free in every way, *to live.* Christ has taken our hope forward, into the very presence of God, perfectly setting our scope to a rode that is long enough, strong enough, and stretchy enough to keep our anchor securely in place, but still allow us to move as needed.

Excuse the diversion from the sailing metaphor, but remember in Top Gun, when Cougar lost the edge and turned in his wings because he was holding on too tight? Don't hold on too tight. Be thankful that Christ has given your anchor line the proper scope, and placed your hope right at His Father's feet. You have to be free to swing on your rode, or you might end up on the rocks.

Prayer: Dear Heavenly Father, we praise You for giving us Your Son as our High Priest! Without Him our hope, our anchor, might be misplaced, thinking that in our own strength and wisdom we could hold onto righteousness. Only when we look to Jesus to set our anchor properly, is our faith and our hope secure! AMEN

JUNE 10

Trivia

"A text out of context, is a pretext for a proof text." (Pete Briscoe)

Each Saturday night for the last couple of months of pandemic 2020, there has been a family trivia game played out online via *Zoom*. We have pitted our extended family, from Maine to Texas to California, against another extended family that I believe populates New England for the most part. I don't know them. My brother and his wife know them. My brother, his wife, their kids and their spouses congregated in rural coastal Maine earlier in the year than usual, taking advantage of the built in "social distancing" that God has already provided in the area.

My brother and I were made for trivia games. As children we would spend hours pouring over the best gift our parents ever gave us: The World Book Encyclopedia! (For the Millennials, these were *actual physical books* with 22 alphabetized volumes that had articles on everything! Okay, similar to *Wikipedia*, but no "search" function and actually fact checked before printing!) I am not sure how our parents passed it down to us, but anyone who knows us today will tell you that our thirst for knowledge has not dissipated in the least!

Now, some would argue that a collection of "facts" stored in your temporal lobe does not constitute "knowledge." I would agree wholeheartedly, but I would also contend that it is at least *closer* to knowledge than having a temporal lobe virtually devoid of any facts at all! *Zoom* trivia does at least, clearly illustrate the principle that facts in context are certainly more meaningful, useful, and thus easier to remember. For instance, if I give you four bars of a song, you may or may not be able to identify it. If I add the lyrics that accompany those four bars, your chances increase. If someone else in the family takes those four bars and sings beyond them to the chorus for which the song is named, well, now you are 'cooking with gas' as my dad used to say!

A couple centuries ago, historians tell us, the bible was studied more intently and much more widely than it is today. Remarkably, virtually every home in America had a copy of the Bible in some form. Often, in the absence of any other books, it was the source for learning not only scripture, but how to read and write as well. And these were bibles printed on actual paper, like our World Books! There was no search engine, only a concordance at the back. There was no button you could press to bring up a myriad of different commentaries that scrolled along with the text as in apps like *Olive Tree, Blue Letter Bible, OpenBible, Bible or Logos,* just to name a few. Still, people studied.

There are those who will quote you Bible trivia. There are those who have memorized facts, lists, verses, prophecies, miracles, you name it, and more power to them. But be wary of anyone who quotes a verse and either can't tell you where it is from, or worse, can't tell you in what context it was written, especially if they are using it to prove a point. There are an infinite number of examples, but here are two well known verses. Romans 8:28 is often quoted without the following verse, because 'predestination' is seen as controversial. Likewise, Ephesians 2:8-9 is quoted without reference to verse 10, especially by those who wish to separate works from faith.

I am not terribly adept at memorizing Bible verses word for word, as many are. But I'm okay with that, because it seems to me, a bit of an anachronism anyway, since today we have scores of different translations at our fingertips. What I learned during seminary, was that *knowing the story that surrounds a verse*, and roughly where to find it in the average 1800-2200 page Study bible, made it much more useful than simply knowing the single verse and its exact reference.

Whenever you have a few moments not dedicated to some task, working at the frenetic pace that I am afraid many of us apply today, sit down with your iOS device and download one of the apps I mentioned. If you already have a favorite scriptural source, sit down with it. Think about your emotional state at that moment. What is happening or just happened in your life, that has made you feel the way you do at that moment? Are you happy? Sad? Anxious? Exhausted? Angry? Frustrated? Thankful? Whatever comes to your mind, use the search function in your chosen app, or if you only have a bible in your lap or a digital translation on your iOS device, then Google that emotion. For instance, Google, "What does the bible say about being frustrated?" You'll be amazed at what happens!

Take any of the verses listed, go to them, and read at least the full chapter in which they occur. If you have the time or the inclination, choose any of the Study notes in your study bible or on the app you are using, and read what it says about that verse and the surrounding verses. It might take you 10-15 minutes, total. Finally, pray for the Holy Spirit to help you interpret what you have read and apply it to your particular circumstance.

The bible is full of fabulous stories of romance, intrigue, empire building, wars, regime change, you name it! Every aspect of life is addressed in scripture. Who knows, a little Bible study might even help you with Zoom Trivia, unless the categories are One Hit Wonders from the '60's, World Series Winners in the '50's, Asian Rivers, Insects of South America and NeoClassical Architecture in Wales.

"Trivia games are designed to make us feel better about the random, useless facts that are all we have left of our education." (Chuck Palahniuk)

"The brain may die, but my compulsion for useless trivia lives on!" (Molly Harper)

"There is no such thing as trivia in a strategic mind." (Toba Beta)

Prayer: Dear Heavenly Father, we love you! Thank you for Your Word, and for all the people down through two millennia who have studied it, translated it, and written it down, so that we might go to it for whatever

we need! Holy Spirit, slow us down long enough to treat the Bible not as a collection of trivial facts, but as the revelation of God and what He wants for us that it is! AMEN

JUNE 11

Siblings

"Definition of Siblings: children of the same parents, each of whom is perfectly normal until they get together." (Sam Levenson)

What can I say about my brother? I mean, you know, that even children would be permitted to read. ☺ They say that siblings are the only enemy you absolutely can't live without! I am the younger brother. That means there has never been a time for me, when there wasn't a "first born" somewhere nearby or in the conversation. Down through the millennia, first sons have been the heirs to titles, to land, to money, to privilege. Second sons, on the other hand, have always resented it, from Biblical Jacob cheating his older brother, Esau, out of his inheritance, to the prodigal son who left in anger knowing that his older brother would get the lions' share of the inheritance. It would seem that the second sons had reason to complain of unfairness, until we see that God often favored the second son over the first, as with Isaac and Ishmael, Jacob and Esau, Perez and Zerah, Joseph and Reuben, and even Solomon over his unnamed older brother who died as an infant.

While the scriptural principal behind this trend might well be Christ's proclamation that the first shall be last, the fact remains that in this life, when the chips are down, your sibling is always there for you. There is no question that while growing up, my brother often took the heat as the elder, even if I was the instigator of whatever mischief had occurred. While it seemed my big brother beat me in every competition, he was always available to play again, even after I repeatedly claimed he had cheated, or I had flipped over the chess board, or whatever horrible little brother things I did that I can't now recall! When I felt threatened at school, there was always my big brother to look out for me. Later, through college and medical school, whenever I ran into a sticky wicket, he was there to get me out. Even today, both in our mid-sixties, I know that if everything falls apart in my life, I will always be able to turn to my brother.

I've watched this with my own children. Now grown, the girls have an almost physical need to get together from time to time. Many of my son's escapades while a teen, have only recently come to light because his sisters had his back, and together they made sure the parental units never had a clue! All our kids lived through the emotional trauma of becoming a blended family, and it's clear they depended on each other, always having each other's backs.

My wife is an only child. I am probably not speaking out of turn when I say one of her regrets has been the lack of a sibling, even when she sees our daughters or my brother and I going at it!

Siblings are special. It's not just blood. They've often experienced not only the same upbringing, but the same cities, moves, schools, churches, and sometimes even shared friends, and hand me down clothes, toys, bikes, you name it. Siblings have shared memories.

Christians certainly understand this, having been adopted into God's family as sons and daughters. (Ephesians 1:5; Romans 8:15) This quite naturally makes all believers brothers and sisters, and it is used as a term of endearment and deep respect throughout the New Testament. (Romans 7:4; 1 Corinthians 1:26; Galatians 1:2; 3:15) While siblings are naturally rivals, having competed for their parents' approval and attention, they are also a constant that can be turned to throughout one's life. My mother was very close to her little brother right up until his death, as was my father to his little brother. Siblings are for life.

If you are blessed enough to have a brother or a sister, make sure that you let them know from time to time that you wouldn't have it any other way. If you are estranged from a sibling, "un-estrange" them right now, today, or at the latest, tomorrow! Don't go through life holding a grudge or refusing to forgive a sibling. In the end, you've caused yourself suffering and lost an invaluable resource.

Christ calls us to love God and love each other. Scripture repeatedly refers to that "each other," as brother and sister. God did that for a reason.

"If you mess with a big sister, remember there is always a younger crazier sister behind her...that's who you don't wanna mess with!" (Anonymous)

"My brother is my best friend until he tells on me. Then he's my brother." (Anonymous)

"Brotherhood—man's oldest competition. Sisterhood—man's oldest cult." (Anonymous)

> *Prayer: Dear Heavenly Father, thank You for our siblings! We love them in a unique way. They remain one of the constants in our lies, and constants are often comforting. Thank you for adopting all who love Christ into Your family, so that we might have the rights and privileges of being the sons and daughters of the Almighty God! Whom shall we fear indeed? AMEN*

JUNE 12

Shake It Off

"I stay out too late, got nothin' in my brain, that's what people say, mmm, hmm,
That's what people say, mmm, hmmm...
But I keep cruisin', won't stop movin', It's like I've got this music in my mind,
Sayin' it's gonna be alright!
Cause the Players gonna play, play, play and the Haters gonna hate, hate, hate,
Baby, I'm just gonna shake, shake, shake, I shake it off. I shake it off!

In 2014, the already wildly popular Taylor Swift, released a song she co-wrote with Max Martin and K.J. Schuster, titled "Shake It Off." The song and music video became one of the most popular ever released, by anyone, at any time. How does a pop tune, aimed primarily at adolescents to young adults, become one of the most played ever?

Less than a year before, "Let it Go," another incredibly popular song performed by Idina Menzel as the Princess Elsa, in the Disney musical *Frozen*, had already swept to the top of the charts with every child in America, and before long, every child in the world, knowing the lyrics! How is that even possible?

Well, if you'll excuse the pun, they both struck a chord! All of us have experienced hurt because of what someone else said about us, or thinks about us. Even those mature enough to realize that sticks and stones might hurt their bones, but words are never *supposed to hurt*, find that they nevertheless do. People can hurt your feelings with what they say to your face, or what they gossip about you behind your back. Then you can hurt yourself yet another way, by holding onto those things with bitterness and anger.

Interestingly, the scriptures instruct us to avoid all three. The bible tells us repeatedly that what comes out of our mouth is dangerous, difficult to control, hurtful, and reveals our heart. (James 3:3-10) Furthermore, it tells us specifically that gossip comes not out of the Fruit of the Spirit, but from the flesh, stirring up conflict and separating friends. (Proverbs 16:28; Galatians 5:22) Lastly, the bible tells us that our mental health and happiness depend on letting go of bitterness and anger. (Ephesians 4:31) When hurt is dwelt upon it turns to anger, and anger to a desire for revenge, and revenge acted out, makes us no better than the one who injured us initially. (Romans 3:10-20)

So, what should we do when people hurt our feelings with their comments, gossip or even actions? *SHAKE IT OFF!* One way is to lose yourself in the joy and energy of music and dance! It's hard to be bitter when dancing! Taylor Swift suggests that the players, the haters, the heartbreakers, and the fakers aren't gonna change, so just forget about them and go on with your life, enjoying every moment as the gift that it is! *LET IT GO!!* Princess Elsa says to turn away, slam the door, she no longer cares what people are saying about her; let the storm rage on, the cold never bothered her anyway!

Next time you find yourself stewing over some hurtful comment, or hear about something negative said about you behind our back, remember that other's opinion of you really has no bearing on your happiness. Only God's opinion matters, and He's already shown you how much He loves you through Christ! He is the one that made you and He thinks you are AWESOME, "fearfully and wonderfully made!"

"The truth is, unless you let go, unless you forgive yourself, unless you forgive the situation, unless you realize the situation is over, you cannot move forward." (Steve Maraboli)

"Bitterness and resentment only hurt one person, and it's not the person we're resenting." (Alana Stewart)

"Let go of resentment for it will hold you back. Do not worry about what could have been, what is to come is what matters." (Leon Brown)

Prayer: Dear Heavenly Father, we love You! When You first hear our prayer in the morning, remind us that it is Your opinion that matters and not any others. If we act justly, seek mercy and walk humbly, we know that we are on the right path and the criticism of others need not be hurtful if we just let it go! AMEN

JUNE 13

Pink LlamaCorn

"Enjoy the little things in life, for one day you will look back and realize they were the BIG things! (Anonymous)

One of my daughters who lives about 30 minutes away, has spent the last several months dealing with the 2020 Pandemic by home schooling our 8 year-old grandson and 6 year-old granddaughter. While there are many joys in seeing a part of their lives normally spent in the classroom, it is a grueling task in many ways. For all those moms out there trying to suddenly become teachers and at the same time do their own jobs, we salute you! When there wasn't enough time in your day to begin with, it seems an almost insurmountable task to all of a sudden have to deal with all the hassle of remote learning in terms of not only curriculum and teaching, but wifi connectivity etc. etc. Still, the kids need "down" time, which is harder to find when in many places in the country they can't just go outside and play due to Corona virus.

So, when our daughter wanted to bring the kids over to swim, on a day when I was off and school was "out," we readily agreed. The kids love the pool, and could spend hours in there making up games. But they are also siblings, so naturally bickering over the inflatable alligator inevitably arose. There are, of course a myriad of ways to handle this situation, and probably better than their grandfather's approach. But once we were reduced to the threat of removing them from the pool if they didn't stop fighting, (and thus egregiously hurting ourselves since the adults actually finally had some time to sit and visit while they splashed about,) I decided as the "Papa" that we would remove them from the pool so we could all go to Walmart and get another floating toy. The American solution, right? You're thinking, "Oh good, throw money at the problem... buy more 'stuff' after all the railing I've done against acquiring 'stuff!'"

Before setting out, we looked at the offerings online, of course. I've never seen Allie, the six year-old, quite as excited as when she spotted the large pink floatie which evidently was a combination of a Unicorn and a Llama! (Two of her favorite things!) When we arrived, the parking lot was full of cars and the store with people wearing masks, all enjoying the recent relaxation of 'shelter at home' regulations. I warned Allie and Liam as we negotiated the aisles, that they might not have exactly what they wanted in stock. But when we found the right aisle, by sheer dumb luck, there was the pink LlamaCorn in a big box, right at Alllie's eye level! They were both jumping out of their skin! I'm sure there is joy all around us all the time, but their faces would be preserved in my memory forever when I told them they could lug the box to the front, and along with the goggles their mom found, we flew threw self-checkout. Total time in Walmart from car doors open to back in the vehicle: 12 minutes. You gotta love America!

If possible, the joy only intensified once my genius grandson Liam, suggested using the leaf blower to blow up the LlamaCorn, since we had no pump that would fit. He pumped and the creature grew and grew and grew. The rest of the afternoon, they dove onto, flipped over, hid under, splashed across, and laughed constantly, completely neglecting the poor alligator. But the fighting had stopped.

Ecclesiastes 11:9 tells us, "You who are young, be happy while you are young, and let your heart give you joy in the days of your youth!" Yes, you can criticize this old grandfather for reaching for the credit card to solve a small problem, but the LlamaCorn was a remarkable buy at $20, and had we done anything you could normally do, (but NOT in a pandemic,) the price of admission would have been far greater for the four of us. Okay enough rationalization. The point is an easy one. Christ came so that we might live more abundantly, leaving guilt and shame behind, knowing we are forgiven. That abundant life comes directly from doing what He told us: loving each other. A little bit of love can bring a huge amount of joy! Okay, so we do have a giant pink LlamaCorn floating in our pool for an undecided amount of future time. But the smiles on those faces for hours is what life is all about. It's the little things. We could have flown them to Europe and done the classic tour and they might never have had memories as happy as the pink LlamaCorn.

The next time you can bring that kind of joy to anyone, for any amount of time, do it. Trust me, you'll get just as much out of it as they will, plus you have the extra knowledge of knowing that Jesus is smiling along with them!

> *Prayer: Dear Heavenly Father, thank You for the stages of life! It is Your wisdom that brings us the simple, memorable pleasures of youth and shares them with grandparents! The joy of our young ones brings back memories of our own carefree years, and that, added to the pleasure of helping to provide those memories for our children and grandchildren! Pretty good design God! AMEN*

JUNE 14

Hither and Yonder

"Strategy equals execution. All the great ideas and visions in the world are worthless if they can't be implemented rapidly and efficiently. Good leaders delegate and empower others liberally, but they pay attention to details, every day. (General Colin Powell)

Yonnie. In a roundabout way, she was responsible for the tremendous blow to my forehead at 4:30AM that Monday morning. The more direct cause lay in my position at the time, lying under the steel desk, with my head about six feet from the cow theoretically under my supervision at the time. I had only been asleep for an hour or so when something struck the sole of my feet, instantly propelling me into a sitting position. Unfortunately, the desk didn't quite allow adequate clearance for the sitting position, and thus the fierce blow to my head only microseconds after my foot was insulted. I uttered several expletives, college students being particularly adept at this form of communication. I slid myself angrily out from under the desk and looked up, way up, at the face my assailant, who unfortunately was 6 foot 6 inch, Dr. Denton Cooley, famous heart surgeon, and my boss at the time.

"Are you supposed to be watching my cows?" he snapped. I decided this wasn't the time to remind Dr. Cooley that they weren't *technically* his cows.

If you are at all confused, add to the scenario that this scene is playing out on the third floor of the Texas Heart Institute in 1977. I was a premed student at Rice University, across the street, trying to earn a few extra bucks at night by taking readings on the cows who were implanted with total artificial hearts. It was five years before the device would be placed into Barney Clark at the University of Utah, and thus a fierce competition was playing out at various institutions across the country. My job was to record the Swan-Gantz catheter readings, administer antibiotics, feed, water and otherwise nurture the two cows whose natural hearts had been replaced with plastic ones operated pneumatically. There were a number of less famous cows throughout the nation prior to Barney Clark.

The Utah team had calves (little cows for non-Texans) living for hundreds of days more than our cows, and actually outgrowing their hearts. Or moos had a nasty tendency to die of sepsis or get sacrificed in the interest of drug studies for companies who in large part funded the research. But that meant our cows had many more holes in their chests for hoses and IVs and opportunities for infection. College students who fell asleep on the job did little to advance our competitive status in the research.

While Dr. Cooley caught me snoozing, he allowed me to rise to my feet and fill him in on the night's events. He made it clear that errors in drug administration, or catheter readings, could lead to faulty data or worse, the premature loss of a cow. That would translate into millions of dollars in lost grant money, which in turn meant that people could lose their jobs, which down the road could mean that sick people would lose their lives!

Attention to detail matters and attention to detail is part of doing a job diligently and doing it well. Recall that Paul's letter to the Colossians instructs us to do just that: *"Whatever you do, work at it with all your heart, as working for the Lord and not human masters."* (Colossians 3:23) Remarkably, "the Lord" is even higher up the scale than a cardio-thoracic surgeon! We have God-given talents. Don't waste them. When you go to work each day, ask the Holy Spirit to remind you that anything less than your best is an insult to the Lord.

Oh, Yonnie. Yonnie is short for Yonder. Hither and Yonder were the two Harlequin Great Danes belonging to Dr. Norman, the heart surgeon directly in charge of the lab. He left one there over night for security. Yonnie was 200 lbs and looked down on me when her forepaws were on my shoulders. Her growl was similar to what you would hear from a Russian T-72 tank as it maneuvered over a berm right before crushing you into oblivion. She preferred the couch. I slept on the floor beneath the desk.

"A man's accomplishments in life are the cumulative effect of his attention to detail. (John Foster Dulles)

"There is the flash in the pan, the sudden success. But continued success is totally dependent upon tremendous attention to detail. (Frederick Lenz)

Prayer: Dear Heavenly Father, we love You, because You first loved us. You spared no effort in our creation and in providing the means to our salvation through Christ's perfect life and redemptive death. Remind us as we work, that we are ourselves nothing short of miraculous, and it behooves us to utilize our gifts to maximum effect in order to bring Glory to You! AMEN

JUNE 15

Be Prepared

"But in your hearts honor Christ the Lord as holy, always being prepared to make a defense anyone who asks you for a reason for the hope that is in you; yet do it with gentleness and respect." (1 Peter 3:15 ESV)

Englishman Robert Baden-Powell published the first edition of his *Scouting for Boys* in 1908. It was originally a self-help manual regarding tracking, wood-craft, and the powers of observation. Its intent was to foster self-improvement and self-discipline in young men so that they might be of increased benefit to the Empire, as dutiful citizens of the Crown.

The well-known and oft quoted motto of the Boy Scouts is *"Be Prepared."* Baden-Powell later expanded on this, further defining the slogan to include the following.

1) *Be Prepared in mind* by having disciplined yourself to be obedient, and also by having thought out beforehand any accident or situation that might occur, so that you know the right thing to do at the right moment, and are willing to do it and

2) *Be Prepared in body* by making yourself strong and active and able to do the right thing at the right moment and to do it.

You know by now, that my family sails. Any sailor can tell you that racing success, cruising success, and just flat out survival on open water, all depend on being prepared. And, barring a crew who are younger, stronger and more fit than yourself as the skipper, you need to be prepared in both mind *and* in body! Now, admittedly, my Catalina 350 in Texas has bi-directional power winches, and both a self-furling main and genoa, not to mention an inboard diesel and autopilot, so that my preparedness in body need be somewhat less, now that I am in my 60's, than it was in my 20's! Nonetheless, the principle still applies, (and the Greenwich 24, Ensign, Tartan 37 and Dark Harbor 17 that our family sails in Maine all have power-*nothing!*) In fact, the preparedness of mind overlaps that of the body, so that, for example, failing to remember to open the seacock for water intake to your diesel engine causes it to over-heat and thus become only a very heavy, not very useful, piece of metallic ballast!

Now, there are lighter examples of not being "prepared," while sailing. Like the time *Tuffy*, the miniature Schnauzer, launched himself over the side of *Fledgling*, the classic wooden, gaff-rigged, Dark Harbor 17, in Maine. Both the dog and the boat are owned by my uncle, who was sailing by himself at the time. Ignoring peril to both himself and his boat, my uncle dove into the frigid water just northeast of the Howard Ledges, pulling for the now frantic Schnauzer, while *Fledgling* sailed slowly away, the sheets having at least been released by the quick-thinking skipper. Despite the quick-thinking however, the wind still took the sailboat far enough away that he and *Tuffy* had to be hoisted from the water of the Reach by a passing pleasure cruiser. As they motored in pursuit of the "not under command" *Fledgling*, the couple who owned the cruiser were kind enough to say nothing about the fact that my uncle had been sailing *au naturel*, and simply handed him a large towel to both dry and cover himself. Admittedly, the dog was *au naturel* as well, but this was somewhat more expected of a Schnauzer.

Christians are called upon to be prepared as well.

First, Christ said we would be known by our fruit, meaning it is the way we act that identifies us as Believers. (Matthew 7:16) When people ask us about our lives, our stories, our worldview, our attitude, our joy: we need to be prepared to explain the Gospel to them! (1 Peter 3:15)

Second, Christ warns us to be prepared for His return, because we will know neither the time nor the place. (Mark 13:32-37) If we abide in Him, He will abide in us, and we will be prepared whenever He ushers in the New Heaven and the New Earth! (John 15:4; 1 John 2:28; Revelation 21:1-2)

Lastly, Christ has prepared a place for us! Our Savior has promised us that in God's house there are many rooms, and one of them will be ready for us when the time comes, when Christ returns to take us with Him.

Luckily, while we might be *au natural*, naked in the flesh as the day we were born, we will be clothed in the righteousness of Jesus, and able to stand before the Father unashamed! (Isaiah 61:10)

Remember, every day, that being prepared in mind, body and spirit is always the key to success! We need to keep physically fit, we need to keep in a supportive community of faith, we need to get familiar with our Owner's Manual, the Bible, and we need to talk to the Father whenever and wherever we think of it!

Prayer: Dear Heavenly Father, we love the life You have given us! None of us wants to leave this world, and we know You have imbued us with that desire for life! But we will be prepared for that day when the Son returns and we will all go to a better place even than this beautiful earth! But before that day, and with the help of the Holy Spirit, we will remain prepared to give a defense of our faith and explain the love of Christ to others who still struggle under the burden of guilt and shame. AMEN

JUNE 16
Legal U-Turn

"Trust in the Lord, and do good...Delight yourself in the Lord, And He shall give you the desires of your heart. Commit your way to the Lord, Trust also in Him... Do not fret-it only causes harm." (Psalm 37:3-8 NKJV)

One of the very most powerful men in the world pulled off to the side of the road for safety. He was crying so hard that his tears were compromising his vision on that dark August night in 1973. The man was an attorney and a former US Marine. He was a tough, take no prisoners, be sure to return fire kind of guy. He was a man whose entire life was ruled by the belief that the "ends justified the means." He also happened to be the recently fired White House Special Counsel to President Richard Nixon, and the Watergate scapegoat for the infamous gang of Nixon's inner circle, which included Haldeman, Erlichman and Dean.

Chuck Colson was as low as you could get. The incredibly intelligent, industrious and overwhelmingly ambitious, young, superstar, with the Ivy League pedigree, the former Marine turned honors graduate from George Washington Law School, then the dirty tricks wizard of Richard Nixon's ascension to the Presidency, was in the midst of a spectacular fall from the pinnacle of power. Hounded by the press as the secret Nixon Oval Office tapes were sought, Colson had stopped into the home of Tom Phillips whom he had met a few years previously when his law firm had been courting Raytheon. Phillips had told him then, that he had accepted Christ, and it had radically changed his life! Colson was skeptical then, and skeptical this time, until Phillips talked with him about C.S. Lewis's *Mere Christianity* with its irrefutable logic, and read aloud Chapter 8: "The Great Sin of Pride." Colson found himself filled with shame as he heard a description of his prideful, ruthless, self-righteous self in those words. Phillips took him through Psalm 37, and then prayed with him.

Colson recalls an energy flowing into him suddenly and identifiably while his friend prayed. He felt a wave of emotion that brought him to tears. Phillips gave him his copy of *Mere Christianity,* and told him to expect a call from a friend of his named Doug Coe. Then he left. It was after his sobs became uncontrollable that he pulled over to the shoulder. There he prayed, "God, I don't know how to find you, but I'm going to try. I'm not much the way I am now, but somehow I want to give myself over to you." He related the above to Eric Metaxes, his longtime friend and biographer, "I hadn't accepted Christ. I didn't know who He was. My mind told me it was important to find out first, to be sure that I knew what I was doing...only something that night came into me and urged me to surrender-to what or whom I did not know." (*Seven Men, Eric Metaxes, Chapter 7)* He told only Patty, his wife and in the coming weeks he read voraciously, as he would his entire life. He took notes throughout *Mere Christianity.* Then, several weeks later, in an isolated cottage on the coast of Maine, he asked Christ into his life.

The rest as they say is history. Chuck Colson was convicted of felonies related to Watergate and sentenced to three years in Federal Prison. Prior to incarceration he was befriended by a group of powerful men in Washington, all of whom belonged to a Christian men's group called simply, The Fellowship. Contacts from there and repeated epiphanies in prison, led him to the understanding that God had a greater purpose for him. One night after parole was denied and his son was arrested on a drugs charge, Colson was convinced by one of his Fellowship friends, to literally turn all his problems over to God. Chuck prayed a prayer of thanks and praise to the Lord for leaving him in prison, for losing his license to practice law, even for his son's arrest, knowing that God had a higher purpose. Colson tells Metaxes that this simple prayer changed everything from that point onward.

Not coincidentally in his opinion, the-hard nosed judge that had sentenced him to the maximum, decided to commute his sentence to time served and he was released only days later. Colson went on to dedicate the next four decades of his life to the nurturing of his Prison Fellowship Ministries. The program spread worldwide to more than 100 countries and hundreds of thousands of participants and volunteers. Colson went on to be a much sought after evangelical speaker. He authored many books including, *Born Again, How Now Shall We Live?, Loving God, The Good Life, The Body, The Faith* and many others. His radio program *Breakpoint* had 8 million listeners daily. He founded the well-known ANGEL TREE, to get Christmas presents to families of prisoners; the JUSTICE FELLOWSHIP, devoted to criminal justice reform; ECT (Evangelicals and Catholics Together), promoting understanding and teamwork in missions; INNER CHANGE, in Texas prisons with the help of his friend President George W. Bush to ease re-entry into society; and the CENTER FOR CHRISTIAN WORLDVIEW, to teach the only perspective that Colson knew could rescue and make sense of a hurting world. The list goes on and on.

Chuck Colson passed away in 2012. He was a modern-day 'Saul to Paul' transformation, going from amoral, prideful bully, to humble, loving servant, who dedicated the rest of his life to improving the lives of society's forgotten, and bringing them the joy and peace of Christ.

Next time you think you aren't good enough, or moral enough, or smart enough, or life has got you too far down, remember Chuck Colson. The last words he wrote were, "I want my funeral to be joyful. I don't want people to be sad because I believe with every ounce of conviction that death is a homecoming…it's the culmination of life. It's a celebration!"

"Never give in—never, never, never-in nothing great or small, large or petty—never give in except to convictions of honor and good sense." (Charles Colson)

Prayer: Dear Heavenly Father, we love you! Let the Holy Spirit help us be bold enough to literally turn everything over to You! How our lives could change if we only would! Thank you Lord for Your servant Chuck Colson who showed us that no matter how far we are from You, we can make a legal U-Turn, accept Your gracious gift of Christ's forgiveness and get our lives back on track! AMEN

JUNE 17

Marriage of Christ

"Let us rejoice and be glad and give Him glory! For the wedding of the Lamb has come, and his bride has made herself ready. fine linen bright and clean was given her to wear." (Revelation 19:7-8 NIV)

One of the greatest rewards of having been an Ob/Gyn for 40 years is witnessing the rejoicing of the parents at the birth of each new child, always slightly different, always very special! One of the rewards of having gone to seminary is officiating at weddings and witnessing the joy of couples and their families. But it's also fun to see the emotion on the faces of all those who are remembering their own nuptials as they watch! In fact, several days ago, I had this pleasure once again, presiding over the marriage of one of my medical partner's daughters.

God created both of these joys, birth and marriage, and they are woven into the scriptures which reveal His character. As Nicodemus learned from Christ Himself, both the incarnation of Christ, God born fully human, and the re-birth of Believers, are central to the Gospel. Likewise, wedding analogies are used throughout both testaments signifying God's love and faithfulness to us, despite our own repeated infidelity!

Over and over again man has turned away from God, and over and over again, God has forgiven us, as told throughout the Old Testament. We have prostituted ourselves repeatedly, like Hosea's wife, Gomer, turning away from our Creator to worship almost anything else you can think of! God, after our endless unfaithfulness, finally let us have it our way, and the Chosen people ended up largely destroyed, dispersed or in exile. (Hosea 8:7-8) But like Hosea, our God would go to unheard of extremes to get us back, because He never stopped loving us just that much!

First, God gathers His people back from exile. (Isaiah 54:5-8) Second, He courts us, His intended bride. Traditionally, in biblical times, the Groom brought gifts to his fiancé's family, wooing her through them. God does exactly this with His gifts to us of faithfulness, righteousness, goodness, love, and compassion. (Hosea 2:19-20) Third, God provides the means to wash us before the wedding, for that washing is a ritual purification and cleansing, always done before a wedding ceremony. God knows we are filthy inside and need His righteousness! He washes us clean with the forgiveness He won for us on the cross. He washes us clean with His own blood. He then sends us the indwelling Spirit as a final promise of the wedding to come, a sign of our engagement! One day, the wedding will finally take place in heaven, where we the church, join with our bridegroom joyfully and eternally, at the marriage supper of the Lamb!

Some people have trouble with the concept of God sacrificing His son for us. Some have trouble with the imagery of being washed clean in His blood. For those just exploring the Christian faith, and for those new to their faith that find these metaphors disturbing, perhaps you could start by viewing the whole course of Biblical history as one long courtship! God loves us more than we can imagine. Really. Just imagine how powerful the Creator of the Universe is! Everything He does would be of a magnitude and perfection far beyond what we could even begin to understand. So maybe picture that giddy love of the engaged couple, planning on spending an eternity together, and whose engagement culminates in a blow-out fantastic wedding celebration, with the best friends, the best band, the best food and the best cake you could ever imagine! You think God doesn't know how to have fun? Think again. He's spent all our eons on earth planning this shin-dig! GET READY TO PARTY DOWN FRIENDS!

"Love never gives up, never loses faith, is always hopeful and endures through every circumstance." (Corinthians 13:7)

"When you make sacrifices in marriage, you sacrifice not to each other, but to unity." (Joseph Campbell)

"Love is not something you feel. It's something you do." (David Wilkerson)

> ***Prayer: Dear Heavenly Father, thank You that Your love endures despite our faithlessness! Thank you that Your love is the greatest love man has ever been offered and could ever know, and we need only say "Yes," and You shower us with faith, peace and love and the anticipation of being honored guests at the wedding supper of the Lamb! AMEN***

JUNE 18
Reducing Sail

"Martha, Martha, you are anxious and troubled about many things, but one thing is necessary. Mary has chosen the better portion." (Luke 10:40-42 NIV)

There are huge advantages to living in the 21st century, no question. But along with the tremendous advances in technology which allow ease of living, transportation, and increased life expectancy, come stresses never before experienced by man. Everything in our Western society is ***fast!*** In America we are even more intense than in Europe, no less the Far East. We might live longer, but there are quite a few of us who never stop to smell the roses until they're piled on our caskets!

When you're sailing, you have to be aware and knowledgeable about wind, weather, currents, hazards, as well as the integrity and function of your vessel. One thing a sailor knows to do, and it's now easier than ever before, with smart phones and weather apps, is to be prepared for a "big blow." Where we sail on Lake Texoma and on the Maine coast, the winds can be gusty, even on sunny days. But a squall can also show up suddenly on the horizon, and then race down upon your position with alarming speed. *Reducing sail* is the answer.

There are many ways to decrease the size of the airfoil that the wind contacts. If you ***anticipate*** a coming blow, you can ***reef*** the mainsail with ties which allow only a portion of the sail to be raised. The same can now be accomplished on modern cruisers with roller-furling of the mainsail into the hollow mast. But the most common way to accommodate a high wind, is to roller-furl the triangular sail in the front of the mast, called the jib.

The key is to be prepared. The sailboat caught in a sudden squall which has not reduced sail, can meet with disaster in a number of ways. They can lose their mast, they can tear their sails, but worse they can be swept onto the rocks or even capsize.

If you are going *full tilt* at your work life 24/7, you won't be prepared when the squall comes over the horizon. When a family member falls ill, when your son gets arrested, your daughter has an unplanned pregnancy, you get demoted, lose your job, or your spouse finds someone who has more time and energy for them; well, then you might be dismasted, or you might even capsize and sink.

Starting tomorrow, ***slow down!*** Reduce your sail! Apply it to every aspect of your life. Don't drive as fast. Don't stay at work as late. Delegate. Accept a lower income. Take more vacation. If you're my age, ease into some type of retirement strategy. Spend more time with your family and you'll know them better and they'll know you better. That way, when the whitecaps start to froth, and the wind begins to howl in the rigging, you'll be ready. You reduced sail, and you did it in time!

Christ understood this. Martha didn't until He explained it. They would only have Jesus on earth a little while and Mary knew to treasure that time. Well we only have each other on this earth a little while too! Reduce your sail skipper.

" Do not toil to acquire wealth. Be discerning enough to desist." (Proverbs 23:4)

"The world is passing away, along with its desires, but whoever does the will of God abides forever." (1 John 2:17 NIV)

Prayer: Dear Heavenly Father, we love You! Thank You for the drive to do our best that You have given to us, but let Your Holy Spirit remind us that "doing our best" doesn't mean frantically working to acquire more wealth, but instead means taking every opportunity to slow down and show Your love to those around us. AMEN

JUNE 19

Cats and Dogs

"One who is faithful in a very little is also faithful in much, and one who is dishonest in a very little will be dishonest in much." (Luke 16:10 ESV)

I like cats. I like dogs. We've had both, off and on over the last sixty years. Those of you that have had both as pets may have noticed one certain truth: dogs are not cats, and cats are definitely not dogs.

There is an old expression: "Dogs have masters, cats have servants." Now, I know there is no way I won't get in trouble with some of you for this devotional, but there's a lot of truth to that expression. Our Tuxedo rescue, *Sterling,* is a big boy. He's a fully armed (not declawed) indoor-outdoor cat, and we're not sure, but we think the neighborhood coyotes run and hide when they hear the flap fall on his cat-door. He wears a GPS on his collar so we can find him if he sneaks out at dawn or dusk, because we forgot to lock the cat door during those dangerous hours. You can just see how *annoyed* he is when we come to find him on those occasions, mystified as to how his people seem able to find him wherever he hides along the creek.

But, like many cats, he's a lover too. He sleeps on the foot of our bed as long as it suits him, and if we forget to put him out in the kitchen at 10 PM, he reliably attacks my foot at 1:38 AM, eliciting a forcible ejection usually accompanied by an actual swift kick launch from the bed. *Sterling* will crawl onto your chest when you are lying down or into your lap when sitting on the couch and purr loudly in supreme contentment, right up until the instant he suddenly tries to take your hand off at the wrist in his abrupt escape maneuver. Cats will play as well. *Sterling* will hockey stop treats thrown across the hardwood floor. He will stalk a fur mouse on the end of a long felt string attached to the end of a flexible plastic stick held in your hand. He will bat a white ping pong ball around the floor or in his circular cat-toy that sits on the floor. But he will do it....until he doesn't want to any more. He's on and off like a light switch in every area of his life.

Buddy, our last dog, was a Shepherd mix, rescue, who followed our teenage girls home one day fifteen years ago, when they were running in the rain. *Buddy* was playful too, but he played whenever I wanted him to, in addition to trying to get me to play when he wanted to! He would fetch; he would wrestle a stick; he would come, stay and sit on command; he would run next to my bike in the neighborhood; he would sit up in the passenger seat and hang his head out the window of my truck; he would lay across the transom when we sailed; he would run to the door when I came home, absolutely *overwhelmed with joy* that I had returned to him! In the evenings, he would sit at my wife's feet and rest his head in her lap, or lay on our breakfast room window seat and lay his head on the sill and watch the world go by. I only saw him growl twice: once when a stranger yelled at me out biking, another when a pit bull stray we had taken in temporarily, growled at me in his presence. Buddy passed five years ago, but Windsor, our new standard Labradoodle, is gentle, loving, smart, and equally devoted to his people. (AND he doesn't shed! :)

Dogs and cats both have lovable qualities. But dogs are *loyal servants who know their master's voice!* Our cat rarely acknowledges his name, and then only when there is food at the other end of the call. Our dogs come on command *just because it makes them happy to make us happy!* In fact, it's hard to escape the conclusion that our dogs actually *love us.* A dog will sacrifice his own safety for yours or your children's. There are thousands of examples. Hard to find many examples of cats doing that, ever.

I'm not sure this is a good analogy or not, but I really think we Believers ought to be a little more like dogs than cats. ***We need to listen for the Master's voice, and when we hear it, we need to follow commands.*** We follow those commands not because we get a treat in reward, but because we love the Commander! (We do have an advantage over dogs in that the commands are written down and we can read them.) Dogs are genuinely *excited to see you!* They are excited to see you whenever you show up, not just around mealtime. Do you think maybe we ought to be *excited* to pray, to worship in community, to see the Lord's work around us, as we witness His people serving others in need? Do you think maybe we ought to *defend our faith* when it comes under attack by a relativistic, secular world?

Be more like a dog. Wag your tail and bark a little when you see your Master!

"His master said to him, "Well done good and faithful servant. You have been faithful over a little: I will set you over much. Enter into joy of your Master." (Matthew 25:21 ESV)

Prayer: Dear Heavenly Father, we Love you! Forgive us that we sometimes greet you like a cat, pleased for a moment, but then jumping away and trying franticly to escape from You! Let Your Holy Spirit guide us into faithfulness, serving You ought of the sheer joy of being loved, and loving You back! AMEN

JUNE 20

Doxology

"Praise God from Whom All Blessings Flow, Praise Him all creatures here below; Praise Him above ye heavenly hosts; Praise Father, Son and Holy Ghost." (Thomas Ken 1637-1711)

I grew up attending a Presbyterian Church, but had I been in any other mainline protestant denomination, I still would have memorized the words above and the tune that accompanies them by the age of five! Known as the "Doxology" from the Greek *doxa* meaning "glory," and the Greek *logia* meaning "saying or word," it has been sung, usually after the collection of the offering, for over 350 years. It reminds us that we are but stewards of our wealth and possessions, and that all blessings, all good and perfect gifts, come from above! (James 1:17)

Thomas Ken was a Church of England bishop when in 1673 he wrote a prayer manual for the students of Winchester College. In it, he penned three different hymns, each to be sung in the morning, evening and if you were awake, at midnight. He ended each of his hymns with the words which would eventually become known as the *doxology.* According to William J. and Ardythe Petersen in *The Complete Book of Hymns*, Ken eventually became well aware that it was often difficult to sing a hymn of praise after a long hard day. He knew, because he would have some of the longest and hardest days one could have in years to come.

Orphaned as a young child, he was raised by his stepsister's husband, a well-known author and scholar. At age 15, Thomas entered Winchester College, then obtained a fellowship to Oxford where he earned a BA, was ordained in the Anglican Church, and then earned his MA at age 27. He led a succession of Anglican churches on the Isle of Wight, then in Hampshire before resigning in 1672 in order to return to Winchester as chaplain to the

Bishop. Charles II appointed him Chaplain to Princess Mary, wife of William of Orange while they resided at the Hague. However, Ken very shortly, insisted the Prince's cousin make an honest woman of the girl with whom he was currently sleeping.Not surprisingly, he lost his position. Surprisingly for the time, he kept his head, and returned to England, where he immediately became one of the King's chaplains.

Residing in Winchester once again when King Charles II brought his mistress there on a visit, Ken objected vociferously and refused to allow his mistress to sleep under the same roof. Charles actually recalled this two years later and insisted that he would have only that bold little priest that had refused him, as his Bishop. Ken was at Charles' death-bed shortly thereafter.

The new King was James II, a Catholic, and in 1687, at age 50, Thomas Ken was once again in trouble. He was confined to the Tower of London for refusing to sign King James II's "Declaration of Indulgence." This proclamation was supposedly intended to promote Freedom of Religion in Britain, but also served to promote the King's despised, Roman Catholicism. He was acquitted at his trial, but then found himself in trouble again, when protestant usurper William of Orange came to power after the Glorious Revolution. Thomas Ken and others, although Anglican, refused to swear William allegiance, believing it dishonorable since they had already sworn allegiance to James II. He lost his bishopric, but once again, managed to retain his head and went into retirement.

The familiar *Doxology,* sung to the tune of the *Old 100th,* is purported to be the most sung Christian verse in history. Thomas Ken wanted his students at Winchester to know that praising God at every hour of the day, was not only appropriate, but good for them. So it remains 250 years after he put pen to paper.

While it may be easier to "praise God when morning gilds the sky," and "your heart awaking cries," (Anonymous 1828,) Thomas Ken knew the value of praising God at the end of a hard day as well, no matter your circumstance. In fact, the *Doxology* has been sung for centuries *right after tithing,* in recognition that all we have really belongs to God the Father. If you grew up in a tradition other than protestantism, Spotify *Doxology.* I found 28 versions immediately, all sung to variations of the Old 100th. It's a tune that's hard to get out of your head! GOOD.

"Shout for joy to the Lord, all the earth. worship the Lord with gladness; come before him with joyful songs. Know that the Lord is God. It is He who made us, and we are His; we are His people, the sheep of His pasture. Enter His gates with thanksgiving and His courts with praise..." (Psalm 100 NIV)

> *Prayer: Dear Heavenly Father, why do we so often forget to praise You? All of our troubles, all of our pain, all of our fears, are as nothing when we look at a star filled sky or the open ocean! Spirit remind us to value every breath, every wonder that surrounds us, and praise the Father morning, noon and night. AMEN*

JUNE 21

Get Help!

"God is our refuge and strength, an ever present help in trouble. Therefore, we will not fear, though the earth give way and the mountains fall into the heart of the sea, though the waters roar and foam and the mountains quake with their surging." (Psalm 46:1-3 NIV)

I was nine years old and living in Houston, Texas. We lived in a newly constructed house on a residential street northwest of town, where many other lots were still vacant, or construction was ongoing. Houston is hot. Kids spent most of their time running around barefoot in cutoffs with a t-shirt, or no shirt, in the summer. The barrancas that led to the bayous, the vacant lots and the construction sites were all fair game for play. It was a different time, and parents let their children wander farther from home than they do today! My friends and I would ride our bikes down to the creeks and hunt for turtles, frogs, and often snakes; we would explore vacant lots and look for whatever treasure we could find on construction sites, when the workers were off.

One Saturday morning, while having a water gun fight in and amongst the 2 X 4s of a newly framed house, I managed to step on a board and drive two four inch nails through the bottom of my foot. I distinctly remember seeing them poking through the top of my foot, and thinking wow, I didn't even know this could happen! Remarkably, I didn't fall down immediately, but called for my friends to come over. When they saw the blood and the nails protruding, they screamed at me not to move, and one ran to get help. But I didn't listen. I panicked and yanked my foot up off the board. Unfortunately, that caused me to lose my balance and my injured foot came down on the same two nails once again, impaling me now in four places rather than two! This time I screamed, yanked my foot off again, and ran the several blocks home!

The rest is a blur except for a clear memory of lying face down in the doctor's office and having the misfortune to see the long needle with a syringe full of either anesthetic or antibiotic, right before he plunged it into the bottom of my food and moved it all around!

We live in a "me" world where every advertisement of every product glorifies your independence, strength, and ability to make your own decisions, and "go it alone." This even extends to the prevailing view that you can "make your own truth," and that "right and wrong" are just relative terms. Every part of this is wrong from the Christian Worldview! We seek to be *dependent* on our creator, whom we *trust completely* because of the love He has demonstrated for us through His Son. God makes it clear that the knowledge of right and wrong is layed out in scripture and imprinted on our conscience. It is not subjective, nor is truth.

I could have avoided four nails in my foot. I could have listened to my parents and a) not played on construction sites, b) worn shoes c) listened to my friends when they told not to move. I cried for help and then didn't listen. I have a feeling a lot of us cry for help and then don't listen. We may not listen to our loved ones, and we for sure don't listen to God much of the time, especially if we don't like what we hear. Remember, all men wish to serve God, but mostly in an advisory capacity!

I guess what I'm getting at is that all of us find ourselves in tough spots sometimes. All of secular society tells us to rely on *ourselves* and extricate ourselves from every predicament we encounter. "Pull yourself up by your bootstraps" and all that! *As Christians, we are called to do exactly the opposite.* Next time you find yourself euphemistically with two nails through your foot, look to your friends; look to your family; and look to God in prayer and scripture for the help and advice you need! That way maybe you can avoid four nails in your foot.

"The name of the Lord is a strong tower; the righteous run into it and are safe." (Proverbs 18:10 NIV)

"The Lord is a refuge for the oppressed, a stronghold in times of trouble." (Psalm 9:9-10)

"But they who wait for the Lord shall renew their strength; they shall mount up with wings like eagles; they shall run and not be weary; they shall walk and not faint." (Isaiah 40:31 ESV)

> *Prayer: Dear Heavenly Father, why do we forget the Helper that indwells us and turn to our own understanding when we get in trouble? Remind us everywhere we look of Your presence Lord, and keep our thoughts close to You so that in our times of need we turn naturally to You in prayer and to Your Word, and to our brothers and sisters for advice. AMEN*

JUNE 22

Washed in the Blood

"For God so loved the world that He gave His only begotten Son, that whoever believes in Him should not perish but have everlasting life." (John 3:16 NKJV)

Twenty eight years ago I was sitting on the dock at our lake house on Cypress Springs in east Texas. I had a fishing pole wedged under my leg, a good book on my lap, and our Labrador sitting at my feet. The kids were screaming as usual, bouncing on the trampoline just up the hill. There were a few sails on the Lake and more than a few Sea-doos. In short, it was a beautiful, lazy, summer Saturday, until the timbre of one of the screams took on a distinctly different pitch.

The dog turned and went barking up the hill to the house, and as I turned to see what was making the racket, the first scream was joined by another, but this one hollering my name! I bounded up the steps to the open back door and I still remembering seeing the floor of the mudroom completely covered in blood, and I mean completely. My 4 year old son was lying on the linoleum floor screaming as loud as a human can scream through sobs, and his mom had a beach towel wrapped around his lower right leg. My five year old daughter was standing in a soaking wet bathing suit with a towel pulled up over her chest, also crying but not quite as loudly as her brother.

I took a quick look under the blood soaked towel, re-applied pressure, picked him up in my arms and said, "Everybody in the truck. Kelly, you're up front with me." My wife jumped in back and I handed Andy over to her, and she immediately re-established pressure on the wound which simply welled up through your hands. We careened the 4 miles to the East Texas Medical Center, a 10 bed hospital with an "Emergency Room." As we pulled into the parking lot, unbelievably, there was a life flight helicopter on the lawn with its rotors turning.

We dashed inside, past the little check in desk, where a clerk made a futile attempt to slow us down. The ER doctor came running up in scrubs. I relayed what I had been told in the truck. My kids had been trowing buckets of water on the trampoline and jumping. When Andy ran inside to pee, he slipped on the utility room floor, and his bare right foot slid under the razor sharp sheet metal edge of the washing machine, slicing through skin, muscle, and maybe tendon, down to the bone. Evidently, the only thing that bleeds like the head is the foot. The tiny ER had a recent gunshot wound (Life Flight on lawn,) a heart attack, and a near drowning of a ten year old, all there at the same time, and the ER doc was overwhelmed. I told her this kid needed stitches, but that I could do it. An administrator told me even with a Texas license, I couldn't sew Andy up there without privileges. The ER doc turned to her and said, "You can go home now. We got this."

She turned to me and asked, "What do you need?" I told her just a table, someone to hold my son down, good light, 1% lidocaine with epi, and several different sutures. She called to Carl, an older but very sturdy looking janitor who would use his bulk to fixate Andy, face down, on one of the treatment tables. The ER doc then returned to gettin the gunshot victim out to the helicopter.

Andy was calmer, but didn't handle the lidocaine injection all that well. Through his tears he kept saying, "Daddy, do you know how to do this?" "Sure," I replied! "But I'm not having a baby!!!" says my 4 year old son, the critic.

Most parents of even one child, have had moments like this, where you just do what you have to do. Luckily, no tendons were severed, and although I got the bleeding stopped and the skin back together, had a plastic surgeon done the repair like I did, he probably would have been sued!

The point is that you would do ANYTHING for your child! A parent's love is ***absolutely unconditional.*** So, that being a given, what would it take for you to allow your child to be ***crucified*** in order to save others? It's hard to wrap your mind around it, isn't it? ***That's*** how much your heavenly Father loves you! When you look at one of your children and know you would gladly step in front of a train for them, that's a shadow of the magnitude and quality of the love we are talking about. Paul's language in Romans 8 and 9 in terms of our being adopted as sons and daughters, must not be taken lightly. Next time you feel threatened, or locked out, or unloved, remember who's your daddy!

"But God demonstrates His own love toward us, that while we were still sinners, Christ died for us. Much more then, having now been justified by His blood, we shall be saved from wrath through Him!" (Romans 5:8 NKJV)

Prayer: Dear heavenly Father, we love You because You first loved us. We praise You that You have made us equal sons and daughters of the Creator, worthy of the sacrificial love that even we as humans, may know from our families. AMEN

JUNE 23
Origins

"The Heavens declare the glory of God; and the firmament shows His handiwork. " (Psalm 19:1 NKJV)

My first degree was in biology from Rice University, long before those I attained in medicine and theology. That college degree came only twenty years after Watson and Crick described the building blocks of life in the DNA molecule. Many believe, including Christians, Jews, Muslims, agnostics and atheists, that the genetic transmission allowed by these and related compounds, coupled with "natural selection" of environmentally favored characteristics through random mutations, explain the development of advanced life forms on earth, including humans. Many others, in all the same groups, do not. Still others, believe that God created the universe and everything in it, and certainly could have used a process of evolution if He desired, given that the Creator would, by definition, be outside of time. Famous geneticist and evangelical Christian, Dr. Francis Collins, director of the Human Genome Project and head of the National Institutes of Health, certainly felt this was the case. He wrote *The Language of God* about the human genome largely in defense of that position.

Dr. Collins relates in his introduction, that in 1916 researchers asked biologists, physicists, chemists and mathematicians whether they believed in a God who actively communicates with humankind and to whom one may pray and expect an answer. Forty percent said they did. In 1997, the same survey found the same percentage of believers across the fields of science, despite the phenomenal liberal relativism found across American college campuses, and the commonly held erroneous belief that scientists are all atheists.

When Lee Strobel interviewed Walter Bradley, PhD., (Texas A&M University Department of Biology) about the common objection to faith that contends evolution has made God unnecessary, he countered with multiple points. The true Achilles heel of macro-evolution is the origin of life, in his opinion. Famous scientists like Haldane, Urey and Miller contend that early life arose spontaneously from a "pre-biotic soup." But NASA has proved definitively that no such soup ever existed! The methane, H2 and ammonia necessary for their building block theories to reflect reality, simply did not exist in the early atmosphere; only H20, NO2, and CO2. Did life evolve by chance arrangement of these molecules? Even proponents of evolution agree that 400 million years from cooling to life is not nearly adequate time for random assemblage of the simplest protein, no less DNA or the cell membrane! Could amnio acids have come together just because of their bond affinity? Mathematically disproven. Do some molecules have self-ordering tendencies like ripples in the sand or ice crystals, which would allow them to form complex molecules like a protein? Examples in nature are orders of magnitude too simplistic for this to be the case. Could the building blocks have come from space? Same problem: realistically requires intelligence for assembly. Could building blocks have come from ocean floor heat vents? Same problem: assembly. Even Carl Sagan, the great atheist astrophysicist, said *any information string* broadcast from space would prove intelligent life. Really? **Estimates are that the information string contained in a single cell would fill 30 volumes of encyclopedia, and yet skeptics claim this doesn't imply an intelligence behind its creation.**

Scripture is crystal clear on one thing: God created the heavens and the earth and everything in it! (Genesis 1) Some day science might be able to tell us how, but whether or not that day comes, doesn't change the facts, and doesn't change my opinion. Look around you. Just look. You don't even have to see a baby born. Just watch a flower open, or an Eagle fly, or the sunset, or the waves roll in, or the motion of the constellations. Don't be a dummy.

"For since the creation of the world, His invisible attributes are clearly seen, being understood by the things that are made, even His eternal power and Godhead, so that they are without excuse, because, although they knew God, they did not glorify Him as God, nor were they thankful, but became futile in their thoughts, and their foolish hearts were darkened." (Romans 1:20-21 NKJV)

Prayer: Dear Heavenly Father, we love You! We praise You for the wonders all around us that make even the most skeptical person of intelligence realize the foolhardiness of denying Your existence! We ask Your Holy Spirit to guide us when we enter into conversations with the lost, providing the patience and the words to turn them into seekers of the Truth. AMEN

JUNE 24

Lighthouses

"Behold, the days are coming, says the Lord, when I will make a new covenant with the House of Israel and the house of Judah... this is the covenant that I will make with the house of Israel after those days, says the Lord: I will put my law in their minds, and write it on their hearts; and I will be their God, and they shall e My people." (Jeremiah 31:31,33 NKJV)

There are 65 lighthouses along the coast of Maine. The ones that still function are automated, and for the most part owned by the U.S. Coast Guard. There are many lighthouses now however, which are privately owned, and those families often occupy them as their summer residences. Pumpkin Light is one of these and sits off the end of Little Deer Isle on Penobscot Bay, marking the western entrance to Eggemoggin Reach. That means it is directly across the Reach from our house. For all of my 64 years, the first thing one does on arrival, is to walk out in front of the house and gaze at Pumpkin! It is a view that hasn't changed for well over 170 years, as long as you don't look toward the Deer Isle Bridge built "recently" by New England standards in 1939.

But something has changed. For all of my life and most of my parent's, there has been no light at night in the light tower of Pumpkin Isle. The lighthouse was established in 1854, but went "offline" if you will, in 1933, having been automated for its last three years. Why have the lighthouses gone dark? The answer is of course there is a better way to know where the hazards are today. First there was radar and floating automated bells and lights, but now every ship is equipped with GPS. Where once the stars were necessary to navigate, now only a satellite! The knowledge of your position and heading is now "internalized." Stars and lighthouses were external guides. Today the source of needed navigational information can be held in your hand and its right in your boat!

The change is analogous to what happened to Old Testament Jews: where once they looked to their priests and the Torah for guidance, now the laws and precepts are written on the hearts of the believers! (Jeremiah 31) Jesus' incarnation, birth, perfect life, sacrificial redemptive crucifixion, and subsequent victory over death in resurrection, led directly not only to our assumption of His perfect righteousness by grace, but also to the indwelling Holy Spirit! That indwelling Spirit is our GPS! Yes, there have been endless analogies to Christ as the guiding light, and thus to metaphors about the lighthouse of the Lord. And it is true that He is our light. But that light is now an *inner light*. We no longer need a human priest to intercede for us in a Tabernacle or a Cathedral. We abide in Christ, and He in us, via the Holy Spirit. The prophet Jeremiah makes the promise of the New Covenant very clear. God will forgive our iniquity and be our God, if we will be His faithful people; and we will have His law in our minds and written on our hearts! We will *know Him* without even being taught, and we have the Holy Spirit to help us understand the scriptures.

Like the view of Pumpkin, Synagogues and Cathedrals are beautiful to look at, unchanging for lifetimes, but the *people are the church*, and we have been changed. We are now saved by grace through faith in Jesus, and He sent the Spirit to indwell us all. That's the change on the inside. The Light shines from within. Guidance is now and forever readily at hand.

"For all who are being led by the Spirit of God, these are the sons of God." (Romans 8:14 NIV)

"In the same way the Spirit also helps our weakness; for we do not know how to pray as we should, but the Spirit Himself intercedes for us with groaning too deep for words…" (Romans 8:26 NIV)

Prayer: Dear Heavenly Father, When we think of the Light that is Your Son, and we visualize a distant lighthouse warning us of danger from the hidden rocks, let the Holy Spirit speak up and remind us that the light of Christ is now inside us as well. When we feel lost and alone, and the storm is too violent and dark for us to see, we can be led by the GPS in our hand, the light on the inside, the Helper You sent to us! We praise You Father, that Your plan included a way for You to abide in us, and we in You, through the Spirit. AMEN

JUNE 25
Original Names

"As for Me, behold, My covenant is with you, and you shall be the father of many nations. No longer shall your name be called Abram, but your name shall be Abraham; for I have made you a father of many nations." (Genesis 17:4-5)

Names are interesting. When you've delivered as many babies as I have, you've had many opportunities to see young parents select their children's names. Often the name honors one of the new grandparents, or more commonly a great-grandparent. There is often a family surname included as a middle name. The first name often carries a special meaning, the first blessing of sorts. This name might reflect their ethnic origin, their religious beliefs, or simply the hopes they have for their child. When the child grows, they often alter their name. This may be rebelliously as teens, or thoughtfully as adults, or still, in some cases, because of marriage. But the individual's choice of Michael over Mike, or Patricia over Pat, or choosing to incorporate both their maiden name and their new husband's name, are all decisions that invariably accompany *change*.

Bands frequently have name changes that the public knows nothing about because they weren't famous with their original names. *Maroon 5* was once *Kara's Flowers; Destiny's Child* was *Girl's Time; Van Halen* was remarkably *Rat Salad; Pearl Jam* was *Mookey Blaylock; Nirvana* was *Pen Cap Chew* (Sorry, but I love that one!) *Led Zeppelin* was *The New Yardbirds; Black Sabbath* was, incredibly, *Polka Tulk Blues Band; Kiss* was *Wicked Lester; Coldplay* was *Starfish; The Grateful Dead* were *The Warlocks; Boyz II Men* was *Unique Attraction; The Who* was *The High Numbers;* and *U2* was *The Hype; The Bee Gees* were *The Rattlesnakes; New Kids on the Block* were *Nynuk;* and finally one of my personal favorites, *The Red Hot Chilly Peppers* were *Tony Flow and the Miraculously Majestic Masters of Mayhem!* The list could be much, much longer.

When people undergo a change so significant that it alters their perception of themselves, then either they or someone else sees fit to change their designation as well. Their name changes. In the Bible Abraham became Abram, Sarai became Sarah, Jacob became Israel; Simon became Peter, and Saul became Paul. There are many other examples, but in each a significant change has occurred in their relationship to God and to others. For thousands of years infant baptism, or in some traditions, Christening, has been the time when people of the Christian faith officially give their child a name. This is also the time that Christian families pledge themselves to bringing their children up educated in the faith. In many places such as Africa, the Middle East, India and the Far East, conversion to Christianity in adulthood is often accompanied by a change of name as well. That's because at the moment of conversion, when Christ is accepted and the Holy Spirit indwells, we are reborn! We become a new creation! (2 Corinthians 5:17; Galatians 6:15)

In the west, Christians do not often change their names after their acceptance of Christ. For some, raised in a Christian home, it was what they always believed. For others, while they may remember the exact circumstances and timing of their rebirth, a name change just isn't part of our culture. But, nevertheless, being born again as a Christian does change the way we view the world and the way the world views us. While God has loved us all from the start, it changes our relationship to Him as well. We are now forgiven, saved by grace through faith in the risen Christ! Once we were slaves to sin, condemned to death. Now we still sin unfortunately, but we have been granted the righteousness of Christ and have been offered an eternal reunion with the Creator! That's cool enough to warrant a new name in my opinion.

We may actually have a new name, for all we know! After all, we get new bodies after Christ returns. (1 Corinthians 15:44) The Bible tells us that God knows us by name! (Isaiah 43:1; Jeremiah 1:5; John 10:3,14; Psalm 139:1) What a reassurance to know that the unimaginably powerful force behind the Creation of the universe, knows your name personally!! That's a good thing to grab a hold of the very next time you feel unimportant, insignificant, or frightened of evil. Remember being a child on the playground and resorting to "My dad can beat up your dad?" (Come to think of it, that was probably exclusively a boy thing.) Well, it's something for Satan to keep in mind anyway, when he decides tempting you is a good idea.

Prayer: Dear Heavenly Father, we praise You that You know our name! Adopted as sons and daughters through Christ, perhaps you even have a new name for us that reflects the change inside of us! However we are called in Heaven, the certainty that You know Your sheep, that You will leave the ninety nine to rescue even one of us, is all we need to face whatever challenges lay before us! AMEN

JUNE 26

Farrier

"I have no need of a bull from your stall or goats from your pens, for every animal of the forest is mine, and the cattle on a thousand hills..." (Concerning sacrifice Psalm 50:9)

Your level of familiarity with the title of this devotion may well be determined not only by your level of education, but where you grew up and reside currently. There are occupations in this world that are carried out in such a way that they rarely meet the general public's eye.

We were on a shuttle bus from the brand-new gorgeous terminal at the Louis Armstrong International Airport in New Orleans, to the rental car center. Virtually all the occupants were wearing the ever-present 2020 Pandemic face masks, currently required for air travel. One moment before the bus pulled away from the curb, a final passenger came bounding through the double doors, put her two rugged looking bags on the rack and took the only seat remaining, next to my wife and me. She was a tanned, fit, mid-30's, strawberry blonde in a pink sweatshirt and jeans. Her ebullient demeanor was easier to assess than everyone else's, because she wore no mask. It was obvious from her open and friendly face, that a mask on her would have seemed a crime against nature.

We commented briefly on the degree of misinformation about Covid-19 across the country and how the world seems to have forgotten the original intent of wearing a mask, which was to prevent droplet exposure to others *if you were symptomatic*. We told her she didn't have to mask for us, we only had them on to make others feel comfortable at this point. We established that she was only in New Orleans for a one-night stay, and that she travelled a lot with her job. Holding onto the metal pole on the shuttle, we all noticed she had a similar bruise to my wife, on her right thumb. The etiology of my wife's injury was unclear, but our new friend told us about each scar on her hand, and which part of the pig had caused it! Some were crush injuries from their incredibly powerful bite, others were tusk injuries. Hmmmmmm.

Turns out Emily, that was her name, travels the world teaching a technique for calming and subduing pigs, cows and horses while working on their feet! As a Farrier, she was trained to shoe horses, but over time her specialization became hoof care for all of them. She had lots of pictures on her phone. Some of them were harder to look at than mine from surgeries! For two decades she has been a traveling hoof care specialist, treating pigs' hoofs, tusks, ears and eyes, as well as providing foot care for horses, mules, donkeys, goats, sheep, chickens and even dogs and cats!

Now, some of you might think that Emily's particular occupation is mundane, but I'm telling you she had an enthusiasm for what she does that would absolutely knock your socks off! (There's a foot joke in there somewhere.) The point is, she is an example of exactly what God wants us to do when He tells us to *"work heartily, as for the Lord and not for men." (Colossians 3:23)* Whatever you do, we are encouraged to do it with an awareness of God's character reflected in us, and awareness of His presence. *No matter what your occupation, your work is important to God!* If we learn nothing else from the pandemic of 2020, it's that literally *everything is connected*. The 'ripple effect' of each industry and service affected, is remarkable. In the same way, if you work in the factory that makes wooden pallets and wake up thinking you wish you did something *important*, something that *served others*, consider that your pallets carry the vegetables on the trucks, that carry the fresh produce to distributors, who pass the pallets on to more trucks that take the food to stores so that people can buy them, bring them home, serve their families, and keep their children healthy and growing!

Emily trims nails on pigs' feet. Those are God's pigs. Just like the cattle on a thousand hills. Get up every morning and plan to work as for the Lord. Do your best as though He were standing right in front of you. Because He is.

Prayer: Dear Heavenly Father, we love You! We know You have given this earth into our care; all the plants and animals and oceans and atmosphere. All our jobs are important to You! We ask Your Holy spirit to encourage us each day to remember that when our work seems boring or unimportant, that we are all interconnected and each small task done correctly, is useful to man as a whole and service to You. AMEN

JUNE 27

Back Pain

"Therefore, we do not lose heart. Even though our outward man is perishing, yet the inward man is being renewed day by day. For our light affliction, which is but for a moment, is working for us a far more exceeding and eternal weight of glory, while we do not look at the things that are seen, but the things that are unseen. (2 Corinthians 4:16-17)

I have what you would call a "bad back." While I've had several back and neck surgeries on intervertebral discs, all of which were "successful," I continue to intermittently collapse on the ground screaming when I have crippling lower back spasms. (I understand some 50,000,000 Americans have similar issues.) Over the last five years, QiDong and Yang Style Tai Chi every single morning, have strengthened my core and markedly decreased the frequency of these episodes. However, bending and turning to pet the cat this morning caused a twinge which is gradually tightening through the day.

I don't have crippling migraines, or insulin dependent diabetes, or a major birth defect, or dyslexia, or leukemia, or lymphoma, or a colostomy, or renal failure, or heart failure, or need an organ transplant, or a hip transplant, or you name it. But still I find a way to feel sorry for myself intermittently, and think internally how "unfair" it is that I have to deal with this, when other people have no problems with their backs! Really? I mean REALLY?

The now famous evangelist, motivational speaker and author, Joni Eareckson Tada, dove off a dock into Chesapeake Bay at age 17, and was instantly paralyzed from the neck down. I'm sure she would *love* to be able to feel some back pain! Paul reminds us in our opening verse, that we should view life from an eternal perspective. Our physical and circumstantial pain is only transient, and viewed as nothing compared to the "weight of glory" accrued in heaven by the nature of our response to those difficulties. **Tada said this perspective used to infuriate her!** She would never walk, never even use her hands, never feel what everyone else felt, and God thinks that's "light and temporary?" But after her fifth year of quadriplegia she began to understand how her accident was beginning to work for her good and God's glory: ***she was becoming more Christ-like!***

In her book, *Making Sense of Suffering,* Tada defines suffering as having what you do not want and wanting what you do not have. How we deal with that is directly linked to our attitude about God and how He works in our lives. Suffering can sanctify one individual, and in another breed only anger and self-centeredness. Understanding that God is Sovereign, and will work everything for good for those who believe, can shape an attitude that molds a more Christ-like character. (Romans 8:28; Ephesians 1:11-13; Isaiah 45:5-7)

Tada points out that afflictions have many effects on us and the Bible outlines them. They increase our awareness of God's sustaining power (Psalm 68:19,) they force dependence on God (2 Corinthians 12:9,) they break our spirit, humbling and emptying us, so that God may pour His healing onto the broken hearted and submissive (Psalm 51:17,) they drive us to discernment, to scripture and to obedience, allowing us to see things from God's perspective (Psalm 119:66,) and they weaken us so that we must lean on God's grace, discovering

His strength, and bolstering our testimony about His Grace!

Suffering helps us learn the mind of Christ, who Himself learned obedience through suffering. (Philippians 2:5-7) Suffering allows the life of Christ to show up in our lives, as we die to ourselves and our wants and wishes. (2 Corinthians 4:10) Suffering teaches us that God is more concerned with our character than our comfort! God can use our adverse circumstances to foster character qualities. (Romans 5:3-4; Hebrews 12:10-11)

Joni Eareckson Tada shows us that Christ, who could have altered the plan, did not exempt Himself from suffering. Do we somehow get a pass? Matthew 10 tells us a student is not above his teacher. *God has uses for our affliction and they are good ones! Seeing them is difficult, and takes time, study, and prayer.* But her testimony is a shining example of Romans 8:28. As frustrating and unfair as our own difficulties may seem to us at times, it is helpful to remember that God really, really, can and does, work all things together for good for those who love God.

Yes, my back hurts. But it makes me grateful for what I *can feel!* Yes, my back hurts, but it reminds me to help others whenever possible, because I know they are hurting too! Yes, my back hurts, but I can use it to understand a little tiny bit about how God can use affliction, and then to tell you about it! AMEN

Prayer: Dear Heavenly Father, thank You that You sent Your Son, not only for His perfect life, example and teaching, but as awful as it sounds, so that He could suffer and die for us. Our Lord knows what it means to suffer. Through it He showed us obedience, and through obedience demonstrated His love, just as we can. Thank God for His gift of eternity! Believing that in our heart makes suffering a thing we can endure and still use to help others! AMEN

JUNE 28

Skeet

"Even a child makes himself known by his acts, by whether his conduct is pure and upright." (Proverbs 20:11 ESV)

Yesterday morning I took one of my son-in-laws and my eight year old grandson skeet shooting. My son-in-law was a lieutenant in the US Navy and has some familiarity with guns, but little with shotguns and skeet. My grandson had no experience, but boy, was he excited to get some!

It was a hot, breezy, June morning in Texas, with a few clouds and quite a bit of haze, but nothing to dampen Liam's enthusiasm. Watching your grandson grow up is not quite the same as watching your son grow up. I think it's mainly because you see your son everyday, and he's not always thrilled, particularly as a teenager, at his interactions with dad; but you see your grandson less frequently, and he would be glad to see you even if you'd just been sprayed by a skunk!

I've recently watched this grandson go from being the usual unfocused, constantly moving, constantly loud, often inattentive, 4 to 7 year old, to a young man maturing right before my eyes! Last night we watched his Taekwondo lesson. He not only did as instructed, was determined with his technique, but volunteered to help straighten up the equipment at the end. When we met at the skeet range west of Dallas yesterday, I wasn't quite sure what to expect. The move from video games to a very serious sport involving lethal weapons is not to be taken lightly, and I was a little nervous about how well it would all go.

Long story short, (don't you love it when people say that and the story goes on for another 20 minutes) it went swimmingly! Liam listened intently as I discussed safety rules with him, ear and eye protection, went over checking the safety, holding the gun properly, pointed at the ground, loading the chamber, closing the spring loaded breech, then loading the subsequent shells, releasing the safety, positioning for firing, sighting, and calling out, "Ready," and then "Pull!" I fully expected, in his excitement, that he would swing the gun barrel toward us, or drop the weapon, or forget to release the safety, or drop the shells on the ground, or catch his finger in the spring-loaded action bar! None of these things happened. He was perfect every time. His actions were considered, measured, and no steps were omitted. Well, actually hitting one of the skeet was omitted, but his father and I almost completely omitted that step as well!

There is a tendency today, with our culture firmly in the grip of relativism, personal independence, and focus on self, for parents to believe that just letting kids "do their own thing," minimizing instruction and boundaries, is always the right choice. Parents tend to "go along" with their kids demands, evidently in some effort to "be their friend." Well, it's not the right choice if doing their own thing means killing someone with their car, or harming themselves with drugs, or derailing their life early on with poor decisions on sex, or in this case, perhaps blowing their foot off! There is a **right and a wrong** way to go when driving, making health and recreation decisions, dealing with the opposite sex, and yes, handling a lethal weapon!

Yesterday, there was joy reflected in everyone's smile, grandfather, father, and son. Why? Because this young man had a father and mother who avoid provoking their children to anger, but are bringing them up in the discipline and instruction of the Lord. (Ephesians 6:4) Even though the skeet field is only one small instance, my son-in-law and I were training Liam up in the way that he should go, and we both commented that he won't soon forget today and the lessons he's learned. In fact, even when he's my age, he won't forget where to point that gun and to check the safety! (Proverbs 22:6)

I'm just so darn proud of him, I had to write this today! Not once did he express the slightest frustration at being unable to actually connect with a single one of those fast flying orange discs! He knew that would come with time and practice, just like so many other skills in life.

Hopefully, reading this you either have children or plan to, and if you haven't or have been unable to, then find a way to immerse yourself in some kids' lives somewhere. Volunteer to read at school, help in the classrooms or on the playground of your local elementary or junior high school, coach a sport you may know nothing about initially, teach Sunday School, volunteer in scouting, cheerleading, drama, even if only to help with the scenery. But find a way to be around kids. They can benefit from your kindness, your wisdom, your experience and your guidance, but I guarantee that you'll get more out of it than they will!!

"Behold, children are a heritage from the Lord, the fruit of the womb a reward." (Psalm 127:3 ESV)

"A refusal to correct is a refusal to love; love your children by disciplining them." (Proverbs 13:24 Message)

Prayer: Father God, thank You that You have seen fit to give us children! What we once were ourselves, You have given us the opportunity to shape. As Your children ourselves, we too may be shaped by You through Your word, and through our sisters and brothers! Let us show the world that there is a right and a wrong, that You make it clear in the Bible, and that the children who come to understand that truth through our instruction, will be the ones who grow into adults who truly do live abundantly! AMEN

JUNE 29

Quiet

"Lord, my heart is not haughty, nor my eyes lofty. Neither do I concern myself with great matters, nor with things too profound for me. Surely, I have calmed and quieted my soul, like a weaned child with his mother; Like a weaned child is my soul within me." (Psalm 131: 1-2 NKJV)

There are two phrases which, in my mind, have always been linked: '*back to nature*' and '*be still.*' We live in an increasingly frenetic, shifting, bouncing, unsteady, and most of all, loud and noisy world! The noise may be audible, or it may be only a term to describe the avalanche of information with which we are bombarded every minute. You can try to stop watching the evening news on TV, but you'll have trouble getting away from all the stories they tell in 30 second sound bites, because those, along with a thousand other shards of information, will accost you every minute of the day, unless you, and all those around you, throw your smart phones in the ocean!

We were in Glacier Bay, just off the coast of Alaska, several years ago. Incredibly lucky, we were able to witness a glacier 'calving' into the ocean, as a piece of ice, that our guide assured us was the size of a ten-story building, separated from the top of the ice cliff and slipped 'silently' into the freezing spring water some four miles away. All of us on the cruise ship could eventually hear the thunderous roar as a muted 'boom' rolling across the surface of the sea, over twenty seconds later. What at first appeared as an almost gentle event, as if in in a slow-motion silent movie, was then revealed, as the powerful disruption of the status quo that it truly was, once the sound arrived!

Pick the scariest part of the scariest movie you can think of; the part where you would cover your eyes, if you were ever convinced to watch it again. Now, watch it with the sound off. Even the worst circumstances are radically altered with the removal of sound.

How do we put ourselves in that posture of humility and receptiveness and wonder of which the Psalmist speaks? How do we 'quiet our hearts?' What do we do in order to 'hear the still small voice of God?' (1 Kings 19:12) Can God even 'be exalted' before we become 'still and know that He is God?' (Psalm 46:10)

For me the answer lies in nature. For me the answer lies in sail. Rarely, we sail with music playing. Sometimes, we sail with muted conversations taking place. But more often, and always when I sail by myself, the only sound is the wind in the rigging, the spray hitting the hull, and the water rushing past the keel and rudder. That peace, that calm, that simplicity, that immersion in God's creation, quickly overwhelms and quiets my soul. The immensity of the ocean and sky, the power of the wind and waves, the dot that I realize I am in reality, washes over me in the form of humility. There is no time when I am more receptive mentally to the voice of God; not audibly, but as the urging of the Spirit within.

For you, it might be hiking a nature trail. Or biking. Or kayaking. Or fishing. Or the beach. Or the mountains. Or simply sitting in your yard under a tree with only the wind chimes and the birds to fill in the sound. Whatever you have found works for you, take time. Maybe a few minutes per day, but certainly a longer span hopefully measured in hours, each week. 'Silence is golden,' not just because holding your tongue is often the better choice, but because if you're always talking, and people around you are always talking, even if that talk is coming to you via the likes of Instagram, Facebook, Twitter, or Vine, it may be very difficult indeed to hear that still small voice.

"Silence isn't empty. It's full of answers." (Anonymous)

"Nature is pleased with simplicity, and nature is no dummy." (Isaac Newton)

"Adopt the pace of nature. Her secret is patience." (Ralph Waldo Emerson)

(In every walk with nature, one receives far more than one seeks." (John Muir)

> *Prayer: Dear Heavenly Father, we love You and we want to communicate with You. We praise You for the magnificence of the natural world around us! How unsurprised we should be that it is in the midst of it, rather than our man made cacophony, that we can hear Your voice. AMEN*

JUNE 30
Traffic

"Gratitude is the appreciation of the things that are not deserved, earned or demanded; those wonderful things that we take for granted." (Renee Paule)

In my adult life, I've lived in three major metropolises: Houston, San Francisco and Dallas. One thing they all have is traffic. Lots of it. Enough for everyone! Today I had an experience however, that was *literally mailed to me* by God, that relates to traffic.

Last weekend, my wife and I flew to Lubbock to see my daughter and her family. The previous week we had flown to Baton Rouge to see my mother. Not too long prior to that we had flown to San Antonio to stay at a B&B on Canyon Lake and explore the Hill Country. ONLY the TSA in Lubbock felt it likely that I would bring the plane down with my one inch Swiss Army keychain knife, with convenient toothpick, tweezers and scissors. (Really all an adult male needs for proper grooming.) In any event, I ordered the $14.95 replacement from AMAZON, which of course miraculously, arrived 14 hours later. Not as miraculously, they had shipped the wrong knife, in a very UN Amazon type move.

If you've never returned something to AMAZON, you need to do it; even if everything's perfect with your order. You need to do it just to fully understand why anyone who tells you NOT to buy AMAZON stock is living under a rock. I went to the Orders dropdown on the AMAZON app on my phone; clicked on Return or Replace, clicked on Wrong Item Shipped; hit Next and took a screen shot of a QR code. I then drove 1/4 mile to our nearest UPS store, where a very pleasant, but still pandemic masked recent Richardson High School graduate said hello, scanned the code with his gun, handed me an instantly printed receipt, and instructed me to have a nice day! I was in the store maybe, MAYBE, 35 seconds. America.

But to get to the UPS store, I have to turn south on a six lane road, three in each direction. I crossed to the left turn lane, put on my blinker, and waited. And waited. And WAITED. Why? Because there was traffic. Lots of it!! Hallelujah!! If ever there was a sign of approaching normalcy in a pandemic, it's TRAFFIC! For the first time in my remembrance I was HAPPY I had to wait in traffic!!

Once again, the good Lord helped me to see what I had never clearly appreciated before: traffic. Traffic means quite simply LIFE. People are out and about, doing whatever it is that they needed or wanted to do! YAHOO!! Now when I have to wait in traffic, I can do what my mom always did, and still does: she looks around her and imagines she can tell you the life story and circumstance of everyone sitting in their vehicles just by their appearance! Suddenly, I could appreciate what a wonderful thing it can be to live in community! People going about their business, but waving, smiling, letting you turn. All of them ALIVE and interacting with each other! (Do you think ants or bees understand how good they have it?) It was a stunning, wonderful realization, and it came to me via an exceedingly rare, incorrect, AMAZON shipment.

"I will give thanks to you in the great assembly; among the throngs I will praise you!" (Psalm 35:18 NIV)

"Rejoice always, pray continually, give thanks in all circumstances; for this is God's will for you in Christ Jesus." (1 Thessalonians 5:16-18 NIV)

Prayer: Dear Heavenly Father, thank You that You made us a people who thrives in community! How simple it is for us to overlook a gift and interpret it as affliction! I give praise to You that there can even BE traffic, having experienced a pandemic in the modern world. Lord, open our eyes. Open our ears. Let us appreciate the wonder of Your works! AMEN

JULY

JULY 1

Killing of Innocents

"'Get out of here baldy!' He turned around, looked at them and called down a curse on them in the name of the Lord. Then two female bears came out of the woods and mauled forty-two of the boys." (2 Kings 2:23 NIV)

I read a fascinating book recently entitled, *Death in the Long Grass,* by Peter Capstick. Capstick was a big game hunter in Africa for more than three decades. While specializing in lion and elephant, he divides his book into chapters titled for each type of game he has hunted, Lion, Elephant, Cape Buffalo, Hippo, Crocodile, Rhino, Snakes and finally "Underrated Killers." I am what you would call, an 'animal lover," and as such, have often felt that shooting any animal who was not likewise armed with a high caliber rifle, was not only unfair, but quite possibly immoral. I confess, I have hunted myself; dove, duck, and only once deer, but always justified the action by eating my prey afterwards. I think what bothered me was thinking of my targets as "innocents."

Mr. Capstick spent much of his professional career hunting man-eating lions and rogue elephants, animals you soon find out are anything but 'innocent.' They kill 200-500 people each per year as a very low estimate. Capstick estimates the number at ten fold that, rural deaths and government reticence re tourism, accounting for the disparity. Hippos, for instance kill at least 3,000 people per year and those are only the ones witnessed. Of course, you can make an argument that even when a lion seemingly kills out of 'revenge' and not hunger, we cannot assign human moral judgments like 'guilt or innocence,' to him. But if it was your child torn apart by a lion, you might not think 'innocent' was the best word to describe the big cat.

One of the objections to the veracity of the Bible, and the morality it purports to teach, is that it seems replete with stories of 'innocents' being killed. Admittedly, there are multiple chapters in the Old Testament which relate tales of the Chosen People sweeping into villages and killing every man, woman, child, and even their livestock, directly at the command of the Lord! Saul is even rejected as King by the Lord, for sparing an enemy King and his livestock. (1 Samuel 15:9-11) To some, God's very character seems capricious, unjust and vengeful.

In our opening verse, the prophet Elisha is evidently teased by some children for being bald, and he calls down a curse which leads to their deaths at the hands of two bears! Really? This is the God whose love is unending? Well, yes, as a matter of fact, it is. Because people who object to what appears to be violence against innocents in scripture, are often only vaguely aware of the whole story, and seemingly oblivious to Evil as a real entity and enemy. The people destroyed in these Biblical histories are people whose entire cultures had specifically, purposefully, turned away from God, after being warned repeatedly that it would meet with their downfall. The blood of their children was on the heads of their ancestors who practiced evil, and taught their children to practice it as well, that is when they weren't sacrificing them to a pagan idol!

Often the Hebrew is mis-translated, as well. While the KJV and NIV translate those who tease Elisha as "little boys or children," the actual Hebrew word, *na'ar,* means "youths," as in the NKJV, and is used to mean "teens," 238 places elsewhere in the bible. If forty two were killed, there had to have been an angry teenage gang surrounding the prophet at the time. Ever dealt with a totally amoral street gang? It presents a slightly different picture than a class of 3rd graders teasing an old bald guy!

Note also that repentance, in the Old Testament, always leads to mercy. Look at the city of Nineveh in the book of Jonah for instance. (Jonah 3:5-8) God is not cruel, but He is unequivocally just.

We as Christians are encouraged to always be prepared to give an answer for the hope we have. (1 Peter 3:15) Giving an answer means being capable of defending the scriptures in light of what you know to be the true character of God. For example, the killing of innocents should be abhorrent to all. Understanding that it is *most abhorrent* of all, to God, is at the core of our faith.

"I will praise You, O Lord, among the peoples; I will sing to You among the nations. For Your mercy reaches unto the heavens, and Your truth unto the clouds." (Psalm 57:9-10 NKJV)

Prayer: Dear Heavenly Father, You have shown us Your overwhelming mercy when, by Your Grace, You offered us forgiveness and salvation through faith in Your Son and His sacrifice. We praise You for being unchanging, and realize that some things we don't understand are part of Your Divine purposes, and always consistent with the character You have revealed to us through Christ. AMEN

JULY 2
Horse Play

"And forget not that the earth delights to feel your bare feet and the winds long to play with your hair." (Kahlil Gibran)

Recently, my wife and I were blessed to have a patient offer us the use of their house in Crested Butte, Colorado. Even though it was toward the end of June, the temperature dropped below freezing each night and there was frost on the long grass in the field outside our bedroom window. When I awoke this morning, I lay in bed and watched the Big Dipper gradually give way to the grey light filtering over the Butte, directly to our east. As the brilliant golden sunlight ignited the tops of the mountains to the north, with the valley before us still in shadow, I caught a glimpse of what appeared briefly, to be a puff of smoke in the distant field. Then it was gone.

I got up and moved to stand right at the window, gazing at where I had seen the disturbance, and sure enough, moments later it was there again! A jerky brown movement caught my eye, and I exclaimed to my still half sleeping wife, who by the way, is not a huge fan of bright light in the morning, that I thought I saw some deer out in the distance. I went to the kitchen and grabbed the binoculars.

When my brother and I would get in trouble as children, I can still clearly hear my father's voice, "You two, quit horsing around!" Well, I've never been privileged to own a horse, so my dad's expression didn't really mean much. In the last 60 years, my only exposure to horses other than at a rodeo or race track, was watching my daughter ride at a nearby stable until she was about 13 and lost interest. My riding experience was confined to sitting astride a wide, bumpy animal, who followed the tail of the horse in front of it, while we meandered through this National Park or that.

But when I raised the binoculars and looked out over the frost covered field, I saw not deer, but six horses, literally frolicking in the grass, only catching the bright yellow sun on their heads and shoulders when they reared high up, pawing their hooves in the air. I could hear their neighing only in my mind due to the distance, but I could clearly see that the puffs of "smoke" had been frost, blasted into the air by their frenzied whirling and bucking, augmented by their visible breath. Now, as already acknowledged, I know nothing about horses. But I know as sure as the sun rises in the east, that these animals were joyful! They were playing, not fighting. They twirled and pranced and danced and then ran in tight little circles, only to come back and momentarily rest their necks against each other. They were brown and white, white, black and brown, and their coats glistened in the new sunlight.

Watching them, just watching them, filled me with joy as well! The wolf hours had been particularly bad at 3 AM when I lay there partially awake, worrying about the future. I worried about money, about changing roles in my practice, about patients, about my nurses, about the health of family members. I'm worried that I may have forgotten some of the things that I worried about! Its easy to talk a good game, you know Matthew 6:28-32 and all that, but the wolf hours get me too.

It's the next verse that I sometimes forget. *"But seek first the Kingdom of God and His righteousness, and all these things shall be added to you."* (Matthew 6:33 NKJV) I awoke worried, I sat down to my coffee with a smile on my face. Why? Because God sent me those horses. God gave us a magnificent canvas that stretches across the heavens and around the world and painted it in with creatures that live fascinating lives! Yes, His Kingdom is coming when Christ returns, and yes His Kingdom is also here now with the Spirit dwelling in each of us. But as Paul told us in Romans 1:20, His invisible attributes, and thus the character of His Kingdom, are clearly seen in the things He has made! Like horses. Playing in the frost. "Horsing around!"

I finally understand what my father meant. But he meant it as a behavior we needed to curtail. I see it as a behavior we need to emulate, from the real horse players! Put your cares behind you and make the time, give yourself the space, forgive yourself the work slightly delayed, clear your mind, and go out in the frost and whirl and dance and rear and snort and spray some frost around! Imagine how good you'll feel when just my watching it from 200 yards away turned my day around! And when you're breathing hard afterwards, you'll be amazed at the creative solutions to your problems that just pop into your head! Why didn't I think that before?

"It is a happy talent to know how to play." (Emerson)

"The intuitive mind is a sacred gift and the rational mind is a faithful servant. We have created a society that honors the servant and has forgotten the gift." (Einstein)

"Whoever wants to understand much, must play much." (Gottfried Benn)

Prayer: Dear Heavenly Father, we love You! We praise You that You surround us with wonders, magnificent creations of Yours, the contemplation of which allows us to share in the joy You must have in their creation! Spirit, remind us every day to play a little, to soak up the sun and the wind and the waves, and whirl and prance as the horses do! AMEN

JULY 3

Charging

"Those who wait on the Lord shall renew their strength; they shall mount up with wings like eagles, they shall run and not be weary, they shall walk and not faint." (Isaiah 40:31 NKJV)

I am always surprised at the number of patients who have a smart phone, but it's dead or nearly dead. I know because they open it to make a note, show me a picture of their kids, exchange contacts or whatever, and then venting their frustration, note audibly that their "stupid" phone is dead or almost dead.

This came to mind because one of the most essential items that my wife and I always bring on a trip is the car charger for our phones. Most cars nowadays actually have a USB port so no adapter and no Apple block is even necessary. We also have portable chargers good for several full charges, which we use on long flights. But most days, I am simply commuting to and from the hospital. I plug the phone into the charger even before I turn the car on as part of a routine. The 20 minute ride is usually adequate to completely charge my iphone.

But while my iphone is charging, and attached to the car via Bluetooth, it is the conduit for the DAB or Daily Audio Bible podcast which I have mentioned elsewhere. What struck me tonight as interesting, is that my phone is charged twice per day and very rarely do I find myself in a circumstance where it has lost power. So am I. Because I use it on the same commute in which it is charging, to listen to DAB, every single day! As Brian Hardin is wont to say frequently, thousands of us gather everyday around the "global campfire" to soak up God's Word. Just as my phone is recharged in the car, my strength to face another day of other people's problems, added to my own, is recharged as well!

People drink protein shakes, kale shakes, they eat raw eggs, they do all manner of things to recharge their physical health in the mornings! Why would anyone think that your Spiritual-self needs nothing? Why would anyone think that neglecting your emotional and spiritual health would be any less damaging than neglecting your physical health? If you just get into the habit of listening, or reading, the scriptures every day, even if only for ten minutes, I guarantee you will find yourself gaining strength emotionally every day! Once you discover that both testaments of the bible are really one continuous revelation of God's love for us, of His constant care for us, of His plan for us, of His equipping us, of His forgiveness of us, of His Salvation offered to us; well then, it's very hard to feel unworthy! In fact, you'll simply feel re-charged!

"And the God of all grace, who called you to His eternal glory in Christ, after you have suffered a little while, will Himself restore you and make you strong, firm and steadfast." (1 Peter 5:10 NIV)

Prayer: Dear Heavenly Father, it is so easy for us to become weary and discouraged with our daily responsibilities and intermittent downfalls! Teach us first that Your teachings are worthwhile and the key to peace, joy and strength on a daily basis! AMEN

JULY 4

Independence Day

"For we know that our old self was crucified with Him in order that sin's dominion over the body may be abolished, so that we may no longer be enslaved to sin... For sin will not rule over you, because you are not under law, but under Grace." (Romans 6:6,14 HCSB)

One of my favorite scenes in all sci-fi movies is the penultimate one from Independence Day, in which the President of the United States, played by Bill Pullman, gives a stirring speech about the challenge that lies before them in defeating a more powerful alien invader.

"Mankind. That word should have new meaning for us today. We can't be consumed by our petty differences anymore...we will be united in our common interest. Perhaps it is fate that today is the Fourth of July, and you will once again be fighting for our freedom; not from tyranny, oppression, or persecution, but from annihilation! We're fighting for our right to live, to exist; and should we win the day, the fourth of July will no longer be known as an American holiday, but as the day when the world declared in one voice, 'We will not go quietly into the night! We will not vanish without a fight! We're going to live on. We're going to survive. Today we celebrate our independence day!'"

Paul, in his letter to the Romans, gives very nearly the same speech! Man has been threatened with the annihilation that is death, ever since his first rebellion against his creator in the Garden of Eden. It matters little whether you believe there was a literal garden, but only that you understand a great gulf arose between man and God with man's disobedience, and nothing could breech that gulf except the offer that the Father made in sacrificing His Son to pay for our sins! If we accept that incredible undeserved gift, then in fact we are saved and have avoided annihilation. The Evil One, Satan, will do everything in His power to blind us to the reality of Christ as the one embodiment of truth, and the only avenue to life!

The offer is open to all mankind! We no longer need be enslaved to sin. The voluminous laws once written down to guide God's people also clearly demonstrated that righteousness could not be found there, because perfect obedience was impossible for everyone. The righteousness necessary to be reconciled to God is ONLY found in the perfection of His Son, and His sacrifice on our behalf, bestows that righteousness on us, even while we were still sinning!

Every day is Independence Day for believers all over the world! We have "won the day" as Bill Pullman says, and we won it on the cross! That means that every day from the moment you accept Christ onward, you are no longer defenseless against Satan. Yes, we still sin. We are not perfect. But we don't *have to sin* any longer, and we won't *want to sin* any longer once we give free reign to the Spirit that dwells within us!

"It was for freedom that Christ set us free; therefore keep standing firm and do not be subject again to the yoke of slavery." (Galatians 5:1 NIV)

"For the wages of sin is death, but the free gift of God is eternal life in Jesus Christ our Lord." (Romans 6:23 ESV)

Prayer: Father God, thank you for setting us free! How easy it is for us to grasp the joy in victory over the tyranny of a despotic English King, and yet difficult to see that victory over death, a much greater prize, is within reach of everyone on the planet! Lead us to spread the Good News by both word and action, Lord. Help us to show others what freedom really looks like on this American Independence Day! AMEN

JULY 5

Greener

"And He said to them, 'Take care, and be on your guard against all covetousness, for one's life does not consist in the abundance of his possessions." (Luke 12:15 ESV)

We've been looking at zero lot line, gated, lock and leave type houses lately. We're both in our mid-60's and the large house with yard and pool on a creek in which we raised four children, simply seems almost a waste, with just the 2.25 of us.(*Sterling*,the cat, passed; Windsor the Labradoodle 1/4 human) Admittedly, its nice to have the pool, playroom, and simply *more space* when the grandkids come over, but it doesn't seem critical. The 'no maintenance' part seems the most attractive part of a potential move!

We found a great place, on a green space, no lawn, vaulted ceilings, master bedroom down, in a gated community, 30 years newer than our house, but still twenty years old. Smaller, and at first appraisal considerably more money than our house, (location, location, location,) I drove back to snoop around on my own, now that we had the gate code! (Shhhhh!!) Exploring the exterior in detail I noted the 20 year old A/C units, the beginnings of rot under the large deck, the constant humming sound of the nearby freeway, which I had previously taken for the sound of the creek. There's really no place to park on the small cul-de-sac if you have a gathering, the two car garage is listed as 'oversize,' but I would say only if both of us drove Mazda MX-5s, and the kitchen window looks at a blank brick wall five feet away.

There is nothing really, that we don't like about our house, except the upkeep and the guilt of living in a space large enough for four or five homeless families. It's roughly similar to my continuing to offer my wife a new car when the one she has, a ten year old Lexus, has nothing wrong with it and only 50k miles on it! There are places to live and livings to make and lifestyles to have elsewhere, by the ocean, in the mountains, all of which sound like they might be "better."

Jesus had some advice on this point. In fact He and His dad thought it was a good enough idea to make it the 10th and final commandment! Thou shalt not COVET. "Covet" means not just to want something, but to *long for it, to convince yourself that you must have it, you need it!*. It's not legitimately needing a new house because yours leaks and floods when it rains; it's convincing yourself that you really *need* a new house because you love the way it looks, inside and out, and possibly even because you have friends with the same type of high ceilings and zero lot line that you love! Maybe you just love the way it *makes you look!*

There's an old expression, *"The grass may look greener on the other side of the hill, but that means there is more to mow!"* Learning to be *content* with what we already have is one of the keys to peace, as the apostle Paul discovered. (Philippians 4:11-13) He tells us that he knows how to be content with a lot, and content with a little. The secret? *"I am able to do all things through Him who strengthens me."* This is one of the most incorrectly applied quotations in scripture. It doesn't mean you can leap tall buildings at a single bound. The Greek word *autarkies*, translated *"strength,"* is used only here in the entire bible. The Greek Stoics used it to mean self-sufficient in all circumstances. But Paul uses it to mean *divine sufficiency*, for it is Christ who allows him to be satisfied whether in plenty or in want.

The Chosen people ended up in exile because it proved impossible for man to "keep *all* the commandments," and every promise from God was dependent on the perfect compliance needed to become righteous. The recognition that living under the law only points to all our sin, left the door open for God's grace, expressed in the undeserved forgiveness He offers us through Christ's redemptive death on the cross. How do we not covet? We all still sin, that is clear, even though we no longer have to do so. So how do we not covet? **We call on the divine strength offered to us through our faith in Christ. We depend on the Holy Spirit to remind us that we have the power to be content with what we have, because the power offered through God's indwelling us,**

is quite frankly, immeasurable!

Next time you think you *need, you long for,* that new phone, car, house, partner, job, or transfer, make sure it isn't just wanting. God has no objection to our having the things we want, nice things, useful things, even pretty things. What God abhors is our feeling like we ***have to have what belongs to someone else****, or one just like it,* whether that's a possession, wealth, or another person!

Working hard and acquiring possessions is alright, just don't make it the *object of your hard work.* Draw on God's power through ***prayer***, the next time you see something that someone else has, that you really thing you need to have as well. Just bringing it to the Lord, is the most important step.

Prayer: Dear Heavenly Father, we ask that You bring to our minds the 10th commandment when we set out to possess something new! Prayer and patience will bring the right answer, as You see into our hearts! And we know that You have written the law on our hearts already. We live not under the law, but under Grace. We know Lord, that this doesn't mean we can ignore Your instructions, only that Jesus is the only man who has ever lived a perfect, sinless life, and drawing on His power is what we need in order not to covet. AMEN

JULY 6

Chick Fil-A

"You are to labor six days but you must rest on the seventh day; you must even rest during plowing and harvest time." (Exodus 34:21 HCSB)

If you're an American and you're not a vegetarian, it's very likely you've eaten at Chik-Fil-A. It's also likely that you've *forgotten* that they are closed on Sunday until you pulled into the drive-thru and noticed you were the only car there. S. Truett Cathy, the founder, was a Southern Baptist from Hapeville, Georgia. Originally it was the *Dwarf Grill and later the Dwarf House* until re-branded as Chik-Fil-A in 1967. Cathy, much like all of us who grew up in the 40's and 50's would never even assume that *any business* was open on Sunday, or Thanksgiving or Christmas or Easter!

In the time of the 2020 Pandemic, certain businesses have been deemed "essential." Oddly enough, the liquor industry was one of these. But in the 1970's, even as the "Blue Laws" restricting businesses on Sundays were being gradually repealed, the prohibition against liquor sales stayed firmly in place. The Blue Laws or Sunday Laws have been repealed in almost all of the states now. Originally they were enacted to allow the free practice of, and attendance at worship services, and to ensure some weekly rest for everyone. Labor unions and the US Supreme court have always supported Blue Laws whenever challenged, but as the national culture has become more an more secular, legislatures were forced to respond to those who felt there should be no restriction on Sunday businesses.

Sunday (or Saturday) as a day of rest called the 'Sabbath' didn't start with government regulation, but with the Word of God. Whether God's six days of creation were 24 hours apiece, or if those days were 1/2 billion years apiece, is inconsequential with regard to His command which reflects His own choice to rest after 6 days. The parallel to His own experience remains intact. God understood that constant work without rest is bad for us. It's bad for your physical, mental, emotional and spiritual health. The Sabbath (from the Hebrew Shabbat, meaning 'cease') was made for man (Mark 2:27) at Creation. (Exodus 20:8-11) Believers, both Jewish and Christian, are commanded to remember the Sabbath *and keep it Holy.* So not only must we not work, but we must keep the day Holy, and most denominations have chosen to honor that by scheduling worship on Sundays if Christian, and Saturdays, if Jewish.

Unfortunately, for some, the very act of "going to Church" can become a chore. Some church obligations take literally all day, from multiple hours of worship, to meetings, to service organizations, to bible studies, to youth groups etc. etc. If you find yourself attending worship because you feel you "have to," then you need a break! Go to the lake, hike in the woods, get out into nature somewhere and in that time talk with God! He listens no matter where you are. I love our worship services, but some times in the year the only time we have to get out on the water and sail is Sunday...so we do!

God commanded you to *rest from your labors* and keep the Sabbath Holy. While Sabbath means "cease," we shouldn't forget that "Holy" means "set apart." Yes, we honor God through worship. But we also honor God by keeping the day of rest sacrosanct and untouchable. That doesn't necessarily always mean communal worship.

Worship the Lord because you want to, because you need to! Do it with other like-minded individuals, because its joyous! But don't let it be a box to check off like journaling, or tithing, or quiet time, or anything else that becomes a chore in itself because you feel "obligated." Going to church because you think you should is the very opposite of keeping the Sabbath Holy! The seventh day is to recharge your batteries. You might usually plug into worship. But you can plug into a morning in the park with your dog too! (It IS God spelled backwards, right?) You could read the paper at your leisure, curl up with a good book, stroll through a Farmer's Market, go to a movie, have brunch with the family, or simply enjoy a "good brisk nap" as Garfield always said!

"Sunday is the golden clasp that binds together the volume of the week." (Longfellow)

"Sunday Checklist: Do Nothing. Chill." (Anonymous)

"Sunday. Take it slow and let your soul catch up with your body." (Anonymous)

Prayer: Dear Heavenly Father, thank you for giving us the day of rest! While You deserve our praise every day, You have given us a reminder of Your Blessings in a day where we can slow down, do the things we enjoy, and in the process come to the startling realization every week that we have You to thank for every good gift! AMEN

JULY 7
Essentials

"In essentials unity. In non-essentials liberty. In all things love. (Augustine)

We belong to a "Life Group," which meets regularly for lunch and fellowship after worship on Sunday afternoons. Several couples have been part of this group for twenty years or more. We've been in it for about ten. Currently, it's make-up is seven married couples, ranging in age from late forties to mid-sixties. We all belong to the same non-denominational evangelical Christian church, but we all come from varied church backgrounds. Some have been divorced and have blended families. Some were raised in mainline protestant denominations, some were raised Roman Catholic, some were raised in non-denominational churches.

We rotate our homes for each gathering, and the host usually provides the meal. "Life Group" is a term derived from one of our church's mottos: *Experiencing Life Together,* and it inspired the title of the devotional series you are reading right now. Life can be difficult for everyone, from all walks of life, and from all socioeconomic and ethnic backgrounds. While we usually decide on a discussion topic, or a series of them, whether they be devotionals, a book, the last sermon, or a video series, we spend much of the time laughing, eating, telling stories, catching up on each other's children and now grandchildren, and sharing all aspects of our lives. We share our joys, our sorrows, our worries, (increasingly our health issues,) and we pray for each other together.

True, we have some doctrinal differences, but we all believe *"we are saved by Grace, through faith, in Jesus Christ alone."* That's what we in Christian Theology would call an "essential." Certainly, we could also include people in our life group who do not agree on that point, who are in fact "seekers," but we simply don't have anyone in that category at the moment. How, when and why baptism is different in different traditions can be debated. How, when and why communion is celebrated differently in different churches can be debated. How the church views sexuality can be debated. How we view the problems with race relations can be debated. How worship should be conducted with respect to liturgy, music, the message, can be debated. All different political views can be debated. The relative strength of football teams can be debated! The sole owner of an Android phone in the group can be teased mercilessly and his sanity debated! In all these things, liberty!

But, most important is love. (1 Corinthians 13:13) The reason there is so much laughter is because there is always love. Love is the *real essential!* God made us to live in community. That's part of what is so hard about the 2020 Pandemic. "Social distancing" is just not woven into the genetic make-up of most Americans! But even through this struggle, our Life Group has hung together, apart, with digital assistance like FaceTime and Zoom!

If you are trying to negotiate the vicissitudes of life alone, you need to make it your priority to fix that! If there is no church which you attend regularly, find one! Pick the closest one, if you have no denominational preference. Most Christians are familiar with Augustine's words, or at least the principle, that there is unity in the essentials. As C.S. Lewis, author of *Mere Christianity* and the *Narnia Chronicles* said, 'just walk down the hall, look at all the doors with different church names on them, open one, and then after you go in, stay there!' There are loving people in every church! Give anyone you pick a chance to alter your life! After you find a church, ask about smaller groups right away. Christianity is modeled after family! (Romans 8:15; 9:4) That's why Paul tells us we have been adopted into Christ's family as sisters and brothers. It's harder to feel part of a family if the family has hundreds or thousands of members! Once you join a small group, commit yourself to being "all-in!" The more you give the more you will get, just like in every other aspect of life!

"Let us consider how we may spur one another on toward love and good deeds, not giving up meeting together, as some are in the habit of doing, but encouraging one another—and all the more as you see the Day (Christ's return) approaching." (Hebrews 10:24-25 NIV)

"Finally, all of you be like-minded, be sympathetic, love one another, be compassionate and humble." 1 Peter 3:8 NIV)

> ***Dear Heavenly Father, we thank You that we may view our fellow Christians as family, regardless of their ethnicity, socioeconomic background, or nationality. Life alone would be excruciating, and as the world becomes increasingly secularized, it helps immensely to do life together with other Believers! Lord, for those who have not found a close group of people to support them, love them, guide them, and listen to them, we pray that the Holy Spirit works in others to include them! AMEN***

JULY 8

Hidden Blessings

"Behold, it was for my welfare that I had great bitterness; but in love you have delivered my life from the pit of destruction...(Isaiah 38:17 ESV)

My wife and I have a few favorite shows, and near the top of the list is BBC's, *Call the Midwife*. No, it's not because I've delivered babies all my life. It is, I suppose, because the show tenderly retells the true story of a young nurse in poverty-stricken Poplar, East London, in the 1950's. Nurse "Leigh" works alongside the experienced Nuns of Nonnatus House, with whom she abides, as do several other young nurses. The tales of their inter-relationships and the cases they take on, reveal the beautiful confluence of faith and medicine.

The story is narrated by Vanessa Redgrave as elderly Nurse Leigh, remembering events now decades in the past. This episode was about a dying old man who once had seven children, but whose five sons, one daughter and his wife had all succumbed to tuberculosis. His only surviving daughter left the Public House that her father owned and operated, when she was in her early 20's, to make a life for herself and to escape her heart broken and bitter father. Absent for six years, and pregnant by a man who had left her once he learned of the child, she returned to her father's bedside when informed of his ill health. She hid her pregnancy with a corset at work, ashamed and afraid she would lose her meager job in a typing pool, which paid barely enough for her to survive.

Her father's heart failure was terminal and becoming rapidly more critical when she arrived. To her dismay, her father had nothing but mean-spirited, cutting things to say to her, ostensibly for leaving him heart-broken years before. She tried to explain it had all been too much for a young girl, that she had lost her whole family as well, but the jibes from him and silent anger between them, remained. Nurse Leigh then convinced the young woman that she was all her father had left, and he undoubtedly loved her despite the bitterness he displayed. She needed to tell him he was going to have a grandchild before it was too late!

She did, and the old man changed in the twinkling of an eye, determined to cling to life until the child was born, no longer angry with his daughter. She agreed to stay with him, and a short time later went into labor and delivered in a room above the Public House, aided by the nurse and the Mother Superior of Nonnatus House. The old man held the baby in his arms, noted out loud it was a shame that he was about to leave just as the little one arrived, ships passing in the night, and admonished the newborn to take care of his mother. He breathed his last with his daughter just coming into the room, and the baby on his chest.

When the old man's will was read, he had left everything, including the Public House, to her. In it, he remarked that she was the most important thing in the world to him and always had been.

How is it that a loving Lord permits the deaths of almost an entire family to disease, breaks the hearts of the father and his only surviving daughter, permits their estrangement, his heart attack and heart failure, and her unwed pregnancy? Well, how many times must we recall that God's ways are not our ways and His thoughts not our thoughts? (Isaiah 55:8) How many times must we forget that He has plans for us, plans for our welfare for good and not evil? (Jeremiah 29:11)

Love between a father and daughter restored. A family line that will live on through the grandson. The lost family sweetly remembered by father and daughter together at last. The daughter's welfare secure, wrought by the love expressed in her father's will, written long before, when she thought he had hated her. Hidden blessings.

Laura Story, one of my favorite singer-songwriters wrote a beautiful ballad called simply, *Blessings:*

We pray for Blessings. We pray for peace.
Comfort for family, protection while we sleep,
We pray for healing, for prosperity. We pray for Your mighty hand to ease our suffering.
All the while, you hear each spoken need, Yet love is way too much to give us lesser things.
'Cause what if your blessings come through raindrops, What if your healing comes through tears,
What if a thousand sleeplessness nights are what it takes to know you're near?
What if the trials in this life are your mercies in disguise?

We pray for wisdom, your voice to hear. We cry in anger when we cannot feel you near. We doubt your goodness. We doubt your love.
As if every promise from your word is not enough.
All the while, you hear each desperate plea, And long that we'd have faith to believe......

Prayer: Dear Heavenly Father, oh that we could have faith in the darkest hour to truly believe that You have a plan, that You love us and want the best for us, but we just can't see it! Use Your Holy Spirit Lord to grant us the patience if we have not the wisdom, to wait and see. We need simply believe and wait on You Lord. It sounds so easy. Thank you that You showed us Your heart through the suffering and death of Your precious Son so we can be assured that You get it Lord. You get it! AMEN

JULY 9

Silence

"And they sat with him on the ground seven days and seven nights, and no one spoke a word to him, for they saw that his suffering was great." (Job 2:13 ESV)

Because of the hope that we have as Believers, and because we are encouraged always to be ready to defend our faith and give a reason for that hope, sometimes we speak when we shouldn't. If you have ever experienced a personal tragedy that literally 'came out of nowhere,' and in fact seemed totally, 'unfair,' then you know that a well meaning acquaintance tossing Bible verses your way doesn't help much. In fact, it can give you a big push right through the first Kubler-Ross stage of grief, which is denial, and launch you quickly into anger. While that anger may have been diffuse and growing, suddenly it becomes pointed and directed. Directed right at God! Not exactly the effect you were hoping to achieve.

This week I had the following brushes with grief. I sat on the edge of the bed with a patient of my partner's who had just had a Cesarean section for a dead baby at term, with no obvious cause. She had been an infertility patient, and this had been an IVF conception. A few days before I spoke on the phone with the husband of a woman who died 30 hours after a minor surgery. It seemed unlinked to her procedure or anesthetic, but instead, to her incredibly high risk status, having had previous heart attacks and strokes. Nevertheless, her family was devastated. Also this week I had to console a patient whom I had just informed had a significant genetic defect with her unborn child. And as usual, I had to inform two different patients of their cancers, one breast and one uterine. Most think an OB/Gyn spends all his time buried in buttercups and roses, delivering happy, healthy newborns to ecstatic couples. Not always.

Job's friends, Eliphaz, Bildad, and Zophar, start out on the right track, sitting quietly with Job in his anguish. But then they start theorizing erroneously, that this must be his fault, for only sinners suffer catastrophic punishment from

God. Incredibly, when you try to make someone feel better in the midst of tragedy by telling them of God's wonderful plan for their lives, you're likely to have a cup of hot coffee thrown in your face. There is a time for everything, and postulating about how God works, or even stressing that he loves the aggrieved, can be a monumentally bad idea.

When someone is struck with unexpected tragedy and you wish to be a comfort, there is exactly one thing you should do: make them know you are available and say nothing. Just be present. Even offering to pray for them initially may not be the best idea. Pray for them anyway. You only have to share it with God, not them. There's nothing wrong with expressing your sorrow for their loss, but then stop talking. Just be there. Offer to stay as long as they want. Sit with them. Tragedy has to be processed over time and its a little different for everyone. Take your signals from the patient. Prayer works and it works from wherever you do it! If they ask you to pray with them, that's totally different. Otherwise, still pray for them, but do it silently. God is always listening.

"Rejoice with those who rejoice, and weep with those who weep. Be of the same mind toward one another...do not be wise in your own opinion." (Romans 12:15-16 NKJV)

Prayer: Dear Heavenly Father, we love You because we know with certainty that You loved us first!! We know that You are a merciful God and we know that You want what is best for Your people! But we also know that as much as people hate the term, we DON'T HAVE THE BIG PICTURE, only You do! We know that You can take bad things happening and turn them for good, we only need wait in faith. We will pray for those in anguish, but recognize that they need time to adjust, and consoling/counseling them in the midst of their grief might best be postponed. AMEN

JULY 10
Fear

"When I am afraid I will trust in You, In God, whose Word I praise, in God I trust; I will not be afraid. What can mortal man do to me?" (Psalm 56: 3-4 NIV)

We in America are living in a time of fear. Not many would dispute that. We have a pandemic that no authority seems to know best how to combat, which leads to dispute not only on the right approach, but who has authority to curb our individual liberties. We have a breakdown of civil authority stemming from race riots that have damaged the cause of those who would peacefully continue to work for change. Now, both of these crises have become politicized as we come into a bizarre Presidential election like none we have ever encountered in the past. The very fabric of our society, from traditional constructs and institutions of law and order, to professional and college sports, to all forms of entertainment indoor and out, is fraying around the edges and threatening to come completely unraveled. America is living in a time of fear, no doubt about it.

But there is an answer for fear. The answer is to see clearly, to understand the characteristics of right and wrong, and to know where to find the truth. Our pastor once told of finally going to the optometrist and getting properly refracted. It opened a whole new world of clarity to him! He was so excited, that he made a pair of glasses for his wife too! NO, that's not what he did. What he did was make her an appointment with the optometrist. The change in his life that he wanted to share with the one he loved, allowed him to know to Whom she should go for help, to find clarity!

We need help. Fear about societal changes, parenting, schooling, work, relationships, our health and a myriad of other things cause not only sleeplessness but distinct physiologic changes that are detrimental. Weight gain and loss, cardiac arrhythmias, increased pain, immune system failures are all well recognized consequences of chronic fear states.

Once we accept that we are afraid, what do we do? Do we listen to Dr. Phil and practice the Golden Rule, learn to say 'no,' do we watch Dr. Oz, take more Omega 3s, get organized and stop arriving late? We could do all of these, and sometimes different steps might help a little for a while. But there's another option.

Pastor Pete Briscoe, author and podcaster on ***Telling the Truth,*** recommends this: ***Dive into the Bible***. He says there are three types of people described in Romans 1: **Hedonists** who stiff arm God, and trade the truth for the lie of idolatry; **Finger pointers** who pass judgment on others with contempt for God's kindness; and **Do Gooders** who live by a stringent set of rules that they want everyone to follow, though they fail themselves. Sounds awful. But we have met the enemy, and they are us! (Romans 3:9-10)

Christ came for the average Joe, not especially for the learned scholar, or the righteous priest, or the government authority, although He came for them as well. The angels appeared to the poorest of the poor on that hillside in Bethlehem; the illiterate, filthy, social outcast, the physical laborer, the shepherd. the first words out of their mouths were, *"Fear not!"* (Luke 2:8-10) Did they mean don't be scared out of your mind because a host of angels just appeared over your head in the night sky, or did they mean something more? The very next words out of the angel's mouth were these, *"I bring you good news of great joy that will be for all mankind!"* Of all the hundreds of thousands of words in the bible, (783,137 KJV if you ever wondered!) these are the ones that should catch your attention!

The Good News is quite simply that you never need to be afraid again. Never. How does that sound? The God who created the universe, more powerful than the mind of man can possibly conceive, ***loves you personally,*** so much that He sacrificed His only Son, and if you only believe in Him, you will never die but have eternal life. (John 3:16) Think on that the next time you find yourself really afraid. What's the worst that can happen? What do we fear more than illness, pain, separation from loved ones? Death. Guess what? For those who believe, ***the worst cannot happen, ever, under any circumstance!***

What then can mortal man do to me? Hah! As the British say, "pish posh!"

"Fear not, for I am with you; be not dismayed, for I am your God. I will strengthen you. Yes, I will help you. I will uphold you with my righteous right hand." (Isaiah 41:10 NKJV)

"My sheep hear my voice and I know them, and they follow Me. And I give them eternal life, and they shall never perish; neither shall anyone snatch them out of My hand." (John 10:27-28 NKJV)

> ***Prayer: Father God, we trust You, but we need to trust You even more! When fear warps our perspective, alters our physiology and often our treatment of others, Holy Spirit point us to the truth. Point us to the answers in Scripture, right there in front of us! AMEN***

JULY 11

Losing Your Life

"And he who does not take his cross and follow after Me is not worthy of Me. He who finds his life will lose it, and he who loses his life for My sake will find it." (Matthew 10:38-39 NKJV)

For most, these are some of the hardest words in scripture, both to fully understand and to act upon. What sort of paradox is this? If you find your own life, you lose it? If you lose your life, you find it? Following Christ means "taking up the cross?" Today's western culture is all about "finding oneself," celebrating the wonder of me, prizing our own independence and self-reliance! How on earth can these words of Christ make any sense at all?

Perhaps an easier way to think of "losing your life" rather than actual physical death (which could also apply to Christian discipleship,) is *getting yourself out of the way.* That means subjugating your own wants, temptations and tendencies to idolize things other than God. It means allowing the Holy Spirit to work through us! It means that following Christ, "discipleship," demands *desiring what He wants* more than what we want! And what *does* Christ want?

He told us through the profit Micah, and then He told us Himself on multiple occasions. *"And what does the Lord require of you, but to do justice, to love mercy, and to walk humbly with your God." (Micah 6:8 NKJV)* Then Jesus told us the Greatest Commandment of all, *"You shall love the Lord your God with all your heart, with all your soul, and with all your mind…and the second is like it: you shall love your neighbor as yourself."* If you do justice (act fairly) love mercy (have compassion) and walk humbly (having the mind of Christ as in Philippians 2,) then you *are* loving the Lord with all your heart, soul, and mind! In order to truly do these things, you cannot possibly be focused on yourself. You are in fact *denying yourself*, renouncing your own central importance. If you do the opposite, if you live for yourself, refusing to submit to the tenants of Christian discipleship, you may be a high roller in this life, but you'll be denied the next.

Jesus demands death to oneself, and thus the symbolism of the cross, which all in the time of Christ knew to represent a most horrific, painful and shameful death. We use the expression "well, that's her cross to bear," as though Christ meant suffering through a difficult, awkward or tragic circumstance. Not so. The phrase found both in Matthew 10 and 16 (Mark 8:35; Luke 9:24 as well) means painfully dying to oneself and in that sense all true Christian disciples bear the same cross.

Yes, there have been thousands of Christian martyrs down through the centuries who literally died for their faith. And yes, we all know missionaries who have denied themselves the "good life" in America to live for decades among poverty stricken third world cultures. But Christ wants *every follower* to *lose his life in order to find it*. For some of us there may have been a turning point when we hit rock bottom, lost in addiction, or crime, or failed relationship, or job loss. We may have felt the pain of losing the "good" life we had in a dramatic way and then suddenly realizing what was really important. Others of us have been blessed with family, jobs, security, and wealth, without any traumatic fall, but that very "success" in life may lead to pride in our own accomplishments, and that leads to self-absorption, the very opposite of denying oneself.

Renouncing your old self, self-denial, doesn't refer necessarily, to resisting the desire to buy a new car, or house, or clothes, or whatever. Scripture has no problem with material possessions. The problem comes when those become your identity, when those become the most important things to you. In being reborn as Believers, we can say *"I have been crucified with Christ; it is no longer I who lives but Christ in me; and the life which I now life in the flesh I live by faith in the Son of God, who loved me and gave Himself for me." (Galatians 2:20 NKJV)*

Losing your life sounds bad, but it's the opposite for the Christian. Wake up every single morning and ask the Lord how you can be of service to others, and thus to Him! That mindset, refreshed throughout the day, *is what losing your life means*. Peace and joy flow out of one thing only: glorifying God in all that you do. Do that by loving. Period.

Prayer: Dear Heavenly Father, we love You because You chose to love us by coming to live among us, sacrificing for us, forgiving us, redeeming us. Nudge us daily to get out of the Spirit's way, to deny ourselves so that we might do Your will, having the mindset of Christ, and in humility put the needs of others before ourselves, loving them as we are commanded. AMEN

JULY 12

Home

"Oh, but anyway Toto, we're home. Home! And this is my room and you're all here. And I'm not gonna leave here ever, ever again, because I love you all, and oh Auntie Em, there's no place like home!" (Judy Garland 1939)

The London East End was made up largely of what was called the 'Docklands' in the early 1950's. It was an incredibly poor district dedicated to hundreds of six story 'tenements' that were teeming with life in very close quarters. Almost all the men worked 15 hour shifts at the docks in some capacity or other, and the women raised the babies that never seemed to stop coming prior to the advent of birth control.

The tenements were constructed in squares, with a center courtyard, and balconies running completely around the interior on every floor. The flats themselves consisted of three rooms usually, dividing off each other. The tiny kitchen held a gas stove and a pantry cabinet, usually just a corner of the the main room, which also had a stone sink in the corner with running cold water. There were two bedrooms, often for a couple with six to ten children. Flush toilets were just being installed in the first part of the decade, situated next to the stone sink in the main room due to the plumbing. The lack of privacy was considered insignificant compared to the convenience of not carrying a chamberpot downstairs to empty in the courtyards, or tramping down the stairs in the dark to negotiate your way to a lavatory shed which up to 500 people might have shared.

Living was close, the courtyards the center of social life, but the balconies full of running children, hanging laundry and gossiping neighbors. Washing machines were unknown to the poor and tumble driers had yet to be invented. The vast majority of the populace had never been out of East London. In fact, most lived their entire lives within a few blocks of where they were born. In short, it was a beehive of social activity populated by the very poor, but the menfolk were almost all employed and life was possible on a subsistence level. Distractions consisted mostly of pubs, dog racing, dancing, movies, and brothels, and yet church was almost always the center of social life and uniformly attended. Oddly, there was a strict morality within the social structure of the docklands, with divorce unheard of, unwed mothers a distinct rarity, the streets safe at night, and for the most part violence confined to the domestic variety.

In the late 50's and early 60's, the tenements, thought a huge improvement in the early 20th century, became an embarrassment to the city of London. 'Slum clearance' began in earnest and families would receive a government notice that their home was being demolished in a few weeks, and they were being 'rehoused' to a flat several miles away, with a proper bathroom and central heating. The process devastated the community! In the words of Jennifer Worth, who described the East End in detail in her fabulous memoir *Call the Midwife*, "what good is a flat with a bathroom if you never see your grandchildren again!" Slum clearance completely shattered the extended family which had always lived within easy walking distance of each other. The elderly often died in the transition, completely unable to adapt to a radically different way of life. Every facet of life from the pub to the church to your neighborhood grocers were now often extremely difficult to access or for some, impossible.

There is a lesson here and I think it might be as simple as ***'home is where the heart is.'*** It didn't matter that conditions were objectively 'awful' in London's East End in the 50's. What mattered to people was that it was *home,* and with the unconditional love of family, one can be happy in any circumstance. Our Kenyan boy Jacob, whom we have supported through World Vision for 15 years now comes to mind. He is always beaming in his photos, accompanied by his beaming parents, despite the impoverishment of the village you can see in the backgrounds!

The world can be an awful place indeed, with wars, pestilence, and ethnic hatreds as we are still seeing today. But Christians understand that we are visitors here. Our forever home is with our Lord, and it is in His Kingdom. He loved us first, and we abide in Him. Our brothers and sisters in Christ love each other through His power. Adopted into God's own family, we can be content, we can be happy, in any place on earth, and we can call it home, even if temporarily, along as the ones we love are there with us. The physical structure could be poor, but the structural integrity of our home lies in the heart turned toward our Savior.

"The rains came down, the streams rose, and the winds blew and beat against the house; yet it did not fall, because it had a foundation on the rock." (Matthew 7:25 ASV)

"Unless the Lord builds the house, the builders labor in vain." (Psalm 127:1 NIV)

Prayer: Father God, we love you. We love our brothers and sisters, and we thank You that our home is wherever their love is found. It is such a blessing that we are never alone, never without shelter, as long as we abide in Your Son. AMEN

JULY 13

Ants, Termites and Bees (Oh My!)

"For as we have many members in one body, but all the members do not have the same function, so we, being many, are one body in Christ, and individually members of each other. Having then gifts differing according to the Grace that is given to us, let us use them..." (Romans 12:4-6 NKJV)

I once saw a video of a large outside church picnic, over one thousand people in attendance, taken from a drone high above the crowd. Photo-shopped later to color code each decade of life represented, you could easily see in time-lapse that the younger colors were in constant motion and the older colors in decreasing motion with advancing age. Were it not simply a picnic, but a job site, one might more easily have seen the division of labor, and the similarity to an ant hill. The same seemingly random, vibrating, movement could be seen, with random more direct contact and antennae exchange of information.

Ants are, in Lewis Thomas' words, "so much like humans it's an embarrassment." (*Lives of a Cell*) They farm with aphids as livestock which they herd and fungi as their crop. They launch armies into war, they use chemical weapons, weaver ants even utilize child labor, engaging their larvae as shuttles to help weave their thread used for fungi farming! They are constantly in contact and sharing information, for as individuals, they are essentially helpless, a few neurons strung together. But together, in a mass of thousands, they act as a single organism, planning, calculating and effecting societal actions.

Termites similarly seem to grow smarter as they gather together. Individually, they pick up and transport pellets randomly; but put thousands together and they build them into multiple pillars that they eventually turn toward each other and connect, constructing complicated crystalline vaulted chambers!

An individual bee might be out in the clover collecting sugar, directed there by the dancer that gave him the appropriate GPS coordinates if you will, (no idea how they do this,) but in the hive under construction they collectively resemble viruses within a cell, building walls made of row after row of polygonal chambers until the hive is complete. Eventually, every hive population splits almost exactly in half, one group leaving with the old queen and one group staying with the new. At the moment of this swarming, the bees resemble a giant cell undergoing mitosis.

Herring are known to exhibit thousands of individuals moving in exact synchrony, sudden turns and curves communicated as if by magic, not unlike some species of flocking birds. But all of these examples have one feature in common: individuals virtually helpless alone, but part of a new effective, powerful creature together.

Christians are like this, not surprisingly. We are creatures created by the same God, with gifts that work better in concert than apart! Paul makes it clear to the Romans, that each of us must identify our gifts and take full advantage of them. One might have the gift of speech but another the diligence to research the material for him to deliver. One might have the gift of patience, and be able to teach the young, while another might have the gift of humor and be able to entertain them! One might have the gift of listening, and be an effective counselor for others, while another might have the gift of healing and be able to intervene on the physical behalves of others. The list of how Believers can help each other is endless, but the conclusion is clear: together we are better than alone. While Christ is the head, the rest of us are the body, and it is through the hands and feet of the church that Christ works in the world! (Romans 10:15; 1 Corinthians 12:17; Ephesians 4:16)

God commands us to gather together regularly to commune with each other as well as worship. We may draw strength from prayer and study, but we benefit in even greater ways from community. (Hebrews 10:25) In a quiet moment today, think about how your community of believers might benefit from your gifts, and give thanks for those around you whose gifts have benefited you.

"From whom the whole body joined and held together by every joint with which it is equipped, when each part is working properly, makes the body grow so that it builds itself up in love." (Ephesians 4:16 ESV)

Prayer: Father God, we love You. We are blessed that Christ is the head, giving each member of His church, each part of His body, direction and purpose to spread the love of Christ throughout the world. Let us not forget that together we are much more able to accomplish this task than apart. AMEN

JULY 14

Thin Ice

"Then the disciples came to Jesus in private and asked, 'Why couldn't we drive it [the demon] out?' So Jesus said to them, 'Assuredly I say to you, if you have faith as a mustard seed, you will say to this mountain Move from here to there,' and it will move; and nothing will be impossible for you." (Matthew 17:19-20 NKJV)

Growing up in Chappaqua, New York, about 35 miles north of the city, we used to skate on Duck Pond, just off Quaker Road, every winter. This was back in the day when there were no skating rinks, only rivers and lakes that froze over in the winter. Ice needs to be at least 4 inches thick, uniformly, before it is safe for skating. That means at least 2 weeks of overnight temperatures *below 0 degrees Fahrenheit not Centigrade!* In case you don't think there is any global warming happening, in the 1960's we would easily achieve this level of cold by every Christmas; today it is rarely cold enough all winter to skate on Duck Pond.

Ice can look solid enough but have varying thicknesses. Current, wind, daytime highs, shade from overhanging trees or hills that block the western sun over part of the pond, all can make for variable thickness. Skating on ice too thin and falling through in a pond can be disastrous. If the water is deeper than you are tall and your muscles are temporarily paralyzed by the intense cold, you can sink just long enough for the current to take you away from the opening, and then its "Goodnight Irene!"

You can have tremendous faith that the pond is frozen enough to skate on, and yet fall through if it's too thin at any point. Similarly, you can be quite nervous, even scared and have very little faith that the ice will support you, but if it's thick enough it will!

That's what Jesus was trying to tell His disciples who failed to cast out the demon. It's not the strength of your faith that matters; it's the strength of the object in which you have faith! The disciples had so little faith, not in their own abilities, but in the power of Christ, that they found it impossible to exorcise the boy suffering seizures since early childhood!

That's a bitter pill to swallow for some of us! The disciples, who lived with Jesus and heard His teaching everyday STILL didn't get it. Perhaps we have the advantage of looking at the resurrection through the rearview mirror, but still it is remarkable.

"I believe, help my unbelief," was the cry of the of the boy's father, in the telling of this same story in Mark. (Mark 9:23-24) Jesus told him, " If you can believe, all things are possible to him who believes!"

Next time you have doubts, don't castigate yourself. Instead, ask the Spirit within you to help with your unbelief! All of us struggle from time to time, especially in difficult or tragic times. All have doubts. All feel their faith is too weak. BUT IT'S NOT. The One in whom you have faith is the Creator of the Universe. He is strong enough to move mountains, because He is strong enough to create worlds! If you have only the tiniest amount of faith that the ice will hold you, and its 10 inches thick, it will hold you!!

"The name of the Lord is a strong tower; the righteous run into it and are safe." (Proverbs 18:10 NKJV)

"It is the Lord who goes before you. He will be with you; He will not fail you or forsake you. Do not fear or be dismayed.) Deuteronomy 3:18)

Prayer: Lord God, we love You! We only need look around us, at the ocean, at the mountains, at the night sky, to appreciate the immensity of Your power! Then all it takes is a little faith in the reality of You and Your love for us, and Your unfailing love will deliver! AMEN

JULY 15

The Tower

"The name of the Lord is a strong tower; the righteous run to it and are safe." (Proverbs 18:10) NKJV

In 2007, we took a two week driving trip around all of Ireland, first the Republic and then Northern Ireland as well. We arrived in Dublin on a Monday morning, and then made the spectacular drive down through the Wicklow Mountains National Park, then Glendalough, Aughavannagh, Baltinglass, Carlow and finally to Kilkenny, where we spent our first night in Ireland.

It was raining lightly with a mist over everything green in the early afternoon when we came down a hill into Glendalough. The town is no more than a few two lane (well...two lane for Ireland, 1.3 lanes in the US,) that cross in a vale at the edge of the great forest. Within a hundred yards of both Saint Kevin's Church and the Glendalough Cathedral, is the round tower, rising 33 meters into the air. Built in the 10th century, it has stood on this monastic site for over 1,000 years. Naturally, it was closed on Monday. With the rain, and a destination to reach the first night, we merely passed by and marveled at what we perceived to be an oddity. Incredibly, and uncharacteristically, I failed to look it up and read about it in one of our several guide books.

The next day, after a wonderful night at the Zuni Hotel, we explored surrounding Kilkenny. We walked across the Old Mart Road bridge and crossed the River Nore, heading west. Just on the other side, rising next to the Cathedral Church of St. Canice, was yet another round tower! Over the course of the next two weeks we would come to learn that round towers were a not uncommon site in Ireland. We climbed the one at St. Canice and took some spectacular pictures of Kilkenny. We noted the fire escape like metal stair we had to climb first, just to reach the stone arched door of the tower situated some 12 feet above ground! Then we ascended the narrow spiral stair within, reaching a tiny platform some 60 feet into the air.

The Celtic for these towers is "*cloigtheach*" and means literally "bell house, although the nearly identical "*cloichtheach*" means stone bulding, of which there were virtually none before the Norman invasion of 1170 AD. Almost always found in the vicinity of the village church, the tower doors reliably faced the west door to the church or monastery. While the elevated doors of the towers, reachable only by ladders which could be retracted, seem defensive in nature, they were also architecturally critical. These tall round stone towers were strong enough to be gale resistant, and the thinking is that a ground level door would have considerably weakened the tower. By the 12th century there were at least 120 such towers in Ireland, but today only 20 remain in almost perfect condition. Legend has it that these towers served as immediate refuge once the watchman atop alerted the villagers of marauding invaders such as Vikings. More likely, they were actually bell towers used for alerts, announcing the hour, and cross country communication.

But for the first time, I had a better understanding of the biblical references to "running to a strong tower for safety." Once you've actually seen, touched, and climbed a stone tower that has stood against the elements for over a thousand years, you can sense its strength, its solidity, its permanence. These are characteristics of our God! Our God is not a hollow God that blows down in the wind of change. Nor is He weak and temporary like the idols of the Canaanites! Our God is a tower of strength. Solid. Permanent. Trustworthy.

Next time you are afraid of well, anything, remember Who your God is! He's not going anywhere, and you can rest in the shadow of His might, a stone tower that enfolds you and protects you from the elements of secular change and of those who would do evil.

Prayer: Dear Heavenly Father, we love You, and we know that You first loved us! And while we think of You and of Your Son and of the Spirit as loving, compassionate and full of Grace, let us not forget that You are a strong tower! We can depend on You when the enemy comes against us. It is only through submission to Your might, that we can resist the devil and he will flee. (James 4:7) AMEN

JULY 16

Summer Fruit

"But the fruit of the Spirit is love, joy, peace, patience, kindness, goodness, faithfulness, gentleness, self-control. Against these there is no law. (Galatians 5:22-23 NIV)

We had a Pastor who used to exclaim that "but" was his favorite word in scripture, over the giggles of the pre-teens and the looks askance of the visitors. When you see a "but" in the Bible, it's the author begging you to read the previous verse. Doing so helps you avoid the worst scriptural sin of bible believing Christians: taking a verse out of context.

In this case, the previous 2 verses give examples of the "works of the flesh," which clearly contrast with the following "fruits of the Spirit." So, big deal right? First, is the list of "do nots," and that is followed by the list of "do's." Seems simple enough. Except that's **wrong**, and not what Paul is saying at all. Go back one more verse. Galatians 5:19 starts with another "but." "*But if you are led by* *the Spirit, you are not under the law."* So, now what is he saying? Something about the law? Well, we have another "but," right? So go back to verse 16-18. *"I say then, walk in the Spirit, and you shall not fulfill the lust of the flesh. For the flesh lusts against the Spirit, and the Spirit against the flesh; and these are contrary to one another,* ***so that you do not do the things that you wish!"***

The Fruits of the Spirit are well known, and appear on memes and posters all over the place. In fact, they are posted over the inside of the door to my office at work. They are so omnipresent, that they start to take on the feel of "The Nine Commandments" for appropriate Christian behavior! But Paul's entire point is that those in Christ, who have accepted His gracious gift of forgiveness, *are no longer under the law.* That means specifically that the nine Spiritual Fruits are NOT a list of rules to try and follow in our own effort, because we know that we will fail as we always have. In fact, we will exhibit the behaviors he calls the works of the flesh. That is the sinful nature of man that reigns in non-believers, an inability to resist doing the works of the flesh, whether they be sexual immorality, addiction, idolatry, hatred, jealousies, selfish ambition, envy, murder or any of those listed in verses 19-21.

Paul is telling us, just as Christ did when He said the world would know His followers by their love, that if we would only allow the indwelling Holy Spirit to work through us, the fruits of the Spirit are exhibited naturally. These are not a list of "do's" anymore than the previous verses are a list of the "don'ts!" Believers have crucified their old nature with Christ, and it is no longer they that live but Christ in them! (Galatians 2:20) Before we were reborn, we were slaves to sin, now we have a choice! If we choose not to submit to the Spirit, then we will look to the world exactly like everyone else. That's how Christians get labelled as hypocrites.

These are not Fruits of your own handiwork. These are not things you get credit for through superior effort. These are the qualities exhibited by your new *character*, because now you abide in Christ and He in you! (John 15:4) Since these are not rules or laws to live by, there is a better way to think of them.

Use the Fruits of the Spirit as a barometer, because believe me, the people around you will! If you find yourself not being gentle, or kind, not feeling at peace, then you are not letting the Spirit do His thing! In short, you are no longer *abiding* in Christ. Rather than making a New Years type resolution that you will "try to do better on these fruit things," immerse yourself in scripture, prayer, quiet time, and get back on track. When you note your own barometer falling, your friends have noted it too. God wants us in community. Go to a good friend with what's happening in your life. Get their insight as well. Have them pray for you.

It's easy to have your barometer fall at this writing, with the pandemic, social unrest, and political tension. When your ears pop due to the falling pressure, maybe go read the whole book of Galatians and open the door to the Spirit again!

Prayer: Dear Heavenly Father, we love you. Keep us self aware enough to realize when we are blocking Your Holy Spirit. We want the people around us to see the Fruits of the Spirit and yearn to have them as well. Then they are receptive to the Good News. AMEN

JULY 17

The Chosen People

"For not all who are descended from Israel [Jacob] are [the true] Israel; and they are not all the children of Abraham because they are his descendants [by blood]... That is, it is not the children of the body who are God's children, but it is the children of the promise who are counted as [Abraham's true] descendants." (Romans 9:6-8 AMP)

As a child, and before I had studied the scriptures in any detail, it always bothered me a little that even though God supposedly loved us, we weren't "The Chosen People." All through the Hebrew Bible, our Old Testament, there are references to the Israelites as "the Chosen People." Well, who are we then? Chicken scratch?

Paul explains to us both in Romans 9 and Galatians 3, that God's promise to Abraham was clear, that through his descendants "all the families of the earth shall be blessed!" (Genesis 12:2-3) Paul clarifies for us *"Therefore know that only those who are of faith are sons of Abraham. And the Scripture, foreseeing that God would justify the Gentiles by faith, preached the Gospel to Abraham beforehand, saying, 'In you all nations shall be Blessed."* (Galatians 3:7-8 NKJV)

So, it turns out that God ***did pick us! We are part of the Chosen People as well!*** It is not our ethnicity, or whether our males are circumcised, that makes us descendants of the promise to Abraham, but instead our faith in God! This has huge implications for your everyday lives! Isaiah 48:10 KJV says *"I have chosen you in the furnace of affliction."* What does it mean to us to be chosen?

Charles Spurgeon tells us that when poverty is at your door, let it in! God is already in your house. He has already chosen to stand with you! Sickness comes knocking? Well, alright then, come right in because God has already chosen me! Don't forget that Christ in you and you in Him, means that the helper, the Spirit, is right there with you in the midst of your poverty and sickness. You are never alone. Is there anything intolerable as long as you don't have to face it alone? We may not be able to see Jesus physically, but we can hear His voice. We know He is telling us that even when we are walking through the valley of the shadow of death, we need not fear evil, because *He is with us!*

Remember how bad it felt not being picked by either captain to be on the 2nd grade dodge ball team? God picked you. You are Chosen! Rejoice in it!

Prayer: Dear Heavenly Father, thank You for picking us! Knowing that You have made us a part of Your family and that we have all the rights and privileges that go along with that, can reassure us in any circumstance. Bring it on! god's on my team! AMEN

JULY 18

Sufficient Grace

"Concerning this thing I pleaded with the Lord three times that it might depart from me. And He said to me, 'My grace is sufficient for you, for My strength is made perfect in weakness.' Therefore, most gladly, I will rather boast in my infirmities, that the power of Christ may rest upon me." (2 Corinthians 12:8-9 NKJV)

I have a bad back. News flash. If you've been reading DOING LIFE from the start, you know this already. No, it's not lymphoma like my son-in-law. No, it's not Parkinson's like my partner's wife. No it's not life long psoriasis like my cousin. Yet still, it chaps me! My diagnosis technically is "flat back syndrome" and it means my lumbar spine has no curve, and thus fails to act as a shock absorber for my spine. That leads to multiple ruptured discs and that leads to severe back spasms that can drop me to my knees with no warning whatsoever, despite preventative exercises and multiple surgeries. I have dealt with this since age 17, just shy of 50 years. In that time, yes, I have prayed for it to be healed, or at least to never require yet another back surgery, or have debilitating spasms keep me from work, sailing, or time with my children and grandchildren. Thus far I have received exactly the same answer to prayer that Paul received: nope.

What does "My Grace is sufficient" mean anyway? No one knows if Paul's "thorn" was physical or not. It could have been malaria, migraine, epilepsy, or even sciatica like me! It could have been constant temptation. In any event, it was an affliction that Paul could not overcome on his own, and for which he repeatedly begged God to remove. But eventually Paul came to realize that Christ's divine power is more evident to all, against the back drop of human weakness! Instead of removing the problem, Christ instead gave him grace. Grace means the unmerited favor of God. In this instance, it meant that Christ had given him *contentment*. Despite the continued affliction, Paul would be content to carry out his work despite the pain.

There is another clue in verse 12:7, both at the beginning and the end. Paul believes the "thorn in his side" was given to him "lest he be exalted above measure." The original Greek to this phrase, according to the ***Bible Knowledge Commentary***, may be translated, "to keep me from being conceited." The Grace given him transformed Paul's outlook about every difficulty he would encounter. Paul's own weakness, as exacerbated by whatever this thorn might have been, allowed God's supernatural power to be repeatedly on display and bring glory to God, not to Paul!

Whatever my ability to bring comfort and solace to my patients, the glory belongs to God, not to me. Intermittent pain is a reminder of my limitations, my humanity, in the face of God's awesome power on display all around me. There have been many instances when I was dependent on a cane and a brace, and moved very slowly indeed, and yet various clinical emergencies all worked out for the best despite my infirmity!

God's grace is illustrated and magnified in the poverty, trials, infirmities, temptations, aggravations and failures of believers! All of us know believers who bear up under tremendous personal burdens, truly believing that all things work together for good, and knowing in their hearts that out of apparent evils, true blessings will eventually result. They know that God will either deliver them from their affliction quickly, or if not, will support them in it for as long as He deems it necessary for them to endure it.

The patience of believers, waiting on the Lord in strength, proves the power of divine grace! The integrity of a ship's hull is not truly known until tested by the storm. How can Paul be joyful, actually revel in his affliction? Because the more difficult our path, the more clearly we can illustrated to others the all-sufficient grace of God!

Prayer: Lord, forgive us when we whine about our difficulties. We realize You have encouraged us to bring everything to You in prayer, but give us clarity to understand a greater purpose when your answer for the time-being is "no." When we power through, remind us that we need to give you the Glory and not a misguided self-congratulations. AMEN

JULY 19

Know the Tides

"The wisdom of the prudent is to give thought to their ways, but the folly of fools is deception." (Proverbs 14:8 NIV)

There is an old expression in the south: "You can't see the stumps when the water's high!" Now, while that originally applied to tree stumps in southern, man-made lakes, which are notorious for flooding during heavy rains and drying up in drought, it certainly applies in tidal waters as well. The only difference for the Reach, and surrounding waters of Coastal Maine, might involve substituting the word 'rocks' for 'stumps." Our old cottage is named "Gull Rock," because of the laughing gulls that are a constant feature of the six foot diameter boulder that lay 200 feet in front of the house. That is, when it's exposed. At high tide it is quite invisible, as are the gulls. The implication is that in the absence of visible obstructions protruding above the surface, one would seem to have 'clear sailing." Sailing too close to the cottage at high tide would disprove your assumption. During the course of our daily lives, we may be oblivious to impending dangers, whether at work, in our families, or in our relationships with those in both, unless we have some awareness of what is going on at a "deeper" level. But when the tide goes out, the dangers that were there all along become obvious, and often too late to avoid disaster.

While the expression's literal meaning seems obvious, its figurative one is somewhat less so. Whether in business, tech, medicine, or sports, there is a deeper inference. When things are going well, one sometimes gets careless about barreling ahead, even throwing 'caution to the wind!' In small business, if profits seem steady, there might be a tendency to ignore the inherent risks of the enterprise, inviting financial disaster once circumstances change. In medicine, if you are over-confident in your facility with a relatively new procedure, you might tend to get cavalier about its usage, until one of the less frequent complications rears its ugly head. In your marriage, after years of routine with little to no conflict, you may start to take your mate for granted, forgetting entirely how difficult it might be to *actually live with you!* It is likely there are signs on the surface that should suggest what trouble might lurk below, but in complacency, you overlook even the obvious ones.

Life circumstances will arise for all of us where an awareness of the "tides" might well prove useful, if not down right critical. There's an another old expression, *"You will never see the words 'I wish I'd spent more time at the office!'* on a headstone. That is of course, because for virtually all of humanity, it is our families that matter the most to us. Married or single, old or young, East or West; while there may be cultural differences, humans are fundamentally wired to care about and long for, the company of their families. For most of us, our parents were our first safe harbor. In their presence, we didn't feel that we had to watch our backs. For some of us, an older sibling would share that role as well. Later, we would provide that safe harbor for our own children, and after they have grown, we often provide it in turn, for our aged parents. While different cultures have subtle differences with respect to familial inter-relationships, all seem to be structured around the unconditional love of a parent for a child, and to a varying extent, a reciprocal respect and even veneration of our parents and elders.

Knowing the "tides" in your life then, has much to do with paying attention to your family! It is far too easy to get caught up in the rat race for job advancement, higher pay, greater authority, or even to be beat down by the drudgery of a job that is necessary for survival, but in which you seem to have no hope of advancement, such that you miss life as it slips by you faster and faster! When a parent tells me about how much they love to be around their 6 or 7 year old son or daughter, and I tell them jokingly that they might want to journal these moments for later, I am only partially kidding. In retrospect, I spent far too many hours at the hospital on call, writing, seeing patients, and running a business, than I would have liked. Some can see the possible effects of their absence in the self-confidence and coping skills of their own adult children. Life goes by quickly, and if you are not present in the moment, *every moment,* you can find yourself totally surprised when you run aground on a falling tide!

If your family only gets a cursory look before you rush off to work, and perhaps for a few moments after dinner when the kids are ready for bed or doing homework, or heading out with friends, it is like heading into a coastal bay with no knowledge whatsoever of the tides. There may be all sorts of hidden obstructions in the water that will become unavoidable when the water level falls. With the child who barely gets by at school, but nevertheless does get by, you might totally miss his sense of frustration and eventual futility. The early diagnosis of an attention deficit, visual difficulty, or auditory processing troubles, might have averted later emotional problems emanating from the overlooked physical/neurological one.

The teen who pulls away and even rebels against you and your spouse, might be doing so as a normal part of teen evolution, but attention to the tide might have warned you to a deepening depression, lack of self esteem and deterioration of motivation, that could lead to physical danger in the form of alcohol, drugs, and high risk behavior.

With a spouse whose workload is beginning to overwhelm them, perhaps both inside and outside the home, lack of "tidal awareness" may cause you to either miss the signs, or misinterpret their actions, such that your relationship deteriorates into parallel tracks just when your partner needed your support the most! A spouse with no emotional support, no "quality" time where you listen, will unfortunately frequently turn to someone else for that support.

Entire books have been written on every type of flawed human relationship and their potentially disastrous outcomes. But almost all of these scenarios could have been averted by one's "awareness of the tide." Awareness stems from watching, listening, and learning. My father, who was an outstanding sailor and cruiser, once failed to combine all three when he ran aground on a falling tide in Winter Harbor (a story for another time!).

Believers thankfully, have an infallible reference when it comes to the most important aspect of their entire lives: their families! First and foremost, the Bible uses the analogy of a family for our relationship with God, and does so hundreds of times. The Creator is 'God, our Father.' Our Savior Jesus Christ is both His only begotten Son and at the same time a member of the Trinity of God the Father, Son and Holy Spirit. In our receiving of the gift offered through Christ, and His sacrifice for the forgiveness of our sins, we are granted adoption into the intimate family of the Creator of the Universe!

"See what kind of love the Father has given us, that we should be called children of God; and so we are!" 1 John 3:1

"For you did not receive the Spirit of slavery to fall back into fear, but you have received the spirit of adoption as sons, by whom we cry, 'Abba! Father!'" Rom 8:15

"For all who did receive Him, who believed in His name, He gave the right to become children of God." John 1:12

> *Prayer: Dear Heavenly Father, we praise You Lord that You saw fit to give us families to love and be loved in return. Keep us watchful Lord, aware of the "tides" in our own lives. Pride can convince us we are doing so well that we completely miss the fact there are hazards lurking just below the service. Remind us Father, that when we see no gulls, it's probably because they have no safe place to stand. AMEN*

JULY 20

Lions and Tigers and Bears

"We're off to see the wizard; the wonderful Wizard of Oz! We hear he is a wiz of a wiz; if ever a wiz there was; If ever, oh ever, a wiz there was; the Wizard of Oz is one because; Because, because, because, because, because; Because of the wonderful things he does!" (Ray Bolger, Judy Garland,The Wizard of Oz, 1939)

Our granddaughter Allie, saw a mouse in the middle of the dirt path on the way down to the cove yesterday. We were all heading out for a sail on an

"MBD" (Maine Blue Day) when she spotted the little grey fella standing frozen in the midst of the trail, whiskers twitching, clearly unsure what to do. As she approached with loud exclamations of wonder, he finally made the right choice and scampered off into the brush.

But the event prompted a discussion of animals seen during vacation thus far, including two white tailed deer, a bald eagle, bunnies, a star fish, part of a lobster, and multiple crabs. But understandably, her greatest concern was for the possibility of seeing a bear, which she had been told were seen in the past on the long dirt road down to our cottage on the water. We assured her it would be rare to see one during the day and we were quite safe. She remained a bit unsure I believe, and quoted her bear mantra, "Black: fight back; Brown: lay down; White: say goodnight!" The discussion, while walking down the dappled, sunlit path on a breezy, cool, Maine morning, inevitably led to our singing the classic lyrics above!

We are all off to see the Wizard in a way, aren't we? We journey through life's adventures in the hope that one day we will stand before the Great and Powerful One, the One who is both judge and Savior. Along the way, we face all manner of difficulty, things that could swallow us up completely, just like lions and tigers and bears! But all those creatures hunting us from the shadows are really just shapes of fear: fear of the unknown, fear of change, fear of the new. Those fears can paralyze us, keep us from our potential, destroy the pursuit of our dreams.

But with faith in our Savior, and ultimately faith in His promises, we learn that we really have nothing to fear! Jesus, is the Light of the World, and where He is present there are no shadows for the creatures of fear to lurk! More than that, we learn that our companions in life, our fellow believers, our family, stand next to us, there to help us through, just like the scarecrow, the tin man and the lion!

"Be strong and courageous! Do not fear or be in dread of them, for it is the Lord, your God who goes with you. He will not leave you or forsake you." (Deuteronomy 31:6 ESV)

Prayer: Dear heavenly Father, we are eternally grateful that You sent Your Son to be the light of the world! Fear of the creatures that track us in the dark dissipates in Your presence! When fear of the unknown assails us Lord, let Your Holy Spirit work through us to support our brothers and sisters, turning those lions and tigers and bears into little more than a frightened grey field mouse! AMEN

JULY 21

Fumes

"For I will satisfy the weary soul, and every languishing soul I will replenish." (Jeremiah 31:25 ESV)

Yesterday, I was motoring across Deadman's Cove in our inflatable Typhoon, my grandchildren, six and eight, on the small bench seat. We were taking a last spin around the cove, inspecting the sailboats at their moorings, swinging around the rocky point to pass in front of the cottage and give a wave to their mom (my daughter) and Grammy (my wife) before we lost the last of the evening light. Liam took the throttle of the 2.5 Hp Yamaha for a few moments, (the main incentive, I believe, for his joining our little expedition!) The little engine hesitated at one point, enough for me to take the throttle back, put it in neutral and take a look at the prop to clear the seaweed we had just run through. It seemed to be unobstructed however, and I really thought nothing of it when the motor ran smoothly again in forward. We returned to the cove, Allie excited by the bumps as we rocketed over the surface at a blistering 3 mph.

As we made the sweeping circle to come upwind to the floating dock, I throttled back as usual. We approached at dead slow, and just as I routinely reached for the deadman switch to cut the engine, it died on its own! We eased sideways up to the dock, I grabbed ahold, and first Allie and then Liam with the painter in hand, climbed out onto the dock. Liam said, "Wow Papa, I didn't see you pull the red cut off thing!" I hadn't. Weird. I tried to start the engine again and got nothing from the very reliable brand new Yamaha; an excellent engine, albeit one without a gas gauge. I took off the cap and sure enough, bone dry!

I can promise you that I know what it feels like to be operating on fumes. In residency we pulled 36 hour shifts, and believe me, we were running on fumes every time we headed back to our apartments, falling asleep at every red light. You might be running on fumes at your job. It may not be fatigue; it might be frustration, or stress, or boss, or client related issues. For those younger, it might be school related: projects due, team problems, overloaded problems, or plain "I don't get it," issues! The thing about running on fumes, even when you don't realize that's what's happening, is where you happen to be when you run out of gas completely!

For a boater, there's no better place to be than the dock! The dock represents your link to the world of solid ground, to safety, to home. In life too, you need the security of knowing you can make it back to the cove and up to the dock. For people of faith, that's what the Savior is all about! When we're out of gas and dead in the water, it turns out *we're right beside the dock,* and all we have to do is reach out a hand, stabilize the boat and climb to safety! Christ is *always available* through prayer and the presence of the Holy Spirit. We're *never* caught out on the sea in a storm when we run out of gas! With Jesus right at hand, it's as though we are always coasting right up to the dock! Consider that the next time you flat run out of gas. You're not on the open sea alone. Your faith keeps you right near the dock!

"He gives power to the faint, and to him who had no might he increases strength." (Isaiah 40:29 ESV)

Prayer: Dear heavenly Father, we love you. We love that you loved us first and loved us so much that You gave us Your Son, an ever present help in trouble! When we're out of gas, when life has us on our knees in the bottom of the boat, You're right there at our side, our secure dock, always waiting with a place to tie on to! AMEN

JULY 22
Ubiquitous

"Where can I go from Your Spirit? Or where can I flee from Your presence? If I go up to the heavens, You are there; If I make my bed in the depths,You are there. If I rise on the wings of the dawn, If I settle on the far side of the sea, Even there Your hand will guide me,Your right hand will hold me fast." (Psalm 139:7-12 NIV)

Maybe every physician has experienced this, but I know for a fact that obstetricians experience it all the time. I'm talking about four people in labor, distributed from eight to thirty hours in, and they will ALL deliver within 5 minutes of each other! It happens over and over and over and the only problem is that you have to be in four places at once! Just four.

This probably happens to everyone in all walks of life, I just feel more stressed and sorry for myself, than I do for everyone else. Needless to say, I simply cannot be four places at once, and everyone in my profession has had the experience of "missing" a delivery. While in my hospital there are more than enough competent nurses to handle routine situations, it is still disappointing for the physician, and probably sometimes, at least a little disappointing for the new mom when we run in just in time to deliver a bouncing baby placenta! (Of course, she has the actual new baby to compensate!)

Lucky for us, God doesn't have this problem. Theologians use three terms to describe God's cardinal characteristics or attributes: omnipotence, omniscience and omnipresence. The latter of these means He could do four deliveries, or four billion deliveries, simultaneously. Omnipresence means ubiquitous; the ability to be present everywhere at the same instant in time. First of all God is Spirit, and limitless in form. Furthermore, He is outside of time, since He created it. He is all powerful and all knowing. That means He knows what you need and when you need it!

Thinking of God's attributes always reminds me of Jim Carey in *Bruce Almighty*. He quickly realizes that responding to billions of prayer requests per minute, even using a computer, even answering ALL YES or ALL NO, proves to be simply impossible. And that underscores just one single aspect of God's attributes.

So, don't ever catch yourself thinking God is too busy for your little problem, or isn't listening, or isn't present. He isn't too busy, He is listening, and He is present! "Ubiquitous." Great word for Words with Friends as long as you can find an "ous" out there. But also, a really reassuring quality of our God.

"The eyes of the Lord are everywhere, keeping watch on the wicked and the good." (Proverbs 15:3 NIV)

"For where two or three are gathered in My name, there I am with them." (Matthew 18:20 NIV)

Prayer: Thank you Father! We praise Your Name knowing that You see into all our hearts, have the power to save us and lead us, and are miraculously always present in our moment of need! AMEN

JULY 23
Blowing It

"Then they cried to the Lord in their trouble, and he delivered them from their distress." (Psalm 107:28 ESV)

It was early morning in Maine. The sun comes up about 4:30 AM and I come up with it. Not everyone does, but for some reason I do. I'm just not one for lying in bed while awake. To be honest, I am usually awake a bit before the sun, and here in Maine, that's due to the song of the wrens, then robins, and then the blackbirds, all of whom start to sing before the sun reaches the horizon. (Nickel knowledge: 'nautical dawn' is when the sun is 12 degrees below the horizon and the sailor can distinguish the horizon; 'civil dawn' is when the sun is 6 degrees below the horizon, the sky becomes colored, blue if clear, orange or red if cloudy.)

Once downstairs with coffee in hand, and fire lit, if you sit on the porch and listen, you'll hear the occasional early lobster boat, but every few minutes you'll hear other noises coming from the water. If early enough, you will often hear the mournful, unmistakeable, wail of the loon, long before the gulls make their appearance. If you pay attention, you may also hear a short bark or grunt from the water, interspersed with the cry of the loon. Then if you're particularly lucky, that morning, you'll occasionally hear a *chuff* or a *snort* along with the subtle sound of water moving rapidly. The loon, the harbor seal and the Atlantic dolphin, are all common inhabitants of Mid-Coast Maine, and they all have something in common: they spend a whole lot of time under water. All subsist on fish, and all hold their breaths for ridiculously long periods, usually longer than one minute and often 3-5 minutes! While the exhalation of air by the loon immediately upon breaking the surface is essentially inaudible, the snort of both seal and dolphin are often startling in their suddenness and volume.

The dolphin, like both the baleen and the toothed whales, breathes through its 'blow hole.' The *blow* that one can hear and see, is air forcibly exhaled immediately upon surfacing after a dive. You can see it for long distances in winter, because the warm water vapor in the exhaled air condenses instantly when it contacts the cold air. Something about the sudden urgency of that first breath, conveys our own desperation to breathe! One of the scariest experiences of my life came when I was about five or six. I was in a neighborhood pool when another older kid held me under water. I guess he thought I was playing as I thrashed about in a panic, but I hadn't taken much of a breath before he forced me under as a 'joke.'

All of us find ourselves under water, holding our breath from time to time. Whether it is work, marriage, parenting, or even in 2020, pandemic related, all of us find ourselves desperate for a breath now and then! If you've ever been forced to hold your breath a little too long, especially under water, you know the incredibly sweet relief of that first gasp when your lungs exhale the foul air, and then rapidly inhale the life giving freshness of clean *air!*

For me, when life holds me under for a little too long, that fresh air comes in the form of scripture. I suppose to the secular that may sound impossibly trite, but to the believers, you know of what I speak. When I need a breath of fresh air, I reach for the Psalms. Try it. The theme is not only God's awesome power, but also His goodness, expressed in poetry and music. There are psalms of lament, of praise and of wisdom, as well as others. But there are specific ones that encourage, like 3,4,8,9,16,19,20,23,27,29,30,34,37,46,51,55,84,91,100, 107,121,127,147. (Benefit of seminary, what can I say?) Pick any one of these and meditate on it when you feel like you desperately need to *blow*, as the Cetologists say!

"I keep my eyes always on the Lord. with Him at my right hand, I will not be shaken." (Psalm 16:8 NIV)

"The Lord is my light and my salvation-whom shall I fear? The Lord is the stronghold of my life-of whom shall I be afraid?" (Psalm 27:1 NIV)

"Taste and see that the Lord is good; blessed is the one who takes refuge in Him." (Psalm 34:8 NIV)

> ***Prayer: Father God, we love You! Thank you that You are that breath of fresh air that we desperately need when life has held us under too long! AMEN***

JULY 24
Blessings

"Blessed are the poor in Spirit...Blessed are those who mourn...Blessed are the meek...Blessed are those who hunger and thirst for righteousness...Blessed are the merciful...Blessed are the pure in heart...Blessed are the peacemakers...Blessed are those who are persecuted for righteousness sake..." (Matthew 5:3-10 NKJV)

There are many times in life when each of us feel far from God, or sad, or shy and withdrawn, or like we are desperately trying to do what is right and failing. There are indeed times when we show compassion for others, when the best in us comes out, when we bring a peaceful resolution to someone else's strife, and yet even these require that someone be hurting or fighting. And yes, there are times when others speak ill of us, when we are only trying to be loving. Sometimes, it seems that if it weren't for bad luck, we'd have no luck at all!

But look closely. These are the times, when the Author of Salvation sat on a mountain above a huge crowd of every type of sinner and downtrodden, and told them who are the *Blessed*. The Aramaic word our Lord used, rendered in Greek was '*makarios*' and it means fortunate, happy, or well off. Incredibly, Jesus tells us the definition of happiness in these seven sentences! (Theologians regard verses 10 and 11 as benedictions upon the people described in the preceding seven Beatitudes.) The whole seven describe the perfect *character*. Charles Spurgeon says he knows of 288 different opinions of ancient philosophers on what constitutes *happiness*, and none hits the mark, but Christ does in just these few sentences! He calls the Beatitudes "the ladder of light" ascending from the poor in spirit to the pure in heart and peacemaker. And yet, Spurgeon says they are a descent in human terms, for the Beatitudes mark "deepening humiliation and growing exaltation." As men become more Christ-like, rising in their divine blessing, they sink in their own esteem. Recall Philippians 2 and the mind of Christ!

Note also that *makarios* is in the present tense. The Beatitudes aren't giving you a list of ways to behave for which you will only be rewarded in the future, but character traits that develop as you become less and less "poor in Spirit," which breed joy, and happiness, right now! Even the poor in Spirit can rejoice in their fledgling faith, having just experienced Grace, just as the peacemaker can rejoice in resolving disputes with humility! Our opening verses omit the actual blessings, but only identify who are the Blessed. Read the entire passage, and note that the Blessing for each character level, is tailored to that particular rung on the "ladder of light." So, the poor in spirit inherit the Kingdom (by Grace!) while those who mourn are comforted, etc.

Not unlike the parables which our Lord loved to use in teaching, the Beatitudes are steeped in paradox. Seven times Christ tells us of characters which start in poverty and end in persecution, and yet are "happy" beyond all others! How like the Rabbi! He grabs our attention and makes us think! The Beatitdues remind us of the Fruits of the Spirit, once again. They are not a list of "do's" but a list of 'states of being' as we surrender to the Savior and allow the Spirit to work progressively, more and more, through us. The world will indeed know us by our love, but they won't love us, for what they don't have! As the happiness of the believer increases with his sanctification, his progressive Christ-likeness, his ascent up the ladder of the Beatitudes into the 'Son' shine, the persecution of the world will intensify. But that will not rob us of our joy, because we know that we are not of this world. Instead, we are in the words of B.B. King, "riding with the King!"

Prayer: Dear Heavenly Father, through Your Spirit, remind us daily that it is no longer we who live, but Christ Who lives in us! He is the source of our happiness and contentment. Joy comes with each step as we gradually become more Christ like, manifested in the characteristics on the ladder of the Beatitudes. As we become more comfortable with prayer, more stimulated by scripture, more aware of Christ around us, it will be manifested in our love and our humility. AMEN

JULY 25

Carry On

"When vandal hordes ride down ready to eat me alive, those bullies and toughs fall flat on their faces. When besieged, I'm calm as a baby. When all hell breaks loose, I'm collected and cool...." (Psalm 27:2-3 The Message)

There's an expression that was produced as a motivational poster placed throughout London during the Nazi bombings of WWII (the *Blitz*), that in recent years has undergone a resurgence in popularity. *"Keep Calm and Carry On!"* The phrase now occurs on t-shirts, coffee mugs, and variations of it on a thousand different memes. Maybe the world has never seen devastation as widespread, as lethal (85 million killed) as WWII, but there are still plenty of stresses to power through from viral pandemics, to state sponsored terrorism, to race riots, to nonstop vitriolic political accusation. But, the phrase can be applied on a personal level for all of us as well.

Recently, I could NOT find the fifth piece out of 54, needed to assemble a gas grill for my mother. Now the directions, as they are wont to be nowadays, had NO WORDS at all, in any language. They were drawings, that sometimes sufficed, but often failed miserably in their rendering of 3 dimensional objects intended to be fastened together in a particular orientation using 4 X A screws, 4 X D washers, and 2 X B screws all of which were theoretically available in the impossible to open, inadequately perforated, plastic and cardboard and foil Fort Knox packaging material! All of the standard frustrations, like trying to screw on a nut with the pictured end wrench, when in fact, it is recessed, and quite impossible to do with an end wrench, could have been overcome if the DANG THING weren't MISSING a piece!!! As I became increasingly angry and disgusted, I evidently became louder, more demonstrative in my discard of packaging and tool selection, and might possibly have even said some bad words! Luckily, (or not,) my wife and 91 year old mother were both witnesses of my diatribe. Being the good wife that she is, she simply asked if she could see the directions. I may have 'tossed' them in her direction while I pointed out that the pieces were numbered with stickers and NUMBER 5 was not there!

Long story short, much to my chagrin, no part was missing. I had placed #2 between #1 and #3 just as instructed and needed the identical #5 to go between #4 and #6; the only problem being, as my lovely bride pointed out, the piece I had identified as #2, was in fact #8. Once I identified the correct #2, I found the matching #5. (Your honor, my only defense is that #5 did not in fact have a sticker, although it was the mirror image of the correct #2.)

As a surgeon, I can remain calm in some of the most harrowing medical emergencies, and have done so in the past. But putting together a grill, or altering a sailboat rigging, or having a political discussion, or following my wife's directions while driving, can all become heated!! Why on earth is that, when daily I succeed in staying composed with regard to the worldly issues enumerated above? Perhaps because I too often ignore the verse that follows our opening verse. Psalm 27:4 says, *"I'm asking God for one thing, only one thing: to live with Him in His house my whole life long. I'll contemplate His beauty and study at His feet. That's the only quiet secure place in a noisy world..."* (The Message) Maybe this dove-tails with another popular meme, *"Keep the main thing the main thing!"*

There is actually no reason for those who have the risen Christ *abiding* within them, to ever have a hissy fit over trivialities! But I have a feeling I am not the only one that does so from time to time. When you find yourself pretty sure you are missing piece #5, take a breath, sit back, and count your Blessings! In my case, I had a family for whom to put together a grill, a house outside of which to grill, the wherewithal to afford a grill, and the income to buy food to cook on the grill! Taking the time to pause, breathe and thank God, even

I *might* have noticed that the piece I thought was #2 was just way too long to match the picture!!!

"Abide in Me and I in you. As the branch cannot bear fruit of itself unless it abides in the vine, neither can you unless you abide in Me." (John 15:4 NKJV)

"The one who knows much says little; an understanding person remains calm." (Proverbs 17:27 The Message)

> *Prayer: Dear Heavenly Father, we know that You made the seas, and that only Your voice can calm them. Christ was the ultimate example of calm under pressure, and with Your Holy Spirit abiding in us, let the power that calms the seas pass through us. With Your strength Lord, let us stay calm and carry on, no matter the obstacles or controversies or frustrations before us. AMEN*

JULY 26

Only Words

"The Word of Life appeared right before our eyes; we saw it happen!...The infinite Life of God Himself took shape before us. We saw it, we heard it, and now we're telling you so you can experience it along with us, this experience of communion with the Father and his Son, Jesus Christ." (1 John 1:2-3 Message)

There's an expression I imagine all of us have used from time to time: *"I wouldn't have believed it if I hadn't seen it with my own two eyes!"* The implication is that information obtained through the written or spoken word carries a certain amount of weight, undoubtedly related to what is known about the source, but that physical presence at the occurrence in question, where all five senses can come into play, lends the maximum credulity.

Perhaps the most famous example from the scriptures is the story of the disciple, Thomas, who like many of us, simply wouldn't believe that Jesus Christ had miraculously risen from the dead, even though he had been witness to multiple other miracles! (John 20:25) This is something that God understands well. It is one of the reasons that the Trinity manifested itself in the incarnation of Christ, so that He could be physically present and live among us as one, wholly man, and wholly God, at the same time. We could read the Sermon on the Mount, and take it as good advice, but the fact that Jesus spoke it, was crucified *on our behalf*, and then raised from the dead with over 500 eye-witnesses, leading to countless testimonies as to its veracity, leaves us much more likely to believe, than simply reading a story.

Steve Brown, author of *Scandalous Freedom,* tells the story of a young woman who became overwhelmed for many reasons, and chose to leave her husband and two children. She ran away to the other side of the country. He called her repeatedly and begged her to come home, telling her over and over that he still loved her. She refused. Finally, he got a relative to watch the kids and booked multiple flights across the entire U.S. to get to her. When he showed up at the door of the place she was staying, she fell into his arms and agreed to come home. When he asked her why she wouldn't come earlier, she said, *"When you kept calling me, it was only words. But then you CAME!"*

So it is with our Savior! He didn't just send a message, or even send a messenger, **He came Himself**, to redeem us personally!! That should make the Gift we don't deserve even harder to refuse! Think about that today, if it crosses your mind that maybe He doesn't love you because of who you are, or what you've done, and then remember that He CAME!!!

"For God so loved the world (YOU) that He gave His only begotten Son, that whoever believes in Him shall not perish but have everlasting life!" (John 3:16 NKJV)

Prayer: Dear Heavenly Father, we love You and we know that You love us, for one simple reason, YOU CAME! AMEN

JULY 27

Oh Hell

"Therefore, there is now no condemnation for those who are in Christ Jesus, because through Christ Jesus the law of the Spirit who gives life had set you free from the law of sin and death. For what the law was powerless to do because it was weakened by the flesh, God did by sending His own Son in the likeness of sinful flesh to be a sin offering. And so He condemned sin..." (Romans 8:1-3 NIV)

One of the objections to Christianity, is that it is difficult to believe in a God who would consign people to hell for all eternity. The thinking goes, if He is truly a loving God, He wouldn't be so mean-spirited and vindictive to so many. Really?

J.P. Moreland, PhD, philosopher, theologian and Christian apologist at Biola University in La Miranda, California, reminds us that *"Hell is the forever monument to human dignity, in that it demonstrates God's respect for our freedom of choice, and even respect for those image bearers who deny Him, and yet He still declines to annihilate them."* The point is that nowhere does the scripture, or any quotation of Christ ever state that God consigns sinners to hell. In fact, just the opposite is true: He offered His only Son as a sacrifice to forgive everyone who wants to be forgiven, so that they might be redeemed and have a loving relationship with their Creator once again! No, God doesn't send people to hell to be tortured, people send themselves to hell.

D.A Carson, prominent Canadian evangelical scholar and author from Trinity Evangelical Divinity School summarized his view of hell to Lee Strobel in *The Case for Faith*. *"Hell is not a place where basically good people go who just didn't believe quite the right thing. Hell is separation from the love of God for all eternity! [This is the fate] of those who deny their creator's very existence, and STILL want to be the center of the universe themselves!"*

Interestingly, "Oh hell," as an interjection, is a full utterance despite having no subject, verb or object, according to Professor of linguistics, John Lawler. It is the sort of thing you exclaim when you've made a mistake, or another has, and in that occurrence you view it as the "displeasure of Fortune." (One of my ancestors preferred the expression, "Blasphemous fate that has dealt me this blow...." in place of the blatant curse word, hell!) But the implication reflects our general mis-use and mis-understanding of hell. We are not consigned to this place called hell by fate, or by God as vengeful punishment for sinning or mis-behaving. We consign ourselves to an eternity of misery because we could have been in the loving presence of God, but by making ourselves the center of our worship, we denied ourselves that opportunity! Remember the older brother in the story of the prodigal son? He was angry that his father threw a party for his ne'er do well younger brother's return, when he viewed himself as a dutiful son that ought to be rewarded. He was so self-righteous that he refused to come to the party and partake of the food, wine and festivities even when his father begged him!

Don't worry that the price of sinning is going to hell forever. We all sin. Jesus paid the price for your sin, nailed to a cross 2,000 years ago! All you have to do is believe, and accept His forgiveness and be redeemed! If you choose not to come to the party; if you choose to refuse the gift offered to you, explained to you in detail in the bible, even though you are undeserving; well that's on you! God won't keep you out of the light. Only you can do that.

"Then Jesus spoke to them again, saying, 'I am the light of the world! He who follows me shall not walk in darkness, but have the light of life." (John 8:12 NIV)

Prayer: Dear Father God, we know that You have offered us a way back to You when we are undeserving! All we need do is believe and accept Your offer of forgiveness and eternity in the light of your presence. We believe Lord. Help our unbelief, as we pray for those who have not made a choice. AMEN

JULY 28

East From West

"For I will forgive their iniquity, and their sin I will remember no more." (Jeremiah 31:34b NKJV)

Did it ever occur to you what a big deal it is for God to forget something? I mean it's no problem for me. I delivered a baby yesterday, and everything went well. When I saw the couple again today on rounds, admittedly wearing face masks for 2020 Covid-19, she asked about her follow up visit and I told her to make an appointment in 6 weeks with me or whoever in my group was her primary doctor. She looked at her husband and then at me and said haltingly, "You're my primary doctor." Oops. My memory of people is *strongly* tied to facial recognition, cause I am *terrible* with names.

On the other hand, I have no trouble remembering all the times I have messed up as a physician, as a husband and especially as a father. I have crystal clear memories of multiple scenes in which the audience would have no trouble identifying me as the bad guy. How is it that I find it nearly impossible to forget my past failures, in all my life roles, and yet the one omniscient intelligence in the universe (well, outside of it technically,) is capable of doing exactly that? His love for me is so great, that He gave up His only Son as a price for my sin, and now, even 2,000 years later, my faith in Christ by His Grace, means that even my failures yet to come are already forgotten and forgiven by my Father!

Psalm 103:12 tells us that, "*As far as the east is from the west, So far has He removed our transgressions from us.*" Removed from us, means our that sins, our screw-ups, our abject failures, are no longer stuck to us! God sees us only clothed in the perfect righteousness of Christ! How cool is that?

So next time you're beating yourself up about past mistakes, keep in mind that your loving Father in Heaven *doesn't even know what you're talking about, no less holding them against you! He has forgotten them! Poof!* You may have trouble forgiving yourself for past transgressions, but choosing to follow Jesus means that the only One that matters, the only Judge in the end, has already forgotten whatever you did, and it won't be held against you! Thank heavens! Literally!

Prayer: Father God, thank you as we do everyday for the decision to send Your Son to live among us, show us perfection, die in our place, for our sin, and make it possible for You to forget every bad thing we have ever done or will do, because when You look at us, You only see Him abiding in us and we in Him! AMEN

JULY 29

What Are You Doing?

"Do all things without complaining and disputing, that you may become blameless and harmless, children of God without fault in the midst of a crooked and perverse generation, among whom you shine as lights in the world..." (Philippians 2:14-15 NKJV)

Wow, does that sound like it was written this morning, or what? "*In the midst of a crooked and perverse generation.*" Well, we have that down pat in America, don't we, where self-service, self-focus, self-promotion, self-conceit, independence and self-centeredness rule the day! These are not looked at pejoratively in today's society, they are *celebrated* in advertising, movies, television, and political rhetoric!

The reason so many people view Christians and church goers as hypocrites, is they see the way we live. Paul says right before our opening quote, "*Let nothing be done through selfish ambition or conceit, but in lowliness of mind let each esteem others better than himself.*" *(Philippians 2:3 NKJV)* There is nothing wrong with providing for your family. There is not even anything wrong with working hard, whether in a dual income household or single, to have money to buy some nice things, or maybe go some nice places with your family.

But there is something wrong if you are known to others as the hard charging, upwardly mobile scraper, who will do anything to get ahead, including dishonesty, defaming others, and positioning yourself for success at the cost of another's failure. And even this doesn't mean Christ thinks it is wrong to compete, and compete to win. What's wrong, is working in your own strength, with no attention to God, no dependence on a relationship with Christ, and doing it specifically so you will look better than someone else, because you think that will make you feel successful! What's wrong is thinking your "peace" and "happiness" depend on buying the things that the advertising world bombards you with every second of every day. The ads tell us that contentment lies in a bigger house, or a re-modeled kitchen, or a brand new car, or flashy outfits, or thousand dollar suits.

The world convinces you that the deeper relationships and the approval we all desire, can be bought.

There's a saying that "money may not buy you happiness, but it will buy you a boat big enough to sail right up next to it!" The expression is tongue in cheek! The times you'll want to remember on your big boat are the same times you'd remember if you'd grilled out in the public park next to the marina instead. The laughter of friends and family, the stories they tell, the love that they share; that's what will stick in your memory. Your friends won't remember the leather covered seats, or the size of the engines, or the fact that you had no boat at all and only a public park in which to entertain. They'll remember the fact that you invited them and you had fun.

Doctors doctor every day. Lawyers practice law. Writers write. Musicians play. They all get up every morning and do what they love, or are good at, or are trained to do. The act of doing, is what makes them what they are. A doctor isn't really a doctor if he only has the degree, and then goes to work for an insurer reviewing claims. A lawyer isn't really a lawyer if he goes to work as a sales director, even though he has the J.D.

Faith works in a similar way, and this is what James was trying to say in his New Testament epistle. Christ tells us they will know we are His by our love. James tell us they will know *our faith is real*, if we act like it! That's what "faith without works is dead," really means! When we lend a hand to the downtrodden, whether in a mission setting or simply helping a friend who's fallen on hard times, people see it. When we are the peacemaker in a debate at work that starts to get nasty, people see it. When people notice that we never have a negative word to say about someone not present, and in fact defend those not present, people see it. When you get the tough assignment at work, the thankless task, and do so quietly and without expecting any reward, people see it.

People are often passionate about what they do. We can be passionate about our faith by falling more and more in love with Jesus every day! When you live in such a way that you are depending on God for renewed strength, for direction and trusting Him with the outcome, people see it.

"Let this mind be in you which was also in Christ Jesus, who being in the form

of God, did not consider it robbery to be equal with God, but made Himself of no reputation, taking the form of a bondservant, and coming in the likeness of men. And being found in appearance as a man, He humbled Himself and became obedient to the point of death, even the death on a cross." (Philippians 2:5-8 NKJV)

Prayer: Dear Heavenly Father, direct Your Holy Spirit to work through us Lord, so that, to the greatest extent possible, all that we do brings glory to You rather than ourselves. Re-kindle the fire of passion in us for our Savior! Let our greatest happiness come not from exalting ourselves and increasing our position of power, but by humbling ourselves, serving others willingly, and thus having a greater influence on those around us than any amount of worldly success could offer. AMEN

JULY 30

True Love

"I wish that I could have gone with him to Korea. Then I could have shared the horrors, shared whatever hurt him so badly. If had, then maybe I could share his pain now. Perhaps it would halve the pain. That's what love is. Carrying each other's pain." (Jennifer Worth)

We live in a "what's in it for me" culture. Perhaps that's why so many relationships fail. Gary Smalley wrote a bestseller some thirty years ago entitled, *"If Only He Knew."* It's about how to love your wife. But specifically, it's about how to love your wife *sacrificially*, the way Christ loves His bride, the church. Jesus was God incarnate for a reason, so He could experience our temptations, emotions, physical sensation, and yes, share in our pain. God didn't have to do anything like what He did with His only Son. There's no "God handbook" that said, as the Creator of the universe, He had to suffer in pain and humiliation, and then die a horrific, excruciating death on a cross. He did that because He loves us so much, and wants us to come back to Him, so much, that He was willing to do *anything*, no matter how painful, to offer us redemption, to offer us a way back!

Paul tells us throughout the New Testament, that we "are saved by grace through faith." True, our salvation only depends on us believing in Jesus Christ as the Son of God, and accepting the gift of redemption, even while we are undeserving. But just as Christ suffered the physical and emotional pain of mankind voluntarily, so too, the Believer is called to die with Christ, die to the law and die to our old selves, in order to be born anew. "Dying to your old self," can be extremely painful as you give up a self-centered focus to your life and start to put the best interest of others before yourself. (Philippians 2:3-4)

That's what the quote above is speaking about. A young wife in 1954, pregnant with their first child, in poverty stricken East London's Poplar District, watches her young husband suffer with horrific anxiety, nightmares and lack of self-confidence; a result of PTSD from his battlefield experience during the Korean War. Love to her, meant sharing her husband's pain in an effort to diminish it for him. The love Christ speaks of is this type of sacrificial love. It's the kind of love Gary Smalley speaks of in his advice to married couples. Christ tells His disciples, *"Greater love has no one than this, to lay down one's life for his friends." (John 15:13 NKJV)* Paul explains further in Romans, *"Scarcely for a righteous man will one die; yet perhaps for a good man someone would even dare to die. But God demonstrates His own love toward us, in that while we were still sinners Christ died for us." (Romans 5:8 NKJV)*

True love means easing another's burden, even if it adds to your own. The *Sannibel Success Story,* that my father carried folded in his wallet for 70 years, defined success as , *"Knowing that even one life has breathed a little easier for your having lived."* It might be a tremendous idea to start with your spouse and children, and from there you can build outwards. When you see someone needing help, don't wait to be asked, help them! When you see a problem developing in a relationship, look for the answer in the mirror, it's often right there in front of you. Try to see things from another's perspective, and after you've tried that for a while, try seeing that same person from God's perspective. God made them, and loves them just like He loves you. Shocker.

Prayer: Dear Heavenly Father, thank you that You wanted to experience life from the perspective of the ones You created! Lead us to love our spouses, families, and eventually all whom we can, sacrificially, putting their benefit before our own. AMEN

JULY 31

100 Pounds of Clay

"He took a hundred pounds of clay, and then He said, "'Hey listen! I'm gonna fix this world today, Because I know what's missin'!' Then He rolled His big sleeves up, And a brand new world began. He created a woman....and lot's of lovin', for a man! Whoa-oh-oh, yes He did." (Lyrics by Bob Elgin; performed by Gene Mc-Daniels 1961)

My older brother used to be a cardio-thoracic surgeon. He's retired now, but he spent his professional career preventing people from leaving this world, while I spent my career bring people into it. Soon after retirement, he became more interested in pottery, or specifically, "throwing pots," as some say in the craft. Of course, he also improved his sailboat racing skills and at the same time climbed the national rankings of duplicate bridge players. But pottery seems best to fit the skill-set of an accomplished surgeon. He made all the beautiful coffee mugs for his son's restaurant in Blue Hill, Maine. He's made all manner of vase, bowl, cup, and container that one could imagine.

But as skilled as he has become, and as skilled as he might one day become, he'll never be able to make anything as magnificent as a woman! Oh, he can make a mug whose handle is exactly configured to match your grip. But that pales in comparison to making a helpmate who learns to know you and your needs better than you know yourself. The Hebrew word used in Genesis 2:20 is *ezer,* and it means *to succor.* 'Succor' means to help, assist or aid, but it also means to shelter, protect, relieve or provide a remedy. Well, isn't *that* interesting! I bet some of you Cro-Magnon men out there thought *you* were the one to do all the sheltering, protecting and providing of remedies! Turns out that when God says you are designed to leave your fathers and mothers and cleave to each other, forming one flesh, that He had more of an equal partnership in mind!

Okay, some of you Biblical scholars out there will note that scripturally the lyric to the 1950s hit song above, is slightly inaccurate. Genesis 2:22 tells us that God caused man to fall into a deep sleep, and he took one of man's ribs, out of which He fashioned a perfect helper for man, and called her *woman,* because she came out of man. But hey, the *rib was made from clay (Hebrew word 'apar' meaning dust or clay, Gen 2:7)* and I can tell you as a man and a physician, that there's a whole lot more to a woman's body than a rib, so I can easily believe He used just about a hundred pounds of clay for the rest of her! Note that after He fashioned her, God *brought her to the man.* She was a gift. The perfect gift, suited exactly to fit his needs physically and emotionally. (Genesis 2:22b)

Some Christians believe strongly that the literal creation story took place in the Garden of Eden. Other Christians, like Dr. Francis Collins, director of the NIH, the Human Genome Project, and the author of *The Language of God,* feel just as strongly that evolution over millions of years was the mechanism God chose to create man and woman. What is central however, is that GOD DID IT, and I have to tell you, I think He did one *heck of a job* on the girl thing!

No, my brother may be getting to be quite the accomplished potter, but God needn't worry about the competition. I think Yaweh throws the most wicked fine clay around! Next time you get angry with your wife, remember a couple things. First, the Creator of the Universe made her perfectly, specifically to suite your needs. Second, He didn't just leave her under a tree, He brought her to you as a gift! Third, He intended her to protect, shelter and problem solve, roles that you are designed to fill together. Fourth, His intent was for you to love each other sacrificially, forsaking all others, like Christ loves the church. (Ephesians 5:25)

Treat her like the most precious gift you've ever received, and wives, you do the same with your husbands, because I promise you, nobody's ever gonna take a hundred pounds of clay and come anywhere close, ever again.

Prayer: Dear Heavenly Father, direct Your Holy Spirit to keep us mindful every day that our mates are the most perfect creations fashioned by You specifically to match our needs! Remind us also that our spouses are fragile, like pottery, and if we shatter them, they can't ever be replaced. AMEN

AUGUST

AUGUST 1

Texting

"I like when texting someone becomes routine, like it's not normal if you don't talk to each other all day." (Anonymous Meme)

This will sound absurd to some, but we had to *write letters on paper and mail them* when I was young! The phone was too expensive to talk to someone far away like a grandparent, and for my parents as children, the phone wasn't even an option. No, we had to put pen to paper, write the letter in cursive, then put it in an envelope, place a stamp on which we had purchased at the store, and then depend on the postal service to deliver the missive some several days later! But the paper itself was a relatively modern and a huge technological step forward!

Parchment (animal skin) pre-dated paper by several thousand years, followed by papyrus (thick sheets made from the pith of the papyrus plant) first made in Egypt @ 2500 BC. "Paper" as we know it wasn't made from processed milled plant and textile fibers until @200 AD in China. Five hundred years later the process spread to the Islamic world, but it wasn't until 1250 that paper "mills" using waterwheels were designed in Spain, and then not until the mid 19th century that wood pulp became the fiber source for mills in England and the United States. An American (not British) postal service, didn't exist until Benjamin Franklin was appointed the first Postmaster General just prior to Independence in 1775. So, to communicate within the USA, we mailed letters as the only option, until the advent of the telegraph in 1840. Shortly thereafter, in 1843, the first FAX machines were invented, if you can believe that, and perfected for trans-oceanic use by 1865! (11 years before the telephone was invented!) At that time, it was called an "Electric Printing Telegraph" machine.

So, telegraph, FAX, then telephone, added to our ability to communicate, but the letter was still the gold standard for detailed longer messages until the advent of the computer, then the "internet," and of course finally, "e-mail." Still, until the 1990's, e-mail was largely slow, "dial-up," and only marginally quicker than mailing a letter! E-mail improved as cell phones and access to the internet improved, both in speed and reliability. But as early as 1984, a German engineer typed out the first 160 character message in a completely different format, proposed his system to another engineer from French Telecom, who then developed a proposal for the Group Special Mobile, which met in Oslo in1985. This "texting" process was developed on a laboratory level, but finally in 1992, a young engineer with the SEMA GROUP in the UK, used a personal computer to send the message "Merry Christmas" via the Vodafone network to a friend at a party specifically organized to celebrate the auspicious event! It was one of the very first SMS text messages sent outside a laboratory setting. By 1994, the Finnish had a commercial option to add texting to your phone. The rest is history.

Now, I can't even get my adult children to answer the phone at all! I can hardly get them to check email. Only texting gets through. Texting is wonderful, but before the use of "emojis" there was really no way at all to express the tone of the speaker. The mood, whether humorous or deadly serious, was often confused. Additionally, messages are short via text, and rarely contain the full explanation that an email might, or heaven forbid, that an actual letter might!! Even your own family might express their love for you only via an emoji or number code.

While you are more likely to get right through to the intended party with a text, it's nowhere near as effective as prayer! First of all, God ALWAYS gets the message, because He's always awake. (Psalm 121:4) Second, He knows what's in your heart without any words. (1 Samuel 16:7) Third, the Holy Spirit intercedes on our behalf, even when we don't know what to say! (Romans 8:26-27) Finally, the Lord knows what you need before you even formulate the thought! (Matthew 6:8)

Now, that's more efficient than text for sure! Don't spend any time at all worrying about what or how to pray: just talk to Him in your head!! And talk to Him in your head, *whenever the Spirit moves you,* so to speak. You don't even have to worry about auto-correct, or how lost SIRI can be!! Try it. You'll start to use it all the time, just like our opening quote. Pretty soon you won't feel comfortable unless you talk to God throughout the day!

"The Lord does not see as man sees; for man looks at the outward appearance, but the Lord looks at the heart." (1 Samuel 16:7 NKJV)

Prayer: Dear Heavenly Father, thank You that You are always there for us, that You neither slumber nor sleep! Remind us Spirit that we can pray by just thinking whatever we want the Lord to know; and even if we don't know the right words to say it, He knows our heart and You, Holy Spirit will intercede on our behalf! AMEN

AUGUST 2

Imposter Syndrome

"Before I formed you in the womb, I knew you!" (Jeremiah 1:5 NKJV)

I read an article in the local paper this morning about a young woman who is now a successful paleontologist. But as a young Latina college student, Lydia was so lacking in self-confidence that she was convinced she wasn't smart enough to be on a science track. Her doubts multiplied to the point, coincident with courses like calculus II, organic chemistry and physics, where she developed what psychologists call, "the imposter syndrome." People so undermine their own perception of their abilities, that they become convinced they really don't belong in their chosen endeavor.

Certainly, I have many colleagues who have confessed that they *still* suffer from aspects of this, even after decades in medical practice. Sometimes in the middle of a surgery it will suddenly dawn on you exactly what you are doing to another human being, and doing it with a very sharp knife in your hand! Even if its only momentarily, it crosses your mind that maybe you're not really *good enough* to be doing this!

Thankfully, we can pause and reflect on the fact that our Creator knew us before we were born. He knew *exactly* what He was doing! Believers don't have to undermine their own confidence by doubting their self-worth, because we know that our value is inestimable! God created us, loved us so much even when we were defiant, that He sent His Son to save us by dying on a cross! If that doesn't make you feel worthy, I don't know what will!

When you feel the *Imposter Syndrome* creeping up on you, do what I suggested in an earlier devotional: do like Dory in *Finding Nemo*. Just keep swimming, just keep swimming!!! Keep doing what you are trained to do, and whenever you want, just *think* your concerns to the Lord. You'll be amazed where and how the answers will come to reassure you!

For Lydia, the answers came through a caring mentor who pointed her in the direction of several projects that emphasized her strength, which turned out to be fossil prep. Working on dinosaurs with her hands had been her dream since childhood! Once her confidence was restored, the rest of the academics all fell in line. Now years later, she is an ambassador for the IF/THEN Initiative, managed by the American Association for the Advancement of Science, which seeks to advance and spotlight women in STEM fields. (Science, Technology, Engineering and Mathematics)

Not to be too repetitive, but "remember who your daddy is!" You are indeed a marvelous creation!

"I will praise You, for I am fearfully and wonderfully made!" (Psalm 139:14 NKJV)

Prayer: Dear Heavenly Father, we love You! We must remember that all of our self doubt and anxieties are a sort of slap in Your face!! You made us to be who we should be, and once we strike out on a path, You will make sure that we have what we need to follow it! AMEN

AUGUST 3

Rollercoaster

"Can anything separate us from Christ's love?...I am sure that nothing can...not death, life, angels, or ruling spirits. I am sure that nothing now, nothing in the future, nothing above or below us—nothing in the whole created world—will ever be able to separate us from the love God has shown us in Christ Jesus our Lord." (Romans 8: 33-34, 38-39 ERV)

When I left the office today, and the last patient had been seen, I had an opportunity to experience one of those things that makes it all worthwhile! A patient of mine for the last twenty years or so invited me to come to her home and take a picture with her kids, all six of whom I had delivered personally! Well, in my 35 years of practice, the double hat trick was a record for me! I drove the short distance to her house and we spent twenty minutes laughing while we tried to herd her kids into one picture. They ranged from nine years down to 8 weeks, and it was exactly like herding cats…laughing, giggling cats!

The older kids had all drawn me thank you cards, and they all reportedly helped make the lemon pie they presented to me. It would be hard to imagine a bigger smile on my face as I drove away! Thirty seconds after I pulled from the curb, my nurse texted to say that a patient of mine needed to be induced the following morning when I would be on call. She had come into triage, in Labor and Delivery, at 33 weeks pregnant with no sense of movement all day. The triage nurses couldn't find a heartbeat. Sono confirmed that for no discernible reason, she and her husband were about to experience the worst thing a parent can go through. I would, once again, for the umpteenth time, experience it with them.

My emotional high, shared with the mom and her six kids whom I had delivered, vaporized in an instant! I had seen the woman with the stillbirth in the office, just six days before. Medicine is like that, often an emotional rollercoaster. One minute reveling in the happiness of a beautiful family, another feeling the anguish of a young couple who had dreams for their young daughter, who now had only sorrow and questions.

When bad things happen in medicine, it's very hard not to wish desperately that somehow you could have done something different to alter the outcome. I had seen her the previous week. Should I have picked up on something? Was there some clue about what was about to occur? The parents of a stillborn, or any other reproductive disaster, question their own role in the same way. Unfortunately, they sometimes become convinced that something they did caused this to happen, all the way from a glass of wine to exercising too hard. Some even feel they might be being punished by God for something they've done in the past.

I'm sure it applies to other walks of life as well. For example, there are many times for all of us, when we walk away from an exchange, regretting our role immediately. We might think, often erroneously, that we could have avoided a bad result had we only reacted or said something differently. In short, regret can end up being tied to guilt, and guilt is a poison that can quickly begin to erode your self-worth. Guilt will make you feel unloved in a heartbeat.

In these situations, it's always a good idea to hit the pause button and bring it to God! Why? Because through the Word, through prayer, through supportive friends, you will be reminded that nothing can separate you from the love of Christ! The reason the Gospel means "Good News" is that Christ's sacrifice has purchased your freedom; freedom from guilt, freedom from shame, freedom from the tyranny of a forever failed march under the law!

Yes, I feel pain for the couple's awful ordeal. I feel somehow responsible, as do they, even though the evidence doesn't support that conclusion. But any feeling of guilt is short lived. Even had I done something, or failed to do something that led to a loss as bad as this, I know that I was forgiven 2,000 years ago on a hillside outside of Jerusalem, by a God that loves me more than I can imagine! The best I can do, is anything within my power to make sure that this young couple knows it as well.

Prayer: Dear Heavenly Father, we love You. How Blessed we are that You have assured us absolutely nothing can separate us from Your love! Life may present us with all sorts of curves, but we need not question our worth, because you have made it clear we are each priceless in Your eyes! AMEN

AUGUST 4

Shock Collar

"Choose for yourselves, this day, whom you will serve, whether the gods which your fathers served that were on the other side of the river, or the Gods of the Amorites, in whose land you dwell. But, as for me and my house, we will serve the Lord." (Joshua 24:15 NKJV)

When our kids were little, I wanted them to have a dog. I grew up with a dog, and I felt all kids ought to experience the unconditional love of man's best friend, while at the same time learning some discipline, such as that involved in picking up poop. My wife was less enthusiastic. The consequence was a black lab puppy named "Connie" because it was short for "controversy."

In any event, Connie was about 10 months old, and our son Andy was only a little more than a year older than the dog. One morning I was sitting in the breakfast room looking out on the back yard, when I noticed Connie behaving strangely indeed. She would scamper along nose to the ground as usual, but then suddenly drop to the ground like a rock. A moment later, she'd be up, but only get about 10 feet before dropping to the grass again. Each crash to the ground was accompanied by a brief, but audible yelp!

I headed around the corner to go through the living room, intending to get to the back yard through the porch, where I found my 2 year old son, Andy, giggling uncontrollably as he pressed the remote for Connie's shock collar every few moments, watching his large puppy intently!

There are people who honestly think that is our relationship with God. Seemingly random destruction all around us caused by an unfeeling deity. Others think that God holds the remote alright, but He fully understands the connection between the button and the shock, and uses life circumstances to control our actions just like Pavlov and his dog! There is a term for this called "theological determinism," and it was held by some very famous preachers, like Jonathan Edwards in 18th century New England. He felt that every move you made was pre-determined, right down to when you washed your hands!

Scripturally, it is clear that while God is indeed Sovereign, He has given us all a choice. The discussion of His foreknowledge and the topic of Calvin's perspective on predetermination are complex topics. Knowing that God doesn't function like Connie's shock collar, is not complex. God gave His people the law as a way to identify sin, and no human since the Garden has ever lived, who could keep the law perfectly; that is, until Jesus Christ. God sent His Son to live a perfect life, die in our place, and impart His perfect righteousness to all those who believe, so that we could return to God. All we have to do is make the choice to receive the gift, even when we don't deserve it! That's how much He loves us! As the famous mathematician Blaize Pascal expressed, "to believe, there is much to be gained, to not believe, there is everything to lose!"

"For God so loved the world, that He gave His only begotten Son, the whoever believes in Him should not perish but have eternal life." (John 3:16 NKJV)

"Behold, I stand at the door and knock. If anyone hears my voice and opens the door, I will come in to him and eat with him and he with me." (Revelation 3:20 ESV)

"But to all who did receive Him, who believed in His name, He gave the right to become children of God..." (John 1:12 ESV)

Prayer: Dear Heavenly Father, we love You because You first loved us! In loving us, You have given us freedom to choose our own way, for simply controlling our response would not be love at all. Thank you for letting us be free! AMEN

AUGUST 5

Whistle

"Whoever dwells in the shelter of the Most high will rest in the shadow of the Almighty. I will say of the Lord, "He is my refuge and my fortress, in whom I trust." (Psalm 91:1-2 NIV)

While we're on the subject of collars, our cat has a special collar. Right next to the clasp is a grey plastic box about 1.5 X 3/4 X 1/2 inches. It's made by a company called *Whistle*, and it's a quite sophisticated GPS tracker. Pretty sure it was really designed for hunting dogs, maybe so you can know when they've cornered a bear and you can run in the opposite direction! But in our case, it simply lets us know where our very large tuxedo cat is at the moment, where he's been recently, and even how much walking he's been doing that day.

That may seem silly, even on an indoor-outdoor cat, but we have coyotes in the creek, hawks overhead, and garbage trucks zipping down the alley, all of which hunt domestic felines at dawn and dusk! When *Sterling* sneaks out, either when the sun's just coming up or just going down, because we're coming into the garage, or we forget to put his cat door down, or he just doesn't return from an afternoon gecko hunt, then we check *Whistle* on the cell phone. It will show us where *his collar* is at that moment, unless he is within a defined 150 foot radius of the center of our house, in which case it merely displays an uploaded photo of Sterling's face within the green circle, and the statement, "*Sterling is home.*"

We've trekked out in our pj's with flashlights more than once, when we recognized that one of us forgot to close the cat door, or he made his escape some other way. Finding him is easy with the GPS, much to his obvious dismay.

Getting him to come to you is a bit tougher, and requires cat treats and a quick hand. But more often, we just wonder where he is, and are reassured when we see his portrait within the green ring, and that statement that confirms he's within wifi range, and thus at "home."

There is a feeling of calm that comes over us instantly, whether from *Whistle's* reassurance, or as it did years ago when the hall light would suddenly go out, confirming that our teen was safely home. That calmness is associated with home, because home is where the family is, and the family will protect its own. Home means safety to most.

Our home, as believers, is wherever Christ is! And we know where He is, because He promised that He would abide in us if we abide in Him! In other words, Christians need never fear, because they are never alone! Family is always right there with them! We are sheltered by the Almighty in every endeavor. The type of security we get knowing that we are *always at home* with our Savior, is much more than mere physical safety, because in Him we have eternity, regardless of what happens to us physically!

"The Lord is my light and my salvation—whom shall I fear? The Lord is the stronghold of my life—of whom shall I be afraid?" (Psalm 27:1 NIV)

Prayer: Dear Heavenly Father, thank you that wherever we are, whatever our circumstance, we are home with You! AMEN

AUGUST 6

Two Step Identification

"I am the Good Shepherd; I know my sheep and my sheep know me—just as the Father knows me and I know the Father—and I lay down my life for my sheep." (John 10:14 NKJV)

When I arrived at the hospital this morning, I needed my photo ID to scan into the parking lot. I needed a different ID to open the power glass doors on the lower level. Then I needed to scan myself through the door to the controlled access area. Then I had to open the double doors to the L&D area, controlled by camera access, with my ID on a scan pad. Then I had to badge into the doors to the OB OR area, which I have to pass through on my way to the lounge, for which of course, I also need a badge to enter! In case you weren't counting, that's six times my ID was verified before I could get to the coffee pot!

In the lounge I can access our patient census through the desktop computer there. I have to sign in, with a 12 digit password including a number, capital and special symbol (which they force you to change every 90 days.) After I printed my census, I pulled out my iphone to look something up from our office chart, on one of the patients in the hospital. I entered my 4 digit pin, then opened the EMR app, then had to enter a Username and Password (which had to be exactly 14 characters, including spaces, and use a symbol, capital and number.) When I got on the Staff elevator, I had to badge swipe before I could press a floor. On the 5th floor, I remembered I had to make a transfer from one account to another at my bank. That required the PIN for my iphone again, 2 step verification at the bank, including Username, Password, and then enter the TEXT code sent to me at that moment.

In the first ten minutes I had been at the hospital, I was required to prove my identity twelve times, (well, 13, I had to go DOWN the elevator after rounds!) Isn't it nice that the Creator doesn't need that kind of verification? Try getting in to see your city's Mayor, or your state's Governor, or a Congressman or a Senator, or the President, or just getting on a plane, without at least two forms of ID! Scripture tells us that God knew you even before He formed you in the womb! (Jeremiah 1:5) That means that He knows you much better than you know yourself! And once you've accepted Christ as your personal Lord and Savior, you'll never have to identify yourself to Him; He knows His sheep and His sheep know His voice. (John 10:3,27)

Do you remember the opening song to the TV show, *Cheers*? Why did everyone go to that bar? Because there "everybody knows your name." Do you remember a time in your life when things weren't going well, and you did what we all long to do from time to time: you went home? Why? Because somebody at home knew you. Your mom or your dad or your siblings just *knew you*, and understood how to support and encourage you. It's like that, but more so, with our Lord. He knows you and He already knows what you need. That's just like home.

Dear Heavenly Father, we love you, and we know that You know us better than anyone, because You're the one who knit us together! And because of that, Your Son knows us too, knows our voice, and will always see us coming, welcoming us home with open arms! AMEN

AUGUST 7

There's Been a Gate Change

"I write these things to you who believe in the name of the Son of God that you may know that you have eternal life." (1 John 5:13 ESV)

I'm one of those people that leaves for the airport a little early. Well, okay, a lot early! The potential of missing my flight makes me anxious, probably inordinately so. I'm not sure why really. I mean it could be that, even though I fully understand the physics of Bernoulli's principle and the purpose of the camber on the wing, a large tin can that weighs roughly 185,000 lbs. *simply should not hurdle through the air at 500mph with me in it!* So, there's that. Then, if I miss the flight, I guess then I have to go through all the additional anxiety of booking another flight and trying to get to that one on time! Or, one of my favorites. You've been stuck in traffic, had your bag searched by TSA, and just made it to the gate in time, when your phone vibrates. It's a notification from your airline: your gate has changed! Not just a little. Your gate has changed to the other end of the *next* terminal! In short, forget it, you ain't gonna make it.

Now, take a moment, close your eyes, and actually *feel* the physical manifestations of the anxiety you know you would experience when you get that gate change notification. Your pulse is up a little. You might be a bit tremulous. Some people even have a little tightness in their chest or shortness of breath. Just a momentary panicky feeling.

Now, imagine that you are one of the billions who don't know what the end game is; I mean the end game to the whole thing, to life! They may have a religion, they may not. They may have a vague concept of what their purpose is on earth, they may not. Even with a religion, other than one centered on Christ, they have a set of rules, a pathway to follow to the top of the mountain, and they have no guarantee that the missteps they inevitably make along the way, won't disqualify them from the next life, the next level of existence! That's an anxiety that is with them *every time they lie awake* and think about what they've done, or not done, or maybe should have done. That's an anxiety that's with them every time they contemplate their mortality and their approaching, unavoidable, death.

Believers *will always make it to the airport on time!* Believers *will never experience a gate change!* Paul tells us in his letter to the Romans that "there is no condemnation for those in Christ Jesus." (Romans 8:1) Once we have chosen to accept the gift of salvation by grace through faith, no amount of missteps can keep us from an eternity with the Creator. That's what Christians call the "assurance of faith." It means no matter when your Uber arrives, even if you have a flat tire, even if the traffic is bumper to bumper, even if the TSA searches your bags, even if your gate changes, you will *always make it with plenty of time to spare!*

Prayer: Father God, we are so grateful that You have chosen to send the Savior so that all we need to do is believe, in order to find our way back to You! We know we will mess up along the way, but we also know that You will not condemn us for any of it! We are assured, that we who accept Christ, will soon be with You no matter what, and it will be forever. AMEN

AUGUST 8

Infidelity (Not What You Think)

"I gave faithless Israel her certificate of divorce and sent her away because of all her adulteries. Yet I saw that her unfaithful sister Judah had no fear; she also went out and committed adultery." (Jeremiah 3:8 NIV)

The term *infidelity* has come to mean only one thing in our Western society: sexual betrayal. People associate the word with committing adultery in a sexual sense, i.e. married individuals having sex with a partner who is not their spouse. Clearly, from both Old and New Testament proscriptions, adultery is a sinful act. Under Mosaic Law, it was punishable by publicly stoning the accused to death. Under Grace, it is a forgivable sin like all others. But still, its severity is such that both the prophets (see especially Jeremiah, Ezekiel and Hosea,) and Christ, use *adultery* as the metaphor for Israel's continued unfaithfulness in turning to idol worship and the false Gods of the peoples around them.

But the word *infidelity* comes from the Latin *infidelis,* meaning lack of faith or disloyalty. When Christ speaks of a "wicked and adulterous generation," He is not referring to sexual sin, but to a total lack of faith in God, the Father. (Matthew 12:39) So how does infidelity apply to us on a daily basis, in the sense that Jesus uses it?

My maternal grandfather had a saying He used frequently when I was growing up: *"An anxious Christian is a confusion in terms!"* As we face the challenges of daily life, when we fail to put God first, if we get bogged down in worry about how we will make it from day to day, ***that's infidelity.*** Oswald Chambers, author of *My Utmost For His Highest,* goes so far as to claim that, *"Jesus sums up common sense carefulness in a disciple as infidelity!"* He was referring to the famous passage in the Sermon on the Mount, in which Jesus admonishes us not to worry. *"Do not worry about your life, what you will eat or drinker about your body, what you will wear." (Matthew 6:25 NIV)* He wants us to abandon forethought, because worrying about the details of our lives means we don't think our God is attentive enough, or big enough, or competent enough, to handle our concerns day to day! That is a lack of faith. That is *infidelity.* Christ said the things that would choke out the growth of His Word, were *"the cares of this world!"*

Next time the details of your life present themselves for action, make your first action turning to God. Leave it at the foot of Your Savior. What good is it having a Savior if You don't let Him be that?

"But the worries of this life, the deceitfulness of wealth and the desires for other things come in and choke the Word, making it unfruitful." (Mark 4:19 NIV)

Prayer: Dear Heavenly Father, instruct Your Spirit within us to steer us toward You FIRST when we start to fret about the details of our lives! It's not in planning that we fail, but in troubling our hearts over worrying that our plans are wrong or might come to nothing! Keep us in faith Father. Guard us from everyday infidelity. AMEN

AUGUST 9

Love God

"'Teacher, which is the greatest commandment in the Law?'" Jesus replied, 'Love the Lord your God with all your heart and with all your soul and with all your mind.'" (Matthew 22:37 NIV)

We don't generally think of "love" as something you do on command. Try telling a Red Sox fan to "love" the Yankees, or an OU Sooner to "love" the Texas Longhorns. Good luck. So how is anyone supposed to just "love" God because Jesus (i.e. God) tells you to? While that seems almost impossible to just turn 'on,' the second part of His answer almost seems possible: *"And the second is like it: Love your neighbor as yourself."* Why does the second seem more possible than the first? Well, maybe because we have experience loving ourselves! It only gets tougher when you realize Jesus was talking about loving your neighbor whether you *like him* or not. Not to mention the small sticking point clarified in the parable of the Good Samaritan, that is, that literally *everyone* is your neighbor!

So how do you just manufacture feelings in order to "love" God? We can't see Him. People just beginning to seek Him will tell you they certainly can't hear Him, or feel Him, or touch Him; so how on earth are we supposed to love Him with all our heart, soul and mind? Well, the best thing to do when you're not "feeling it," is act as though you were! The prophet Micah tells us exactly how we are to do that: Act justly, love mercy, and walk humbly. (Micah 6:8 NIV)

Ask yourself, if I really *did love God,* how would I act? Well, first of all you would ***fear God***, in the Hebrew sense of holding Him in awe. If you hold God in awe, you will find yourself in a state of mind to ***obey Him***. If you obey God, then you will love others by serving them and putting their interests above your own, right? Well guess what? That's exactly what Deuteronomy 10:12 tells you to do.

C.S. Lewis points out in *Mere Christianity,* that none of us have devout feelings all the time, but that doesn't really matter. Why not? Because *feelings* are not what God really cares about. The love God expects, is an act of will, more than an emotion. While our feelings may wax and wane, we can be assured that His love for us does not! Recall that God doesn't even remember our sins and has separated them from us as far as the east is from the west! The Hebrew word, *hesed,* permeates the Old Testament with over 248 instances. It refers to God's faithful love, favor or grace. He says He loves us *all the time.* I think He means it. So, we need to *act like* we love God all the time, because loving like He wants, is an act of will. When you act in a certain way, the feelings follow.

"Therefore know that the Lord your God, He is God, the faithful God who keeps covenant and mercy for a thousand generations with those who love Him and keep His commandments…" (Deuteronomy 7:9 NKJV)

> *Prayer: Dear Heavenly Father, we love You, even if we're not feeling it from time to time! We ask that Your Spirit guide us to walk humbly and obediently, remembering that God's faithful love applies to all of His creatures, and we need to remember that in our dealings with others, as a first step toward behaving in a way that leaves us more and more in love with God everyday. AMEN*

AUGUST 10

Panhandlers

"But this I say: He who sows sparingly will also reap sparingly, and he who sows bountifully will also reap bountifully. So let each one give as he purposes in his

heart, not grudgingly or of necessity; for God loves a cheerful giver. (2 Corinthians 9:6-7 NKJV)

I don't know about where you live, but in our neck of the woods around the Dallas-Fort Worth area, there are people begging at almost every large intersection, especially those close to freeway off ramps and underpasses. It's hot in Texas, and these folks seem to be out there with their grocery carts full of worldly possessions, their cardboard signs and their camp chairs, from dawn to dusk. Most are disheveled, obviously unbathed, often cachectic, some physically handicapped or wheelchair bound. If luck is a thing, these people appear to be down on it.

Yet, we all know some are organized. Some are merely shills, employed by those who would take advantage of the generosity of strangers with a small army of beggars working for them. Some of these "panhandlers" as my grandfather called beggars, certainly have the look of those hooked on alcohol or perhaps other illicit drugs.

Frequently, I have heard acquaintances and even friends, who have commented on what a blight they are; that they ought to be removed; that it's all a scam anyway and they certainly wouldn't be caught giving them any money. After all, they're just going to head to the nearest liquor store with anything you give them.

Maybe.

An awful lot of them must have the best make-up artists in the world though, because they sure look as though they have absolutely nothing, not even a sustainable portion of health. What if they are working a scam? What if they are part of an organization to take advantage of the generous spirit of a few? (You won't see so many people rolling their windows down that these unfortunate souls have trouble getting to all their donors in a light cycle!) Even if part of an organized effort, I seriously doubt if their "salary" amounts to much and I am pretty sure the "benefits" don't exist.

Maybe we could all think a little more about the homeless in this time of pandemic. Imagine if you had a blue collar job that vaporized in the economic downturn. Your skills may be as limited as your education was. Now you have no income. None. Zip. And what if you have no family? Lots of people don't. You don't have to be crazy, or a drug addict, or an alcoholic, or a criminal, to end up at an intersection with a sign. You just have to have been living on the edge. When you fall off that edge, how do you climb back up if you have no way to bathe, have no new, or even clean clothes, and no way to even go look for a job?

You certainly don't need to feel obligated to give money, or a coupon, or a sandwich, or a Big Mac, to the filthy soul on the corner. But if you're a believer, you darn well better be giving money to *someone or some charity* in need! But you say, give a man a fish and he eats for a day, but teach him to fish and he eats for a lifetime! Really? Next intersection you come to, just hop out and teach the barefoot, toothless, smelly, filthy, individual some life skills, you know, before the light changes!

But you give to several charities and you tithe at church! Great! How do you know how much to give? Luckily, Christ tells you in the parable of the widow's mite…GIVE IT ALL. Okay, she might have given all that she had, but a good rule for any of us that do have a comfortable amount, is give enough that it's more than you can spare! That means there ought to be things you want to spend money on that you really can't, because you gave away that much. *Charity* doesn't just refer to tax-deductible 501c organizations either. When a friend, a relative, a neighbor, or an employee is in distress, that may demand your generosity as well.

Make no mistake, loving your neighbor means acting charitably, and those with saving faith will do so without hesitation! Jesus says His own will be known by their fruit. (John 15:1-6; Matthew 7:16) People who don't give a little more than they feel they can spare are already acting faithlessly, because they are worried about their own financial security! Remember, "an anxious Christian is a confusion in terms."(Matthew 6:25)

Every time you help someone down on their luck, you will feel your Savior smiling at you. I guarantee it, because every time you give them food and drink, you give it to Him. (Matthew 25:35-36)

> *Prayer: Dear Heavenly Father, we love You! You have been more than generous to us with only the breath in our lungs, the shade of a tree, and the blue of the sky! Remind us Spirit, that Christ would have us do one thing only, love Him by loving others. Just as loving a spouse calls for sacrifice, so does loving a stranger down on his luck. AMEN*

AUGUST 11

Pot of Gold

"Like the appearance of a rainbow in a cloud on a rainy day, so was the appearance of the brightness all around it. This was the appearance of the likeness of the Glory of the Lord! (Ezekiel 1:28 NKJV)

Rainbows are truly ephemeral things. We see them usually only for moments at a time, and even then only infrequently. When we do see one, it is often only a portion of the arc, sometimes duplicated faintly, but often coming and going and returning within moments. They seem to be right there in front of us, and yet we can't touch them! They seem, in short, magical!

What's more, its exceedingly difficult to follow one to it's intersection with the horizon, exactly what the Leprechauns of Ireland were intent on centuries ago, when they hid their treasure there to prevent the Viking hordes from stealing it! This of course, is the origin of the legend that a pot of gold lies at the end of every rainbow.

I was biking the other evening and took a picture of a fabulous double rainbow, and I messaged it to a few friends and my children. One acquaintance asked if I had found that pot of gold? My son, a pilot, immediately texted back a photo of the very same rainbow as he was seeing it, several thousand feet in the air! His angle was opposite to mine, and that meant he was looking at the 1/2 of the arc that appeared hidden in cloud and invisible to me. The picture was spectacular! It arced down from the heavens accompanied by a wide swath of brilliant yellow light, set against dark clouds behind.

Rainbows in our culture have come to be a symbol of diversity, with political interest groups, coalitions, t-shirts and memes, all bearing the image of this perfectly curved splash of all the colors. Scripturally, bible readers associate reference to the rainbow with Genesis 9:13-16 where God places it in the sky as a reminder of His covenant with earth, that He will never again destroy it with flood.

But the reference in Ezekiel is the one I want you to think of instead! Each time a rainbow fills you with wonder, (even those of you who like to analyze the science behind moisture in the air and refraction of light etc etc) remember that the prophet Ezekiel likens it to the appearance of God Himself in all His glory! Let the rainbow be a reminder of God's omnipresence, of His over-arching protection, for those who love Him, and accept the rain as a gift! The refraction of light that allows us to see the full spectrum of colors is a momentary glimpse into the nature of our God! There are seven colors in the rainbow, the Hebrew number for completeness. (Red, orange, yellow, green, blue, indigo, violet.) He is magnificent, indefinable, and His presence encompasses all that is, because He is the Creator of the Universe! Let your next rainbow remind you not of treasure, or destruction in flood, but instead remind you of the Glory of the Lord and that all good things do indeed come from above! (James 1:17)

"If your life is so blue, then pick another color from the rainbow." (Anonymous)

"The way I see it, if you want a rainbow, you've got to learn to put up with the rain." (Dolly Parton)

"And when it rains on your parade, look up rather than down. Without the rain there would be no rainbow!" (G.K. Chesterton)

Prayer: Dear Heavenly Father, we praise You for giving us this magnificent reminder of your presence! When we suffer in the rainstorms of life, You gift us with this image of Yourself as the storm passes, making sure we don't forget Your promises and protection! AMEN

AUGUST 12

Open Window

"Don't you know that as long as you do what is right then I accept you? But if you do not do what is right, watch out! Sin is crouching at the door, ready to pounce on you! You must master it before it masters you!" (Genesis 4:6-7 The Voice)

This morning my wife was introducing me to an Instagram channel called # wildliveplanet. One of the first videos I saw was a parked SUV with the rear window open, and a yellow lab leaning out of it to sniff a Bengal Tiger! Next thing you know the tiger has leapt into the car through the open window! It reminded me of a video several years ago of a "drive through" wild life reserve in China where first one and then a second woman, exit their vehicle, presumably to get a closer look, and get dragged into the underbrush in the mouth of a tiger! Neither survived.

I've watched our cat, Sterling, go through his set, look left, look right, wiggle haunches and pounce routine a hundred times. The dead squirrel on our porch this morning, is testimony yet again, to just how fast a cat can pounce! Leaving your window open with your dog hanging out of it with a Bengal Tiger prowling close by is not a good idea. Getting out of your vehicle to take a closer look at a tiger is a bad idea. Getting out of the vehicle after your friend has already been taken by a 600 lb cat, is an even worse idea!

Moses uses the word *rabbis* (crouching) to graphically communicate how close we are to making fatal mistakes. The Evil One is right there, waiting patiently to take advantage of our too often rampant selfishness, or even our simple lack of caution. For Cain, it was jealousy over Abel's acceptance by God, and succumbing to the temptation to kill his brother that led to his downfall. For us, it might be the pastor who meets to counsel the attractive young woman, distraught over the husband who has just left her...and closes his office door. It might be the traveling sales person who stays in the chain hotel, who knows that that big screen TV can show him things for a few dollars that he wouldn't watch while on vacation with his wife. It might be the college freshman who knows she needs to study, but instead agrees to accompany her new friend to a bar late at night...then wakes up with a terrible headache, next to a naked man whose name she doesn't even know. It might be the recovering addict who has been clean for two years, but who goes to visit an old friend at his beach house, knowing full well that this friend was still into "the life."

My mother used to say what a lot of mothers have always said, "Nothing good ever happens after midnight!" We humans are susceptible! The Spirit is indeed willing, but the flesh is weak. (Matthew 26:41) Why leave the window open when there's a tiger right outside? Why get out of your car for a "closer look" when the thing you want to see has both the will and the power to take you down?

As believers, we need to take care not to put ourselves in situations where sin, crouching at the door, can easily pounce. Use common sense! Yes, it is a dying commodity, but most of us know our own weaknesses and could take steps to avoid those temptations if we were just conscious of the danger! It is true that we live under grace, and our sins are forgiven, but that doesn't mean we should make it easier for ourselves to sin! As Paul tells us in Romans, living under grace, though forgiven, means we should sin less not more, for we died to our old selves when we were crucified with Christ! We are no longer slaves to sin! We now have the power to roll up the window, to stay in the car, and to slam the door in the face of the crouching lion!

"No evil dooms us hopelessly except the evil we love, and desire to continue in, and make no effort to escape from." (George Eliot)

"A man who gives in to temptation after five minutes, simply does not know what it would have been like an hour later. That is why bad people, in one sense, know very little about badness. They have lived a sheltered life by always giving in!" (C.S. Lewis)

Prayer: Dear Heavenly Father, we want to do what pleases You! Knowing the Spirit is willing to resist the Evil One but the flesh is weak, direct Your Spirit to strengthen us, and to make smart decisions when it comes to avoiding a Satan who is always ready to pounce! AMEN

AUGUST 13

Rerouting

"Life is unpredictable. It changes with the seasons. Even your coldest winter happens for the best of reasons. And though it feels eternal, like all you'll ever do is freeze, I promise spring is coming and with it, brand new leaves." (Erin Hanson)

Most of the time I love my GPS devices. Chart, compass, slide rule, protractor, have all been replaced by GPS dependent chart plotting software like Navionics, useable on any iOS device. In my truck, Google or Apple Maps are both available to not only guide me to my input destination, but make me aware of everything from gas stations, to restaurants, to pharmacies along my intended route.

Despite the advantages of audible commands (I've chosen an Australian woman as my preferred navigator,) and an easily visible, well lighted map with inset that indicates just how far my next turn is as I approach it, I *still manage to mess up* from time to time! Now, often I try to blame some aspect of the system, like not loud enough, told me too late, indicated an exit when the road merely turned, etc. etc. Sometimes I purposefully take the wrong route just out of "innate cussedness" as my father used to say!

When things go wrong in life, there's a tendency to blame our navigator as well; that would be God. When we find ourselves possibly in the wrong career, possibly with the wrong partner, possibly in the wrong city, or house or apartment; possibly with the wrong boss, possibly with a body that keeps betraying us in injury or disease; possibly with the wrong parents who are alcoholic, or abusive, or never around. Well, these are God things, right?

My guess is, much like my truck's GPS, the wrong turns in life are a result of either not listening to or understanding the navigator, or intentionally acting contrary to what the navigator advised! But you know what's great about Google, Apple, Ways, Magellan, Garmin, or Tom Tom? When you screw up, they don't give up on you! God has the same feature. Instead of just turning away from you, God will offer you this simple phrase, "Re-routing." Your Creator will use the obstacles in your life, the poor decisions you've made, the injuries, the heartbreak, the abuse, and consider them road construction, accident sites, or just wrong turns, and then lead you in another direction! That's where the expression, "when a door closes, God always opens a window," comes from.

In the Bible, when Abram and Sara couldn't conceive and were forced to bear children through their maid, God gave them Isaac in their old age. When Moses became a murderer and a fugitive on the run, God gave him a new direction and a new purpose, to bring His people out of slavery in Egypt. When

Joseph's brothers threw him in the well and then sold him into slavery, God gave Joseph a new position, new purpose, and he saved all of Egypt and his brothers. When David took Bathsheba in adultery and then had her husband Uriah murdered, while he paid a price with his descendants, God still gave him a new path and an heir in Solomon. The list goes on and on.

If you feel lately like everything in your life is heading in the wrong direction, rest easy! God will not abandon you by the side of the road; He's *re-routing*! You however, will still have to pay attention and listen for His direction. It may come to you in the night, or through the Bible, or through another book, or through a friend, or through what seems to you at the time as an accident! But God's love is faithful. Remember He neither slumbers nor sleeps. He knows right where you are, how you got there, and how to get you out of whatever situation in which you find yourself.

"Just when the devil tries to steer me in the wrong direction I learn how powerful God's GPS really is. Evil will not re-route my journey! God has mapped my success to the final destination." (Carlos Wallace)

> ***Prayer:** Dear Heavenly Father, thank you for the Holy Spirit whose constant presence nudges us in the right direction, even after we've made a wrong turn! AMEN*

AUGUST 14

I Hear You Knocking, but....

"You went and left me long time ago, Now you're knocking on my door. I hear you knocking, but you can't come in. I hear you knocking, go back where you been!" (Pearl King/Dave Bartholomew; Performed by Fats Domino)

Most people have probably heard that in order to be a Christian, you simply have to invite Jesus into your heart! There's even a famous book entitled, *My Heart, Christ's Home*, by Robert Munger. Sounds easy, right? But an awful lot of people are perfectly happy to just crack the door a little and ask his advice, then slam it closed again! Inviting the Light of the World into your home sounds like a great idea, until as the comedian Michael Jr. puts it, "you suddenly realize that your house is a MESS!!"

Letting the Light into your house might just reveal a whole lot of things that you've worked so hard at keeping in the dark! I mean, it's okay maybe if Jesus comes and sits in the "good room." In Michael Jr.'s set entitled, *Bring a Friend*, he explains that the "good room" is that room in your grandmother's house that is just perfect! All the good china and silver on display, the furniture covered with plastic except Sunday; and it always faces the street. It's the room people can see through the windows. That's the part of you that you are willing to let the world admire!

Jesus did say he would come to the door and knock. If anyone who hears His voice will simply open the door, He will gladly come in. (Revelation 3:20)

But, Jesus also said He came for sinners not the righteous. The Great Physician comes for the sick, not the healthy. (Matthew 9:12) So if you've got a drug problem or an alcohol problem or a porn problem or a gambling problem or a fidelity problem or a gossiping problem or an anger problem or a holding a grudge problem or any other thing you don't want anyone to know about, remember this: God can see through your roof and Jesus can see through your door! HE ALREADY KNOWS AND HE LOVES YOU ANYWAY! (Romans 8:1)

So when you hear Him knocking, don't be like Fats Domino and just decide that He can't come all the way in! Throw open the door and let Him pick His way through your messy house. His love will teach you how to love, and you'll have the whole place cleaned up in no time!

Prayer: Dear Heavenly Father, we love you! If we love You, why don't we trust You enough to let You see every room in our messy house? Remind us Spirit that there is no condemnation in those who are in Christ Jesus! Help open the door for the light of the Son, so all the things we wish to hide can be exposed and cleansed from our hearts! AMEN

AUGUST 15

Pet Peeve

"A fool shows his annoyance at once, but a prudent man overlooks an insult." (Proverbs 12:16 NIV)

Some of you may be old enough to remember *The Newlywed Game* with host Bob Eubanks. Four couples were asked questions about each other, they would write the answer on a card, hoping that they responded the same as their new spouse. The idea was to see which couple already knew each other the best. It led to some funny moments, as you might imagine! But if you asked my wife, "What's your husband's #1 pet peeve?" she'd get it right every time. "It's people that don't do their job, Bob," would be her correct response.

What I've actually discovered over time, is that the *real truth* is, I get annoyed when people don't do their job *the way I think they should!* That, as you can see, is quite a horse of a different color. Not doing their job would be their problem. Not doing their job the way I think they should....well, that's my problem.

When the TSA searches my bag and takes my key chain Swiss Army Knife; when the software designers change where the appropriate clicks are on the Electronic Medical Record; when the Amazon packager sends the wrong size, or color, or item altogether; when the pharmacy won't fill the prescription I ordered for any number of reasons; when the WiFi won't work as it should; when the rattle in the car can still be heard after the shop has had it three times...the list is quite literally endless!

If you find yourself getting annoyed at how other people's efforts don't meet your standards, you're in danger of being in a constant state of annoyance. It turns out, the entire world is not designed to rotate correctly on its axis solely for my pleasure! Yes, sometimes people make mistakes. But sometimes the only mistake is that I don't like the result, even when no mistake was made! That leads to a lot of annoyance, which, let's face it, isn't too different from low level anger.

Staying focused on our actual purpose, glorifying God, while keeping our eyes fixed on the "author and perfecter of our faith," alleviates this disastrous state of affairs! (Hebrews 12:2) *Our job* is to love others as we love ourselves, even sacrificially as Christ loved the church. That would seem to exclude being angry at the TSA agent for following the rules, even if I think the rules are silly.

So I have a new Pet Peeve: people who have my former Pet peeve! If I am going to act justly, love mercy, and walk humbly with God, (Micah 6:8) I have to forgive the Amazon packager who put the wrong color item in the box! Whew! I feel better already.

> ***Prayer: Dear Heavenly Father, help us remember that if we judge others, You will judge us using the same standard! (Matthew 7:1) Annoyance at others' efforts is nothing more than exactly that type of judgement. Have Your Spirit tweak us every time we are tempted to judge rather than show compassion. AMEN***

AUGUST 16

Restoration

"...the Lord restored his fortunes. In fact, the Lord gave him twice as much as before!" (Job 42:10b NLT)

Many people know the story of Job, even if they aren't from the Judeo-Christian tradition. God agreed to allow Satan to test the faith of Job, the most righteous and faithful of all the men on earth. Satan took everything from him: his land, his wealth, his family, even his health! His friends who came to support him, turned on him instead, convinced that he must have egregiously sinned against the Lord for all these calamities to fall upon him.

But Job never lost his faith that God would rescue him. Yes, he eventually became impatient, and yes he eventually became angry, but he always acknowledged God's Sovereignty. Job knew he came into the world with nothing and would leave with nothing, and anything that happened in-between was just as much a gift from God as his every breath had been. (Job 1:21)

Through these devotionals we have reviewed several lives where it seemed all was lost, but turning to Jesus restored their purpose, their joy, and magnified their effect in the world. Joni Eareckson Tada, paralyzed from the next down as a teen, became one of the most effective evangelists of the 20th century, as did Chuck Colson after serving time for his role in the Watergate scandal that destroyed Richard Nixon's presidency. Eric Liddell refused to compete in the 100 yard dash, in which he almost certainly would have won Olympic Gold for

Great Britain, but the race was held on a Sunday, the Lord's Day of Rest. While Liddell lost his chance at being the "fastest man in the world," he went on to be fulfilled as a missionary in China, and eventually, as one of the most famous testimonies to faith in history. Eric Bonhoeffer refused to knuckle under to Nazi pressure. He made sure the Lutheran Church of Germany condemned the persecution of Jews and the handicapped. He first gave up his job, then family, then freedom and finally his life. But his story of courage and faith has literally inspired millions!

God has a plan for those who love Him, to heal and restore. Whether it is our health, our livelihood, our families, our relationships, or even our freedom, trusting in the Savior to do just that, leads to remarkable results! Was Tada's paralysis reversed? Did Chuck Colson avoid prison and derision from many? Did they let Eric Liddell run the race on another day? Did Bonhoeffer avoid execution? No. None of these things happened, and yet there is no question that in every case their faith restored them to joy and peace, and God used them to bring the same, to literally millions and millions of others!!!

Look beyond your closer circumstances. Look beyond your affliction, poverty, or heartbreak. Keep your eyes fixed on Jesus and leave it all at the foot of the cross. (Hebrews 12:2) He will come through for you! It may not be in the manner or timing of your choosing, but that's why we depend on the One with the bigger picture, the One who made the picture in the first place, to work everything together for good! Thank God!!

"Therefore, we also, since we are surrounded by so great a cloud of witnesses, let us lay aside every weight, and the sin which so easily ensnares us, and let us run with endurance the race that is set before us, looking unto Jesus, the author and finisher fo our faith, who for the joy that was set before Him endured the cross, despising the shame, and has sat down at the right hand of the throne of God." (Hebrews 12:1 NKJV)

Prayer: Dear Heavenly Father, let us remember that our Lord, Your Son, laid down His Godhead and suffered and died in our place, that we might share the joy of eternity as Your children! No calamity that befalls us is beyond the reach of Your mercy and Your restorative power! Use us Lord, to advance Your Kingdom on earth, in any way You se fit! AMEN

AUGUST 17

Mercy

"And what is it that the Lord requires of you, but to do justly, to love mercy, and to walk humbly with your God?" (Micah 6:8 NKJV)

You'll note we've referenced our opening verse multiple times before, because it's important. The Prophet Micah answers the eternal question of what exactly are we supposed to be doing here? But what does it mean to "love mercy?" Certainly, we all love mercy for ourselves, but what does it mean to *love mercy* for others? Mercy is generally thought of as kindness, the opposite of cruelty. Mercy is universally thought of as "good" and cruelty as "bad." Most of us like to think of ourselves as kind, and it is quite easy to convince oneself that this is, in fact, the case. After all, there is no definitive action required to prove or disprove a supposition when we are only trying to convince ourselves, right?

Mercy and Grace are often confused. *Mercy* means not receiving what you do deserve, i.e. punishment of some sort; compassion for the powerless, even though they are guilty of an offense. God's forbearance and forgiveness of sins is in fact merciful. But *Grace* means the unmerited favor of God, by definition, on one undeserving. It is in fact, a *gift*. Rather than a withholding of deserved negative consequences for offense, as in mercy, Grace imparts a positive blessing on the undeserving, as in Salvation. God was merciful in withholding the death penalty for our sin, but graceful in granting us salvation through faith.

Micah tells us that God wants us to love *mercy*, and that means *forgiveness*. It doesn't just mean viewing oneself as *kind*. It is far too easy to write off our other sins as inconsequential, as long as we can tell ourselves, "Well, I generally have my heart in the right place!" Forgiveness is part and parcel of mercy, and that means the uncomfortable state of forgiving those who have wronged us, (Matthew 6:14), or those whom we perceive to have wronged us! That is the first requisite step in loving one's enemies, is it not? (Matthew 5:44)

C.S. Lewis in *The Problem of Pain*, contends that we think ourselves kind and virtuous, when in fact we are simply happy! He says it is easy to imagine oneself kind or merciful, but less so, chaste, or temperate, or humble!

In order to *love mercy* as Micah tells us, it is necessary to ***actually actively forgive*** those we dislike, because we feel they have wronged us in some way. That involves letting **them know** that you forgive them as well! Turns out, its not as easy as just imagining yourself kind!

Prayer: Dear Heavenly Father, we ask that Your Spirit work through us when we don't have the strength ourselves to show mercy to those who have wronged us! We know that once we forgive however, the burden will lift from ourselves even more than from those forgiven. AMEN

AUGUST 18

Fake It Till You Make It

"You have heard that it was said, 'Love your neighbor and hate your enemy. But I tell you, love your enemies and pray for those who persecute you...and if you greet only your own people, what are you doing more than others? Do not even pagans do that?" (Matthew 5:43,47 NKJV)

Everyone has people in their lives who just drive them to distraction. Let's face it, some people are, well, *jerks!* Have you every really tried to love someone that wishes you harm? Maybe there is someone going behind your back to damage your reputation with falsehoods. Perhaps someone is suing you for something that was not your fault, something with which we in medicine are all too familiar. Maybe you just have an inconsiderate neighbor, whose dog never shuts up, or whose yard is a mess and doesn't care, or who parks so you can't get out of your own driveway! Perhaps a relative has turned cold toward you or a former partner is trying to steal your business. There are a million reasons to hate.

When we try in our own power to go from hatred to love, I can tell you, it doesn't often work. But there are steps to take while you honestly pray for this person and you invite the power of the Holy Spirit to be your ally in the process. It starts with an expression you may know, that my grandmother frequently employed, "You catch more flies with honey than with vinegar!" C.S. Lewis put it this way: "Do not waste a moment bothering with whether you 'love' your neighbor; simply *act as if you did!* As soon as you do, you will discover one of the great secrets of life. When you are behaving as if you loved someone, you will presently come to actually love him! If you injure someone you dislike, you will find yourself disliking him even more!"

There have actually been studies that show reproducibly, that if you intentionally smile more, you will gradually get happier! The same principle applies. Treating people lovingly naturally causes them to change their behavior toward you, and an UN-vicious cycle begins! The only exception is when you are behaving in a loving fashion primarily so people who know of your true dislike, will *think better of you.* If you forgive someone so that they, and others, will admire your character, rather than to please God, they will see right through you. ***Self-promotion is the death of charity.***

So, in today's parlance, ***"Fake it till you make it,"*** applies to dealing with those you dislike as well. Give the Holy Spirit an opening and He will jump right in! Try it. You'll like it.

"Be careful not to practice your righteousness in front of others ***to be seen by them.*** *If you do, you will have no reward from your Father in heaven. " (Matthew 6:1 NIV)*

> ***Prayer: Dear Heavenly Father, have Your Spirit strengthen us as we seek to behave lovingly toward those whom we dislike and who dislike us in return! We know we can ACT anyway we decide to, changing our hearts will follow with the aid of Your Spirit! AMEN***

AUGUST 19

Christian Violence or Violent Christians

"Not everyone who says to Me 'Lord, Lord' shall enter the Kingdom of Heaven, but He who does the will of my Father in Heaven!" (Matthew 7:21 NKJV)

Unfortunately, labelling an individual, society, or culture as *'Christian,'* has very little clear meaning. The difference between the authentic believer who has made Christ His personal Lord and Savior, and the merely cultural Christian, can be as wide as the east is from the west! This leads to yet another objection to the moral validity of Christianity; it has been the purveyor of world-wide violence that has led to the loss of millions of lives in the last 2,000 years! How can Christ be the legitimate literal incarnation of God when such horrific bloodshed has occurred in His name?

The simplest answer to this common objection is to recall that famous quote of the Hindu pacifist Mahatma Gandhi: *"I am liking your Jesus very very much! It's just your Christians I don't care for!"* How does the Christian account for the four Crusades from the early 11th to the late 12th centuries when hundreds of thousands of Muslims were slaughtered? How about the Inquisitions in France and Spain in 1093, 1472 and 1546, when hundreds of thousands were tortured and executed for *not professing* Christ as Savior and the Pope as His immortal representative on earth? What about the Salem Witch Trials in America, or the six million killed in the Holocaust while a misguided church stood by, submitting to the xenophobic Nazi insanity? The answer of course, is that evil is committed by man, not by Christ!

Much good has come out of Christianity, despite the mis-guided, power hungry men and women who have falsely professed faith down through the centuries. The faith spread across the known world in just the first few centuries, if for no other reason than that Christians were remarkably kind, compassionate, loving, and selfless, even in the face of phenomenal persecution! Christianity has given mankind hope, purpose, and dignity, for all who wish it, not just a few, as taught in ancient Greek philosophy. *Imago dei,* the concept that we are all made in the image of God, came out of the Judeo-Christian tradition. Incredible works of art, architecture, and science, as well as institutes of education, came out of Christianity, including the now secular institutions like Harvard, Yale and Princeton. New ideas about personal liberty, conscience, truth and humility all had Christian origins in the Middle Ages. Literacy came to Europe, the Americas and Africa all through Christian Missionaries.

Next time someone rejects "Christianity" because of bad Christians, you might point out that professing a cultural faith and behaving like it, are and always will be, two very different things. Don't throw the baby out with the bath-water, especially when the baby in question is Jesus! Encourage them to read perhaps, the Gospel of John, then Romans, then Ephesians, and ask if there is anything written there, to which they object? It will help them see that Mahatma Gandhi had a point.

Beloved, let us love one another, for love is of God; and everyone who loves is born of God and knows God. He who does not love does not know God, for God is love!" (1 John 4:7-8 NKJV)

Prayer: Dear Heavenly Father, we love You because You first loved us! Let our actions speak louder than words! Let them know us as His by our fruit Lord, and not just by our teaching. AMEN

AUGUST 20

Disoriented

"Let the morning bring me word of Your unfailing love, for I have put my trust in You. Show me the way I should go, for I entrust You with my life." (Psalm 143:8 NIV)

Every morning I get up at 5:15 AM, do my Qigong exercises, my Tai Chi, and then head for the coffee pot. But on my way to the kitchen, I pass through our living room, which at that hour is only lit by the light in the 110 gallon corner fish tank. Normally, I glance at the sleepy fish (just beginning to move about) and continue on my way to the elixir of life. But this morning, our 18 year old Blood Parrot Cichlid, the Dowager of the tank, was swimming *exactly* upside down! I can promise you, this just doesn't look right, even for a large orange fish who is pretty much disc-like. Additionally, she seemed to be ascending and descending rather randomly, bumping into plants and rocks and other fish indiscriminately. In short, she didn't know which way was up!

My pilot son has explained to me some of the facets of IFR (Instrument Flight Rules,) which are always in effect for airline pilots, but for private pilots, only when they can't see the horizon, due to conditions like clouds, rain, snow or fog. Similarly, I've been disoriented driving a car in a rain storm, and on a sailboat in a thick fog. A modern automobile in a rainstorm, a boat in the fog, or a plane in the clouds, all have instruments that use some combination of GPS, sonar, radar, compass, and gyroscope to help them regain their orientation.

We can be disoriented too, both physically and emotionally, even when not traveling, but where are our instruments? (NOT disorienTATED, which doesn't exist…oops, pet peeve coming through again!) What are we supposed to do when we've lost our orientation because we've lost our job, or lost our health, or lost a loved one, or we're trapped in a vicious cycle of addiction? What does my Blood Parrot Cichlid do when her swim bladder over inflates? Hmmmmm……

Well, I still went and got my cup of coffee before returning to the fish tank. I opened the top and did what I always do: I sprinkled their flakes on the surface and closed the lid. There is always a flurry of activity as the thirty or so different fish, rainbow colors and varied sizes and shapes, head for the surface. The Dowager hesitated, started to swim *up, which was down for her,* but when she reached the surface and took the first flake, she flipped! Once she began to feed, or orientation returned!

Christians demonstrate the same phenomenon! How are we fed? We are fed by the Word of God! When we've lost our moral compass, when we're struggling with depression, when we're anxious over the immediate future because we've lost our income, or we've been abandoned, or we've received a terrible diagnosis, how do we get re-oriented? We feed on the Word and more often than not, we find that we've suddenly flipped! Its not that absorbing God's User Manual will instantly make all our problems disappear, but it will put them in perspective…every time! Once you have your circumstance in perspective, once you have your gaze fixed on Jesus where it should be, you will find that the horizon will stabilize right in front of you! You regain your confidence to fly on!

When you don't know which way is up, head for the flakes on the surface: open your bible.

"Trust in the Lord with all your heart and do not lean on your own understanding." (Proverbs 3:5 NIV)

"for god is not the author of confusion, but of peace..." (1 Corinthians 14:33 NIV)

> ***Prayer: Dear Heavenly Father, we love You and we need Your Word to orient us everyday!! Have Your Holy Spirit nudge us when we forget where to look feeling lost! AMEN***

AUGUST 21

Turbulence

"The wisdom from above is first pure, then peaceable, gentle, open to reason, full of mercy and good fruits, impartial and sincere. (James 3:17 ESV)

When you walk down the gangway, stand in line at the end, slowly move forward and board a modern jetliner, you do it because you have faith that it will take you from where you are to where you want to go. Is it blind faith? No, because you know similar flights occur successfully thousands of times every day. You might even know some of the physics involved, some of the pilot's training, some of the engineer's perspective who designed and built the aircraft and its engines. Your faith is not in conflict with reason, it is aligned with it!

So why is it then, when the fasten seat belt light comes on in mid-flight, the Captain asks that everyone return to their seats, and you fly into the first of what could become severe turbulence, that your pulse goes up? Why are you all of a sudden nervous? And if the lights flicker, and the turbulence snaps open some overhead bins, or knocks someone off their feet, you may actually become scared to the point of panic? It's because your imagination takes you to the worst case scenario, no matter how unlikely. It's your emotions that are reacting, not your capacity to reason at all.

The person who thinks reason and your faith are in conflict, simply doesn't understand your faith! Christians don't just swallow a wild story because it gives them the eternal life that they crave. Their faith is based on reason. Anyone who thinks our faith is mythological or irrational hasn't read the book of Romans. They don't know Saul turned Paul, the consummate lawyer. They haven't read Acts and the way he reasoned with both those seeking and those trying to destroy the fledgling faith, as he had done once himself.

Hundreds and hundreds of people saw the risen Christ. The empty tomb is impossible for critics to explain. Literally millions of people can testify to their personal experiences with Christ having changed their lives. The study of the origins of the universe as well as the origins of life both lead inexorably to the inexplicable. When the evidence leads to the supernatural or miraculous if you will, a true adherent of reason follows where the evidence leads.

There are many books exploring the relationship between reason and faith. The point is that they are really never in conflict, because the latter is based on the former. It's only when our emotions and imagination take control of us that our faith falters. When we are emotionally upset, reason can go out the window, and along with it, the faith based upon it.

When the going gets tough, the tough get going…to God! It's only reasonable! The One who created you, and the world you live in, is the One to trust. That's in whom you put your faith, because you became convinced by your own study, when you were not under duress, that the Gospel is true.

When the plane starts shaking, remember why you believed in the first place. That hasn't changed.

Prayer: Dear Heavenly Father, Your Word sets out every reason why we should believe! It is the Evil One who would have us believe our faith is fantasy. Faith and reason have no quarrel, only faith and our own fears, insecurities and emotions. Holy Spirit take us back to Romans, take us back to Hebrews, take us back to the prophets whose predictions hundreds of years before were fulfilled in Your Son, and set our hearts at ease. The Gospel is true! AMEN

AUGUST 22

Jesus' Little Brother

"'Is not this the carpenter, the son of Mary and the brother of James and Joses and Judas and Simon? Are not his sisters here with us?' And they took offense at Him." (Mark 6:3 ESV)

Michael Jr. is a well known Christian comedian who has a skit about what it must have been like to be Jesus' Lil brother. He points out how many times James must have heard comments like, "Why can't you just be more like Jesus, man!" But poor James was just James, not 'James Christ.' Michael Jr. says that at the very next banquet when they ran out of wine and Jesus had left early, everybody turned and looked at James. Can you imagine how the dude felt? He couldn't even make Kool-Aid. How about when James would follow his big brother around everywhere like little brothers do? Michael Jr. says he bets one time, James almost drowned! Imagine when James had problems and he went to his parents for help; they would probably say what anyone would say, "Well, WWJD, James. I mean son, what would Jesus do?"

Many of us know what it's like to be the little brother. The eldest son is the bomb right? I mean he's inherited the name, the power, the land, the money, all down through the ages! Who's going to be King of England, right? I mean, it's certainly not Harry.

But the quote above comes from Jesus' return to the town in which he was raised, Nazareth. When he started teaching in the local synagogue, the people questioned His authority. They recognized Him not as the Messiah, not as the Savior, not even as a scribe, but just the kid who was the poor carpenter's son! So much for being the first son on that occasion!

By grace however, it doesn't matter what your birth order or gender when it comes to inheriting the Kingdom of God! We are all brothers and sisters of Christ, all children of God, once we have believed and accepted the gift of the Gospel! We are all equally valued by God, no matter how small or alone or lost we perceive ourselves to be! Jesus is the Good Shepherd who will leave the ninety-nine to rescue the one! (Luke 15:3-8)

We are all blessed to be the little brother or sister of Christ! I for one am happy to follow Him right back to the Father and into eternity, even if I can only drink the wine and not make it out of water!

Prayer: Dear Heavenly Father, we love You! There is no better feeling than knowing we have been adopted into Your family and earned the right to call You Abba! AMEN

AUGUST 23

I Wish I Could!

Ross: "Is there any way you could maybe come over and help us put together our new furniture?"

Phoebe: "Oh gosh! I really wish I could, but, well, I don't want to!" (Phoebe on Friends, 1994)

Have you ever told a little bitty white lie when you wanted to get out of something? A friend invites you to a lecture on a week night; an acquaintance invites you to their Juice Plus neighborhood event; your church group is going to a movie that you've seen (and didn't like); your mother-in-law wants to come stay the week; your best friend in high school just wants to meet over coffee to tell you about their new job (which you know from someone else is selling whole life insurance!)

We've talked a little about White Lies before (see January 5th) and the fact that they seem to be a situation of the "ends justify the means." You make up an excuse, rather than telling the truth and risk hurting your friend's feelings. There are several problems with this, not the least of which is that every time your ruse "works" you get more used to telling little untruths. Then it gets easier and easier to tell slightly bigger untruths. Then you start to tell even bigger untruths to protect yourself, not really someone else.

Here's an idea: be Phoebe next time! Why does literally everyone *love* Phoebe? Because she sees nothing wrong with telling the exact truth *all the time*. Lying, even a little, damages your reputation in the eyes of others, and eventually will damage your perception of yourself. So take the little hit. Tell your high school friend, "No thanks, I really have no need for insurance." Then sit and enjoy your coffee at home on the porch with your dog.

"If you always tell the truth, you never have to remember anything!" (Mark Twain)

"I'm not upset that you lied to me. I'm upset that from now on I can never believe you. (Nietzsche)

"Lying lips are an abomination to the Lord, but those who act faithfully are His delight." (Proverbs 12:22 ESV)

"No one who practices deceit shall ever dwell in My house; no one who utters lies shall continue before my eyes." (Psalm 101:7 ESV)

> ***Prayer: Dear Heavenly Father, have Your Spirit prick us every time we are tempted to tell a little lie and help us find the right way to tell the truth gently. AMEN***

AUGUST 24

Time Heals All Wounds?

"It has been said, 'Time heals all wounds.' I do not agree. The wounds remain. In time, the mind, protecting its sanity, covers them with scar tissue, and the pain lessens. But it is never gone." (Rose Kennedy)

Rose Kennedy would indeed be likely to know. Tragedy has hovered over the Kennedy family for generations, long before the President and his brother's assassinations, and long afterwards. Most psychologists would agree that the pain of loss, the pain of mistreatment or abuse, the pain of failure, may lessen with time, but they are always there beneath the surface.

But what if you are the one that caused the pain? What if you did cruel things to others in your past, even as a child? Did you lie to get out of trouble? Did you mistreat an animal? Did you belittle and make fun of a classmate because of their appearance, or speech, or size, or ethnicity? Does time lessen the gravity of those offenses? Are the sins of your youth, now that you are grown and realize the error of your ways, forgiven by the passage of time?

What? Did you think God would just forget *everyone's* sin? Did *you* forget that God is outside of time, and fifty years ago for you is the same as today or fifty years from now for Him? But didn't David say, quoting God, *"As far as the east is from the west, So far has He removed our transgressions from us."* ? (Psalm 103:12) The author of Hebrews in 8:12 said, *"For I will forgive their wickedness and remember their sins no more."*

Remember, that a text out of context is a pretext for a proof text! Psalm 103:11 says, *"So great is His mercy* ***toward them who fear Him."*** Believe me, that ain't everyone! Then in Hebrews 8:10-11, it makes clear that those whose sins God forgets are those with whom He made the New Covenant! The New Covenant is made with those who believe in Jesus as the Son of God, who died for the forgiveness of their sins. It is His blood on the cross that blots out their sins, not Father Time!

Just as old wounds are never healed by time, old sins remain as well, unless you decide to choose Christ as your Savior. Your worthiness, your record of sin, just like all of us, is not the stumbling block to your salvation. The Good News is that all you have to do, is admit your sin, plan to turn things around, and accept the gift offered on the cross, even though you are undeserving. Then the love, peace, joy, and freedom from shame and guilt you experience, will be the thing that lessens the pain of old wounds, even those inflicted by you upon others!

Prayer: Dear Father, thank you for forgetting my sin in exchange only for my faith in Your Son! There is nothing that feels better than starting with a clean slate, when born again! AMEN

AUGUST 25

On Tap

"I know your works, that you are neither cold nor hot. I could wish you were cold or hot. So then, because you are lukewarm, and neither cold nor hot, I vomit you out of my mouth!" (Revelation 3:15-16 NKJV)

I was standing at the kitchen sink this morning at 5:30 AM, filling the bucket with water to replace the evaporative loss of just two days, from the corner fish tank in the living room. I tested the water with my finger and it was ice cold, so I moved the lever a bit and tested again until it was lukewarm; just about right for the fish! I recall thinking how easy it was to go from cold to lukewarm to hot, with just the touch of a lever.

So what on earth does Christ mean in his letter transcribed by John to the Laodicean church recorded in the third chapter of Revelation? What's wrong with a lukewarm church? Is Christ criticizing spiritual weakness? If so, why would he say he would rather they were hot ***or cold?*** A little background is helpful here. You can read this as Jesus telling them they need to be fully on board, or their contribution is less valuable. But there's more to it than that!

In the ancient Roman Province of Asia, (modern day Turkey), the town of Laodicea was literally a suburb of Collossae, some sixteen miles distant. Just to the south was another large town called Hieropolis, which was famous for its healing hot springs. The water in Collossae was from deep natural caverns, and was ice cold. So, while the water in the springs of Hieropolis was hot and excellent for bathing, the water in Collossae was cold and good for drinking! But Laodicea had no natural water source of its own. The water in Laodicea was *piped in* via aqueducts from both Collosae and Hieropolis, and by the time it reached the town and mixed in its cisterns, it was lukewarm! It was good for neither drinking nor bathing, and this was Christ's point! The Laodicean church was really good for *nothing,* because they were doing *no good works at all!*

Jesus wasn't criticizing the Laodiceans for a lack of enthusiasm. We're all human. We can't be enthusiastic all the time. But, we are to do *some good works, and* when we do, we are to work as though it were for the Lord! (Colossians 3:23) We can at least be *reliable.* The cold water was always good for drinking, and the hot water always good for bathing. *But the lukewarm water was good for nothing!* That means if you volunteer for a service organization, show up! If you tithe, that means tithing, not something close. If you feed the poor, feed them every time you are scheduled, not just when you feel like it.

"Whatever you do, work at it with all your heart, as working for the Lord, not for human masters." (Colossians 3:23 NIV)

Prayer: Dear Heavenly Father, forgive us for our inaction! As James noted, faith without works is dead! How can we tell others of our love for Christ and then not do what He commands? AMEN

AUGUST 26

Behind Enemy Lines

"And the great dragon was thrown down, that ancient serpent, who is called the Devil and Satan, the deceiver of the whole world—he was thrown down to earth, and his angels were thrown with him." (Revelation 12:9 ESV)

Usually it is in childhood that we hear of legend or myth and have the distinct tendency to believe it might be true. Then as we grow older, learn more of the world, become rational and reasoning, we reject the improbable fairytale as the mythology it is. The power and existence of Satan, horns, pitchfork, tail or no, was just the opposite for me! As a child, first learning Bible stories, I totally bought into the Creation Story, Abraham and Isaac, the whole Moses deal, Joseph and the multi-colored coat, the incarnation of Christ, His crucifixion, even with some doubt, His resurrection. But the devil? I never thought Satan was real. Even as a child I thought he was just a metaphor for our own disobedience.

But as an adult, as my reasoning powers grew, and I began both to read about and witness spiritual warfare, I started to believe that *there is* a war going on! There is a battle between the forces of good and the forces of evil, not unlike a Star Wars scenario, but happening on a spiritual plane of existence that we cannot literally see. As I learned of the horrors of the Crusades, the Inquisitions, the Holocaust, the Khmer Rouge, the Nigerian genocide, just to name a few, I became convinced that there was evidence for this battle, and that men chose under whose influence they wished to be, Satan or Christ.

But as C.S. Lewis points out in *Mere Christianity*, the battle between Good and Evil is not between two equal and independent states, but it is instead a Civil War! Satan is a created being, created by God according to scripture, and then thrown to earth as punishment for his rebellion! Christianity holds that the Evil One was created good, but then became evil, leading a persistent revolt against the powers of a loving God, never ceasing in his efforts to turn men away from faith and love of their Creator. The world is his dominion now, having been ejected from the Kingdom of Heaven. We then, as it turns out, *are behind enemy lines* throughout our entire lives! We live in territory occupied by the enemy. But the King has come to shore in the person of Christ, disguised first as a baby and then as a humble carpenter's son. Christ calls us to participate in a worldwide strategy of sabotage, foiling the efforts of Satan at every turn! When we worship together, it's as though we are receiving secret orders and an intelligence briefing rolled into one. Lewis says the Evil One will call on our conceit and our self-centered sense of importance to convince us that church is unnecessary, and thus cut us off from the reinforcement of fellow believers as well as critical intelligence briefings!

Let us not forget daily, that we are operating behind enemy lines! Believers need each other to negotiate the trip wires, pits, and booby-traps placed by Satan! Don't "go it alone!" If you're not in a strong community of believers, find a church and visit this Sunday! When you do, you may find the intelligence report eye-opening, and the love you feel around you replenishing!

Prayer: Dear heavenly Father, we love You! For some reason we find it easier to accept Your Son as Savior than we do Satan as destroyer! Holy Spirit, make us sensitive to the presence of the Evil One that we might take precautions, moving carefully but confidently to place our Lamp on a Lamp stand, dissipating the darkness around us, in which Satan lurks! AMEN

AUGUST 27

Mooring

"God is our refuge and strength, a very present help in trouble. Therefore we will not fear, even thought the earth be removed, and though the mountains be carried into the midst of the sea; though its waters roar and be troubled..." (Psalm 46:1-3 NKJV)

If you are vigilant, you've listened to NOAA, you've checked the radar, you've noted small craft warnings, and you've looked at the sky that morning and the previous night, then you, the experienced sailor, know when to stay home. But even the most conscientious mariner will occasionally be caught out on the water when a squall seems to come out of nowhere. You may see the virga in the distance and a darkening sky and think that it's too far to be a concern. Then your attention is elsewhere, seemingly for a moment only, and suddenly the wind and the waves are upon you!

Hopefully, you are always ready for this eventuality, and in less than a few minutes you drop, or at least reef your main, roller furl a portion of your jib, and if you are close enough, you head for the barn! On Eggemoggin Reach where we sail in Maine, we head for our mooring in Deadman's Cove. A mooring is a line that ends in a woven eye, permanently fixed to both a floating buoy, and a chain, which leads to a very heavy cement block on the sea floor. Usually, there is also a winter-stick attached to the buoy line, with a small float and a fiberglass rod which sticks straight up out of the water. As you come into the mooring, your mate (literally, for me, i.e. my wife) is responsible for lying on the foredeck and grabbing the winter stick, and then hauling in the rope which leads to the larger line, which is the one with the eye in it, that you then bring under the bow pulpit, through the chock, and secure around the bow cleat.

Sounds simple, right? But in a high wind, heavy sea, and other boats nearby, missing the winter stick as you come up into the wind can be dangerous if not disastrous. So, you might think the skipper's abilities are important, and they are, but the mate's responsibility is significant. In other words, you need someone you can really *rely on* up front when you are coming into a mooring!

From Psalm 46, you might think Christ is our mooring, the thing that keeps us safe, off the rocks, and steady in the storms of life, and so He is. But He also gave us a helpmate in our spouse, who must be *absolutely reliable*. That spouse, you will find in hard times, is often the one who picks up the winter stick, and makes sure you are securely fastened to the Lord! Of course, it can go both ways. Your wife may be at the helm in a bad time, and it is you who grabs the stick from the pitching foredeck. Either way, God designed marriage so that we could help each other be secure in our relationship to God. The Holy Spirit may well work through the counsel of your spouse when you are adrift, or nearly so!

Each day, if you have a spouse, make sure you are up for picking up that winter stick! Make sure they can depend on you no matter the weather conditions in your lives. Your spouse is a *gift from above*, and you would do well to remember it each and every morning when you wake up! Believe me, you don't want to miss your mooring in a blow!

"And the Lord God said, 'It is not good the man should be alone; I will make him a helper comparable to him...Therefore a man shall leave his father and mother and be joined to his wife, and they shall become one flesh. (Genesis 2:18,24 NKJV)

"Therefore, do not be unwise, but understand what the will of the Lord is...give thanks always for all things to God...submitting to one another in the fear of God." (Ephesians 17,20,21 NKJV)

Prayer: Dear Heavenly Father, we love You! Thank you that You designed us so that we become one with our spouse, knowing we can rely on them to lead us to You, when we falter in our faith. AMEN

AUGUST 28

Traffic Lights

"Do not think that I came to destroy the law or the prophets. I did not come to destroy but to fulfill....Whoever therefore breaks one of these commandments, and teaches men so, shall be called least in the Kingdom of Heaven..." (Matthew 5:17,19 NKJV)

A few years ago I had travelled to Austin, Texas for a medical convention. This was back in the pre-Uber days, so I had taken a yellow cab from the airport to my hotel. Making small talk along the way, I discovered that my cabbie was an immigrant from Pakistan, along with his wife and two children. I asked him what it was that he most liked about America, now that they had lived here for almost five years. He answered immediately, "I like your red lights!" Wow!

I thought to myself. I sort of hate red lights. "I'm surprised," I exclaimed. Most Americans complain about red lights. He was shocked. Why would we complain? He explained, "When traffic stops at the red light, the traffic crossing can move safely. When the light turns green, we may proceed safely. It is a beautiful thing, is it not? Where I come from no one pays any attention. It is very dangerous. The streets are lawless. I cannot go to the corner store at night to get my aged mother goat's milk, because of the fear that someone will realize I have that money and hit me on the head!"

Yes, we Christians live under grace, not under the law. But it is a mistake to think that means the law is bad. Paul tells us to submit to society's authorities and rules. (Romans 13:1-2) Is the law a bad thing? Absolutely not.(Romans 7:7) It is the law of Moses that caused man to recognize his own sin, and to realize that no human effort would enable him to keep the law perfectly. The laws of man provide for civil societies. They are not bad, just because we are forgiven and live under grace!

So, next time you are sitting in the heat and traffic at a red light, maybe you are late for work or a meeting, maybe you feel you like you have caught every single red light along your route; then pause and say a silent prayer thanking God that you live in a place that has traffic lights and millions of people who agree to obey them!

"For it is not the hearers of the law who will be righteous before God, but the doers of the law who will be justified." (Romans 2:13 ESV)

"Be subject for the Lord's sake, to every human institution…for this is the will of God, that by doing good you should put to silence the ignorance of foolish people." (1 Peter 2: 13-15 ESV)

> *Prayer: Dear Heavenly Father, we thank you for order. We thank you for societies that exist in peace around the structure of law. We realize we cannot keep God's law, nor man's law perfectly, and that we are forgiven, but we also realize that following the law allows all of us to live together freely and peacefully. AMEN*

AUGUST 29

Dry Chemical

"Therefore, as God's chosen people, holy and dearly loved, clothe yourselves with compassion, kindness, humility, gentleness and patience. Bear with each other fan forgive one another if any of you has a grievance against someone. forgive as the Lord forgave you. And over all these virtues put on love, which binds them all together in perfect unity." (Colossians 3:12-14 NIV)

I was making coffee in the kitchen of our medical office the other morning, and as I waited on the Keurig my gaze fell on the fire extinguisher hanging on the wall nearby. After "doctoring" (ha!) my coffee, I walked over to have a closer look. It was a dry chemical extinguisher, and the instructions for use were printed right on the front. Attached to the neck of the red canister by a thin wire was a green tag with months and years printed on it. The current year and a date two months before were punched. Someone had inspected the extinguisher and checked its pressure.

While the fire extinguisher's presence and up to date readiness were reassuring, it also reminded me that emergencies like fires actually do happen! If we had a fire, I might be the only person who had read the instructions and even knew where the fire extinguisher was located!

People around us have emergencies all the time. Sometimes they actually are physical; a fire, a car wreck, storm damage, injury or illness. Sometimes they are entirely psychic; a death in the family, a break up or divorce, a failed exam, a job change, or a job lost. But there will be many opportunities in life for you to be the dry chemical! Often just being nearby and available to the person affected is all that is needed. Sometimes you may combine that with offering to do whatever they can think of that might help. Less often, and perhaps after a time, they may ask your advice or at least be open to your council. Sometimes that may only mean reassuring them that one foot in front of the other is all that's expected for now.

It turns out that love is our dry chemical. When people are obviously having an emergency, love means being available and being ready to help! You make sure that you'll actually function in love by keeping yourself up to date! The community of believers to which you hopefully belong, regular study of scripture, prayer and worship will do just that! Without any one of them, your ability to function in an emergency may decrease like the pressure in that dry chemical extinguisher.

Prayer: Dear Heavenly Father, we love You!! We want the Holy Spirit to keep the love of Christ present in our lives at all times, so that we might let You work through us compassionately to help those in immediate need! Thank you for Your Word, our friends, our churches, and the ability to talk to You personally in prayer whenever we want!! We'll stay ready! AMEN

AUGUST 30

Reminders

"Know that you are the perfect age. Each year is special and precious. For you shall only live it once. Be comfortable with growing older!" (Louise Hay)

Today would have been my late father's 93rd birthday. When he turned 80, I asked him what it was like? He thought for a moment, and then said, "I guess it was about like 70." I said come on dad, what was 70 like? Again he looked contemplative, and said, "Really, I guess about like 60." Now I just felt like he wasn't trying! Okay dad, what was 60 like? (I was 52 at the time.) He got a little twinkle in his eye and said, "Nothing like 50 son, cause everything goes to hell after 50!"

I think I've told you that story before, but its okay because it bears repeating. In the physical sense, dad may have been right. My wife and I were laughing the other morning because neither of us could remember getting up in the morning when nothing hurt! When you're young, you just take your body for granted. You just don't think about the fact that the laws of entropy apply to your muscles, sinews, bones and organs!

A few weeks ago, our grandchildren were reading the Shel Silverstein poem, SICK, out loud and it seems apropos here.

I cannot go to school today! Said little Peggy Ann McKay

"I have the measles and the mumps, A gash, a rash, and purple bumps,

My mouth is wet, my throat is dry, I'm going blind in my right eye.

My tonsils are as big as rocks, I've counted sixteen chicken pox,

And there's one more, that's seventeen, And don't you think my face looks green?

My leg is cut, my eyes are blue, It might be instamatic flu.

I cough and sneeze and gasp and choke, I'm sure that my left leg is broke!

My hip hurts when I move my chin, My belly button's caving in.

My back is wrenched, my ankle's sprained, My 'pendix pains each time it rains.

My nose is cold, my toes are numb, I have a sliver in my thumb, My neck is stiff,

My spine is weak, I hardly whisper when I speak, My tongue is filling up my mouth.

I think my hair is falling out, My elbow's bent, My spine ain't straight,

My temperature is 108! My brain is shrunk, I cannot hear, There's a hole inside my ear.

I have a hangnail, and my heart is…what?

What's that? What's that you say? You say today is SATURDAY?

Ha-ha, G'bye. I'm going out to play!

Sometimes, in my mid-60's, I feel just like Peggy Ann McKay in the morning. But you know what? Every joint that creaks, every back muscle that spasms, every digit that's numb, every toe with gout, every bout of reflux, every knee that screams, believe it or not, **reminds me** of what a gift my body has been and that I better do more to take care of it! I am grateful to be here at all, even if a few of the parts need to be oiled more frequently!

Age brings wisdom, to some extent, to us all. Part of that is a creeping up of gratitude, I think. Things that we took for granted most of our lives become more precious in our sight, as they always should have been, really. Pain in your back is really nothing as a price to pay for hearing the laughter of your grandchildren as they read a Shel Silverstein out loud!

"He will renew your life and sustain you in your old age." (Ruth 4:14 NIV)

"Wisdom belongs to the aged, and understanding to the old." (Job 12:12 NIV)

"Grandchildren are the crown of the aged…" (Proverbs 17:6 NIV)

Prayer: Dear Heavenly Father, we love YOU and we know that Your love for us is steadfast and will carry us through our old age and our infirmities. Thank you that you have given us these marvelous machines we call our bodies, and give us the mental fortitude to work to preserve them! And finally Lord, thank you for grandchildren, that we can relive the carefree years of our youth in their laughter! AMEN

AUGUST 31

In the Response

"God isn't in the events Jenny. He's in the response to the events... " (Jennifer Worth)

The young nurse, Jenny, had been dating the architect, Michael, for several months, when they had their first real argument. It was in the mid-1950's and things moved a bit slower then. He had planned a vacation for them, away at the beach, at a small hotel. She was excited, but right before the weekend planned, a friend of her boyfriend intimated that he planned on only one room for the two of them. She was furious, let her boyfriend know of her anger, but not clearly why she was so upset, and then she cancelled the weekend, leaving him dumbfounded.

Later that same day, the young architect was on a third floor scaffolding that collapsed. He survived, but lost his right foot, and had multiple compound fractures. At his bedside in the hospital, Jenny realized the error of her faulty assumption, reassured Michael that she would stand by him forever, and the loss of a foot meant nothing to her! They kissed and parted full of love and hope and excitement again.

The next day, she was summoned to the hospital emergently. Michael had "taken a turn for the worse." When she arrived winded, after biking furiously for miles in London's East End, she was told he had just passed. Her response was zombie like. She was furious with God, with herself, probably even with him, for dying! Unable to function, the Mother Superior of Anglican Nonatus House, where Jenny worked as a midwife, held her in her arms and told her quietly the words of our opening quote.

When the events are tragic, humans cycle through Kubler-Ross' stages of grief, from denial to anger to bargaining to depression to acceptance. The time and depth to which one enters these stages vary, but their existence rarely does. Jenny wouldn't get over her cataclysmic loss immediately. But she might get through her anger without extinguishing her faith by understanding the words of the Mother Superior.

I find there is sort of an "Old Testament" misunderstanding in Christians. Too many believe that when tragedy strikes it was planned by God or that He made it happen as punishment for misdeeds. Christ debunks this directly in the story of the Tower at Siloam. (Luke 13:4-5) Stuff happens! It's a fallen world of our own making! When we stop blaming God, but turn to Him instead for direction in our response to the storms of life, we reap the beauty of our faith! His love for us will conquer all our tragedies! Our time on earth is but a blink of an eye compared to the eternity we have been given by Grace.

Jenny decides she cannot work in her current state. As she prepares to go on sabbatical, she runs into an old Jewish woman, survivor of the holocaust, who had blamed herself for surviving when so many others perished. Her self-imposed guilt had left her unable to leave her daughter's meager apartment for 12 years! But, the birth of her first granddaughter finally brought her out into the sunlight. Nurse Jenny had helped her and her daughter through the pregnancy, and the old babushka remembered her when she saw her on the street, and had heard of her tragedy. She crossed the street to say a proper 'goodbye.' Holding the sobbing nurse in her arms, she whispers these words from experience and faith, *"You will feel better than this. You must just keep on living until you feel alive again."* (See DOING LIFE January 13, February 8, March 14) Good advice.

"Blessed are those who mourn, for they shall be comforted." (Matthew 5:4 NKJV)

"He heals the broken-hearted and binds up their wounds." (Psalm 147:3 NKJV)

"I called on Your Name O Lord, from the depths of the pit. You heard my plea: 'Do not close your ears to my cry for relief.' "You came near when I called You, and You said, 'Do not fear.'" (Lamentations 3:55 NKJV)

Prayer: Dear heavenly Father, we love You! How Blessed are we that You are faithful, that You are always there for us, that You have promised us eternity! We know that we can always lean on You when troubles come, when the sun seems always behind a cloud, and that You will stay by our side until the sun returns!! AMEN

SEPTEMBER

SEPTEMBER 1

No Take-backs

"[David] said, While the child was alive, I fasted and wept; for I said, Who can tell whether the Lord will be gracious to me, that the child may live? But now he is dead, why should I fast? Can I bring him back again?" (2 Samuel 12:22-23 NKJV)

Remember being a kid and when someone said or did something mean to you, you would say, "Take that back!" Or, maybe closer to home, you can remember something you said or did, perhaps not just as a kid, but more recently, that you wish with all your might you could take back! When we do something we ought not do, which often involves hurting someone else, the effect on others is almost always something you can't just 'take back.'

We believers know that we are forgiven, right? Through Christ, our sins are forgiven past, present and future. Scripture tells us He remembers our sins no more, right? Separates us from our sin as far as the east is from the west, right?

But the consequences of your sin are not so easily erased! The fervent attempt to undo with prayer alone, what we have done, is futile. King David realized this. His adultery with Bathsheba, his murder of her husband Uriah, had inescapable consequences! Yes, he confessed and repented at Nathan's behest. Yes, the Lord forgave him. But the damage his sin had caused was not undone with prayer and would affect his family for generations. He understood that once his son by Bathsheba was dead, no amount of prayer would undo the damage!

When Christians sin, which they do every day, (if not virtually every minute), they know they are forgiven. There is freedom from guilt and shame in that forgiveness, it is true, and that's a Blessing! But your sin often hurts another deeply, and just because God forgets your sin, doesn't mean the person that you injured will! Your sin ***does have consequences*** even if forgiven. So as Paul tells us in Romans 6:15, we should not feel free to sin simply because we live under Grace and not the law! We are no longer slaves to sin, but slaves to Christ! Just because there is "no condemnation in Christ," doesn't mean at all that your sin doesn't have serious consequences to yourself and others! If you murder someone and are forgiven by God, they are still dead, their family still devastated, and you're still in prison!

So, next time you think about saying or doing something mean-spirited, whether to someone's face or behind their back, remember, there are no 'take-backs.' Prayer won't necessarily undo the hurt you cause. Yes, bring everything to the Lord in prayer and all things are possible with God, but don't assume God's forgiveness means you get off Scot free with the people you hurt. Usually, there are no 'take-backs."

Prayer: Dear Heavenly Father, we love You! We are beyond grateful for the forgiveness you shower on us even though we are undeserving, but Spirit remind us that our actions have consequences nevertheless.

Remind us that sin may be forgiven, but can still hurt us and the people around us! It should give us pause when we are about to give into a temptation, and that weakness will lead to another's pain. AMEN

SEPTEMBER 2

Fans in the Stands

"Therefore, since we are surrounded by so great a cloud of witnesses, let us lay aside every weight, and the sin which so easily ensnares us, and let us run with endurance the race that is set before us, looking unto Jesus, the author and finisher of our faith..." (Hebrews 12:1-2 NKJV)

You could write a book, and believe me many will, about the bizarre twists and ripple effects that have accompanied the Pandemic of 2020-21. One of the strangest, is to see professional sports teams competing on television, as always, but before nearly empty stadiums, viewed only by cardboard cutouts of people filling the first 10-20 rows of seats! Here in Dallas, both the NBA Mavericks and the NHL Stars are involved in playoff series capping an abbreviated season, played before empty arenas. In all likelihood, the Tokyo Olympics, delayed to summer 2021, might well involve empty arenas as well.

Football, basketball, baseball, hockey are all experimenting with canned crowd noises in addition to cardboard cutouts! Why on earth would they go that much trouble? The reason is simple: athletes perform better when they are being watched! There is something about the very nature of athletic competition, the desire to win, the desire to complete a task, the desire to do one's best, that is augmented by the presence of witnesses. Is it fear of embarrassment? Is it anticipation of the accolades showered upon the victor? Is it internal, the reaching of a goal for which one has sacrificed that is all the sweeter when witnessed and verified? Maybe its a little of all of these.

The author of Hebrews understood this as well as the Commissioner of any sports endeavor. The Greek word for "witness" is *uaptus*, pronounced "martus" from which we get the English word, "martyr." The witnesses spoken of in Hebrews, are the deceased individuals who bear testimony to the power of faith and to God's faithfulness. As we travel through this life on earth, we are aided by the knowledge, and written testimony, of those who have gone before us! In one respect, it's possibly the perspective that, "Well, if he or she can do it, so can I!" In another, it's the recognition that no matter what the obstacles and tragedies they faced in their lives, their faith led them to a glorious final reward, an eternity in heaven, that now allows them to cheer on those who come after!

So, remember each day, as you deal with the vicissitudes of life, that others of the faith have seen their trials through to a successful completion, and they are pulling for you as you do the same. Keep the faith, baby! Our professional sports teams may be encouraged by the *appearance of a crowd* rooting for them, but you have a crowd *invisible to others* pulling for you, and the Savior sits in the stands with them!!

Prayer: Dear Heavenly Father, we love You!! Thank you that Your is faithful, that You keep Your promises to us, and that after we have finished the race, we will be surrounded by others who have done the same and we can cheer on those who have come after us! AMEN

SEPTEMBER 3

Air Conditioning

"There will be a shelter to give shade from the heat by day, and refuge and protection from the storm and the rain." (Isaiah 4:6 NKJV)

We live in Texas. I've lived here for 47 of my 65 years, and four of those not here, were in the "almost Texas" state of Oklahoma. I spent my first nine years in Pennsylvania and New York. Summer meant sunshine and daytime highs of 75. In second grade I thought summer was just *fantastic!* Then in 1965 my dad was transferred to Houston. In July. No kidding. And mom's Volkswagon had no AC. Even as an eight year old, I knew immediately that something was *seriously wrong.*

Except for high school in Tulsa, I lived in Houston from second to eighth grade, and then for some unclear reason, returned to Houston for college and medical school. Driving my '69 GTO back and forth to Tulsa, I used 4/80 AC (4 open windows at 80 mph,) and the dorms had 'water chillers' which really wasn't *quite AC* either. We used to rate the misery of June-September in terms of required showers/day; never less than two and often four to five! Luckily, when you suffer from the heat and humidity in Houston, the mosquitos are always available to take your mind off of it!

In the 21st century of course, most of us in Texas go from our air-conditioned home to our air-conditioned car to our air-conditioned office. But when the power goes out after a storm and you're in a building where the city codes don't allow the windows to open, well, it's not so *bueno!* You can buy a used car with a rusted through body, bald tires, a bad muffler, no radio, but if the AC works, hey, it could be a bargain!! Despite the ubiquitous availability of AC, homes with big trees and shade have prices that reflect that feature. In short, it's often just too darn HOT in Texas in the summer!!

When your life starts to heat up, you look for the same thing you do when the forecast heats up: a place in the shade! The demands on our time and emotions in the fast paced, interconnected world in which we live, can cause us to overheat at the office or at home. If our radiator blows, it can scald loved ones, co-workers and even ourselves!! Shade brings immediate relief; temperatures at least ten degrees cooler. There's a reason that the prophet Isaiah describes the dwelling place of God as a place where you can find shade from the heat of the day. (Isaiah 4:6) He is there, reliably, a great tree planted by water, "that has no fear when the heat comes." (Jeremiah 17:8 ESV) I like the visualization of a giant redwood or ancient oak for God. Immutable, immovable, powerful, secure, full of life itself and yet freely giving life-giving shade as well. Our God is big enough to give you shelter from the noon day sun, or from a downpour!

So, when you are about to have a melt-down, pause and take it to the One who made you; the One who sent His Son for you; the One whose Spirit dwells within you. He can, and will, cool you down and get you thinking again! Pray, read your Bible, call your friends, rest in the shade of His love for you for an hour, a half-day, maybe even take a day off. Take time to get out of the heat. He's always available. Unlike the AC in your building, His power never fails.

Prayer: Dear Heavenly Father, for those of us all over the world that live through the broiling heat of summer and understand the analogy, thank you that when our problems heat up, You are always there to provide for shade and a chance to cool down! AMEN

SEPTEMBER 4

Hove to

"Be still and know that I am God." (Psalm 46:10 NKJV)

One of the fascinating things about sailing, is that unlike motoring, or snow skiing, or driving, or jet skiing, or water skiing, or cycling, or riding a scooter, or just about any other means of travel, there is no intrinsically obvious way to easily STOP! A sailboat is to some extent "at the mercy of the wind." If it's blowing, you're going! Now, of course this assumes you have sails up, and sheeted in, not just flying in the breeze! But even then, the breeze will find a way to move your boat with even the motion of the free sails and the wind effect on the hull. Once you are sailing, whether beating toward the wind, reaching across it, or running away from it, your boat will be moving if there is wind! *Unless, you take advantage of the ONE place a sailboat can never go: directly into the wind!*

We've taught a little basic sailing in earlier devotionals, and hopefully you remember that while a sailboat can turn into and through the wind, so that now the wind is on the opposite side of the sails than it was when you started your turn (called tacking,) it cannot point its bow directly into the wind, and stay there, simply because of the physics involved. However, if you back the jib or foresail in a maneuver called 'heaving-to' you can bring a sailboat to a complete halt quickly, even in a stiff breeze.Originally, I had described this maneuver here in detail, but upon review, forget it! Just trust me.

There are lots of reasons to hove-to. The wind may be getting too much for your craft, you may have a man (or a dog) suddenly washed overboard, you may need to go below for some reason like an instrument check or perhaps you need to go forward to attend to some rigging that has failed. In any event, the ability to stop, is as important a skill to a sailor as it is to the downhill skier!

The ability to STOP is important in all walks of life! You may be working yourself to exhaustion on a project, you may be in an escalating argument with your spouse or a child, you may be pursuing something that everyone but you realizes is unreachable, you may be teetering on the edge of an addiction, you may be tempted to cheat on your taxes, on your business partner or on your spouse. JUST STOP!! Hit the PAUSE button. Stop and listen. Believers soon realize that God is always right there next to you, listening, ready to guide, but you have to STOP and give Him your attention!

Now, we have noted before that "a text out of context is a pretext for a proof text," and I don't want to misuse this one. The Psalmist quoted in our opening is addressing those enemies of the Chosen People who continually assail them, warning them that to make war on them is to make war on Him. But I think the passage applies to our circumstance as well. When you get out of control, either in an argument, or even driving yourself over the edge, you are warring with God in a very real way! You are imago dei, made in His image, and when you fly off the handle, party to excess such that you are inebriated with drugs or alcohol, argue in a mean spirited way with your loved ones or colleagues, gossip about another in any way, use expletives or disparaging marks about other people or groups of people, well, you are staining the image of God that you are!

What the Psalmist is saying applies: STOP! Even when you are simply overworking, you are hurting the One who Created you and Loves you more than you can imagine! When you finally, stop, maybe try and listen, for that still small voice that Elijah heard. (1 Kings 19:12) It is there.

Prayer: Dear heavenly Father, forgive us when we forget from whence we came! You have made us in Your image and we blur that reflection when we hurt others or ourselves! Let us be a light to the world, not a shadowy distortion that misleads and undermines the faith of others. AMEN

SEPTEMBER 5

Mud Puddles

"We start out so enthusiastic about life, so entertained and delighted by the very nature of things. But the newness fades; we grow jaded or exhausted, and we begin to lose some vital appreciation for the possibilities inherent in the day." (Marianne Williamson, from Keep a Sense of Adventure)

I was given a collection of essays on my fiftieth birthday entitled, "*Fifty Things to Do When You Turn Fifty.*" I picked it up the other morning, for the first time. I am sixty five. Oops. I had thought it a list of things like see the Grand Canyon, the Eiffel tower, parachute once, climb a mountain etc.etc. and I think at the time I thought it too depressing to contemplate a bucket list that would still be long at my funeral. But I discovered this morning, that the book is actually a marvelous collection of essays by fifty famous authors, on *attitude* more than anything else! For instance Garrison Keillor, the incredible creator of the *Lake Wobegon* stories, advises one to stop bellyaching...no one cares that you're getting older! You should "lose the ponytail, start telling the truth, and stop having dinner with people you don't like!"

But many of the essays speak to the more serious truth that as we finally acknowledge our mortality, our search for answers turns inward rather than outward, and mid-life can mark the beginning of a certain kind of enlightenment. We eventually realize that our generation is not going to usher in a new earthly utopia, and that the massive cruelty we had hoped to eradicate is still in the world. It is disillusioning. In the words of Marianne Williamson, "disillusionment is actually a good thing, because it means you were laboring under illusions before, and this is the beginning of spiritual insight."

Paul tells us much the same thing, when he encourages us to test all things and determine what is good, in his letter to Thessalonica. (1 Thessalonians 5:21)

For the Believer, many things start to make much more sense as we move through mid-life. One begins to see what is meant by a "fallen world," but one also comes to appreciate the validity of all the aphorisms like "the best things in life are free," and "youth is wasted on the young!" It's much easier to understand that love is the only thing that matters once you've lived long enough to have experienced both the loss of it, and its effect on others. Then its much easier to understand why God would sacrifice His only Son for our salvation, because no other act could demonstrate love like that! And a God who would love us like that, and would give us life on this earth, surely wants us to experience it in all its fantastic facets!

So at sixty five, I can look *backwards quite a distance* to fifty, and analyze the choices I've made. We can gradually dissipate from mid-life into old age, or we can purposefully choose a kind of spiritual rebirth, and through it perhaps understand better both our relationship to our Creator, and the myriad of opportunities that still remain, and will, until we draw our final breath.

Williamson wrote her essay on turning fifty while her teenage children splashed and laughed in mud puddles in the yard. She decided she would rather rejoice in the fact that her kids were happy, than worry about the way the mud might ruin her bath towels. AMEN

"This is the day the Lord has made; let us rejoice and be glad in it!" (Psalm 118:24 NIV)

Prayer: Dear Heavenly Father, we love You, and we know that You first loved us and demonstrated it with the the life and death of the Messiah! Keep us mindful of the fact that we were saved for a reason, though undeserving. Loving each other is what You want. Love lets us see good in every direction, and rejoice in it, even in the midst of a fallen world! AMEN

SEPTEMBER 6

Something is Wrong

"Something is radically wrong....the American church today accepts grace in theory, but denies it in practice...Personal responsibility has replaced personal

response. We talk about acquiring virtue as if it were a skill ...The emphasis is on what I do rather than what God is doing...our scrambling for brownie points, our thrashing about trying to fix ourselves while hiding our pettiness and wallowing in guilt are nauseating to God and a flat denial of the doctrine of Grace...Something is radically wrong." (Brennan Manning, The Ragamuffin Gospel)

I attended a private prep school on scholarship. I worked hard to graduate at the top of my class. I attended Rice University on a National Merit Scholarship. I worked hard to get into medical school. I attended Baylor College of Medicine. I worked hard to graduate at the top of my class, and then attend the residency program of my choice. I attended UCSF for my residency. I worked hard to become the administrative Chief Resident, and then be in a position to practice wherever I chose. I began practicing in Dallas, Texas, became involved in our local church, and I worked hard teaching Sunday School, singing in choir, serving as an Usher, getting on the Board of Elders at a young age. I even eventually attended seminary and strove to excel in every class! So what? **So what?**

Do you see a pattern? Everything I did, I did in my own strength, striving to ***achieve,*** striving to ***earn*** each position so that I, others, and I dare say, God, might respect me more and more! There is nothing wrong in striving to achieve per se, unless some portion of your motivation is improving your stature in the eyes of others, forgetting that for the Christian, everything we do is to be for the Glory of God! And there is definitely, something wrong, when your desire to achieve confounds your faith, and you become convinced that more service, more Bible study, more quiet time, more mentoring, more teaching, more appointments, more ***anything*** will slowly build your righteousness to the point where you actually ***deserve*** what God has to offer! **You will never achieve that righteousness and you certainly will never deserve it!**

It took failures in parenting, marriage, professional practice, and finally participation in first, a Grace filled church, and second, a Grace filled seminary, before I *finally got the point of the Ragamuffin Gospel* quoted above*!* The beauty of our faith, the central tenant of it really, is that God loves us immeasurably, as His creation, even though we will never, ever, deserve it! We will never be able to earn His love for the simple reason that ***we already have it!*** We will never achieve righteousness through piety, no matter how sincere and fervent. That's what it means to live under ***Grace,*** and not under the law. There has only been one sinless life lived, one person who kept the law, and allowing Him to live in us, allowing ourselves to be clothed in His righteousness, is the only avenue back to a Creator that we started denying right there in the Garden!

Salvation isn't for those who **earn it!** Salvation isn't for those **good enough to get 'in!'** Salvation is a gift for all the Ragamuffins like us, as Brennan Manning would say. All I achieved with my decades of striving, other than a skill with which to make a living and perhaps help some people from time to time, was the final realization of my own failures! Once I started learning to allow the indwelling Spirit to live through me; once I started taking my dilemmas, my anguish, and even my joys, and laying them at the foot of the cross; well, then I experienced the freedom Paul talks about in Galatians! If you don't feel like doing your Bible study tonight...don't! There are no demerits in God's eyes! He wants you to do your Bible study because He wants you to learn about Him so your relationship with Christ can grow; not because you need to check it off your list!

So, if you are anywhere in your Christian walk and recognize yourself in the opening paragraphs, ***CHILL DUDE!!*** The physician comes for the sick, not the healthy, the Great physician comes for the sinner, the downtrodden, the exhausted, the depressed, the failing, the ones who have given up. But remember, the sinner may just as easily be the proud, the successful, the self-concerned, the one who has a false sense of righteousness!

Try to do this: love better and have Christ help you through the Holy Spirit. Pray for help to love others, even people that make you mad, who you don't want to love. For some, you'll need to love by forgiving. Once you realize that freedom from your own guilt, shame, and fear have been given to you by the Grace of God through faith in Christ, who forgave you, you'll find it much easier. Believe it or not, it can even be **fun**, because you feel better and better every day!! Then suddenly, *something is very right!*

"Now the Lord s the Spirit, and where the Spirit of the Lord is, there is freedom." (2 Corinthians 3:17 NIV)

"So if the Son sets you free, you will be free indeed." (John 8:36 NIV)

"Live as free men, but do not use your freedom to cover up for evil; live as servants of God." (1 Peter 2:16 NIV)

Prayer: Dear Heavenly Father, thank you that You saw fit to love us, to offer us eternal life in Your presence, when we did and can do nothing whatsoever to deserve it! What a love is that! AMEN

SEPTEMBER 7

Hidden at High Tide

"When you pass through the waters, I will be with you; and when you pass through the rivers, they will not sweep over you." (Isaiah 43:2 NIV)

I took a week off from the summer heat to go back to the coast of Maine for one more week at the end of August. Yesterday, we took our 51 year old Greenwich 24, *Adagio,* out for a sail on the Reach. It was a gorgeous MBD. (Maine Blue Day.) It just so happened that when we headed out at about 1PM, it was just shy of high tide. We were on a close haul, starboard tack, heading straight from the cove toward the north tower of the Deer Isle Bridge. My cardiologist daughter, orthopedist son-in-law, and at that particular moment, Great White Shark grandson, Henry, (who was bearing teeth and chomping with claws up, which I believe was a cross between a Shark and a Grizzly) were accompanying me.

The bridge is a smaller, yet exact replica of the Golden Gate, built the same year, 1939, by the same designer. Its delicate arches, are painted green, but are often a golden glow in the rays of the sun, that literally takes the breath away. The view is so stunning in fact, that it's regrettably, extremely easy to forget the large rock about 150 yards off the coast, exactly in a line between Deadman's Cove and the bridge. My grandfather forgot it in Fledgling, fifty years ago. My father forgot it in Malachite, thirty years ago, and I very nearly forgot it last week! About 300 yards from its concealed location (exposed and easily avoidable at low tide) I remembered my ancestors' errors. I pulled out my iPhone, switched on Navionics, and there, *exactly* on the red line marking our instantaneous heading, was the menacing tiny red and black starburst indicating a hazard visible at all but high tide! Too shoreward to head down, my crew assisted with a rapid tack, while the Great White switched sides of the boat in his father's lap.

It's easy to forget the errors of our fathers, and the lessons they learned, especially when we are transfixed by the dazzling glow of the future before us. The Chosen People made that mistake hundreds of times over, and it led to their ultimate exile and near complete annihilation. Our elders have much to teach us, for they have made all the mistakes that lay before us already! Many eastern cultures have seemingly learned this, to their advantage. When you have the opportunity, when the pandemic finally allows it, spend time with some older people whenever you can, whether in a retirement facility or with your own parents and grandparents still living on their own. Many of the hazards of which we are blissfully unaware can be exposed by the wisdom of our elders with a little effort. History will repeat itself as reliably as the tide, if we aren't careful.

"Likewise you who are younger be subject to your elders." (1 Peter 5:5 ESV)

"Listen to advice and accept instruction, the you may gain wisdom..." (Proverbs 19:20 ESV)

"Honor your father and your mother, that your days may be long..." (Exodus 20:12 ESV)

> ***Prayer: Dear heavenly Father, let Your Spirit lead us to humility and a posture where we can be receptive to the lessons learned by our elders! Thank You for the structure of our families, that we have the opportunity to help those who come after with our own experience. AMEN***

SEPTEMBER 8

A Bear's Behind

"Ask the animals, and they will teach you, or the birds of the sky, and they will tell you; or speak to the earth, and it will teach you, or let the fish of the sea inform you. Which of these does not know that the hand of the Lord has done this? In His hand is the life of every creature and the breath of all mankind." (Job 12:7-10 NIV)

We recently returned to Coastal Maine for a week to be with another of our daughters and her family. When I sat down to write this, we had been at the cottage for only two days. Thus far, we had seen the following: bald eagle, osprey, seagull, barn owl, black backed woodpecker, gray jay, chickadee, northern raven, dove, hummingbird, chimney swift, cardinal, waxwing, meadowlark, whip-poor-will (heard), wild turkey, belted Kingfisher, loon, coot, and crab, starfish, urchin, mackerel, porpoise, harbor seal and finally deer, raccoon, porcupine, chipmunk, squirrel, field mice (in the house, not in a field), hare, and a BEAR!

My son and I were returning from Blue Hill, and came around the corner on the dirt road down to our cottage. It was 11:15 AM on a sunny , warm, day. Evidently the very large black bear we almost ran into, felt it was a good time to eat blueberries or whatever else had her in the middle of the road at that moment! Luckily, she glanced at us over her shoulder, and beat a hasty retreat down the road for about 20 yards before veering off into the thick underbrush. Andy and I were struggling to get our phones out of our respective pockets, but we were no where near fast enough.

Forty eight hours in just one rural part of America, and I saw at least thirty four different creatures, all with their unique God-given, appearance, behavior, habitat and culture. Any one of them individually, could have kept my attention for hours, but as it was, collectively, they kept me ooing and aahhing from one wonder, right to the next! Have you ever walked right behind a porcupine? It's well, hilarious! They are just not very good walkers, waddling from side to side, tail going in a circle, and in no hurry whatsoever! I guess they know their own secret pretty well! I know my brother's Labrador, Bouncer, had to have procedures under general anesthesia TWICE to remove those quills, two years in a row, before he learned their secret!

Some people look at the stars and conclude that there must be a God. Others just look around them, and reach the same conclusion. It's hard to conceive of, but I guess some people also look up at the night sky and conclude, that gee, I guess this is all random and so are we! Some I suppose, have little sense of wonder at all. Maybe city dwellers are at a disadvantage being surrounded by man-made things which totally pale in comparison to God-made things! True, they have people at which to wonder, but that just doesn't catch your attention like a bear's behind! If you don't normally have the opportunity, or you don't normally take the time, find a way to get out into nature this weekend. Even if its a bike ride, or hike in a city-surrounded nature preserve, or a park. Keep your eyes wandering and pay attention. The absolutely *miraculous surrounds you*, if you will only look for it!

You'll know when you find it, because it will make you stop and wonder as well. You'll wonder something like, "*How is that even possible?*" What you are actually feeling, is called, *awe*, and in translated biblical Hebrew, it was called, *fear.* The more you feel that 'awe' the more you will come to appreciate that the hand of the Almighty is all around you. As soon as you truly believe that, you are at the doorstep of comprehending the universe.

"The fear of the Lord is the beginning of wisdom, and knowledge of the Holy One is understanding." (Proverbs 9:10 NIV)

"God shows His anger from heaven against all sinful ,wicked people, who suppress the truth by their wickedness. They know the truth about God because He has made it obvious to them." (Romans 1:18-19 NLT)

Prayer: Dear Heavenly Father, we love You! Thank You that You have left so clear an indication of Your reality and Your presence every where we look! Encourage us to point out Your presence to others! AMEN

SEPTEMBER 9

Something Untoward

"Have I not commanded you? Be strong and courageous! Do not be afraid; do not be discouraged, for the Lord you God will be with you wherever you go." (Joshua 1:9 NIV)

I always leave for the airport early. I have mentioned this. My rationale is simple: you never know when something untoward might happen! When you are leaving the cottage in Maine for instance, you could have a flat, or run into fog, or get behind one of those impossibly slow gravel trucks, right?

Last week, my wife Pat, daughter Kelly with her husband Ian, and I, along with 3 year old grandson, Henry, headed up the dirt road to the coastal two lane at 0345 dark. Negotiating the long series of narrow, hilly, and in Henry's parlance, "squiggly" roads, to the Bangor Airport takes 75 minutes, if everything goes perfectly. Our flight to D.C. then on to Dallas took off at 0600. I drove our rented Chevy Tahoe between 40 and 65 mph for the most part, careful to have my left fingers always on the control for the bright lights. Oncoming traffic was rare at that hour, but one always had to be extremely vigilant, not only for the curves, but for the other guy who might have few good reasons to be out at that hour. My mom always claimed that "nothing good ever happens after midnight."

About 1/2 hour into our trek, I was accelerating after a yield, where our road merged into another on a curve. I was going maybe 50mph, when suddenly in the arc of those bright lights, looming out of the dark, were cables strung across the road like a 10 foot high barbed wire fence! I slammed on the brakes and we skidded to a stop with the downed power cable literally lying across our hood, and another stretched across our grill. There were sparks coming out of the trees to our left. I quickly slammed into reverse and backed out from under the cables, all of us shaken. The lines hung across the entire road and shoulders, completely obstructing any path forward or around. I hit the flashers, and only moments later, another car came up behind and thankfully pulled over rather than barreling around us to certain disaster. My son-in-law and I exited the vehicle just as another set of lights approached from the north, I reached back in and flashed our brights again while Ian waved frantically over his head to warn them. My daughter whipped a sleepy Henry out of his car seat, and with my wife, ran to the far side of the road, avoiding a potential nightmarish pile-up. Thankfully, this next on-coming car stopped in time as well, putting his flashers on for any that were to follow.

None of it made sense. There was no rain or wind, even though we had seen moments before, what I thought were flashes of lightening over the tops of the trees. The power lines hung across the road from two intact poles, but then, just as we gawked at the *top half* of a power pole hanging in mid-air back to our left, the woman from the car behind us screamed that there was something in the ditch off to that side! We ran over and there was a still smoking inverted pick up truck, wheels slowly revolving. We screamed for my wife to call 911, requesting police and an ambulance. This is *very rural Maine*, and we had no idea how long it would take for help to arrive, or even if we'd have a signal. Ian and I used light from our cell phones to climb down through the thick brush, along with the woman from the car behind us, where we discovered a truck lying on its crushed roof, windows blown out, and on hands and knees with heads inverted, we could just make out a tangled, blood soaked driver. There appeared to be no one else in the vehicle. The door was impossible to open.

The other woman stripped off her vest and laid it across the shattered glass, so Ian could crawl in through the inverted window. The driver only moaned when we tried to talk him into extricating himself. He seemed either dazed, or more likely, and correctly as it turned out, thoroughly inebriated. Somehow, my orthopedic surgeon with the metastatic lymphoma son-in-law, grabbed the driver under the arms and dragged him backwards over the inside of the roof and out into the ditch. I helped move him away from the smoking vehicle up onto the embankment. There, a quick and bloody neuro assessment assured us that he wasn't paralyzed, despite the fact that his appearance indicated he took the brunt of the impact with his now, virtually unrecognizable face.

Astoundingly, a volunteer fire fighter, flashing lights on the dash of his private truck, arrived shortly thereafter. Within another five minutes ambulance and fire truck arrived from the north, obstructed by the wires and unable to get any closer than several hundred feet. About the same time, two men drove up and asked if that was a silver Ram pick up overturned in the ditch? When we affirmed that it was, they sheepishly noted that this was their friend whom they had parted with a short time ago, and he had definitely been drinking. Ian ran up and informed the paramedics that they would need to roll a gurney under the wires to get to the injured man, but that his injuries appeared not immediately life-threatening.

Having done all that we could do, and now with multiple cars lined up on both sides of the wires, we reloaded the grandson, climbed aboard the rented Tahoe, apparently undamaged by the wires, and began searching Google maps for another way across Hancock County, since for over forty years this was the only route to the airport of which I was aware! My daughter found a circuitous route over an even smaller country road that led us back to the "main road" through Bucksport. We eventually arrived at Bangor International with 15 minutes to spare, and remarkably made our flight!

It was only a short time ago that I noted we are sometimes called upon to *be the fire extinguisher* in the face of unexpected tragedy! Certainly, my son-in-law demonstrated both super-human strength and calm, in rescuing this unfortunate man, who brought about his own near demise. Recall, that I said the *dry chemical* in our fire extinguisher is love. Ian didn't have to run down that embankment under sparking power lines to a smoldering vehicle and then risk his own life somehow dragging a 200 lb man from the wreckage on all fours. He did it for love; for love of life as a gift, for love of his fellow man, for love of right over wrong. You would be hard pressed to convince me that God didn't put Ian in our car so that *exactly* the right person would arrive first on the scene and use calm reassurance and his own medical knowledge to prevent an accident from becoming a tragedy. Even if God wasn't in the event, as we've said before, He was certainly in the response!

Our faith strengthens us for times like these because it molds us into the kind of person that God wants us to be! For my money, Ian showed us a pretty darn good *imago dei, the "image of God."*

For myself, the Lord was with me indeed, for it is truly miraculous that I saw those wires and stopped in time! You never know when something untoward might happen on the way to the airport.

Prayer: Dear Heavenly Father, we are grateful that You have given us Your Spirit and that we have the opportunity to mature into men and women who allow that Spirit of love to work through us to the benefit of others, in every situation! AMEN

SEPTEMBER 10

Acts of God

"He after all, loves each of us-good and evil, kind and cruel. He causes the sun to rise and shine on evil and good alike." (Matthew 5:45 Voice)

As I sit down to write this evening, there are over 35 wildfires burning from southern California all the way to northern Oregon. For the first time in anyone's memory, the sky over San Francisco was dark orange in the middle of the day, with smoke so thick it looked like fog obscuring views of the bridges and downtown buildings. In some parts of the Bay Area, ash swirled through he sky like snow. One national reporter filed his story from the back of a pick up rolling through a town in Oregon that simply didn't exist anymore. It was completely incinerated, cars abandoned in the middle of the road where their tires then melted to the pavement. Over 14,000 firefighters are struggling to contain the flames.

More than one person has described the fires as "apocalyptic." Insurers typically describe natural disasters as "Acts of God." The flooding in the Houston area from Hurricane Harvey was described as "flooding of Biblical proportions," and the consequent destruction as an "Act of God." Tsunamis that sweep away villages, mudslides that do the same, homes destroyed by lightening, earthquakes that swallow homes and highways, all described as "Acts of God." The implication is that these things could not have been caused by man, nor reasonably avoided by man, and therefore, no one is responsible. This of course means no one is *liable* in our incredibly litigious society. So, if you can't blame man, there's only one Guy left, right?

Anthropologists tell us that many ancient religions evolved specifically in response to natural disasters, concluding that if one worshipped and sacrificed to the correct God, perhaps disaster could be avoided in the future. Thus, Gods from those whose purview was crop growth, to battle, even to fertility, became part of the mythologies of Assyria, Greece, Egypt and Rome. If the Gods could be appeased, they could be angered as well, and people began believing that natural disasters were caused by the relevant God as punishment. Philosophers and theologians in the past used the term "natural evils," but since the scientific revolution, following the Renaissance, vengeance from multiple Gods has taken on the quality of fairytales.

Yet, as Rabbi Harold Kushner famously asked in the 80's, *"Why then do bad things happen to good people?"* There is still a reflexive response, especially in the West, that some divine force must be behind tragic events, and certainly tragic events on the scale of a tsunam, earthquake or pandemic! But it doesn't take very long for many who examine the question of God's culpability in all this, to notice that natural disasters seem not to discriminate between the innocent and the guilty!

What then is the answer? The answer is what that old Russian Babushka said on *Call the Midwife,* which we alluded to last month: "God is less in the events than He is in the response." When someone in the crowd asked Christ what sin had been committed by those crushed under the falling tower in Siloam, or what evil had those Galileans committed, who were butchered by Pilate while worshipping, Christ responded that they had done nothing to deserve their horrific deaths. It just happened. (Luke 13:1-5) When He was teaching about loving your neighbors in the Sermon on the Mount, Christ pointed out that God causes the sun to shine on the evil and the good alike, and causes the rain to water the fields of the righteous and the fields of the sinner. (Matthew 5:45)

So when there is flooding along the Mississippi or in the Gulf, when there are wildfires engulfing the West Coast, when there's a tsunami that threatens Hawaii, when there's an earthquake in San Francisco, or even when there's a viral pandemic wreaking havoc across the globe, God is more likely in *our response,* than in the event. Christ tells us repeatedly that God is love, and we have only to love God and love our neighbor with everything we've got, to have met the demands of the Greatest Commandment . (Mark 12:29-31) That means when trouble comes to good people, the rest of us need to help.

When you see pictures of the devastation wrought by fire on the West Coast, don't shake your head and wonder why God would allow it, wonder instead how Christ would have you be one of his witnesses, and help those affected.

Prayer: Dear Heavenly Father, we love You and we KNOW that You love us! Let Your Spirit guide us when we become misguided, and decide to blame You for our fallen world's disasters, or blame those affected for whatever sin they must have committed to bring this on, for Your Son told us Himself that this is not the way it works! Remind us of JOB ONE: LOVE EACH OTHER. AMEN

SEPTEMBER 11

Remember What?

"Only give heed to yourself and keep yourself diligently, so that you do not forget the things that your eyes have seen and they do not depart from your heart all the days of your life; and make them known to your sons and grandsons." (Deuteronomy 4:9 NIV)

It is hard to believe that as of this writing, any young person under 24 has no memory of the horrors of 9/11, and probably anyone under about 30 has no clear memory of the events surrounding it. (I noticed last year, that the 79th anniversary of Pearl Harbor went virtually unmentioned on any of the US news broadcasts for December 7th.) The danger of course, lies in the forgetting of history.

We are living through a tumultuous time in America, with the Pandemic dragging on, the economy suffering, political vitriol like we have never known, widespread demonstrations over racism largely overshadowed by the violence interjected by those that would destroy our republic and replace it with anarchy. Certainly since my birth in the mid-50's, we have never known division like this, even during the anti-war demonstrations that eventually brought an ignominious close to the Vietnam War and shortly thereafter to the resignation of a President.

Now, more than ever, we need to remember Pearl Harbor, remember 9/11, and not in order to focus on our amoral enemies who would kill and destroy in a mis-guided attempt to advance their own culture or religion, but in order to focus on the aftermaths! In the words attributed to General Isoroku Yamamoto in the closing scene of the film *Tora, Tora, Tora!* *"I fear all we have done is to awaken a sleeping giant and fill him with a terrible resolve!"*

That resolve is the outcome of national tragedy that makes those events the lynchpins of history, not the loss of lives, tragic though they may be. What we need is people to remember 2020 as the time when the country pulled together to help each other through the economic chaos in the wake of the Pandemic; to remember 2020 as the time when all Americans acknowledged that prejudices remain in society and we needed to redouble our efforts to continue the remarkable progress that had already come about in race relations since the mid 20th century; to remember 2020 as the time when Americans stopped assassinating each other's characters because of their political stances, and instead started listening *to all ideas* and then compromising whenever necessary to bring about a more perfect union!

Moses understood the importance of history, the importance of passing on the wisdom born of previous failures and subsequent triumphs! As we remember 9/11 and mourn for those who were lost and for those who lost loved ones, let us also remember that like Pearl Harbor, the towers collapsing did indeed fill us with a terrible resolve, and the domestic reflection of that was a uniting, a patriotic resurgence that brought us all together as Americans, overlooking our racial, ethnic, religious and political divides and instead viewing our phenomenal diversity, seen no where else in the world, as our greatest strength!!

Prayer: Dear Heavenly Father, we love You! Just as You have written Your law on our hearts as Jeremiah tells us, inscribe in our hearts the memory of the feeling when we all pull together for a common goal! That unity opens channels for the expression of love for our fellow man which have been closed by rancor and division. AMEN

SEPTEMBER 12

Full of Trouble

"Man who is born of woman, is of few days and full of trouble. He comes forth like a flower and fades away; he flees like a shadow and does not continue." (Job 14:1-2 NKJV)

In the last few years I have had the following occur in my extended family and close friends at church: death from metastatic pancreatic cancer, squamous cell cancer of the ear canal and of the eyelid, a fatal fall from a motorcycle, a broken wrist, a broken hip, cancer of the thyroid, metastatic lymphoma, a fatal car wreck, death after a fall, death from metastatic breast cancer, hip replacements, liver failure and transplant, a baby with a major chromosomal error, death from complications of heart surgery, death from ALS/Parkinson's disease, loss of a business, wealth to poverty, loss of jobs, and the list could well go on and on.

The remarkable thing is that any one reading this could undoubtedly make a similar list just from their "inner circle." This life is full of trouble indeed; always has been and always will be. Once the new Christian gets over the "honeymoon" period in their love of Jesus, they rapidly discover that all of what He taught us is true, including the fact that this life will be painful and full of sacrifice! Life does not become a bed of roses for the believer, unless you want to consider it similar to walking barefoot through that bed and enduring the thorns!

But, if our days were not full of trouble, if we didn't realize that our loved ones are only on loan, if prosperity followed us continually, if there "were not at least a few clouds in the sky," as Charles Spurgeon used to say, we would certainly begin to do exactly what Christ warned us against: we could too easily start to love the things of this world! The recognition that we are not above adversity will keep us humble, and humility you will recall, is precisely what God requires of us! (Micah 6:8) Every time man decides that he can "do it himself" and has "no need of God," he invariably proves himself a fool. Both our prosperity and our health are, unfortunately, transient. *"Naked I came from my mother's womb, and naked I will depart. the Lord gave and the Lord has taken away; the name of the Lord be praised!"* (Job 1:21 NIV) *"Do not store up for yourselves treasures on earth, where moth and vermin destroy, and where thieves break in and steal. But store up for yourselves treasures in heaven…"* (Matthew 6:19-20 NIV)

All of us have a tendency to see affliction as our trials in this life, but prosperity and good fortune, perpetually, can be a "fiery trial" in themselves according to Charles Spurgeon: *"Affliction, though they seem severe, In mercy oft are sent."* Recall the DOING LIFE on the song *Blessings*, by Laura Story. *"We pray for blessings, we pray for peace, comfort for family, protection while we sleep. We pray for healing, prosperity. We pray for Your mighty hand to ease our suffering. But all the while You hear each spoken need, but love us way too much to give us less of things. But what if Your Blessing comes through raindrops, what if Your healing comes through tears? What if a thousand sleepless nights are what it takes to know You're near? What if trials of this life are Your mercies in disguise?"*

Don't let this be a downer. It's a spiritual reality check! **If you are living your life confident that you have no need of any help, really from anyone, because you've got it under control; well, you're for in for a shock, one of these days.** Our Savior is all about relationship. He wants You to trust Him with your losses and trust Him with your wins! It's all a gift remember? Job had that part right for sure. Remember, it's not so much that God is in the events that befall you, it's that through you, your response can be a light to others; a light that directs them to Him!

If you're in the midst of a bad time in this 2020 Pandemic year, if the hits just seem to keep on coming, thank God that His offer is eternal! We are promised a life of no more tears, no more sadness, forever! That's a good deal! I'd seriously consider taking Him up on the offer if you haven't thus far!

Prayer: Dear Heavenly Father, we love You! We trust that You want only what is best for us, even if it doesn't seem good for us at the time! The disease that leads to resolve, the poverty that leads to perseverance, the loss that leads to a new appreciation for what we do have; all are gifts from above, Blessings in disguise! AMEN

SEPTEMBER 13

Puppy Training

"Love suffers long and is kind, love does not envy; love does not parade itself, is not puffed up; does not behave rudely, does not seek its own, is not provoked, thinks no evil; does not rejoice in iniquity, but rejoices in truth; bears all things, hopes all things, endures all things. Love never fails." (1 Corinthians 13:4-8 NKJV)

We were supposed to pick up our new Labradoodle puppy today, but due to my call schedule, we can't make the trip to Houston until September 24th. Both my wife and I are excited, although should it all go south, this is decidedly my fault! Her contention was that our four year old Tuxedo cat was a *compromise*, not a *step*. (We lost our dachshund and our shepherd mix within six weeks of each other about five years ago.) Out of sacrificial love for me, and in order to make me *just stop it,* she finally acquiesced.

Be that as it may, I have now read four puppy training books in the last few weeks, including those by Cesar Millan, the Monks of New Skete, and Claudia Kaiser. They have extremely similar approaches, founded on a dog's "pack mentality," and the mutual love and respect in the optimum man-dog relationship.

My daily "ah ha moment" occurred while reviewing the bullet points I had made during my reading! (I was a medical student: we highlight, underline *and* make notes when reading *anything!)* The puppy training bullet points and the famous love passage in 1 Corinthians, read very similarly. Not in the same order or exact wording, but still. Hmmmmm, mutual love and respect! Go figure!

Take these for example:

1) BONDING: go for long exploratory walks together, side by side

2) HOUSE BREAKING: Never scold for an accident; just clean up with no comment (human variant applies to any minor mess ups at home)

3) NAME ONLY: associate NAME only with praise, or to get other's attention

4) FEED: one person prepares, other holds back; when bowl is set down, then call out COME.

5) SIT/LAY DOWN: hold treat above nose and say SIT as he does it, then lower treat slowly right in front of his nose onto massage or exercise table, he will lay down, as you say lay down. (Human application: use your imagination)

6) BITING: Stop game immediately and walk away; be sure to make up 30 minutes later

7) RESTLESSNESS: quiet petting in crate (bed) and say EASY softly

8) RIDING IN CAR: always assist into the car, but never lift hind legs (Human application: Okay, maybe just the first part)

9) WALKING ON A LEASH: when walking together, if puppy starts to pull ahead, stand still and say nothing until leash relaxes; say SLOWLY and then proceed together. (Human application....skip the leash entirely)

10) DESTRUCTIVENESS: keep fragile things out of reach; if caught in the act, grab puppy and go elsewhere to play favorite game or give favorite toy. If destructive when left alone, be sure adequate exercise given twice/day.

11) COME: attract attention with excitement in your voice and body language; say COME HERE as he approaches, then give treat! Practice at successively further distances

12) STAY: body language and voice should be peaceful; have puppy sit. Stand still right in front of him for a moment, then praise and give treat. Make sure he gets rewarded for staying. Gradually increase time and distance: walk up and down next to him, walk in a semicircle, then a circle, then eventually out of sight. He should be lying down for this level.

13) LEAVE IT: when you want him to drop something, never try to take it away by force; offer him an attractive exchange instead. When he finally drops it, say LEAVE IT and give him the toy or treat. NEVER run after him or he will refuse to drop it and treat it as prey!

14) BARKING: when he/she starts barking DO NOT YELL or respond! Wait for him/her to STOP barking and then give a treat immediately! Never respond to a barking dog, only to his/her cessation of barking.

15) HEEL: proceed together and entice puppy to the side you desire with a treat held at your side; when puppy goes for the treat walk quickly forward and say HEEL! After a few meters have him sit, and give him the treat. (Human application: avoid the actual voice command HEEL!)

15) OVERALL TRAINING: remember everything you do is "training" to your puppy! Remain consistent in the signals and body language you give. Mutual respect is the key to the relationship. LISTEN to what your puppy is telling you by gradually improving your understanding of the dog's language. Remember, the dog doesn't actually speak your language. She/he is much more attuned to scents, body language, emotional tone, and only after all that, words.

Enough said.

"I would like to be with you right now and change my tone of voice, because I don't know what to do about you." (Galatians 4:20 NIV)

"Speak evil of no one, avoid quarreling, be gentle, show perfect courtesy toward all people." (Titus 3:2 ESV)

"A soft answer turns away wrath, but a harsh word stirs up anger." (Proverbs 15:1 ESV)

"But the fruit of the Spirit is love, joy, peace, patience, kindness, goodness, faithfulness, gentleness, self-control..." (Galatians 5:22-23 ESV)

Prayer: Dear Heavenly Father, why is it we read books on how to treat 'man's best friend' and yet fail to realize that You gave us our 'best friend' in the Garden, when you gave us our mates! Few people put the degree of intensity and study and preparation into loving their mates well, as they do into how to love their dogs! The principles of mutual love and respect that flow from the Spirit, catalogued in both 1 Corinthians and Galatians 5, apply to all members of the 'pack!' AMEN

SEPTEMBER 14

Sorry for the Convenience

"Watson, come at once if convenient. If inconvenient, come all the same!" (Arthur Conan Doyle as Sherlock Holmes)

This morning I had entered the hospital ground floor planning on rounds on the 4th and 5th floor. The staff elevators were sitting ominously, with their doors already open, no indicator lit by the button outside, no hint of recent activity. I walked into the right one hesitantly, (not really liking elevators, even when I know they are working) and pressed '5.' Nothing. Then I pushed that cryptic hieroglyph for 'close.' Again, nothing. Not even a lit button on contact. A lab tech walked on and I said, none of the buttons do anything. She said, 'Hmmm,' and then tried multiple buttons herself. (*Really?*) Same result. We then proceeded to the public elevators on the other side. Nope. The patients on 4 and 5 were evidently doomed to live out the rest of their lives in the Perot Women's and Children's Hospital.

She walked away, but I tried my badge on the electronic door lock to the stairwell. *Voila! A way up!* The late comedian Mitch Hedberg, had a joke about a broken escalator. He said he ran into one at the subway and there was a sign across the bottom that said, *"Out of Order. Sorry for the inconvenience!"* Inconvenience? The escalator just **became** stairs! How cool is that? The sign should say *"Sorry for the convenience!"* I was inconvenienced by the elevator not functioning, but I neglected to be grateful for the staircase! The stairs offered me much neglected, but needed exercise. It offered me a few moments of quiet to contemplate the day ahead. It offered me a way to get where I was going, protected from the brutal heat outside. In short, what a God-send the stairs were!

We are so conditioned to instant gratification that we forget to be grateful for the blessings all around us! We have to *wait* three minutes for the microwave? The rental car's sound system won't pair to my bluetooth and I have to *find* a radio station by turning a dial? The cottage in Maine has no electricity, so I have to *build a fire* to keep warm? There's a DETOUR on your route to work and you have to drive two miles out of your way, throwing your planned schedule off by multiple minutes? OUTRAGEOUS!! Its enough to raise your blood pressure, up your pulse, what a hassle!

Modern inconveniences would hardly be considered as such, only a few years ago! After all, recall that my grandmother was *most grateful* for both hot and cold running water actually *inside* the house! Little high tech things that don't work have taken on the descriptor as 'First World Problems,' and so they are. The next time you suffer the outrage of having to stop the **microwave**, puncture the film covering, and heat for yet *another* two minutes, you might be grateful that you don't have to go wring the chicken's neck and then de-feather it, before building a fire, hauling the water from the stream, boiling it and cooking it, as just the *first step* to a complete meal!

So, sorry for the convenience! These first world problems help us learn to be grateful for the bigger things, developing that patience part of the Fruits of the Spirit, and controlling our anger! Look at inconvenience as divine opportunity!

"Patience is a virtue, possess it if you can, seldom found in woman, never found in man!"

"Rejoice in hope, be patient in tribulation, be constant in prayer." (Romans 12:12 ESV)

"Be angry, but do not sin; ponder in your own hearts on your beds..." (Psalm 4:4-5 ESV)

"Whoever is slow to anger has great understanding, but he who has a hasty temper exalts folly. (Proverbs 14:29 ESV)

Prayer: Dear Heavenly Father, we love You! Let the little frustrations we encounter every day, the little inconveniences, be a reminder of Your great mercies and a lesson for our attitudes! AMEN

SEPTEMBER 15

No Internet

"If then you were raised [from the dead] with Christ, seek those things which are above, where Christ is, sitting at the right hand of God. Set your mind on things above, not on things on earth." (Colossians 3:1-8 NKJV)

After my usual morning ablutions and exercise, my routine is to make final edits on this devotional, transfer them to email, and then send them to you! Unless, as happens from time to time, there is no internet. The usual confusion ensued a few mornings back: there was a strong wifi signal, but no internet attached to it. Discussion with wife followed. The functioning modem displays a green light, conveniently located by the floor boards underneath the chess table in my office. The light on the modem was a non reassuring red. The modem restarted after it was unplugged and then plugged back in, and the only effect was the red light turning white…and then… back to red, all while I was on all fours on the hard wood floor in my underwear. (It gets harder with age to attain this position and then the upright position, even after doing Tai Chi.) My wife texted me at the hospital thirty minutes later that she had fixed the problem using her phone to go to the internet providers' website. The light was green again.

We are all so used to cellular service on our phones which automatically kicks in when there is no wifi signal, that losing internet signal to my iMAC, which has no cellular connectivity, borders on a national emergency for me! The significant editing I had done on that particular morning, led to a final draft that could not be emailed as mentioned, but also couldn't be transferred to my iPhone for transmission, for the same reason! I took a picture of the screen with my phone, then copied the changes into the appropriate file on the phone, using big fingers on little keys for quite a few minutes, and then used the phone to copy and paste into gmail, and then sent it from my phone to you guys.

Connectivity, it would appear, is important for humans in society! It is especially important for people of faith. The remarkable thing about the power of the indwelling Spirit, which we are given by Grace, when we hear and believe the Gospel, is that we as believers are *always connected to the Lord*, even when we feel like we aren't! You can pray silently whenever and wherever you find yourself. But if you are really feeling disconnected and out of sorts, then follow the advice of scripture and find a quiet place (Matthew 6:33), maybe right after getting up in the morning. (Psalm 63:1) Read a short passage from the Bible out loud. Often the Psalms, the Gospels, or the epistles of the New Testament, are best when you feel far from God. Read the passage several times until something in it strikes you. Then take a few moments to think about why God thought it important that you understand whatever caught your attention. Once you've thought about it, pray. Tell the Lord what you're thinking. Ask Him to clarify your thoughts and trust Him to direct your path for the rest of the day. Ask Him to empower you through the Holy Spirit to be a light to the world for Him today. Thank Him. Tell Him why you love Him.

When you take time to re-connect, you can turn the light from red back to green! And you know what that means: it's go time!

"O God, You are my god; Early will I seek You; My soul thirsts for You…" (Psalm 63:1 NKJV)

"I have called upon You, for You will hear me, O God…show me Your marvelous lovingkindness by Your right hand…(Psalm 17:6 NKJV)

"Do you not know that you are God's temple and that God's Spirit dwells in you?" (1 Corinthians 3:16 ESV)

Prayer: Dear Heavenly Father, we love You! Thank You that You have chosen to dwell within us through Your Spirit, so that we can never truly be disconnected from You and Your Son! It is indeed a wonderful feeling to know that we are never alone! AMEN

SEPTEMBER 16

Mathematics

"Woe to those who call evil good and good evil, who put darkness for light and light for darkness, who put bitter for sweet and sweet for bitter..." (Isaiah 5:20 NKJV)

My father always taught me there was a right way and a wrong way. He meant both a correct way to do a thing, and also a correct way to think about things. In short, he espoused the belief that wrong and right, are in fact *not* in the eye of the beholder, but clear in their meaning from both a theological and an ethical standpoint. In a way, ethics is like math. Two X two will *always* equal four. You can't just decide that it equals five from your own perspective, for the simple reason *that 2 X 2 doesn't equal five.*

When I was taking physics at Rice University, we were often challenged to work out a problem's solution mathematically, demonstrating how to arrive at the correct answer, which was a given. When your calculations failed to reach that known correct answer, you went back, found your error, corrected it, and then proceeded to complete the equation required. That means by definition, that going back and correcting your error was the *progressive* thing to do, even though you went *back to do it!*

We live in an angry, frightened, mis-guided America today, whose citizens have been duped in large part, into believing that light is dark and dark is light, if you simply want it to be! This is what our college professors advocate as *moral relativism,* and to some extent, it finds its recent roots in the self-focused "I'm okay, You're okay," perspective of the late 1960's. People started equating civil disobedience of misguided government policy with resistance to all authority, from parents, to teachers, to the church, to local, state and federal authority. It became mainstream to believe that seeking after your individual ambition and desires was paramount, even to the exclusion of the common good.

In fact, It's *never okay* to burn down other people's businesses, break their store fronts and loot them, beat up individuals in the streets, vandalize public buildings, or even to tear down statues that belong to the public, even if you are angry about an injustice or a history of injustice. Anyone who believes that such action is okay, is in fact an anarchist, and has no place in a society based on law, order and due process. Believing that wanton destruction and injury is morally justified, is simply *not right.* (Titus 3:1-2)

Charles Colson, the famous Watergate conspirator turned Christian evangelist and prison reformer, contended that Harvard University was incapable of actually teaching Ethics, because they had abandoned a belief system based on the existence of absolute truth, and thus right and wrong for them had become only relative, dictated by appearances and consequences. Western civilization has enjoyed 23 centuries of progress founded on belief in a transcendent system, even if not always Judeo-Christian, but which guided our conduct. But after the thoughts of Camus and Sartre entered American consciousness in the mid 20th century, with the contention that God is dead, life is meaningless, and right and wrong are relative, then the only route to peace and happiness became *experiential*, entirely through one's own efforts. Relativism and individualism then saturated American College campuses, and the beliefs of its graduates.

But the truth is that *gratification of self leads to the inevitable destruction of character.* The social contract unravels. Colson often pointed out that if there are no shared values, there can be no ethics.

When you watch the news on TV or an app on your phone, or heaven forbid, actually read a newspaper, pay attention to the way in which individual desires, goals, preferences, and actions are presented. Self concern, whether in 'news' or advertising, saturates the airwaves and is always portrayed as virtuous. Valor, honor, compassion, self-sacrifice, find little or no place in the news-feed.

True *progressive thought* does not lead to dismantling the institutions of society, in a mis-guided worship of self, for that leads to chaos, destruction and anarchy. We know this, because *it has always done so in the past! True* progressive thought is going back to the foundation of those institutions, finding those things that we can all agree upon were errors as a society, and then working together to correct any mistakes we might have made in our calculations. Ethics isn't philosophy, it's arithmetic!

"Likewise, you who are younger, be subject to your elders. Clothe yourselves, all of you , with humility toward one another, for God opposes the proud but gives grace to the humble." (1 Peter 5:5 ESV)

"Do not be deceived, bad company ruins good morals." (1 Corinthians 15:33 ESV)

"For whoever knows the right thing to do and fails to do it, for him it is sin." (James 4:17 ESV)

Prayer: Dear Heavenly Father, we love You! Let Your Spirit guide us to demonstrate our love for You by loving others. Help us to recognize, that loving others means doing what is right, and teaching our children to recognize what is right and what is wrong is our obligation. Thank You that You have written Your law on the hearts of man so that there can be no excuse for evil, because all mankind knows what it looks like. AMEN

SEPTEMBER 17

In the Eye of the Hurricane

"Rejoice in hope, be patient in tribulation, be constant in prayer." (Romans 12:12 ESV)

I made rounds a few days ago on all my partners' patients, including my own, since it was the weekend, and that is our routine. As an ObGyn, visiting in-patients can mean joyous postpartum visits with their new baby in the room, anxious postpartum visits with their new baby in NICU, or devastated postpartum visits with a stillbirth. Antepartum patients may just be waiting to deliver with pre-eclampsia or diabetes, or premature rupture of the membranes; or even bigger problems. Gynecology patients usually just had a major surgery. So weekend rounds run the full gamut of possibilities.

That morning I visited with a partner's patient, admitted months prior to her due date, with a baby not growing well due to a rare genetic syndrome that, if it survives, will have some varying degree of cognitive disability, certain brain defects, autism, cranio-facial abnormalities including cleft lip and palate, dwarfism, and some degree of blindness, just to name some of the features.

Her husband was absent, and there could be no family gathered due to the never-ending pandemic of 2020. I knocked on the door, pushed it open slowly and found her sitting up in bed, laptop on top of her lap, oddly enough! She gave me a cheery hello, and I introduced myself. We talked about the current state of her fetus' evaluation, the different teams of physicians involved, the uncertainty of outcome but the certainty of significant difficulties. Her moveable meal table had both a bible and a daily devotional sitting on top of other papers. While obviously anxious about next steps, possible outcomes, variable timing, future effects on their family and time, (they have a toddler at home,) she clearly was realistic about the severity of the situation but hoping for the best! Both the number of bookmarks and the state of the cover communicated that the bible was anything but ornamental to her.

When I left her, the verse above occurred to me. Here was a couple in the eye of the hurricane! Swirling around them a world-wide pandemic, a needy toddler at home, a baby on the way with guaranteed severe problems, and those were only the things that I knew of! Here was a circumstance that all would categorize as legitimate for the category of tribulation. Yet everything about her demeanor and discussion indicated a hope that was clearly tempered by realism. And finally, I have no doubt that this couple was in constant prayer and I hope there were other family and friends praying consistently as well. Of course God knows our needs before we voice them because He sees into the heart. (1 Samuel 16:7; Matthew 6:8,) But it's also clear that He fervently wants our prayers. Why? Because He knows it's good for us and it builds our relationship with Him, which is what it's all about, in the final analysis. Hope and prayer. Both good things to cling to in the eye of a hurricane, when you have a Savior that can calm the sea with a word!

"For the Lord sees not as a man sees: man looks at the outward appearance, but the Lord looks on the heart." (1 Samuel 16:7 ESV)

"For the Father knows the things you have need of before you ask Him." (Matthew 6:8 NKJV)

"'Why are you fearful o you of little faith?' Then He arose and rebuked the winds and the sea and there was great calm." (Matthew 8:26 NKJV)

Prayer: Dear Heavenly Father, we love You! We trust You! We know that You see into our hearts and will arrange things to work together for good for all of those who love You, even if on Your timetable and not ours! AMEN

SEPTEMBER 18

Brand New Life

"They say a person needs just three things to be truly happy in this world: someone to love, something to do, and something to hope for." (Tom Bodett)

We are going down to Houston to pick up our new labradoodle puppy next week! Between my wife and I, we have had 13 dogs over our 64 years, all of whom have been rescues of one sort or another, except for one little pure bred Dachshund we had for 12 years. Our new labradoodle is from a breeder, but there is intentionality: we have grandchildren with allergies, we'd like to skip the shedding, and well, we're 64, and we wanted to have the breeder pick the "calm" one from the litter!

But despite having had four children and three grandchildren, we are *almost* as excited at this impending arrival! (Sterling, the cat, seems somewhat less so.) The breeder sent a video, and from that data and her description, we have named the little guy *Windsor*. We are a sailing family, and the word was used in Old English as a place name for a location with a "windless." The windless, among other things, is used to weigh anchor when a sailing vessel is getting underway. Windsor also happens to be the name of the House of Windsor, of which the much admired Queen Elizabeth II is a representative, as well as the name of several towns in the Labrador/Newfoundland/Nova Scotia region of Canada, where my wife's Scottish ancestors arrived, and of course, where Labrador Retrievers originated!

What the *heck* is it about *puppies* that just melts the hearts of even the most jaded individuals? Is it their innocence while still having a penchant for mischief? Is it their sheer cuteness and playfulness? Is it their need for care and protection and guidance? Is it the knowledge that they will grow to reward a caring owner with unconditional love, affection, and loyalty? Is it all of these? I think a new puppy fulfills all of Tom Bodett's criteria for true happiness. Puppies are definitely someone *to **love***; training them is without a doubt, a very big something ***to do***; and finally that long term unconditional love relationship, is clearly something ***to hope for***!

I've had this exact same feeling before! No, it actually wasn't at the impending birth of children or grandchildren, as wonderful as those were and no doubt, will be again, in the future. Now, don't judge me, but *this is the feeling I had as a new Christian in college, forty-five years ago!* Being "born again' is truly a mystery. It's the same confounding phenomenon that perplexed the Pharisee, Nicodemus, such that he asked Jesus how a man could possibly be born again when he was old? (John 3:1-16) Jesus' response, that in order to see the Kingdom of Heaven one must be born of the water and the Spirit, has led to many interpretations, two of the most accepted being 1) that "water" birth means biological birth, and Spiritual birth means the gift of salvation in Christ or 2) the "water" birth refers to John the Baptist's ministry in baptism and Spirit refers to the indwelling of the Holy Spirit of Christ. Either way, the old self dies with Christ the man, and the new self is raised with Christ the Lord, indwelling! (Galatians 2:20)

What greater ***hope*** is there than eternal life, resurrection from the dead? What greater ***love*** is there than the sacrifice of God's child to save the whole world? (John 3:16) What greater work ***to do*** is there than to spread the good news of the Gospel through loving our fellow man and telling him why we do?

Tom Bodett is exactly my age. He's an author, actor and radio personality, and I know nothing of his personal beliefs. But I can tell you that his philosophy of happiness fits right in with the hope that we Christians espouse! No ***wonder we're so excited about the coming of Windsor!***

Prayer: Dear Heavenly Father, we truly love You!! Use Your Holy Spirit within us to rekindle that excitement at the prospect of new life! Remind us of the joy that awaits us no matter our trials on earth! Thank you that You reminded me with something as simple as the arrival of a new puppy!! AMEN

SEPTEMBER 19

It's Evitable

"Our new constitution is now established, and has an appearance that promises permanency; but in this world nothing can be said to be certain except death and taxes." (Benjamin Franklin)

I participate in a fair amount of WWF (not World Wrestling Federation, but Words With Friends!) One of the things I, and my most frequent opponents, have learned, is that occasionally, you find yourself so hopelessly behind, even with many letters left, that your demise is unavoidable. In short, you Resign, because the outcome is *inevitable*. Many games have this aspect as a common accompaniment of the competition, whether chess, poker, or boxing. Deadly competitions, known as wars, have this as a feature as well, demonstrated by millennia of surrenders from General Cornwallis in the American Revolution, General Lee in our own Civil War, to the Japanese and Nazis in WW II. Surrender comes when the realization of the inevitable, makes the further loss of life even more absurd than the rationale for the original combat!

In modern language however, we almost always hear the negative form of the adjective. *Evitable* is just as much of a word, and means exactly the opposite of *inevitable*. Evitable means *avoidable*. Benjamin Franklin might indeed be correct about taxes. Avoiding them can lead to one enjoying years of solitude at the government's expense, in which to contemplate the folly of tax fraud!

No, it's the other half of the assumption that is in fact incorrect! *Death is totally evitable!* This is the basis of the hope to which Christians hold; that is, the promise of eternal life! (John 3:16) For the believer, this is not merely a fairytale, but a reality founded upon historical observation of the Risen Christ, (1 Corinthians 15:6) and upon the Word left for us, that records God's Promise of Salvation as a free gift for those who turn to Him in faith! (Ephesians 2:8-9; Acts 16:30-31; Acts 4:12; John 5:24)

When absolutely everything seems to be going wrong; when you feel like, if it weren't for bad luck, you'd have no luck at all; when you've lost a loved one, a friend, a job, a relationship; this is when the followers of Christ put their faith on display. This is when those who know Jesus as Savior, are buoyed up by His unfailing love, His permanence, His strength, His compassion, His righteousness, and His promise of bringing us home to the place where there are no tears and no sorrow!

So, sorry, Benjamin! I love your sayings almost as much as those of G.K. Chesterton and Winston Churchill, but you only get partial credit on this one, dude!

Prayer: Dear Heavenly Father, we love You, because You first loved us! Thank you that You demonstrated this love for us through Your Son Jesus Christ, and in so doing, removed the curse of death from those of us who have faith! Thank You that you have made that end that many men fear completely evitable! AMEN

SEPTEMBER 20

Coming Home

'The rains came down, the streams rose, and the winds blew and beat agains the house; yet it did not fall, because it had its foundation on the rock." (Matthew 7:25 NIV)

We arrived back in Dallas after a week in rural Maine visiting my mom, (in her nineties and still building her own fires, cooking her own meals, walking the dirt road, caring for her little dog), and sailing with other relatives for a peaceful, much cooler week.

But while we were there, Hurricane Laura slammed into the Texas-Louisiana Coast as a Category 4 storm, outpacing even Katrina from fifteen years ago. While landfall was in marshy, less populated areas, small cities like Lake Charles were devastated. Still, life goes on. On the SkyLink from our arriving terminal to the one at which we had parked on departure, we spoke with a woman and her teenage daughter. I had noted that the teen's shoe was untied and the trailing laces *almost* became trapped in the teeth of the escalator as we approached the train level, and this initiated our conversation.

The mom said they lived in Lake Charles, and when the time came to evacuate they had moved to a shelter in a high school. They had grabbed a few possessions as they hurried out the door, but had inadvertently left the daughter's new iPhone behind! After the storm passed, they had tried to fly out, but the airport was destroyed and closed indefinitely, so they just kept on driving to Dallas, where FEMA had directed them. She cheerfully related all of this, including the fact that her home had a tree on it, "well, through it, actually," and they would just deal with it when they got home! She was at DFW Int'l to get her daughter on a plane to see her dad in St. Louis. "The good Lord saw us through alright! Just another adventure!"

We were struck by her attitude. In a time when people are even more tense than usual, liable to explode into road rage for someone who cuts them off in traffic, or go off on somebody because they weren't wearing a mask (recall Pandemic 2020), this woman viewed the destruction of her home as a *blessing* because they were all safe.

You see Christ wasn't talking about an actual structure in Matthew 7, He was talking about *attitude,* an attitude of faith! Faith in the unfailing love and eternal promises of the Savior, keep your life and your family's foundation secure. Home is where the heart is, right? If your heart is Jesus' home, Jesus the cornerstone, then you have built your life on the rock, and a little thing like a Category 4 Hurricane can't even touch it!

Prayer: Dear Heavenly Father, We love You! How simple and joyful and peaceful our lives could all be if we would only build our homes, set our hearts, on the Rock! AMEN

SEPTEMBER 21

The Good Shepherd

"...just say the word and my servant will be healed. For I am also a man under authority, with soldiers under me; and I say to this one, 'Go!' and he goes..." (Matthew 8:8-9 NASB)

Recently, I was reading C.S. Forrester's 1955 classic, *The Good Shepherd.* I knew it would be excellent, because as a boy who grew up in a sailing family, I had read all of the famous *Horatio Hornblower* series by the same author. But the real impetus for picking up this novel of historical fiction, was the recently released 'major motion picture' as they say, entitled *Greyhound,* produced, directed and starred in, by Tom Hanks. It is based closely on the 1955 novel. Hanks wanted to do justice to the so called *Battle of the Atlantic,* perhaps the most critical and longest contested theatre of WW II, but to date, the least depicted in popular media.

Hanks plays the American U.S. Navy Commander, George Krause, a 42 year old experienced officer, but as yet untested in battle, in command of the USS Keeling. She was the flagship of an international four destroyer escort, which was tasked with guarding a 32 ship supply convoy. The menagerie of different ships, varied in size, configuration and speed, was crossing the Atlantic to the British, who in 1942 were desperate for fuel, food, medical supplies and clothing. Unfortunately for the Allies, the Nazi submarines, known to hunt in what were referred to as 'wolf packs,' lurked beneath the surface, waiting to pounce on any allied ship, sending a series of torpedoes that could and often did, send huge supply ships and their doomed crews, plummeting toward the frigid, dark, bottom of the Atlantic ocean, over two miles below the furious waves of the surface.

Krause was a deeply religious man, not only praying on his knees by his bunk every morning and evening, but frequently calling scripture to mind in the course of each and every pitching, rolling, grey, freezing spray, of a North Atlantic day. A radar contact, 15 miles in the distance, representing a possible Nazi U-boat on the surface for air and battery recharge, brought to mind 1 Peter 5:8. "*Be sober, be vigilant; because your adversary the devil, as a roaring lion, walks about, seeking whom he may devour...*" Vigilance was brutally difficult with exhausted crews, and too few destroyers, and yet, if neglected for a moment, could lead to the deaths of hundreds in a moment.

The young Commander gave radio orders quickly, authoritatively, positioning both his shepherds and the sheep they sought to protect, despite the knowledge that the other destroyers were Polish, British and Canadian, and captained by older men, who had all been in battle, whereas he had not. He marveled at their devotion to duty, and our opening excerpt crossed his mind. It was an excerpt from the story of the centurion in Matthew 8. The young Roman commander from Capernaum, had a servant lying paralyzed at home, and sought Jesus' intervention. When the Lord offered to follow him home, the centurion famously refused, saying that as a military man under orders, he knew that when he gave an order it was followed, and the Centurion believed in his heart that Christ had power over life itself, and merely needed to say the word and it would be done, even without Jesus' physical presence at the servant's bedside.

The other captains had faith in him, in the unified chain of command, in the power of the Allies, working together to defeat the closest enemy to Satan himself that the world had ever known. Their obedience was complete, without hesitation, without thought to their own peril, because *they trusted in the Good Shepherd* who commanded the USS Keeling. Krause too would put his trust in His own commander, Jesus Christ, and do so over and over, despite the horrific vicissitudes of battle on the high seas.

We all face hardships every day, some small, some nearly overwhelming. We've been given the Holy Spirit to dwell within, and if we'll allow Him, He will bolster us against temptation, lead us away from the crouching lion waiting to pounce, and remind us of the centurion's faith, immediate, unhesitating, and confident, that the Good Shepherd with just a word, can see us through!

Prayer: Dear Heavenly Father, we love You! Part of that is trusting You, even when the wolf pack gathers in the gloom. One word from You, and the devil will flee! One word from You, and no matter if life in this world continues, our home with You is never ending and persists right there on the other side of our last breath! AMEN

SEPTEMBER 22

I Believe in Me

"Complete self-confidence is not merely a sin; complete self-confidence is a weakness." (G.K. Chesterton)

I may have previously alluded to the fact that G.K.Chesterton, the early 20th century British philosopher, journalist, humorist and theologian, is one of my favorite writers. The creator of the *Father Brown Mysteries,* he is much more than simply the absolute master of logic and paradox that he is universally acclaimed to be. He is perhaps, with C.S. Lewis, who admired him greatly, the greatest Christian apologist of the last millennia.

In the quote above from the introductory chapters of his seminal work, *Orthodoxy,* he is responding to the comment of a prominent publisher and acquaintance who remarked about a third party, *"That man will get on; he believes in himself."* Chesterton's immediate response was not only is the one who believes primarily in himself suffering from a dangerous weakness of mind and character, he is in fact destined for the lunatic asylum! The publisher objected that he knew many men who believed in themselves and yet were not in asylums. Chesterton, who was always making a point, often with hyperbole and humor, not surprisingly, had a retort for the publisher: *"Oh yes, you would know of them. Like the drunken poet from whom you wouldn't accept a dreary tragedy. He believed in himself. Or the elderly minister who's epic writings led you to hide in a back room, he believed in himself...Actors who can't act, believe in themselves. Debtors who won't pay believe in themselves. It would be much truer to say that a man will certainly fail, because he believes only in himself! Believing utterly in one's self is a hysterical and superstitious belief...* "

The exasperated publisher then asked Chesterton, *"Well, if man is not to believe in himself, in what can he believe?"* He replied, *"Well, I shall go home and write a book in answer to that question!"* Thus was born the 155 page tome, *Orthodoxy,* published in 1908. The very foundation of Christian doctrine rests with Original Sin. Man chose not the righteousness with which he was bestowed at Creation by a loving God, but instead chose to reject his Creator, going his own way, trusting in his own choices and strength to get him what he wanted out of life. In today's parlance, *"How's that workin' for ya?"* The entire story of the Bible, revealing both the nature of God and the nature of man, answers the question.

On his own, man ultimately goes astray and fails. Peace, happiness, and the true *success* that comes from sacrificially helping others in love, is the purview of those who believe in something outside of themselves. It belongs to those who trust in the Lord. There's a reason the scriptures speak of those who hope in the Lord soaring on wings like eagles! (Isaiah 40:31) God takes ordinary people and does extraordinary things through those who have faith. The bible is replete with examples, from Abraham, Isaac, Joseph, Moses, Samuel, Isaiah, Jeremiah, Elijah, Ruth, Daniel, and the likes of David the shepherd boy, right down to John the Baptist, all of the disciples, and Saul turned Paul, just to name a few!

Self-confidence is not a bad thing, when it's based on the recognition that everything we are, God made us to be. Yes, we are 'fearfully and wonderfully made,' (Psalm 139:13) but a relationship with the One who did make us, is the only way to achieve our true potential.

"I have set the Lord always before me; Because He is at my right hand, I shall not be moved." (Psalm 16:8 NKJV)

"Trust in the Lord with all your heart, and lean not to your own understanding; In all your ways acknowledge Him, and He shall direct your paths." (Proverbs 3:5 NKJV)

"Orthodoxy had as much influence on my spiritual direction as any single book... it's one of the few books I go back and re-read." (Philip Yancey)

> ***Prayer: Dear Heavenly Father, we love You! Thank you that You have made us as we are, but keep us mindful every day that our strength, our identity, our potential, are all dependent on believing in Our Savior, not in ourselves. AMEN***

SEPTEMBER 23

Lion Haired Bunny

"But ask the beasts and they will teach you; the birds of the heavens, and they will tell you...Who among all these does not know that the hand of the Lord has done this? In His hand is the life of every living thing..." (Job 12:7-10 ESV)

Initially, I wasn't sure I could write a devotional about a type of rabbit. But then I reflected on the pleasure my entire office staff got today, out of intermittently peaking at the "definition of cuteness" instagram account, "stinkycouch_bunnyboy." One of my patients was surviving work at home in the pandemic by acquiring a unique pet. She researched and bought a chameleon! A significant expense with all the equipment and supplies involved, she was distraught when he crossed over the rainbow bridge only days after his acquisition! She then went on Craig's List looking for another pet, and discovered the wonders of a *lion haired bunny!*

Her new pet was litter box trained in only two days, and is perhaps the cutest house pet I have ever laid eyes upon! My patient recently travelled across the country with him and was told by the airlines, in no uncertain terms, that a rabbit could not travel in the cabin. My patient then went to another counter to check in, and introduced her small furry pet, confined to her carrier, as ah...ah... ah...kitten! That, it turns out, is totally fine with the airline!

Videos of this tiny little lion are absolutely hilarious and addictive! He pops up all over the house, totally unexpected, destroys nothing, endlessly entertaining, uses the litter box and, despite his name, turns out to not be "stinky" at all!

A *devotional* is intended to be the *setting apart*, usually of a small portion of time and meditation, to a sacred purpose. If we all set apart a little more time to truly appreciate the wonders of God's handiwork, and to thank Him for its endless diversity, from starlit night to orange sunrise, (Psalm 19) from snow covered peaks to white sand beaches and crystal blue seas, from whale to giraffe, from elephant to Labrador, and yes, from lion to lion haired bunny, we'd have a little less time to be hateful to each other! Next time you have a mean spirited thought about a person espousing the position of another political party, or the guy who puts his bulk trash in front of your house, or the guy who shamed you for not wearing a mask when you were out walking your dog (Pandemic 2020 again,) think about *Stinky* the couch bunny, and maybe just smile for a while! Trust me, when you're smiling at thoughts of a lion haired bunny, and you acknowledge the wonder of the Lord's handiwork, it's contagious, and *that*, for my God, is sacred.

"The heavens declare the Glory of God; the skies proclaim the work of His hands." (Psalm 19:1 NIV)

"How many are your works, Lord! In wisdom you have made them all; the earth is full of your creatures. There is sea vast and spacious, teeming with creatures beyond number-living things both large and small." (Psalm 104:24-25 NIV)

> ***Dear Heavenly Father, we love You! With all our daily worries and strife, how blessed we are that You send us lion haired bunnies!! Holy Spirit, remind us that lion haired bunnies are with us by Grace, yet another of Your good gifts from above, for which we are grateful yet undeserving! AMEN***

SEPTEMBER 24

Leadership

"He sat down and called the twelve, and said to them, "If anyone desires to be first, he shall be last of all and servant of all." (Mark 9:35 NKJV)

I believe I have mentioned the Labradoodle we are picking up TODAY down in Houston! YAY! I may also have mentioned the four different books on training a puppy I have read as well. Two themes run throughout all of them: 1) Use only positive reinforcement and 2) establish yourself immediately as the alpha, the leader of the pack. To be the leader, according to Cesar Millan, you have to be the one to do everything *first!* For instance, you *never* let your dog precede you through any door, going in or out; you *never* let your dog eat before you, but make him wait while you eat *something* right in front of him, before you put his bowl down; and you *never, never,* let your dog walk in front of you when on a leash (or a *lead* as the Brits say!)

In other words, the conventional view of *leadership* applies in the dog training world just as it does in human society. The *leader* is the one who goes first, and the follower trails behind. The *leader is in front,* so the one being led can keep their eyes on him, right? The leader is the one who wins the race, who comes in first, whether running on a track or a candidate in an election, right?

Well, like so many other assumptions, Jesus turns this one directly on its head! When the disciples embarrass themselves by arguing about which of them will be called *greatest* in the Kingdom of Heaven, Christ makes it clear that whoever really wants that honor, must voluntarily decide to be the very last, the lowest, the one who serves everyone else! In other words, *leadership isn't about talent, it isn't about skills, its about love!* Once again, love turns out to be at the root of our Savior's instructions for us.

So when you're taking your pooch for a walk, who's leading who? You have to admit, from a pack standpoint, the bow wow will see you as the leader if you do *everything* before and in front of him. But, who loves you better than your dog? Who wants to do anything possible to serve his master? *"He shall be last and servant of all."* Hmmmmmmm, God may have made man before dog, (Genesis 2:19) but the dog might just be a quicker study!

"For even the Son of Man came not to be served but to serve…" (Mark 10:45 ESV)

"If I then your Lord and Teacher, have washed your feet, you also ought to wash one another's feet." (John 13:13 ESV)

"Do nothing from rivalry or conceit, but in humility count others more significant than yourselves." (Philippians 2:3 ESV)

Prayer: Dear Heavenly Father, we love You! We live in a world of competition, of ambition, of emphasis on cultivating our own strengths, on winning; let Your Holy Spirit give us openings not to win out over another, but to help another win out, even if at our own expense! AMEN

SEPTEMBER 25

Your Crowd

"As Jesus reclined at the table in the house, behold, many tax collectors and sinners came and were reclining with Jesus and His disciples. When the Pharisees saw this, they asked His disciples, 'Why does your teacher eat with tax collectors and sinners?' "(Matthew 9:10-11 ESV)

I happen to live in a mostly politically conservative state, in a mostly politically conservative city, in a mostly politically conservative neighborhood, with mostly politically conservative colleagues and friends, in a mostly politically conservative "Life Group" formed out of an evangelical church with mostly politically conservative members. Oddly enough, I am mostly politically conservative.

But I am a physician, and I have many politically liberal patients and not a few colleagues and nurses who would certainly never label themselves conservative. I interact with these people daily and make an effort to keep an open mind about social, economic, racial, and political issues in general. Even so, I would say that my wife and I are usually found in the company of like minded individuals.

The problem with that, in my experience, is that if you are always surrounded by people of the same opinion, same socioeconomic circumstances, same ethnicity, same level of education, you can start to *'believe your own press'* as it were. (Some of my friends were *horrified* that I would even waste my time watching the Democratic National Convention on TV!) You can start to lose sight of the fact that God loves vegans just as much as paleo people; God loves African Americans just as much as Irish Americans or Mexican Americans; Gay people just as much as straight; slow people just as much as intelligent; Democrats just as much as Republicans...not kidding! (Galatians 3:28)

Jesus didn't have this problem. He was Jewish, and a Rabbi. He was *expected* to *act righteously,* and that meant hanging out with the *right* people. But He didn't think like the religious elite, the Pharisees and the Scribes, who were experts on the law. They made it their life's goal to adhere to every statute, and who, in keeping with that goal, *wouldn't be caught dead* hanging out with a sinner, or *worse,* a Gentile! Christ came as a *Savior,* and He was Jewish, so He did hang out with His own people, but He also spent time with anyone who needed saving! (Matthew 9:12) He even hung out with prostitutes and tax collectors, the latter of which were renowned for lining their own pockets, cheating even the poor out of what little they had! Though the religious elite of His culture couldn't see it, ***all men are sinners and fall short of the glory of God!*** (Romans 3:21-24)

Christians can be confused by Christ's example, when the Apostle Paul quotes the pagan writer Menander to the Corinthians, "*Do not be deceived: Bad company corrupts good character.*" (1 Corinthians 15:33 NIV) But remember, our former Pastor's mantra about scripture: **"A text out of context is a pretext for a proof text!"** Paul was talking about false teachers; men who claimed knowledge of God, but in fact were ignorant. He was warning the Corinthians not to be deceived. He wasn't warning them to avoid the average Joe who sinned, because that would be *everyone!*

Here comes the broken record: God instructed us to do TWO THINGS! How hard is that? You don't even have to write them down. I mean, its just TWO THINGS, right? **LOVE GOD AND LOVE EACH OTHER!** Well, that's impossible unless you a) forge a relationship with God and b) expose yourself to the company of people who need your love! Remember what Jesus told us all, "*Love your enemies, bless those who curse you, do good to those who hate you...For if you love only those who love you, what reward have you? Do not even tax collectors do the same?*" (Matthew 5:44,46 NKJV) The only way to love those who aren't like you, and don't hold to your opinions, is to hang out with them sometime, and LISTEN to their perspective. You never know what you might learn. Evidently Christ found something worth loving in Matthew, and he was the man, the tax man!

Prayer: Dear Heavenly Father, we love You! At least we say we do; but if we do, we need to do what You ask of us! (John 14:15) Let the Spirit move us to engage people different from us; different in appearance, in opinions, in social status, in beliefs, in preferences, and encourage us to listen more than we speak! Who knows what might happen? AMEN

SEPTEMBER 26

Make Over

"He had no beauty or majesty to attract us to Him, nothing in His appearance that we should desire Him. He was despised and rejected by mankind, a man of suffering and familiar with pain. Like one from whom people his their faces He was despised, and we held Him in low esteem." (Isaiah 53: 2-3 NIV)

Recently I watched from across the street, as a young man, presumably with severe cerebral palsy, was walking down a busy sidewalk. His gait was tortuous, his facial expression distorted into a grimace, his arms held partially bent, yet rigid, with his fingers out-stretched not like a salute, but randomly in different directions, with the same awkward rigidity as his arms and legs. People moving the opposite direction would stare briefly, then completely unconsciously, like automatons, navigate a wide arc around him, even brushing against the storefront on one side or bumping into people coming the other way in an effort to leave him a wide berth. After staring briefly, each of these people would look away, averting their eyes. Their discomfort, just being near the man, was palpable, even from across the street. Ironically, the background to this scenario were several huge billboards advertising hair products, a major motion picture, "body sculpting," and *Peloton*. All featured extremely attractive, barely clad models.

An alien visitor from another world would conclude immediately that our *appearance* was the essence of our being; the very thing we prized the most. The sad reality, is that for many of us, this may not be too far off the mark!

But when God made mankind in His own image, presumably spiritually and physically, He chose to be incarnate, in a body that scripture assures us, was very unattractive indeed. He could have been the image of Adonis! He could have been someone who put Blake Shelton or Chris Hemsworth to shame! Instead, He chose to appear as someone whose face causes us to turn away. Why? Why would He do that? Did He do it just to make unattractive people feel better?

Maybe He did it so people would LISTEN to Him more than just stare at Him. Maybe He did it because He wanted people to understand that He came as the Son of Man, a servant, not a Greek God, to put on a pedestal. But I think He did it mostly because outward appearance just wasn't that important to Him. It's not important because He sees into our hearts, and is really not concerned with appearances. (1 Samuel 16:7; Psalm 44:21) He wanted us to see beyond the surface as well.

Perhaps next time you see someone whose appearance scares you, or makes you feel uncomfortable, instead of looking away, or moving away, you could approach them with a smile and say hello? You never know what might happen.

Prayer: Dear Heavenly Father, we love You! Remind us from time to time, that the artist's rendition of the Savior down through the centuries fails to reflect what the prophet Isaiah told us of His appearance! Remind us in the midst of a society that values looks enough to en-

courage our spending large portions of our income to alter what You gave us to begin with, that its what's in our hearts that You see, and what's in other's hearts that should matter most to us! AMEN

SEPTEMBER 27

Ash in the Air

"Dear Children, let us not love with words or speech but with actions and truth." (1 John 3:18 NIV)

A week ago we were in Fort Collins, Colorado for our nephew's wedding. It was a joyous occasion as weddings tend to be; a chance to catch up with relatives we hadn't seen in quite some time; a chance to tell stories on the young bride and groom as both sides of their new families got to know each other. The rehearsal dinner was at the home of my wife's brother, a large tract of land, surrounded by horse ranches, the back of which looked over the nearby Rockies.

But this particular weekend, the mountains, only five miles away, were a blur through the late afternoon haze. Like a smaller version of the devastation wrought in California where literally millions of acres have burned, there was a fire up in the pass only 15 miles from the wedding, where 330,000 acres have already burned. The smoke lay over Ft. Collins like a blanket, and we were told only days ago, when the wind had come from the west, it had snowed ash on everything, leaving cars coated in the grey powder, and people grateful for the masks they already wore for the pandemic.

We stayed at the Hilton nearby, a large beautiful hotel with a 10 story high atrium. But every time we got on one of the glassed elevators, we could see lines of burly young men, and even occasionally women, maneuvering through the lobby, returning in the evening, heading out in the early morning, all clad in high boots, yellow overall trousers, and suspenders over their blue -T-shirts. They were firefighters. Volunteer fireman from all over the country. Some from full-time forces, but many from small town volunteer units that left skeleton crews behind in order to face the massive threat in the west. Just last week in Dallas, we had a funeral for a 61 year old mother of four and grandmother of eight, who died fighting the LNU Complex Fire in Napa. She didn't have to go there. She went because she had a skill set that could save other people's lives. She went *because* she was a mom and grandma, and knew she could help keep other families intact. She went out of love.

People talk a good game about loving their neighbor. People get hung up on exactly who their neighbor is, like the priest and the Levite in the parable of the Good Samaritan. (Luke 10:30-37) But Jesus makes it pretty clear who your neighbor is and what it means to act neighborly: your neighbor is anyone who needs help, and acting neighborly is simply to give it! The one who shows mercy is the one who loves his neighbor. This discussion in Luke began, you will recall, when one of the scribes asked Jesus what he must do to inherit eternal life? Jesus merely answered his question with a question. (After all, Jesus *was*

Jewish!) "*What does the law say?*" Jesus asked. The man responded, "*Love God and Love your neighbor.*" Jesus told him he was correct, and shared the story of the Good Samaritan to answer the scribes follow up question of "*but who exactly is my neighbor?*"

The tired young people with the determined looks on their faces, but the ready smiles, knew the answer far better than the scribe who needed the parable to understand. If you leave your home and your family, cross the country, and then risk your life hiking through 120F temperatures, blowing flames, falling trees, and incinerated towns, you already know who your neighbor is.

When you pray today, thank God for people like these firefighters. Thank God that there are people who understand that as a society, there is no way to go forward without sacrificing to help each other. It's too easy to forget in this tumultuous time of fires, floods, hurricanes, rioting, and viral pandemic, that the love of Christ is all around us, flowing through regular people who are willing to die to help people they don't even know. We saw many types of love in Fort Collins. We witnessed the joining of lives by two young people in love and dedicated to each other; we witnessed the love of their family and friends, and we witnessed the brotherly love of firefighters from far away. Love is still the answer. Always will be.

Prayer: Dear Heavenly Father, we love You! Let your Holy Spirit work within us and stir us not just to exhortation of Your Promises, but stir us to action whenever our skills can alleviate the suffering of a neighbor. AMEN

SEPTEMBER 28

Growing Out

"Be doers of the word and not hearers only, deceiving yourselves. For if anyone is a hearer of the word and not a doer, he is like a man who looks intently at his natural face in a mirror. For he looks at himself and goes away, and at once forgets what he is like." (James 1:22-23 ESV)

While attending our nephew's wedding recently in Colorado, I was thinking about why it is that people cry at weddings? (More specifically, why do *I cry* at weddings?) Witnessing two young people, obviously totally enraptured with each other, express their love for each other publicly, proclaiming a lifetime commitment, is touching indeed. Certainly, those of us who are married remember our own nuptials, and maybe we all see the ceremony as a right of passage of sorts, growing up as it were, from childhood under the authority of their parents, to adulthood, under only the authority of God.

Coincident with the wedding we attended, was the impending arrival of our new puppy in a few days, and we examined from afar, the multiple labradoodles and goldendoodles found in our exploration of Fort Collins. My thoughts turned to the challenges of a new puppy, needy not unlike a new baby; and then to my grandchildren who at 8 and 6, very much want a pet. If their parents acquiesce, they will undoubtedly have hours of pleasure in store for them, but also they will face new responsibilities in caring for another living creature that is very much dependent on them!

When you think about it, we really don't "grow up" as much as we "grow out!" The toddler transitions from a completely *me* centered world in which he discovers his own independent existence, to the child who may learn, perhaps through a pet, that they are capable, and in fact designed, to care for the needs of others. By the time they are grown and marry, hopefully they have come to realize that the *other* is in fact even more important than the *me*, and marriage gives them the paradigm in which to develop a *sacrificial love*, putting the needs of another human consistently higher than their own.

The process of *sanctification* for the Christian, reflects this very same progression. If sanctification is *becoming more Christ-like*, and Christ came not to be served, but to serve, then growing up as a Christian is really *growing out* as well! We die to our old self when we are crucified with Christ, leaving our self-centeredness in the grave. (Galatians 2:20) Then we rise as a new Christian, led by the Holy Spirit who is the epitome of self-sacrificing love. We gradually grow outward into the world around us, extending the love of Christ and the message of Grace to all! That's what the Fruit of the Spirit is all about...growing outward!

"I have been crucified with Christ and I no longer live, but Christ lives in me." (Galatians 2:20 NIV)

"But the fruit of the Spirit is love, joy, peace, patience, kindness, goodness, faithfulness, gentleness and self-control." (Galatians 5:22 ESV)

Prayer: Dear Heavenly Father, we love You! Guide us each day through Your Spirit to look beyond our own needs and desires, to grow outward so that the needs of others outweigh our own. Help us to help others Lord, first, to see the need and second, to act. AMEN

SEPTEMBER 29
Slumber

"From whence comes my help? My help comes from the Lord, Who made heaven and earth. He will not allow your foot to be moved; He who keeps you will not slumber. Behold, He who keeps Israel shall neither slumber nor sleep." (Psalms 121:1-7 NKJV)

You can pretty much tell when you're watching a movie, whether an old western, a modern crime drama, or science fiction, that when the guy who was supposed to take the second watch falls asleep, something *really bad* is about to happen! It's the same feeling you get when watching a horror movie, and all the teenagers decide the best way to handle the situation is to split up and meet back in the garage!

There is a traditional hymn that quotes Psalm 121, and one of the lyrics intended is "*He sleeps not, nor slumbers.*" Our high school church choir however, had to abandon a planned performance of it, when it always came out "*sleep snot nor slumbers*" in rehearsals! But the immature humor of a group of teenagers at least imprinted the passage on my brain forever. I was never very good at memorizing scripture word for word, even in seminary, but this one became hard to forget.

As an obstetrician, I know a thing or two about exhaustion, and believe me, I treasure sleep like a Maine blue day with a fair wind for sailing! I also know that everyone gets exhausted from time to time, physically and emotionally. Everyone who works hard stumbles and falls occasionally. Sometimes we have all the good intentions in the world, but fatigue overcomes us and we simply can't concentrate any longer. We just lose our capacity for vigilance.

But those of us of faith, those of us who trust Him, know that our strength will be renewed! Our strength will come from the Creator of the universe; the one who created the heavens, and yet is a shepherd to His sheep. He is vigilant. He is ever watchful for us. If we wait patiently for the Lord; if we put our hope in the Lord; if we know that we can expect His help, it will *always* be forthcoming in HIs time and in His fashion!

"See the sovereign Lord comes with power, and He rules with a mighty arm...He tends His flock like a shepherd: He gathers the lambs in His arms and carries them close to His heart..." (Isaiah 40:10-11 NIV)

"The Lord sees everything you do. wherever you go He is watching." (Proverbs 5:21 NIV)

Prayer: Dear Heavenly Father, how comforting to know that when we are simply too tired to go on, too tired to keep our eyes open, You maintain the watch! Whether physically or emotionally exhausted, if we put our faith in You, You will give us rest and renew us refreshed, having kept Your Spirit awake and watchful over us! AMEN

SEPTEMBER 30

Too Good

"If you think you are standing strong, be careful not to fall." (1 Corinthians 10:12 NLT)

Just last week we learned of yet another evangelical pastor of a megachurch in Dallas who has resigned. The reason he gave: "I have sinned." So he judged himself, and found himself wanting? For two millennia there has been a pervasive misperception in Christendom. That misperception is that Christian leaders are somehow "cleaner" somehow "purer" than the rest of us believers. The truly unfortunate aspect to this misguided perspective, is that seekers then look at Christians, and conclude that they just aren't "good" enough to join this exclusive God club. That of course undermines the very Gospel itself; it betrays the offer of grace extended to all. The very meaning of grace is that we are offered forgiveness when we are undeserving! Part and parcel of this distortion, is that Christian leaders start to believe their own press. They start to believe that they really are just a little closer to Christ, just a little bit purer, just a little bit more devout, just a little bit more faithful, than the flock they are supposed to be leading.

Paul warns of this error. A man too confident of the grace he knows has been extended to him, too proud, may start to think that he cannot fall at all. That's what our opening verse means. He starts to think that the temptations before him can be resisted in his own strength because of the "special status" he has been granted by the assurance of his salvation, and possibly the misplaced adoration of his followers as well. Or sometimes, he just becomes so adept at rationalization that he concludes his sins aren't really all that sinful in the final analysis!

Our opening verse above, is less well known that the one that follows it: "*No temptation has overtaken you except such is common to man; but God is faithful, who will not allow you to be tempted beyond what you are able, but with the temptation will also make the way of escape, that you may be able to bear it." (1 Corinthians 10:13 NKJV)*. Note that it says, "God is faithful." But you can't avoid temptation at all, if you start trusting in yourself and your position, and you forget to trust in the Lord. Over and over I have heard people misquote this text, saying "God won't give you more than you can handle." Scripture never says that. In fact, it repeatedly says the opposite. You are *always* given more than you can handle, *on your own!* That's why God requires of us, faith! Verse 13 means that *God will provide* you an escape, not that you may do so in your own ability!

So there are two errors here. The first error is the lay person's belief that Christian leaders have some special status; that they are somehow less susceptible to the temptations of this world, and are thus somewhat "better." This leads to the seeker thinking he/she may not be "good" enough to become a Christian. But it also leads to disillusionment and charges of hypocrisy when a pastor or elder is found to be sinning.

The second error is that pastors may start to believe the same fake news! The assurance of hope which all Christians share, becomes distorted into an assurance that they will somehow be able to avoid sinning like the rest of us! Nothing could be further from the truth, and when they discover they are only human, their fall from grace seems all the more catastrophic.

Yes, Paul tells us that Grace does not mean a license to continue sinning. (Romans 6:1-2) Yes, Paul tells us that leaders are held to a somewhat higher standard, and they should be. (1 Timothy 3:1-7; Titus 1:6-9) But he also emphasized, as did Christ, that we are not to judge, lest we be judged, (Matthew 7:1) and that there is no condemnation for those in Christ Jesus! (Romans 8:1)

Being born again, means that the indwelling Holy Spirit is available to help us *if we will only allow Him!* In fact, the very act of becoming more Christ-like, of sanctification, could be described as permitting the Holy Spirit to manifest itself through us, to a greater and greater extent every day!

So when you hear a story about a pastor who has "fallen," perhaps he began to think, in today's verbiage, that he was "too big to fail" and thus gave in to some repeated temptation. Or maybe he legitimately recognized a growing false pride in himself. It may well be best for the church if he no longer holds a position of leadership, as outlined by Paul. But he, like us, should remember what Grace is all about. Christ is pretty clear, "if we can't forgive others, nor will our father in heaven forgive us." (Matthew 6:14-15) That's what we need to show the seeker. That's also the grace we need to show ourselves, our brothers and sisters, and even our leaders.

Prayer: Dear Heavenly Father, we love You! Just as Your love for us has granted us undeserved forgiveness, so too must we allow the Holy Spirit to work through us to forgive not only our leaders who sin, but also ourselves! AMEN

OCTOBER

OCTOBER 1

Too Bad

"A moderately good man knows he is not very good: a thoroughly bad man thinks he is all right." (C.S. Lewis)

Our country has been torn by violent demonstrations since this last spring. As if the burden of the 2020 Pandemic, along with all of its hardships and losses were not enough, a select few individuals across the nation have hijacked the legitimate peaceful protest of those who seek for racial justice, and instead have been using it as an excuse for the wanton destruction of property, physical violence against those who oppose them in any way, and even the senseless murder of some.

Perhaps they are funded by powerful individuals who, for unclear reasons, seek a state of total anarchy. Perhaps not. But no matter their true motivation, people who randomly steal and destroy and threaten and injure others with impunity, are felt by many to be simply *evil*. Those of us who hold to a code of ethics in which random violence is completely unacceptable, find the actions of these few, virtually inexplicable.

C.S. Lewis, the author of both *The Narnia Chronicles* and of *Mere Christianity*, says that far from inexplicable, their actions are quite logical. A man can understand the nature of sleep while awake, but not while sleeping. You can see mistakes you've made in a math problem when you are thinking clearly, but while making them, you cannot see them at all. You can understand what it means to be drunk when you are sober, but much less so when you are inebriated. And thus our opening quote. The average man, indeed, knows that he is not altogether good, but the thoroughly bad man thinks himself quite all right!

Believers, as they move along the path of sanctification, becoming more Christ-like, have greater and greater understanding. As you get better, you can recognize what evil remains within you! But if you are steadily getting worse, progressively becoming more and more evil, then you understand your badness less and less. Lewis says in summary, *"Good people know about both good and evil; bad people know about neither!"*

We can reach only one conclusion then, and that is, that *only more right can extinguish wrong!* There is a reason that God wants us to love others, even when we dislike them, or dislike what they do! Because if we simply hate them, and treat them with angry disdain, nothing improves for them or for us! I'm not suggesting you go hug a rioter. Many, I am sure, will simply not listen to reason. But everyone, perhaps even the mostly bad, can at least see love demonstrated and understand its effect on others. We as believers have to set the best example we can in terms of grace.

Remember the song, *"What the World Needs Now?"* The lyric goes, *"What the world needs now, is love sweet love; it's the only thing, that there's just too little of!"*

Evil men aren't inexplicable at all. They are simply "blinded by their hatred," as the expression says. The best we can do for the man headed down that road, is allow the Spirit within us to guide us toward loving our fellow man whenever and however possible, and then there is at least a small chance that he will make a u-turn and head down a different road! Then we can pray that the moderately bad man can yet see both good and bad and understand the difference.

"But I say to you, Love your enemies and pray for those who persecute you." (Matthew 5:44 ESV)

"Do not repay evil for evil or reviling for reviling, but on the contrary, bless, for to this you were called, that you may obtain a blessing." (1 Peter 3:9 ESV)

Prayer: Dear Heavenly Father, we often find evil hard to understand. But realizing that those descending into the abyss may not be able to see what is happening, helps. Lord, enlighten those who destroy and injure randomly, such that they might see that there is a better way for everyone, including themselves. AMEN

OCTOBER 2

Negotiation

"For by grace you have been saved through faith, and that not of yourselves; it is the gift of God, not of works, lest anyone should boast." (Ephesians 2:8-9 NKJV)

So, with a new labradoodle puppy at my feet, you may be stuck with dog training analogies for a while in these devotionals, at least intermittently! Windsor made very quick work of sit, lie down, and come. All of these behaviors were in response to the positive reinforcement offered by a treat and lots of praise. But wearing a collar and walking, even forward just a few steps, is not coming so easily. He uses "sit" now as a way to imitate a mule that has no intention of going anywhere when that leash is on! In short, everything about training him is a negotiation. He behaves properly, and he gets a treat. He disobeys, no treat.

Many Christians down through the ages have, unfortunately, believed that their relationship with God worked on a similar paradigm. Many a man in a foxhole has prayed "Lord, if you just get me out of this one, I'll never (smoke, drink, gamble, cheat, fight, etc etc) again!" We negotiate.

This is the way the Pharisees viewed man's relationship to God as well. They just believed they were better at it than everyone else. Whoever keeps the most of the 613 Laws of Moses, gets the Scooby-snack, right? If righteousness, and thus acceptance by God, is based on keeping the rules, i.e. legalism, then the ones who keep the rules the best, get Blessed. That blessing may include material circumstance, or for those who believed it, an afterlife of no cares.

This is why they despised Jesus so intensely. By presuming to announce that God loves *everyone*, (preposterous!) He was undermining their superiority, and thus their authority to hold people to the letter of the Law. (Matthew 12:11-14) Their "religion" was itself a never ending negotiation. The Good News, the Gospel Truth, is that this conception of God's intent is completely and utterly false! Jesus came to the average man and woman, who were just struggling to make a living, and sinning off and on, along the way! That would be *all of us*, not the paragons of Christian virtue or the masters of theological knowledge. All God requires of us is faith; faith that He loved us enough to send His only son to pay the price for our continued disobedience!

One more dog thought. Our dog's obedience is indeed a negotiation from our standpoint, and, I would imagine, from his. *But our dog's love is not. It is unconditional.* It is not based on the number of treats we give him or withhold. Once the bond is formed, his love persists, even when we mistreat him. That's what the bible calls *hesed* in Hebrew, meaning "faithful love."

So, when you find yourself in that foxhole, with shells bursting all around you, instead of striking a deal with God to save you, take a moment to thank Him for *already saving you* 2,000 years ago. If you then let the Holy Spirit empower you to quit cheating or smoking or drinking or whatever, *great! But God is not a vending machine where you put in 4 units of repentance and He doles out salvation!* Salvation is a free gift, even when you've done nothing to deserve it other than believe!

"What if God was one of us? Just a slob like one of us? Just a stranger on a bus, trying to make his way home?" (Eric Bazilian and Rick Chertoff)

> *Prayer: Dear Heavenly Father, we love You! When we are under fire at work, in our marriage, with our kids, or literally on the battlefield, remind us that loving You is all that is required! There is no negotiation. You won't save us in exchange for any certain behavior. You've already saved us out of Your inconceivable love for us! AMEN*

OCTOBER 3
You Might Be Right

"Honestly, I think there is nothing more stressful than arguing with someone when you know they're right!" (Jennifer Worth)

My mother told me long ago that the secret to a happy marriage was learning when to pause, and then say one particular phrase when enjoined in marital conflict: "*You know dear, you might be right.*" Of course most of us, when in the midst of battle, are quite confident that the other party is *definitively wrong!* After all, that's why we're fighting in the first place. My mother's advice, I believe, was intended for just this circumstance. Unfortunately, once this phrase has been used once or twice, your spouse will begin to sense the distinct possibility of some insincerity. Eventually the ploy will be of no use whatsoever!

But what if it's not intended as a ploy? What if you pause whenever arguing with your spouse and consider a few basic facts. 1) Your opponent is sane 2)

Your opponent is intelligent 3) Your opponent is sincere 4) Your opponent loves you and finally 5) You love your opponent! Hmmmmmmm. This might lead to your listening more carefully to whatever point they are trying to make. This might lead to your seeing things more from their perspective. If you do this, it even brings up the harrowing possibility that you might be *wrong!* And if you're in the wrong, there's a pretty good chance, that your spouse is in the *right!*

Jesus felt there was no place at all for anger in discourse. Two people can argue a point intellectually, but becoming angry with the other party, especially if your spouse, is completely unacceptable. He so disdained it, that He warns your offerings to God won't be received until you make up with whomever you are angry. (Matthew 5:21-25) Wisdom literature in the scriptures is not surprisingly, just as clear on the point. *"A gentle answer turns away wrath, but a harsh word stirs up anger." (Proverbs 15:1 NIV)* So is Paul, in his New Testament epistles. *"A servant fo the Lord must not quarrel but be gentle to all, able to teach, patient in humility..." (2 Timothy 2:24 NKJV)* Certainly James understood the destructive power of the tongue in an argument. While he acknowledged that we all stumble in this regard, he drew the analogy between the tongue and the bit in a horse's mouth, the rudder of a huge ship, even the spark that can start a forest fire! (James 3:2-7) James actually concludes that no man can tame the tongue, but we *can effect a change of heart!* (James 3:8-12;)

So maybe my mom's advice about *"You might be right,"* should be taken seriously if not literally. Not the words necessarily, but the attitude they represent. The reason words can be *so hurtful* is that they usually come from the heart, as Jesus points out to the authorities. (Matthew 12:34-36) If you find yourself fighting with a loved one and perhaps saying things you wish you hadn't, then perhaps a change of heart is in order, even if you can't always control the tongue.

Perhaps truly acknowledging to yourself, before a discussion elevates to a full blown fight, that you know, they *just might be right,* will help you control your tongue!

Prayer: Dear Heavenly Father, as James tells us, out of the same mouth should not come both praise to You and cursing of our neighbor! Direct Your Holy Spirit to give us pause whenever we get angry, to recognize that everyone has their perspective, and sometimes the other person's might be a better way to look at things! AMEN

OCTOBER 4

Is There Hope?

"You are the light of the world. A city that is set on a hill cannot be hidden. Nor do they light a lamp and put it under a basket, but on a lamp stand, and it gives light to all who are in the house." (Matthew 5:14-15 NKJV)

Two of my colleagues were having a discussion in the surgeons' lounge the other day, after watching about five minutes of national news from the flat screen TV hanging on the wall. The spot had only been a rundown of the headlines: more fires devastating California and Oregon with entire towns incinerated; more rioting in Portland; more demonstrations spreading once again in response to a months old case of police shooting a person of color by mistake, in their own apartment; two more hurricanes hurtling toward the Gulf Coast; Covid-19 surging again across Europe and in many states of the US; one party accusing the other of trying to fix the upcoming Presidential election; the media claiming the current President refuses to guarantee a peaceful transition if he loses.

The conversation went something like this:

Doc A) Shaking his head, "The world is going to hell in a hand basket. It makes it awfully hard to believe there's a loving God up there! Why would an all powerful God let this kind of crap go on?"

Doc B) I don't know. Maybe it's all part of the big plan.

Doc A) Well, I want no part of a God who burns up towns and starts riots so He can show us we need to be rescued!

Afraid I had to jump in at that point. I pointed out that neither of those perspectives held water theologically. God is good. He is good *all the time!* (Psalm 34:8) That is at the core of our faith as Christians. That means that God doesn't purposefully give your son-in-law leukemia, so you can draw closer to Him when you beg for healing. He doesn't set up political and racial hatreds in our nation so that we are forced to turn to Him as our last chance. And it certainly doesn't mean that every disastrous headline is because there is no God at all! The type of thinking my two friends demonstrated either denies the existence of God altogether, or perverts his role to that of the pyromaniac who sets the fire only so he can arrive in a cosmic firetruck and save the day!

God can and does turn evil to good for those who believe. (Romans 8:28) He can and does take the worst of circumstances, like attempted fratricide, human trafficking, slavery, blackmail, drought and famine, and use them for good, as He did with Joseph. (Genesis 50:20) But God didn't throw Joseph in the pit to begin with; his brothers did, and there is no doubt that the idea for it came from the Evil One.

But Jesus is the Good Shepherd who laid down His life for ours. He came and sacrificed Himself so that Satan, the thief, could not kill and destroy any longer. He came that we might have life abundantly. (John 10:10-11) Our freedom from shame and guilt coupled with the indwelling Holy Spirit, enables us to resist Satan and force him to flee! (James 4:7) The joy and peace that result, comprise that abundant life promised.

The world is only a hopeless mess as long as it refuses the free gift offered to it by its creator! That hope must be communicated to the world by those who understand; by those who get it; by those who believe; because they are the light in the darkness! Satan lurks in the dark, but he has no where to hide when the light of Christ disperses the darkness! (John 8:12) That light is love for our fellow man. If we loved each other as we might through the fruit of the Spirit, the headlines would have no rioting, political vitriol, or angry individuals spewing hatred; and the only news of natural disaster would be of how people came together to meet the challenges selflessly.

Bad things happen to good people because sometimes bad things happen, (Luke 13:4-5) or because the devil is always working to destroy (John 8:44);

but not because God caused them to happen. The abundant life promised comes through our response to disaster and tragedy, and the only hope for this dark world, is through spreading the Light. When one truly understands how much they are loved by God, not only can one roll with the punches, but they are compelled to spread the Good News.

Prayer: Dear Heavenly Father, we love You! Guide us to recognize opportunities for helping others understand they are not alone, and that the Light of the World is standing ready to dissipate the darkness of their early morning terrors. The world is not without hope, it is simply ignorant of where to find it! AMEN

OCTOBER 5
Uncertainty Redux

"Trust in the Lord with all your heart, And lean not to your own understanding; In all your ways acknowledge Him, and He shall direct your paths. Do not be wise in your own eyes." (Proverbs 3:5-7a NKJV)

It doesn't happen as frequently anymore, with the existence of modern navigational aids, but when you are sailing on open water you can go from confident of your position to uncertain, very quickly indeed. Uncertainty of position in a sailing vessel is the step right before disaster. If you are uncertain of your coordinates on the map, then you are at the mercy of what you can see. At night or in a fog, you may be able to see very little. Even on a clear day when you can see distant landmarks, their actual identity and distance are easily misjudged, especially in waters like coastal Maine with rocky shoreline that looks identical on each of a thousand islands. The feeling is uncomfortable to say the least, and sometimes, as in thick fog with no GPS or RADAR, downright terrifying!

Uncertainty happens in life as well, and can leave one with the very same feeling, ranging from uncomfortable to paralyzing fear. (See June 1: Uncertainty) Maybe you're in your late fifties and just lost your job. Maybe you've just received a diagnosis that could go either way, in terms of your survival. Maybe you are recently separated and facing a probable divorce, with all its attendant uncertainty in terms of children, houses, income, cars, household possessions, and even legal fees. Maybe your plans for graduate school didn't work out and suddenly career goals are looking very different. Maybe you've just been discharged from the military, can't find a job with the skills you've learned, have no family support and find it almost inconceivable that you are staring homelessness right in the face! There are unlimited scenarios for uncertainty in life. That's why having one thing of which you are certain, is critical.

Both scripture and experience have taught me that no matter how messed up, confused and scared life gets, knowing that I am loved and valued immeasurably, by the most powerful force in the universe, is more than adequate solace. (John 3:16; Romans 5:8; Isaiah 41:10; 1 John 4:16) The biggest part of being loved by God is the certainty that He has your best interests at heart, and even if you just can't see your way clear of your present circumstance, the One that loves you will never give up on you; will always be there for you, no matter what! (Proverbs 3:5-6; Numbers 23:19; Psalm 86:15; 117:1-2; 118:1-29; Lamentations 3:22-23; Romans 5:8; Ephesians 2:4-5) Finally, God's steadfast love and power are coupled with His wisdom! Prayer brings answers on which we can depend; on which we can be certain. (Proverbs 1:7; 2:6; 3:6-7; Isaiah 40:28; James 1:5; 3:17; Romans 11:33)

So when you're uncertain; when you're making that list on legal paper of Pros and Cons; don't forget to pray and ask for guidance. It's there for those who believe it's there. And after you pray, be as patient as possible. God, who is by definition out of time, never promises to respond on our timetable, but you can be certain that He will respond!

Prayer: Dear Heavenly Father, we love you! We sometimes forget that your love for us is unmatched and completely reliable. You see into our hearts and know our needs effortlessly, since you are indwelling through the Spirit! Remind us of this Lord, when we face the terror of uncertainty. Your power is infinite, Your wisdom reliable, and Your love undeniable. AMEN

OCTOBER 6

Cast Off

"But someone will say, 'You [James] have faith and I have works.' Show me your faith apart from your works, and I will show you my faith by my works." (James 2:18 ESV)

Have you ever had the chance to work with someone who was "great on paper" but not so much in practice? Unfortunately, we see this in medicine frequently. When I was an intern at UCSF I worked with residents from all across the country. When I saw a Baylor College of Medicine ring on the hand of another doctor in the ER, I was confident of his/her clinical abilities under stress. It happened that my medical school stressed practical application as well as academics. By the time I graduated, before my internship even started, I had already delivered hundreds of babies, placed dozens of central IV lines, tapped chests and bellies for fluid, placed chest tubes, and performed CPR. But some of the residents from vaunted academic medical schools on the East Coast, that shall remain nameless, were absolutely hopeless when it came to even starting an IV, no less placing a chest tube!

Some Christians are like that. They've memorized bible verses, they attend bible study, they go to church regularly. But have you ever *seen them* actually help someone? Could they tell you if you asked them, how the light of Christ shines through them to the outside world? To the doubters? To the questioners? To the hungry? To the lost? To the downhearted? To the poor?

Sometimes this isn't an indictment of their faith, but only their initiative. Sometimes it is an indictment of their faith, because they're the same person who is mean to subordinates, ridicules his children, humiliates his wife and *then goes to bible study.*

Two groups of people talk a good game, but show nothing of Christ. The first group may simply be timid. They may pray for guidance, sense the right thing to do about it, then are simply too unsure to proceed. The other group are the Pharisees. The hypocrites. They are the ones James would claim have no faith, because they have no works.

If you find yourself in the first group, still on your mooring in the cove, sails raised, course plotted, but unsure about heading out; then *cast off!* The next person who needs a friend, the next person who needs emotional or financial support, the next opportunity you have to serve whether at a food bank or at a women's shelter or whatever, *just go for it! Cast off!* You can always head back to the cove if need be, but you'll never know the joy of *exercising your faith* unless you put your back to winching in that sheet and trimming your sails!

James is the brother of Christ. He knows of what he speaks! He never said good works would earn you righteousness and thus salvation. He only said that if you truly have faith, it will be demonstrated in your works! (James 2:17) Drop the mooring line dude! Pick a heading and go for it! You won't be sorry.

Prayer: Dear Heavenly Father, forgive us for our temerity, and our lack of confidence. It is so easy to doubt our capabilities forgetting completely that the Holy Spirit will guide our steps and work through us! Even Moses and Isaiah doubted their ability to do what their faith demanded, so you are in good company, but remind us when we balk at "getting involved" that "getting involved" is exactly what Christ would have us do! AMEN

OCTOBER 7

Anticipation

"Such is the state of life, that none are happy but by the anticipation of change; the change itself is nothing; when we have made it, the next wish is to change again!" (Samuel Johnson)

My wife and I are both hard on the edge of sixty-five; Medicare age; the magic moment; the traditional age for 'retirement;' the time to consider down-sizing; the time to appreciate the ever growing number of grandchildren; the time to spend helping aging parents; the time to finally 'get in shape', to try and stave off the new pains that arise each morning! One would think that the changes were tapering off, right? I mean college, graduate school, marriage, children, moving, more graduate school, different business partners, different offices, new techniques and equipment in the operating room, and new rules from the medical bureaucracy; it has to end right?.

But the cycle has begun all over again with my children, finally out of graduate schools, making their livings, having their children, moving, new jobs etc. etc. It's the endless 'circle of life' to quote one famous lion! But interestingly, as much as I have told myself that I "hate change," I have anticipated almost every one of them with excitement and the promise of something new!

Samuel Johnson, as usual, is pretty darn perceptive! All of us have experienced at least the slight 'let down' after the anticipation of wedding/and honeymoon, followed by dirty dishes and garbage that needs to go out! The new job turns out to have someone over you that you certainly wouldn't have picked; the new office nurse turns out not to fit your practice; the new jacket you bought for a certain someone as a gift turns out "not to be her color;" it turns out that the trailers for the "blockbuster movie" you waited for, for months, were the only decent scenes in the entire film; even the new wifi you installed turns out to not reach the living room and the flat screen, which is why you bought it in the first place! There is indeed a lot to be said for anticipation. But the actual change often turns out not to be up to par with the build up! Maybe that's why I feel like I hate change, because the change is so often a let down after what we thought it would be.

What a Blessing that our God is not like that! He is the same yesterday, today and tomorrow! (Hebrews 13:8) The Lord God is the Alpha and the Omega, who is and was and who is to come. (Revelation 1:8) Every good gift and every perfect gift is from above, coming down from the Father of Lights, with whom there is no shadow of change. (James 1:17) All things were made through Him. Nothing was made without Him. (John 1:3) God, Jesus and the Holy Spirit are completely reliable! Reliability means consistently dependable in judgment, character, performance and result. (That means then, that God's essential character is unchaining, not necessarily that He can't change His mind! (See Genesis 9:15; Jonah 3:10; 2 Kings 20:1-11) The Lord is, in a word, trustworthy. (Psalm 18:30; 19:7; 33:4; 111:7; 1 Timothy 1:15; Revelation 21:5)

Change may not be quite the fun that anticipation is in our everyday world. But with our faith, the joy of anticipation is matched by the promised change in us, but the lack of it in our Savior. Risen with Him, we are reborn in this life, but we will also one day be present with the Lord in a place with no tears, no shame, no guilt, no anger, no hatred, and no prejudice! And we who believe in the Gospel can look forward to death with the anticipation of new bodies in a new world where there is no more pain. That doesn't mean Christians *want* to die, for we have the same tenacity to live the life we were given that anyone does; but we do have that joy of anticipation that others lack!

Now, Samuel Johnson had it mostly right. But my guess is that he never had an Australian Labradoodle; because I think the change is just as good as the anticipation!

Prayer: Dear Heavenly Father, thank you for Your promise of Eternal New Life through Your Son, and for the change we experience right here on earth once we accept the Gift of Salvation bought for us on the cross. Let the change in the way we live and treat our brothers, reflect Your unchanging love and unchanging character! AMEN

OCTOBER 8

Your Purpose in Life

Q: "What is the chief end of man?"

A: "The chief end of man is to glorify God and to enjoy Him forever." (Westminster Shorter Catechism Question 1)

I was raised a Presbyterian. The Catechism is really a course of study wherein questions about life are addressed by appropriate scripture. The word "catechism," means a summary or exposition of doctrine, and is traditionally used in *catechesis,* or the teaching of youth and adult converts to Christianity, by memorizing a series of questions and their answers. The form is Epicurean, based on the teaching technique of the famous Greek philosopher, Epicurus, in the late 4th century BC. I knew the chief end, or purpose, of man, by the time I was ten years old. What I didn't know until much later, was how I was supposed to figure out my *specific individual purpose* in bringing about Glory to God! Many feel that finding their specific purpose is harder than they had expected.

Growing up I wanted to be a weatherman like my dad in the Army Air Corps WWII, a policeman, an astronaut, a veterinarian, and then, only by my third year in college, a physician. (My parents always thought I would be a lawyer, since I like to write, and I *certainly* like to talk!) But as I went through medical school, I liked every subject we had, and every clinical rotation we did. I finally selected the specialty which allowed me to play with the most toys in the operating room, do primary care stuff in the office, and take part in the miracle called, "birth."

I've watched my children go through a similar stop, start and turn process as they found their way to careers as well. So how did they *select* a career to fulfill their individual purpose in life, one that would help man glorify God? I think they all gravitated toward whatever they were passionate about initially. But you can be passionate about music, and yet not hold a tune to save your life. (My mom for example...sorry mom.) You can be passionate about sports, and lack the coordination to make purposeful contact with any kind of ball, ever! **So eventually you settle on the passion which intersects with your God given capabilities!** My son is a gifted musician and pursued a music education in college. He is extremely coordinated, able to have laser like focus, which certainly made him good at both multiple instruments and video games. While he was good at those, it turned out one video game had always turned him on more than the others: Flight Simulator! My son is now a commercial pilot and flight instructor. He eventually found the intersection of his capabilities and his passion! All of kids went through similar fits and starts before becoming a cardiologist, a counselor and in many ways the toughest career, a full-time mom!

When the crowds wanted to know what they should be doing in order to do the work of God, Jesus answered simply, *"Believe in the One He has sent."* (John 6:29b) Wowzers! That's pretty clear. Believe in the Good News of Christ the Savior, and everything you do will glorify God! Couple that with the Greatest Commandment, *"Love the Lord your God...and love your neighbor,"* and you have the prescription for your purpose in life! God's plan for you is to use the capabilities He has given you to love and benefit those around you! You use those capabilities with the most enthusiasm and to the best effect, when you apply them in an area about which you are passionate!

So if some path really lights your fire, really gets you excited, *and* your gifts make you good at it, you've found your specific purpose! Living it to the fullest then, by definition, glorifies the God who made you and gave you your gifts! Acknowledging the source of your gifts will then allow you to spread the Good News as well! See, not so hard after all!

> *Prayer: Dear Heavenly Father, we love You! We praise You with the effective use of our gifts in our areas of passion! Let others benefit from our lives, and let us not forget to give credit where credit is due, to You Father, the giver of all good gifts! AMEN*

OCTOBER 9

Lean In

"For I am the Lord, your God who takes hold of your right hand and says to you, 'Do Not Fear." (Isaiah 41:13 NIV)

Last week my wife was out of town for a few days, I had a week off, and it was just me and Windsor, the Labradoodle pup, batching it. I knew we should be doing something constructive one afternoon, so I fell into my chair with the dog at my feet, and watched a Will Smith movie!

In it, one of the character's fathers was explaining to the young soldier that fear was actually an asset; you just need to *lean into it*. After the movie was over, that line stayed with me, and I thought about my own experience. I remembered that even though I had always done well academically, like most people that ended up in medical or law school, I had been terrified before each big exam. I used to cough all the way across campus (my nervous tell!) In medical school and residency, every time I started a new rotation, I felt an amorphous sort of fear, even though past experience would suggest I had nothing to fear. During 35 years of private practice and teaching, each new talk to give, each new procedure, each new instrument, each new technique in the operating room, could produce this unsettling feeling.

Let's face it. Fear is often just another form of uncertainty about what's going to happen in the future. Fear of the dark, fear of aging and death, are really all the same fear: fear of the unknown. When I was a child, I remember my dad taking my hand in the breakers off Cape Cod's Nauset Beach, without which each wave would have swept me under. When my kids were small, I did the same for them, whenever they were in danger or whenever I even sensed their fear.

But, with dad holding my hand, eventually *I could power walk into those breakers!* Over time, I learned how to turn sidewise, lean toward the curling wave, and have the water and the foam rush around me while I stood firm. I ended up doing the same thing through my graduate education and medical practice. I leaned into my fear. My dad and mom weren't there to hold my hand anymore, but it was held nevertheless.

Jesus tells the disciples, *"Take courage. It is I. Do not be afraid,"* as they saw Him approach, walking on the water. *(Matthew 14:27 NIV)* God is present, and one of the advantages of faith, is that those with it, can feel His presence. Stepping judiciously into whatever you fear is the only way to discover if there is really something of which to be afraid. People without faith can try to do that as well. But, I have seen patients face extremely difficult circumstances for decades, and I promise you that those who have faith, are very much better equipped.

So, whatever your fears, consider that God made you to be productive and forward moving, using the gifts He has given you to help others. I'm not saying you ought to take selfies on the edge of the Grand Canyon! Use common sense, one of the gifts incorporated in your God given intellect! But when you are unsure of the outcome, but sure you need to move forward, remember your Savior isn't just *near,* He's *indwelling.* Let the Holy Spirit hold your hand if need be. He's right there.

> *Prayer: Dear Heavenly Father, we love You! Thank you that You can always be relied upon as both a refuge and our strength! You gave us fear for a reason; to keep us safe from things like lions and falling and traffic! But when we only fear the unknown, we can know for certain that You go with us, and that Your plan is always good for us in the end! AMEN*

OCTOBER 10

Who's Will?

"For it is God's will that by doing good you should silence the ignorant talk of foolish people." (1 Peter 2:15 NIV)

It's a Saturday in late autumn and remarkably you and your wife have nothing specific planned. The children are grown and busy with their own kids, and those kids don't have a single sporting event today! You decide its a good idea to ask your spouse what they would like to do this afternoon? You might say something like, "Oh, I don't know. I was kinda of thinking that kicking back, having a beer and a pizza and watching football on TV would fit the bill!" Your wife might look at you and say something like, "Well, I s'pose you could do that. But there's a really cool event at the Convention Center, all about landscaping your own backyard with cheap things like large rocks and gravel! You want to give that a try?" In a word, you might respond with, "No." Sometimes what we want to do conflicts directly with the desires of the one we love!

Well, sometimes it seems that our will conflicts directly with the *One* we love, as well! It's not very hard for us to truly desire God's will, when it happens to be exactly what we want! But what about when it's not? What about when you know you should act lovingly to a co-worker, but they just absolutely drive you to distraction? What about when you know you need to stay in a job you dislike for right now, because your family needs the stability and the income? What about when you know you need to honor your father and mother, but your father is a relapsed alcoholic and your mother is an enabler? What about when you know your marriage is in trouble, and you really need to work on it, but instead you flirt with the new secretary at work and stop for a drink on the way home just to avoid whatever conflict might await there? You know God's will, because you know what's right, but it's not what you want to do.

But there are times when you truly don't know what is in God's plan for you. Do you take this job or another? Do you take the scholarship for one school, or take on more debt to go to the one you think would be better for you? Do you break up with your girlfriend or boyfriend because it isn't perfect, and look for another? Is it finally time to retire, or is continuing to work better for everyone? You can dream up as many scenarios as there are people. Here comes the broken record for the hundredth time: "What is it that God requires of you?" The prophet, Micah asked this question rhetorically, and answered, "to act justly, to love mercy, and to walk humbly with your God." (Micah 6:8) An expert in the law asked Jesus what was required of him for eternal life. Jesus asked him in turn, "What is written in the law?" the man responded, "Love God with all your heart, soul, strength and mind, and love your neighbor as yourself." Jesus responded, "Do this and you will live." (Luke 10:25-28)

The task you don't like, the relationship with people who just rub you the wrong way, the job that doesn't gratify, but pays the bills for now; these are times when you need to pause, rather than just reacting reflexively. God has told you that He, a) loves you (John 3:16,) b) wants what is best for you (Jeremiah 29:11,) c) will work all for good in the end (Romans 8:28,) d) commands your obedience (John 14:15,) and finally, e) commands that you love Him and love others as yourself. (Matthew 22: 37-40)

Keeping each of these five points in mind, pray for wisdom. Wait for the answer. Don't be afraid of making the wrong choice if you are a believer! Faith grants you the indwelling Spirit, and if you trust the Lord, the Spirit will spur you to the right decision. Thank God we don't have to make tough choices alone! Thank God for His Word, because it makes His will clearer than we ever expected!

Prayer: Father God, when we struggle with trying to discern your will for our lives, let us not make it harder than it is! It is not always that either of two choices is right or wrong, as long as our direction is guided by trust in You and understanding of Your desire for us overall! We will choose the path that glorifies You best, in the use of our gifts to alleviate the suffering of others! AMEN

OCTOBER 11
Joy from Adversity

"I have been entrusted with a box that has the Hope diamond inside! The box may not be that attractive to others, but when you open it, you see the most dazzling beauty!" (Emily Colson)

Those of us who lived through the Watergate scandal of the early 1970's will remember Chuck Colson, an attorney who was part of President Nixon's inner circle, and who was subsequently convicted of Federal crimes and sentenced to several years in prison. (See *U-Turn June 16)* Through that experience, which led not only to his becoming a Christian, but eventually to a huge international prison ministry, Colson became one of the best known Christian evangelists of the 20th century. He describes this as a signature paradox: out of his prison experience came a challenge, and meeting that challenge turned out to be more fulfilling than anything he could ever have imagined! He concluded that true joy and freedom comes from obedience to one's calling, not from following one's immediate desires with no restrictions.

Our opening quote is from his daughter Emily, who's son Max was born autistic. The strain on their marriage led to a divorce and the bright horizon she looked to after college, happy marriage, and a successful job, was replaced with a sky of deep darkness and threatening storm clouds. Chuck himself went into a deep depression, grieving for his daughter. But Chuck says his daughter fought back every step of the way, once she conquered her initial "paralyzing fear." As a single mom, she worked to find additional funding for the special school he required. She went through all the difficulties of being a single mother but with the added "burden" of Max's diagnosis.

But gradually a remarkable thing happened. Colson says his daughter's own personal faith deepened and she developed an iron-strong character. Others describe her as "radiant and constantly filled with joy!" Putting her writing and art career on hold, she invested almost all of her time and energy into Max. People who know her, will tell you that she has never once voiced a complaint or expressed the "unfairness" of it all. The opening quote is her description of her own life. She isn't just an example of someone who overcame adversity, according to Colson, in his book, The Good Life. She is an illustration of how one can find true joy in their calling, even if it evolves from difficult circumstances. Her calling wasn't to reach the top of a profession, but to care for someone limited in almost every way except his capacity to love! Pursuing that calling with all her energy led to a person truly joyous and free, not depressed and trapped.

The bible of course, is replete with such stories. Out of Abraham and Sarah's long infertility came Isaac; out of abandonment, adoption, and being a fugitive for murder, came Moses; out of human trafficking, false imprisonment, and threatened execution, came Joseph; from a poor shepherd boy, despised by his older brothers, sent to fight a giant, came King David; there are many more!

We've talked of the chief end of man before. The Westminster Catechism says it is making sure that everything we do is to the glory of God. How do we do that? We use our God given gifts in whatever endeavor we undertake, to comply with the two things Jesus told us specifically were the most important: love God with everything we have, and love our neighbor as ourself. *When we do that, joy and peace follow*, even if we must come through extreme adversity in order to accomplish it.

No, it doesn't follow immediately. Tragedy is tragedy, for all of us. But some shut down, let their gifts go fallow, turn away from God in anger and disappointment. But some realize that God isn't the bad guy. In fact, he's the very definition of the good guy, who will always be available for you, always love and support you, and in point of fact, already laid down His life, specifically to save yours! The people that come to this realization, despite incredibly difficult circumstances, will find a joy that many will never experience!

"Consider it a sheer gift, friends, when tests and challenges come at you from all sides. You know that under pressure your faith is forced into the open and shows its true colors. So don't try to get out of anything prematurely. Let it do its work so you become mature and well-developed, not deficient in any way. If you don't know what you're doing, pray to the Father. He loves to help!" (James 1:2-5a Message)

Prayer: Dear Heavenly Father, we love You! Direct Your Holy Spirit to strengthen and re-direct us when we feel we are about to crumble under the burden of our misfortunes. Help us to realize that our characters are tempered in the furnace, and that applying the gifts you have given us through adversity will see us through to the other side where we find a joy we had not thought possible! Grant us patience Lord, to wait on You! AMEN

OCTOBER 12

Self-Conceit

"There is no fault which makes a man more unpopular, and no fault which we are more unconscious of in ourselves. And the more we have it ourselves, the more we dislike it in others!" (C.S. Lewis)

One of my anesthesiologist friends and I were talking in the surgeons lounge a few days ago. He was aghast at one of the younger Ob/Gyns, who when asked by the circulating nurse to place a Foley Catheter in the bladder, responded that she couldn't help, because she didn't know how. This may mean nothing to the lay person, but it would be analogous to an astronaut who had trained for 10 years for a shuttle mission in all its technical complexity and intricate aerodynamics telling the CapCom in Houston that everything was GO on the launch pad, but they couldn't lift off because he wasn't sure where the ON switch was!

Now, the interesting part of this is that the physician in question took umbrage at the anesthesiologist's incredulity. She began reciting her vaunted education at East Coast schools, her scores on her Boards, etc. etc. I had the same experience forty years ago at UCSF. I happened to go to a medical school that provided extensive hands on experience to medical students. We performed spinal taps, thoracenteses, put in all manner of central lines, chest tubes, intubated patients, performed bone marrow biopsies, you name it. But we weren't in the "Ivy League." Many a time at 2 AM in the ER I would witness an intern telling us essentially how smart he/she was, but then they couldn't draw blood successfully.

The same happened with UCSF medical students as those in the Ivy League. UCSF was an extremely competitive medical school and undoubtedly everyone there was indeed, exceptionally smart. But one night at midnight, attending an eclamptic in DIC (seizing and bleeding out) as the third year Ob/Gyn resident, I asked a senior medical student to run down to Radiology and get the patient's chest film. We were quite frankly, knee deep in alligators at that point, with several emergencies ongoing. He looked me straight in the eye, refused the request, crossed his arms and leaned against the wall. *"I'm not sure I see how that will contribute to my education!"* Needless to say, we found a way to contribute, by altering his future career path. But a smug attitude, self-conceit on display, is possibly the most off-putting characteristic a person can exhibit.

Christians are to take on the mind set of Christ, which as we are told specifically in Philippians 2:2-4 by Paul, and many times by Christ Himself (Matthew 20:28,) is *humility,* the exact opposite of pride or self-conceit. People think of sexual immorality, drunkenness, greed, anger, lying, cheating, stealing and the like as the essential vices, and yet the bible teaches us that pride is worse than all of these bound up together. In fact, when you think about it, self-conceit is *exactly what leads* to all the other vices. Once you start to think of yourself as better than others, and in fact so much better that the rules of civil behavior don't apply to you, then you are in a position to commit every sin imaginable and feel it is simply your right to do so!

The startling realization is that we are all guilty of self-conceit from time to time. This is especially common in those who are either highly educated, trained or just rich, no matter how they came to be that way. When your socio-economic station in life is elevated far above the "common" man, you can start to think of yourself as somehow "better" than the rabble. Christ was by nature, very God and very man, and yet He comported with sinners and "low lifes" of every type. He constantly taught His disciples that the way to please God was in serving others, as He did, not in following a set of rules. The first shall be last and the last first.

The next time someone is telling a story, and it occurs to you that a similar thing has happened with an *even more* remarkable outcome, keep it to yourself! One up-man-ship is the most visible form of self-conceit. I know because I have been guilty of it myself. It's cliche, I know, but WWJD?

Prayer: Father God, looking at ourselves is perhaps the hardest thing to do for all of us. Let Your Holy Spirit within us tweak us whenever we start to behave in a way that puts our own interests ahead of the interests of others, for this is the pattern of self-conceit. Allow us to be repulsed by our own behavior when we start to "toot our own horn," in the common vernacular, and remind us that we are to take on the mind of Christ who sought nothing more than a way to serve. AMEN

OCTOBER 13

Stay Different

"And do not conform to the pattern of this world, but be transformed by the renewing of your mind. Then you will be able to test and approve what God's will is; His good, pleasing and perfect will." (Romans 12:2 NIV)

There's an expression here in Texas that everyone in the state is familiar with: *Keep Austin Weird.* Now, Austin is the state capital of Texas, and so it's where most of the politicians live or at least hang out a lot. It is also the home of, and the central campus for, the University of Texas. You might think 50,000 college students and a bunch of politicians might be enough to make a city weird, but I don't think that's really what the expression means.

Red Wassenich died right before the Pandemic of 2020-21. He was the librarian of the Austin Community College for more than thirty years, and wrote many best selling guide books to the Austin area. It was during his call on a local radio station pledge drive in 2000, that he coined the expression, "Keep Austin Weird." It was subsequently adopted as the official slogan of the Austin Independent Business Alliance and has been mimicked by many cities including Portland, Louisville and Indianapolis. What did he mean exactly?

Austin has a personality all its own, evolving from its small town feel but terrible traffic, its 6th street bars, dives, live music and outdoor cafes as well as its symphony, its wealthy lakeside communities and even its tiny house neighborhoods. Austin is a city that wants to be a small town and a metropolis at the same time, that offers tax breaks to Toyota and Amazon and yet fights to keep big business out with zoning! It's a great place to raise kids, but also to retire. It's home to Bible churches and LGBTQ communities, country music artists and classical symphonies, to rap and hip hop, the seat of State Law enforcement and a welcoming town for protests. Austinians are fiercely proud and protective of their city even with all its paradoxes.

Christians have something in common with those from Austin. They were decidedly weird in the first century. They preached the teachings of Jesus Christ, a poor carpenter executed for blasphemy at only 33. He espoused love for your enemies, rather than hatred. (Matthew 5: 43-44) They preached to turn the other cheek when assaulted, rather than fighting back and extracting an eye for an eye. (Matthew 5:38-39) They taught that followers of Christ would be viewed as righteous in God's eyes, even though they sinned, and be granted eternal life after death. (John 3:16) They proclaimed to a desert people that anyone who drinks well water will soon be thirsty again, but those who drink the water Christ gives them, will never thirst but have eternal life. (John 4:14) They preached that those who follow Christ are not of this world, but belong to the Kingdom of Heaven and only sojourn on earth. (John 18:36) They told people they were truly free, even as a Jews occupied by Rome, because they had died with Christ on the cross, who had forgiven their sins, and were then reborn free from all guilt and shame! They were now righteous before God, not from following the Law of Moses, but from following the Son of God! (Galatians 2:15-21)

Now, all of that was *really weird* in the first century! What's even more weird (weirder?) is that nothing has changed by the 21st century! The Christian who lives his life empowered by the indwelling Holy Spirit, who's goal is to serve rather than be served, to love rather than be loved, to lift others up rather than themselves, and to work in everything to the Glory of God, is definitively viewed as *weird* by an increasingly secular world!

So, if the company you keep ever makes you feel weird because of your faith: congratulations!! You are on the road to becoming more Christ-like!! Keep it up! Keep Yourself Weird just like Austin. Stay different.

> *Prayer: Father, we know Your Son Jesus was decidedly different. Different to the point that He was ridiculed and despised by His own people! So when we feel awkward because our faith doesn't seem to match the attitudes of those around us, give us the strength to STAY WEIRD and not conform to the pattern of this world! AMEN*

OCTOBER 14

In the Pocket

"The angels of the Lord encamp around those who fear Him, and He delivers them. Taste and see that the Lord is good: blessed is the one who takes refuge in Him. (Psalm 34:7-8 NIV)

I live in Texas. That means we have only one real pastime, and that means the same one in all four seasons: football. In fact, during the Pandemic of 2020-21, which ripped the economy apart, separated families, brought international travel to a standstill, and even became a political piñata, Texans really only cared about the virus' effect on one thing: football! So at the moment, I am stuck in the hospital on call, with several patients in labor, watching college football on TV.

Switching from game to game, I always notice the same thing for these offenses. Those teams which have a front line worth paying for (oops) seem to be able to provide the quarterback with a pocket that he can actually step into and depend on. Sure, some QBs get creamed when they make the ill considered decision to fade back and then step out of the pocket, but the ones who step into that pocket when it doesn't collapse, tend make awesome plays over and over. They have no fear of the "blind side" because their left tackle is just as good as their right tackle.

People of faith never have to step out of the pocket...ever! We are assured that if we resist the devil, he will simply flee from us! (James 4:7) Agnostics and atheists misunderstand this promise. It doesn't mean at all that we believers will have no hardship. It doesn't mean that we will escape tragedy in this life. It doesn't mean we won't lose loved ones, or lose jobs, or even lose our health. It means that the Evil One, who is bent on one thing only, separating us from God, will fail! Steadfast faith in the face of adversity *drives Satan to distraction!* He may blitz you from the safety or middle linebacker position, trying to convince you that whatever bad thing has befallen you is somehow God's fault! He wants to convince you to step *out of the pocket of faith* and try and solve your problems on your own, without any direction and protection from the Holy Spirit! I promise you, planning your own escape from that blitz rather than staying in the pocket, will find you curled up on the ground, thrown for a considerable loss!! (Proverbs 16:9)

When things aren't going the way you would like, instead of getting mad at God and deciding you can fix things in your own power, lay them at the feet of your Savior, step into the pocket, and wait for the opening He will provide!

Prayer: Dear Heavenly Father, we love You! If only we could learn to trust You, to step into the pocket rather than retreating and trying to escape out to the side, we can throw the long ball and move the chains, rather than huddling on the ground for a loss! Faith means depending on You to keep Satan at bay, and then we can resist his temptation of pride in our own ability and depend on You to keep the pocket intact! AMEN

OCTOBER 15

Exploit the Joy

"Whoever welcomes one of these little children in My name welcomes Me; and whoever welcomes Me does not welcome Me but the One who sent Me" (Mark 9:37 NIV)

The last of my daughters to become pregnant is now expecting! The cat is finally out of the bag, so to speak, so I can mention it here. But the manner in which the cat was released is illustrative.

My middle daughter and her husband decided, as many couples do, to wait until viability before they informed the world of the upcoming expansion to their family. But when they decided to tell their 8 year old nephew, Liam, and 6 year old niece, Allie, the children of our eldest daughter, they made a game of it! Everyone who lives in town (sister Kelly, husband Ian and cousin Henry unfortunately in Lubbock) came to Grammy and Papa's house for dinner Friday night. Shawn and Allison, the expecting couple, had earlier set up a scavenger hunt for the kids. Allison even carried an untouched glass of wine when she welcomed her older sister, Ashley, at the door, to throw her off the scent!

The kids had multiple stations to find, marked with a flag, and in each was a card in an envelope with a rhyming clue, borrowed in part from Dr. Seuss. At each spot, one of the kids would read the poem out loud. Locations ranged from the big aquarium in the living room, to a tall oak outside (requiring a boost for Liam to reach the card,) to a window seat upstairs, and finally to the refrigerator in the kitchen. The final poem card was under the ribbon around a cake box. When the kids opened the box, there was a final note and an ultrasound picture! Needless to say, neither had any idea what the picture was of, but the note ended with "news that will fill you with glee, Shawn and Allison are having a baby!"

The brief video of this last step in the reveal, would not only make the likes of The Grinch and Mr. Scrooge smile, but is the very reason that Christ said what He did to the Disciples above! Yes, children can be noisy and hyperactive and exhausting, but they are also full of wonder and awe and joy at simple things, and all of that is infectious!

At the time of Christ, and really until the last century, many societies treated children, at best, as insignificant, even if necessary. Quite frankly, the neonatal to childhood mortality rate was as high as 50%, and people just made more children when they didn't survive. If they did survive, they were expected to work from an early age, and to remain silent in the presence of adults unless spoken to. But Jesus wanted people to understand the significance of the preceding verses: *"Anyone who wants to be first must be the very last, and the servant of all."* Children were the most insignificant members of society, even less valuable than slaves. By welcoming the children into His arms, He showed the love of God for all. Similarly, Jesus rebuked the disciples when they sought to keep the children away, whose parents were seeking a blessing from Him. The disciples thought them a nuisance, but Christ told them they represented the Kingdom of heaven! (Matthew 19:13-14) Why? Because the last shall be first!

But I know that's not the only reason. Because I watched not just the children's faces on Friday night, but all the adult faces watching them! Children aren't naive so much as they are filled with the light of new life! Everything is new to them, and they have no inhibitions about showing the joy that discovering every facet of God's wonderful creation brings to them!

You may not have children, or your children may be grown and you are yet to have grandchildren, or you may be of the age where even your grandchildren are grown, no matter! Find a way to suffer the little children to come unto you as well. ***Exploit their joy for yourself!*** Let them remind you how phenomenal the world is by the joy they find in things you have long since thought of as mundane! Watch a three year old and a toad, or a caterpillar, or a butterfly, or a flower, and I guarantee you'll remember how good it is to be alive and how grateful you are to the Creator!

Prayer: Dear Heavenly Father, we love You! Thank you that show us Your love in the cycle of marriage, birth, babies, childhood, (even teens,) and finally adulthood, just to start all over again! Jesus showed us that even the least of us is not only worthy of Your love, but first in the Kingdom of Heaven! Finally, thank you for the wonder that children demonstrate openly in the world around us! Too often the cares of this world divert us from the joy that even the simplest aspects of it hold for those who will stop and view them as a child. AMEN

OCTOBER 16

Surfing the Internet

"A joyful heart is good medicine, but a crushed spirit dries up the bones." (Proverbs 17:22 ESV)

There is no question that a person of good moral character can get into all sorts of trouble surfing the internet. But scrolling through a particular topic, whether on FB, Instagram, Twitter, Vyne, you name it, can be a *very good* thing for your demeanor and your general health! I'm talking of course about funny animal videos. The only real risk to them is not to your moral fiber, but to your continued employment, if you happen to get hooked while at work.

You probably have noted the significant new addition to our family named, Windsor, the labradoodle, from earlier devotionals. I posted a video of him being chased, literally around the front yard, by our 4 year old Tuxedo cat. It opens from a perspective behind and above the cat as he drops into his hunting, "I'm about to pounce" posture, twitching tail and all. The labradoodle is facing him on the lawn about 6 feet away, and makes the ill advised move of belly crawling even closer to the ready to spring feline! A wee bit shocked when he pounces, Windsor beats a hasty retreat and then circles the yard with Sterling the Tuxedo in hot pursuit! It is impossible not to laugh or at least smile when you see it! I know this from FB responses to the post!

There are reams of scientific data suggesting that smiling actually changes your mood for the better, even if you think initially that there is nothing to smile about! So joy leads to smiling, but good evidence suggests that smiling can actually lead to joy as well!We know that a healthy attitude fosters good health, and the opposite holds as well. "Heart" in our opening Proverb refers to the mind, and science has proven repeatedly that a positive outlook hastens healing. A "crushed spirit" means the same as it does today: depression and ill humor. "Bones," during the early Iron Age, when Solomon was thought to have recorded much of the biblical wisdom literature, referred to the entire body. "Fat bones" meant health and "dry bones" meant sickness and deterioration. All this simply means that King Solomon understood that God thinks happiness is good for our health!

So, if there seems to be nothing to smile about in this 2020 Pandemic, forest fire, protest/riot, furloughed, restaurant and theaters closed, Presidential election year, you need to get on your smart phone, (not while driving,) and scroll through YouTube's Funny Cat Videos, or Funny Dog Videos, or Animal Bloopers. (If for some incomprehensible reason animals are not your thing, then scroll through YouTubes of Tim Hawkins or Michael Jr. or Mary Ellen Hooper; same effect!) Even 3 minutes will change your outlook for the day!

Prayer: Father God, what would life be like without humor? Thank you that the creatures over whom we were given dominion, may not only love us unconditionally, as our pets do, but force us to smile even on our darkest days! AMEN

OCTOBER 17

Spiritual Muddle

"Simplicity is the secret of seeing things clearly. The Christian does not think clearly for a long while, but he ought to see clearly without any difficulty." (Oswald Chambers)

My wife has a sign over our breakfast table that reads, "SIMPLIFY." One of my late father's favorite acronyms was, "KISS: Keep It Simple Stupid!" Philosophers and theologians are all familiar with Occam's Razor: "Given multiple possible solutions to a given problem, the simplest is usually correct."

So why is it that so many Christians seem to find themselves in, to use Oswald Chamber's words, "a spiritual muddle?" We read, we think, we pray, we discuss endlessly, we compare and contrast beliefs with others, and yet we still find ourselves confused about all sorts of aspects of our own faith, not to mention others. In intellectual matters, thinking it through, researching it, bouncing it off of others will often clarify a problem and its solution. In spiritual matters however, Chambers says, "we will simply think ourselves into cotton wool!" Why?

Because the fear of the Lord is the beginning of wisdom (Psalm 111:10; Proverbs 1:7;9:10,) not depending on our own intellect in spiritual matters! *"Trust in the Lord with all your heart, And lean not to your own understanding; In all your ways acknowledge Him, And He shall direct your paths."* (Psalm 3:5-6 NKJV) If we are not to depend on our own intellect, how do we begin to trust the Lord? It's simple: obedience! Once we simply decide to obey, then the will of the Lord for our lives becomes remarkably clearer! The spiritual haze begins to clear!

Don't misconstrue this with legalism. It doesn't mean that the one who keeps the most rules is the most righteous! Our righteousness comes from Christ, whose blood washed us clean of sin (1 John 1:7); and in accepting Him, we put on his righteousness like a cloak! (Isaiah 61:10; 2 Corinthians 5:21) No, ***obedience means a posture of the heart***. It means simply obeying Christ's command to love God with everything you've got and to love your fellow man as you love yourself. (Matthew 22:34-40) It means, in the words of the prophet Micah, to do justly, to love mercy, and to walk humbly with your God! (Micah 6:8) The only way to do this is to stay focused on Christ, "the author and finisher of our faith." (Hebrews 12:1-2)

So when doubts start to overwhelm your faith; when you've read and studied and discussed; when you've faced a crisis and feel your prayers have gone unanswered; don't think quite so hard! Your mind will turn to "cotton wool!" Instead, just concentrate on loving, and all of a sudden your personal theology will clear up remarkably quickly, like fog at noon on the seashore when the wind comes up and the sun is high!

> *Prayer: Dear Heavenly Father, we know You meant us to study your Word, discuss it, pray about it! But its a lot; and there's a lot written about it! Remind us when we start to get confused about what it all means, and even if its all true, that we need only to concentrate on loving and all will come clear again! AMEN*

OCTOBER 18

The Gap Remains

"Nothing can fill the gap when we are away from those we love [or they are taken away] ....It is nonsense to say that God fills the gap; [when a loved one is lost] He does not fill it but keeps it empty so that our communion with another may be kept alive, even if painful." (Dietrich Bonhoeffer)

Unfortunately, I have been asked too many times by patients who have lost a child, or a spouse or even a husband, when the pain will go away? The answer of course, is that it doesn't go away; we simply learn how to live with it. At first this seems unacceptable. Why shouldn't we be able to fill that gap in our lives with something or someone else? Why shouldn't a new focus, a new love, time itself, heal the wound? Why won't God take the pain away when we ask earnestly?

One of my patients about ten years ago, had two boys, 4 years and 18 months old. On a random Saturday afternoon, she dashed into the house to answer the phone and her husband, not realizing she wasn't there, went to the garage via a fence gate to get a tool for the backyard. The two children were unsupervised for roughly three minutes. In that time, the 18 month old climbed onto the AC unit, over onto the adjacent above ground pool cover, and fell through an opening at the edge, drowning before his parents returned. I had never seen grief like theirs. She was literally almost catatonic. We did what we could, hooked them up with therapy, and despite our prayers, felt the chances for the family to survive intact were small.

But I underestimated the power of prayer and a woman's strength. Gradually over the next year she pulled out of it. Her love of her older son and her husband prevailed. They went on to have two more children, and volunteer to help other moms and dads who have lost a child.

When you ask her how she got past the pain she'll tell you something like she didn't; its always there. She just learned to live around it, because that hole, that pain, *is her lost son*. If she were actually able to fill that gap with love for another child, or a job or a charity, well then, in an odd way, she would lose him all over again. So paradoxically, as Martha Hickman points out in her classic work <u>Healing After Loss</u>, *"Our ability to love and care is not limited to some finite number, so that taking on a new love means replacing an old one. Time does not expand, but love does—as with a parent who has three children, and then another. What was once loved and cherished is not replaceable."*

If you have lost a loved one, don't believe a new love is a betrayal, or is taking the place of the lost person. The love we feel for the lost will persist, and its place will simply remain that "gap" in our lives, as it should be. So we *will feel better* over time. We *will handle the pain* of that loss better, though it won't be gone until we are united with Christ in a new world. Our affections and attention and time and effort will, and should be channeled into new places, for if we failed to do that and became sullen, introverted and cheerless, we would be wasting the precious gift that is the rest of our lives!

"Blessed are those who mourn, for they shall be comforted." (Matthew 5:4 NIV)

"He will wipe every tear from their eyes. there will be no more death or mourning or crying or pain, for the old order of things has passed away." (Revelation 21:4 NIV)

Prayer: Dear Heavenly Father, we love You! We are blessed that the capacity to love is unlimited by time or space, like You Father! Loves we have lost are never replaced. The pain may remain in the gap that is left, but with the help of the Holy Spirit, we go on, we keep growing outward, finding new people to love and new circumstances to be a Blessing to others! AMEN

OCTOBER 19

It's the Little Things

"Unexpected kindness is the most powerful, least costly, and most underrated agent of human change." (Bob Kerry)

It's a disappointment to me that people are so surprised by a little kindness. In our busy society with people rushing from one thing to another, head down, concerned with their own agenda, it just takes people totally unawares when you are even nice to them. A case in point involves the book I just mentioned the other day, Martha Hickman's fabulous classic, now forty years old, entitled *Healing After Loss*. The inspiration for this much loved daily devotional, was the tragic death of the author's teenage daughter, when thrown from a horse on a family vacation.

When my father passed away in 2014, he and my mom had been married for 64 years. An anesthesiologist friend of my heart surgeon brother gave her a copy of Hickman's devotional around the time of the funeral. Mom subsequently recommended it to me. Even years later I find myself driving and just on the edge of calling out "Hey Siri, call Dad," multiple times per week. The thoughts in this little book reflect my own almost every time. Anyway, I decided to buy them 30 at a time, and simply give them to patients of mine who are hurting from a recent loss. I've had to reorder every month for several years now.

The remarkable thing is how touched almost every single patient is; that I would even care about their loss, no less *give* them a book? Almost all of them ask, "*You're **giving** this to me?*" Our culture accustoms people to being pushed repeatedly to buy things like extensions on their car warranty, for which they have no need whatsoever; not to receiving an unsolicited gift out of compassion! I've mentioned this before, but next time you are in say, an airport bathroom, and someone who speaks no English is cleaning the toilets, thank them with a smile and give them not a dollar, but $20! It will brighten their week, maybe their month, and they will remember it forever! You might say that this doesn't advance the case for Christ when His name is never mentioned! I don't think that's true.

Christ wants us to love each other, and when we demonstrate that, even to total strangers, it can gradually change their hearts. It changes them so that their hearts are receptive to the Gospel and the Holy Spirit! The individual who lives a life of drudgery from day to day, viewing each sunrise as just another challenge to stay alive, often sees little for which to be thankful. That one unsolicited act of kindness may be all it takes to open their eyes to new possibilities; new possibilities like the existence of a loving God who would make the ultimate sacrifice just to bring people back to Him!

Don't miss your next opportunity to show a little kindness: leave a generous tip and write on the receipt that this waitress's service was the best you've ever had; give that $20 bill to the unsuspecting janitor; tell the person on the IT help line, the one with the heavy Indian accent, that you sincerely, really, really appreciate their help; ask that person at work whom you just can't stand being around, if there's anything you can do to help them right now, or simply tell them everyone's noticed they are doing a great job; give someone who needs it your umbrella; offer to walk a co-worker to their car after dark; bring a flavored ice water out to the men working on the phone lines behind your house! If you keep your eyes open, there are thousands of opportunities every single day to show people the love of Christ without saying a single word. Try it.

"Be kind to one another, tender hearted, forgiving one another as God in Christ forgave you." (Ephesians 4:32 ESV)

"Therefore encourage one another, build each other up..." (1 Thessalonians 5:11 ESV)

"Anxiety in a man's heart weighs him down, but a good word makes him glad." (Proverbs 12:25 ESV)

Prayer: Dear heavenly Father, we love You! Direct your Holy Spirit to lead us to those moments where we can simply be kind, and possibly change someone's life forever. AMEN

OCTOBER 20

Mess up or Cover UP

"If we claim to be without sin, we deceive ourselves and the truth is not in us. If we confess our sins, he is faithful and just and ill forgive us our sins and purify us from all unrighteousness." (1 John 1:8-9 NIV)

I witnessed the maturation, or sometimes, lack there-of, of our four teenagers! All are grown now with careers and young children of their own. But as teenagers they all made some poor decisions that could be written off to lack of experience, lack of awareness re consequences, peer pressure, rebelliousness, or perhaps just general lack of cerebral development! All of these mis-steps were expected at some point, understandable and forgivable.

Had any of them made the decision to lie about their mess-up later, it would have been a much more serious error than the initial offense! Sneaking out the window at 1 AM is not nearly as serious as lying about it afterwards. Wrecking the car is not nearly as serious as lying about the circumstances afterwards. Drinking alcohol when you're not permitted, and not of age, is not nearly as serious as lying about it when confronted with the evidence. Using a fake ID is not as serious as lying about how you obtained it in the first place. You get the idea.

Hypocrisy is really just a more pervasive version of lying. The hypocrite is essentially lying to he rest of the world, all the time. He wants the rest of the world to see a version of himself that he knows is false. They get so used to it, that they start to lie to themselves as well, believing their own press, as it were.

Jesus dealt very differently with the self-conceited hypocrite, as opposed to the average sinner. He could frequently be found in the company of tax collectors, liars, cheats, and prostitutes, but assured all that they would enter the Kingdom of Heaven before any one of the Pharisees. (Matthew 21:31) For Jesus came to those in need of salvation, not those who were sure they needed no such thing! While having dinner at Levi, the tax collector's house, in the company of all manner of sinner, the Pharisees asked why on earth he associated with the likes of them? Jesus overheard the question and answered, " It is not the healthy who need a doctor, but the sick. I have not come to call the righteous, but the sinners!" (Mark 2:17)

When the Pharisees questioned His healing of the demon possessed man who was blind and mute, Jesus called them a "brood of vipers," so evil that nothing good could ever come out of their mouths! (Matthew 12:34) Later, when addressing the Pharisees and Scribes in front of a crowd including the disciples, He delivered the famous "Seven Woes." Jesus called them plainly, hypocrites, but also went on to refer to them as blind guides, blind fools, who ignore justice, mercy and faithfulness, while priding themselves on giving a tenth of their spices to the Temple! (Matthew 23:23) He accused them of cleaning the outside of the cup and dish (Appearance) but inside are self-indulgence and greed!(Character) He called them "white-washed tombs" righteous appearing on the outside, but inside they are dead and unclean.

We ALL sin. We all fall short of the mark! (Romans 3:23) We have all turned away. No one is righteous! (Romans 3:10-12) It is those who think themselves righteous because they 'keep" the laws, and those who pretend to be righteous even though they know they aren't, who deny in their hearts the reality of the gift offered through Christ, and will end up separated from Him forever! We who recognize that we sin, want to turn around, and accept Christ as our Lord, will be the ones who find themselves saved and born again to a new existence! (1 John 1:8-10)

Prayer: Dear heavenly Father, we trust You! We depend on You. Let our understanding of Your Majesty function to keep us humble every day, and in that humility, recognize our own sinfulness. No one is righteous, not one, except for The One in whom we place our faith! Thank You that You have offered His righteousness to us while still sinners, so that we might return to You! AMEN

OCTOBER 21

Are You Worthy?

"He Himself bore our sins in His body on the tree, that we might die to sin and live to righteousness. by His wounds you have been healed." (1 Peter 2:24 ESV)

You're probably tired of hearing about our Labradoodle Windsor, but he's really a very good boy. If you give him the command to "sit," or "high five," or "lie down," and he does it, well then he deserves a treat, right? If on the other hand, he just looks up at you, cocks his head to one side, and acts as if you have either lost your mind or are speaking Swahili, then no treat, right? That's what it means to be deserving. If you behave in a certain way, then you will get rewarded. If you behave differently than that, you not only get no reward, you might even get punished. That would be "undeserving."

So, if you're a sinner; maybe you've cheated, lied, embezzled, had an abortion, committed date-rape, hit your spouse, stolen from a store, stolen a car or a stereo, have addiction issues to alcohol, drugs, hookers, porn, gambling, or maybe you're just self-centered and downright mean, you name it; well then, no reward for you right? I mean, aren't Christians rewarded because they're "good" people? If you find yourself in that sinner group, you're just not worthy of salvation, right? Would a church even want you to be a member? The "good" people who follow the rules, never commit crimes, have few bad habits, and treat most everyone with love and respect, surely they're worthy of the sacrifices Christ made!

This of course, is the wisdom of the world, and the reason God tells us repeatedly in the scriptures not to trust it! (Psalm 3:5; James 4:4; 1 Corinthians 1:19-20; 3:19)*Worthiness* and *deservedness* are often confused. Christ died for us *while we were yet sinners!* (Romans 5:8) "Yet sinners" is the old English way to say that we are all still sinning at the moment we are saved by putting our faith in Christ! Our *worth* is defined by that very faith. God sees our worth in Christ and Christ in us, and that's how we attain the righteousness required to come into the Father's presence. It has nothing whatsoever to do with what we *deserve*. What we *deserve* is death! Every one of us! (Romans 6:23)

So, if we constantly sin and are "undeserving" of reward, what determines our worth? True, the believers' value, their worth, their very identity, is found in Christ Jesus. But what is the worth of any man that God would care enough to sacrifice His only Son for them? Why does God pay attention to mankind at all? God is not only aware of man's plight, separation from Him, even if self-inflicted, but He gave man dominion over all of the earth and all the creatures that live upon it! (Psalm 8:1-8) In fact, *"God so loved the world that He gave His one and only Son, that whoever believes in Him shall not perish but have eternal life."* (John 3:16 NIV)

So the next time you think you're not worthy of God's love or Christ's sacrifice, you're thinking like the world; like the Evil One wants you to think! If someone tells you don't deserve God's love, they're RIGHT! You don't! What you deserve is death and that has been man's ultimate reward since the rebellion in the Garden! However, if you think you're not *worth* God even troubling about you, you are dead WRONG! You are made in His image, and He's the one who has determined your worth is not simply high, but inestimable!

Prayer: Dear heavenly Father, Thank You that You chose to give us Christ rather than the death we deserve! Thank You that You made us in Your image, and although we may have tarnished it with rebellion, we haven't erased it! As such, You see us as worthy of Your extreme and unfailing love! AMEN

OCTOBER 22

Disqualified

"If you declare with your mouth, "Jesus is Lord," and believe in your heart that God raised him from the dead, you will be saved." (Romans 10:9 NIV)

Sailboat racing has a lot of rules. I mean a whole lot. The U.S. Sailing Racing Rules are outstripped only by the World Sailing Racing Rules. There are 91 RULES, divided into seven PARTS. Each rule under each part is divided into SECTIONS for that rule, i.e. Rule 63.1 Rule 63.2 etc. Usually a numbered rule has 4 sections. Each section is divided into sub-sections, such as Rule 63.1 (a) Rule 63.1 (b) etc. and there are usually four of those. So there are really, give or take, 728 actual rules. The rules section is preceded by DEFINITIONS AND BASIC PRINCIPLES, which believe me, if you are a layman with respect to sailing, you might find the most difficult part to comprehend of all! The assumption, is that you already speak the unique language of those who operate sailing vessels. That means you know the difference between a sheet and a halyard, a stay and a spreader, a gunnel and a transom, a windless and a winch, windward form leeward, a jibe from a tack, the tack from the clue, the clue from the peak, the leach the foot, the foot from the luff, a topping lift from a downhaul, etc. etc. You get the idea. After the Rules Section comes the APPENDICES A-T, sort of like a Bill of Rights added to the US Constitution, and governing variances such as Wind Surfing rules, Scoring, Team rules, Radio use, Logos on sails, Protest committees etc. etc.

Now, when it comes to *actually participating in a sailboat race,* you have to not only know how to make the boat move most efficiently, using wind as your only source of power, but you have to *know the rules by heart*! For example, *fetching* meant a pretty girl to my grandfather. It means going to get the ball and bring it back to my dog (sometimes,) but in sailboat racing it means when "*she (all sailboats are feminine) is in a position to pass to windward of a mark and leave it on the required side without changing tack.*" While that is a definition and not a rule, if you pass around the mark on the wrong side you may be penalized or even disqualified. You also have to comply with *mark-room,* which is leaving space for another competitor to sail on a proper course close to the mark, to leave a mark on the required side, and finally to round the mark as necessary to sail the course. If another skipper feels you did not comply, he may file a protest, and if found guilty by a committee afterwards, you may be disqualified. (Of course, mark-room for a boat does not include room to tack unless she is overlapped inside to windward of the boat required to give mark-room and she would be fetching the mark after her tack. *Believe it or not, that is perfectly clear to every member of my family!)*

The Israelites of the Old Testament only had 613 Laws of Moses, 115 less than those with which the sailboat racer needs to comply! The Pharisees and the scribes, made it clear to the Chosen People that failure to comply with these Laws would make them unclean in the eyes of the Lord, and atonement for each one of these sinful failures required sacrifices that were handled by the priests. But God made it abundantly clear through the prophets, that no man could comply perfectly with the Law, and thus no man could make himself righteous before Yahweh, the Creator God! (Isaiah 53:6)

Compliance with all the rules in racing can be difficult, but complying with all of the Laws of Moses was impossible. While you might get disqualified from a sailboat race when you make a mistake, you were *always* disqualified, as far as God was concerned under the Old Covenant, because God recognized that His people were simply going through the motions of the sacrificial system, assuming they were forgiven, when none of their behavior actually changed. (Jeremiah 9:25) There was no *repentance*, no true desire to correct their behavior. No one is righteous. (Romans 3:10-12, 20) The price for that was death, ever since the Garden of Eden.(Romans 3:23)

So, as prophesied for centuries, (Isaiah 40:1-5; 53) God sent a Savior, in the form of His only Son, who would be fully man and fully God, live a perfect sinless live, die on the cross as the perfect sacrifice for all our sins, be dead and buried, and then rise again to reign in Heaven for eternity! By simply believing in Him, we become cloaked in His righteousness, die to our old selves, and are re-born with the Holy Spirit indwelling us! (Galatians 2:20) Not only are we promised eternal life, but we are free! We are no longer slaves to sin, destined to always round the mark the wrong direction or cross the start line too early or fail to give our brother room at the mark! ***And we can never be disqualified!*** (Romans 8:1) Christ died for us ***while we were yet sinners.*** (Romans 5:8) This doesn't mean we will never make mistakes; we will, because we're only human! (Romans 3:10) But the indwelling Holy Spirit means we desperately long to do the right thing! We want to do it because we know that God so loved us that He gave us our Lord and Savior in whom we live and breath and have our being! (Acts 17:28)

If you think that you are disqualified because of your sins, because you look back and view yourself as just a flat out bad person; or you feel you've lost your qualification because even after accepting Jesus, you sin; then you just don't understand Grace and the Gospel! We don't have a set of rules to keep like the Israelites or like competitive sailors. All we have is Jesus. Nothing more. And nothing more is required. When you are in Him and He in you, trust me, you qualify!

Prayer: Dear Heavenly Father, we love You! We praise You and we worship You for all of creation, but specifically for loving us enough to save us through the Cross of Jesus, when all we deserve is death, the ultimate disqualification! AMEN

OCTOBER 23

Just a Sec!

"See what kind of love the Father has given to us, that we should be called children of God; and so we are! The reason why the world does not know us, is that it did not know Him." (1 John 3:1 ESV)

Like a lot of physicians, I can get pretty intense sometimes; pretty focused; essentially trained to shut out extraneous input and concentrate on the task at hand. I am sure this "quality" was honed through years of determined study from prep school, to college, to Medical School. This tendency to shut out interruption then developed further in the operating room where concentration might mean the difference between a good outcome and a bad one. Unfortunately, an intolerance to interruption may not serve as well in real life as in the operating room.

One of the best books I have ever read was entitled, *Deep Survival,* by Laurence Gonzales. His father was a bio-physicist in the Texas Medical Center in Houston, where I had gone to medical school. Frederico Gonzales, his father, had the left wing of his B-17 shot off over Dusseldorf at 27,000 feet during WWII. The plane broke apart, all 10 crew were killed, but Gonzales rode the spiraling hunk of steel to the ground where it crashed through the roof of a barn. He broke nearly every bone in his body, but survived the rest of the war in a German prison camp. Laurence grew up wondering why it was that some people survived horrific accidents and others did not. Was it just chance, or were survivors different somehow? The answer has to do with aspects of fight or flight, the power of emotional highs, and the ability to be hyper-focused when need be, and open to outside stimuli when need be, and never confusing the two.

Many of the stories in this book related the deaths of people who didn't have to die; they simply became so focused that they brooked no interruption at all; took in no outside information, even terribly relevant information, if it disrupted their attention to achieving their goal. Mountain climbers that ignore approaching storms; pilots that ignore air traffic controllers; skiers that ignore clearly posted warnings; and hundreds of examples of those who ignore interruption so that they can attain an anticipated intense emotional high, like landing safely on an aircraft carrier or reaching the summit of a mountain!

Shutting out interruption worked well for me in studying medicine, but it didn't work quite as well when my small children needed my attention. It didn't work quite as well when my grown children needed my attention either! (See DOING LIFE January 1) It certainly doesn't work too well in a marriage. It turns out, intolerance of interruption doesn't work very well as a Christian either!

Jesus wants us to love God and love each other right? Well, its hard to love another if you won't pay any attention to him or her because you're too busy with whatever it is you're busy with! All of us tend to get hyper-focused and busy at our jobs. While our jobs are important to feed and clothe our families, they're not so important that you forget the Greatest Commandments! Interruptions by people who request our attention could be annoying and insignificant, true. But they could also be opportunities to demonstrate the love of Christ, which you would have missed entirely if you have isolated yourself either physically or emotionally or both, so that you have become unapproachable to others! In loving them by helping and attending to them, you nudge them in the direction of knowing the loving God you worship!

BE AVAILABLE for the Holy Spirit to work through you! How many times in your life have you said, "Just a second!" to a co-worker, to a subordinate, to a member of your family, and then either turned the second into an hour, or more commonly, forgot that they had approached you at all! Focus is good, to a limit. Focusing to the point where it excludes the human needs of others can become a disaster! Next time someone interrupts you with a need or a question, unless you are defusing a nuclear device with 110 seconds left on the timer, STOP what you are doing and see how you can help! Treat them as you know you should treat your own children whom you love fiercely! It will change your life, and possibly the lives of the people with whom you interact, for the better!

"When the Lord saw that he turned aside to see, God called to him out of the bush, 'Moses, Moses!' And he said, 'Here I am!' (Exodus 3:4 ESV)

"And I heard the voice of the Lord saying, 'Whom shall I send, and who will go for us?' Then I said, 'Here am I! Send me!' (Isaiah 6:8 ESV)

"Then the Lord called Samuel. Samuel answered, 'Here I am; you called me?' … Speak for Your servant is listening.' (1 Samuel 3:4,10 ESV)

Prayer: Dear Heavenly Father, we love You! Direct Your Holy Spirit within us to view interruptions as opportunities to show Your love that simply show up unexpectedly; rather than viewing them as annoyance! AMEN

OCTOBER 24

No, He Didn't

"Or those eighteen who died when the tower in Siloam fell on them—do you think they were more guilty than all the others living in Jerusalem?"

"I tell you no! But unless you repent, you too will all perish." (Luke 13:4-5 NIV)

Recently an acquaintance related a horrific story. While she was speaking with a friend on the phone, she actually overheard her murder during an attempted car-jacking. Apparently, the woman who died was extremely well thought of by everyone who had ever had contact with her. She had a devoted husband, loving children, neighbors and friends who adored her, and a history of charitable work that would impress Mother Teresa. She was killed by a group of teens, evidently completely lacking in a sense of right and wrong, who incredibly, struck again elsewhere the following day, which eventually led to their capture.

My friend remarked at the end of her narration, that she just didn't understand "Why God would take a person like her? It just makes no sense!" Indeed, there are "senseless" tragedies that happen in our fallen world every minute of every day. In fact, one of the most famous books of the twentieth century, Rabbi Harold Kushner's, *Why Bad Things Happen to Good People*, sought to address this very issue. His conclusion had more to do with the "tapestry" of God's overall plan and our inability to see it as He does. While it's true that God has a plan *for good* for those who love Him, and we may not be able to see it in the midst of tragedy, that ***does not mean that He caused the tragedy!*** (Jeremiah 29:11)

So when my friend asks why God would **take** a person like her, my answer is, ***"No, He didn't!"*** While this discussion can lead one down a serious theological rabbit hole, since Job acknowledged that *"The Lord giveth and the Lord taketh away,"* only those adherents of theological determinism believe that every single event is orchestrated by God. When we try to make sense of tragedy in terms of our faith, we must first remember the *nature of God* and one simple truth: ***God is love.*** (Ephesians 2:4; 1 John 4:7) Yes, God is omnipotent, and yes God has power over life and death, but we live in a fallen world since the first man rebelled against Him, and Satan has dominion over the earth! When bad things happen, it is just not theologically sound to *blame a loving God who wants more than anything to bring us into a relationship with Him!* (John 3:16; John 1:10-13; Romans 5:8; Hebrews 11:6)

When someone asked Jesus if the 18 who died when the tower fell in Siloam were worse sinners than others and thus were taken, he answered essentially, that their deaths were accidental. When Jesus healed the man born blind and was asked who had sinned to cause this, the man himself or his parents, Jesus responded that no one had sinned. His blindness only served as an opportunity for the mighty power of God to be displayed in the healing! (John 9:2-3) Paul explains in his letter to the Romans, that God works everything together for good for those who love Him! (Romans 8:28)

When your son-in-law gets lymphoma, when your dad dies of Parkinson's, when your teenager dies in a car wreck, when you lose your pregnancy, when your spouse dies of pancreatic cancer, thinking that God is responsible for it, is ***exactly what Satan wants!*** How better to have you turn on your Creator than to make you believe He is responsible for the worst thing that has ever happened to you?

Next time someone asks why God took someone away in a senseless tragedy, you might remember, that to believe God did that is, in fact, senseless itself! God is so personally in love with You that to believe He would purposefully hurt you is scripture turned upside down! Don't believe it. Did He kill your loved one? ***No, He Didn't!***

"I am convinced that neither death nor life, neither angels nor demons, neither the present nor the future, nor any powers, neither height nor depth, nor anything else in all creation, will be able to separate us from the love of God that is in Christ Jesus our Lord." (Romans 8:38-39)

Prayer: Father God, we love You because You first loved us. No thought of You "taking anyone too soon" makes any sense, Lord. We know of Your unfailing love and turn to You as a source of refuge in tragedy, not as the source of the tragedy! AMEN

OCTOBER 25

I Got this

"The Lord of hosts has sworn: "As I have planned, so shall it be, and as I have purposed, so shall it stand." (Isaiah 14:24 ESV)

Thirty four years ago I bent down to pick up a sock and my back "went out." Any of you who have bad backs understand that the phrase "went out" is totally inadequate as a descriptor of the paralyzing pain and immobility that drops you to the floor unable to move, often for hours. I had ruptured my second disc, the first having been thirteen years before that, playing high school basketball. Unfortunately I was only several months into my new job as a physician with Walnut Hill Obstetrics in Dallas.

I ended up in the hospital, and one early morning was awaiting surgery when a nurse came into my room and said, "Time for your enema!" I responded, "No, way. That is not part of this!" I insisted on seeing the order in the chart. She then brought the chart and showed me the order, written not by my neurosurgeon, but by my new senior partner! This I was to learn, was exactly his sense of humor!

I remember distinctly being rolled down the hall on a gurney, watching the fluorescent lights pass overhead, and thinking how helpless I was. I had absolutely no control over my circumstances. Had the nurse not relented, I might even have had to submit to a most uncomfortable practical joke! Now, as I rumbled down the 6th floor hallway, I thought to myself, "What if they roll me into the elevator shaft and the elevator isn't there?" Okay, I might have already had a few pre-op meds.

The point I am trying to make is that feeling like you have no control is an extremely uncomfortable feeling; and purposefully ceding control to another is even worse! When you get on a commercial jet, you cede all control for your safe transit to the crew. When you zip line in Costa Rica, or ride up a chair lift in Crested Butte, you are ceding control to the operators and the people that maintain the equipment safely. When you go on a trip and your spouse is driving 75mph on a freeway or even a two lane state highway, you've ceded control for your life to the other person. These things may not be that hard to do, unless you maybe start thinking about them a little too hard! When they asked Alan Shepherd what it was like to sit on the launch pad on top of a Mercury Redstone rocket, he replied, "How would you feel if you were sitting on top of 100,000 lbs of explosives inside a rocket whose every part was assembled by the lowest bidder?" That's ceding control!

Our Lord is Sovereign! That means He is in control of the whole shootin' match! Yes, He has granted us free will to make our own decisions, to make our own choices, but eventually we learn that trusting in Him is the only decision with a reliable outcome!(Proverbs 16:9, 33; 19:21) And while it is hard to cede control of our lives to *anyone else*, it is *essential* that we recognize our ultimate dependence on our creator, and that omnipotence and omniscience have real meaning! (Psalm 135:6; Isaiah 45:7) The remarkable thing to me, is that as difficult as giving up control is for all of us, once you begin to do it on a daily basis, you find it not only easier, but desirable. It works on a physical level when you delegate tasks to others and find it vastly improves your life, and on every level, when you take your worries, your fears, your regrets, your confusion, and lay them at the foot of the Lord!

Of course, the clay pot isn't really "ceding control" to the Potter, because the potter had control all along! But it is the recognition, that we are not *really ultimately in control* that brings not fear, but relief! *Fear of the Lord*, of course means holding God in awe, not being scared. When we hold God in awe, when we understand His sovereignty, when we feel His reassuring presence and power, then we can give ourselves a break! When you are at the end of your rope, at work, at home, or literally scaling El Capitan, there are no sweeter words to hear than, "It's cool, I got this!" when help arrives!

Well, a sovereign Lord means that every moment of every day, when you find yourself going to pieces, backed into a corner, or simply exhausted, all you have to do is call on Him and you'll feel those sweet, sweet, words wash over you: ***"Don't worry, I got this!"***

"The salvation of the righteous is from the Lord; He is their stronghold in the time of trouble." (Psalm 37:39 ESV)

"Then they cried to the Lord in their trouble and He delivered them from their distress." (Psalm 107:28 ESV)

Prayer: Dear Father, all of us have trouble ceding control of aspects of our lives to others. What a Blessing that when we learn of Your power and love, and recognize You are always available and always in control, our lives take on a peace that we could otherwise never know! AMEN

OCTOBER 26

Debbie Downer

"Therefore encourage one another and build each other up, just as in fact you are doing...(1 Thessalonians 5:11)

On May 1, 2004, a new expression entered the American Lexicon. "Debbie Downer" was introduced as a character on Saturday Night Live, played by Rachel Dratch. The sketch was so popular, that the term came to apply to anyone whose negative comments constantly make other people feel bad, or reliably dampens the mood of an individual or group of people.

In one skit at Disney World, a family seated together is excited about the breakfast special of steak and eggs, Debbie Downer exclaims that ever since mad cow disease surfaced in the US, knowing it can live in your body for years before ravaging your brain, she's not taking any chances! A moment later when her cousin remarks that Tigger hugged her at the door, and she thought she would cry she was so excited, Debbie Downer pipes up with the fact that Roy of Zigfried and Roy, wasn't doing so well after his own tiger attacked him and left him brain damaged and paralyzed! You get the idea!

Whatever the rationale for its use, scripture is pretty clear about how God feels. Putting others down, either discouraging them right to their face or undermining them behind their back, is a reprehensible action in the Lord's eyes. In fact, James tells us, in an extended passage, that our tongues are really windows into our souls. Not only can we do great damage with our tongues, but the language we use reflects who we really are. He refers to the tongue as *"a restless evil, full of deadly poison. With the tongue we praise our Lord and Father, and with it we curse human beings, who have been made in God's likeness. Out of the same mouth come both praise and cursing...can both fresh water and salt water flow from the same spring?" (James 3:8-11 NIV)*

Whenever and wherever it is possible, if you are standing around the water-cooler at work, in your TV room watching football with the guys, or out to lunch with the girls, when you hear Debbie Downer's voice, particularly if the effect is to discourage someone or put someone down with their comments, steer the conversation in the opposite direction! If there is just no way that you feel you can do that, then at least tell the others you really don't want to be a part of it, and walk away. Remember, Edmund Burke famously exclaimed, *"The only thing necessary for the triumph of evil is for good men or women to do nothing,"* and as my grandmother famously said, *"If you can't say anything nice, then say nothing at all!"*

> *Prayer: Dear Heavenly Father, We love You! When we find ourselves bad-mouthing someone else, forgetting that they are not only Your creation but made in Your very image, have Your Holy Spirit startle us into self awareness and put a stop to it! When we hear others doing the same, let us be bold enough to either directly correct another, or at least move the conversation in another direction! AMEN*

OCTOBER 27

Locker Room

"Do not let any unwholesome talk come out of your mouths, but only what is helpful for building others up according to their needs, that it may benefit those who listen." (Ephesians 4:29 NIV)

October

In recent years there has been another nuance added to the comments made by the Debbie Downers of the world referenced in yesterday's devotional. I am referring to the torrents of foul language often heard publicly nowadays. Maybe I have just become too fussy in my mid 60's, but not only do I witness this intermittently in my own work environment, but it seems to be commonplace among the tail-end of the Gen Xers, and the norm among many Millennials and Gen Zers. It is almost like a societal version of trash-talking on collegiate or professional football fields. It's what my father used to call, "locker room language."

Whenever we go out to a restaurant that is somewhat trendy with younger folks, just walking through the parking lot and then finding our way to our seats, we overhear conversations where every sentence is laced with multiple "f*** yeahs," or "Sh** , that's f***ing ridiculous!" Perhaps it's due to the general deterioration in literacy that has accompanied the loss of the written word. Texting has replaced even e-mail, such that the skill of letter writing is virtually extinct. But this can't be the entire explanation, for it is not simply the lack of articulation in modern spoken language that is so obvious, but the infusion of a non-stop stream of vulgarities. There was a time when a "swear word" was used in special times of stress, like when you just smashed your thumb with the hammer, or the bookshelves you were hanging collapsed to the floor in mid-installation! Not that it was excusable even then, but it was at least understandable. The word "expletive" means literally, a meaningless exclamation to "fill up space." And a new generation has chosen to "fill up space" with the worst vulgarities imaginable? Why? Does it make the speaker feel more "in with the in-crowd" as we said in the 60's? Does it make them feel tough, or superior, or confident somehow?

What we **do know** is how it makes their Creator feel! *"Let there be no filthiness nor foolish talk nor crude joking, which are out of place, but instead let there be thanksgiving." (Ephesians 5:4 ESV)* Christ Himself addressed the issue, recorded in the gospel of Matthew. *"It is not what goes into the mouth that defiles a person, but what comes out of the mouth, this defiles a person!" (Matthew 15:11 ESV)* In Luke the Lord says, *"The good person out of the good treasure of his heart produces good, and the evil person out of his evil treasure produces evil, for out of the abundance of the heart his mouth speaks!" (Luke 6:45 ESV)* It is not just advice to avoid injuring someone else's sensibilities. God takes an extremely dim view of those whose speech is careless and especially if injurious to others. There will be a time, on the Day of Judgment, when Christ returns, when every person will be called to give an account of every careless word they have ever spoken! (Matthew 12:36)

Solomon had a lot to say about what my mom used to call, "potty mouths." Proverbs 19:1 says, *"Better is a poor person who walks in his integrity than one who is crooked in speech and is a fool."* In Proverbs 10:32, *"The lips of the righteous know what is acceptable, but the mouth of the wicked, what is perverse!"*

Saint Paul made it pretty clear as well, in his letter to the Colossians, *"Now you must put them all away: anger, wrath, malice, slander, and obscene talk from your mouth." (Colossians 3:8 ESV)*

The bottom line is this: your words are significant, even if you think they aren't. Maybe you've fallen into the habit of using expletives in normal declarative sentences, essentially for no reason that you can identify? Maybe you think it isn't hurting anyone, so who cares? But you'd be wrong. What comes out of your mouth reveals your character to others. When you use words carelessly, it's yourself that you are hurting. So quit it.

Prayer: Dear Heavenly Father, We love You! In praising You, remind us that You have made us in Your image, and everything we do that tarnishes our character tarnishes Yours! Forgive us Lord when we speak carelessly; when we take Your name in vain of course, but also when we use coarse vulgarities simply because others around us are doing the same! AMEN

OCTOBER 28

Far from the Shallow

"Tell me something girl. Are you happy in this modern world? Or do you need more? Is there somethin' else you're searchin' for? I'm falling. In all the good times I find myself, Longin' for change, And in the bad times I fear myself..." (Stefani Germanotta)

Yet another remake of the classic movie, *A Star is Born,* was released in 2018, starring Lady Gaga and Bradley Cooper. Viewers that were expecting the same fare as they received with Barbra Streisand in 1976, Judy Garland in 1954 or even Janet Gaynor in 1937, were in for a pleasant surprise! The powerful voice and universally admired originality of Lady Gaga (Stefani Germanotta raised in the Upper West Side of Manhattan) brought new life to the modernized tragic love story, and also a Grammy and Academy Award winning original song, *Far From the Shallow.*

Most of us spend much of our lives just staying afloat, staying right near the surface, so we can at least breathe. Whether we asphalt roofs for a living, lay rebar in foundations, stand behind a cash register, argue cases in court, or take others' lives in our hands in an operating room, we might very well come home exhausted most nights. There might be few moments of discussion over the dinner table. There probably will be an hour or two of TV. There might even be some exercise, working out on a Peloton or walking the dog. What there usually isn't, is time or energy for many "deep" conversations. We get in the habit of staying near the surface, or maybe just "in the shallows."

Unfortunately, developing this habit inadvertently, has a tendency to condition us in such a way that staying "in the shallows" is the only place where we're really comfortable. Believers in this circumstance, are robbing themselves of the kind of fellowship that scripture tells us we desperately need! All of us sin. All of us tend to carry some burden of shame or guilt, even though we know intellectually that we were freed from this on the Cross of Jesus. James, the brother of Jesus, tells us that we need to confess our sins to each other so that we might pray for each other. (James 5:16) Dietrich Boenhoffer, author of *Life Together,* urges the same. If you only discuss last night's football scores or who you liked on The Voice, you're never going to make it to that deeper level!

If you're not in a small group of some sort; a Life Group out of your church, a Bible study, a book club; even a group as intimate as a regular golf foursome, a bowling team, or a card game; then get in one! Even if you do, it's hard to share the most intimate issues with even a small group. You may need to concentrate on a relationship with one or two others with whom you can confide, and who can hold you accountable in the future. Sometimes it can even be a sibling with whom you want to cultivate a closer relationship.

Everybody needs someone they can trust completely when they're far from the shallow! Yes, of course, hopefully you can and will go into the deep with your spouse. But you usually need someone else as well. The marital relationship is so central to most of or lives, that sometimes we need a more objective perspective than our spouse. Our opening lyrics ask if you're happy in this modern world, or are we searching for something more? Well, newsflash: we're all searching for something more, because we were made that way! Pascal called it "a God shaped vacuum in the heart of every man." Christians believe that only Christ can fill that hole. And scripture tells us that our Savior wants us to serve each other, love each other, and in so doing, love God.

You'll never fill that hole if you stay superficial, right on the surface. Christ wants a personal relationship with you, and that is facilitated best by like-minded close friends with whom you can share all aspects of your faith and your day to day life. What you need is to move **far from the shallow;** swim into the deep with someone whose close, reliable friendship you have developed, so that it becomes second nature to confide in and help each other!

> *Prayer: Dear Heavenly Father, We love You! We understand the best way to show that is by loving each other! Any love relationship, to be long-lasting and solid, means we can approach each other with our guard down. That kind of vulnerability comes only from being able to confide in each other, knowing we are doing so with no fear of judgment. Use the Holy Spirit within us to glorify the Father through every relationship where we move far from the shallow! AMEN*

OCTOBER 29

Rest in Peace

"Forgiveness is not about the other person, it's about you! It's not about making peace with others; it's about making peace with yourself." (Dr. Heather Violante)

As we approach Halloween in America, signs bearing the acronym R.I.P. have been popping up on front lawns throughout our neighborhood. The Latin phrase, *requiescat in pace,* means "may the deceased rest in peace." The phrase first began appearing on gravestones in the eighth century in Western Europe, and was in wide use by the 18th century. The particular beliefs of the Roman Catholic church gave rise to this prayer, that the soul of the one who has died might find eternal peace in heaven.

Interestingly, it is those of us left behind who are often not at peace with the loss of a loved one. Too often those important to us, especially close members of our family, die before we have taken the initiative to resolve all sorts of issues. Then, while the deceased might *requiescat in pace,* we may be left with regrets and remorse over whatever we said or didn't say. Too often we feel that the one who passes had injured us in some way, and while it may have been long ago, we've maintained a grudge the entire time. The failure to forgive has no effect on them now, even if somehow we thought we were hurting them back, by our failure to make amends. No, instead the only one not at peace... is us! Hanging onto bitterness often leads to depression, and sometimes even to self-destructive behaviors like fits of rage, and the use of drugs and alcohol.

Scripture has a lot to say about bitterness and the failure to forgive. Of course, the best known of these is found in Matthew 6:14: *"For if you forgive other people when they sin against you, your heavenly Father will also forgive you. But if you do not forgive others their sins, your Father will not forgive your sins."* The Apostle Paul instructs the Ephesians in no uncertain terms to put away all bitterness, wrath and anger, and specifically to forgive each other. (Ephesians 4:31-32)

In the letter to the Romans, he urged them not to be overcome by evil, but to overcome evil with good. His specific prescription for doing so was to repay no one evil for evil, but instead to forgive them! (Romans 12:17-21) The Old Testament book Leviticus, instructs the people not to bear a grudge, but for them to love their neighbor as themselves. (Leviticus 19:18)

So, R.I.P. may be written on the headstone, but it's the people left behind who are meant to read it! Make your peace with whomever you feel might have wronged you in the past. Forgiveness is the only way for *you* to move forward! Forgiveness doesn't mean you condone or even excuse another's bad behavior (or your own bad behavior!) It only means you are acting generously and in a compassionate way. Forgiveness is the only way you will heal, move on and remain productive. It will allow you to gradually dissipate the anger, frustration, and resentment, which has seeped over into other areas of your life! When you finally choose to forgive, you will find yourself increasingly at peace where there was none before.

Do yourself a favor. Forgive the one who has gone, even if only after they've gone. Just let it go! Its the only way you'll rest in peace yourself!

> *Prayer: Dear heavenly Father, We love you! We love you because You loved us first...and how did you demonstrate that? By forgiving us! Let the love of Christ suffuse us and empower us to forgive those we feel have wronged us! Yes, it may make them feel better, or they may already be gone, but it will certainly put us at peace and allow us to move on with the business of life and glorifying Your name in all that we do! AMEN*

OCTOBER 30

Assumptions

"If others tell us something we make assumptions, and if they don't tell us something, we make assumptions to fulfill our need to know and to replace the need to communicate." (Miguel Ruiz)

A classic psychology experiment demonstrating the power of false assumptions is the "9-dot problem." A grid of 9 dots, 3X3 on a side, is the starting point. The only instruction is to connect all 9 dots using only four straight lines. The false assumption of course, is that the lines must remain confined to the "box" defined by the dot matrix square. Without the insight that you are operating under a false assumption, you could work on the puzzle till the cows come home and never come close to a solution!

Relationships between people suffer from the same unproductive false assumptions, particularly about motive. Let's say I suggest to my wife that we go out to a Mexican restaurant, instead of eating at home tonight. If my wife's response is clipped, her face set in a frown, and she avoids making eye contact with me, I will undoubtedly start to get upset myself! This is coupled with rapidly rising righteous indignation, since I *know* my intention was nothing but good! Never mind my assumption that I must have done something, the very state of annoyance *I think I observe* in her facial expression and actions, is *in itself,* an assumption! If in fact, her demeanor is entirely because she had just finished a conversation with her 91 year old aunt who, my wife believed, was unjustifiably rude to her when she was only trying to help, then all of my assumptions were patently incorrect! The annoyance I then felt would only serve to escalate the severity of our disconnect! None of this was necessary, if instead of *assuming motives,* I had simply asked my wife if something was wrong!

Certainly, 1 Corinthians 13:4-7 was tailor-made to apply to the above situation. *Love is patient, love is kind,* alone would have rectified this situation, even with the false assumptions. *Love is not self-serving or easily angered,* again, both applicable here. *Love keeps no record of wrongs;* even if my false assumptions had been true, they should have had no effect on how I treated my wife in return. *Love does not delight in evil, but rejoices in truth;* failing to ascertain why my wife was acting the way she was, put me on the defensive, perceiving malicious intent, rather than seeking the truth. Finally, love *always protects, always hopes, always trusts, always perseveres.* Both trusting and protecting my wife would mean that I *always assume loving motives* rather than the opposite!!

Christians are intended to treat *everyone* as though they are better than themselves, not just loved ones. (Philippians 2:3) Making assumptions about anyone's motives without communicating our concerns, causes us to jump to conclusions. We then *act as though our own conclusion is the truth*, then, misunderstanding the other person's actual intent, we take it personally! We in fact, take offense! Then we react from a defensive posture, often striking out with words that are hurtful, rather than helpful. It's a gentle answer that turns away wrath, not a sharp retort! (Proverbs 15:1) Paul's point in Philippians is that Christ would have us act out of humility, as He did. When we act from a position of self-absorption or self-conceit, we can easily see faults in others, but are blind to our own. (Matthew 7:3-5)

So when that truck comes up behind you and sits right on your bumper on the freeway when you're already going 10mph over the speed limit, don't just assume he's a jerk. He might be, but he might also have a kid who was just in a car wreck, and he's trying to get to the hospital before his child heads into surgery!

Prayer: Dear Heavenly Father, We love You! Let Your Holy Spirit lead me to a humble, listening state of mind, so that I can speak in love rather than react defensively to an offense that probably never even really occurred! Help me act, not RE-act! AMEN

OCTOBER 31

All Hallow's Eve

"Shadows of a thousand years rise again unseen. voices whisper in the trees, "To-night is Halloween!" (Anonymous)

If you grew up in America, you have some memory of Halloween as a child. I lived in the Northeast until age 9. That meant October 31 was usually pretty brisk, with a chilly breeze moving the treetops in the moonlight, the lawns carpeted with colored leaves, the smell of apples and spice in the air. We were bundled up, if not in winter coats, at least heavy sweaters and scarves. But Halloween meant two things to me above all others: The Wizard of Oz, which came on TV only once per year, and of course, a paper grocery sack full of more candy than it was a good idea to eat! (I remarked to my son once, that I never even knew the Wizard of Oz (1939) was filmed in color until I was in high school. He said, "How could that be? Don't you remember that Munchkin Land is in color when Dorothy opens the door?" "Not if you're watching on a black and white TV!" I explained. (He had no idea black and white TVs ever even existed!)

It was only after I became a father myself, that I became aware of the concerns of many Christians, when it comes to Halloween. "It's a Pagan holiday, celebrating death, and horror, and all kinds of evil!" they complain. Hmmmm. Let's set aside for a moment that Christmas and Easter *might have been* assigned to their current calendar dates by Pope Constantine in the 4th century, specifically because it would make them coincide with various winter and spring pagan celebrations. "Hallowe'en"(1745) is actually a contraction of "Hallows' Even," *even* being the Scottish word for *eve*. It began as the time set aside in the Catholic liturgical calendar, specifically to remember the dead, including saints or *hallows*, martyrs, and the faithful who have passed away. Certainly, it was never intended to be a "celebration of evil."

The ancient Gaelic festival of the fall harvest known as "Samhain," (Old Irish for *summer's end*) may have been Christianized by the early church, and morphed into Halloween, but that is disputed. It was celebrated in Ireland, Scotland, Wales and the Isle of Man. This would however, explain many customs such as pumpkin carving, bobbing for apples, costume wearing, etc. Samhain was set at the midpoint between the summer equinox and the winter solstice. The celebration was on the evening before, because for the Celts, days both began *and* ended at sunset! People believed this was a *liminal time*, which not only marked the line between the light of summer and the dark of winter, but also the boundary between this world and the Otherworld.

On this night, the boundary *thinned*, so that *fairies or Spirits* from beyond the dead, could more easily enter our world. They were called *Aos is*, and were both respected and feared. People widely believed the souls of the dead would return home for this one night a year, and places were set at table and food left by the fireplace to appease them. Bonfires and divination games to predict the future were commonplace. *Mumming and guising* began in the mid 1500's, where children would go house to house singing songs, wearing costumes, and receiving gifts of food. Scholars believe the tradition started with the children mimicking the *Aos si*, by wearing disguises and receiving treats, as a way to appease the spirits and guarantee that livestock (and their families) would survive another winter!

While Halloween certainly has been commercialized in the United States, (not unlike the Day of the Dead in Latin cultures), many countries around the world still have church services on All Hallow's Eve, when prayers are said for the souls of the dead, followed by the lighting of candles on the graves of the dead. Death has always been frightening to man since time began, so it's not hard to see how Halloween became associated with spooky decorations, costumes and even horror movies! There is something in the human psyche that craves being scared from time to time, as the time honored tradition of ghost stories around the campfire testifies. Maybe scary stories serve to emphasize the safety found in numbers, whether friends or family. Maybe scary stories and movies help delineate reality from imagination? Once they come to an end, we breathe a sigh of relief, just as one does when awakening from a bad dream, flooded with relief.

In any event, the combination of dressing up, heading out with friends, and getting candy, is an exciting and fun time for children! As Bible believing Christians, rather than side-lining our kids and making them feel excluded, perhaps we can permit them to have fun with their friends, still teaching them the history of the holiday, emphasizing that remembering our loved ones who have passed is a *good* thing! We can teach them that *Christ is the light of the world* and dissipates all darkness, as symbolized by the candle in the pumpkin! (John 8:12) We can explain that our loved ones who have passed are now with Jesus for all eternity, (John 10:28-30; 1 John 5:11) but fear of Jack-O-lanterns, witches, black cats, and ghosts, all come from long ago rituals and beliefs that we know are not true, and we can reassure our children of just that!

Christmas trees, Santa Claus, Easter bunnies, and Easter eggs all have little to do with the birth and death of Christ, even if symbolic value has been applied later, and yet there is little outcry to ban them! Besides, I've know a lot of 2 year olds who think Santa is plenty scary!

Prayer: Dear Heavenly Father, We love You! Help us to keep the main thing the main thing! Our children need to know that we find our identity in Christ Jesus, that He lives in us and we in Him, because we believe that He was conceived by the Holy Ghost, born a man, lived a perfect life, and died on a cross as payment for our sins! He then rose from the dead, and rules both from Heaven and from within us! Scary stories and movies can be fun, but kids need to understand that they are just that, stories! Let Halloween be fun, but also a time to honor our ancestors who have passed. AMEN

NOVEMBER

NOVEMBER 1

Profanity

"Be diligent to present yourself approved to God, a worker who does not need to be ashamed, rightly dividing the word of truth. But shun profane and idle babbling, for they will increase to more ungodliness." (2 Timothy 2:15-16 NKJV)

I was listening to Brian Hardin's *Daily Audio Bible* podcast on the way to work a few days ago. I probably listen to the 20 minute reading of scripture and Brian's brief discussion afterward about 90% of my commutes. He had recently begun 2 Timothy and I became aware that I was sort of tuning it out. After all, this is my 12th or 13th year through the bible with him, as well as several other times in light of my years in seminary, and I just wasn't focused on more guidelines for establishing church structure and offices.

Of course, the personal letters to Timothy, whether actually written by Paul or one of his followers, offer much more than my unfair mental characterization as a guideline to church organization! Although confessing my failure to focus on the scripture being read, as mentioned, the opening verse above suddenly grabbed my attention and shook me! We are, in America, experiencing societal tremors the likes of which haven't been seen since the Civil War! We are in the midst of racial strife, political infighting and vitriol, a younger generation seemingly entitled and lacking a sense of personal responsibility, the disintegration of the American family, the wanton disregard for any sort of civility in our discourse, natural disasters from hurricanes to wild fires to tornados of unprecedented frequency and severity, and a pandemic different from any the country has ever encountered! If ever there was a time for faith; if ever there was a time for people to pull together; if ever there was a time to set aside our differences and unite to preserve our union, it is now!

Instead, from the top of each political party's ticket, all the way to the bottom, what we hear mostly, is character assassination. I have not seen ONE political commercial that laid out the candidate's plan for any problem on any level. All I have seen are negative ads about the opponent. This is now so prevalent, the candidate they *want* you to support isn't even mentioned in the ad except at the end where they add the tag "So and so approves this message." Well, they ought to *all disapprove these messages!* It's almost a dark farce with each side accusing the other of sowing division while they are both busy sowing division. These nasty, negative, assaults on personal integrity of the opposing candidate are utilized whether the supposed topic is climate change, race relations, the Supreme Court, taxation, or approaches to Covid-19. We as a nation of individuals need to *JUST STOP IT!*

What the author of 2nd Timothy says, is happening right before our eyes! Profane and idle babbling *is leading to more ungodliness!* The word "profane" means 'not pertaining to the sacred,' or more simply, 'that which is secular.' The

Greek word is *bebelos,* and it means common, public or ungodly. Profanity isn't just using swear words. It's speaking in a way that Jesus would find abhorrent. Think bout that. As people of faith, we need to stand up and put an end to this kind of talk whenever we hear it. If where you work, whether in person or streaming due to Covid-19 restrictions, you hear character assassination, you need to object, or at least make it clear that you'll have no part in it. If you are active on social media, eschew the horrific vitriol in what passes as "political discourse." If you are tagged, or get dragged into a conversation like this, rather than immediately "taking a side" you could comment that if the discussion isn't handled in a civil manner, respectful of all parties, then you're out!

Remember what Paul told the church in Ephesus. *"Do not let any unwholesome talk come out of your mouths, but only what is helpful for building others up according to their needs, that it may benefit those who listen...Get rid of all bitterness, rage and anger, brawling and slander, along with every form of malice!" (Ephesians 4:29,31 NIV)*

Prayer: Dear Heavenly Father, We love You! Please let the Holy Spirit within us stop us cold each time we are becoming profane! Remind us not what would Jesus think if He were standing here listening, but remind us instead that He is standing here listening!! AMEN

NOVEMBER 2

No Pressure

"No one can come to Me unless the Father who sent Me draws him." (John 6:44 ESV)

"And when He [the Holy Spirit] comes, He will convict the world concerning sin and righteousness and judgment..." (John 16:8 ESV)

Have you ever had a frustrating experience trying to convince someone of something that you know to be correct, but they either just can't see it, or plain refuse to see it? It can happen in all walks of life. It can happen when arguing an approach to a surgical problem with another physician; it can happen when arguing a structural engineering approach with an architect; it can happen when arguing the best approach to a legal position with a client; it can happen when arguing the best financial approach to housing with your spouse; it can happen when coaching pee-wee football and arguing for a certain approach with a parent whose sole concern is their child, when your concern is all the children!

When I was a newbie Christian during college, I thought it could happen when trying to convince someone of the truth of Christianity and the life saving transformation of accepting Christ. This perception was reinforced by a well meaning fellowship group that measured the success of evangelism with the number of "saves!" As a young adult in years to come, I was bombarded by televangelists in the 80's and 90's who espoused the same score-keeping method of evaluating effective evangelism!

During my time in seminary, I was exposed not only to Grace, and its true meaning, but to the realization that it isn't and never will be, ***my*** responsibility to bring people to faith! Whew! Thank God! It turns out that God takes responsibility for that Himself! He only gave us two tasks remember? Here's that 8 track tape stuck on replay again: ***Love God and love each other.*** That's it! That's the whole ball of wax; the whole enchilada! You just love your brother, and by that I mean anyone you run into, and the Big guy will handle the rest! The Holy Spirit is a real live person and 1/3 of the Trinity, and he's *living in you as a believer!* That means He will give you the words to speak when you don't know them, and He will use the love and compassion that you show others to draw them to the Father as He wills! (Luke 12:12; John 14:26; 16:13 ESV)

So, the pressure is off! You won't be responsible for any quota of reborn Christians when the roll is called up yonder! The only thing you will be held accountable for is your love (or lack of it.) Did you feed the hungry? Did you give water to the thirsty? Did you clothe the naked and house the homeless? Did you have compassion on the sinner (like yourself?) Did you forgive those that harmed you?

Just love! Leave the recruiting to the Front Office!

"All scripture is breathed by God and useful for teaching, for reproof, for correction, and for training in righteousness." (2 Timothy 3:16 ESV)

"The Holy spirit will give you the words to say at the moment when you need them." (Luke 12:12 Voice)

Prayer: Dear Heavenly Father, We love You! Thank you that You are the One who has sent His Son to offer us a way back to You, and that You promise to draw those whom You will to yourself! We have only to love, and through our love show people the love and freedom and peace that comes through faith in Christ as our Savior! AMEN

NOVEMBER 3

Election Day

"Though they were not yet born and had done nothing either good or bad, in order that God's purpose of election might continue, not because of works but because of Him who calls..." (Romans 9:11 ESV)

Many of you in America are just on your way out to vote today. Many of you may have voted early. But all of us hope to have some clearer course in the near future, during this monumentally confusing time of political vitriol, natural disasters, racial upheaval, economic uncertainty and pandemic fears. November 3rd looms out of the darkness like a beacon of hope, no matter where you stand. All of us hope we can take a breath afterwards, rather than the process dragging on for weeks as it could if the contests are close.

Since 1792, the states had been allotted 34 days, from November 1st until early December, in which to pick presidential electors. But in 1845, congress named the first Tuesday in November as Federal Election Day, codifying it in statute for the first time, though at least near that day had long been the preferred time for national elections. The harvest was safely in and yet the severe winter weather that could keep people from the polls had not yet descended on the north. 1845 was also the year the new technology of the electric telegraph came into widespread use, and elections that were spread over days to weeks would allow some regions of the country to know the outcome from other regions, before they voted.

Christians have an "election day" too, but exactly when that is has been the source of controversy for at least four hundred years! John Calvin, (1509-1564) the French born Swiss theologian, had five religious principles attached to his name posthumously, which for centuries people have taken to be the core of "Calvinism." Calvinists believe in 1) ***Total Depravity:*** mankind can do nothing good to earn God's favor, and in fact acts out of evil constantly; apart from God's grace, he can do nothing to save himself. 2) ***Unconditional Election:*** God chooses whom He will save before their births and without regard to their choices or actions. 3) ***Limited Atonement:*** Christ died only for the elect, the believers, not for everyone. 4) ***Irresistible Grace:*** Grace is unmerited favor, and once God selects you to receive it, you cannot resist it. 5) ***Perseverance of the Saints:*** People who are predestined, called, justified and saved, cannot lose their salvation for any reason.

Jacobus Arminius, (1560-1609) a Dutch reformed theologian, had a different take on the role of man's free will than John Calvin, and his followers (called Remonstrants) formed the religious philosophy known as "Arminianism." Arminius felt that every person could either choose faith and accept God's grace, or choose to resist it. He believed that Christ died for everyone's sins, but only believers were forgiven. The Arminians also felt that despite having been saved, an individual could lose his or her faith and fall so far from God as to lose their salvation.

So, some Christians believe their "election day" happened before they were even born. Others feel their "election day" is the moment they choose to accept Christ and the Spirit elects to become indwelling.

Anyway you look at it, one thing is clear: God is the one who does the accepting! Both Calvinists and Remonstrants believe that the Holy Spirit calls us to faith. Whether He calls only the ones who are pre-selected, or the ones He knows choose to believe, He still delivers the ballot in the form of an invitation, and you either vote for Christ as your Savior or you don't! Either way, at some point in your life you go to the ballot box! God may have picked you to respond to Him before you were born, or He may not have. Your election day may have been long ago, or on the day you ask Jesus to be your Savior. Either way, this particular election has eternal consequences!

When you cast your vote today in the American elections, just remember that politicians come and go; policies come and go; prosperity comes and goes, peace comes and goes, even health comes and goes. But The Savior came to stay. He is the Alpha and the Omega, the first and the last! He may rule from Heaven at the moment, but He's present in the form of the Spirit in each one of us, and as Paul said in his letter to the Romans, nothing, absolutely nothing, can separate us from the love of God in Christ Jesus! (Romans 8:38-39) So when you start to get all upset about the outcome of the election; just don't! Believers are abiding in Christ and He in us, so we need to keep the main thing the main thing! (John 15:4-9)

While standing up for what you believe is important, with the Creator of the Universe firmly in your corner, and firmly in charge, it makes the Paris Accord, the Iran Nuclear Deal, Russian intervention, the development of the Covid vaccine, the federal taxation rate, even aging Presidents, just not as important.

Prayer: Dear Heavenly Father, We love You! We ask Your Blessing on this nation who through all her ups and downs, has persisted in protecting the freedom to worship You! Remind us Lord, as we face each national crisis, that ultimately we are only visitors here, and our time here is as nothing compared to an eternity with Christ! That ought to help us Keep Calm and Move On! AMEN

NOVEMBER 4

Keep Calm

"Life goes by so fast! Enjoy it. Calm down! It's all funny. Next. Everyone gets so upset about the wrong things! " (Joan Rivers)

It's the day after the American Presidential election. I write these several weeks ahead, so I have no idea of the outcome. If it's anything like the previous fifteen elections in my memory, (Geeeezzzz,) about 1/2 of you will be elated and the other 1/2 bordering on panic! Don't.

Sometime in the last couple decades, the British WW II expression *"Keep Calm and Carry On,"* started showing up again. (See *Carry On, July 25)* It originates with a British motivational poster distributed in 1939, to encourage the English population as the Nazis began to sweep across the Continent. In fact, it was never widely distributed, but was rediscovered in a small bookshop in 2000, and has since made it, and variations thereof, to millions of t-shirts, mugs, posters, you name it!

The worldwide popularity of the poster swept a globe shaken by 9/11 and the subsequent wars and waves of radical Islamic terrorism. As Wiki notes, it evoked the Victorian belief in British stoicism, "stiff upper lip" and all that! Few know that the poster was the last of a three part series. The first read, *"Your courage, Your cheerfulness, Your resolution will bring us Victory."* The second read, *"Freedom is in peril, Defend it with all Your Might!"* But the British were facing annihilation from an overwhelmingly powerful enemy, led by a maniac who was evil incarnate.

We face important issues today as well, some very broad indeed, affecting every corner of the world, like the environment. But the election held yesterday isn't the same as facing Hitler across the Channel, no matter what the media tells you. Those who react in the extreme; the loud voices at either end of the political spectrum; the ones the media loves because they make you buy and watch; rather than those who act with thought and moderation, are the ones terrifying everyone! If we join them, their dire predictions just might come true! Instead, we need to *keep calm*. I saw a Covid mask last week with the inscription, "*DEFUND THE MEDIA.*" I can't think of a better idea!

Christians should know something about keeping calm. We may not be able to find humor in *everything*, like Joan Rivers did, but we can certainly appreciate those who can, when we watch something like SNL! (Okay, don't defund *all* the media! *Seinfeld, Friends and SNL* must remain untouchable!) We *do* get upset about the wrong things. *We ought to be upset about anything we are doing that might be hurting someone else. We ought to be upset about any missed opportunities to show others by our love and compassion, the nature of the Lord we serve!* We ought to be upset with ourselves over any grudge we continue to hold onto. We ought to be upset about each time we react in a decidedly unloving manner toward our spouse, or child, or co-worker.

But I suspect that this day will find Americans needing to Keep Calm and Carry On with respect to our democracy as well. We need to have faith in the Lord. We need to have faith that the remarkable foresight of our Founding Fathers, that has seen us through thus far, will once again triumph over the boisterous noise of those who have forgotten that a house divided against itself cannot stand.

> *Prayer: Father God, let Your Spirit work powerfully in all Believers today in America. Guide us to reason. Guide us to compassion. Guide us to love those with whom we disagree. Guide us to remember that all people, no matter their color, ethnic origin, or opinions were made in Your Image. Only with Your help can be sure to Keep Calm and Carry On! AMEN*

NOVEMBER 5

The Problem of Pain

"I have told you these things, so that in Me you may have peace. In this world you will have trouble. But take heart! I have overcome the world!" (John 16:33 NIV)

Man, in his search for meaning, has had a moral, theological, ethical dilemma, as old as the concept of a deity itself. If God is good and loving and at the same time all-powerful, why does He permit those He created in His own image to experience pain and suffering? It is a conundrum that has kept many an agnostic seeker from faith, and at the same time solidified the absence of faith in the atheist. While we touched on this issue with *No, He Didn't, (October 24)* we only addressed the fallacy that God *specifically* purposes the pain of loss. Blaming God for the misfortunes that befall all of us, is admittedly, one part of the problem. Negating His very existence because His purported character would seem to eliminate the possibility of pain even being allowed, is the bigger issue.

Philosophers and theologians have wrestled with this since the time of Socrates, Plato, and Aristotle, five centuries before the birth of Christ; and man undoubtedly, at least contemplated these issues, thousands of years before that. One of the most cogent treatments of this issue in the last century was certainly that addressed by our old friend C.S. Lewis, the one time atheist, become Christian apologist and, first Oxford, and then Cambridge professor of Medieval and Renaissance literature. He is perhaps best known for his works, *Mere Christianity* (a compilation of his WWII radio broadcasts,) and *The Narnia Chronicles,* penned in the 1950's. He published the short book, *The Problem of Pain,* in 1940, as the war in Europe was really getting under way.

God created mankind with free will, and in Lewis' estimation, most of our suffering is due its misuse. We are extremely adept at inflicting pain on each other. The remainder, due to disease and "natural" disaster, have long been thought to have their origins with Satan, and this is supported, to a great extent, by scripture. (Luke 13:15-16; Matthew 8:28-40; Mark 9:17-29, to name just a few.) We Christians are called first to repentance, and then, in accepting the forgiveness purchased on the cross by Jesus, we are reborn. (John 3:3) Dying to our old selves, we *submit our will to Him.* (Galatians 2:20) Submitting to the will of another, even God, is always hard, and often painful. Lewis contends that our pain in this life facilitates this submission in three critical ways.

First, suffering destroys the *illusion* that all is well! Those who hold to this illusion will never turn to God. Second, only when we lose some of what God has given us will we ever be able to *recognize* how much we need Him. Only then does it become clear that we can never do life successfully, "on our own." Third, only when we find that doing God's will *is painful,* can we recognize it as His will and not our own! If we are doing something we love to do all the time, how do we know it's God's will for us, or simply what we want instead? That doesn't mean that doing God's will is always painful, just that when our actions lead to our own suffering and yet we persist, God's will is more likely the motivation, rather than our own.

Suffering is not "good" in and of itself, but in suffering two good things may result: the sufferer *submitting to the will of God* and the compassionate observer striving to *relieve the suffering of another* with acts of mercy. Lewis also purports "that tribulation is a necessary prerequisite for redemption, and suffering won't end until the entire world is redeemed or the world becomes unredeemable!" Perpetual happiness and security would teach us to love the things of this world, and Christ is very clear that this is a fatal error! The world rejected Christ, and it will reject His followers too. (Romans 12:2; John 15:19; 17:14; 18:36; 1 John 2:15) God grants us moments of happiness in love, in nature, in our work; but we know that the absence of tears, the absence of pain and fear and sadness and loss, will only come when He returns and the entire world bends the knee! (Romans 14:11;Philippians 2:10)

Job teaches us all of this, as well. He progresses in his suffering, from initially blaming God, believing he is being unjustly punished; all the way to repenting of his arrogance and pride, and finally *submitting to God's will for him no matter what it might be.* He decided, after God challenged him face to face and made perfectly clear the relative power and position of the Creator and the created, (Job 38) that ***he could trust God in all situations, even if he*** *didn't comprehend the reason for his circumstances.* (Job 42:10-17) God then restores everything he has lost and more! Only suffering led Job to this level of faith, and eventual peace and joy!

Jesus sent His Holy Spirit as a "helper," and that means He is available to help whether you are suffering or on top of the world! God is *always in the response*, but not always in the event. Theorizing on why a misfortune has befallen you is usually a waste of time, (unless of course, you brought it on yourself; and then you weren't just the "fall-ee" were you?) When you're getting pulled under in the whirlpool, even if you have no idea why, that's the time to submit and look to the One who quieted the storm with the wave of a hand! (Matthew 8:23-27)

> *Prayer: Dear Heavenly Father, We love You! Remind us even in the midst of our suffering that You are Sovereign! Teach us as You schooled Job, that You are ultimately in control and we can do nothing wiser than trusting You no matter how dire our situation might seem! AMEN*

NOVEMBER 6

Do Tell

"But the fruit of the Spirit is love, joy, peace, patience, kindness, goodness, faithfulness, gentleness, self-control..." (Galatians 5:22-23 ESV)

Normally we think of the word "tell" as meaning to verbally communicate something. But when you get a facial tic every time you have a straight or better in Texas Hold'em, they call that a "tell" as well! Until the advent of electronic sensors, sailors were extremely dependent on "tell-tales." The tell-tale is a strip of fabric, or now commonly plastic, that is attached at one end to a stay, the leech of the sail, or the surface of the foresail near the luff. The other end hangs free and blows back horizontally either parallel to the apparent wind direction when flying on a stay or the leech of the mainsail, or fluctuating in a way that helps adjust the headsail when on the jib near the luff. (Okay, sailing terms again. You get the point. They tell you about the wind so you can adjust your sails and direction appropriately!)

People have 'tells" as well, about their characters. Recall that James warns us that the tongue is a potentially lethal weapon and difficult to control. (James 3:1-11) Christ Himself, tells us that what comes out of your mouth reveals what is in your heart! (Matthew 15:18) Paul tells us in his letter to the Ephesians, that the only thing that comes out of our mouths should be to build others up! (Ephesians 4:29)

So the words that we say, reveal our characters, but, is it just our speech which reveals character? Galatians 5:22-23 lists the fruits of the Spirit. These are the character traits that naturally flow from the Believer who allows the indwelling Holy Spirit to guide her and thus work through her. These are not qualities we must work to achieve, but instead "fruits" of what lies within, shaping every aspect of our identity and character. Note that right before this famous verse, Paul lists examples of the "works of the flesh," meaning those things that come naturally to the man or woman who does *not* have the indwelling Spirit! He lists fifteen things *for starters*, from jealousy, anger and divisiveness to drunkenness, orgies, and envy!

We Believers live under Grace. We are saved by Grace, through faith, are we not? (Ephesians 2:8) So we can't *work* to *achieve* the fruits of the Spirit. What we can do is love. True 'love' is itself, one of the fruits, but the Greek word here is *agape*, and it means benevolence, charity and good will. Submitting our will to the Father's will, immediately available to us via the indwelling Spirit, leads to a charitable, loving character, because that's who He is! Loving others, and loving God through a closer and closer relationship in prayer, study of the Word, and fellowship, will inevitably lead to your greater expression of the Fruits!

As you develop a progressively closer relationship with your Savior, you will fulfill the Great Commission without conscious effort! How? *"By this everyone will know that you are My disciples, if you love one another." (John 13:35 NIV)* Let the "tell-tale" that flies over your head be each and every one of the Fruits of the Spirit, and people will know to whom you belong!

Prayer: Dear Heavenly Father, We love You! Help us free the Holy Spirit to act through us, loving all those around us, even if we dislike them! It is only by loving that people will know we are Yours, and only by loving that they will be able to witness the Fruits of the Spirit instead of the works of the flesh that are on display all around! AMEN

NOVEMBER 7

Paradox

"I am a bundle of paradoxes. I believe and I doubt, I hope and get discouraged, I love and I hate, I feel bad about feeling good, I feel guilty about not feeling guilty, I am trusting and suspicious, I am honest and I still play games. Aristotle said I am a rationale animal; I say I am an angel with an incredible capacity for beer!" (Brennan Manning)

It's a good thing, a really good thing, that God promises He keeps no record of my wrongs! God is love, right? (1 John 4:8) And love keeps no record of wrongs! (1 Corinthians 13:5; Psalm 103:12) I talk a good game. I write these devotionals drawing on my seminary education and my forty years of experience as a physician, right? I try to do the best I can with my patients, but then I come home one night and I'm a jerk with my wife. I pray about loving even my enemies and then find myself sort of hoping a certain attorney gets Covid-19 and...! I'll sit in the hot tub with a bourbon, really enjoying it at the end of a long day, and then feel sort of bad because I ought to be doing my patient's labs on the computer, or heck, maybe even writing one of these! But then like Brennan,

I realize I don't really feel guilty at all, until I feel guilty about not feeling guilty!

Christianity is actually *radically different* from what most people think it is. That was the impetus for books like Brannan Manning's classic *Ragamuffin Gospel*, and more recently, Andrew Farley's *God Without Religion*. ***Grace is the key!*** Christ died for us while we were yet sinners! (Romans 5:8) It isn't the "good" people who get saved and go to Heaven and the "bad" people who go to Hell! This is exactly the misperception that led to 2,000 years of failed efforts to follow the rules for Old Testament Israel, and many would say, to another 1500 years of much the same for Christians up to the Reformation. Grace means *"unmerited favor."* God loves us so much as His creation and image bearer, that He sacrificed His only Son, who literally gave Himself up, as punishment for our sins, *even though we were all still sinning!* No one *deserved* the Father's love. No one *deserved* the love of Jesus. No one *deserved* the Holy Spirit's help. ***We were forgiven, and given new lives, out of the Father's great love; no other reason!***

Now, once we accept the gift of forgiveness, we are saved by that grace, through our faith in Jesus. We are crucified with Him, and we die to the Law. We are no longer slaves to the perpetual sin that the Law made clear! We live as slaves now to the Spirit, not to sin; but that doesn't mean we don't still sin! Sanctification is, in a very real sense, the ongoing battle between our own natural proclivity to sin and the extent to which we allow the Holy Spirit within to guide us. Paul discusses this in detail in Romans, and especially Romans 7:14-25.

So a big part of forgiveness starts with forgiving ourselves! God isn't some score keeper in the sky with Jesus as the plate umpire! Instead, He's a Father who loves us passionately and boundlessly! Loving Him back should come easy, but it means loving ourselves and loving others, and we desperately need the Spirit's help with that! That's WHY Jesus promised to send a Helper after He ascended to Heaven! Yes, we are saved by grace through faith, but if that faith were adequate for us to do it all ourselves, we wouldn't need a helper!

Next time you find yourself feeling guilty about not even feeling guilty, think about it for a moment! One thing the Cross did for sure, was free us from guilt and shame! We all still mess up. Over time you will mess up less, and that is the process of *sanctification*. In the meantime, when you find yourself in the same kind of paradoxes that Mr. Manning, Mr. Farley, and Dr. Thurston do, stop, throw up a prayer about it, and let the Spirit know you are willing to love your way out of whatever mess you've created! After all, that's really all we *can do!*

Prayer: Father God, we believe, help our unbelief, Lord! No one can live the perfect life that Jesus did, but at least we are no longer forced to sin, because now we live under Grace and not the Law! Holy Spirit, help us as Jesus promised You would: give us the strength to love others and to love our own sometimes miserable selves! AMEN

NOVEMBER 8

Jesus Take the Wheel

"Jesus, take the wheel. Take it from my hands. 'Cause I can't do this on my own. I'm letting go. So give me one more chance, and save me from this road I'm on! Jesus take the wheel!" (Brett James et al.)

I was blessed to have one of those memorable days a couple weeks ago. It was Saturday, and I was heading up to the boat on Lake Texoma, just to run the engines, and set the thermostat on the heater, just in case our current cold snap was followed immediately by an unexpected freeze, as it seems like we in North Texas *ought to expect* by now! It was also to be the Labradoodle pup's second trip to the boat, but possibly the first where we would actually leave the dock! I texted my daughter to see if either of her kids would like to come. I was delighted to find that while Liam, the eight year old, had a birthday party to attend, Allie, 6, was *beaucoup* enthusiastic! (Of course, this could have been more Windsor-labradoodle related than Papa related!)

While it was chilly, the sun was out and there was only a light breeze. I hadn't planned on actually sailing, just motoring a little to get the dog used to the boat moving, but Allie and I decided to unfurl at least the jib, and cut the engines once we were well clear of the marina. After a while spent reassuring the puppy, Allie asked to take the wheel. When she was really little, several years ago, she would only feel reassured if I stood behind her and held the wheel with her. Remarkably yesterday, she remembered "Auto" referring to the autopilot, from last year. At age 4 to 5, she had no idea she was being assisted by the autopilot when she took the wheel, but she had since learned, both from observation and trial, that steering a 14,000 lb. boat was not as easy as it looks! Consequently, she was well aware that the autopilot had control, while she moved the wheel only the small amounts that the system allowed. Rather than being frustrated by the lack of freedom, she was reassured that everything was ultimately under control!

The song above, which Carrie Underwood made famous, relates the same experience that all believers can have in this life. Yes, God designed man with free will; and yes many feel that our free will is what allows us to make the decision to accept or reject Jesus Christ as our Lord and Savior. But all believers know that trying to steer our way through the storms of life on our own, is a formula for disaster! We may have plans that come from the heart, but the Lord graciously determines our actual steps! (Proverbs 16:9; 19:21) This concept has made into our modern lexicon from an old Yiddish expression, *"man plans, God laughs!"* Throughout our lives we make plans about where we want to go, what we want to do, and with whom we want to do it. But things frequently don't turn out exactly as we had expected! The person of faith, *consults with God all along the way,* rather than making plans that might otherwise come from, well, perhaps too self-concerned a place. The believer also plans without the limitations of the secular, for he knows that with God, all things, even outrageous things, are possible! (Matthew 19:26) There will still be surprises, things that God has in store that we didn't anticipate, but we'll be able to handle them knowing that a Sovereign Lord is at the helm, who wants only good things for us! (1 Chronicles 19:11; Romans 8:28)

So having God's hand on the wheel isn't so much a restriction of freedom, as it is reassurance that no matter what we encounter, our Lord is ultimately in control! We can relax a little! Even a six year old understands that some things are better not handled alone!

Prayer: Dear Heavenly Father, We love You! Thank you that Your hand is always on the wheel with us, even if we sometimes can't see it and aren't aware! That's what the indwelling Holy Spirit is all about! Help us to bring our worries and concerns and indecision to You and leave them at the foot of the Cross! AMEN

NOVEMBER 9

Push the Button

"And when you pray, do not heap up empty phrases as the Gentiles do, for they think they will be heard for their many words. Do not be like them, for your Father knows what you need before you ask Him!" (Matthew 6:8 ESV)

Thirty years ago, when my mother and my late father were about my age now, they went on a fun trip to San Antonio. As is often the case, ever since HemisFair in the 60's, like most tourists, they booked a hotel on the famous River Walk. Having both grown up in New York, but having lived in Texas off and on for 10-15 years or so, they were somewhat familiar with a Texas twang, but less so with a Mexican accent. One morning they were descending to the Lobby in the elevator, and ask the man inside which button to push, since the lower level buttons were confusing in their labelling. He responded politely, "Ponce reever." My mother said, "Excuse me?" He repeated, "Ponce reever, ponce reever!" Again they failed to understand until the man reached over the luggage carrier and pushed the button marked, 'RIVER."

Like most families, there are little stories like this one which all of us refer to intermittently with a chuckle. But have you ever thought about elevators and their reliability? You walk into a steel box suspended, almost always, at a definitively lethal height above ground, press a button, and *every single time* it takes you to exactly the floor you requested! *Every time.* Barring the extremely rare malfunction, if you end up on the wrong floor it's because you *selected the wrong floor.* We live in a world where we are *used to getting exactly what we asked for instantly!* When you push your Apple remote while Netflix is highlighted, you get Netflix; while Hulu is highlighted, you get Hulu. When you type in your password on your laptop, it opens to the screen which corresponds to everything you have on that desktop and in the cloud. When you open Google Maps on your iPhone, and type in a destination, it gives you a choice of routes instantly, including which one to select for fastest arrival. The list is endless. In fact, in the USA, when any one of a myriad of modern conveniences we enjoy everyday fails to function properly, we call it a "first world problem!"

It's no wonder that we sometimes feel like our prayers have gone "unanswered!" We are conditioned to expect immediate gratification of our desires and in exactly the manner we anticipate. It turns out prayer doesn't work that way! But wait, you say, doesn't Jesus promise that if we ask, it will be given to us? ***Not exactly.*** What He says is that ***IF*** you believe that you will receive it; (Mark 11:24) ***IF*** you abide in me and I in you; (John 15:7) ***IF*** we trust the indwelling Spirit; (Romans 8:26; Ephesians 6:18) ***IF*** we pray humbly and in secret; (Matthew 6:6) and ***IF*** we pray that God's will be done; (Matthew 6:9-13) ***THEN*** you will receive His answer!

Sometimes we forget that God is not an elevator. He doesn't just do what we say, go where we want, stop and go when we tell Him to! He is the potter. We are the clay. Not the other way around. It would do good to remember that. Job figured this out eventually. Elijah figured this out eventually. David figured this out eventually. Even Jonah figured it out eventually! Why does Christ want us to "pray without ceasing?" (1 Thessalonians 5:17) Does He want us standing in the elevator all day long just riding up and down pushing buttons? He wants us to pray unceasingly because He wants a relationship with us, and He knows that it is good for us! He already knows what we want before we ask, (Matthew 6:8) and He will respond to those who believe Him on His own timetable and in His own way! (Isaiah 40:31; Psalm 27:14; Proverbs 3:5; Lamentations 3:25; Romans 12:12)

Prayer: Father God, we know intellectually that the Holy Spirit communicates our needs to You even when we have no words. Help us to feel it Lord, and to wait on Your response, and to realize that Your YES answer to our prayer may not look at all like we expect it to! We will trust in You Lord, and know that Your response is always in our best interest, however it might look to us at the time! AMEN

NOVEMBER 10

Light of the World

"Your Word is a lamp to my feet and a light to my path." (Psalm 119:105 ESV)

Our hospital recently installed motion detectors along all of the hallways, and in all of the restrooms of the physician office building. That means that when I am on call and needed emergently in Labor and Delivery, I roll out of the Murphy bed in our office, pull on my scrubs and shoes, and hustle down the hall toward the elevator. Now, when I do that, the overhead fluorescents light up sequentially beginning about 20 feet in front of me. I remember thinking how neat it was that the hospital would convert to this, of course to be more economical, but also to keep us from stumbling in the dark. They could have just left the office hallways dark. To be honest, it was kind of spooky at first, but still very cool! Then it became routine. When it became routine, it became expected. Now that it is expected, I rarely think about being grateful for it anymore!

Believers have the Lord to light their way, every minute of every day and night; through every shadow, in every dark closet, in every dark forest, through every storm, through whatever plans Satan has, and through every night, moonlit or not! (John 8:12) The verse above tells us that "God's Word" is what lights our way, and so it does! But let's not forget the beginning of the Gospel of John! The Word **IS** God! The Word **IS** Christ! The Word **IS** the Holy Spirit! Trust in the Lord and ***He*** will disperse the darkness of your darkest hour! (Isaiah 60:19-20; Micah 7:8) What does Romans 8 tell us? All things work together for good for those who love Him; if God is for us, no one can stand against us; and nothing can separate us from the love of God in Christ Jesus! Those who once walked in darkness have seen a great light! (Isaiah 9:2) Christ disperses the darkness of your soul! The light of salvation, offered on the Cross through the Grace of God, shines bright indeed!

Pretty reliable lighting system, huh? When I walk down the hall in the hospital though, the fluorescents aren't lit up 200 or 100 or even 50 feet ahead. They're only lit up enough that I can see my next few steps! God can be like that. (Psalm 18:28; 27:1) Remember that too. Don't think God isn't pulling His weight if He doesn't lay the whole five year plan out for you in day one! One step at a time, one day at a time. (Psalm 32:8; 37:23; Proverbs 3:5-6;16:3,9; Isaiah 48:17; 58:11; Jeremiah 10:23; Romans 12:12) Slow and steady wins the race.

Prayer: Dear Heavenly Father, We love You! Thank you that the dark which causes us to stumble, causes us to lose our way, causes us to hurt ourselves and others, will never again be a cause for fear! Our trust in You is complete; our faith in the One who created light is the most reliable defense against darkness that there is! AMEN

NOVEMBER 11

Ladders

"Have this mind among yourselves, which is yours in Christ Jesus, who though He was in the form of God, did not count equality with God as thing to be grasped, but emptied Himself by taking the form of a servant, being born in the likeness of men." (Philippians 2:5-7 ESV)

I don't care for ladders. There are probably several underlying reasons for this dislike, but chief among them is that I don't care for heights either, and one seems to lead to the other! The other day I was post call and we had a meeting set up with our AC/Heating guy. This by the way, is almost *never* a get together just to receive good news.

Of course, it turned out we had serious heating unit problems which could easily be fixed for just under a bazillion dollars. But before receiving this good news, I had watched our service man first carry a ladder up to the second floor, and then use it to climb into the cramped space in the attic through which he could access one of the guilty units. When I brought him water 30 minutes later, it was his descent that struck me! Except for the fact that it gets me lower, I think I hate descending even more than climbing! But he zipped down that ladder like it was a water slide at the park, and then he could speak to me face to face about just what needed to happen in order to rescue us from the extremes of Texas weather.

How just like Jesus to come down to my level and rescue me! I doubt if Chris felt like Jesus that afternoon, since I'm sure the dollars involved seemed like bad news. But overall, having been to impoverished portions of India on a mission trip, the hefty price was well worth the reward of the miracle called "central heating and air!"

When you really look closely at all the world's systems of faith, there is *exactly one*, where God comes to us, rather than the other way around! In both Judaism (0.18%) and Islam (24.1%), the other two monotheistic religions, one must adhere to a set of behavioral rules which govern not only prayer, but every aspect of life, in order to *possibly* earn God's favor and go to Him in the afterlife. (For example the Five Pillars of Islam and the Mosaic Law of Judaism.)

Hindus (15.1%) have literally 33 million gods, of which most people can name only a few. But these few gods are clearly manufactured of wood or plastic, felt not just to be images of, but the actual gods themselves! Each of these gods must be appeased in various ways in order to win a favorable reincarnation in the next life.

Buddhism, (7%) is really more a set of interpreted philosophies, with no one "God" as the object of worship, based loosely on the teachings of Gautama Buddha in the 6th century BC. Most of their traditions include the goal of overcoming personal suffering and the cycle of death and rebirth by attainment of Nirvana. This may include developing the "perfections" or virtues, observance of moral precepts, meditation, taking refuge in Buddha etc.

Adherents of Sikhism, (0.3%) the only Indian religion that could be qualified as "monotheistic," worship the shapeless, timeless, One, the Creator. Its founder Guru Nanak, stressed spiritual development as expressed in everyday moral conduct. He advocated living an active, creative and practical life of truthfulness, fidelity, self-control and purity. While the tenor of this belief system is clearly attractive, it is nonetheless another of the "do" religions, where one's behavior dictates how far one can climb the "ladder."

Christians, on the other hand, are offered salvation merely by *believing* (Romans 10:9) that God would love us so much, that He came *down the ladder to us* with the incarnation of Christ! This is a major part of the peace and joy enjoyed by Christians! Not only are we free of the guilt and shame of our own sinfulness, (1 John 1:9; Romans 8:1) but we are free of the guilt suffered by those who adhere to belief systems emphasizing perfect obedience to a set of rules. Jesus offers a love relationship where our every *desire* is obedience! Our peace is magnified by our *assurance* not only in an eternal afterlife in the presence of God Himself, but also an eternity free of tears, pain and suffering! (Revelation 21:4) That is the miracle of the Gospel!! While we were *still sinners*, God chose to offer us the free gift of salvation instead of the death that our sin deserved! (Romans 3:10-20) He *came to us, and offered us the perfect righteousness of His Son,* knowing that we could never climb the ladder back to Him after our rebellion! Hallelujah!! don't even have to step on one of those ladders I dislike so much!!

Prayer: Dear Heavenly Father, We love You! How Blessed we are that simply by accepting Your offer in Grace, we may be saved for all eternity! Thank you for the Holy Spirit that we might have a constant Helper as we strive to be more Christ-like, not because we are required to, but because we want to out of love for our Savior! AMEN

NOVEMBER 12

Memories

"I even I, am He who blots out your transgressions for My own sake, and I will not remember your sins!" (Isaiah 43:25 ESV)

I have discovered in my mid-60's, that I often have no problem remembering something I memorized 40 years ago in medical school, but momentarily forget my best friend's name when introducing him! In fact, my wife and I have a rule that when we can't remember that British band from the sixties with the bowl haircuts and named after a Volkswagen and an insect, we give ourselves FOUR MINUTES before we panic! Interestingly, I also have very clear memories of each of the times I have screwed up royally in my life. Pretty sure you could throw a lot of the behaviors associated with those times into my personal big bucket of sins! It is sometimes hard to keep in mind, when wallowing in a combination of guilt and self-pity, that my Savior forgave my sins on a hill outside of Jerusalem two thousand years ago!

While memory of our sins tends to be crystal clear, God has not only forgiven us, but *He no longer remembers our sins at all!* That is pretty incredible when you stop and really think about it. God is omniscient, omnipresent, all powerful, and the Creator of the Universe. He *can't remember? Really?* It almost seems like this falls into the semantic trap posited by the atheist when he asks if "God can make a rock that He can't pick up?" But scripture is pretty clear about it! It's not just the passage in Isaiah, it's all over the place. *"For I will be merciful toward their iniquities, and I will remember their sins no more." (Hebrews 8:12 ESV)* On top of that feel free to look up Jeremiah 31:34; Hebrews 10:17; Acts 3:19; 1 John 1:7-9; Romans 8:1! When God decides to do something, there are no half measures! In Isaiah, God promises to forgive the sins of Israel, despite the fact that their hearts were not in their sacrifices, and their sins had wearied God! He forgave them *"for My own sake..."* meaning out of Grace, not because they deserved forgiveness. In Jeremiah, God expressly mentions the New Covenant that He will make with His followers, in which the Law will be written on their hearts, and He will forgive their iniquities. Hebrews 8-10 explains specifically how the New Covenant will be mediated through the perfect sacrifice of the High Priest, Christ the Lord.

When my patients' aging parents are progressing into dementia, they tell me the process is excruciating. But in the end, they find their parents are often completely at peace. Remembering nothing, everything is new, and none of the pain remains!

Remembering our sins may happen automatically, and we can only diminish the pain by reminding ourselves of the promises our Lord has made, and rekindling our belief that we will never be condemned. But God has no issues like ours, because at the moment we are washed clean by the blood of Jesus, He has no recollection whatsoever that we ever sinned! All He sees is one He created whom He loves and who loves Him back!!

Prayer: Father God, as hard as it is to conceive of, we trust that You remember our sins no more! Perhaps You grow tired even listening to us reiterate them when You've told us already that we are forgiven! But we are thick Lord! Thank you for Your patience with us! AMEN

NOVEMBER 13

Sufficient Grace

"Three times I pleaded with the Lord about [the thorn in my flesh], that it should leave me. But He said to me, 'My Grace is sufficient for you, for my power is made perfect in weakness.' (2 Corinthians 12:8-9 ESV)

Our church has supported a mission seminary in India for more than twenty years. This school, and the organization that runs it, trains house-church pastors for the surrounding area. In this particular Indian state, there are over 100 million people, but the Christian population may be counted in the thousands. Our leaders there, both men and women, work incredibly hard on barely above subsistence wages. The message of the Gospel is frequently not well received in Hindu villages, who for thousands of years have worshipped a panoply of idols they think of as gods. Not to mention, these villages may be hundreds of miles from the city in which the organization is headquartered, and the village pastors use motorbikes or even bicycles, to negotiate the "roads" through the heat and insects, monsoon season or dry, covered in mud or caked with dust. As if that weren't enough, there is subtle, as well as not so subtle, persecution from the Hindu state.

Yet, every time a team from our church in Dallas visits, including the time that my wife and I visited several years ago, we found our partners there were filled with joy! They were literally exuding the peace and freedom that comes from giving their lives to Christ! While our partners in India live a life with no luxuries, still they are better off physically than the thousands who live in the slums of Mumbai. But, yet again, when we visited the local pastors and the corrugated 1-2 room aluminum huts lining muddy alleyways there, which their congregants called home, we found not the despair we in the West might expect. Instead, we found the same joy and peace simply radiating from these people, even when on the brink of starvation, that we experienced with our own mission leaders. One of our leaders had a serious motorcycle accident several years ago. Doctors in India couldn't repair his leg so that it would ever bend again at the knee. No one has ever heard a complaint from this man.

How are these things possible? How can people be *content* with their hardships and afflictions? Because the words in the passage above are more than just words, for those who keep their eyes fixed on the Cross. Remember, *Grace* means unmerited favor. We are saved *by Grace through Faith*. (Ephesians 2:8) Whatever the thorn in Paul's side, and most interpreters believe it was physical, Paul learned that Christ's Grace was sufficient. In other words, God's glory is best displayed against the backdrop of human weakness. Since the chief end of man is to glorify God and enjoy Him forever, (Westminster Catechism), our continued faith, compassion and love shown toward others in the face of our own adversity and affliction, maximizes our ability to glorify God!

There's nothing wrong with asking God to cure us of an affliction or rescue us from poverty or difficult circumstances, and in some instances God may choose to do so. But often God will use the Holy Spirit within us, simply to gracefully grant us contentment with our lot, and then we can continue to love God and love others as we are led by Him. Note that even Philippians 4:6, often quoted as a reference to support bringing anything to God in prayer, promises that the response will be *the peace of God which passes all understanding,* not necessarily what we request! Paul learned to be content in all circumstances; *that* is the meaning of v.4:11, that he *"can do all things through Him who strengthens me!"*

Prayer: Dear Heavenly Father, We love You! Teach us what Paul learned Lord! Teach us to be content in all circumstances knowing that Your love is unchanging, and our hope of salvation is sure, no matter our trials in this life! AMEN

NOVEMBER 14

Naked

"There are certain horrific moments in life when the only way to fix an awkward situation is to be awkward." (Roshani Chokshi)

I published a book on changing healthcare in the USA in 2008 entitled *Disrobe Completely*. The name reflected the instruction given 30 times per day by my nurses when ushering patients into an exam room. "If you would disrobe completely, put this gown on so it opens in front, like a vest, put the paper sheet across your lap and have a seat on the end of the table, and the doctor will be with you in a moment." First of all, 80% of women put the gown on so it opens in back despite the instruction. A full 20% leave their underclothes on, apparently not catching the "completely" after the "Disrobe."

In any event, if I am caught up and on time, I often listen through the door for the sound made by the table paper, indicating that the patient is now seated and by definition, ready for her exam. A couple of years ago, I followed this routine, making a cursory knock on the door as I opened it, announcing that I had heard the "telltale crinkle of paper!" My patient was standing in the center of the room, facing the door with the phone to her ear. In her other hand was the gown, not yet adorning her very naked torso! I backed out of that room like a dog with his nose in a hornet's nest, crying out, "So sorry, I'll be back in a moment!"

When I re-entered several minutes later, my patient was seated with the gown on and the sheet across her lap as instructed. She looked up at me and queried, "How many times do you think you've seen me naked?" I had delivered all four of her boys over the last 25 years. "I don't know, maybe … a hundred?" She laughed and said, "And yet *vertical nakedness* remains totally different from *horizontal nakedness*, doesn't it?" I readily agreed! Oddly enough in this scenario, it was I who was embarrassed, not the one who was bare-assed! (That's a pun btw) And yet, with just a few words, she had *rescued me* from embarrassment!

Christians have a special responsibility when they encounter a situation embarrassing for someone else; we need to make them feel better despite the awkwardness of the situation! The Apostle Thomas experienced this at least twice, as did Peter, multiple times! Thomas told the Lord that the apostles had no idea where He was going to prepare them a place, in John 14:5-6. Jesus told him essentially, well, if you had known Me, you would understand. But *from now on, you know God, and you have seen Him!* (Like, "don't worry about it. You'll do better in the future!) Even so, it was Thomas who later wouldn't believe that the Lord had risen from the dead, until he saw and touched the Lord's wounds! Jesus could have just let him swing in the breeze when He appeared before them, but instead He let Thomas put his finger in the wound, and told him simply, "*Do not disbelieve but believe.*"(John 20:27)

Peter, as we all know, was frequently a mess! Talk about embarrassing. First He told Christ He didn't really have to die (that ended with a '*Get behind me Satan.*' I used to think that was mean, until I understood Jesus *really was* talking to Satan, not Peter!) It was Peter who got the heebie-jeebies and lost his faith when walking on the water, and sank before Jesus pulled him out! (Talk about embarrassing.) It was Peter who denied knowing Christ three times after He was arrested. (John 18:15-27) How did Christ react? Did He worsen Peter's lot with his fellow apostles by chastising him and embarrassing him further? No, Christ told Peter in front of everyone, that He would build His church on him, and changed his name right there to Peter, "The Rock!" (Matthew 16:18)

There is a tendency when people are caught in an embarrassing situation to laugh at them, perhaps even with others. We can laugh, as long as the one embarrassed is laughing as well! Otherwise, loving another means doing what we can to alleviate their mortification; perhaps sharing that the same has happened to us, or reassuring them that no one saw or no one thinks a thing about it! You never know the next time you're gonna have a friend with lettuce in their teeth, right? They would much rather you informed them in a whisper than have you join in a mysterious group laughter!

Prayer: Dear Heavenly Father, We love You! Remind us through your Spirit that it may not be funny if we're the only one laughing, as my mother used to say! Help us always to be compassionate, even in situations that people might find funny; remembering how it would feel if we were the ones in the same circumstance! AMEN

NOVEMBER 15

Stonecutter

"I will give thanks to You, for I am fearfully and wonderfully made; Wonderful are Your works, And my soul knows it very well!." (Psalm 139:14 NASB)

I don't know about you, but it seems there are more and more days when I get up and look in the mirror, and *"Fearfully and wonderfully made,"* are not the first words that come to mind! It could be age, I suppose. Or some days, it's just the feeling that well, I don't know; maybe the feeling that I just could have done *more*: more for others, more for my family, more for me, and yes, certainly more for God!

You may recall my mentioning the *Tao of Pooh,* by Benjamin Hoff, in the past. I have been a Winnie the Pooh guy since I was four, and all things Pooh fascinate me. Pooh, as those of you familiar with Christopher Robin's stuffed bear will recall, is the creation of A.A. Milne. He lives in the Hundred Acre Wood with his friends Rabbit, Piglet, Tigger, Owl and Eeyore. Pooh is a Bear of Very Little Brain, but despite this, seems to be the one who always unwittingly comes up with the solution to all manner of problems and predicaments. In the ebb and flow of Pooh's day to day existence, Benjamin Hoff saw, somewhat tongue in cheek, living examples of Taoist philosophy. *Tao* is the Chinese word for *way, path or route,* and *Taoism* is the Eastern philosophy which has grown out of the study of the natural order of the universe. This natural order must be discerned not as a concept to be studied intellectually, as much as knowledge obtained through the experience of simply living life from day to day. That in itself, fits well with the lifestyle of a Bear with Very Little Brain.

Pooh contemplated his Usefulness many times, just as all of us do. Recognizing our own value can take many years, even though God knew it the moment He made us! Hoff tells us the story of the Stonecutter in the *Tao of Pooh.* It seems one day a stonecutter was passing the house of a wealthy merchant and through the gate saw the luxury and many possessions, and wished that he could be a powerful merchant too. Instantly he became one, and while he had the power of his wealth, he was envied and despised by all those less wealthy. Then one day a high government official passed his house being carried by soldiers in a sedan chair and with everyone bowing low as he passed. The merchant wished he had power like the government official, and guess what, he instantly became a powerful government official! But one day, he became hot and sweaty in his sedan chair, and despite power over people who hated him, he thought he would rather be the sun overhead, unaffected by the heat. Poof, he became the sun! But then one day his powerful rays were blocked by a huge black cloud and he wished he could be that cloud instead. Instantly, he became the cloud, but he flooded the roads and fields with his downpour and the wind blew him away. Then he wished to be that powerful wind, and he was, destroying entire villages and anything in his path. He was hated by everyone! Finally, he blew up against a giant rock that was completely unmoved by all his power. He wished he could be as strong as that rock and poof, he became the giant rock, weighing many tons and seemingly indestructible. But soon he felt something starting to unbalance him and he heard the clang of metal on metal below. He looked down, and there, easily cutting into his side, was a stonecutter! Pooh eventually came to recognize his God given usefulness to all his friends, just as the stonecutter came to recognize his.

Not all Eastern philosophy is incompatible with Christianity. Why do we, and all his friends, love Pooh and follow him faithfully through the woods, when he's so obviously a Bear of Very Little Brain? Because in the final analysis, brains are not the answer. Brains can do important things, but abstract cleverness separates the thinker from reality, according to Hoff. Our world is in desperate shape because ***"too many people think too much and care too little!"*** Eventually we won't survive that trend.

The world thinks that contentment with what one has is a shoddy excuse for a goal, when power and wealth can be achieved with a clever application of the intellect. Christ teaches exactly the opposite, (Matthew 6:19-20) and while there may be a way to look at Pooh as a Taoist example, Pooh exemplifies many Christian principles as well. Pooh never overthinks things. He looks *inside for the guidance he requires*. Christ didn't leave the believer alone when He ascended to the right hand of God; He sent us the Spirit to live within and help us find our way. (John 14:16,26) Pooh finds his joy and his contentment in the love that he shows to his friends, and the love showered upon him by Christopher Robin! We followers of Christ learn to be content in all situations, because that contentment comes from the joy we have from loving others, being loved, and in our eternal salvation! (Hebrews 13:5; Philippians 4:11) No circumstance in the Hundred Acre Wood could ever cause Pooh to lose the love of Christopher Robin; and no circumstance in this world can separate us from the love of God in Jesus Christ! (Romans 8:38-39) Pooh may not think too clearly when working out the occasional problem, but he is never in doubt about Christopher Robin's unconditional love for him! In that he can be assured, for he is fearfully and wonderfully made!

If Winnie the Pooh can figure that out, as a Bear of Very Little Brain, surely when we look in the mirror and perhaps doubt our own worth, we can figure out that if the Creator of the Universe made us in His image, and then sacrificed His own Son to save us, despite our continual rebellion, maybe we're selling ourselves a little short when we doubt our usefulness!

Prayer: Dear heavenly Father, We love You! Have the Holy Spirit help us to see more clearly in the mirror if we think we see too many flaws to be useful! How blind can we be to not see our value when we contemplate the unconditional, unimaginable love that You have showered upon us through Grace alone? AMEN

NOVEMBER 16

Misunderstood

"Now this is our boast: Our conscience testifies that we have conducted ourselves in the world, and especially inner relations with you, with integrity and godly sincerity."

One of the unintended consequences of being in my mid 60's writing this, is the songs that run through my head are often from...well, the mid-60's! Fifth grade is about when we started listening to the radio, and by 8th grade or 1969 for me, we knew every word to every top 40 song! Today, if asked the name of any song or the one hit wonder that recorded it, I guarantee you I will draw a blank. But start singing the first 3-4 words in tune, and I'll finish the whole song for you! That happened this morning with a song recorded by the *Animals* in 1965, which I heard driving in to the hospital. It's called:

Please Don't Let Me Be Misunderstood.

"If I seem edgy, I want you to know, That I never mean to take it out on you.
Life has its problems and I get my share, And that's one thing I never mean to do.
Cause I love you, Oh, oh, oh baby,
Don't you know I'm human. I have thoughts like any other one.
Sometimes I find myself Lord, regretting Some foolish thing I've done!
I'm just a soul whose intentions are good!
Oh, Lord, Please don't let me be misunderstood.

All of us have experienced being misunderstood. We say or do something at which someone, often a loved one, takes offense. We know our own motivations. We know no harm was intended. We may know full well that we were speaking or acting out of stress totally unrelated to the person with whom we are speaking. But we have to remember; in fact, we have to *assume*, that others are making their own *assumptions about our motives!* The problems arise quickly, because knowing in our hearts that we are innocent with respect to intent, we typically get *defensive*. While the image might be too graphic, humans react just like cornered animals when they get defensive...they lash out! Pretty soon we are in a flat spin just like Maverick and Goose in Top Gun! It becomes unrecoverable and a crash is inevitable! (Note: In recent years, this has clearly become the norm in U.S. political discourse!)

If instead, you allow the Holy Spirit to guide you, the Fruits of the Spirit (Galatians 5:22) will obviate this sort of problem. Why? Because peace, gentleness, kindness and self-control are four of the characteristics by which you are known, correct? When you are being misunderstood, self-control is key. Utilizing self-control effectively, you won't become defensive and you won't lash out. In fact, *stop* talking and LISTEN to the one who feels hurt by your words or actions! (James 1:19; Proverbs 18:2) Then gently, after some thought, slowly, explain your intent, and voice your understanding of how you might have stated whatever you said, more clearly. (Proverbs 15:1; Proverbs 29:20)

In the words of Winnie the Pooh, *"If the person with whom you are speak-*

ing appears not to be listening, be patient! It may be that they simply have a small piece of fluff in their ear!" Or more likely, the fluff is in *your* ear!

> *Prayer: Father God, help us remember that listening is of far more importance in a conversation than trying to make our own point! We may well be misunderstood because of a false assumption by the one with whom we are speaking, but it is our responsibility to clear that up, gently, lovingly, kindly, thoughtfully, and slowly, just as much as it is for all of us to avoid assuming motives in the first place! AMEN*

NOVEMBER 17

The Branch Alone

"Remain in Me as I also remain in you. No branch can bear fruit by itself; it must remain in the vine. Neither can you bear fruit unless you remain in me." (John 15:4 NIV)

Earlier this summer, we took a ten day vacation in Maine. It was wonderful to see family, enjoy the spectacular coast, get out on the water, take hikes in the woods, and just breathe! When I returned however, I experienced the same thing many of my colleagues have noted, and it happens to all of us every time. Just a couple weeks away and you have to *think* about the name of the instrument you reach for in a surgery, or you even to have think about what the next step is! Recalling each one of your myriad passwords for your own computer, the office's EMR, the hospital's EMR etc. etc. suddenly takes an effort, and a moment. This phenomenon occurs with the younger physicians as well, so it's not just a getting old thing!

It turns out that medicine is one of those things in which you have to immerse yourself, surrounded by others who either have a similar role to yours, or interact and support you in hundreds of ways, in order to function at your full potential! In other words, when you've been on your own, even for a short period, you quickly realize that you can't be away from "the source" for very long and continue to function! It reminded me of the verse above.

What, after all, does "remain in me," really mean? It means faith in the Savior, right? But what does it mean practically? It means prayer, studying the Word, communal worship, and service. That's how you maintain a relationship; by staying involved on every level possible! You don't have to worry about the "and I in you part," because Jesus is completely faithful and trustworthy...He won't be going anywhere if He says He's staying with you!!

When you are in love with someone, you long to be with them! You have no desire to go it alone. You can feel in the deepest part of you that "going it alone" no longer works! Jesus is the vine, and being the branch by yourself won't lead to anything for anybody, not even yourself! Stay connected! Talk to Him! Read your mail from Him! After all, He wrote you a very long love letter! Talk about Him to your friends! Sing about the two of you together! Worship Him with the people you love. A branch without a vine is, well, just a stick!

Prayer: Dear Heavenly Father, We love You! How on earth do we forget to tell you that? How do we forget to share that? How do we forget to read your letters to us? Remind us Spirit, that loving doesn't mean separating ourselves from the object of our adoration with silence; or by ignoring the one we love day after day! Help me to start every day anxious to invite my Savior to work through me and end every day thanking Him for showing me how that happened! AMEN

NOVEMBER 18

One Day At A Time

"Therefore, do not worry about tomorrow, for tomorrow will worry about itself. Each day has enough trouble of its own." (Matthew 6:34 NIV)

When I wrote this, two of my partners had gone home the day before, positive for Covid-19. With over 100,000 patients in our records, losing 28% of our physicians instantly, for two weeks, was well, concerning to say the least! My schedule for the following day, as of 6 PM on the day my colleagues went down , was 24 Gyn patients of my own, 51 OB patients of one of the physicians out, 3 labor inductions, 2 scheduled cesarean sections, and responsibility for covering Labor and Delivery, the floor and the ED. Hmmm. In short, it was a scenario literally tailor made for "worrying about tomorrow!"

The expression "one day at a time," is well founded. Living life that way, is recommended by our Creator over and over in scripture. The Israelites, released from slavery in Egypt, spent years traipsing across the desert, with no natural, reliable, source of food or water. Yet, God provided them with water out of a rock, and manna on the ground, each and every morning! They were forced to literally live one day at a time. (Exodus 16:1-34) He instructed them to eat all of what they collected each day. God wanted them to *trust* in HIs care for them, but some refused to listen. They would save food "just in case" for the future. While they no doubt thought this harmless, instead of a ready supply of food they ended up with rotting maggot filled garbage. "Just in case" what? "Just in case" God doesn't keep His word? *That's what worry about tomorrow means to our God.* Lack of faith. One of my maternal grandfather's favorite expressions was, ***"A worried Christian is a contradiction in terms!"***

Psalm 68:9 is often used as an illustration of the daily benefits of faith. *"The Lord deserves praise! Day after day He carries our burden, the God who delivers us. Our God is a God who delivers; the Lord, the Sovereign Lord, can rescue us from death."* God makes it clear that His blessings come *daily.* Some days He parts the sea for us, others He just gives us a drink and some shade! God carries our burdens, not only with the promise of salvation, but with His loving kindness, forgiveness, gentleness, as well as physical provisions. Each new day, we should be delighted at the way He shows up! And our God *delivers,* takes on a new meaning during the pandemic of 2020 doesn't it? No matter what, we can depend on our God showing up with the goods! We may be in situations where there appears to be no way out, and God will show up lighting the way down a path you didn't even know existed before today!

My nurses made calls late into the evening, rescheduling, cancelling, rearranging. The next morning I showed up early to a schedule that looked essentially normal. My first official act was to assist on a C-section where the baby was a surprise back down transverse lie which could never have been delivered normally, and required two experienced surgeons to even deliver abdominally. The baby was fine. My second official act was an emergent unexpected cesarean on a woman who just showed up in triage abrupting (placenta separating.) The baby was fine. Both these babies and possibly their mothers, could have died had we not been here early and ready to go for the horrendous day I had anticipated! Hmmmmmm.

I slept like a rock last night. Why? Because I wasn't really worried about today. God provides the light to see one day at a time. All we have to do is **believe it**, and our lives are instantly filled with a bit extra of that peace and joy we keep talking about!

Prayer: Dear Heavenly Father, We love You! Perhaps there is a good reason Your Son told us to pray first, "Thy will be done," and then "Give us this day our daily bread." We need to trust that Your will is always that we be provided for daily in every way required. Our part is only to believe it! AMEN

NOVEMBER 19

Never in Doubt

"But let him ask in faith, with no doubting, for the one who doubts is like a wave of the sea that is driven and tossed by the wind." (James 1:6 ESV)

Today is my mother's 92nd birthday. She has 100% of her snap, all of her humor, a surprising amount of her mobility and is the epitome of the "can-do" attitude that characterizes the Greatest Generation. She has one other quality: she's one of the best spellers I've ever known! She may not be able to carry a tune to save her life, but she could spell her way out of a tight spot in a New York minute! Happy Birthday, mom! Evidently, the ability to spell is not transmitted genetically. I once famously bet my brother $100 that "facade" was in fact an entirely different word from the one pronounced "phasahed." I just knew the common word for the front of a building was "fay-cade," while the word spelled "phasod" was the French word for it anglicized. I am not entirely sure, but I believe I still owe him that money.

Members of our life group from church have previously characterized me as "*Often wrong, but never in doubt!*" I am almost positive it's not a compliment. It's the "often wrong" part I take issue with of course. I'm good with the "never in doubt!"

It would be nice if we Christians were never in doubt, but then again, if that were the case, I'm not sure where "faith" comes in! Most of us would agree that we find ourselves identifying with the father of the epileptic boy in Mark 9, who cried out to Jesus, "*I believe! Help my unbelief!*" So what does the brother of our Lord mean by the opening verse? Are we all then, like a wave of the sea, driven and tossed by changing attitudes and beliefs? Don't verses James 1:7 & 8 then make it even worse? The person in doubt will receive *nothing from the Lord*, since he is *double-minded, and unstable in all his ways?*

These verses always worried me. I have doubts. Does that mean God ignores my prayers? Does it make Philippians 4:6 invalid for people like me? The Greek here is of some help. The word "doubting" in verse 6 is diakrinomenos, which means "vacillating." In verse 8, the words "double-minded" in Greek are literally dipsychos, which means "two-souled." James wants us to understand that you cannot be all over the place, staggering like the inebriated, not knowing your mind with respect to your faith. It is not the strength of your faith in question, for Christ told you that faith the size of a mustard seed could move mountains! (Matthew 17:20) It is instead, the very existence of faith that is in question with the one driven and tossed by the environment. We must believe that our prayers can be answered, (Mark 11:24) or there is no sense in praying at all! John Calvin, in his commentary, feels that James is referring first to the unbelieving (doubters) who are unstable because they swell with pride and confidence of the flesh at one moment only to crash to the depths of despair, when things go poorly. They are often hypocrites, who claim belief but act otherwise. Expositors Commentary, refers to the "double-souled" as those who are entirely indecisive, claiming they believe in one moment and not in another. Their indecisiveness makes them ineffective in their personal, business, social as well as spiritual lives!

Calvin contrasts these unstable ones, with those who ask *in faith*, who are of one mind, believing that Christ is the Savior, even if their faith varies in its intensity from time to time. The father who cried, "I believe, help my unbelief," was not vacillating in his faith, only confessing that he felt it inadequate and wanted it *strengthened!*

So when you come to the Lord with your burdens; when you lay your troubles and worries and fears at His feet; don't make the mistake of thinking because you don't understand it all; because you sometimes question the power of your own belief; that His power is in any way affected! The point is that *you believe enough* to come to Him! The doubt James speaks of is not strength of faith, but absence of it; otherwise Christ's metaphor about the mustard seed makes no sense at all, and one thing you can rely on with our Lord is that what He says, *makes sense!*

So, HAPPY BIRTHDAY MOM! I failed to inherit the spelling part, but I guess I got the never in doubt part!

Prayer: Dear Heavenly Father, we believe, help our unbelief! Believing means not being of two minds! We may falter in our understanding, and falter in the strength of our faith, but we know that Your Grace is real! We know that we have been saved! It is only our limited comprehension that stands in the way of perfect faith, and we do know that only One has lived that perfect life and had that perfect faith! Help our unbelief, indeed! AMEN

NOVEMBER 20

Helpless?

"God gave us a spirit not of fear, but of power and love and self-control." (2 Timothy 1:7 NIV)

Watching the national news the other night, it was impossible to miss the background milieu of fear. The national anchor opened the thirty minute segment emphasizing how horrific the USA's total of 250,000 Covid related deaths is, and the prediction that it could easily reach 400,000 by Christmas. They showed footage of overwhelmed hospitals in Iowa, and dire predictions from nurses on strike outside one of them. Then they spent a long segment on a purportedly healthy woman in her thirties who barely survived Covid after being on life support for two months. There was footage of her intubated, then in a wheelchair, then doing PT. The program went on to cover Pfizer's announcement of a vaccine that was 95% effective across all age groups in a study of 40,000, but then the reporters emphasized that state Governors were setting up *their own* committee's to study its safety and effectiveness, the implication being we cannot trust the FDA. They showed footage of the deep freezers necessary to keep the vaccine cold enough and stressed the logistic nightmare this presented, and that *only* 20 million doses may be ready by the spring! There was no mention of the other vaccines soon to be available in even larger numbers.

Next they took less than 30 seconds to cover the 737 Max being deemed safe to fly, releasing 800 grounded aircraft in the USA alone; but 2 minutes to air difficulty with software patches; 2 minutes to air a statement by the wife of a man killed in the Ethiopian disaster last year that she would *never* fly any aircraft made by Boeing; and then 30 seconds to explain how to get off a flight booked on a 737 Max.

It is no wonder that much of the country is depressed, anxious, and many, staying sequestered in their own homes, terrified! Feeling *helpless* means believing you cannot possibly survive your current circumstance, and furthermore, that there is no one available to help you! It means you feel you are no longer in control of your own situation. Unfortunately, much of the media spin plays into this every day, emphasizing the negative in every story, such that *any normal person begins to feel helpless!*

Specific to this situation, the rapid widespread resurgence of the Covid 19 virus is presented as *terrifying,* rather than a problem we can successfully address. Understanding that the morbidly obese, very old, immune suppressed and chronically ill are primarily, albeit not exclusively, the group most at risk of serious illness, seems to escape the headlines. Perhaps the media heads think that putting all these numbers in perspective will cause people to act too cavalierly? But the actual facts are what one desperately needs to combat that feeling of helplessness and fear. Fear is primarily of the unknown, so that the impartial facts are essential to defeating it! With regard to the pandemic, yes, people who are healthy and young are at *low risk,* and true, that is not the same as *no risk*. But perspective is important to combat hysteria in any situation, including a pandemic.

The situation *is* serious. No denying that. But we as a nation, *are far from helpless,* nor are individuals without control of their own circumstances. Those of us that work in healthcare, who have much higher exposure than the average person, and yet not contracted it ourselves, are evidence that hand washing, social distancing, wearing a mask when logical, and avoiding gatherings that easily spread the virus, are effective weapons which all of us can wield. We merely need to form the resolve to do so, *together,* as a nation!

The announcement of safe effective vaccines being produced is *good news;* not the contrary. The news that major airlines will fly a modern miracle of technology again, is *good news,* not the contrary!

Christians have a distinct advantage! We have been given a Helper who is indwelling! We by *definition never find ourselves helpless! (John 15:26; 16:7)* The Holy Spirit's role for the believer is comprehensive. He comforts, He is our advocate, He is our intercessor, He is our supporter, and He is ever present and available at all times! As in our opening verse, we have the self control to act responsibly in a pandemic and the loving desire and the persuasive power to lead others to do the right thing as well!

We forged a nation through Revolution, salvaged a nation through Civil War, welcomed millions of immigrants and integrated them into the fabric of our society, preserved a nation in two World Wars, sent men to the moon, outlasted a Communist atheist Empire, and developed mind-boggling new technologies. As you wake up and face another day, find a way to step up and lead. Wear a mask inside, keep your distance, wash your hands, avoid close gatherings indoors. Volunteer wherever possible, financially or in person, to care for the hungry and unemployed and homeless, and show everyone that the pandemic *can be controlled,* if we get back to the spirit that acknowledges, "WE REALLY ARE ALL IN THIS TOGETHER."

Prayer: Dear Heavenly Father, We love You! Thank You for loving us enough to provide us with the Spirit! Let those of us of faith stop squabbling over politics and show our neighbors that fear dissipates when we understand that we do have control of our own circumstances, and we need only to exercise it! Help us Lord lead others in what most perceive to be uncertain times, but which we know with certainty to be under Your Sovereign hand! AMEN

NOVEMBER 21

Betrayal

"Whenever you stand praying, forgive, if you have anything against anyone, so that your Father who is in heaven will also forgive you your transgressions. (Mark 11:25 NASB)

It is unfortunately the nature of humanity that if you live long enough, you will one day feel the sting of betrayal. It may be a friend, it may be a coworker, it may be your boss, your sibling, your boyfriend or girlfriend, or it may even be your spouse. Somehow the pain of betrayal cuts much deeper, much quicker, right to the marrow; more than the damage inflicted by an enemy. The very nature of the concept of *trust* is the security of knowing that the person in whom you trust will *always have your back,* and certainly never injure you *behind your back!* When we suffer the shock of such an injury, when we at least recover our breath and realize that somehow we have to go on, then we face a choice. We can carry the pain and the bitterness for the rest of our lives, or we can somehow learn to let go, and maybe do more than survive; maybe even feel happy and able to trust again.

Forgiveness seems impossible right after betrayal. In fact it even feels outrageously wrong at the time! But we have to reach deep into ourselves and recognize what we all know to be true: forgiveness is more healing to us even than to the one forgiven! The easiest thing to remember is Matthew 7:12, the verse that has come to be known as the "Golden Rule." As hard as we try, it is likely at some time we may betray a friend as well, even if inadvertently. The forgiveness we would then crave, is what God would have us bestow on those who have betrayed us. It is so much easier to say than to do, as David reveals in Psalm 55, where he sings of the anguish of a friend's betrayal.

Christ of course, didn't just suggest that we forgive those who betray us; He seized the opportunity to do so before, during and after the cross! His disciples *ran away* when the going got tough. Peter even *denied Him three times* after His arrest, just as the Lord told him that he would! Peter was no doubt terrified, and fearing for his own life, he did what we might all do reflexively. But can you imagine the shame that Peter felt, weeping aloud after his denial? But Jesus had *already forgiven him,* hadn't He? He had not only washed his feet at the Last Supper, but He had already promised to build His church on Peter the Rock, knowing he would deny Him!

On the Cross, Jesus famously asked His father to forgive those who had called for and then had Him crucified, recognizing that they simply hadn't understood the colossal mistake they were making! Think about the Resurrection. Paul says in 1 Corinthians 15:17 (ESV), *'And if Christ has not been raised, your faith is futile and you are still in your sins!"* Jesus died on the cross as penalty for our sins. It was His Resurrection that assured our forgiveness, and triumph over the age old penalty of death! Romans 4:25 says that Jesus was, "*delivered up for our trespasses and raised for our justification.*" Justification means we are made "right" before God. Christ's perfect life and perfect atoning sacrifice for our sins, was rewarded with the Resurrection, the proof of our forgiveness and justification.

So great, you think. I'm not Christ! Well, none of us is. Each of us, including myself, have had opportunities to forgive in our lives that we passed up, of which we now wish fervently we had taken advantage. But Believers *really do have the indwelling Holy Spirit as a Helper!* The problem is we fail to call on Him in our hour of need. When you are betrayed; when you are hurt like you didn't think was possible; you need time to recover. You need time to put all of your life in perspective. When you've given yourself time to mourn, time to catch your breath, then remember that Christ is there waiting for you. Pray then that the Spirit will lead you gradually, to do that one thing that will release you from your daily anguish: forgive! When it finally happens, you'll understand why God tells you to do it over and over, just as He has done for us. It's hard to believe in the moment, but many have lived through betrayal, forgiven, worked hard, and come out the other side with stronger relationships!

Prayer: Dear Heavenly Father, We love You! We know that You loved us first...how? By forgiving us our sins, past, present and future! It's hard Lord, seemingly impossible, to forgive those closest to us who betray us! But when one day we do, we are flooded once again with that peace that You've promised that goes beyond our understanding. AMEN

NOVEMBER 22

The Bris

"Some men came down from Judea and were teaching the brothers, 'Unless you are circumcised according to the custom of Moses, you cannot be saved.'" (Acts 15:1 ESV)

First, everyone should watch *Seinfeld,* Season 5 Episode 5, *The Bris*. Even if you've never seen a single episode; even if you don't care for the show, (in which case you need more help than I have to offer) even if you don't watch television at all; you need to see this episode! As an obstetrician for just shy of forty years, I have performed roughly 3500 circumcisions. While there has been a slight decrease in frequency in the United States since the American Academy of Pediatrics first posited in the late '80's that it might not be medically necessary, still, in our hospital system here in Texas, at least 90% of newborn males are circumcised. Now, I know we have touched on this topic earlier in the year, but some additional points are worth mentioning.

God instituted the ritual of circumcision on the 8th day of a male child's life as a sign of the covenant between Himself and His Chosen People. (Genesis 17:10) But with the incarnation, life, sacrifice and resurrection of Christ, a New Covenant was established between God and the people, and *anyone* who believed would be the "spiritual" offspring of Abraham and thus incorporated in the Chosen People. Circumcision was a sign of the Old Covenant under which the people were to abide by the Law of Moses. This proved impossible. Paul described that Law, whose existence made sin clear, as the "Guardian" until Christ came, at which time we would be justified by faith alone. *"But in Christ there is neither Jew nor Greek, there is neither slave nor free, there is no male or female, for you are all one in Christ Jesus. And if you are Christ's, then you are Abraham's offspring, heirs according to the Promise."* (Galatians 3:28-29)

In the verse from Acts above, we see that some did not understand that in Christ, we are justified by Grace through Faith, and adherence to the Law was not what brought salvation. They insisted that to become a Christian, you must first be circumcised. Jeremiah had prophesied hundreds of years before that when the Savior came, the Law would be written in the peoples' minds and on their hearts. (Jeremiah 31:33-34) They would no longer be under the Law, and nor would Gentiles seeking the Lord. They would not need to adhere to Jewish ritual in order to be part of God's people. This controversy led to the famous Jerusalem Council decision which followed the verse above. Circumcision would no long be a requirement to be a follower of Christ and the One true God.

So today, when Christians consider circumcision for their sons, we can make the decision on the basis of cultural preference, personal hygiene, uniformity in the family, but not as a requirement for being a Christ follower. Most of Christian Europe has not adhered to circumcision for centuries, nor have many other parts of the world. It is a requirement for faithful Jews and followers of Islam, but that very fact emphasizes their divergence from Christianity! Christ died that *all might be saved*, simply through faith! For Christians, circumcision, or the lack thereof, can now be a reminder of a practice that once was meant to single out God's people, but now brings to mind the New Covenant, where all believers of every race, creed, color, and gender can come to Christ, *"just as they are."*

> *Prayer: Dear Heavenly Father, We love You! Thank You that You welcome everyone into Your Kingdom, solely on the basis of faith, without regard to outward signs, or any other distinction between peoples! Remind us Spirit, as we encounter all sorts of people in our daily walk, that God loves them just as much as He loves us! Perhaps thinking about circumcision might remind us what's important and what isn't in the eyes of God! AMEN*

NOVEMBER 23

Finishing Well

"Better is the end of a thing than its beginning, and the patient in spirit is better than the proud in spirit." (Ecclesiastes 7:8 ESV)

I can't recall a year in my lifetime that needs to finish well, more than 2020! From politics on a street-fight level, to wild and widespread forest fires, to devastating hurricanes, to rioting and looting in a bewildering misguided response to racial injustice, to a viral Pandemic that claimed more than a quarter of a million lives in the USA alone; this has been a year that people will wish to *not* remember!

This is a season when tensions often run high over trivial disagreements, as families gather from far and wide to celebrate three major holidays within five weeks! Parents are often stressed by children at home, and grandparents who need accommodating. The hassles of travel, decorating, preparing larger than usual meals, selecting and purchasing gifts, juggling work projects around time off, all combine to occasionally wear tempers thin and lead to outbursts that we really wish hadn't happened! The Holidays are usually ripe for kerfuffles. *And all this is in a normal year!*

As 2020 comes to a close, we are certainly stressed, but perhaps for less trivial reasons than usual. Thousands will have empty chairs at Thanksgiving and Christmas, that they didn't expect to have empty. Millions have elderly parents and grandparents who are in some type of assisted living and Covid has kept them isolated, depressed, and often with worsening disorientation and overall health. The stress of large family gatherings has been replaced by *the much worse stress* of not being able to gather at all, as the Pandemic once again decimates travel, and prudence keeps most of the population at home. All of the preparations for both Thanksgiving and Christmas seem disjointed and maybe even half-hearted, where the shopping malls will be largely empty, where there will be no parades, no packed football stadiums, no parties with wings and beer and chips to watch playoff games that once seemed so much a fabric of our lives that nothing could alter them.

Most of us can't even remember New Year's Eve 2019, and why we might have longed for the new year! Surely we started out with high hopes, which came crashing down for all of us in the spring. But as Solomon says in Ecclesiastes, it is better to finish well than to start well! The bible tells us that Saul started out as an expert on the Law of Moses, dedicated to the mission of stamping out the fledgeling Christian faith. After meeting the risen Christ however, Paul (once Saul) sets out on a lifetime of foreign travel, largely on foot, to communities which beat him, jailed him, and repeatedly sought to kill him. But he finished the race! (2 Timothy 4:7) Despite his trials, with the power of the Holy Spirit, He was instrumental in leading enough of the known world to Christ over roughly thirty years, to result in 2.4 billion believers today!

We've had a rough year. Some rougher than others, but virtually all have been directly impacted in some way. It's time to finish well. It's *important* to finish well. We need to focus on the only thing we are called to do: love each other! We need to do it even if on FaceTime! We need to be generous, even in a time of diminished income or job loss. We need to be forgiving to relatives and friends who may have hurt us in the last year. We need to encourage those who have lost more than we have. We need to make clear to everyone that we are giving *thanks to God* during Thanksgiving, because we truly believe every good thing comes from above! (James 1:17)

Finally we need to prepare ourselves to celebrate the coming of the Savior! Perhaps in this year when stores are closed, when more people are staying home and not gathering so readily, we can actually focus on helping everyone to understand what Grace really means! The reason for the Season has never been more relevant or needed! God loves us *so much* that He gave us His only Son so that we could find our way back to Him! That's a big deal. Concentrating on that and praising Him is the best possible way to finish well!

Prayer: Dear Heavenly Father, We love You!! Thank you for always being immediately available in these times when running the race seems so tough indeed! Help us to finish 2020 well Lord, loving extravagantly! Guide us to listen well to those who disagree with us politically, and listen well to loved ones rather than getting in a fuss! Help us to bring You Glory in the way we are seen to treat others, that they will know us by our fruit! AMEN

NOVEMBER 24

Shifting

"There is a time for everything, and a season for every activity under the heavens." (Ecclesiastes 3:1 NIV)

When people say that they have heard I am a violinist, I tell them, "Oh no, I wish that were the case, but actually I have simply played the violin for the last five years. I would call myself perhaps a "beginning intermediate," player, but I am not sure my teacher would be so generous!

While a violin has only four strings, it also has no frets. That means your fingers must learn exactly where to be placed in order to achieve the correct tone. The further one reaches up the finger board toward the purfling (the edge of the instrument's body) the higher the pitch of the note. But since we only have four fingers on the strings, and 3/4 of the notes couldn't be reached with your pinkie without moving your entire hand, the violinist can move, or shift positions, up the fingerboard as needed. The position of the hand is where the hand hovers to place the fingers on the desired correct pitches. There are usually five positions spoken of, but virtually all the notes can be played by shifting up to the second and third positions.

But for the beginner, shifting is difficult. The hand must move smoothly and rapidly to each new position and the fingers have to be placed exactly, quickly, firmly enough, and without touching other strings. Furthermore, once the notes in first position on the G,D,A, and E strings become second nature, it is hard to assign your fingers to the new notes of a new position, mentally! In short, shifting needs to be learned, and practiced by repeating the motions over and over again.

Shifting in life can be even harder. We tend to get wrapped up in our work or schooling, focused on achievement or acquisition, and we lose the ability to slow down and smoothly shift positions to the notes in our lives that are actually the most important. (Matthew 6:19; Hebrews 13:5) Our challenges at work may keep us in high gear physically and emotionally, and then we forget to stop when we come home to spouse and family, or have an afternoon or weekend off. We need to be reminded that there are not only seasons in life, but in a way, seasons in every day! It takes a conscious effort to learn where our "fingers go" when we shift from home to work to home again, *even if we work from home and don't change locations physically!* There needs to be a time for work, a time for play, a time for each relationship, including our relationship with the Lord!

Jesus understood this. Frequently He would draw away from the crowds, and sometimes even the disciples, in order to commune with His Father and to be alone with His thoughts. (Mark 1:35; 6:46; Luke 6:12) He took time to preach publicly, (Matthew 13:1-3) but also time to teach his disciples privately. (Luke 9:18) He took time to relax and have meals with his closest friends, but also he took time to travel to those in need. (Luke 19:5)

Think about your day yesterday and practice any shifts that come to mind tomorrow! When was your last date night with your spouse? (Ephesians 5:25; 1 Peter 4:8) When was the last time you spent time *alone* with each of your children or grandchildren? (Proverbs 17:6) When was the last time you took the time to stop and thank the people that help you every day, whether at home or at work? (Ephesians 1:15-17) The more you practice shifting to find the right pitch in your relationships, and yes that means prayer and study as well, (2 Timothy 3:16) the better your every day performance will be!

Remember, when the tourists on the street in New York City asked, "How do you get to Carnegie Hall?" The answer was, "Practice, practice, practice!"

Prayer: Dear Heavenly Father, We love You! Let Your indwelling Spirit help us to shift up and down the fingerboard every day, practicing just the right tones for work, play, study and prayer! Learning to shift means learning to love others and You Lord, better and better! AMEN

NOVEMBER 25

Queen's Gambit

"As iron sharpens iron, so one person sharpens another." (Proverbs 27:17 NIV)

The 2020 Pandemic drove an awful lot of people to streaming entertainment, since for much of the year, and across much of the world, the customary date night became a thing of the past. One of Netflix's original series was called, *The Queen's Gambit*. The story is about a girl named Beth Harmon, raised in an orphanage in the early 60's, after her single parent mother committed suicide by head on collision while Beth was in the back seat. The girl thinks a bit differently than the other girls, and learns to play chess on the sly, from the kindly old janitor in the basement. Beth is adopted as an adolescent, by an alcoholic woman who wanted her, and her husband, who definitively, did not.

The "Queen's Gambit" turns out to be a standard chess opening that involves two pawns working together, one of which is often sacrificed. She will employ this tactic in the most important game of her life 10 years later, when playing the Russian World Champion in Moscow. I play chess, but not at all well. I have never developed, and may not in fact, have the innate capacity, to see many moves ahead, as a good chess player must. Most think of chess as a silent, solitary game, one mind pitting its two dimensional capacity vs an opponent's, as well as the clock. Harmon had an extraordinary ability to visualize an entire chess game and its critical moves on the ceiling of her room, while lying in bed. She could play entire games in her head. But the culmination of the Queen's Gambit reveals a much deeper human truth. Human beings *never function at their very best*, when they go it alone!

One would think after her string of victories, working her way to the top, that no one could ever play chess better than she! But twice she loses to the World Champion, once in Mexico City and once in Paris. It gradually dawns on her that he takes every adjournment, every day between games, to consult with friends of his who are fellow expert chess players. That has not been Harmon's way. When others relax before a match, she is studying books of previous games relentlessly. The final match in Moscow, finds her again on the brink of inconceivable loss, and the Champion adjourns the game after hours, to be continued the following day. Harmon is at a loss as to what to do, when she encounters an old friend who has a surprise! (Spoiler alert!) Once in her hotel room, he gets on the phone, and all her old chess friends from years past have gathered in New York, studied the moves published in the New York Times from the day's match, and combine their formidable intelligence to give her advice on options. The little girl from the orphanage, taught by the janitor, wins the day!!

We live in a Western Society that absolutely *worships individualism!* The very founding of America is structured around freedom, liberty, opportunity, to accomplish on our own, however we desire! This individualistic milieu has led to further concentration on self in the latter half of the 20th century, resulting in a culture that is very much "me" oriented. We've spoken before how this can lead to self-absorption and the pride that is the true origin of all sin, but it also leads to the misperception that, like a two year old, *we can do it ourselves!!*

This is not what scripture teaches! Two heads are always better than one! (Ecclesiastes 4:9) As our opening verse implies, friends make us better. Friends have different gifts than our own, and when they are combined, they can accomplish more than one can alone. Camaraderie also simply breeds happiness! Man is not meant to be alone. Peace and joy may be found in momentary solitude, but not over any length of time! If you are facing the challenges in your life alone, FIX THAT. Get bold and join a group at work, or church, or a sports team, or a choir, or a dog walking club! Get connected, even if you are shy and think you can't, or self-confident and think you don't need to! Beth Harmon found out that even extraordinary intellect and dedication are no match alone, for a team of like minded individuals!

"Individual commitment to a group effort—that is what makes a team work, a company work, a society work, a civilization work!" (Vince Lombardi)

"Coming together is a beginning. Keeping together is progress. Working together is success." (Henry Ford)

Prayer: Dear Heavenly Father, We love You! Thank you that you made us creatures that crave each other's company! Thank you that You gave us all different gifts and different needs, so that coming together, in work, or as the Body of Christ, is the only way that really works, and certainly the only way to peace and joy in this life! AMEN

NOVEMBER 26

Life Blood

"Indeed, under the law almost everything is purified with blood, and without the shedding of blood there is no forgiveness of sins...So Jesus suffered outside the gate in order to sanctify the people through His own blood." (Hebrews 9:22; 13:12 ESV)

I did well in medical school. I could have gone the route of my roommate: ophthalmology. Certainly, I would have avoided a whole lot of encounters with blood over the last forty years! But, as I often say in delivery, (with a cockney accent, which is critical) "Its a bloody bizness, buh sumbahie ga ta do eet!" Besides, every believer knows there's life in the blood, right?

Just twenty minutes ago I delivered the third baby to a long term patient of mine. Shortly after dad cut the cord and mom had the baby on her chest, with the placenta yet undelivered, I slipped a needle into the cord and collected about 100cc of the baby's cord blood. This blood would be shipped off, separated, and the "stem" cells harvested and stored in freezers at -130C, indefinitely. Originally, these stem cells were used in place of bone marrow transplants, if the child one day developed rare blood cancers or anemias. More recently, stem cells are being used for regenerative medicine. Their immunomodulatory characteristics may help with autoimmune disease of all types from diabetes, to Crohn's, to Multiple Sclerosis, Lupus, and many more. Studies show they may help with autism, head injury, deafness, Alzheimer's and spinal cord injury. One day soon we hope to be able to expand their numbers and even use them to stimulate growth of replacement organs! This stuff got real for me when my son-in-law was diagnosed with lymphoma right before the onset of the pandemic. Hopefully it won't ever be needed, but if his chemotherapy were to fail, they could still use my grandson's cord blood, which they banked at his birth.

Scripture tells us there is life in the blood, and certainly that is true physiologically, but it's true spiritually as well! Without blood, we would have no oxygen carrying capacity and no organ could function. No blood, no life. But God also made it clear after the Garden, that man's only hope of forgiveness lay in the shedding of blood that accompanied sacrifice. That sacrifice included the surrender of their most precious possessions: their unblemished animals. No blood, no life. But the people quickly let this become an empty ritual. With no repentance in their hearts, they continued to sin, even while offering sacrifices which had become meaningless.

But God's eternal plan of redemption had always centered on coming to live among us as *Emmanuel, God with us*. Jesus became God incarnate, lived a sinless life, and then took on our sin with the shedding of His blood on the cross. But Jesus rose from the dead, and there was life in the blood once again! Faith in Him alone became the only requirement of salvation and an eternity with God!

When we gather at Thanksgiving to share with each other the things for which we thank God, think about what it meant for Jesus to shed His life's blood on that cross. We sometimes mention the "cross" so cavalierly. We wear it on t-shirts and jewelry and place nice, clean, shiny, ones above our places of worship. We shy away from contemplating the agony of those hours that our Savior spent hanging on a blood soaked post, *saving us*! The price He paid is almost beyond comprehension. The righteousness required to come before God could never be achieved in our own effort, as the Law clearly showed us. We are saved by Grace, unearned, through our faith in the Lord, who took the hit for us on that tree outside the walls of Jerusalem 2,000 years ago. There *is life* in the blood, and *that* is something for which to be very thankful indeed!

Prayer: Dear Heavenly Father, We love You! As we gather whatever family we can in this pandemic year, keep us mindful of what it meant for Your Son to shed His blood on that cross. Our salvation is indeed free, but didn't come at all cheaply! We thank You Lord, over and above all our Blessings, for the chance to be born again, righteous in Your sight and worthy of saving! AMEN

NOVEMBER 27

Enlightenment?

"'Let a man build a roof over his head, and he thinks he has created the universe.' So it has sometimes seemed with the current effort to manage alone, without God's council or enablement." (Morris Inch PhD)

As we approach the Holiday season in this crazy political, pandemic year of 2020, many people who are facing the death of a loved one, the loss of a job, physical and social isolation, and possibly economic desperation, wonder exactly what there is to be thankful for? It made me stop and wonder just what "enlightenment" has done to us?

Morris Inch, PhD, a professor of Biblical Studies at Wheaton and the author of *A Case for Christianity*, lays out the Enlightenment succinctly. The revival of classical learning in the 14th century that was the "Renaissance," led inevitably to the "scientific revolution" of the 16th century, which in his words, "ushered in the Modern Era." Humanity displaced God at center stage. Reason triumphed over faith, viewed at once as antiquated and superstitious. Man was encouraged to achieve his full potential as an individual! "Humanism," with man as the measure of all things, and "Secularism," with humanity and its activity forming the basis of the correct worldview, have completed the modern stage on which we all live. Darwin's evolutionary theory left man as little more than a very complex animal derived from the same building blocks as all creatures. Man was in essence, no longer King of the Hill put in place by God, but instead merely the conqueror of lesser evolved species. Pride has allowed man to place himself at the center, with no transcendent deity in existence.

A universe scientifically proven to have a starting point, the origin of life inexplicable, phenomenally precise tuning of the universe on every level to allow our existence, a moral code that seems remarkably uniform across cultures, the miraculous spread of the Gospel with its implausible story of an incarnate God who took the world's deserved punishment on Himself and then conquered death, and the personal revelatory experiences of billions of individuals, still fail to convince the secular of God's existence!

Paul put it this way in his letter to the Romans, *"Instead of believing what they knew to be the truth about God, they deliberately chose to believe lies.So they worshipped the things that God made rather than the Creator Himself..." (Romans 1:25 NIV)* Despite the position of the secular, faith is no less an essential for the humanist than the theist. Both believe. Both form a worldview that seeks to make sense of the facts. Literature is replete with examples of brilliant men who have concluded that belief in God is both reasonable and consistent with the findings of science as it advances. Men and women exemplary in their command of both science and letters like G.K. Chesterton, Dietrich Bonhoeffer, C.S. Lewis, Ken Samples, William Craig, Gary Habermas, Joni Eareckson Tada, Hugh Ross, Fazale Rana, Eric Metaxas, Timothy Keller, and NIH director Francis Collins, just to name a few off the top of my head, all have faith in God and trust in science.

So, as we enter this season of Thanksgiving, let us renew our efforts to pull ourselves out of the quagmire that human effort alone has made of the world! If we were all but to adhere to the Greatest Commandment, because we all believed it was a divine imperative from the Creator, literally *all of our problems* could be resolved! ***Love God, love each other.***

We all have plenty to be thankful for if we just look around and see the Blessings bestowed on us every day! We live in a country that permits us to worship our Savior, and we see His gifts every moment of every day from sunrise to sunrise! From the warmth of the sun on your face, to a moonlit path under a starry sky at night; from the family members who cherish you and you them, to the people with whom you work and serve; from one more day drawing breath and using it to ease the suffering of another; from the joy of reading a book, or sharing a movie, or sharing a meal (soon without a mask); from the exhilaration of a hike, or a climb, or a swim, or yes, a sail or just time playing fetch with your dog, there is so *much to be thankful for!*

"Enlightenment" has truly come for those of us who have concluded that *"theism is not explicit in anything but implicit in everything," (Borden Parker Browne)*, and there is never enough time to thank God for every good gift that comes from above! (James 1:17)

Dear Heavenly Father, We love You! We ask Your Spirit to keep alive in us every day, the thankfulness that we express in this season! Truly understanding that You loved us first, changes our worldview from one centered on ourselves and striving to achieve through our own efforts, often at the expense of others, to one in which we recognize Your Sovereignty and instead serve to love and serve as You have shown us, as the road to peace and contentment. AMEN

NOVEMBER 28
Hedgehog

"If you're lucky, a dog will come into your life, steal your heart, and change everything!"

"A dog is the only thing on earth that loves you more than he loves himself."

"To err is human, to forgive canine."

"Having a dog will bless you with the happiest days of your life and at least one of the worst days."

"If I had a penny for every time my dog made me smile, I'd be a millionaire."

"Thorns may hurt you, men desert you and sunshine turn to fog; but you're never friendless ever, if only you own a dog."

Actually, it wasn't the hedgehog I had my eye on at first. It was a large, fat, yellow, brown and orange, chicken! My wife on the other hand, was partial to a medium sized purple elephant. That's when we checked to make sure the aisle was empty, lined up all our top choices and let Windsor choose. He went right for the...long green dragon! What? What on earth is he thinking? The dragon of course, made by far the *loudest squeak!* But our vigorously tail wagging, prancing, flouncing, so obviously excited, happy pup, had made his choice. (I actually snuck in the little hedgehog, mostly because it makes a hedgehog sound rather than a loud squeak...he likes it... a little.)

The day after Thanksgiving began with the rest of the clean up for us. Thanks to that turkey, Covid-19, our usual 12-20 people had been carved down to just 6 adults. Still, we collectively made a remarkable mess, particularly because we threw in my wife's birthday celebration as well. (You know, the one where your big gift is your Medicare Card.) In any event, after the dishes, we got dressed appropriately and took our rapidly growing Labradoodle to Pet Supplies Inc., where they have three huge metal tubs, tethers to attach fido to a rung on the wall, a shower like nozzle that sprays warm water, and a warmed air hair dryer perched on the wall that looks like the vacuum you put money into at a do-it-ourself carwash. If you've ever owned a dog, especially a big one, you know there were a whole lot of laughs that followed! There is nothing quite like a large wet dog, post multiple shakes, trying to "catch" the air from the dryer in his mouth and even with his paws!

The point? A thoroughly enjoyable morning! Sure we had our masks on, but otherwise there was no hint of the viral onslaught. People who don't own a pet might think that washing a big dirty dog was a chore. I guess that's one of the wonderful things about an animal who loves you so perfectly, so unconditionally, so, well, *graciously.* If *grace* means bestowing good will on one who is undeserving, then it's no coincidence that the letters of "*God*" and "*dog*" form a palindrome. Palindromes are words whose inner letters reflect each other. Have you ever noticed that unconditional love is the attribute assigned most frequently to both?

We, like everyone, have all sorts of problems. Troubles at work, troubles in the family; health issues and mental health issues; financial issues; legal issues; aging issues; and of course we all deal with societal issues that seem inescapable. But let me tell you, they *are escapable!* Just go wash your dog. (If you don't have one, *get one!)*

Dear Heavenly Father, We love You! No one who ever had a dog could doubt Your existence; that You would make such a perfect companion for us! Let Your Spirit encourage us each day, to try and view others through the same eyes with which our canine friends see us: forgiving, understanding, patient, loyal, and yes, loving. AMEN

NOVEMBER 29

Advent

"I got to get it! I got to get it this Christmas!! Cause its almost nearly getting close to counting down to Christmas! It's almost time to see the tree light up the town for Christmas! It's 34,026 minutes more... (Broadway show: A Christmas Story, Clarke Hallum)

A lot of people about my age are familiar with the 1983 movie, *A Christmas Story,* based on the 1966 book entitled, "*In God We Trust: All Others Pay Cash.*" It was later made into a Broadway Musical, a song from which the opening quote was taken. The story centers around Ralphie Parker, the nine year old son who wants only one thing for Christmas: a Red Ryder Carbine Action 200 Cartridge Model Air rifle. This, despite the fact that his mother, teacher and even a department store Santa, have warned him that you might just "shoot your eye out!"

Much of the film portrays the growing excitement as Christmas draws closer. The excitement for Ralphie and all the other kids of course, is the prospect of receiving presents! This is the season of *Advent* for all of Western Christendom, and there is growing excitement among believers as well, but our excitement paradoxically, is for a gift *we have already received!*

The birth of Jesus Christ marks the first physical presence of God incarnate. His sinless life, followed by a crucifixion that He suffered as atonement for our sins, led to the greatest possible gift of all: our redemption and resulting justification before our Creator! Our Christmas gift was purchased over 2,000 years ago, and unwrapped the moment we accepted Jesus as Lord and Savior! In that moment we were in-dwelt by the Holy Spirit and granted eternal life!

Advent is the beginning of the liturgical year in most Western Christian denominations, including all mainline Protestant faiths and Roman Catholicism. The celebration dates back to at least the early 5th century. It marks a time of mental and spiritual preparation for the commemoration of the birth of Jesus Christ. The word itself derives from the Latin for "coming arrival." The Greek translation is *parousia,* which usually refers to the Second Coming of Christ in the End times. Advent actually is a celebration from three perspectives: the coming Nativity, the reception of Christ into the heart of the believer, and the Second Coming. No wonder it is an exciting time! Advent calendars, lighting of Advent wreaths, daily devotionals, erecting Christmas trees, are all traditional parts of the celebration marked by the four consecutive Sundays before Christmas Day in the Western church. (Eastern Orthodox churches mark the time with a period of fasting as well, and on a slightly different schedule.)

As a child, I remember getting to open alternate doors of the advent calendar with my brother. The excitement would build a little each day of the month before Christmas, and the calendar would remind us every day what the season was really about! As you move into the Advent Season this week, maybe try to remember Ralphie's excitement when his dad shows him the last hidden present, and he realizes that his dreams have finally come true: its the Red Ryder! Christmas is a time to commemorate the gift given to us, with the joy of giving gifts to others! Think how excited God was when He sent Gabriel and that Host of Angels to the shepherds in the fields outside of Bethlehem! You'll never *believe* what I have for you guys under the tree!!!

Prayer: Father, thank you for the incredible unexpected gift of Your Son!! He told us all we need do is love You and love each other to enter Your Kingdom. Let Your Spirit empower us to be a light to the world with our love this Advent season! AMEN

NOVEMBER 30

Grades

"For by grace you have been saved through faith. And this not your own doing; it is the gift of God, not a result of works, so that no one may boast." (Ephesians 2:8-9 ESV)

Seventeen. A perfectly good number, really. It could be the number of chapters in a book, the age of our tuxedo cat, the number of billions the Federal Government spends every 48 hours, the age at which girls became an all consuming passion for me, the number of games the Dallas Cowboys won in the '93 season, the number of feet at the waterline of our family's Dark Harbor 17, or really any number of things. It was not however, a particularly good number to have written boldly in red across the top of my first chemistry test at Rice University.

I, of course, thought it was the number I had *gotten wrong,* right? I mean I was high school salutatorian, a National Merit Scholar, had never received anything but an "A" on *anything* since that "B" in handwriting in third grade! Surely they were grading on a curve, right? Nope. Flunked it. I flunked it along with everyone else I might add, but that didn't really help at the time. Why? Because I was pre-med. You simply *cannot* receive a grade of "17" on anything and ever expect legitimately to have M.D. written after your name. Denial, remorse, fear, anger all apply here. Elizabeth Kubler-Ross, author of *On Death and Dy-*

ing, would have put this somewhere between losing your spouse and children beneath an overturned cement truck, and the annihilation of all life as we know it from nuclear holocaust. In short, this was not good.

Even if you were never pre-med, most of your life was patterned by reward and punishment growing up. You did your laundry, mowed the lawn, finished your homework, came home by your curfew, and you got rewarded with something tangible, or at worst, at least good will, from your parents. You failed to do any of these or a myriad of other things, and you could end up spanked, sent to your room, grounded for a week, or anything worse that your parents could think up!

No wonder people don't understand that Christianity is based on Grace! It is simply a very difficult concept, particularly for Americans, to accept that salvation, that eternal life, that escaping the death that we all fear deep down, has *nothing whatsoever to do with performance!* The closest we can probably get in our own experience is the love we bestow on our children. No matter how they mess up in life, we may not like them from time to time, but we do love them unconditionally. Christ refers to us as "children of God" and the Creator as "Father" for just that reason: so we have some small hope of understanding! (John 1:12) God chose to send Jesus to mankind to live a perfect life as an example, and then to *literally become sin for us,* and suffer our punishment. God did this while we were still sinning! (Romans 5:8)

If Christianity were reward based, the only thing we would get would be the death we deserve, from constantly rebelling against God! Praise God that His unconditional love frees us from that! Grace is *undeserved* reward. That means that someone feeling like they aren't "good enough" to be a Christian, is an anathema! Christians ***want to be good*** not because they need to follow the rules or earn a reward, but because the love of Christ is within us, and it just wants to keep bubbling out!

The bottom line is that we *all always make the grade,* in God's eyes! We are His beloved! The apple of His eye, as it were! Nothing we can ever do can make Him love us less or love us more! If you just can't bring yourself to believe in a God who would allow suffering in the world, think about a God who loves you even though ***you*** continue to allow suffering in the world!

Prayer: Father God, thank You that You are not about grading our performance, but about loving us and wanting to love others through us! AMEN

DECEMBER

DECEMBER 1

Unchanging

"...Every good thing given and every perfect gift is from above, coming down from the Father of Lights, with whom there is no variation or shifting shadow." (James 1:17 NASB)

A good friend of mine plays the cello about as well as I play the violin. (Let's just say, if we are ever in Carnegie Hall, we'll be facing the stage not the audience.) I went over to his house last week on a Saturday to work on Christmas Carols together. There were several reasons for this: 1) Carols are notoriously easy 2) His wife promised me homemade turkey soup 3) There was at least a chance that the last year might have brought marginal improvement to our duet skills. He's now retired. I'm working only half a day with patients, but still taking nightcall. He's a little older. I'm a little older. We both have some new pains. Some of our kids have new jobs, new marriages, new babies. The Pandemic has altered both our lives as well, just like everyone else. In short, things change. We change.

But my friend was preparing to lead a group of fellow believers in a discussion of one of the characteristics traditionally, and scripturally, attributed to God: *immutability*. Oxford English Dictionary says immutable means, *"not subject or liable to change, unalterable. Not varying in different cases."* Christians who have at least some familiarity with the bible, however, often wonder how that could possibly be the case? Isn't the God of the Old Testament angry and vengeful, and the God of the New Testament the epitome of love and compassion? Didn't God decide to destroy His people Israel for their unfaithfulness, leaving only a small remnant, and decide to replace the Law of Moses with a New Covenant in which only faith in Christ is necessary to attain righteousness adequate to come into His presence? Isn't that *change?*

Everything that we know of ourselves, of animals, of plants, of the climate, the planet we live on, even a universe subject to the forces of entropy, confirms that literally, everything changes! But God is unchangeable, and that along with His eternal attributes, His Holiness, His omniscience, His omnipresence, separate the Creator from mankind. But God is also Spirit and Invisible and *outside of time*. That means that when we say, "But he changed His mind?" we are using an *anthropomorphism*. In other words, we are using human attributes to describe a behavior of the Creator, because we have no other way to express our limited understanding of Him. The scriptures never say that God can't alter His response to changing human circumstance. What they *do say is that God's character is unchanging!* Nothing about humanity or the world we live in is completely reliable. But God is. His purposes never change. His love never changes. We can rely on Him fully and at all times. When we pray, "Thy will be done," we are relying on that will, being for our benefit, without knowing the specifics of His plan for us.

James Montgomery Boice points out in Foundations of the Christian Faith, that a perfect moral being *cannot change by definition*. Any change for the better means He wasn't perfect before, and any change for the worse means He is heading toward sin and imperfection. This differs from the Greek philosophical concept of immutability *(απαθεια)* in their Gods, which meant unchanging and unaffected by any outside force. This they felt kept their Gods Sovereign.

But Scripture tells us that Yaweh, the One God, is unchanging in nature, unchanging in His attributes, but responsive to the plight of humanity. So "vengeance is mine" saith the Lord, and "God is love" are not an anathema, but scriptural evidence of our God's responsiveness. A good Father may punish his children, and still love them. Ultimately, he may judge them evil and rebellious or good and faithful, and the changes in us and our environment are due to a Fallen World, not a changing God.

We can take comfort in knowing that God never differs from Himself! In His love for us, He is always available, always receptive, always willing to listen to us whether we are thankful and praising, or angry and needy! Scripture is about the progressive revelation of God to man, and His ultimate revelation is Jesus Christ. (John 14:7 NIV) Jesus could scorn the Pharisees with seven woes, turn over the money changers tables and yet cry over Lazarus and Jerusalem! God responds to human circumstance, and remains immutable in His nature! (1 Peter 1:20)

Our opening verse says the Father of Lights is without variation or *shifting shadow* (τροπη αποσκιασμα) in the NASB. I love that! Think of dusk and the way images can transform in the growing darkness. Why do you think you saw monsters in the closet when you were three? There is no shifting shadow in God's image. He is unchangeable.

"Let nothing disturb you, Let nothing frighten you, All things are passing, God changes not." (Henry Wadsworth Longfellow)

Prayer: Father God, we shift and change in our expression of love for you and others. Our faith often waxes and wanes. Thank You that You are never changing in nature, in attribute, in loving attitude! You are the only constant on which we can rely! AMEN

DECEMBER 2

Commendable

"For what credit is it when you are beaten for your faults, you take it patiently? But when you do good and suffer, if you take it patiently, this is commendable before God." (1 Peter 2:20 NKJV)

All of us have lived through circumstances that left us feeling as though we were being punished unfairly. I know many physicians, including myself, who have suffered through years of litigation in a malpractice suit, knowing that we had done the best we could in a situation, despite the poor outcome. Dealing with that year in and year out, patiently, while continuing to serve patients, is *commendable*.

There are as many reasons to feel beaten down as there are people. Others have dealt with frightening diagnoses, like my son-in-law with lymphoma at a young age, or worse, they've lost a loved one, seemingly out of nowhere. I saw a patient today whose brother, to whom she was very close, died suddenly a few months ago of a ruptured congenital aneurysm in the brain at age 31. Two months after that, her best friend and college roommate died suddenly of a pulmonary embolus (blood clot to the lungs.) at age 25. How could you not feel you were being punished for no reason? The patient's mother came in today as well, a long time patient of mine. In fact, I had delivered both her daughter and the son that just passed away. Mother and daughter are both teachers, helping students in person and online, continuing to help others through their own personal despair, and the never ending pandemic of 2020. Their dedication is *commendable*.

My daughter and her husband, both physicians, literally work 36 hour shifts caring for patients, most of whom cannot pay for their services, who are either injured severely enough to need surgery, or sick enough from Covid and its complications to require ICU care. They are literally beaten down physically and mentally. Their conscientious devotion is *commendable*.

Across the country this year there are police officers who struggled to serve and protect in the midst of rioting crowds of anarchists who were throwing rocks, bottles, Molotov cocktails, setting patrol cars on fire and looting and burning the businesses of innocent bystanders. Their service in striving to maintain law and order was *commendable*. Likewise, there were people of all colors who protested peacefully, speaking out for racial justice in the face of a series of horrific attacks against unarmed individuals, by bigoted small minded men who should never have been given badges and authority. What they did peacefully, was *commendable*.

Our Savior wasn't crucified because he was a criminal or a bad man. He was crucified because He spoke the truth about the powers that be, and despite living a sinless perfect life, was tortured and killed. But it was God's plan from the beginning that His Son would come to earth, experience what we experience, and then take our sins on Himself, accepting the punishment of death that we deserved. (Romans 5:8) His suffering purchased our salvation. His death atoned for our sins, and we were once more welcomed back into God's presence with the righteousness we received by Grace alone. It seems a gross understatement, but what Jesus did willingly, was *commendable in the Father's eyes*. (1 Peter 2:21) When you lose a child, or your brother, or your best friend, through no fault of theirs or yours, it can lead to bitterness, anger, and a turning away from God and His goodness. If instead, you take the pain patiently, quietly, and continue to do good despite your own personal agony, that is *commendable!*

If you've lost your job, fallen ill, had a loved one fall ill, or worse, lose their life, but you are carrying on through your pain, perhaps faltering, but still clinging to your faith, that is *commendable*! It's easy to believe God works everything together for good (Romans 8:28) when everything is going well. It's when the world is on fire and falling apart that one's metal is tested. If you can hold to the truth of

Romans 8:38, and let nothing separate you from the love of God in Christ Jesus, when everything is falling apart, *that is commendable* in God's eyes!

Prayer: Dear Heavenly Father, We love You! Remind us when we are suffering, to do so as Christ did! Even when ridiculed, tortured and hung on a tree, while He could have called down Gabriel and the whole of Heaven's Armies to vanquish His tormenters, He carried on silently, and faithfully, and obediently! AMEN

DECEMBER 3

You Will Be Found

Have you ever felt like nobody was there?
Have you ever felt forgotten in the middle of nowhere?
Have you ever felt like you could disappear?
Like you could fall, and no one would hear...
When the dark comes crashing through
When you need a friend to carry you
And when you're broken on the ground
You will be found
So let the sun come streaming in
'Cause you'll reach up and you'll rise again
Lift your head and look around
You will be found

(Lyrics from Dear Evan Hansen, by Benj Pasek, Justin Paul)

Some things just have universal appeal. It's hard to find someone who just hates *Finding Nemo, or Little Mermaid, or Lion King*. Writers of movies, Broadway Musicals, and the songs that are woven through them, understand that when they craft stories which touch on emotions that run deep in all people, like family, home, loss, fear, yearning and all facets of love, they are likely to bring in the box office! Well, *Dear Evan Hansen* is no exception. The story line does indeed touch on many of the emotions that are deepest felt, but the songs in the show expand that effect to a level that is phenomenally moving.

The song, *You Will Be Found,* while it beautifully expresses the feelings of the protagonist, will bring tears to everyone's eyes. Why? Why is "being found" so important? The reason is that being *lost*, and being *alone*, are two of the most profound human fears. How many times have you heard someone say they "just don't want to die alone?" Truth be told, none of us really want to live alone either. We are social, interactive creatures, and the difficulty of losing the ability to exercise that natural drive has been highlighted by the pandemic of 2020. But it's not just being alone that we eschew, it's being *lonely*. No one likes to be excluded. No one likes to be laughed at. No one likes to feel unloved. No one likes to feel like they have no direction. No one likes to feel like they have no hope.

Believers understand that Jesus Christ is the Good Shepherd. Jesus sought out the outcast; the ones living on the margins. He was drawn to the ones that didn't fit in. If you are at your lowest right now; you feel lost and alone; defeated and hopeless; He is the one who left the 99 sheep to rescue the 1! (Matthew 18:12; Luke 15:4) All you have to do is do what Evan Hansen suggests, "*Let the SON come streaming in, cause you'll reach up and rise again!*" You are never lost and alone when you remember that the Creator of the Universe loves you and will come and get you if you just look up for Him!

One other thing. This lyric says, "*when you need a friend to carry you.*" Too many people, Christians and otherwise, think of Jesus Christ only as GOD; only as so Superior and Perfect that all we can really do is worship Him. But that's not at all what He says about Himself! He not only tells us that He loves us, but that He wants to call us, *friend,* with all the loyalty, devotion, and got-your-backness that the term implies! (John 15:15) He has been completely open with us, like a best friend does, and shown us *exactly* who the Father is and what is required of us. He won't leave your side, *ever,* if you simply ask Him to stay! (John 15:4)

This Holiday Season, if you're feeling forgotten and in the middle of nowhere, lift up your head and look for the One who's looking for you! Sit down and read, say, the book of Luke. Guess what? *You will be found!*

Prayer: Dear Heavenly Father, thank You that you look out for the lost sheep as well as leading the others! All of us go astray, all of us get down and out and lonely and lost in the dark. Remind us that we only have to lift our heads, and You'll be standing right there with Your hand out ready to pull us up into the light! AMEN

DECEMBER 4

Kindness

"Three things in human life are important: the first is to be kind. The second is to be kind. And the third is to be kind. (Henry James)

"I expect to pass through this life but once. If, therefore, there be any kindness I can show, or any good thing I can do for any fellow human being, let me do it now...as I shall not pass this way again." (William Penn)

I was walking our dog this afternoon along the bike path near our house. It weaves along an esplanade that is bordered on one side by a relatively busy four lane street. There are several intersections with lesser neighborhood roads and no traffic lights. Windsor, our labradoodle, is learning to sit at each intersection before proceeding on command. Today however, exactly like the joke implies, he saw a squirrel, and took off like a shot, across the road on an extend-a-leash. In initially following, I lost my loafer in the road, while reigning him in. The car waiting could have continued after we passed, but instead the man smiled and waved me back to retrieve my shoe. He then complimented Windsor, and commented that when he got even bigger I might be forced to wear tennis shoes.

Another day, I may have told you, a man followed me for at least half a mile, working hard at the pedals, since there was a headwind and I was on an e-bike, just to return my bike lock which had fallen off the back. A little while ago, I was playing fetch with the dog in the back yard and I distinctly heard a rooster crow; not at all a common occurrence in our North Dallas neighborhood. I looked over the fence and across the alley and sure enough, there he stood, on the bank of the stream through Arapahoe Park. I called for my wife to come see. Incredibly, I thought it was a wild chicken, like a wild turkey, right? I'm a city boy. My wife gave me an incredulous look, pulled out her phone, took a picture, posted it on *Next-door,* and quickly found the owner of the escaped pet rooster.

I bought a forty pound bag of wild bird seed this afternoon, lugged it to the register to check out, and the young woman who rang me up, summoned a strong young guy to carry it to my car, without asking if I needed help. (Since I obviously looked like I could use it!)

You probably have to think back no further than earlier today, to recall a small kindest someone paid you. Hopefully, you find it just as easy to remember having done something thoughtful for another yourself. It's not a coincidence that Paul lists *kindness* as one of the nine Fruits of the Spirit. (Galatians 5:22) It doesn't mean atheists and agnostics cannot be kind. It only means that kindness should flow naturally from those of us who are people of faith.

It can make someone else's day and cost you essentially nothing, to be kind in your interactions with others, whether strangers or your own family members. Remember too, "*that a gentle answer turns away wrath, but a harsh word stirs up anger." (Proverbs 15:1)* Gentleness goes hand in hand with kindness. When Christians are reborn, there are attributes to consciously exhibit. Scripture tells us to put on "tender mercies, kindness, humility, meekness, and long-suffering: bearing with one another and forgiving one another…" (Colossians 3:12 NKJV)

Next time you can hold a door, carry a package, let someone change lanes in traffic, let someone go first at an intersection, make a meal for a sick acquaintance, or pay for the meal of the person behind you in a fast food drive through, or any of a million other things; ***just do it. (Apologies to Nike!)***

"I wonder why it is that we are not all kinder to one another…How much the world needs it! How easily it is done! (Henry Drummond)

"Kindness is in our power, even when fondness is not." (Samuel Johnson)

"Kindness is the language which the deaf can hear and the blind can see." (Mark Twain)

Prayer: Dear Heavenly Father, We love You! Help us, Holy Spirit, to look at every person with whom we cross paths as someone deserving of kindness, since they are also someone You love, and are made in Your image. AMEN

DECEMBER 5

The Big Picture

"If you spend your life overanalyzing every encounter, you will always see the tree, and never the forest." (Shannon Alder)

The Sunday after Thanksgiving was cloudy, post rain, not freezing, but that damp, windy, in the 40's stuff, that feels colder than if it really were freezing! You know its going to be a cozy, inside day when both the cat and the dog just sit and look at you inquiringly when you open the door, like "You're kidding right?"

After a morning of virtual church, and then respective projects, the wife settled into her office and I into mine. I was trying to untangle the technological mess I had made of my violin music library when my thirty year old pilot son called. My children text, rather than calling, unless their hair is literally on fire or the sky is falling. But he just wanted to play chess! Turns out we had both independently seen *The Queen's Gambit,* which I spoke of a coupe weeks ago, and had both been doing something vaguely similar to studying chess.

I have a little used, very nice, wooden chess table in my office and Andy and I dropped into the chairs on either side, and remarked on how much fun we had both been having just studying the basics of chess again. The first game ended in a draw after perhaps 20 minutes. The next game, first I, and then Andy, made foolish moves that cost us our Queens, but I prevailed. The next game Andy won handily using a critical *en passant* move to advance a pawn and win another queen, which made short work of my remaining pawns and Knight. The final game was an even match but at a critical point I made a move to save my rook, which I considered very clever, until my son checkmated me with the next move!

Losing at chess is often the ultimate example of "not seeing the forest for the trees." If you give too much attention to your next move and forget to think strategically about the entire game, you are destined to lose. A lot of life is like that. If you know the best thing for you to do in the long run, is for example, take the job and move across the country, but you are too focused on the difficulties tomorrow brings, both logistically and financially, to make it happen, you will end up perhaps not fulfilling your full potential for both contentment and usefulness.

Jesus was a big picture guy. The disciples didn't see the big picture, neither before, nor immediately after the crucifixion. Peter even had the chutzpah to tell the Lord that He wouldn't be arrested, executed, or even rise from the dead! (Matthew 16:21-24) Talk about not realizing that sacrificing the most powerful piece on the board might be needed to win the game!

The "big picture" for the follower of Christ is that believing in Him as the risen Son of God means that you have chosen to accept God's gracious offer of forgiveness through Christ's sacrificial atonement. As such, you take on the Son's perfect righteousness before God, as if you had earned it somehow yourself! That grants you eternal life in God's presence! (Romans 5:8; John 3:16) That means your denomination, your political perspective on a myriad of social issues, your financial circumstances, what other people think about you, how you compare to others with your same age and level of education, whether you live in the city or the country, the south or the north, or whether you end your sentences with a preposition, are all *small stuff.* And in the immortal words of Richard Carlson, *"Don't sweat the small stuff, and it's all small stuff!"*

Salvation by grace alone, through faith alone, in Christ alone, (Ephesians 2:8) is the forest. Day to day, just keep in mind that everything else is a tree.

Prayer: Dear Heavenly Father, We love You! We get so caught up in the details of our lives that we have a tendency to miss the big picture! The rebirth that accompanies our salvation by grace through faith, is what allows us to love God and love each other in the way that you command. Rather than getting paralyzed in the complexity of the details , Spirit remind us to take a breath, step back, and not feel lost by the trees right in front of us, but look to the forest beyond. AMEN

DECEMBER 6

Swaddling Clothes

"And she brought forth her first born son and wrapped Him in swaddling clothes, and laid Him in a manger, because there was no room for them in the inn.Now there were in the same country, shepterdsliving out in the fields, keeping watch over their flocks by night. (Luke 2:7-8 NKJV)

I was probably 20 years old before I understood that the *manger* wasn't the little thatched building in our Nativity Scene on the mantle, but instead the feeding trough for the animals. I was probably 50 years old before I started reading the early Church Fathers and learned that Justin Martyr (100 AD-165 AD), was convinced that Jesus wasn't born in a building at all, but one of the caves just outside the city walls of Bethlehem. Evidence that this was long accepted can be seen in the site of the Church of the Nativity, commissioned and constructed by the Emperor Constantine and his mother, Helena, in 330 AD. It is built literally over the purported cave where our Lord was born. Jerome (342 AD-420 AD), the latin Biblical scholar, spent thirty years working in this cave, believing it sacred, while translating the Bible from Greek into Latin.

Interestingly, the sheep set apart to be used for Temple sacrifice were kept in the fields just outside Bethlehem for a statutory year, through all weather, in all seasons. They were required to be "spotless and without blemish." The shepherds who protected them from theft and predatory animals were specially trained "Levitical Shepherds," even if poor and filthy from constantly living outdoors. The special sheep over which they watched, were birthed in a designated cave, which was kept clean and as sterile as possible before the arrival of each pregnant ewe. When delivered, the new lambs, destined for eventual sacrifice in the Temple, were wrapped in clean cloths, kept in place with torn strips of bandage. The intent was to keep them from becoming "blemished" as newborns, so they would be acceptable for sacrifice.

It's no coincidence that the angel Gabriel, among the Host of Angels who appeared to the shepherds watching the flocks that Christmas night, told them the Savior would be wrapped in the same clothes they used for their newborn lambs, but lying in the manger. The angel was aware that they already knew to what cave they would need to go. The significance of the "swaddling clothes" would not be lost on the Levitical Shepherds. This babe was unblemished and destined for sacrifice! So, the Lamb of God, (John 1:29,36; Revelation 5:6; 7:17) foreshadowed by the lamb that God would provide to take Isaac's place on the altar, (Genesis22:8), would live the perfect life, unblemished by sin, and then be sacrificed for the forgiveness of all our sins, past, present and future!

God has a purpose to everything under heaven! I always felt as a child, how cruel it was that no one would take Joseph and Mary in on a cold winter's night. And while that might still have been true, as God is wont to do, He turned an evil to good once again. Had there been room in a Bethlehem Inn, or room in a Bethlehem heart, the Christ child wouldn't have been born in that well known sacred cave, and wouldn't have been swaddled as He was, just as the sacrificial lambs were wrapped. The symbolism of the Savior's birth as a newborn babe, wrapped in such a way, was evident to the Levitical Shepherds. Undoubtedly, their testimony contributed to our knowing the story today!

Christmas time always finds many alone, many cold, many on a hillside away from the warmth of the fires and the life "in town" as it were. But remember, if you are feeling like one of those, that God chose to come to the lowly, not the social elite, just as His Son would seek out the lowly, the lost, the sick, and the frightened. The message of the Gospel is not just that you can become a new person with the hope of eternity, free from the guilt and shame which all of mankind carries; but that He will always find you where you are, and when He does, you will never be alone again!

Prayer: Father God, we are Blessed that not only have You offered us undeserved forgiveness, You have promised to actually dwell within those who believe, so that guided by Christ, the light of the world, we need never be alone in the dark again! AMEN

DECEMBER 7

Infamy

"Yesterday, December 7, 1941, a day that will live in infamy, the United States of America was suddenly and deliberately attacked by naval and air forces of the Empire of Japan." (Franklin D. Roosevelt)

Many of you may not be old enough to clearly remember the Presidential campaign of 1988, but on September 7 of that year, Vice President H. W. Bush was making a campaign speech, which he opened with, "Today is Pearl Harbor Day, a day that will live in infamy," much to the astonishment of both his campaign staff, and the thousands of Legionnaires to whom he was speaking in Louisville, Kentucky that late summer day. Oops! Moments later he corrected himself.

Now, in the former President's defense, he was a WW II fighter pilot who flew many missions and was actually shot down over the Pacific. We can cut him some slack for a gaff when probably exhausted on the campaign trail. But the day he mis-remembered indeed checked all the boxes for infamy.

Infamy means "deplorable, despicable, shamefully vile, a disgraceful act." Two thousand years ago a deplorable, despicable, vile event took place on a hill outside the walls of a little backwater town in the Roman Empire, called Jerusalem. A man was crucified there who had done no wrong, *ever*, to anyone! His crucifixion lives on in infamy for its cruelty and injustice, but because of who He was, it is remembered as much more than just deplorable . The man was in fact, the Son of Man, and many of those who didn't believe He was "God with us," or *Immanuel*, certainly did, only three days later, when they saw Him risen from the dead!

As we approach Christmas Day, turn your thoughts to the full meaning of the *Advent* season. We celebrate not only the birth of our Savior, but the Grace apportioned to us through His crucifixion. Yes, we normally think of Easter as the time to celebrate Christ's resurrection, and so it is; but Christmas would be meaningless without it! Jesus was fully man and fully God at the same time. Through the backward lens of time, we are privy to knowing His destiny. We know that we only celebrate His coming to us as a babe in Bethlehem, because He would eventually take our sins on Himself, purchase our forgiveness from the Father, and promise to come again when the Kingdom of Heaven becomes a reality on earth.

Pearl Harbor Day is remembered as a time when thousands of innocent Americans lost their lives. It is indeed a day of infamy. But in the immortal words of Admiral Yamamoto, *"I fear we have but awakened a sleeping giant and filled him with a terrible resolve."* As horrible a day as Pearl Harbor was, it ushered in a generation of Americans who would pull together, work together, love together, and first save and then build the greatest free society the world has ever known! Greatness was born in infamy.

Christianity has swept the globe over the last two millennia, now claimed as the faith of over 2.4 billion people! That shameful event remembered in infamy, on that little hill outside of Jerusalem, was the event that reunited believers with their Creator, and saved a world! Greatness was born in infamy.

Mourn those who lost their lives on that fateful day as Christmas approached in 1941; but celebrate the freedom secured in the wake of that day! Mourn the horrific death of Jesus, nailed to a wooden cross as the sun set and the Sabbath began; but celebrate the freedom from shame and guilt offered to the entire world in exchange!!

Prayer: Dear Heavenly Father, We love You! Let us mourn today those who died bravely, unexpectedly, executed in a cowardly way, in 1941, as we mourn the cruel and infamous death of our Savior. We thank You that You can always work all things together for good, as You did for America then and as you do now for all of the believers worldwide who take You up on Your offer of forgiveness and reconciliation. AMEN

DECEMBER 8

Living in the Flesh

"Now the works of the flesh are evident: sexual immorality, impurity, sensuality, idolatry, sorcery, enmity, strife, jealousy, fits of anger, rivalries, dissensions, divisions, envy, drunkenness, orgies, and things like these. I warn you as I warned you before, that those who do such things will not inherit the kingdom of God. " (Galatians 5:19-21 ESV)

People unfamiliar with the jargon used by the evangelical branches of the protestant churches, may actually have no idea of what "living in the flesh means." It can be confusing, especially given that the Hebrew word for "flesh" is used 180 times in the Old Testament, and in the Greek, 142 times in the New Testament, with a total of 14 other uses, translated as "flesh" but actually representing four other Greek words. Flesh may simply mean the stuff of which our bodies are made, as in the famous Galatians 2:20 passage, *"I have been crucified with Christ; it is no longer I who live, but Christ who lives in me; and the life which I now live* **in the flesh** *I live by faith in the Son of God, who loved me and gave Himself for me." (NKJV)* "In the flesh," in this case, simply means the physical body.

But the word "flesh," used in our opening verse above, clearly means something quite different. In fact, the list that follows would seem to imply that "works of the flesh" include every base instinct and behavior of mankind. Not insignificantly, the much better known passage, Galatians 5:22, which immediately follows, contrasts the "works of the flesh" with the "fruit of the Spirit." One more point: frequently, the writers of the New Testament substitute the concept of "worldly" for "flesh-like," and "the world" for the secular, unbelieving, peoples. Statements like *"the world hates you,"* (John 15:19) and "*Do not love the world or things of this world. If anyone loves the world, the love of the Father is not in him,"* (1 John 2:15) bear this out.

So does "living in the flesh" simply mean doing bad stuff, sinning as it were? Not really. The best way to think of it is that whenever you are 'living in the flesh," you are not living in the Spirit! Steve McVey puts it this way in his book, Grace Walk: "Don't think of flesh as skin, but as personal techniques for meeting your own perceived needs, apart from Christ. Your flesh life may not [necessarily] be defiant towards God. Walking after the flesh is simply relying on your own ability instead of God's resources." Relying on our own abilities becomes a liability when we do so *rather* than relying on Christ.

Some religious people rely on their skill and dedication to influence perceptions of them and get the status they want in the church. Others rely on their people skills to advance them in sales, or management, or relationships. Some use their wealth, or appearance, or education in their behavior patterns to try and get whatever they want.

McVey points out that the best synonym for "living in the flesh," might be "self-sufficiency." Americans tend to value self-sufficiency as an asset in life, but Christ abhorred it! Remember He promised to "abide in you if you abide in Me."(John 15:4) Our Savior wants us to be *dependent on Him.* Many of us

Christians, before we understand Grace, think that it's all about what *we can do for God.* We use our talents and abilities to do and make things that we believe will please Him. This despite the fact that it is our *faith* He desires, not our performance! (Ephesians 2:8-9)

Instead of using your own strengths to do *for God*, let God work *through* you! That is what the Fruit of the Spirit is about. If we submit our every need and decision to the indwelling Spirit, whatever flows naturally from that choice will be the Fruits of the Spirit: love, joy, peace, patience, kindness, goodness, gentleness, faithfulness and self-control! The Bible is full of men and women who thought faith alone was inadequate, so they would "help God out," with disastrous results. Abraham and Sarah decided they had waited long enough for a child, so they had Abraham impregnate their maid! Moses didn't think tapping his staff on the rock to get water would *really* work, so he tapped multiple times. The Chosen people thought they knew better than God and decided they would return to Egypt in their own strength, rather than enter the Promised Land that Caleb and Joshua had spied out. When Jesus was arrested in the Garden, one of the disciples drew a sword and cut off the ear of the High Priest's servant, instead of trusting that Jesus was in control. The list goes on and on!

If you want to avoid *living in the flesh*, and being enthralled by worldly things, then keep your eyes on Christ, the author and finisher of our faith! (Hebrews 12:2) That simply means develop your relationship with Him. Study Him, talk to Him, bring Him your problems and your pain, listen for His response, discuss Him with others, and you will increasingly display the Fruit of the Spirit, *naturally* allowing the Savior to work *through you* to the benefit of all around you.

> *Prayer: Dear Heavenly Father, help us resist the temptation to strike out and work for you in a fervor of effort to attain your pleasure and approval. Instead, let Your Holy Spirit awaken in us, such that the Fruits that result will allow us to submit and permit Your Spirit to work through us to accomplish your purposes rather than our own. AMEN*

DECEMBER 9

DEATH INTO LIFE

"Do not ever judge death from what you see. The body is only an empty shell, twitching at times, missing its inhabitant." (Alison Stormwolf)

(Skip this devotional if you are squeamish)

Doing Life for most, rarely involves any intimate study of the opposite, that is to say, being dead. The dissection of a cadaver is a strange and unique experience that left me, as a medical student, with indelible images imprinted on my memory, and a perspective denied the rest of humanity. It is perhaps only in retrospect, that physicians recognize what we have really learned. True, we learn the details of what a marvelous machine the human body is. But we also learn—through its stark absence—that the soul is who we are. When we treat our living patients, it is perhaps their difference from the cadaver, not their similarity, that provides the greater guide for our decision making.

Most of the first two years of medical school involve taking notes and asking questions in a lecture hall. There is, however, some laboratory work. Laboratory work, huh? You visualize glass beakers, Bunsen burners, etched and stained countertops and sinks, bad odors, and just a hint of the gorgeous day outside peeking in through the filthy windows, right? Well, you get partial credit for the odors.

Try thirty naked, dripping, rigid, slippery bodies, reeking of formalin, all lying on metal tables. Now imagine the task of cutting away sequential portions of them for the next six months. Mind you, before walking into this lab for the first time, all of us were fairly close to being normal people. By that I mean the only dead people we had seen were impeccably dressed in open caskets, and the body usually belonged to someone we had held dear. Of course, some of us, myself included, had never even seen that!

None of us had a clue as to what to expect. I clearly remember walking in and seeing the gleaming metal tables and wondering when and where the actual cadavers came into play. (They were inside, and raised to the surface of the formalin hydraulically.) I don't recall which of us had the honor of making the first incisions, but I do recall thinking during the process, that perhaps I had made a very serious error in career choice.

Despite the ghastly appearance of our specimen, with her yellowish- grey, slippery skin the texture of shoe leather, her few wisps of grey hair, the incredible weight of her obese, rigid extremities, and that overpowering odor, we put aside our natural aversion for the task, and began our study in earnest.

I will spare you the details, but over the course of the next six months, our cadaver taught us much about both the human condition and the human body. Obesity became much more of a negative reinforcement for our own health habits, as her liquefying fat made dissection of her corpse infinitely more difficult and repulsive than that of the emaciated old male cadaver at the next table over. The carbonization of her lungs by cigarette tar, the cholesterol plaque in her major arteries, the cirrhotic changes of her liver, all served as potent memorials to the dangers of smoking, overeating, over-drinking, and under exercising.

Perhaps the most pervasive memory, however, was the daily recognition that our "specimen" had been a real live person, in many ways, just like us, only a short time ago. Even those who claim to be agnostics will tell you that this particular medical school experience, perhaps more than any other, impresses one with the mystery of the animating force in humans. For me, it made belief in a supernatural creator the only logical conclusion. But the gross anatomy class also impressed one with the vulnerability of the human body to all of the abuses we regularly subject it to! It is much harder to overeat, smoke, drink too much etc. once you've literally held the result in your hands.

So in studying the dead, we learned to appreciate what an incredible gift our lives are, both spiritually and physically. First, one realizes immediately that the "soul" is very real, for its absence is striking! Second, one understands that when this life is over, followers of Christ will leave this shell behind and rise in a new body for eternity. (Philippians 3:21) Finally, one realizes that America is overweight and suffering from multiple addictions to a greater extent than any other comparable western nation. When we consider that peace comes from loving God and loving each other, let us not forget to love ourselves in the process. It is much harder to love God when you neglect your health, for you are trampling on one of His most magnificent gifts! (1 Corinthians 6:19-20) If indeed, the chief end of man is to glorify God, as the Westminster Catechism teaches us, then we would do well to start with some exercise!! Consider your body a Christmas gift this year, and start taking care of it!

Prayer: Dear heavenly Father, direct your Spirit to remind us daily that we are made in Your image, and destroying our bodies through neglect and addiction is the very definition of loving the world, and not honoring You! AMEN

DECEMBER 10

Standing Rigging

"Fear not, for I am with you; be not dismayed, for I am your God; I will strengthen you, I will help you, I will uphold you with my righteous right hand." (Isaiah 41:10 ESV)

Sailboats are literally covered with ropes, cables, stays, spreaders, lines, sheets, halyards, winches, grommets, metal blocks or pulleys, hasps, deck hinges, dog snaps, straps, clevis hooks, eye hooks, cleats, lifelines, genoa cars, and turnbuckles, traveller, roller furler, to name just a few of the hardware/rigging terms that are part of the regular vocabulary. This of course is in addition to terms related to sailing itself, like main, jib, spinnaker, genoa, mizzen, luff, leach, foot, head, clue, tack (related to the sails); run, beam reach, broad reach, close reach, head up, pointing, tacking, jibing, wing and wing, (sail maneuvering terms); bow, pulpit, running lights, bowsprit, topsides, freeboard, keel, rudder, wheel, tiller, transom, pushpit, toenail, gunnel, grabrail, stanchion, cockpit, salon, mast, boom, downhaul, kicker, vang, and gooseneck, (parts of the boat itself.)

The lines used to raise and control the sails, including those that control the boom, and spinnaker poles, and whisker poles, are called the *running rigging*. But the steel cables, rods, fixed lines and wires that support the mast and keep it upright and perpendicular to the deck, are referred to as the *standing rigging*. Typically, on a modern sailboat, this includes the fore and aft stays, running backstays, the shrouds, spreaders, and inner forestay. The stays are taut cables of equal tension, side to side, fore and aft, and keep the mast upright and sturdy. When the boat is simply *standing still*, rather than *running or moving*, it is the standing rigging holding everything in place. When in motion, it is the standing rigging that transfers the vector forces from the wind filled sails to the body of the boat and through to the keel, as well as keeping structures like the mast from snapping off! In short, without the strength of the standing rigging, a sailboat would simply disintegrate when faced with the forces generated by wind and water.

People can disintegrate when faced with powerful forces that jar them in different directions as well. Death of a loved one, betrayal by a loved one or friend, job stress and even loss, a poor prognosis, child rearing, separation from family, temptations that lead to either addiction or destruction of relationships. Christians learn soon after they become one, that the attributes of God which make Him always available, all powerful, all knowing, and faithfully loving, quickly become our "standing rigging." It is simply not possible to bear up on our own, under the kinds of pressure resulting from the unexpected events which occur in all our lives. Without the solid rock provided by our Savior, we would likely all succumb to anxiety, depression, addiction and even suicide.

This is not to say that non-believers cannot find solace and support in friends and loved ones. But scripture is very clear that depending on other people, just as depending on ourselves in our own power, may be transiently effective, but in the long run is doomed to failure.(Jeremiah 17:5; Psalm 118:8)

Don't face the elements in your own strength. That's like sailing into a squall with loose stays, or worse, no stays at all. Remembering that God is all powerful and all knowing, makes Him a pretty good place to turn to when you need help! The mistake is not realizing that you *always need His help, so turn to Him every day and in every circumstance,* and you'll come through every squall to a calm sea and receding clouds.

Prayer: Dear Heavenly Father, We love You! Thank you that You are with us every minute of every day, through every kind of weather. We can depend on You to transfer every force we face in life, into the vector forces that move us steadily forward, loving You and loving others. AMEN

DECEMBER 11

Total Re-do

"Therefore, if anyone is in Christ, he is a new creation. The old has passed away; behold the new has come!" (2 Corinthians 5:17 ESV)

We, in sequential moments, possibly of insanity, decided mutually, to "re-do" our kitchen, pantry, and utility room. My wife seemed much more attuned than I, to the degree of disruption which we might expect in our daily routine. In short, this type of project, properly done, will transform your family home into the psychological equivalent of, oh I don't know, maybe a bomb shelter in London during the blitz?

There was a month of planning and visitation by an assortment of experts in their fields. Then the actual work began. First, everything in the rooms to be "re-done" had to be removed in boxes and stored anywhere outside the construction zone. How the contents of a kitchen can completely fill our dining room and much of another bedroom is truly beyond me. Next, the new appliances arrived and were installed. Then, the "counter-top people" arrived and ripped out the old counters, back splash and island surface, replacing them with the quartzite, weighing about 70,000 lbs (that's the equivalent of a 767, right?) The vapors from the glue for that procedure drove the dog, cat, and any humans in the area, back into the deeper recesses of the house for 48 hours. Then 46 cabinets and drawers were converted to hidden hinges; which left the sliding drawers within all the cabinets unable to clear the open doors. Thus the drawers all had to be rebuilt as well.

Next, the cabinets and drawers were all removed to be power sanded, molding removed etc. etc. The kitchen was taped off with plastic sheeting in a futile attempt to keep the dust from settling literally everywhere in the house. Taping off the kitchen meant preventing use of the dog and cat doors, access to liter box in garage, access to the refrigerator, microwave etc. Add to unhappy animals under foot, the incessant whine of power tools for 12 hours/day. Once the days of prep were finished, primer was applied, rendering the olfactory assault of the counter top glue a distant and insignificant memory! After days of drying, subsequent coats of paint were applied, cabinets rehung, drawers refitted, and the entire area cleaned meticulously. Finally, all of the stuff that had miraculously been evicted from the kitchen, had to somehow fit back in. Finally, *voila!* A new kitchen is reborn after only two months!

As involved as a kitchen can be, needless to say, it pales in comparison to the complexities of a human being! And yet, a human can be reborn, made a brand new creation, transformed, in a moment, in the twinkling of an eye! (1 Corinthians 15:51 NKJV) The moment we accept Jesus Christ as our Lord and Savior, we are saved by grace through faith. While death was once every man's inevitable price for rebelling against his Creator, in one second that can change forever! Christ took our sins on Himself and paid the price. He did all the work for us; and now that work is finished! No amount of rule following or moral behavior is required for salvation and eternal life, for we could never be good enough no matter how hard we tried! The only requirement is to acknowledge our sinfulness, accept the gift of forgiveness offered through Christ's sacrifice, and allow the Spirit to indwell and guide us from that moment on. As Paul told the Galatians, we have been crucified with Christ, and now it is no longer we who live in the flesh, but Christ who lives in us! (Galatians 2:20)

A total re-do on all or part of a house takes a tremendous amount of work! People who seek to understand Christians often have a misunderstanding that it takes a tremendous amount of work in reforming their behavior, before they have any hope of living a new and better life. They think they just aren't, and can never be, "good enough." That is just completely and utterly incorrect! Christ's "finished work" on the cross means that He did the work for us. Becoming more Christ-like after we come to belief, means allowing the Spirit within us to guide our attitudes and behavior. It's less like work and more like a privilege! It becomes what we desperately *want to let Christ do through us!* If you're reading this and feel lost, alone, or directionless in your life, there is an answer. Jesus can do a "total re-do" on you in the time it takes for you to ask Him for help!

Prayer: Dear Heavenly Father, We love You!! Thank You that Christ has done the work for us, the work we could never do on our own, to make us righteous before You!! Holy Spirit guide us as we seek to help others see there is a way to become new for everyone, no matter what you think of your worth. AMEN

DECEMBER 12

Wake Up!

"You shall love your neighbor as yourself...and do this, knowing the time, that now it is high time to wake out of sleep; for now our salvation is nearer than when we first believed! The night is far spent and the day is at hand!" (Romans 13:9b-12 NKJV)

Windsor, the 4 1/2 month Labradoodle pup, now sleeps through the night on the floor at the foot of the bed. Sterling, the 5 year old Tuxedo cat, sleeps *on the foot of the bed*, right over his head, where he can keep an eye on him. If we forget to put the cat on the other side of the house before we fall asleep, I am awakened at 0237 on the dot, every night, with Sterling biting my right great toe after a high flying pounce. For him, and him only, it is *high time to wake out of sleep!*

As we approach Christmas, it strikes me that our excitement increases daily, just as it did as a child, but many of us find ourselves getting perilously close to the holiday and yet still unprepared! Plans incomplete, presents not yet purchased or at least not yet wrapped, and cards unsent. Paul wants the Romans to understand that every day our *salvation [Lord's return]* is nearer than we might think, and certainly nearer than when we first accepted Christ, and yet we seem unprepared, still asleep to the reality! That being the case, it is high time for each of us to wake up and smell the roses as it were! We need to release the indwelling Spirit, and allow Him to love others through us, and we need to do it *right now*!

Mitch Hedberg was a comedian who died in the early 2000's. He had a joke once where a friend showed him a picture of himself, and said, "Well, you know, that was taken when I was younger!" Mitch responded, "Dude, every picture taken of you was taken when you were younger!" Time never stops moving, even when we're standing still! It only takes a moment to ask forgiveness and receive Christ into your heart, and it will only take a moment for Christ's return. It will happen "in a moment, in the twinkling of an eye, and we shall all be changed," risen and given new bodies for eternity. (1 Corinthians 15:52) That means we need to be vigilant. We need to wake up! Those who claim their faith need to start acting like it! Remember, there are only two things you have to do: love God, and do it by loving your neighbor. Jesus told his disciples they will know us by our love.

As Christmas draws near, we need to get with it! Arrange the food, the decorations, the presents, the cards, the tree! But in the same way, we need to be ready for our salvation: love your neighbor by helping him, love your family by being someone they can trust and rely on; love your co-workers by listening and responding; love your friends by forgiving them and asking if there is anything for which you need to be forgiven; love God by doing all of these, and do it *right now!* When you do, you'll *feel* the joy of Christmas!

Prayer: Dear Heavenly Father, We love You!! Direct Your Holy Spirit to stir within us, and wake us up! Just as the celebration of Your Son's birth draws near, so too does His return, and we need to be ready! Help us Lord to be ready by loving as You command at every opportunity and starting right now! AMEN

DECEMBER 13

Light > Dark

"The people who walked in darkness have seen a great light; those who dwelt in the land of the shadow of death, upon them a light has shined...for unto us a Child is born, Unto us a Son is given..." (Isaiah 9:2,6 NKJV)

One of my favorite things to do (and other's *least* favorite) is to sail at night. All of the ambient noises of the day are diminished or gone. There are no motor noises from other boats, no bird noises, no voices; only the sound of the water slipping by under the hull and the wind in the rigging. But there is a huge difference between sailing on a clear night with a full moon, versus an overcast, starless, night. Surprisingly, it's the changes in sound that make night sailing so appealing, rather than the ambient light. Sailing in the pitch dark, even in waters you know well, used to be, frankly, terrifying, before the advent of GPS. On the other hand, sailing with a full moon, the reflection stretched over the water like the yellow brick road, with stars strewn across the sky like diamonds, is simply glorious! It's the *presence of light* even at night, that makes the experience a pleasant one.

Virtually the same phenomenon can be experienced walking on a rural country road. With moon and stars, it's a startlingly pleasant experience. On a moonless, overcast, windy night, the same stretch of road can be scary . Why is that? Why do we have an innate fear of the dark? It's one of the very first fears we have as a child. Perhaps it's associated with bedtime and our parents "leaving." Perhaps it's associated with the things we imagine in the half light. But some remnant of it remains into adulthood.

Darkness has always been associated with bad things happening. Evil can flourish where it is undiscovered. (There's a reason Darth Vader dressed in black!) But there is a remarkable quality to the physics of light. *Light dissipates the darkness.* There is no way for black to dissipate the light. Why? Because dark doesn't *really exist!* It is the *absence of light.* Light illuminates, enlightens, educates, because it allows one to see. It uncovers evil and exposes it, where it cannot survive.

The Chosen People were led for 1500 years by a religious leadership that just didn't get it. They taught the people that they were to follow a strict code of 613 laws of Moses, knowing full well that it was impossible. The sacrifice of animals for forgiveness, as prescribed by the Lord, quickly became an empty gesture, when not performed out of faith. The priestly leadership became hypocritical, sinning without qualm, while holding exposed sin over others. Over and over again the people turned away from Yaweh, to other false Gods. Truly, they walked in darkness, unable to see what they were doing.

Jesus repeatedly identifies Himself as the light of the world! *"I am the light of the world. He who follows Me shall not walk in darkness, but have the light of life!"* (John 8:12; 9:5 NKJV) Christ was teaching in the courtyards of the Temple during the Feast of the Tabernacles, during which giant oil lamps were lit to illuminate the Temple area for songs and dances of praise. It was done in remembrance of the light of the pillar of fire that led the Jewish people out of Egypt into the desert by night. The world being in darkness symbolized evil, ignorance and sin. Jesus made it clear that faith in Him *is faith in the Father, (John 10:30)* and that this alone, was necessary for forgiveness of sins, and these were granted eternal life! Furthermore, accepting God's gracious offer would result in the indwelling Holy Spirit, and no longer would the people be at the mercy of evil. Walking in the Light of His enduring love would free the people from guilt and shame and the tyranny of sin that formerly, they could never resist!

This Christmas season as you drive around with your family and enjoy the lights; or as you sit by the fire and admire the lights on your tree; or as you look into the night sky for a particularly bright star; remember that Christ has already won the victory over the forces of darkness; from His birth, to His sinless life, to His redeeming sacrifice on the cross, to His victorious resurrection, He is the bright light that dissipates the darkness and eliminates the shadows in which evil flourishes!

Prayer: Father God, as we prepare to celebrate the Light that has come into the world, show us the way to be a light to those around us! Let Your love for us shine through, so that others will be attracted to its brilliance, and they can leave the darkness behind! AMEN

DECEMBER 14

Do Not Fear

"Have I not commanded you? Be strong and courageous. Do not be frightened, and do not be dismayed, for the Lord your God is with you wherever you go!" (Joshua 1:9 ESV)

This year has engendered more fear world-wide than certainly any other in our new century, and possibly even in the last. All fear is similar in one respect: it is due to our inability to know the future. The "fear of the unknown," is really at the core of all fear, whether a viral pandemic that seems to act somewhat capriciously in its severity, or the often suppressed knowledge of thousands of nuclear warheads still functional and only awaiting targeting packages and launch commands! But why are these frightening to us? World wide chaos?

Collapse of the economy? The potential elimination of food and clean water supplies? Violence from those who have little towards those who have a lot?

No, at the base of all fear of the unknown is only one thing for human kind: the fear of death. The belief that everything we hold dear in life, from the love of our families, to a walk on the beach, to skiing down a snow covered mountain, might all disappear forever, in an instant! That's what we're afraid of. That's the monster in the dark of the closet that we spend a lifetime being afraid of and hoping somehow we will never have to face.

As I have dealt with death and dying as a physician, I can tell you one thing that is clear: those with a strong faith have a peace "that passes all understanding." Philippians 4:6-7 tells us to *"be anxious for nothing, but in everything by prayer and supplication, with thanksgiving, let your requests be known to God; and [then] the peace of God, which passes all understanding, will guard your hearts and minds through Christ Jesus."* This peace comes to those who practice their faith by doing the above. These people have a *relationship* with their Savior, and thus, they are never alone. We face death with a calm assurance that soon we will not only be in the presence of the Almighty, with no more pain, and no more sadness; but we will also see our loved ones again! Christians have the same confidence about their believing friends and loved ones who are facing death.

Those who understand Grace, and accept the undeserved gift we have been offered by the Creator, through Christ, are still human. We still get scared from time to time. But we are *never alone.* The Holy Spirit is literally inside us, and we never have far to go for help and reassurance! The Lord doesn't recommend that we have no fear, He *commands it!* In fact, Scripture has the command *"fear not"* repeated 365 times! In other words, He is *instructing us* about what *is true*, not what might happen if we're lucky! *Believe* that the Sovereign Lord has your back, and the Pandemic of 2020 takes on a whole new look! Of course we should be careful. Of course we should follow guidelines. But for Christians, the *worst that could happen is also the best that could happen....we go to be with our Lord!* (Philippians 1:21-26)

Prayer: Dear Heavenly Father, We love You!! We love that you have given us not a Spirit of bondage again to fear, but we received the Spirit of Adoption by whom we cry out, "Abba, Father!" No Father would abandon his child, and we know, nor would You! AMEN

DECEMBER 15

Littlest Angel

"Then the littlest angel put his little box,
With the presents fine and wrapped
And the littlest angel sat alone and cried
For his gift was so meager and bad"

(Mark David/Simon Rady)

Christmas music falls into only two categories for me: 1) Instrumental and 2) Bing. It is possible, if you were born after perhaps, 1990, that you've never even heard of Bing Crosby, but its unlikely for two reasons: your parents and grandparents played his impossibly smooth, deep baritone, every holiday season while you were growing up and, unless you were born on a tiny island in the South Pacific or in the jungle of the Amazon delta, you know the song *White Christmas.* Bing released that song in 1941, just as America entered WW II after the Japanese bombing of Pearl Harbor. It stayed at number one on the billboard charts for 11 weeks. It was the centerpiece of the movie *Holiday,* released in 1942, and then again for *White Christmas,* in 1954. In fact, even as of 2020, it remains the number one selling single of all time!

But there are other gems hidden away in Bing's many Christmas albums. Driving home from the Pooch Hotel today, Windsor riding with his head on the transom between us, the tears welled up uncontrollably as I listened to *The Littlest Angel.* Why on earth did this short story about a four year old angel, who had a little box with his treasures from earth pierce me right through the heart? Two hours later when I played it for my wife, the tears were streaming down my face again. Spotify it. The little boy's box contains a butterfly with golden wings, a piece of a hollowed out log, two shiny pebbles, and the worn out collar from his faithful dog. It was his prize possession and the only thing he had from his brief time on earth.

One day there's a great commotion in the Celestial Realm, and the little angel hears of the birth of the Christ Child. All the angels bring Him precious, beautiful gifts, but he has nothing but his little treasure box. So he gives the Lord the little box that he loves above everything else, and cries because it's such an inadequate gift for the Savior of the world! (I'm crying AGAIN as I write this! Geeezzzz) Despite the piles of sparkling gems that surround the Lord, He picks the littlest angel's box as His favorite! It began to glow brighter and brighter that Christmas night and it soon shone as the star above! Now when you see that star in the great Celestial Hall, you will know that the littlest angel is the proudest one of all!

Luke tells a similar story of Jesus and the poor widow. He saw her putting 2 tiny coins in the donation box at the Temple, while the rich were piling their many gifts in the treasury. The Lord knew that these two "mites" were all the woman possessed! *"Truly I say to you, that this poor widow has put in more than all; for all of these out of their abundance have put in offerings for God, but she out of her poverty, put in all the livelihood that she had." (Luke 21:3-4 NKJV)*

So what is it that brings the tears to my eyes, *every single time?* My analysis of my own emotional outburst is this: there is no purer love than this! It is an unfettered and sacrificial love for Jesus, and exactly the same from Him to the giver of the gifts. Perhaps it makes us cry because we realize through the song, that Jesus *sees into the heart.* (1 Samuel 16:7) Our Lord has asked us only to love God and love each other. When we understand that all our effort, all our performance, all the wealth we attain, all the material riches we can give, mean less than nothing to Him if there aren't blessed with love! All the sacrifices of the Chosen People meant less than nothing to Him when unaccompanied by the love that derives from faith! (Isaiah 1:11-13) God doesn't want our empty sacrifices, He wants our hearts! He wants to know us! (Hosea 6:6)

So why the tears, again? Because I don't have to DO for my Savior, I only have to LOVE. He's the one who DID for me on that cross; all I have to do is accept the gift and love Him and others the way that He asked! If that's not pressure off, if that's not how you spell relief, if that's not freedom, I don't know what is! And to be loved that much…well, it just makes you cry!

Prayer: Dear Heavenly Father, We love You!! We know that You first loved us through Your Son, and it's an indescribable feeling to know that what You want in return for Christ's sacrifice and the forgiveness of all our sins past, present and future, is simply that we return Your love by giving others our most treasured possession, our hearts. AMEN

DECEMBER 16

Gender Reveal

"Do not be afraid, Mary, for you have found favor with God. And behold, you will conceive in your womb and bring forth a Son, and you shall call His name, Jesus." (Luke 1:30-31 NKJV)

"Do not be afraid?" Really? Are you serious? Let's look at the facts.

1. The Angel Gabriel just appears at the well near their house in Nazareth, presumably when she is getting water
2. Mary is 13, maybe 14 years old. "Engaged" in an arranged marriage to Joseph at the time.
3. Gabriel tells her she is "Blessed among women," and God is pleased with her.
4. Then tells her she will become pregnant even though she hasn't had sex yet
5. Tells her it will be a boy
6. Tells her not to name it Jesus, but that His name *will be Jesus*
7. Her son will sit on the throne of his *father David,* when Mary knows full well David is not her fiancé's name nor does he have a throne.
8. He will rule over the House of Jacob *forever*
9. *The Holy Spirit* will come upon her and impregnate her on the authority of God (say what?)
10. Her Son will be called Holy One and Son of God
11. By the way, your old aunt Elizabeth, who's been infertile forever, is also 6 months pregnant!
12. Lastly, says Gabriel, "Nothing is impossible with God!"

Can you even begin to imagine? Do not be afraid? An adolescent, undoubtedly already terrified about the prospect of marriage to an older man whom her parents have selected, is told that she will be pregnant *before they are married.* Furthermore, God will get her pregnant personally! And never mind what Gabriel *says,* the fact of him *just standing there* would petrify any normal person! Can you just feel her mind racing? Who is this? What is he talking about? She'll be pregnant? So when she begins to show, she just tells people that God got her pregnant and they're supposed to believe that Joseph didn't jump the gun? And now she knows *ahead of time* that the baby will be a boy? Who has *already* been named? For real? (She could have the first gender reveal in history?)

As if all this weren't enough, Mary is told Jesus will be the Son of God and sit on David's throne forever? Admittedly, even at 13 she would've known who King David was. How on earth could her son rule all Israel and do it *forever*? Finally, Aunt Elizabeth is pregnant in her old age? What the heck???

But then the angel says ***the words that she decides to accept***. She doesn't have to. She could have gone screaming back to the house like any other 13 year old girl would have done when a strange man approaches her at the well, even if he is glowing! Gabriel tells her simply, ***"For with God nothing will be impossible!"*** Hidden away in what Catholics the world over refer to as "The Annunciation," long before the Nativity Scene we think of as Christmas, is the key to our faith.

It isn't just that what Mary has been told is difficult to believe, *it's impossible, right?* In fact, what part of our Christian faith *is possible?* Christ born of a virgin: impossible. Christ lived a perfect sinless life: impossible. Christ, God Himself, dies on a cross: impossible. Jesus definitively dead and buried, rises from the dead: impossible. Christ passes through walls and ignores space-time limitations in His appearances to the apostles after He is risen: impossible. Christ ascends into heaven weeks later right before the disciples eyes: impossible. Christ comes to live within us as the Holy Spirit, one third of the Trinity: impossible. God the Father, Christ the Son and the Holy Spirit, three in one: impossible.

But Mary says, *"Behold, the maidservant of the Lord! Let it be to me according to your word."* **In faith, Mary accepts the impossible.** That is what we are called to do as Christ followers. In faith, we accept that Jesus Christ is exactly Who He says He is. In doing that, we accept the Gracious gift of forgiveness, undeserved, that His sacrifice offers us, and we become new people! Christmas means we are free of shame, free of guilt, living a life abiding in the Savior that empowers us to love as He loved! IMPOSSIBLE.

Prayer: Dear Heavenly Father, We love You! Thank you that faith itself is a gift from above! (Ephesians 2:8) It is in accepting the impossible that we recognize You as Creator Lord, unlimited by our understanding of what can be done. With faith in You Lord, our ability to love others is without restriction. AMEN

DECEMBER 17

The Star

"When they heard the King, they departed; and behold, the star which they had seen in the East went before them, till it came and stood over where the young

Child was. When they saw the star, they rejoiced with exceedingly great joy!" (Mark 2:9-11 NKJV)

Have you ever been lost in the woods? I mean really lost. Like, you were hiking a trail that became less easy to identify and you struck out on the branch you thought was the real one, and before you knew it, there was no trail at all and you were literally in the middle of nowhere? Even if you had a trail map, you no loner knew where you were on it, so no amount of turning left then right then going two hundred yards, then right again would help you!

People from Maine know about deep woods, fog, rural roads, and getting lost. Two of my favorite comedians of all time are Marshall Dodge and Robert Bryan, who created the Bert and I series of books and recordings based on their story telling days as Yale undergraduates. Popular when I was a child in the 50's and 60's, these stories are as iconic today, for those who love Maine, as L.L. Bean and boiled lobster. *Which Way to Millinocket* is one of my favorites!

"I was standing outside the Sutherland's IGA store one morning, when I heard a flivver approaching down the street toward me. Putt putt putt, sa ha..

'Which way to Millinocket?'

'Well, you can go west to the next intersection and get on the turnpike; go north through the tollgate at Augusta, till you come…well, no. You can keep right on this tar road, it changes to dirt now and again, just keep the river on your left, you'll come to the crossroads…well, no, let me see. Then again you can take that scenic coastal route that the tourists use, and after you get to Rockport….hmmmm…Millinocket. Come to think of it, you can't get they-ah from he-ah!"

What you really need if you are lost, and really should have to keep from getting lost in the first place, is a fixed point to guide you that you can see all the time! Detailed directions, including every turn, get confused if the trip is long, and may be inaccurate to begin with. That's why travelers for eons have been guided by the North Star. That's why God provided the star in the East for the Wise Men to follow. They could see it whenever they looked up.

Jesus says of Himself, *"I am the Root and Descendant of David, the Bright and Morning star."* (Revelation 22:16 NKJV) He is the brightest light in the sky and His coming marks the receding of darkness and the dawn of a New Day for everyone! He states clearly, *"I am the Light of the World. He who follows me, shall not walk in darkness, but have the Light of Life."* (John 8:12 NKJV) All of us are spiritually blind by nature, stumbling around in the dark, lost in a world where evil abounds. There will be plenty of people along the way who offer you different step by step directions on how to get to that state of peace and joy we've talked about. Unfortunately, none of them will get you to Millinocket! In fact, without Christ as your fixed and guiding light, *you can't get there from here!*

When you feel lost, when everything seems to be going wrong, when nothing you do or say turns out the way you intended; you need to look up toward the bright morning star! **He is right there,** every day, waiting to lead you in the absolutely right direction! You'll discover, once again, that you shouldn't sweat the small stuff, and it's all small stuff, as Richard Carlsen famously wrote. Your Salvation is the Big Stuff! Living free from guilt, shame and worry is, believe me, the Big Stuff! Love God. Love others. Fix your eyes on that Morning Star and pay attention to where it leads. If you can see Him, you know where you are, and you can use the map He provided called the Bible!

It turns out you *can get to Millinocket from he-yah.*

Prayer: Father God, have Your Holy Spirit give us a nudge every time we start asking directions from anyone other than Christ! Lots of different routes look like they could be fun and get us where we want to go, but if they lead us in any direction other than toward You, we will surely end up lost in the wood. AMEN

DECEMBER 18

All the Time

"Rejoice always, pray without ceasing, in everything give thanks; for this is the will of God in Christ Jesus." (1 Thessalonians 5:16 NKJV)

I'm almost finished with a book by Peggy Noonan, the famous Wall Street Journal columnist, called *When Character Was King.* If you're my age, and knowing that Ms. Noonan is a political columnist, you can probably guess who the book is about! It is a biography of President Ronald Reagan. No matter what your political leanings, left or right, anyone who knew him or worked with him knew this: he was the genuine article. With Reagan what you saw was what you got, as ironic as that was for a man who started his career as an actor.

When he was first running for governor of California and under tremendous pressure from all sides, he developed horrible, piercing, persistent stomach pain. Eventually seeing a doctor, the diagnosis of peptic ulcer was confirmed. He suffered for a year, taking antacids and altering his diet, but determined to keep it a secret because he viewed ulcers as a sign of weakness and thought others would too.

One morning, after a year or so, he woke up with no hint of pain. He reached for the Maalox, but then decided not to take it. He had several meetings that day and the first was with some conservative backers from North Carolina of all places. When the meeting was over, as the man walked out the door, he paused and looked over his shoulder and said, "Ronnie, I wanted you to know that there is a group of men in North Carolina who are praying for you every day." Reagan thanked the man, but was taken aback. Really, he thought? He had two more meetings with out-of-state groups that day. At the end of each meeting, the primary representative paused as he was leaving to let Reagan know that there was a faithful group of people who were praying for him every day.

Nancy Reagan confirmed 25 years later, in an interview with Peggy Noonan, that from that day forward, Ronald Reagan believed that whether his ulcer had been healed by other's prayers, or whether those prayers simply led him to stop taking his medicine, the power of prayer was irrefutable. When Peggy asked Mrs. Reagan if the President knelt by his bed and prayed at night, she responded, "Oh heavens no. Ronnie prayed all the time, every single day! No matter where He was or what He was doing, He either paused to give thanks when he entered a room, or if he needed guidance at any time!"

I try to converse with God that way as well. But when it comes time to give thanks publicly and out loud, I am often the least articulate of my believing friends. But my nine and six year old grandchildren don't have that problem. Before a meal they will often lead us in their favorite song of prayer. *"God our Father, God our Father, we thank You! We thank You! For our many Blessings. For our many Blessings! Ah-Ah Men. Ah-Ah Men!"*

As you prepare for this Christmas celebration, if you don't pray conversationally with God, or find it difficult to do so, even silently, may I suggest you pause three times tomorrow and pray as Liam and Allie do? Remember, God knows what you want before you ask it! (Matthew 6:8) Articulating your needs aren't nearly as critical as making sure the Father hears you, and knows that He is appreciated!

Prayer: God our Father, God our Father, we thank You! We thank You! For our many Blessings. For our many Blessings! Ah-Ah Men. Ah-Ah Men!

DECEMBER 19
Heartbreak

"The Lord is close to the brokenhearted and saves those who are crushed in spirit." (Psalms 34:18 NIV)

I wasn't sure I'd be able to write about this, or even if I should. But what happened a week ago is certainly part of "Doing Life" for people worldwide. We lost our cat. He was a five year old Tuxedo rescue. We are both devastated. He was my wife's best buddy. A faulty garage door allowed it to remain open with about 6 inches of clearance, which Sterling took advantage of sometime during the night. We found his collar in the alley, which he had slipped out of numerous times in the past, and hoped he was merely out exploring. But my wife knew something was wrong when he didn't come running up out of the creek to the sound of her voice. I went into the hospital and was in surgery when she found him, out near the pond, obviously killed by a predator of some kind and probably a coyote since he was a big tough cat with all his claws. I hurried home after the case. I couldn't let Animal Control pick him up. I went and brought him home. I wanted him home. Then I took him to the Vet for cremation. Turns out it's hard to see patients when you've been crying really hard.

Those of you who have never had a pet, and thus never lost one, probably won't quite understand this. For some families, pets become an integral part of not only daily life, but our emotional well being. Cats and dogs admittedly love differently, but you can feel their affection none the less. A dog may seem like it wants to please you more openly than a cat, but a cat who comes and curls up in your lap or on your chest and purrs his contentment is loving you just the same.

There is no judgment in animals. They don't try to get even when you've wronged them; they just keep loving you! In a very real way, perhaps we love our pets so much because there is no judgment, no condemnation from them.

Paul tried to explain a similar concept in his letter to the Romans. *"There is therefore now no condemnation to them which are in Christ Jesus, who walk not after flesh, but after the Spirit." (Romans 8:1)* Once we accept Jesus, there is no condemnation for us because we are covered by His perfect righteousness. Christ loves us *unconditionally,* for nothing we can do could make Him love us less, or love us more.

Maybe this explains the depth of the heartbreak when you lose a pet that was a treasured member of your family. These animals love us *unconditionally!* Good mood, bad mood, attention, no attention, fed on time or not, they keep wagging their tails and purring on our chests.

There is no question in my mind that God totally gets this. When the Psalmist tells us that the Lord is close to the broken-hearted, he means just that: He gets it. It's not happenstance that cats and dogs have been our companions for thousands of years. Our Creator knows what we need emotionally, and pets have always been one of His ways to bring us that peace and joy that we keep speaking about.

We've lost pets before and it has always been extremely difficult. Losing a pet that we felt we should have better protected is perhaps, even worse. But there is a consolation that we know comes from the Father: love. Jesus felt that the greatest commands were love God and love each other. Scripture tells us plainly, that "God is love," so what we felt for our pets and what they felt for us, is a very, very good thing! (1 John 4:8 NIV) It may be cut short, and with short lived animals it is always shorter than we would have wanted, but that very good thing, that unconditional love we feel from them, is priceless and timeless, no matter how long they are with us!

I was angry with God, briefly, that morning. How could He let this happen to *my wife?* I mourned the cat certainly, but I felt my wife's agony much more powerfully. The anger passed quickly when I opened my phone for another reason and stumbled upon the last picture I had taken. It was Sterling, curled up asleep on the couch right next to where his mom sits. He was happy, and safe, and loved. God gave him to us for just a little while, but the love he showed us and taught us, will last as long as memory lasts. Goodbye Sterling, rest in peace, and thank you God, for letting us share him!

Prayer: Dear Heavenly Father, We love You!! We are blessed that You are the very definition of love and understand our agony when we lose a loved one, even if a pet and not a person. The pain is just as sharp and real. But so is the realization that the pain we feel is so deep, because the joy we experienced while we had them was so profound! AMEN

DECEMBER 20

Joy, Joy, Joy

"Joy to the earth, the Savior reigns! Let men their songs imply, while fields and floods, rocks, hills and plains repeat the sounding joy, repeat the sounding joy, repeat, repeat the sounding joy!" (Isaac Watts)

The Doing Life devotional year was intended to help you come a little closer to finding peace and joy! As the year comes to a close, and we come nearer to Christmas Day, let's take a moment to reflect on just what we mean by "joy?" You'll recognize the second stanza of the most played Christmas hymn in history: *Joy to the World.* It was first printed in England in 1719, and inspired by Psalms 98, Genesis 3 and the above stanza, Psalm 96:11-12. Isaac Watts wanted to express the gratitude of God's people for rescuing them yet again! But this time, rescuing them from the oppression of enslavement to sin; and rescuing not only the Jewish people, but all who believe, and for all eternity!

Interestingly, there is no mention of the birth of Christ, the incarnation, Bethlehem, the Virgin Mary, the shepherds, the wise men, or really thing about Christmas! In fact Psalm 98, revolves around Christ's *return to* judge the earth. So how can it be the most frequently sung *Christmas hymn* of all time? The answer lies not in whether the song is about Christmas, but what Christmas is all about! Yes, we celebrate the birth of Jesus with lights and trees and food and presents and family gatherings and communal worship! But we're not *really just celebrating a birth are we?*

I have delivered literally thousands of babies in my career as an obstetrician. I can tell you that most of the time, thankfully, there is a great amount of joy involved! But that joy, that *happiness,* is not the same thing as the joy of Christmas. The joy that we are all privileged to enjoy through Christ, is the joy of Salvation! It is to experience the **wonder of His love** as Watt's closing stanza emphasizes. What's so wondrous about His love?

Well, first of all, we don't deserve it! He offered His love as an undeserved act of His pleasure in us, despite our continued sin. That's what Grace means. Second, His love is faithful. Even when we rebelled against Him He never gave up on us. Third, His love is eternal. We won't outlast it, ever. Fourth, His love means forgiveness, for all our sins, past, present and future. Finally, His wondrous love means, out of love, *we are born again!* We're not just celebrating the birth of a baby 2000 years ago, we're celebrating that because of that baby, *we all get to start again, loving God and each other, and live forever!!*

Now THAT'S SOMETHING to shout about!! Joy, Joy, Joy indeed!

"I tell you that if these should keep silent, the stones would immediately cry out!" (Luke 19:40 NKJV)

Prayer: Dear Heavenly Father, We love You!! The joy we find in Christ is overwhelming and hard to confine to such a tiny word! When we sing of joy this Christmas, remind us that our joy is not only in welcom-

ing the Savior to be with us, Emanuel; but in the Salvation that His coming brings to us through the cross and the third day! AMEN

DECEMBER 21

Peace

"If we have no peace, it is because we have forgotten that we belong to each other." (Mother Teresa, Nobel Peace Prize 1979)

Have you ever walked in new fallen snow at the top of a mountain? Not the very top maybe, but just below the tree line, on a cold, sunny day. The incredibly blue sky in every direction, the snow blowing gently like smoke, off the top of the drifts, the light wind just enough to make the tops of the pines move. It's not completely silent. The snow crunches quietly under your feet, and the wind is just audible in the tops of the trees. As the sun climbs higher, pieces of snow drop from the trees as the midday melt begins. There are rabbit tracks all around the edge of the tree line, and other tracks too, ones not so easy to identify. The only sounds are those made by the breeze moving the tops of the spruce and the soft crunch of your boots in the powder. There is only one word to describe this sensation: peace.

What is peace? Is it the absence of conflict, whether outside of yourself or inside? Is it maybe the absence of distraction instead; the presence of silence? Is it the absence of public disturbance? Maybe it's really forgiveness; forgiving those that have wronged you, and most of all forgiving yourself for the wrong you know you have done? Is it a relationship with no enmity, between persons or nations? Perhaps *calm* is the synonym for which we are searching?

The Apostle John quotes Jesus as saying, *"Peace I leave with you; my peace I give to you. Not as the world gives do I give to you. Let not your hearts be troubled, neither let them be afraid."* (John 14:27 ESV) Christ doesn't simply mean "peace" as a greeting like "shalom" common for 1st century Jews. Instead He means that His crucifixion would leave His disciples with the Peace of God (Romans 5:1) because their sins were forgiven. The Peace of God would then guard their lives. (Philippians 4:7) The fear of the future and eventual death does not exist for His followers, and they are thus, untroubled. (John 11:33; 13:21; 14:1) *"I have said these things to you, that in me you may have peace. In the world you will have tribulation. But take heart, I have overcome the world."* (John 16:33) So peace is at least the opposite of *tribulation*, [misery and affliction] and Christ promises it to His followers, but not necessarily in this world, but the one to come! The Apostle Paul gives a benediction to the Thessalonians: *"Now may the Lord of Peace Himself, give you peace at all times in every way."* (2 Thessalonians 3:16 ESV) Peace here would seem to mean "contentment" in all circumstances, and clearly it applies to this earthly life. To the Romans he writes: *"If possible, so far as it depends on you, live peaceably with all."* (Romans 12:18 ESV) Clearly this means without conflict, or contention.

But that walk in the snow is what always comes to mind for me, and that's why the image of shepherds in a snow covered field, watching over their flocks under a starlit sky seems peaceful to me. Gabriel and a Heavenly Host appear, undoubtedly lighting up that sky like fireworks, and understandably the shepherds are terrified. What do Gabriel and the Heavenly Host say to them? *"Do not be afraid for behold, I give you good tidings of great joy which will be to all people. For there is born to you this day in the City of David a Savior, who is Christ the Lord......Glory to God in the highest, and on earth peace* (ειρηνη *in Greek), to men on whom His favor rests."* (Luke 2:14 NIV) The Greek, *eirene,* when used by one speaking for God or the Messiah, means "the way that leads to salvation."

Tranquility of the soul comes when assured of salvation through Christ Jesus, such that one is content with his earthly lot, no matter what that might be, holding to the hope of eternity with the Father after this life is through! I quoted Richard Carlsen in the past and I'll do it again! For the follower of Christ, no matter how bad it gets day to day, we don't sweat the small stuff, because we know, compared to the promise of eternity, it really is all small stuff. Truly believing that, brings peace, just like that quiet walk through the mountain snow. That's the gift of Christmas!

Prayer: Dear Heavenly Father, We love You! Let Christmas lights remind us that with the birth of the Light of the World comes the Peace that Passes All Understanding; the calm state of assurance in what the future holds for those who believe! AMEN

DECEMBER 22

Joseph

"Joseph also went up from Galilee, out of the city of Nazareth, into Judea, to the city of David which is called Bethlehem, because he was of the house and lineage of David, to be registered with Mary, his betrothed wife, who was with child." (Luke 2:4-5 NKJV)

When I was in medical school and residency in the late 70's and early 80's, husbands were not allowed in the delivery room. In fact, labor-delivery-recovery rooms, in which the couple stayed together throughout the birth process, had not yet even been proposed. For nearly two thousand years before my residency, men were completely and intentionally, ostracized from the birthing room, and the entire labor experience!

But we can discern from scripture, that Joseph was almost certainly present at, or shortly after, his son's birth, in a sheep cave on the outskirts of Bethlehem. Despite being thus, close to center stage, there is scant mention of Joseph at any point in scripture after that. Earlier, the Gospel of Matthew does tell us what happened when Joseph discovered his supposedly "pure" betrothed, was found to be with child. Adultery was punishable by stoning to death, and an engagement was considered legally the same as marriage. (Leviticus 20:10)

Joseph was legally bound to expose Mary as an adulteress, and turn her over to the religious authorities. Yet, instead, he had decided to divorce her quietly, undoubtedly saving her life. (Matthew 1:19)

Then an angel appeared to him in a dream and explained that the Holy Spirit was responsible for Mary's pregnancy, and that their son would be known as "*Immanuel, God with us!*" There is no specific description of how he handled the news, as is there is with the annunciation of Mary. But we do learn this, that Joseph *did as commanded*, abandoned his plans for divorce, and took Mary as his wife. But he did more than that. The one year betrothal period was to ensure the bride's purity, and if evidence of impurity arose, he could have had the marriage annulled. Not only did he eschew this course, but he immediately took her into his own home, violating every custom of engagement. (Matthew 1:24-25)

There are reams of literature written about the Virgin Mary and the annunciation. There are literally thousands of portraits of Madonna and Child, but virtually none that even include her husband, no less feature him. How are we really to know anything at all about him?

A little closer study reveals that the Bible tells us much more about Joseph than first meets the eye. Matthew 1: 19 tells us that Joseph was a *"just man."* To a first century Hebrew, that means he strives to adhere to the Laws of Moses, and that would, by definition, include "divorcing" his fiancé for infidelity. His hesitation to do just that, speaks volumes about his merciful nature and perhaps even his love, for this girl with whom his marriage had been arranged. When confronted with an angel's command in his dream, instead of disregarding it as only a dream, ***he chooses to believe,*** and do as commanded, ***just as Mary did***. Joseph didn't just say, "yes," to the Lord's command, he lived it out, right in the face of a Hebrew community who undoubtedly scorned them both. He took Mary into his home rather than waiting the obligatory one full year. He followed through, staying at Mary's side throughout the remaining months of pregnancy, on the long, difficult journey to Bethlehem, and through the unexpected delivery in a livestock cave. According to Luke, Joseph dutifully brought his wife and son to the Temple for circumcision on the eighth day, despite the shame associated with the birth.

Three more times Joseph was visited by the angel in his dreams: warned to flee to Egypt; told to return to Israel when Herod died; and finally to settle in Nazareth. Can you even imagine moving to a strange land, with a different language, different customs, different rules, and finding a way to support your family for ten years? Then, ***Joseph, obedient to the end,*** raises Jesus as his own in Galilee.

My pregnant patients have always found it "easier to ask forgiveness than ask permission." They always seem to tell me about the wine they drank *after* they drank it, wanting absolution for their crime! Perhaps that is why it's always easier for Christians to talk about forgiveness than obedience! But Christ says, *"If you love Me, keep My commandments!"* (John 14:15) Joseph did just that.

So don't forget him as you prepare your heart for Christmas! Joseph was dealt cards for which he never asked; and led into a life he could not possibly have planned! Many of you may feel that nothing is going as planned, even to the point of utter despair. Well, nothing at all went as Joseph had planned, but he ***chose to trust God in it!*** When you are looking for peace and contentment, accepting Christ and the direction of the indwelling Holy Spirit, is not unlike believing the angels in Joseph's dreams! Have faith that whatever difficult and unplanned path on which you find yourself, will lead you right into the center of God's will. It might take patience, but believing it, will bring you peace.

Prayer: Dear Heavenly Father, We love You! Turn our thoughts this Christmas not only to Mary and the baby Jesus, but to Joseph, who did as he was told by You, even when it was the farthest thing from his plan. His faith and consequent obedience, was instrumental in the institution of God's plan for the world's redemption! We must have faith that our obedience will forward Your will, as well. AMEN

DECEMBER 23

Wrapping

"Consider the lilies of the field, how they grow: they neither toil nor spin; and yet I say to you that even Solomon in all his glory was not arrayed like one of these." (Matthew 6:28-29 NKJV)

Part of my job involves operating on people. Often that involves both judgment and precision. Over the years, I seem to have become somewhat proficient at this skill set. On the other hand, there are certain skill sets that seem completely resistant to my successful acquisition. Folding my laundry, packing my suitcase, making our bed, dressing the kids when they were little, or virtually any handy-man type jobs required around the house. Oh, I can do all of these, but not at all as well as some others can.

Wrapping presents quite possibly leads the list. I can select the paper, find the tape and scissors, even make a label. But when it comes to actually encasing the gift, no matter the size or shape, somehow it always ends up looking like a one armed blind man completed the task! Thankfully, my wife often provides me with a decorative bag, and then all I have to do is stuff colored tissue paper on top of the gift, and *voila*, I have accomplished the task!

God seems better at wrapping than I. You can start with the lilies of the field, but then you can go down to the plankton, or up to the Milky Way, and find the same startling precision, breathtaking beauty, and flawless presentation! That includes people by the way. We all know what Adam thought of Eve when he first saw her!

But Jesus has even improved on this wrapping! If we are to be presented to the Father, we don't just need to look our best, we need to be perfect as God is perfect. He even told us that, in Matthew 4:28. Well, I got news for you. Ain't gonna happen through your own effort. However, God thought it was a good idea to have His Son live a perfect, exemplary life on earth, but then seal the deal with His sacrifice on the cross, taking all our imperfections onto Himself. In exchange, He offers to *"clothe us in His perfect righteousness." (Isaiah 61:10)*

I have known some really great present wrappers, among them my *daugh-*

ters, (sorry son,) my wife, mother, and sister-in-law. But none of them can come close to that lily in the field; nor can they wrap up a person so well that they are presentable to the Creator of the Universe! You need Jesus for that. You need Christmas.

Prayer: Dear Heavenly Father, We love You!! Remind us at Christmas, that while we wrap and exchange presents in remembrance of the Magi at the birth of Your Son, He chose to wrap us and present us to You!! AMEN

DECEMBER 24
Silent Night

Silent Night, Holy Night
Mindful of mankind's plight
The Lord in Heav'n on high decreed
From earthly woes we would be freed
Jesus, God's promise for peace.
Jesus, God's promise for peace.

(Joseph Franz Mohr, Early 1800's)

I grew up with midnight Christmas Eve services reliably concluded in a darkened sanctuary, lit only by the candles we each held. These were all lit by passing the flame from the Christ Candle in the center of the Advent Wreath, one to each other, until we held a portion of the Light. We would then sing *Silent Night,* in unison, a cappella. There was never a dry eye in the house.

Despite having been written in the German language, *Stille Nacht,* has become one of the most widely recognized Christmas Songs in the world. Pastor Mohr wrote the little poem only hours before a local Austrian Christmas pageant, for which he needed a song that the whole town could sing. But not being a musician, he turned to his choir director and friend, Franz Gruber, and asked him to compose a tune to which the poem could be set, and to please do it in the next three hours!

Many of you know that the original song had six verses, not just the three we sing today. Above is the final verse. While each of the verses tells us of a part of the Christmas miracle, and the "*dawn of redeeming Grace,*" in the third stanza, is where the tears usually begin to flow, I think the final verse speaks volumes as well. Here, on Christmas Eve, we find the definition of "the peace that passes all understanding," (Philippians 4:7 NIV), tucked away in an unsung verse of a favorite carol.

It was God's decision to redeem mankind, despite our rebellion, despite our hatred of each other, despite our turning away from Him, despite the dreadful mess we had made of everything! Mankind's plight was certainly one we needed to own, for we did it to ourselves. But God knew there was only One

Way to bring us peace, One Way to turn us away from evil and back toward His perfect love, and that was through the gift of His Son. Faith in Jesus brings us the forgiveness we need to truly be free of our earthly trials and tribulations! No more shame, no more guilt, no more enslavement to sin!

Look up the last four verses to Joseph Mohr's hastily penned masterpiece. You'll find that Jesus is not only *"Lord at thy birth,"* but that He represents *"salvation for all,"* that He *"embraces mankind,"* and that He is *"God's promise for peace."*

This Christmas Eve when you think of that small, helpless baby, lying in a manger on a cold winter's night, think about what He means for you personally. When you feel small and helpless, and we all do from time to time, know that the Mightiest Power that ever existed chose to come to us in just that way for a reason. He could have appeared in the sky on a white horse with the heavenly host arrayed behind him, flags waving, bugles blowing, armor flashing in the sun! But He didn't. Had He done so, it would have required no faith. It would have promised no redemption, only judgment.

Instead, He chose a silent night in a backwater town at the edge of the Roman Empire, and He made it Holy. Holy means "set apart." This night is different from all other nights. This night, the world stood on the eve of destruction, and instead, it was offered peace.

Prayer: Dear Heavenly Father, We love You!! We can only thank you for offering Jesus to us, by doing as He asks and loving You and each other! We ask Your Holy Spirit this Christmas to flow through us, to blot out our own prejudices. There is so much hatred in the world Lord, nation to nation, political party to political party, person to person, all because we see others as "different" from us! Help us to see others as made in Your image, just as much as we are, because You certainly see them that way! AMEN

DECEMBER 25

A Baby?

"Mary, did you know that your baby boy would one day walk on water?
Mary, did yo know that your baby boy would save our sons and daughters? Did you know that your baby boy has come to make you new?
This child that you delivered will soon deliver you...
Did you know that your baby boy has walked where angels trod? When you kiss your little baby,
You kiss the face of God! Mary, did you know?

(Buddy Greene and Mark Lowry)

If you were God, and You wanted to bring Your beloved children back to You after they had strayed far and wide, how would you do it? I mean, you're the

Creator of the Universe! You could make a pretty big splash in the sky the world round if You really wanted to!! You could arrive on earth as an invincible soldier/king riding Your white Charger at the head of a million angel army, and simply crush the Roman Empire, right? Well, admittedly that would involve eliminating a lot of people who really weren't in on the decision to oppress Israel, but hey, aren't they just collateral damage? I mean this is what the Jewish leaders wanted, right? Isn't it what the people who thought they knew the prophecies of Isaiah and Micah and Daniel and Zechariah, just to name a few, fully expected to happen?

The one tiny little fly in the ointment so to speak, is that those who wanted and expected a God who would send a political/military leader as the Messiah, didn't understand that ***"God is love."*** (Hosea 1-3; Ezekiel 16:60-63; Isaiah 62; 1 John 4:8-11; John 3:16) They totally misjudged the character of God, despite 1500 years of writings laying it out for them. God never had any intention of saving Israel from Rome. He decided to save a remnant of Israel *from herself,* along with *anyone else* in the world who would believe! (Isaiah 45:22; John 3:16; Romans 10:13; 1 John 2:2, 4:14) People would have a simple choice: faith in themselves alone, or faith in the One who created them in His own image. (Genesis 1:27) God wanted to give people the chance to love Him as much as He loved them. He wanted them to do that by loving others. (Matthew 22:37-39)

God understood that the common man would only listen to "one of their own," so He chose to experience our world as the son of a poor carpenter, born in Bethlehem, and raised in the backwater town of Nazareth, as prophesied in the Old Testament. (Micah 5:2) He picked a teenage girl, a virgin, to carry His Son, so there would be no confusion about His lineage.

Have you ever held a newborn baby in your arms? Ever held your own? If you have, then you understand what *unconditional love* means. If you believe in Jesus; if you believe He came, lived, and died, taking on the penalty we deserved for our sin; and in so doing, purchasing forgiveness from the the Father, clothing us in His righteousness; then you understand why the Father calls us His *adopted* sons and daughters, even heirs to His Kingdom! (Ephesians 1:5; Galatians 4:5-7)

There is nothing more lowly, more powerless, more dependent, than a newborn. Jesus set aside His equality with God and *"emptied Himself, taking the form of a bond-servant...being found in appearance as a man, He humbled Himself by becoming obedient to the point of death, even death on a cross... for this reason God highly exalted Him..."* (Philippians 2:7-9 NASB)

Mary did you know? Did she know that one day her baby boy would walk on water, heal the lame, give sight to the blind, calm the sea with His mighty hand? Did she *really understand* that He had walked where angels trod, would one day save us all, would one day make us new? Do we think she really understood that she held in her arms the Great I AM, and that when she bent to kiss his forehead she was kissing the face of God?

I don't think so. I think she knew that something wonderful was happening. I think she knew that a miracle was taking place. I think she knew that she loved that little boy with every fiber of her being from the moment she laid eyes on Him. I think she knew all these things, and I think that's exactly what *every mother knows!*

When He grew into a man; when He changed the water into wine; when He began His long series of miraculous healings; when He raised the dead; when He gave Himself up to His executioners even though He could have summoned Gabriel and His heavenly army to His side; when He rose on the third day and appeared to them all....then she **knew as the disciples knew,** that on that cold December morning, lying in the hay of a manger with the animals gathered around, ***she really had kissed the face of God!***

Read the whole story in Luke. If you've never believed in all that *incarnation stuff,* you know, *God becoming man and all that,* think about this: do you want to believe in a God you've never seen, one who makes you jump through hoops so that one day you *might be good* enough for Him to save, or would you rather believe in a God who decided to become one of us; *Emmanuel, God with us;* who showed us how to love; and who gave Himself up for us, just so we could become part of the family? All anyone has to do is call on the name of Jesus and just accept His gift of salvation. It's that easy.

Merry Christmas!!

Prayer: Dear Heavenly Father, We love You!! It is truly beyond comprehension that You would come to earth, One with Your Son, show us the way, pay the price for our sin and rebellion, and then leave us with the Holy Spirit to help us along the way! Joy to the World indeed! The Lord is Come! Let earth receive her King!! AMEN

DECEMBER 26

Boxing Day

"Come you who are Blessed of My Father, inherit the Kingdom...For I was hungry, and you gave Me something to eat; I was thirsty and you gave Me something to drink...... Lord when did we see you [thus]?...The King will answer and say to them, 'Truly I say to you, to the extent that you did it to one of these brothers of Mine, even the least of them, you did it to Me!'" (Matthew 25:35-40 NASB)

When I was in eighth grade I spent a summer at Ozark Boy's camp in Mt. Ida, Arkansas. One of the activities was learning to box. I knew nothing about boxing, and when they paired us off by height, rather than weight, I thought nothing of it. The counselor tied my gloves on, put in my mouthpiece, and sent my 6'1" 125lb frame into combat with a boy of the same height who weighed 185lbs. All I remember thinking as I sunk to my knees after the first punch, was that you *really do see stars!*

I never knew the term "boxing" could refer to anything else until well into adulthood. Throughout the British Empire, when it really was that, and not simply a loose federation called a Commonwealth, the day after Christmas, or the second day of Christmastide, is known as "boxing day." It happens to coincide with Saint Stephen's day, commemorating the first Christian Martyr who was stoned to death in 36 AD. Until well into the 20th century, servants in homes throughout the United Kingdom, were all working on Christmas day, while their masters celebrated. The next day was traditionally their day off, and was spent organizing charity for the poor and visiting their families. In recent times, it has been celebrated as a public and bank holiday, largely devoted to shopping the after-Christmas sales.

Some believe the term originated in the Middle Ages and references the 'Alms Box' found in the narthex of Christian churches intended as a collection point for donations to the poor. Since the early church, St. Stephen's Day was the time for distributing the contents of these boxes. Alternatively, the term "boxing day" may refer to the custom of giving a "Christmas Box" to postmen, errand boys, and other servants and tradesmen on the first weekday after Christmas Day. This box would contain cash, gifts, and sometimes left over food.

While celebrated in slightly different ways throughout the former British Empire, and as St. Stephen's Day across the Latin Catholic church, (and on a day a few days later in the Eastern Orthodox Church,) the concept is largely the same: *charity from those who have plenty to those who have little*. Whether you think of giving gifts at Christmas as a remembrance of those given to Christ by the Magi, or on a deeper level, as symbolic of the gift of redemption and new life given to us by Grace, through Jesus, Boxing Day is certainly about giving. Charity begins in the heart, and certainly people of any faith or no faith, can be charitable. But for the Christian, charity is not intended as a behavioral option, but as an *outgrowth of the indwelling Spirit*! In other words, as you allow the Spirit more and more latitude to direct your steps, you will become more and more charitable. Why? Because becoming more "Christ-like," in other words, "sanctification," is all about following the greatest commandment, right? Love God by loving others.

Our opening verses make it simple: You want to know how to love God? Love others. You want to know how you love people you don't even know? Be charitable. When you donate money to dig a well in central Africa for people who otherwise would have to walk 20 miles round trip in the heat for fresh water, you are digging that well for Jesus. When you take an evening and help out at the North Texas Food Bank, you are helping to feed....Jesus. It's not that hard.

It turns out that boxing by pairing people of equal height leads to a very short competition. But boxing by giving to people with less opportunity for sustaining themselves, leads to clothing, feeding, and housing the Lord Himself!

So get prepared to go out there and "box" the day after Christmas! My guess is you can find a way to do it with PayPal and a computer! But whether you're boxing by financial support or literally by taping cardboard boxes together, you've found a way to put a smile on the face of God. (By the way, Christ is okay with you designating any of 363 days as "boxing day." He's gonna hang on to Christmas and Easter, if its all the same!)

Prayer: Dear Heavenly Father, We love You! When we pass up an opportunity to help the less fortunate, have the Spirit remind us that it is YOU we are passing by! AMEN

DECEMBER 27

Twelve Days of Christmas

"On the twelfth day of Christmas my true love gave to me, 12 Drummers drumming, 11 Pipers Piping, 10 Lords a leaping, 9 ladies Dancing, 8 Maids a Milking, 7 Swans a Swimming, 6 Geese a laying, 5 Golden Rings, 4 Calling Birds, 3 French hens, 2 Turtle doves and A Partridge and a Pear Tree." (Frederic Austin, 1909)

So, what does one do with that time between Christmas and New Year's Eve? Well, you could play trivia games. Here's one: how many birds are mentioned in *The 12 Days of Christmas?* Don't bother counting, I'll tell you: 23! But did it ever bother you that in this season of celebrating the birth of Christ, the epitome of humility and selflessness, that we sing a song about a woman who instead, is celebrating the ridiculous excess of *stuff,* (including 23 birds) that she received as gifts?

Well, maybe all of you have done this already, but I recently researched the significance of these lyrics, after only about 60 years of singing them (assuming I was singing at four!) An article in the National Catholic Register suggests that the gifts were originally meant as symbols to help children learn about Jesus and the Bible. SNOPES will tell you there is no evidence to support this, and earlier versions of the song even used different gifts in different orders. But I agree with the NCR writer: who cares whether or not the story is accurate? It certainly gives the song more substance as a Christmas Carol. So here goes:

1 Partridge and a Pear Tree: Luke 13:34 Christ gathering his people under wing
2 Turtle doves: Old Testament and New Testament
3 French hens: Faith, hope and charity
4 Calling birds: Matthew Mark Luke and John
5 Golden rings: The Pentateuch or first five books of the bible
6 Geese a Laying: The six days of creation
7 Swans a Swimming: The 7 sacraments
8 Maids a Milking: The Beatitudes
9 Ladies Dancing: Fruits of the Holy Spirit
10 Lords a Leaping: The 10 commandments
11 Pipers Piping: The 11 faithful Apostles
12 Drummers Drumming:12 points of the Apostles Creed

Whether Frederic Austin, a British baritone and songwriter, had this in mind, we'll never know, because if he did, he never documented it. But learning the content of each one of these bullet points would undoubtedly be useful for the new Christian of any age. Let's only do the most important one to my way of thinking: **The Apostle's Creed.** I learned this as a child and the early church used memorized versions of it to spread the Gospel around the known world.

*"**I believe** in God the Father, Almighty, Maker of Heaven and Earth (1), and in His **Only Son**, our Lord, Jesus Christ (2), who was **conceived** by the Holy Spirit, **born** of the **Virgin** Mary (3), Suffered under Pontius Pilot, was **crucified, dead and buried (4).** He **descended** into hell. On the third day **He rose** again from*

the dead.(5) ***He ascended*** *into Heaven, and* ***sits on the right hand*** *of God the Father Almighty (6), from whence He shall* ***come to judge*** *the Quick [living] and the Dead.(7) I believe in the* ***Holy Ghost*** *(8), the Holy* ***catholic church****, the* ***Communion of Saints*** *(9), the* ***Forgiveness of Sins*** *(10), the* ***Resurrection of the Body*** *(11) and the* ***Life Everlasting****. (12) AMEN"*

So, while you wait around for New Years, you can use the eleven days after Christmas to learn the Apostle's Creed, if you don't already know it! Remember, the "catholic church" (not capitalized), means *all believers,* not the denomination. Christians know that, understanding and believing this simple creed, leads to the joy and peace for which we all yearn!

People often ask, "what was the best gift you ever got for Christmas?" For years I thought of my black, 3 speed Schwinn under the tree in 1965! Now, when I sing Austin's jingle, whether the purported symbolism was intended originally or not, I remember that Christmas is all about the very, very bestest, super-duper, fantastic gift I ever got: A Savior!

Prayer: Dear Heavenly Father, We love You!! Let us keep in mind as the Christmas Season turns into the New Year, that Your Son, and the forgiveness of our sins past, present and future, is the one constant in Our lives, the one gift that truly keeps on giving! AMEN

DECEMBER 28

Monday Morning

Talkin' to myself and feelin' old, Sometimes I'd like to quit,
Nothin' ever seems to fit, Hangin' around,
Nothin' to do but frown,
Rainy days and Mondays always get me down!
What I've got they used to call the blues.
Nothin' is really wrong, Feelin' like I don't belong,
Walkin' around, Some kind of lonely clown,
Rainy days and Mondays always get me down!
Funny, but it seems I always wind up here with you.
Nice to know somebody loves me.
Funny, but it seems that it's the only thing to do,
Run and find the one who loves me, the one who loves me...

(Paul Williams for The Carpenters)

Sometimes, Mondays are not my favorite days. Okay, most times. They aren't for a lot of people. Whatever stresses your job entails, you may have just started to relax and breathe, when *poof*......the weekend's over. This feeling of "back to the grind" can be particularly acute after a holiday, especially after Christmas. Even for those of us who really love our jobs. No holiday has the anticipation, the build up, the excitement of Christmas! Vendors view this as an opportunity to hawk their wares through "once a year sales." Stores, malls, streets and entire neighborhoods are festooned with every type of glittering decoration and colored lights. The build up is even built into the Christian calendar, with the observance of the four Sundays of Advent! From right after Thanksgiving, and lately even right after Halloween, the build-up begins.

Then, Christmas is *finally* here! From kids to pets to parents, grandparents, aunts, uncles and cousins, families gather from distant cities to meet, greet and eat at a long table with the Christmas tree and the roaring fire in the background! At least that's the way Norman Rockwell always pictured it for us. Not everyone's Christmas celebration is like that; particularly not in 2020, when the never ending pandemic kept many families from traveling. But it's not like that for many people *every* year, because they don't have that extended family, or that roaring fire, or that tree, or maybe even a roof over their heads. For some, Christmas Spirit is a fleeting thing at best.

Not unlike New Years resolutions, intended for permanence, but which fade within days or weeks, the "Christmas spirit" we always talk of, seems all too often to dissipate just as rapidly. The anticipation is gone and routine sets in. It's almost a let down, right? Don't be surprised if someone cuts you off in traffic Monday morning and then unlike Santa who puts his finger beside his nose, makes an altogether different gesture in your direction!

Believers, true believers that is, not those who view Christmas as an excuse to party, or those who've never been to a church except on Christmas Eve and Easter morning, have something that others don't have. We have "*Someone to run to!*" As Karen Carpenter's crystal clear, beautiful, voice reminds us, *"It's nice to know somebody loves you!"* Here's what that means for followers of Jesus: it's up to us! It's up to US, to keep that Christmas Spirit alive all year long; and we can do it! Why? Because we have someOne to run to! We *know* we are loved everyday!

Last week a man thought I cut him off in a McDonald's double line, you know, where the cars alternate merging after you place your order. He honked his horn behind me and gave me that un-Santa like gesture. So I paid for his breakfast when I got to the window. I never got to see his reaction of course. But that's alright. I know it got him thinking. That's the Christmas Spirit. It's not hard. It's actually kind of fun to spread around. I know I sound like a broken record, but hey, so did Jesus: *Love each other.*

Prayer: Dear Heavenly Father, We love You! We know that You loved us first and keep on loving us, and when things seem like a let down or a grind, Spirit remind us that we are loved! Then its easy to pass on the Christmas Spirit! AMEN

DECEMBER 29

Letting God Down?

"But god shows His love for us in that while we were still sinners, Christ died for us." (Romans 5:8 ESV)

Almost twenty years ago one of my daughters was entering her sophomore year in high school. She did what teenagers do: on a sleep over she and three friends snuck out headed for mischief! Suffice it to say they got caught. My daughter subsequently wrote me a long, literally, tear stained letter. She didn't complain about being grounded. She didn't complain about having her driver's license delayed. The letter was simply an obviously heartfelt apology for *letting me down,* for disappointing me!

All of us do things we are not proud of. I do things that I am not proud of. In fact, I did something I wasn't proud of just yesterday. If you do something you know you really ought not, you also have a tendency to hide it. Then, when you are discovered, for most of us, it's not the punishment we fear; it's not the discontinuation of whatever we were into; it's the disappointment in the eyes of anyone we might have hurt. Oftentimes, when we do something we shouldn't, there is someone we have disappointed.

But here is another incredible thing about Grace: **that someone doesn't include God!** Once you have accepted Christ as your personal Lord and Savior; once you actually have the *indwelling* Holy Spirit; there is *nothing you can do* to make you a disappointment to God! Think about that for a minute. Salvation is a *free gift,* it's not something promised for those that do the right thing more than other people. It's not about *doing* at all! If it were about always *doing the right thing,* then none of us would be welcome back to be with God the Father, because we are all sinners. Christians remember, aren't saints who never sin, they are sinners who are saved!

Grace means that we are truly *free!* If there is nothing we can do to either make God love us more or love us less, then we are free from shame and free from guilt! We are promised that for believers, *there is no condemnation* from God's perspective! Imagine what this means for your life? Yes, you will sin, and yes you may be disappointed in yourself for not allowing the Holy Spirit to guide you more consistently, but *Jesus will never be disappointed in you!* ***You couldn't let Jesus down no matter how hard you try!*** Now there's something to be grateful for as you prepare your upcoming New Years Resolutions!

Prayer: Dear Heavenly Father, We love You!! But OH, how You love us!! Free from guilt, shame and enslavement to sin, let the Holy Spirit have free reign from within to guide us so that we constantly express the Fruits of the Spirit! AMEN

DECEMBER 30

The Puerperium

"So they came in a hurry and found their way to Mary and Joseph, and the baby as He lay in a manger. When they had seen this, they made known the statement which had been told them [by the angel] about this Child.

And all who heard it wondered at the things which were told them by the shepherds. But mary treasured all these things, pondering them in her heart." (Luke 2:16-19 NASB)

Maybe its just because I have been a physician who delivers babies for the last forty years, but have you ever wondered about those first days after Jesus was born? Sure, Mary and Joseph had both experienced encounters with Gabriel, whether in dreams or not, but that had been many months before. Yes, Mary stayed with cousin Elizabeth for three months in the middle of both their pregnancies, and yes, her cousin's baby [John the Baptist] jumped for joy when Mary arrived, spurring Elizabeth to state, "*Blessed are you among women, and blessed is the fruit of your womb...Blessed is she who believed there would be a fulfillment of what had been spoken to her by the Lord.*" Mary then spoke the famous prayer of the Magnificat. (Luke 1:46-55) But then Mary went home to Nazareth. She wasn't present for Zacharias' Prophecy that John would *"go before the Lord to prepare His ways, to give His people the knowledge of salvation by the forgiveness of their sins..."* (Luke 1:76-77)

After the Baby was born in a cave outside of Bethlehem, and the shepherds had left, there was no nursery with a crib, no cradle with down comforters, no breast pumps or bottle warmers or microwave or disposable diapers, or washing machines, or central heating! They couldn't run to Walmart. There were no readily available meals, and no friendly neighbors bringing over casseroles to be warmed. It's not clear that Mary and Joseph *knew anyone at all* in Bethlehem! After all, they had no where to stay.

We do know that somehow, after eight days, Jesus was circumcised, presumably by the local Bethlehem mohel. But when the "days for their purification according to the Law of Moses were completed," they climbed up the hill from Bethlehem to Jerusalem for the Baby to be "presented at the Temple" because He was the firstborn, and by definition "Holy" or set apart to the Lord. It was only now, 40 days later, that Mary heard the words of Simeon's prayer, calling her Baby the "Light of revelation to the Gentiles and the glory of Your People Israel." (Luke 2:28-32 NASB)

No, in the first month after the birth, Mary, a 14 maybe 15 year old girl, had to contend with all the headaches of a newborn with none of our modern conveniences, but none of the comfort and support of her own family either! There was no "grandma" to lend a hand with bathing, and diapers, and feedings and consolation. Mary was undoubtedly in pain, with lacerations after her first delivery, after-birth pains, uncomfortable breast changes and nipple soreness. How did a teenage girl, far from home, in the company only of her older, new husband, possibly manage?

As our December 25th devotional queried, *"Mary, did you know?"* Remember, Mary and Joseph didn't get to see Gabriel and the Heavenly Host who appeared to the shepherds on the hillside that night of her labor. They didn't get to hear the angel proclaim that he brought, *"Good news of Great Joy which will be for all people: for today in the City of David there has been born for you a Savior, who is Christ the Lord."* (Luke 2:10-11 NASB) She was busy, sweating, groaning, and undoubtedly crying out in pain for hours, while the shepherds were busy being terrified and then traveling down the mountainside to find her and her baby. But scripture tells us they related what they had seen to her and Joseph, and she *"pondered these things in her heart."*

This young girl had just been through about the most traumatic thing she could have imagined. She did it without the comfort of her mother, or sisters, or even another woman as far as we know, and was now recovering, possibly still in the cave, for the forty days required of her. She had one dream, the certain knowledge of her virginity, her cousin's words, and the story of a few shepherds, with which to figure out what the heck was going on! Instead of falling apart, she basically, "takes it all on faith!" She ponders the shepherds words, treasures them in fact, and must have consciously decided to carry on and wait for the Lord to clarify His will!

There is much to be learned from young Mary! When we are bewildered by our circumstances, by the lightening speed with which our fortunes can change, and sometimes the sluggish pace of our recovery, we could perhaps think of her. Despite the confusion and terror of her incredible circumstances, she chooses to believe, and wait. **"Believe and wait."** That might even be a better t-shirt than "Be Calm and Carry on!"

Prayer: Dear Heavenly Father, We love You! Thank you for choosing Mary, knowing that her faith would see her through an almost incomprehensible ordeal, to come out on the other side and raise our Savior to adulthood, with love and patience and belief. AMEN

DECEMBER 31

Auld Lang Syne

Should old acquaintance be forgot,
and never brought to mind?
Should old acquaintance be forgot,
and auld lang syne?
For auld lang syne, my dear,
for auld lang syne,
we'll take a cup of kindness yet,
for auld lang syne.

New Year's Eve! It means standing on the threshold of something brand new! For some it means a new start, a do-over; for others it's the hope of continued improvement, or maybe even the end to a downward slide. Perhaps no New Year's Eve has been as anticipated as this one, at least for us baby boomers born after the end of WW II.

We all desperately want to put the Pandemic in the rearview mirror, not to mention a year of political turmoil, pitting neighbor against neighbor and even family members against family members! 2020 was a year of deep unrest with regard to racial injustice. It was a year of horrendous natural disasters. It was a year that kept us separated from loved ones even as they died alone beyond glass partitions, where the last faces they were ever to see, weren't even faces, but masks behind transparent shields. The last human touch they were ever to feel was distorted by latex.

Auld Lang Syne, Robert Burn's Scottish poem set to music and published in 1788, is traditionally sung in all English speaking nations at the stroke of midnight that marks the beginning of the new year. Many are confused by the English translation of the original Scots. The word *should* in the first stanza, is not understood in its common English usage, posing a moral question. The first line doesn't ask, "Should we just forget about old acquaintances?" but instead, "In the event that we should ever forget about old acquaintances...!" *Auld Lang Syne* is best translated, *long, long ago*. So the phrase is really, *"In the event that we should ever forget about old acquaintances and times long ago..."* Finally, the remedy is in the chorus. *"We'll take a cup of kindness yet for times long ago."* In other words, ***"Let's drink to our old friends and times long ago so that we never forget them!"***

While there is always much we would like to forget about the previous year, and especially 2020, there is much we want to remember: old friends that have passed, the people who put their lives on the line every day treating the sick, the friends and family that drew together for work and play, even if they had to ZOOM to do it; the incredible "can-do" spirit and innovation of people in all walks of American life, who faced seemingly insurmountable physical and financial obstacles, and yet still somehow found a way to "surmount!"

I started the Doing Life Devotional exactly one year ago, with the call from my daughter, when she tearfully got my attention with the words, "Dad, Ian has cancer!" He went on to fight his way to remission through seven rounds of chemotherapy, while she worked tirelessly, often 24-36 hour shifts, as a cardiology fellow, caring for Covid patients day in and day out, unable to come home and see her husband or son for months, while her husband was immune suppressed. There are thousands of stories just like hers across the globe.

The point of the daily devotional was to help each of us, on a daily basis, to experience the joy and peace that are promised to us as followers of Christ! While our acceptance of the gift offered to us in grace, the forgiveness of sin that frees us, promises to make us brand new going forward, it doesn't mean we should never look back! If that were the case, Christians would only have the New Testament! Hebrews Chapter 11, the famous "Faith Chapter," reviews those heroes of our faith from Old Testament times who make up that "great cloud of witnesses" cheering us on as we run the race to its conclusion! Looking back through the Old Testament we see God's character revealed, with His unfailing love toward a rebellious people, demonstrated over and over and over!

Believers can look forward to the New Year, knowing that an endlessly loving God has a plan for each of us! But we can also look back on a tumultuous year, and still see untold numbers of instances in which God was obviously moving. Let us pass boldly from the old year into the new, remembering Romans 8:28 as we go, "*And we know all things work together for good to those who love God, to those who are called according to His purpose!*" Happy New Year!

Prayer: Dear Heavenly Father, We love You!! We are Blessed that You have given us Your Word so that we might understand what You have done in the past, and what You have promised us in the future. We ask that You use Your Spirit to guide us in the coming year, keeping us ever mindful that the joy and peace that You speak of comes only through loving each other. AMEN

Acknowledgments

No book comes together solely due to the work of one individual. I wish to thank first the incredible dedication of Jill Voges who took on this project personally while still carrying her workload at Bang Printing and caring for her own family through the pandemic of 2020-2021. Thanks to Brian Jansma and Donald Maloney and all the others at Bang who saw this project through and continue to fill orders efficiently. They dealt professionally and compassionately with my whining about this as well as other projects throughout! A shout-out to Rachel Palmer, the e-commerce specialist at Sheridan, and her entire team. Their competence made the production of the e-PUB version for Amazon Kindle a breeze.

I wish to thank all of my patients who were the first recipients of these devotions by e-mail throughout the trying first year of Covid-19. Their feedback was immensely helpful. Thanks especially to Val and Mike Norris, Lynn O'Shea, Dedra Minor, Bettina England, William Young, Jill Willis, Whitney Field, Linda Koval, and scores of others! We "Do Life" with our Life Group at Benttree Bible Fellowship, and I wish to acknowledge the encouragement, sharing of their own experiences, and consistent prayers. These include Jay and Susan Mays, Mark and Lesa Stuart, Brian and Lorena Locke, Jim and Donna Semens, Darren and Pat Ford, and Kurt and Michele Baxter.

Thanks to both Joann Hummel and Steve Frizell, lead teaching Pastors at BTBF, both of whom shared their encouragement with me.Thanks to Bob Goff, the author of Live In Grace-Walk In Love, who responded to my quires personally with enthusiasm and support. Several of my professors at Dallas Theological Seminary were particularly influential including Dr. Michael Svigel, Dr. Stephen Bramer, Dr. Glenn Kreider, Dr. Stan Toussaint, Dr. Ron Allen, Dr. Elliot Johnson, and most especially Dr. Lanier Burns.

Thanks as always to my partners at Walnut hill Ob/Gyn, Drs. John Bertrand, Jim Richards, Julie Hagood, Jane Nokleberg, Lauren Murray, Hampton Richards and Sooyeon Choi for tolerating the time and concentration it intermittently took away from practice to create the book in your hands. A special thanks to Evelyn Roitenberg, my nurse of 32 years, and to Teresa Spurger, who daily support me and keep me focused.

The impetus for this book came first through anguish, as you read on January 1 about my son-in law's cancer diagnosis. I wish to thank both my daughter Kelly and her husband Ian Ratheal, for their unwavering support! As cardiologist and orthopedic surgeon respectively, they were both immersed in the psychic and physical trauma of the Covid-19 pandemic during their own harrowing adventure, and yet found time and energy to be supportive of my efforts at daily reflection and application of scripture.

Thanks to my wife, Pat. Words are inadequate! Gratitude to all of my children Kelly, Andy, Allison, and Ashley, as well as my brother and his wife, Dr. Scott and Joann Thurston, to Uncle Don and *Fledgling*, and of course my mom, Phyllis Thurston, and her unwavering support for the last 65 years!

Finally, unending gratitude to my Savior, Jesus Christ, who enables and empowers me daily, who has freed me of my shame and guilt! I am literally, eternally grateful!!

About the Author

Dr. Thurston is a Board Certified Obstetrician and Gynecologist in the private practice of medicine at Presbyterian Hospital in Dallas, Texas, with Walnut Hill Ob/Gyn Associates since 1986. He is a former clinical professor at UTSW medical school and has been involved in teaching of students, residents and fellows for more than three decades.

He is a graduate of Rice University and Baylor College of Medicine in Houston, Texas, and completed his residency training at UCSF, where he also served as the administrative Chief Resident. Thus far he has attended the delivery of more than 8,000 babies. He has authored several books including most recently, the 5th edition of 1000 Questions About Your Pregnancy (JT2Books, Inc. 2021)

Dr. Thurston received his Masters in Biblical Studies from Dallas Theological Seminary in 2014. He is an active member of Benttree Bible Fellowship in Carrollton, Texas, where he participates and serves locally in a life group. He and his wife support many organizations including Daily Audio Bible, Water is Basic in South Sudan, Door of Hope in Pune, Maharashtra, India, Impact of Hope, Tamil Nadu, India, Hope Ignited in Conakry Guinea, CRU in Albania, and International Partners operating throughout Europe.

An avid lifelong sailor, he holds a 50 ton Masters license in Sail from the US Coast Guard and has his Captain's license in the Merchant Marine. Dr. Thurston sails a Catalina 350 on Lake Texoma, and a classic Greenwich 24 out of Bucks Harbor Yacht Club on Eggemoggin Reach, Penobscot Bay, Maine. Other interests include singing in church choirs and most recently the Barbershop Chorus, Big D. Dr. Thurston has also been honing his violin skills over the last six years. The tropical fish line up at the glass to listen, but the dog and wife beat a hasty retreat!

Dr. Thurston resides in Dallas, with his wife Pat, and labradoodle, Windsor. He has four grown children and four grandchildren thus far!